Boundaries of Religious Freedom:
Regulating Religion in Diverse Societies

Volume 7

Series Editors
Lori G. Beaman, University of Ottawa, Ottawa, ON, Canada
Lene Kühle, Aarhus Universitet, Aarhus, Denmark
Alexander K. Nagel, Institut für Soziologie, Georg-August-Universität Göttingen,
Göttingen, Niedersachsen, Germany

Processes of globalization have resulted in increasingly culturally and religiously diverse societies. In addition, religion is occupying a more prominent place in the public sphere at the turn of the 21st Century, despite predictions of religious decline. The rise in religious diversity, and in the salience of religious identity, is posing both challenges and opportunities pertaining to issues of governance. Indeed, a series of tensions have arisen between state and religious actors regarding a variety of matters including burial rites, religious education and gender equality. Many of these debates have focused on the need for, and limits of, religious freedom especially in situations where certain religious practices risk impinging upon the freedom of others. Moreover, different responses to religious pluralism are often informed by the relationship between religion and state in each society. Due to the changing nature of societies, most have needed to define, or redefine, the boundaries of religious freedom reflected in laws, policies and the design and use of public spaces. These boundaries, however, continue to be contested, debated and reviewed, at local, national and global levels of governance. All books published in this Series have been fully peer-reviewed before final acceptance.

More information about this series at http://www.springer.com/series/11839

Julia Martínez-Ariño • Anne-Laure Zwilling
Editors

Religion and Prison: An Overview of Contemporary Europe

 Springer

Editors
Julia Martínez-Ariño
Faculty of Theology & Religious Studies
University of Groningen
Groningen, The Netherlands

Anne-Laure Zwilling (iD)
UMR 7354 Centre National de la Recherche
Scientifique
Strasbourg, France

ISSN 2214-5281   ISSN 2214-529X (electronic)
Boundaries of Religious Freedom: Regulating Religion in Diverse Societies
ISBN 978-3-030-36833-3   ISBN 978-3-030-36834-0 (eBook)
https://doi.org/10.1007/978-3-030-36834-0

This Springer imprint is published by the registered company Springer Nature Switzerland AG
The registered company address is: Gewerbestrasse 11, 6330 Cham, Switzerland

Foreword

Depriving people of their liberty and detaining them in secure locations have long been practised in human societies. 'Prison' is a useful way of referring to these locations, but the term conceals an astonishing range of variations in the forms and purposes of detention. The authority to set up and administer most places of detention has been claimed by the ruling groups of monarchies, tribes, military units and – in modern times – agencies of the state at local, regional, national or imperial levels. Nowadays, formal codes of national and international law seek to control prison systems, but there are still wide variations in how the law is implemented in prisons. Moreover, the intended purposes of imprisonment encompass different aspects such as punishment, rehabilitation, therapy, detention on remand, detention pending resolution of requests for asylum, protection from violence against self and others, and prevention of threats to life, property and social order. In addition, prison populations are diverse in terms of, for example, gender, age, ethnicity, sexuality, religion, social class, nationality, type of offence, type of regime and length of sentence. Any attempt to understand the place of religion in prisons must take this wide range of variations into account.

At the same time, it is important to recognise that the term *religion* can have many different meanings depending on the context. Popular definitions refer to beliefs in gods, spirits, supernatural forces or – more abstractly – the 'felt whole'. Other approaches give priority to particular kinds of emotions, experiences, identities and relationships with other people and the world of nature. But the lack of agreement on the meaning of religion is not an insuperable obstacle to understanding *what counts as religion* – especially in the context of prisons. Indeed, one of the most important considerations for research on religion in prisons is precisely how decisions are made and implemented with respect to what is and what is not permissible as religion. This is a recurrent theme in the chapters that follow and is quite distinct from questions about the so-called real meaning of the term.

Religion features to varying degrees in the everyday life of prisons in virtually all jurisdictions in the world, but the countries of Europe present a distinctive 'palette' of reasons for examining them separately and together. For example, European countries were among the first to formalise the place of religion in their prisons, but some of these jurisdictions – notably in Central and Eastern Europe under communism – also imposed strict limits on the space permitted for religion. Europe also contains countries that display either significantly high or significantly low levels of religious affiliation and participation. To complicate matters further, many European countries now contain growing numbers of immigrants and settled communities which identify with religions relatively new to Europe. Historically high levels of migration into and across Europe mainly from parts of Africa, the Middle East and South Asia have started to transform the religious landscape of countries that had previously been closely associated with the Catholic Church or the major Protestant denominations. Moreover, Europe's burgeoning interest in non-theistic expressions of spirituality, forms of non-religion and humanistic philosophies adds to the variety of demands to which prison authorities are expected to respond. Finally, Europe has crafted a distinctive framework of human rights doctrines and prison rules which help to shape each country's ways of accommodating religion in prisons.

In short, religion and prisons are closely interwoven in European countries – both historically and today. Moreover, the complex patterns of their interweaving are varied and changing. The forces that drive these patterns arise partly from the spheres of law, crime, criminal justice and penal policy and partly from the spheres identified with the religious, the secular and the spiritual. The distinctive ways in which these spheres are interconnected vary with each country's particular history of constitutional settlements and upheavals in politics, law and religion. These histories have shaped the thorny issues that face prisons and religions today.

On the one hand, concern is high about issues such as the expansion of prison populations, poor prison conditions, increasing rates of recidivism and rising levels of self-harm and violence among prisoners. On the other hand, there is concern about rapid increases in religious diversity and religious discrimination, cross-generational decline in religious affiliation, the questionable capacity of religious organisations to continue supplying social services in difficult economic circumstances, and declining rates of recruitment of religious professionals. If these issues concerning prisons and religion, taken in isolation, are contentious, it is all the more necessary to grasp how they collide and intersect inside the walls of prison establishments. It is no exaggeration to claim that prisons in European societies are increasingly seen as sites where the place of religion has become highly contentious but also potentially helpful.

The last three decades have witnessed an impressive increase in scholarly investigations of precisely how and why the institution of religion in prisons has been changing in European countries. Indeed, many of the contributors to this volume have helped forge an effective agenda for research on this topic, in some cases comparing prisons with other public institutions. The dominant themes that have emerged from work in this area are also fully represented in the present volume. There is extensive overlap between these themes; but they can be grouped for present purposes under three headings, as follows.

Major Themes

(a) Regulatory frameworks

It would be wrong to suggest that each European country has its own national model of relations between the state and religions which mechanically determines the place of religion in prisons; but there are undoubtedly political, legal and cultural forces which shape the general ways in which prisons provide for the practice of religions. European states also vary in the extent to which their management of religion in prisons conforms to the requirements of international treaties and recommendations such as the United Nations Standard Minimum Rules on the Treatment of Prisoners[1] and the Council of Europe's Recommendation of the Committee of Ministers to Member States on the European Prison Rules.[2] Moreover, the European Parliament keeps prison conditions under review.[3] In addition, decisions made by the European Court of Human Rights continue to put further pressure on states to eliminate structures and practices that are judged to discriminate unfairly against prisoners' rights to practise their religion or beliefs. Nevertheless, a strong case can be made for thinking that the court tends to allow states too much discretion in deciding how to balance the rights of individual prisoners to freedom of religion or belief against the needs of states to limit freedom of religion on the grounds of safety, public order and prison discipline (Temperman 2017).

Indeed, many of the contributions to this volume stress the importance of understanding not only the formal frameworks that govern religion in prisons but also the informal practices whereby prison authorities, chaplains and representatives of religious organisations can all find themselves caught up in disputes and negotiations about the freedom of religion as practised at the level of their local prison establishments. This is particularly important in the countries of Central and Eastern Europe which became fully independent of the Soviet Union in the 1990s. After decades of Communist repression, these countries started to face the challenge of forging a new place for religion in public life – including prisons – while trying to preserve a balance between the power of their revived Christian Orthodox churches and the claims for recognition advanced by other religious groups.

Before the twenty-first century, questions about the regulation of religions in the prisons of Europe attracted very little public or political attention, but this situation changed drastically in the wake of the Islamist-inspired attacks on the USA in 2001 and subsequent attacks in a growing number of European locations. As soon as journalists and scholars began to draw connections between the violent extremism

---

[1] First adopted in 1957, revised in 2015 and now known as the Nelson Mandela Rules. See https://cdn.penalreform.org/wp-content/uploads/2016/07/Joint-statement-Mandela-Rules-PR-July-18-.pdf

[2] First adopted in 2006 and considered for revision in 2017. See https://rm.coe.int/16806f97ab

[3] Policy Department C: Citizens' Rights and Constitutional Affairs. Report PE 583.113. 2017. Available at: http://www.europarl.europa.eu/RegData/etudes/BRIE/2017/583113/IPOL_BRI%282017%29583113_EN.pdf

promulgated by various strands of Islamism and the role of prisons, the spotlight inevitably fell on notions of how to better regulate all forms of religion which might encourage violent extremisms among prisoners. Prisons were identified as places that might help to foment this ideology, to spread it through networks of serving and released prisoners, and to foster the conversion of non-Muslims to extremist versions of Islam. The prison systems in European countries have responded in different ways to this 'securitisation of Islam' by, for example, enhancing the training of security staff, the scrutiny of imams working in prisons, and the surveillance of Muslim prisoners' activities. Some countries have put in place, or strengthened, a formal apparatus for attracting, selecting, training and monitoring Muslim 'chaplains' or other representatives of Islam who visit prisoners.

(b) The framing of religion and religious diversity

A second major theme that runs through most of the chapters in this important book concerns the wide range of strategies adopted by prison authorities for determining two crucial things: the question of what counts as religion for practical purposes and the question of how far to acknowledge the diversity of religions. These questions carry greater weight in prisons than in the rest of society because prisons are spaces where virtually all activities, facilities and material things are subject to close inspection and explicit regulations.

A wide variety of organisations have an interest in how religion is defined in prisons. Religious organisations are active in seeking to defend their members' rights to hold their particular beliefs and to conduct such practices as individual or collective worship, prayer, study and festivals. Prisoners' rights to wear certain forms of clothing, to practise distinctive forms of personal hygiene, to consume particular types of food, to meet with representatives of their religious tradition, and to have access to appropriate kinds of religious literature are all subject to negotiation at various levels of prison systems. This negotiation might take the form of angry confrontations between prisoners and prison guards in the course of everyday interactions. But it can also take place at the highest levels of prison governance where administrators, selected religious representatives and even government officials try to decide, in principle, where the dividing line should fall between religion and non-religion or between permissible and impermissible forms of religion. Points of contention often centre on the extent to which the rights in question are soundly rooted in – and mandated by – clearly identifiable and authentic religious traditions. Other contentious issues concern the selection of organisations that are accepted as truly representative of their faith traditions – and of the many sub-traditions within them.

Yet more questions about the management of religion's boundaries come into focus when discussion centres on the conditions governing access to prisons and prisoners by authorised representatives of religions. These agents include salaried and voluntary chaplains, volunteers, teachers and spiritual assistants. Difficult questions about their selection, appointment, training, monitoring, evaluation, remuneration, status, authority and access to prisoners are refracted by the history and structure of each prison system. Other issues concern whether these various agents are permitted to interact with prisoners who do not share their own religious identity, whether any form of proselytism is permitted, and whether they allegedly incite prisoners to adopt any kind of radicalism or violent extremism. The material conditions in which these religious agents have to work also vary widely between countries – especially with regard to the spaces available for collective worship.

All these concerns about the governance of religion in prisons are heightened in contexts where religious diversity is increasing significantly among prisoners – as in many European countries since the 1990s. The growing presence of prisoners who identify with religious traditions and sub-traditions previously unknown or unfamiliar in Europe gives rise to questions about, for example, the place of Christian churches which had previously been dominant, the recognition as 'religion' of beliefs and practices which appear to be spiritual rather than religious, and the frequency of conversion or reversion from one religious identity to another. In turn, these questions generate moral and legal arguments about equal rights and unfair discrimination in relation to religion in prisons – as well as fundamental objections to what can be seen as the privileging of either one religion over others or of religion over non-religion. In all these respects, prisons represent a microcosm of the European societies in which they function.

(c) Changing forms of religion in prison

The chapters that follow are eloquent testimony to the shifting balance that is being struck in various ways in European prisons between, on the one hand, long-established and, on the other hand, more recently adopted expressions of religious and spiritual beliefs. In this sense, prisons are no different from other social institutions insofar as they reflect continuing changes in how religions, spiritual beliefs and forms of non-religion are being expressed in thought, feeling and practice. The ascendancy of major Christian churches and denominations is declining in many European countries – but not at the same rate in all places – and rates of self-identification with religions other than Christianity and with various forms of non-religion are on the increase. Furthermore, a wide range of spiritual beliefs and therapies which draw their inspiration from many parts of the world, without necessarily having links to particular religious traditions, have also been attracting increasing numbers of practitioners and clients in recent decades. Many of them are associated with the so-called New Age and new technologies of the self.

All these changing forms of religion and spirituality are reflected in the collective life of prisons and of individual prisoners. As a result, prison systems are under pressure to recognise ideas and activities which do not fit easily into long-established frameworks of predominantly Christian chaplaincy. Even in countries where arrangements for collective worship in prisons are fully integrated into routine programmes, it can be difficult to provide times and places for 'alternative' spiritual practices which may require the presence of teachers or practitioners rather than pastors, priests or imams. Moreover, the circulation of print and digital media is central to the practice of alternative spiritual beliefs among prisoners but may be more resistant to control by chaplains or other appointed representatives of religions.

The involvement of religious organisations and actors in the rehabilitation of offenders is by no means new in some countries. In fact, some of the ideas that governed the design and regimes of modern prisons had religious origins. But recent developments have seen a blurring of the line between religious and secular forms of therapy and rehabilitation – to the point where, in some cases, chaplains formally participate in programmes designed to combat offending behaviours and to cultivate positive outlooks (Becci and Roy 2015). In addition, some prison systems allow religious groups to take major responsibility for managing the daily life of selected inmates in areas of prisons set aside for them. Other groups are permitted to function as 'prison ministries' that offer extensive engagement in religious study and practice to those prisoners who commit themselves to living in accordance with underlying Christian values and precepts. Needless to say, there is opposition to these schemes in some quarters; and the secular ideologies governing the public sphere in some countries exclude such schemes. Research is inconclusive on the questions of how far participation in religious activities inspires prisoners to retain their religious interests after release and of the extent to which they prevent offenders from becoming further involved in crime.

These three general themes cut across all the chapters in this timely volume. The contributors demonstrate not only the diversity to be observed in European countries' responses to the changing faces of religion in their prisons but also to the challenges that face all countries experiencing rapid changes in religion and spirituality. The resulting analysis is grounded in empirically rich information as well as critical insights into policies and practices. This is Europe's first systematic, comprehensive and cross-national investigation of religion and prisons.

University of Warwick   James A. Beckford,
Coventry, UK

References

Becci, I., & Roy, O. (Eds). (2015). *Religious diversity in European prisons. Challenges and implications for rehabilitation*. Heidelberg: Springer.
Temperman, J. (2017). Freedom of religion or belief in prison. A critical analysis of the European court of human rights' Jurisprudence. *Oxford Journal of Law and Religion, 6*, 48–92.

Contents

Chapter 1
Religion and Prison: An Introduction

Julia Martínez-Ariño and Anne-Laure Zwilling ⓘ

Abstract This introduction to the book *Religion and Prison: An Overview of Contemporary Europe* provides an overview of the main empirical and theoretical issues addressed in its chapters. Firstly, it argues that a focus on prisons as institutional contexts is productive for the analysis of the presence and governance of religion in various national contexts. Secondly, this introduction highlights the original contributions to the existing literature on religion in prisons and more broadly on religious diversity brought by the different chapters. Thirdly, the introduction briefly explains how the content of the book is organised, before turning to the identification of the main topics that run across the different chapters, including, among others, the importance of historical church-state arrangements and regime changes for the presence and regulation of religion in prisons, and the widespread securitisation of religion in prisons across countries

Religious diversification can nowadays be observed throughout Europe. Immigration from all over the world is one of the driving forces of this transformation. However, changes in the European religious landscape have also happened from within, such as the increase in the relevance of so-called New Age movements and spirituality. All this runs in parallel to the loss of significance of historical majority Christian churches. In this context, most states face new demands for symbolic recognition and the guarantee of the right to religious freedom for every person, irrespective of the religious affiliation. This also affects public institutions, which increasingly cater to more religiously diverse populations. This book focuses on prisons as institutional contexts for observing the presence and governance of religion.

J. Martínez-Ariño
Faculty of Theology & Religious Studies, University of Groningen,
Groningen, The Netherlands
e-mail: j.martinez.arino@rug.nl

A.-L. Zwilling (✉)
UMR 7354 Centre National de la Recherche, Scientifique, Strasbourg, France
e-mail: anne-laure.zwilling@misha.cnrs.fr

© Springer Nature Switzerland AG 2020
J. Martínez-Ariño, A.-L. Zwilling (eds.), *Religion and Prison: An Overview of Contemporary Europe*, Boundaries of Religious Freedom: Regulating Religion in Diverse Societies 7, https://doi.org/10.1007/978-3-030-36834-0_1

The study of religion in public institutions has developed over the years into a well-established research subfield, particularly in Europe. Studies focusing on different institutional contexts have analysed the presence, roles and transformations of religion on the one hand, and on the other hand, how states manage religious differences and differences between religious and secular norms within the walls of such state institutions. This literature has proven very insightful for understanding how religion is governed on the ground and how everyday practices reproduce, reinforce or challenge existing legal and institutional arrangements. This strand of research has also shown how religion takes new shapes in those institutions.

Prisons have attracted increasing scholarly attention since the seminal work of Beckford and Gilliat (2005). By now, an extensive body of research on religion in prisons has developed (Ajouaou and Bernts 2015; Becci 2014; Beckford 2005; Beckford and Gilliat 2005; Beckford 2001; Furseth and Kühle 2011), with some countries offering more possibilities for research on the topic than others. The aim of this book is to contribute to those debates with a rich array of studies analysing the presence and regulation of religion in prisons in Europe (including Russia and Turkey). The wide scope of cases included in the volume adds to the existing work done mostly in Western European countries.

1.1 Why Is It Relevant to Study Religion in Prisons?

Multiple reasons make the study of religion in prisons a relevant focus for sociologists and legal scholars of religion. First, prisons are an interesting context in which to study the actual working of legal and political arrangements to govern religion. As some authors have argued, "(...) prisons afford an exceptionally clear view of state policies regarding the social and cultural diversity of the people for whom they are responsible. In particular, prisons demonstrate the extent to which agencies of the state are prepared to go in recognising, and responding to, diversity" (Joly and Beckford 2006: 3). Focusing our attention on well-defined social contexts, such as prisons, allows us to deepen the analysis of the regulations and negotiations around religion as they happen on the ground, beyond what legal frameworks stipulate. We could, thus, argue that by looking at how religion and religious diversity are dealt with in prisons, we can obtain a good grasp of their governance at a broader level.

Moreover, focusing on the well-delimited context of prisons permits us to observe and study large social and religious transformations on a smaller scale. For example, as shown in the chapters for the different Eastern European countries, the extent to which religion has "returned" in the post-Soviet era varies significantly across national contexts. Examining their penitentiary systems allows us to make more concrete observations about how religion has repositioned itself after the transition to democracy in the post-communist era. In some countries, such as Bulgaria and Romania, the re-Christianisation and resurgence of religion in prisons more broadly is quite evident, whereas in others, such as the Czech Republic, this move is less intense, and religion remains in a rather marginal position. Although this is not new, and research had already shown before that the Czech Republic is one of the most secular countries in Europe (Hamplová and Nešpor 2009; Lužný and Navrátilová 2001), the information provided by the chapter in this book offers detailed insights into how this indifference towards religion looks more specifically. In other words, by investigating religion in prisons, we can analyse how the place and role attached to religion evolves over time, depending on historical and socio-political conditions.

Additionally, focusing on a specific institutional context allows research to capture the influence of concrete "institutional logics" (Thornton et al. 2012) in the governing of religion (Bertossi and Bowen 2014). Institutions develop their own logics that affect the daily life of organisations, including the place allocated to religion. For example, the role or function that religion may play in prisons differs from the role it plays in hospitals or in the army, which can have an influence on the ways in which the institutions govern it. In prisons, for example, religion often helps to keep order, whereas in hospitals it is more often seen as a competing epistemological system with the biomedical model of scientific knowledge, and thus something to keep at the margins of the institution (Griera and Martínez-Ariño 2014).

Finally, another important reason that makes the study of religion in prisons relevant is the fact that, despite the existence of what some have called a kind of European shared model of religion–state relations that includes religious freedom, equality and autonomy of states and religions (Ferrari 1995; Willaime 2009), with slight variations in its application, there are still significant differences, across countries as well as within countries. Therefore, analysing the place of religion in public institutions is a good way of capturing the national as well as the local specificities of the ways in which religion and religious diversity are governed. For example, we can observe differences between previously mono-confessional and pluri-confessional states (Madeley 2003), with the cases of Spain – or Italy – and the Netherlands representing paradigmatic examples of each of the two configurations. In addition, by examining religion in public institutions, we can study how the religious and the secular interact with each other and are constantly negotiated (Cadge et al. 2017).

1.2 What Does This Book Add to the Existing Literature?

One big difference between this edited volume and other works on religion in prisons, such as *Religion in prison: 'equal rites' in a multi-faith society* (Beckford and Gilliat 1998), *Imprisoned religion: transformations of religion during and after imprisonment in Eastern Germany* (Becci 2013), and *De la religion en prison* (Béraud et al. 2016), is the wide range of countries that it includes, some of which have been underrepresented or even absent from the literature so far. This is particularly the case for countries of Eastern Europe as well as Turkey, where little or no research had been conducted before. By providing initial accounts for these countries, the book opens the field to more studies in the future.

This book also differs from other collective works, such as *Religious diversity in European prisons: challenges and implications for rehabilitation* (Becci and Roy 2015). In the latter case, the authors of the edited volume deal with different thematic foci related to religion in European prisons. Thus, although Becci and Roy's volume offers more depth of analysis, our volume offers more breadth. Another interesting characteristic of the present book is that it combines historical, legal and sociological perspectives on the analysis of the situation of religion in prison. By doing so, the chapters show the evolution of formal regulations and administrative procedures, as well as of actual practices on the ground. In addition, by combining these perspectives, the chapters provide a more comprehensive account of the situation of religion in prison in each of the countries. We see our volume as a complementary piece to existing works, all contributing to a better and more nuanced understanding of religion in penitentiary institutions, and of religious transformations more generally.

1.3   What Will the Reader Find in This Book?

The idea of this book came out of a thematic meeting about religion in prison in European countries of the members of the EUREL network held in Strasbourg in 2015. The EUREL network is a network of legal scholars and sociologists working on gathering legal and sociological data on religion and making it available to both a specialised and a general public through the website www.eurel.info. Each member of the network is the correspondent for one country, and is an expert on its religious situation. The correspondents hold a yearly meeting. In the 2015 meeting, each country correspondent presented a short report of the state of affairs in relation to religion in prisons in their respective country. The richness of the material discussed in that working session, and particularly the fact of being confronted with information on countries for which we rarely have concise information about religion in public institutions, encouraged us to broadcast the material gathered in the form of an edited volume.

This book contains a systematic set of chapters addressing the presence, role and regulation of religion in prisons, combining historical, legal and sociological perspectives, and including some references to contemporary public debates. Although authors were required to provide some standardised legal and sociological information on the situation in each respective country, the great variety of situations found across national contexts, on the one hand, and the variety and imbalance in the research available on the topic, on the other hand, resulted in a quite diverse range of chapters.

In some cases, where empirical research has been done extensively for some years now, such as Switzerland, the UK or Spain, studies are very detailed and provide a great amount of empirical information, particularly with regard to the situation on the ground. In other cases, the chapters have a more exploratory character, particularly where no empirical research existed previously. This is the case for

Croatia and Montenegro, for example. Of singularity is the case of Russia, for which only a very short overview is given. Yet, despite the brevity of the report, we deemed it important to include it and thereby, hopefully, encourage some readers to pursue more detailed studies in that country.

Similarly, chapters differ in the emphasis put on the legal and sociological analysis of the situation of religion in prisons. In some cases, such as Belgium, Italy, Norway and Poland, a very detailed account is given of the legal framework regulating religion in prison, whereas in others, such as Denmark and Latvia, the main part of the chapter focuses on qualitative, often ethnographic, accounts of situations in the field, or draws on survey research conducted in the prison milieu, such as in Finland. Also, in two cases (Czech Republic and France), two authors wrote the chapters separately according to their specific expertise (legal or sociological).

Finally, we were unable to find researchers to agree to write a chapter for Andorra, Belarus, Bosnia-Herzegovina, Cyprus, Ireland, Greece, Lithuania, Luxemburg, Monaco, Portugal, Serbia, Slovakia, Slovenia and Ukraine. Hopefully, this book will spark interest in researchers in those countries, and a future volume will be able to include them.

1.4   Common Topics Throughout the Book Chapters

The situations presented in each of these chapters are very much context-specific. The different historical pathways of the various countries have led to quite different situations. Yet, at the same time, it is possible to identify some recurrent topics and trends throughout the chapters. Some are common to most cases, whereas others are shared only by countries in different parts of Europe.

The first common element observed throughout the book is that historical arrangements of church and state relations play a role in the current presence of religion and the configuration of chaplaincy in prisons. This is very evident in the cases where there has been, or still exists, a state church, such as the UK and the Scandinavian countries. By way of illustration, in those cases, the status of chaplains of the majority church tends to remain special (e.g. as state employees). This is clearly the result of the preferential state treatment that some churches have received in history. Many chapters in this book show – implicitly or explicitly – the continuity of traces of both formal and informal forms of establishment (Sullivan and Beaman 2013) that do not necessarily disappear with the constitutional disestablishment of a church. One particularly striking example of the entanglement of religion in secular institutions is the case of the *Monastery* in Swedish prisons, a Christian-based silent retreat programme offered to some prisoners as a path to rehabilitation.

Despite this prevalence of legacies from previous historical arrangements, however, one of the important changes observed is the loss of power of previous religious monopolies. These de-monopolisation processes have changed the ideas of what chaplaincy is, how it operates and what the main tasks developed are. In certain cases, it is possible to observe a process of secularisation of chaplaincy, as shown in the chapters for Denmark and Finland, where chaplains of the previously dominant group adapt and struggle with the new environment. Similarly, some other chapters in this book show how historically dominant churches have developed different strategies, such as getting involved in the legal and administrative management of the detainees' situation, to adapt to new situations. Romania is one such example.

Interestingly, in several historically Christian-based prison systems, chaplains or priests are automatically part of the board of the institution and as such are granted authority on assessing the "moral quality" of detainees and have power over penalties and release. Romania, as mentioned above, is one such case, Italy too. In other cases, though, although chaplains no longer occupy that position officially, they may still have some influence on decisions by their long-lasting experience and permanence in the prison milieu and the legitimacy that these accord them.

Another interesting development that some of the chapters in this book capture is the impact of the regime change in the place of religion in penitentiary institutions. In many of the countries from the former Soviet bloc, both the penitentiary system and the religious field have undergone significant transformations, also reflected in the presence of religion in prisons and the provision of religious care for inmates. The post-Soviet context is one in which religious revivals have been documented after a period of state repression of religion (Froese 2004; Müller and Neundorf 2012; Tomka 1995). Moreover, religion plays an important role in the configuration of national identities in many of the countries in the region (Agadjanian 2006). Prison systems have been restructured and international laws and regulations apply to most of them. However, the ways in which religion is regulated and chaplaincy is organised varies across post-communist countries, as well as throughout time. For example, in Estonia, the first years after the country's independence in 1991 were marked by a "chaotic" situation of prison chaplaincy, whereas since the 2000s there has been a stronger institutionalisation of the service, now managed by the chief of chaplains.

All the countries included in this book report a pluralisation of the religious demand and supply. With the democratisation of many countries from Southern to Eastern Europe over the last decades, the consequent recognition of the right to religious freedom, and the increasing immigration to these countries, religious diversity has become a characteristic of prison systems. This is evident both in the religious profile of prison populations and in the religious services and chaplaincy offered. In this sense, in the countries where reliable statistics exist, such as Austria, Finland and the Netherlands, the diversification of religious affiliations of inmates is obvious. In countries where no official statistics exist, this diversity of religious affiliations is observable in the variety of chaplaincy that is offered. Next to historical Christian churches, religious minority groups are now part of the religious offer in prison. Yet, although in some cases, the type of chaplaincy system follows a "multi-faith" one, as is the case of the UK, in others, with the case of Austria as a paradigmatic example, chaplaincy follows a "tradition-specific" model.

Despite this diversification, in many cases we encounter stratified systems of prison chaplaincy: not all religious groups enjoy the same benefits (either legally or in practice) and these unequal configurations are often the result of monopoly situations and traditions of state–church relations. The position that different religious groups occupy in the prison system is often the result of broader stratified systems of legal recognition of some religious communities. In Germany, specific contracts for prisons exist between the federal regions and the religious groups, with a general contract with the state. Stratification is particularly remarkable in the cases where a Concordat agreement exists for the Catholic Church, which grants specific rights to Catholic chaplains, as is the case for Austria, Spain and Italy.

More or less directly connected to this diversification is the reorganisation and professionalisation of chaplaincy services. The scope of this transformation is not as wide as the diversification of the prison population, and not all cases in this book show evidence of this. However, it is increasingly common for chaplaincy services to be reorganised, as in the case of France, for example, and that the provision of religious care undergoes a process of specific professional training and accreditation. This concerns particularly, but not exclusively, Muslim chaplains, as there is a sense of urgency in some countries, such as France and Denmark, to hire and train Muslim prison chaplains. This strategy falls within the broader umbrella of what has been called the "nationalisation" or "domestication" of Islam (Humphrey 2009; Laurence 2006; Sunier 2014).

However, next to this standardisation and professionalisation found in some of the country cases analysed in this book, one can also observe a general pattern throughout the countries, namely the importance of non-written rules. Examples can be found in almost all the chapters. It seems quite common that next to legal regulations and formal administrative procedures, routines and non-written rules play a role in how religion is handled in penitentiary institutions. In this sense, prison managers appear to be very powerful in defining the extent to which religious diversity is accommodated in prisons. For example, in the Austrian case, although this is not established by law, Jewish inmates from various prisons are allowed to gather together for the big celebrations, as a minimum of ten people are necessary to celebrate in the Jewish tradition. Thus, discretion shapes religion in prisons.

However, there are also more institutionalised accommodation practices in different countries. Not all depends on one person's will. In most countries, clear rules or guidelines establish what kind of practices can be accommodated and how. Food is an example of this. In some cases, it is provided according to religious dietary requirements when inmates request it. In countries like Spain, the extent of accommodation of dietary practices is rather limited: the general practice is to offer menus without pork meat. In other cases, the accommodation of religious requirements goes to a deeper degree, as is the case for food provision in Austrian and Belgian prisons, where Jewish inmates receive *kosher* food prepared outside of prison by the Jewish community institutions. However, the fact that a country is less accommodating regarding certain practices does not imply that it is less accommodative in general. For example, in some prisons in Catalonia (Spain), a learning process has led to a rather open organisation and celebration of Ramadan, with special sweets coming from the Moroccan consulate and the possibility of inmates praying and eating together during the night.

Not a predominant trend, but still relevant to mention, is the increase in the presence of "spiritual" practices and alternative forms of religion, such as in the case of Switzerland, or as has already been shown by others in Spain (Griera 2017; Griera and Clot-Garrell 2015). Other forms of religious innovation are also to be found in the cases presented in this book. In the Swedish prison system, for example, the *Monastery* silent retreat could be considered to be one such change.

Another common trend observed across European prison systems is the increased securitisation of religions, and in particular Islam. This development, mostly observed since 9/11, entails suspicion against religion as well as harsher measures against certain collective practices of Islam, for example. The case of France is paradigmatic, but in most countries throughout Europe securitisation of Islam has meant a more restrictive or, at least, more interventionist control of religious expressions in prisons. Interestingly, securitisation has also translated in some cases into attempts to institutionalise, and therefore control, Islamic chaplaincy. The cases of France, Spain or Austria are examples of this development.

All in all, the chapters in this book display different trends, some of them widely shared, others present only in certain regions or countries. What they all show is that prisons are changing institutional environments where the presence and management of religion is not static. Next to historical arrangement, new developments take place, which leaves the door open to new questions and inquiries.

Acknowledgements The editors of this book would like to thank all the authors, particularly those who made extra effort and conducted research explicitly for this book when no research had been done in their countries before. We are also grateful to the external reviewers, series editors and the Springer personnel for making this project possible, and Roos Feringa for her technical assistance.

References

Agadjanian, A. (2006). The search for privacy and the return of a grand narrative: Religion in a post-communist society. *Social Compass, 53*(2), 169–184.

Ajouaou, M., & Bernts, T. (2015). Imams and inmates: Is Islamic prison chaplaincy in the Netherlands a case of religious adaptation or of contextualization? *International Journal of Politics, Culture, and Society, 28*(1), 51–65.

Becci, I. (2013). *Imprisoned religion: Transformations of religion during and after imprisonment in Eastern Germany*. Surrey: Ashgate Publishing, Ltd.

Becci, I. (2014). Institutional resistance to religious diversity in prisons: Comparative reflections based on studies in Eastern Germany, Italy and Switzerland. *International Journal of Politics, Culture, and Society, 28*(1), 5–19.

Becci, I., & Roy, O. (2015). *Religious diversity in European prisons: Challenges and implications for rehabilitation*. Cham: Springer.

Beckford, J. A. (2001). Doing time: Space, time, religious diversity and the sacred in prisons. *International Review of Sociology, 11*(3), 371–382.

Beckford, J. A. (2005). Muslims in the prisons of Britain and France. *Journal of Contemporary European Studies, 13*(3), 287–297.

Beckford, J., & Gilliat, S. (1998). *Religion in prison: 'Equal Rites' in a multi-faith society.* Cambridge: Cambridge University Press.

Beckford, J. A., & Gilliat, S. (2005). *Religion in prison: 'Equal Rites' in a multi-faith society.* Cambridge: Cambridge University Press.

Béraud, C., de Galembert, C., & Rostaing, C. (2016). *De la religion en prison.* Rennes: Presses Universitaires de Rennes.

Bertossi, C., & Bowen, J. R. (2014). Practical schemas, conjunctures, and social locations: Laïcité in French schools and hospitals. In J. R. Bowen, C. Bertossi, J. W. Duyvendak, & M. L. Krook (Eds.), *European States and their Muslim Citizens* (pp. 104–132). New York: Cambridge University Press.

Cadge, W., Griera, M., Lucken, K., & Michalowski, I. (2017). Religion in public institutions: Comparative perspectives from the United States, the United Kingdom, and Europe. *Journal for the Scientific Study of Religion, 56*(2), 226–233.

Ferrari, S. (1995). Emerging pattern of church and state in Western Europe: The Italian model. *Brigham Young University Law Review, 2,* 421–437.

Froese, P. (2004). After atheism: An analysis of religious monopolies in the post-communist world. *Sociology of Religion, 65*(1), 57–75.

Furseth, I., & Kühle, L. A. (2011). Prison chaplaincy from a Scandinavian perspective. *Archives de Sciences Sociales des Religions, 153,* 123–141.

Griera. (2017). Yoga in penitentiary settings: Transcendence, spirituality, and self-improvement. *Human Studies, 40*(1), 77–100.

Griera, M., & Clot-Garrell, A. (2015). Doing yoga behind bars: A sociological study of the growth of holistic spirituality in penitentiary institutions. In I. Becci & O. Roy (Eds.), *Religious diversity in European prisons* (pp. 141–157). Cham: Springer.

Griera, M., & Martínez-Ariño, J. (2014). The accommodation of religious diversity in prisons and hospitals in Spain. *RECODE Working Papers, 28,* 1–13.

Hamplová, D., & Nešpor, Z. R. (2009). Invisible religion in a "non-believing" country: The case of the Czech Republic. *Social Compass, 56*(4), 581–597.

Humphrey, M. (2009). Securitisation and domestication of diaspora Muslims and Islam: Turkish immigrants in Germany and Australia. *Turks Abroad: Settlers, Citizens, Transnationals, 11*(2), 136–154.

Joly, D., & Beckford, J. (2006). "Race" relations and discrimination in prison. *Journal of Immigrant & Refugee Studies, 4*(2), 1–30.

Laurence, J. (2006). Managing transnational Islam: Muslims and the state in Western Europe. In C. A. Parsons & T. M. Smeeding (Eds.), *Immigration and the Transformation of Europe* (pp. 251–273). Cambridge: Cambridge University Press.

Lužný, D., & Navrátilová, J. (2001). Religion and secularisation in the Czech Republic. *Czech Sociological Review, 9*(1), 85–98.

Madeley, J. (2003). A framework for the comparative analysis of church–State relations in Europe. *West European Politics, 26*(1), 23–50.

Müller, T., & Neundorf, A. (2012). The role of the state in the repression and revival of religiosity in Central Eastern Europe. *Social Forces, 91*(2), 559–582.

Sullivan, W. F., & Beaman, L. G. (Eds.). (2013). *Varieties of Religious Establishment.* London/New York: Routledge.

Sunier, T. (2014). Domesticating Islam: Exploring academic knowledge production on Islam and Muslims in European societies. *Ethnic and Racial Studies, 37*(6), 1138–1155.

Thornton, P. H., Ocasio, W., & Lounsbury, M. (2012). *The institutional logics perspective: A new approach to culture, structure, and process.* Oxford: Oxford University Press.

Tomka, M. (1995). The changing social role of religion in Eastern and Central Europe: Religion's revival and its contradictions. *Social Compass, 42*(1), 17–26.

Willaime, J.-P. (2009). European integration, laïcité and religion. *Religion, State & Society, 37*(1–2), 23–35.

Chapter 2
Austria: Management of Religious Diversity in Prisons

Wolfram Reiss

Abstract The management of religious diversity in correctional services in Austria is currently in the process of a complete overhaul and reorganisation. This chapter displays the current efforts as well as the first results of the development of a new national strategy concerning the management of religious diversity and prison chaplaincy within correctional services in Austria. For a better understanding of the current developments, the chapter starts with an overview of the legal regulations concerning individual freedom of worship and collective rights of religious communities for prison chaplaincy, the current status of religious diversity and the organisation of prison chaplaincy and religious counselling by the legally recognised churches and religious organisations in Austria. Finally, it shows the first results and conclusions of the national revision concerning the management of religious diversity within correctional services in Austria.

2.1 General and Legal Regulations for Correctional Services in Austria

In Austria, the administration of custodial sanctions and the measures of involuntary forensic placements are understood as modern and caring correctional services based on European standards as set forth in the Recommendation of the Council of Europe on European Prison Rules (2006). On average, the 27 Austrian prisons and their 13 outposts have detained 8800 persons over the last few years. Prisoners are divided into three different groups: remand prisoners, convicts and persons in precautionary forensic measures (Federal Ministry of Justice 2016). The key provision of the Act on Imprisonment (*Strafvollzugsgesetz, StVG,* 1969) is section 20 (1): According to this provision, the enforcement of a prison sentence is meant "to assist prisoners in acquiring an honest approach to life that is adapted to the requirements of society,

W. Reiss (✉)
Faculty of Protestant Theology, University of Vienna, Vienna, Austria
e-mail: wolfram.reiss@univie.ac.at

© Springer Nature Switzerland AG 2020
J. Martínez-Ariño, A.-L. Zwilling (eds.), *Religion and Prison: An Overview of Contemporary Europe*, Boundaries of Religious Freedom: Regulating Religion in Diverse Societies 7, https://doi.org/10.1007/978-3-030-36834-0_2

and prevent them from pursuing criminal leanings. Moreover, the enforcement of such sentence is to show the negative value of the conduct underlying the conviction". To achieve these aims, prisoners "are to be locked away from the outside world, to be subjected to other restrictions in their lifestyle and to be influenced by educational measures".

All correctional measures are aimed at (re-) integrating prisoners into society. This can only be successful if each prisoner receives individual support and treatment. Concerning prison sentences lasting more than 18 months, these rehabilitative measures are laid down in the so-called correctional implementation plans (*Strafvollzugspläne*). These plans structure the time in prison and set forth the stages and objectives until release. They are flexible and can be adapted to changes concerning the development of the prisoner at any time (Federal Ministry of Justice 2016). To achieve these aims of reintegrating prisoners into society, a wide range of measures and therapies is offered within the correctional services. These rehabilitative measures and therapies include all forms of influence on prisoners as well as all activities that help to realise the desired aim. The measures differ from one federal state to the other as well as from institution to institution. They depend on the character and size of the institution, and on the persons involved. The rehabilitative measures include different areas such as work,[1] leisure-time activities,[2] schooling and education,[3] therapies,[4] medical treatment, relaxing conditions of imprisonment, development of external contacts and preparation for the release from prison.

---

[1] In Austria, prisoners are obligated to work. This obligation is mentioned in § 44 StVG. In § 45 StVG the state pledges to offer working possibilities.

[2] The term leisure time in the context of correctional services is used for the time of the day that is not work time. As already mentioned above, there is a work obligation for prisoners, but there is no legal claim to work or take part in any activities. That is why only 40–50% of the prisoners have the possibility of working. Furthermore, anyone who cannot work or take part in other therapies or leisure-time activities is forced to be idle in his or her prison cell. In that sense, a ban on working or on taking part in therapies is sometimes used as a disciplinary measure. The legal provisions concerning the occupation of prisoners during leisure time are written in § 58 StVG. In most of the penal institutions, sports programmes offer a wide range of possibilities concerning leisure-time activities. Still, most prisoners spend their leisure time watching TV and playing video games. From the penal system point of view, group activities within the chaplaincy of religious groups are seen as a part of the leisure-time or recreational-time activities.

[3] Especially for younger prisoners and inmates, the educational opportunities within the penal institution are of very high importance. These opportunities can range from learning German to schooling and vocational training, as well as academic studies. The possibilities concerning education differ from institution to institution; the legal provisions are based on § 48 StVG and § 57 StVG.

[4] The treatments can be psycho-educative and/or psychotherapeutic. They offer examinations concerning one's own personality, one's behaviour in life and society, one's offence, as well as interventions during crises. They can take place in forms of individual or group therapies, only for a short and restricted period of time, or on a longer-term basis. The main aims of these treatments are, on the one hand, to stabilise the prisoner and, on the other hand, to have a deepened understanding concerning actions and conflicts, as well as an insight into the process, the reasons and the consequences of one's own acts. The long-term aim is to enable prisoners to live an unpunished life with social responsibility. The different therapies offered are based on depth psychology and cognitive and behavioural therapies, as well as on clinical-sexological and trauma-therapeutical knowledge and methods.

Some therapies and measures are offered by social workers, psychologists and chaplains that have permanent employment or appointment at the institution; others are offered by external suppliers or volunteers. Successful participation in some of the therapies and rehabilitative measures has an influence on the correctional implementation plan. It can influence the appraisal as well as the permission for conditional releases from prison. Other forms of rehabilitative measures are optional possibilities that should help the prisoner to spend the time in the correctional service in a structured and reasonable way. These other forms of measures usually include, in addition to work and different leisure-time activities, religious care.

2.2   Religious Diversity in Prison

As in other states and public institutions, the multi-religiosity and multi-culturalism of Austrian society are reflected in the institutions of the penal system. In many prisons, the number of inmates with a migration background as well as diverse religious and cultural backgrounds is higher than among the general population. At present, inmates are categorised according to the left column of Table 2.1 by their different religious denominations. It is striking that the Austrian system of categorisation of religious communities is neither applied nor based on the academic categorisation of the science of religions. They were developed by chance by wards responsible for entrance recording. Because of this, blurred categorisations are being used,[5] and some of the legally recognised or registered religious communities are missing. For example, the Oriental-Orthodox Churches are not included, even though the Armenian Apostolic Church has had the status of a legally recognised church since 1972.

If the religions and denominations are summarised according to confessional groups, the following statement can be made: most prisoners (43.27%) belong to the Catholic Church, followed by Muslim prisoners (23.65%), prisoners with no religious affiliation (15.74%) and Orthodox prisoners (13.86%). The next groups with a much smaller number of prisoners are the group of traditional Reformed Churches (2.93%) followed by Buddhists, Jews and Sikhs, each of which represent less than 1% of all prisoners. At the end of the list, the affiliates of new religious movements that developed within Christian or Islamic contexts, Hindus, as well as independent Churches are mentioned, with each less than 0.1%. However, it is most likely that these statistics are not correct, as members of the Oriental-Orthodox Churches (such as the Syrian-Orthodox, the Coptic-Orthodox and the Armenian Apostolic Church) that are not mentioned as a separate group within the statistics are probably being

---

[5]The alternatives to choose between being a "Muslim", a "Sunnite" or a "Schiite" is as absurd as the alternatives "Serbian-Orthodox", "Russian-Orthodox", "Greek-Orthodox" or "Orthodox". Additionally, the choice of being a "Baptist" or "Freichrist" is misleading, as Baptists are one of five religious denominations that united to be legally recognised as *"Freikirchen in Österreich"* ("Free Churches in Austria").

Table 2.1 Religious affiliation of prisoners in Austria categorised by denomination

Denomination	Number	Confessional group	Number	Percentage
Roman Catholic	3780	Catholic Christians	3781	43.28%
Greek-Catholic	1			
Muslim	2049	Muslims	2066	23.65%
Muslim–Shia (Islam)	11			
Muslim–Sunni (Islam)	6			
No religious affiliation	888	Non-religious	1375	15.74%
Not specified	331			
Unknown	156			
Orthodox	700	Orthodox Christians	1212	13.87%
Serbian-Orthodox	424			
Russian-Orthodox	58			
Greek-Orthodox	30			
Protestant–Augsburg Confession	196	Christians of Reformed Churches	209	2.39%
Protestant–Helvetic Confession	7			
Old Catholic	6			
Buddhist	27	Buddhists (different traditions)	27	0.30%
Sikh	19	Sikhs	19	0.21
Mosaic	17	Jews	17	0.19%
Yezidi	6	Affiliates of other religious denominations	30	0.34%
Adventist	5			
Hindu	5			
Jehovah's Witness	4			
Freichrist (member of an independent Christian Church)	4			
Baptist	3			
Alevi	2			
Sinti	1			
Total	**8736**		**8736**	**100%**

The statistics in columns 1–2 are based on data that have been provided by the director of the penitentiary academy. It displays the status as of 20 February 2017, and is based on the information collected during entrance registration in the penal institutions. Columns 3–5 were created by the author

counted as affiliates to the Catholic or Orthodox Churches. Furthermore, affiliates to Pentecostal or independent Churches from Africa, Asia or Latin America are probably being subsumed under the Protestant Churches. Additionally, Alevites or Yezidis may be categorised as Muslims if they request food without pork.[6]

---

[6] Many of the inaccuracies Unterberger (2013) observed in the registration of the largest correction institution JA Josefstadt in Vienna (Cf. Reiss 2010a).

2.3   Legal Principles Concerning the Practice of Religion in the Penal System

The right to practise religion in prison is based on two pillars. One pillar is the individual right of the inmate; the second pillar is the collective right of (some of) the legally recognised religious communities concerning religious services for affiliates in penal institutions. The individual's right to practise religion in penal institutions is regulated in §85 StVG:

1. Every prisoner has the right to attend services or other religious events and to receive sacraments. He has the right to communicate with a pastoral counsellor (*Seelsorger*) who is appointed in or admitted to the institution. [...]
2. If a prisoner is honestly demanding permission for a visit by a pastoral counsellor who is not appointed or admitted to the institution, this also has to be given. The governor of the institution takes the decision.
3. If the prisoner asks for pastoral care from a counsellor who is not permanently appointed or admitted to the penal institution, the prison governor is obliged to do his best to search for a pastoral counsellor from the relevant religious community and provide contact with the prisoner for pastoral care. Permission of a pastoral visit has to be given to such an counsellor.
4. Prisoners are allowed to receive pastoral counsellors outside visiting hours during office hours. The topics discussed between the prisoner and the pastoral counsellor are not to be monitored.

The prisoner has the right to attend services and other religious events that take place within the penal institution, as long as no threats to security are identified. The law distinguishes between "appointed" and "admitted" as well as "external" spiritual advisers. This distinction is due to the legal status and the attached rights of the religious communities. Legally recognised churches and religious associations have the right to send pastoral counsellors into state-owned institutions. They can "appoint" pastoral counsellors in either full-time or part-time positions, or include pastoral services in penal institutions within the framework of parish work. In the case of the Catholic Church, this service is paid for by the state and in the case of some recognised religious communities a lump sum is paid to the religious ministry. Most religious communities do not get any reimbursement for their services. Pastoral counsellors that have an "admitted" status in a penal institution are allowed to visit prisoners, if a prisoner is asking for pastoral or spiritual care, without an additional check. Further "external" religious counsellors can be allowed as visitors by the institution, based on an individual decision if the prisoner is asking for it.

The collective rights of six (out of 16) legally recognised religious communities in Austria concerning pastoral care in penal institutions are regulated by six specific laws, which define the general relationship between the state and the religious community (Potz and Schinkele 2016):

1. The Concordat of 1933 between the Holy See and the Austrian Republic,[7] complemented by Supplementary Treaties in the 1960s (*Concordat*).
2. The Federal Act of 1961 on the external legal relationship of the Protestant Church in Austria (*Protestantengesetz*).[8]
3. The Federal Act of 1967 on the external legal relationship of the Greek-Oriental Church in Austria (*Orthodoxengesetz*),[9] as amended in 2011.
4. The Federal Act of 2003 on the external legal relationships of the Oriental-Orthodox Churches in Austria (*Orientalisch-Orthodoxes Kirchengesetz*).[10]
5. The Federal Act of 1890 on the external legal relationship of the Israelite Religious Society (*Israelitengesetz*),[11] as amended in 2012.
6. The Federal Act on the external legal relationships of Islamic Religious Societies 2015 (*Islamgesetz*), replacing the *Islamgesetz 1912*.

Article XVI of the Concordat regulates that the local priest or chaplain has free access to the prisoners if an institutional chaplaincy is not permanently established. Furthermore, Article XVIII states that clerics cannot be asked by courts or other authorities to reveal information about people or things they have received under the seal of official clerical secrecy. This implies not only the obligation to confidentiality, but also the right to refuse to give evidence in court. However, this is only applied explicitly for clergymen.

A similar regulation can be found in the Federal Act of 1961 on the external legal relationship of the Protestant Church in Austria (*Protestantengesetz*). It guarantees pastoral care in the armed forces (§17), in public hospitals and healthcare institutions (§18) as well as in prison (§19):

1. The state has to guarantee the practice of pastoral counselling to Protestant persons in prison by the Protestant Church.
2. As far as a Protestant chaplaincy in prison is established, only clergymen (*geistliche Amtsträger*) that have been appointed in a written document by the Protestant Church can become chaplains in prison. […]

As to religious care in penal institutions, the regulations with regard to the right of confidentiality and the right to refuse to testify in courts are explicitly restricted to clerics (*geistliche Amtsträger*) who were ordained for ecclesiastical ministry. In contrast to the Protestant pastoral care in the armed forces, for which the state has to provide the personnel costs as well as the material costs according to §17 (1),

---

[7] Not only is the Roman-Catholic Church included here but also the following Oriental Catholic or Uniate Churches: the Greek-Catholic and the Armenian-Catholic Church.

[8] Both the Lutheran and the Calvinist Churches in Austria are included.

[9] The Greek-Oriental Churches in Austria include the Greek-Orthodox Church, the Serbian Orthodox Church, the Romanian Orthodox Church, the Russian Orthodox Church and the Bulgarian Orthodox Church.

[10] This includes the Armenian-Apostolic Church, the Syrian-Orthodox Church and the Coptic-Orthodox Church.

[11] Orthodox and Liberal Jewish congregations are included in this Act.

financial support is not mentioned in the legal text. The obligation of confidentiality is regulated in §11:

1. Clerics (*geistliche Amtsträger*) of the Protestant Church shall not be asked to circulate information as witnesses [to courts or other authorities] if they accessed that information during a confession or under the pledge of secrecy.

As to religious care in state institutions, §7 of the *Orthodoxengesetz* refers directly to the *Protestantengesetz*, meaning that the regulations in §11 of the *Protestantengesetz* concerning the pledge of secrecy, as well as in §17–19, concerning pastoral care in the armed forces, in public hospitals, healthcare institutions and in prison, are also valid for Orthodox Churches. A similar wording can be found in §3 of the *Orientalisch-Orthodoxes Kirchengesetz*, which also explicitly applies the rules of the *Protestantengesetz*.

The right to "religious care"[12] for Jews is regulated in §8 of the *Israelitengesetz* of 1890. This is the oldest legal text concerning religious care in prison in Austria that is still valid. Similar to the regulations for the Protestant and the Orthodox Churches, the state guarantees the financing of personnel and material costs for military chaplaincy. Concerning the pledge of secrecy, the regulations for rabbis are similar to those in the *Protestantengesetz* and in the *Orthodoxengesetz*, apart from the fact that there is no concept and ritual of confession in Judaism.[13] Furthermore, the religious dietary laws for Jews have to be considered within state institutions (§12).

Similar formulations can be found in the recently amended *Islamgesetz* 2015, which guarantees religious services in state-owned institutions for Muslims (§11) and Muslim-Alevis (§19). Just as in the *Israelitengesetz*, the state guarantees to cover the costs for both personnel and material only with regard to military chaplaincy.[14] Religious dietary laws also have to be respected within the institutions and §26 guarantees the obligation of confidentiality as well as the right to refuse to give testimony for "religious function owners" (*Religiöse Funktionsträger*) of the Islamic and Islamic-Alevi religious community.[15] Although in both communities neither a

---

[12] The laws concerning Christian chaplaincy always use the term "*Seelsorge*" (literally: "care for souls"), which is a very specific Christian term traditionally associated with an ordained priest who speaks with penitents under the seal of penance. Here, the term "*religiöse Betreuung*' ("religious care") is used to avoid the Christian term "*Seelsorge*".

[13] However, rabbis of all modern Jewish religious movements from Reform to Orthodox have the tradition of an ordination (*Smikha*), which entitles persons after several years of rabbinic studies to give advice or judgement in Jewish law (Levitas et al. 2007).

[14] Although there is a legal distinction between reimbursing costs of military chaplaincy and chaplaincy in other institutions, the state does not cover the personal and material costs of Orthodox and Islamic military chaplaincy. The Orthodox, Islamic and Islamic-Alevite communities receive only a small annual lump sum, which does not cover costs (Reiss 2017, 125–129).

[15] There are two Alevi communities in Austria: the "Islamic-Alevi Community" consider themselves to be a branch of Islam. It has had the status of a legally recognised religious community since 22 May 2013. The other Alevi community considers themselves to be an independent religion. They have the status of a state - registered religious community, which had to register as "Old Alevite Community", as the name "Islamic" is protected by law. It does not have the right to chaplaincy in state institutions regulated in the Islamic law of 2015.

rite of confession nor the status of clerics exists, and although there are no clear regulations concerning conditions for a person to claim to be an Imam, the regulations concerning priests, pastors and rabbis are transferred to "religious functions owners" – a term that does not exist in these two religions.

Concerning the other legally recognised churches, and religious associations with public-law status, such as the Methodist Church, the Old Catholic Church, the Free Churches (*Freikirchen*),[16] the Jehovah's witnesses, the Church of Jesus Christ of Latter-day Saints, the New Apostolic Church and the state-registered religious communities[17] in Austria, there have been – so far – no laws and regulations concerning religious and spiritual care in prison or other state or public institutions. Therefore, these religious communities cannot offer religious care in penal institutions in a proactive approach. They can only apply for pastoral visits if inmates explicitly request one.[18]

---

[16] The term *"Freikirchen"* includes five different religious groups: Baptists, Union of Evangelical communities, ELAIA community, Free Christian and Pentecostal churches and Mennonites; it has been a legally recognised church and religious society with public-law status since 2013.

[17] At the moment, eight religious communities have this status: the Old-Alevite community in Austria, the Baha'i, the Christian community, the Hindu, the Shia Muslims, the Seventh-Day Adventist Church, the Pentecostal Church "Community of God" and the Unification Church. Religious groups in Austria are legally divided into three categories: (a) legally recognised churches and religious societies; (b) state-registered religious confessional communities; and (c) clubs/associations (*Vereine*). Religious communities that belong to the first category have the right to provide religious instruction in public schools financed by the state, and to establish a chaplaincy in state institutions. They receive protection against the secularisation of all institutions (transformation of a society from close affiliation with religious values and institutions towards non-religious values and secular institutions), the right to establish private schools and the guarantee of the state of independent administration of all internal affairs. The 1998 Law on the Status of Confessional Communities (*Bekenntnisgemeinschaftengesetz*) imposed new criteria on religious groups to achieve the status of legally recognised church and religious society, although it allowed previously acknowledged societies to retain their status. New criteria included a 20-year period of existence (at least 10 of which must be as a group incorporated as a confessional community under the 1998 law) and membership equalling at least 0.2% of the country's population (approximately 16,000 persons). State-registered religious confessional communities can apply for the status of a legally recognised church and religious society if they have at least 300 members; they must submit to the government their written statutes describing the goals, rights and obligations of members, as well as membership regulations, officials and financing. The community also has to submit a written version of their doctrines, which must differ from that of any religious group previously recognised. Religious groups that do not qualify for either legally recognised church and religious society or state-registered religious confessional community status may apply to become associations under the Law on Associations (*Vereinsgesetz*; similar to sports or cultural associations). Registered associations are corporations under law and have many of the same rights as state-registered religious confessional communities. The difference is mainly that they cannot apply for the status of a legally recognised church and religious society (Hirnsperger et al. 2001).

[18] However, it is a fact that inmates often do not know about this right. Also, the governors of penal institutions often do not know whom to address with regard to the religious care of religious communities who do not have the status of appointed or admitted religious counsellors.

2.4   Organisation of Religious Chaplaincy[19] for Inmates[20]

2.4.1   Catholic Chaplaincy

From the sixteenth to the nineteenth century, the Austro-Hungarian Monarchy was a stronghold of the Roman Catholic Church in Europe. The edicts of tolerance issued by Joseph II of Austria (1741–1790; r. 1765–1790) in the second half of the eighteenth century allowed for the end of discrimination against religious minorities in the Habsburg Empire. At first, the edict of 13 October 1781 officially enabled the free exercise of religion for both the Protestant Churches of the Augsburg and Helvetic Confessions recognised in the Treaty of Westphalia (1648) as well as the Orthodox churches, albeit with certain restrictions that were only gradually dissolved in the nineteenth and twentieth centuries. On 2 January 1782, an edict of tolerance was issued for Jews (in Lower Austria), thus initiating the process of Jewish emancipation. Jews were allowed to establish schools and to attend universities. They were allowed to engage in professions that had been previously forbidden to Jews and could establish factories. The occupation and later annexation of Bosnia-Herzegovina entailed the incorporation of numerous Muslim and Serbian Orthodox subjects. It was within this framework, that the first laws concerning Protestants, Orthodox, Jews and Muslims were issued. They also concerned military, hospital and prison chaplaincy. However, the historical dominance of the

---

[19] The common term for religious care in German is "*Seelsorge*" (literally translated as "cure or of souls"), and many legal texts in this context speak of "*Seelsorger*" (literally: "curators of the souls") or clergyman (*geistliche Amtsträger*). There is an ongoing debate on whether this term should be used only for Christian denominations with ordained priests and pastors focussing on personal communication, or if it should be expanded to any person authorised by religious communities, even if they do not have clergymen and if they focus more on dietary instruction, evangelisation, religious instruction, missions or meditation. Some suggest using the term "religious care" (*religiöse Betreuung*), "religious counselling" or "religious companionship" (*Religiöse Begleitung*) instead of "chaplaincy" or "pastoral care (*Seelsorge*)" for non-Christian communities. However, in Austrian penal practice, all religious actors are normally called "*Seelsorger*" ("curators of souls"), even if they deny the existence of a soul, like Buddhists, for example. It seems that this transfer of a specific Christian term to non-Christian communities is a similar phenomenon to what happened with "chaplaincy", which was also originally a specific term of a clerical office in the Catholic Church. The author advocates for the terminology "religious care" or "religious companionship" for non-Christian counselling to avoid transfers associated with specific Christian concepts (difference between clergymen and laymen, the rite of the confession, which does not exist in non-Christian religious communities). However, recognising the fact that non-Christian actors are mostly called in penal systems "*Seelsorger*", the term "chaplain"/"chaplaincy" is used here as a translation for "*Seelsorger*"/"*Seelsorge*".

[20] The information provided in this part of the chapter is based mainly on information given by prison chaplains. I have to thank Drs. Christian Kuhn and Joseph Riedl (Catholic Chaplaincy), Drs. Matthias Geist and Markus Fellinger (Protestant Chaplaincy), Ramadan Demir (Islamic Chaplaincy), Gerhard Kisslinger (Chaplaincy of Free Churches), Shlomo Hofmeister (Jewish Chaplaincy), Stefanus Fellinger (Chaplaincy of Jehovah's Witnesses), and Andreas Hagn and Jule Thug (Buddhist Chaplaincy). Also, I have to thank Robert Wurzrainer, who supported me immensely in the collection and translation of this chapter.

Roman-Catholic Church is still reflected in existing structures and financial support by the state.

In all prisons in Austria, there are established permanent Catholic chaplaincies with at least one prison chaplain. In most of the prisons, offices and chapels exist, where Catholic liturgies can be performed periodically, in most cases on a weekly basis. Especially in new correctional institutions, Catholic chaplains have to use multifunctional rooms, which is an unsatisfying solution from the perspective of the priests. 6.5 positions for Catholic prison chaplains are paid for by the government. Some parish priests have contracts with correctional institutions for religious services in addition to their work in the parish for 2–5 h a week, and at least one person for 20 h.[21] Moreover, the Catholic Church covers the salaries of several full-time prison chaplains and two social workers in follow-up programmes after release, as well as the main costs of materials. There are three Jesuits who serve as volunteering prison chaplains without payment. Not all chaplains are clerics. Some are pastoral assistants (who have studied theology like priests, but have not been ordained as priests). The Catholic Church authorises Catholic chaplains in correspondence with the Ministry of Justice. They are under the supervision of the diocesan bishop. Concerning their work in prison, they are subordinated to the regulations of the correctional institution. In addition, there are Catholic laymen who engage in personal visits with inmates. In Graz alone, there are about 30 laymen involved in this service.[22] Since the end of the 1970s, the Catholic Church has run a home and eight care places in managed apartments for 40 ex-prisoners in Vienna and a counselling centre for reintegration into society (*Verein für Integrationshilfe* 2015). This historically grown structure and manpower allow permanent professional religious care in penal institutions that cannot be compared with the service of any other religious community.

The Catholic chaplaincy is seen as an offer for prisoners, their relatives, as well as for people working in the penal institution. In the chaplains, prisoners can find dialogue partners to talk about personal problems as well as to challenge feelings of isolation in prison. The Catholic chaplaincy focusses on several aspects concerning life and crises: to find out one's own resources and possibilities, to reflect upon relationships with others, to talk about conflicts and develop new perspectives and new orientations, as well as to obtain support during personal crises in the case of illness and death of relatives or friends or concerning new relationships and break-ups. The Catholic chaplaincy implies the biblical thought that any person, even a person who has committed a crime and behaved "sinfully" against people or society, is accepted by God and therefore has a chance of a new beginning. In that sense, the

---

[21] With an estimated salary of €50,000 for a full position, this means that the Catholic Church receives an annual support by state for prison chaplaincy of about €350,000–400,000 per annum.

[22] It is a point of discussion if pastoral assistants or Catholic volunteers have the same rights and duties with regard to the confidentiality and the refusal of witness before court as ordained priests. Dr. Christian Kuhn, pastoral assistant in JA Josefstadt (Vienna), holds the opinion that they have this right. Joseph Riedl (JA Graz) thinks that the law guarantees this right only for the content that is revealed in the sacramental rite of confession.

Catholic chaplaincy not only preaches and talks about these thoughts, but tries to actively bring the prisoners closer to this possibility by outright dialogue and social care (e.g. Reiss 2016a, b, c: 78f.)

The Catholic chaplaincy is open for ecumenical cooperation and for prisoners of any nation and religion or denomination. The concept of Catholic chaplaincy includes diverse activities such as the single supervision of prisoners as well as group supervision, dialogue with relatives in prison and outside of prison, church services, meditations, evening prayers, commemorations and funerals, introductory courses to the Christian faith in addition to musical activities. Educational courses include a wide range of themes. Other duties of the Catholic chaplaincy are public relations in church as well as in youth and adult groups and the support of people working in prisons. Furthermore, Catholic chaplains in prison are often seen as reliable experts concerning religious as well as cultural questions and problems, even though they often do not have a special education or expertise in that area (e.g. Reiss 2016a, b, c: 79).

2.4.2   Protestant Chaplaincy

The edict of 13 October 1781 officially enabled the free exercise of religion for the Protestant Churches of the Augsburg and Helvetic Confessions. In 1861, both Protestant churches became legally accepted as a corporation that opened the way to establishing equality with the Catholic Church. Finally, the Federal Act of 1961 on the external legal relationship of the Protestant Church in Austria (*Protestantengesetz*) allowed the establishment of rules for the chaplaincy in prison.

The self-conception of the Protestant chaplaincy is in many aspects similar to that of the Catholic chaplaincy. However, the Protestant chaplaincy places stronger emphasis on the idea that every person is accepted by God and has the chance to change his/her life. This is based on the basic theological concept of justification, which is considered a singular act in which God declares an unrighteous individual to be righteous through Christ's atoning sacrifice alone. Justification is granted to all who exercise faith as a gift from God. The change of life is not seen as a precondition, but as a consequence of faith. Many of the activities, groups and social work carried out by the Protestants are similar to what is done in the Catholic chaplaincy. The Protestant chaplaincy emphasises that it is a religious service not only for prisoners but also for all persons involved with correctional institutions: prisoners and their relatives and families, ex-prisoners, wards, social workers, psychologists, department managers, up to the management team of the correctional institutions. It is understood as professional spiritual and social accompaniment for people who live and work in prison through the cooperation of the state and the Protestant Church. People working in the Protestant prison chaplaincy are authorised by the Protestant Church and approved by the Ministry of Justice. The companionship consists of church services that are open to all prisoners of any confession, religion or *Weltanschauung*, including atheists or agnostics. For example, Protestant chaplains care for African prisoners who are members of Pentecostal or independent churches in Africa. Muslim Friday prayers and gatherings were performed in the multifunctional Protestant chapel in JA Josefstadt before an Islamic prayer room was established in a cellar. Ecumenical and interreligious teamwork is a basic asset. Furthermore, Protestant chaplains offer – for prisoners as well as for people working in prison – individual conversation and dialogue on all relevant topics in the penal institution. This kind of companionship from a Protestant perspective sees the person as a whole and does not reduce the person to his/her status within the institution. These conversations are bound to strict secrecy and have, in contrast to therapeutic conversation, no influence on the correctional implementation plan.

The primary method of Protestant chaplaincy is based on an appreciating approach and active listening of any person, without distinction of status. The whole person and personality is within the dialogue's focus. Owing to this understanding of the chaplaincy, the Protestant chaplaincy strictly refrains from imposing any doctrines and dogmas. However, it offers Bible reading groups or other group sessions for those interested and tries to support people concerning the development of relationships inside and outside the institution. One of the main emphases of the Protestant chaplaincy is encouraging and aiding education by encouraging the prisoners to rediscover their skills and talents and to find possibilities to develop those skills and talents through formation and education (*ARGE Evangelische Gefängnisseelsorge Österreich* 2015).

People working as Protestant chaplains are chosen, among other criteria, on the basis of their theological education and qualifications, as well as their communication skills and competences, which are essential for working in the chaplaincy. The majority of Protestant chaplains are ordained pastors. There is one full-time position for a prison chaplain in JA Josefstadt, and another prison chaplain in a 70% position serving in different correctional institutions, both paid by the Protestant Church. Fifteen are in active church ministries and fulfil prison chaplaincy in addition to their parish work. Individual contracts between correctional institutions and Protestant pastors do not exist. Nine serve as volunteers: two have already retired, others are lectors or community workers in the Protestant Church. Protestant church services are currently possible in 19 penal institutions. Protestants have a private chapel only in JA Josefstadt. In other correctional institutions, the services are performed in multifunctional halls or in the Catholic chapel. Protestant chaplains have their own offices in three prisons. In a general contract between the Protestant Church and the Federal Ministry of Justice, it has been regulated that the Church appoints only clerics (*kirchliche Amtsträger*) and that they all participate in a one-day introductory course in the penal institutions. As an honorarium for the services, an annual lump sum of 14,535€ was fixed in 2004. This was increased to 30,000€ in an amendment of the general contract in 2009. This budget will increase in the future according to the national consumer price index. In addition, the Church received in 2016 a one-off benefit of approximately 4000€ for the care of ex-prisoners, which means that personnel and material costs are mainly covered by the Protestant Church.

2.4.3 *Orthodox Chaplaincy*

The legal principles for the Greek-Oriental Orthodox Churches[23] date back to the *Toleranzpatent* 1781, which explicitly mentions the "non-uniated" Greek Church, the Eastern Churches who are not in union with the Catholic Church. Nowadays, it includes the Greek-Orthodox, the Serbian-Orthodox, the Romanian-Orthodox, the Bulgarian-Orthodox and the Russian-Orthodox Churches.

Russians as well as Russian-speaking persons from the former Soviet Union are – at the moment – the ethnic group that seems to be the most difficult one concerning the integration within prison as an institution. This group also evokes major problems for questions concerning security and violence.[24] There does not seem to be any noticeable motivation from the Orthodox Church to offer religious chaplaincy in prison. This can be specified by the fact that compared with Catholics, Protestants and Muslims, only very few Orthodox priests offer pastoral care in prison. If they do go to see prisoners, these priests mostly have the status of a visitor. Worships are normally restricted to vespers, which can often be celebrated in the Catholic chapels. There are no consecrated altars and icons on prison compounds to celebrate the Orthodox liturgy, even though participation in the Eucharist is of central importance in the Orthodox understanding of religious practice.

This unsatisfying situation concerning the Orthodox Chaplaincy has been discussed by the Orthodox Episcopal Conference for some years now. One of the aims under discussion is to develop Orthodox prison chaplaincy in a similar manner to what is already established within military institutions. Furthermore, it is planned to develop a positive impact of Orthodox chaplaincy in a more international context. As Arsenios Kardamakis, the Greek-Orthodox Metropolitan of Austria, and exarch of Hungary and Middle Europe, pointed out, the Orthodox Episcopal Conference is a reliable partner in cooperation with the state, which already fulfils its duty, as an example, within religious education in schools as well as chaplaincy in healthcare.

Orthodox chaplains are mostly clerics who have studied Orthodox theology. Orthodox prison chaplaincy takes place in individual dialogue and in groups, especially when it comes to liturgical aspects of Orthodox religiosity. Concerning the individual conversations between prisoner and chaplain, the spiritual care and the support in different ways towards developing a personal relation with God are of high importance and one of the main aims. The key focus lies within spiritual

---

[23] The first Orthodox church to be recognised by the State in 1782 was called the "Greek-Oriental Church". Later, other churches belonging to the Orthodox Church family were included and also received official recognition (Serbian, Romanian, Russian, Bulgarian). In many legal texts, the ancient term "Greek-Oriental Church" is still used, although the term (Byzantine or Chalzedonian) Orthodox Church is more common.

[24] In many prisons, they dominate the (prohibited) trade of drugs and cell phones, establish mafia-like structures and an honour code of secrecy. Whoever violates the rules is severely punished. The use of the Russian language and the relatively large number of inmates speaking Russian create a closed community (Schmidt 2002; Hollenstein 2012; Heynisch and Verheyen 2010; Simoner 2010).

supervision in a theological sense. Furthermore, the question of how to deal with guilt and on how to reconcile with God, people and oneself is widely raised.

2.4.4   Jewish Chaplaincy

As there was still only a limited tolerance for Jews after the *Toleranzedikt* of 1782, the Basic Law (*Staatsgrundgesetz*) of 1867 finally accepted the Jewish people as equal citizens before the law. A few decades later, the "*Israelitengesetz*" (1890) put the relationship and interaction between the state and the different Jewish religious communities on a legal basis. Since then, these legal regulations have been valid.

The JA Josefstadt in Vienna has a special situation, as there is a prayer room with a Torah shrine for Jewish prisoners. However, it can rarely be used for ritual and collective prayer as there are not enough religious affiliates in the prison (a quorum of ten Jewish adults is needed for collective prayer). When the important Jewish religious rituals and ceremonies take place, Jewish prisoners from all Austrian prisons have the possibility of getting together and performing their rituals. Even though this possibility is not legally established, it is being exercised. Furthermore, the observation of religious dietary prescriptions concerning Jews is highly respected in Austrian prisons. As most of the kitchens in prison cannot follow strict rules concerning the *Kashrut*, it is regulated that the meals are delivered from outside the prison via the Jewish religious community. The food supply is paid for by the state. Furthermore, there are *kosher* products on shopping lists in the prison shops.

Jewish chaplaincy is mainly based on the Talmudic obligation (Shevuot 39a) of "all Jews being responsible for each other" (כל ישראל ערבים זה בזה). This phrase is the basis of the notion of communal responsibility in Jewish law in general, and it also applies to Jewish prisoners. If a Jew sees another Jew on the verge of sinning, he has an obligation to step in and help. Furthermore, it implies an obligation to all Jews to ensure that other Jews have their basic needs for food, clothing and shelter taken care of. Within the framework of correctional institutions, the first task of Jewish religious care, therefore, is to ensure that Jewish prisoners are permitted to practise their faith by providing the advocacy and religious materials to further that goal. This implies, first of all, the facilitation of the observance of Jewish dietary rules (*Kashrut*), which include complete abstinence from pork and any pork products, the separation of milk and meat, the observance of Shabbat and the possibility of performing individual daily prayers.

The services are directed to all those who are Jewish, without regard for the level of religious observance. However, the Jewish chaplaincy also considers its task to protect Jewish inmates against any kind of proselytism by other religious groups. According to the Jewish concept, God has created man with both good (*Yezer Ha-Tov*) and evil inclinations (*Yezer Ha-Ra*), the two powers or tendencies that pull him in opposite directions. God commands each man or woman to choose the good and right path over the evil and the human has the "ability to subdue the sin which crouches at the entrance of your heart" (Gen 4,7). Everybody has full responsibility for any sin he/she has committed, because God gave them power to overcome sin if they really wish to do so. The return to God and the observance of Jewish law and ethics is the main method of returning to the right path of the Jewish community and society in general. Jewish religious care calls for return (*teshuva*) to God and the observance of the commandments. It focusses on individual conversations with inmates, dealing with the observance of Jewish laws, and personal and social problems. It encourages arguing with God in times of crisis. A biblical example can be seen in the book of Job and the Psalms. This is seen as a difference compared with Christian or Muslim counselling. Sometimes, rabbinic stories of the haggadic Midrashim that display basic human and theological situations play a role in such conversations, besides referring to biblical texts and Talmudic concepts (Cf. Reiss 2010b).

2.4.5   Islamic Chaplaincy

The legal situation of Islam in Austria is very special in Europe, as this religion has been legally recognised since as early as 1912 and has the status of a recognised religious corporation like the Catholic or Protestant Church in Austria. On the basis of the law of recognition of Islam from 1912, a first contract between the Ministry of Justice and the Islamic community, which regulates Islamic religious care in correctional institutions, was concluded in 2010. In this contract, the Islamic community "agrees to commit themselves to cooperate in the religious care for Muslim prisoners, who demand for such religious care" Baghajati (2010). Imams are called "*Seelsorger*" (the same term as that used for Christian chaplains). A good command of the German language and an intermediate school-leaving certificate were fixed as the only binding conditions for the appointment of Islamic chaplains. The Islamic community has to guarantee that candidates obey all correctional and constitutional laws and affirm their commitment to the European Convention for the Protection of Human Rights and Fundamental Freedoms. Islamic *Seelsorger* are bound to maintain absolute confidentiality about any data and information they have learned in their service. Friday prayers and sermons on the occasion of feasts have to be in German, in contrast to the ritual prayer, which can be performed in Arabic. The ministry promised to strive to provide an office, a telephone line and a computer if resources were available (however, this was not fulfilled in most cases). If there are no special rooms already reserved permanently as prayer rooms (this is currently the case in three correctional institutions), the ministry has promised to provide multifunctional rooms for the performance of prayers. Muslim prisoners who fast during Ramadan should be accommodated in the same cells and should be provided with the possibility of heating food after sunset. It was recommended to deliver an annual report about the activities by the Islamic Community to the Ministry of Justice. As honorarium for these services, an annual lump sum of 15,320€ was fixed. Although the increase in this sum was connected with the national price index, this lump sum was increased by an amendment of the contract of 2014 to 20,320€, under the condition that an annual report is submitted before March every year. This sum is also used to fund the introductory course to volunteers offered by the correctional services. This sum has been paid to the Islamic community until the time of writing (April 2017).

In 2015, the 1912 law concerning the legal status of Islam has been revised comprehensively. Although the former regulations were only a contract between the Ministry of Justice and the Islamic community, the right of Islamic religious care in prison is now guaranteed by law (*Islamgesetz 2015*). The concept and the organisation of religious care for Muslim prisoners have drastically changed since then. Islamic religious care is starting to be integrated into penal institutions on an equal basis to that of Christian chaplaincies.

The "Association for the Promotion of Muslim Religious Care in Prison and Correctional Institutions in Austria" was founded. This association, which is linked to the Islamic Religious Community, claims that they have the exclusive right to organise religious care for Austrian Muslims in correctional institutions under the supervision of a general secretary.[25] One of the main aims of this association is to care for Muslim prisoners, to emphasise ethical values and religious education through knowledge transfer, as well as to promote communal life. Spirituality and the reintegration of prisoners into society are further aims that are being developed at present. Furthermore, interreligious cooperation between the different religious groups is supported. Skill enhancements for people working in Muslim religious care is another area in which this association is actively involved ("Islamische Glaubensgemeinschaft in Österreich (IGGiÖ)" 2013).

Thirty-four Muslim volunteers, among them two female chaplains, were as of April 2017 active in serving in almost all correctional institutions in Austria. Owing to other obligations, most of them make visits once or twice per month. In some cases, weekly visits are usual. Only the costs of travelling are reimbursed by the Islamic community using the lump sum of the ministry. All persons working in this field now have a good command of German and have completed theological education.[26] A completely new development towards professional Islamic religious care started in 2017. Since 13 February 2017, the first full position for Islamic religious care was established, serving in four prisons in Vienna. Dzemal Sibljakovic, an imam of Bosnian origin, is paid for completely by the Islamic community, which asked for collections for this service in the mosques (IGGiÖ 2017) The directors of the Islamic prison chaplaincy, Ismail Ozan, and since 2014 Ramazan Demir,

---

[25] However, this is questioned by the Shiite community, which is an officially registered religious confession in Austria. Some Shiite prisoners prefer prison chaplains from their own confession. This claim is indeed covered by §85 (2) StVG, which states explicitly that prisoners have the individual right to demand chaplains of their own confession even if there are no contracts for chaplaincy and a permanent chaplaincy is not established. The individual right of the prisoner is more important than the collective right of religious communities and no religious community can make decisions about the access of another religious community to correctional institutions. A few Shia Muslims are already volunteering as prison chaplains, sent by the Shiite community.

[26] Unpublished interview with Ramazan Demir.

advocated publicly (in vain) for an increase in the lump sum or cost-sharing in the personnel costs, referring to the fact that several Catholic prison chaplains are completely paid for by the ministry of justice. After the attacks on the French satirical weekly newspaper *Charlie Hebdo* in Paris, expectations were high that the financial support could be increased by combining the services of Islamic religious care with deradicalisation programmes. However, these hopes were dashed. The ministry refused to refer to the existing contract, which defines all costs included in the annual lump sum. Also, this combination of deradicalisation programmes and Islamic religious care would endanger the confidentiality of the communication of Islamic chaplains (Rosner 2015).

Many efforts are currently also being made with regard to the better preparation of Islamic prison chaplains. §11 (2) of the *Islamgesetz 2015* states that only candidates who have passed Islamic theological study at the University of Vienna (or equivalent studies), have 3 years of work experience and good command of German can be authorised to serve as Islamic prison chaplains. In the planned Bachelor curriculum, it is possible to choose a module on Islamic Chaplaincy, which informs about concepts of counselling care and a visiting course in an institution. In the Master curriculum, it is possible to choose a module in which rituals, psychological counselling, spiritual care in state institutions and discussions of cases are implemented. Also, information about the organisation of the chaplaincy in hospitals and prisons is included.[27] In addition, the postgraduate centre of the University of Vienna launched in October 2017 three certificate courses: 1. "Basics of Islamic Counselling"; 2. Islamic Counselling in Penal Institutions; 3. "Islamic Counselling in Hospital".[28]

That means that many problems concerning Islamic religious care are gradually solved, and a professional chaplaincy in correctional institutions is being established. A legal foundation was made by the Islamic law 2015. Imams do speak German and they will soon receive a professional education tailored for Islamic Chaplaincy in correctional and other state institutions. They will receive training comparable with the structures of the traditional churches. The structures of Islamic prison chaplaincy are already established, as is the first full-time religious care. However, several challenges still exist. For example, most Muslim prisoners are offered only the choice to have meals without pork, but there are no regulations concerning food that includes pork products, which is – just as for the Jewish community – strictly forbidden in Islam. Also, *halal* slaughtered food is not offered. Further problems and difficulties become apparent sometimes, regarding accommodation and the possibilities of performing ritual washing, that make it impossible

---

[27] The second draft of both curricula was finalised by the working group of the curricula commission on 20 April 2017. The intention is that BA and MA studies can start in October 2017. An Alevite branch will be established later.

[28] These certified courses are tailored to suit candidates who do not meet the formal requirements for the Master courses at University level. In particular, those who already have work experience in state and public institutions or have an interest in such fields can use it for targeted further education and training.

for Muslim prisoners to follow all the religious rules. One major question raised concerning Islamic religious care in prison is the understanding of the Islamic Chaplaincy. At present, the Islamic religious care that has been reasoned and developed mainly refers to the concept of religious instruction and guidance (*Irshâd*), which is based on an asymmetrical hierarchical personal relationship between the instructor/adviser and believers, guiding them to repent and to observe Islamic ethics and rites to reintegrate into the Islamic community and society. On the other hand, some concepts focus much more on psychosocial interpersonal relationships, in which the person is principally accepted regardless of his/her observance of religion and of his/her affiliation to a specific Islamic school. In this concept, the chaplain is very cautious with regard to religious advice or instructions and offers these only if they are explicitly demanded by the dialogue partners (Reiss 2017, 2019). However, a theoretical elaboration of such a concept in Islamic tradition is still missing.

2.4.6 Buddhist Chaplaincy

Even though there is no written law in Austria that regulates the religious care of Buddhists in prison or other state-led institutions, Buddhist care is very well established. From an international perspective, Buddhist religious care in prison has been widespread for a surprisingly long time. For example, Buddhist Vipassana Meditation is established in many Asian countries and is seen and accepted as religious care. In India, this even led to mass meditations with thousands of prisoners. In Austria, the Buddhist religious society has now built a well-organised system of religious care in prisons. It is organised by a working group called "Bridge" (*Brücke*). At the moment, eight persons are actively engaged in religious care in prisons. The way in which religious care is carried out differs from person to person, as well as from institution to institution. Mostly, religious care is performed in the form of individual dialogue, sometimes group meditations are organised if the prison authorities allow them. Group discussions take place in three different prisons at the moment, in which Buddhism, as well as other topics, is being discussed.

The requirements for Buddhist religious care in prison are completely different from the requirements of religious care in Abrahamic religions. For Buddhist religious care, a room of silence is needed, in which people can meditate for several hours without any interruptions. As Buddhist religious care usually takes place in the room for visitors, there is no such possibility in most of the correction institutions in Austria. Furthermore, the conversations between the prisoner and the adviser take place under video surveillance.

At the moment, all the persons involved in Buddhist religious care in prisons work on a voluntary basis with a small budget for materials and travelling costs. Usually, they come to prisons on request only, and they have to be officially registered by the Buddhist society in Austria. However, many prisoners do not even know that there is a possibility of receiving Buddhist religious care.

Individual care mostly consists of individual dialogue as well as the explanation of meditation techniques and their practical performance, depending on the prison's spatial situation. In this context, most activities that challenge the regular daily routine of the institution, such as longer meditations, are often dismissed as they provoke organisational challenges that are not welcome. Several attempts to link Buddhist traditions with different forms of psychotherapy can be noticed with the aim of exercising those new kinds of spiritual care in the correctional services (Cf. Reiss 2010b). Furthermore, the *"Naikan"* method (a structured method of self-reflection), developed at the beginning of the twentieth century in Japan, has become increasingly common in Austrian and German prisons. However, despite its Shin-Buddhist origins and its persistent religious character, this is not considered to be religious care (Reiss 2016a, b, c).

So far, the working group has established guidelines for people working on prison Buddhist religious care. These guidelines have been developed in cooperation with the Buddhist society in Austria. The requirements are, for example, the knowledge of the Buddhist teaching and doctrine, the practice of meditation on a regular basis, as well as participation in meetings and workshops. Furthermore, participation in a one-day course for chaplaincy in prison, offered by the correctional academy, is required to obtain permission to work in prisons.

2.4.7   Chaplaincy of Jehovah's Witnesses

Jehovah's witnesses have been present in Austria since as early as the beginning of the twentieth century. In 1978, they applied for the first time to be officially recognised as a religious corporation. However, the ministry refused to respond to this application, and to the others that followed. Since 1998, Jehovah's witnesses only have the status of a registered religious confession, although they insist on being recognised as a religious corporation and have lodged a complaint with the European Court for Human Rights, which considered, in a decision taken in 2008, the prolongation of the proceedings as an act of religious discrimination. On 7 May 2009, the community was recognised in Austria as a religious community, which includes the right to chaplaincy in state institutions. Nonetheless, there is no special agreement concerning relations between the state and Jehovah's witnesses, nor is there a special agreement with regard to prison chaplaincy.

From the perspective of Jehovah's witnesses, the obligation to religious care and chaplaincy is founded in the succession of Jesus Christ. Chaplaincy is not only seen as a psychological or psycho-therapeutical care for persons, but it is also bound to God's work and in that sense it is regarded as a directive given by God. It is of great importance for Jehovah's witnesses to make people acquainted with God's word as this is considered the only possibility of solving former or current problems, of gaining insight and of changing one's life. It is essential for every individual to have the possibility of gaining this insight. In that sense, the chaplaincy of Jehovah's witnesses is understood as a Christian chaplaincy, as an aid to self-help. One of the aims of this religious care is to help people to change themselves, and to change their lives, to become a useful part of society, leading a life agreeable to God.[29]

Jehovah's witnesses has offered religious care and chaplaincy in prison in Austria for more than 15 years. At present, 24 chaplains are working in 24 different correctional institutions. One of the main requirements for people working in prison care is that they have to be elected as elders within their community. Furthermore, chaplains are trained regularly. The Jehovah's witnesses chaplaincy focusses on visits of individual inmates, but also offers prayer meetings and group discussions. Services in their own kingdom halls, although usual in Spanish or Italian prisons, do not exist in Austria. Furthermore, biblical literature, as well as audio and video material, are distributed to the prisoners. Still, the focus of religious care offered by Jehovah's witnesses is on Bible studies (Unterberger 2012: 90).

2.4.8   Chaplaincy of Free Churches

The fact that Free Churches in Austria were legally recognised only 4 years ago still causes challenges to developing stable and regular chaplaincies in Austrian prisons. This can be seen in Table 2.1 concerning the denominations and the number of prisoners. In Table 2.1, the Free Churches in Austria are not explicitly mentioned in the list, the only denomination mentioned and included in the Free Churches being the Baptists.

Some active members and pastors of the religious groups that are now part of the legally recognised Free Churches had started to offer religious counselling in youth detention centres as early as the 1980s.[30] After some time, they widened their activities, and now also visit regular prisons in different regions of Austria. Religious counselling in prisons usually takes place in the visitor's room, although sometimes they are allowed to talk to prisoners in interrogation rooms. One of the aims of religious counselling by pastors and chaplains of Free Churches is the integral restoration of prisoners, that is their body, mind and soul. This possibility is offered through individual conversation, reading of the Bible, as well as counselling and listening. The final aim is to develop a stable relationship with God and oneself. Currently, there are approximately five members of Free Churches that regularly visit believers in prison. Because the Free Churches are a legally recognised church and corporation of public law with the right to religious care in penal institutions, the communication with the Ministry of Justice is reinforced. So far, there has been no financial aid by the state for the chaplaincy and religious counselling by the Free Churches. The persons involved are not being paid, and rooms for their religious activities are presently still not available.

---

[29] This information refers to an unpublished document by Jehovah's witnesses concerning their self-concept of religious counselling in prisons.

[30] This information has been provided by G. Kisslinger from the Free Christian and Pentecostal church in Austria (FCGÖ).

2.4.9 Other Religious Groups

The list of the religious groups involved in prison chaplaincy described in this chapter is probably not complete. This is because some members of religious communities make only occasional visits at the request of an individual prisoner in a correctional institution for a limited time. Long-term research would be needed in all 26 institutions, because the situation is constantly changing, with the imprisonment, release or relocation of prisoners and the religious actors visiting them. Therefore, it is likely that members of the Oriental-Orthodox Churches also visit prisoners. As Muslim-Alevites are included in the new *Islamgesetz* of 2015 and now have the right to establish religious care, one can assume that they will do so, as they have recently established an Alevite military chaplaincy. The president of the Shiite community is already serving as a prison volunteer chaplain, and a member of the Adventist Church has shown interest in the introductory course to the correctional services. The multireligious character of prison chaplaincy is probably already more diverse than displayed here, and will certainly be expanded in the coming years, because several registered religious communities will have a good chance of being granted legal recognition as religions with the right to establish a prison chaplaincy.

2.5 Current Developments and Challenges

Owing to the changes concerning religious diversity in society that are taking place, the author has conducted several inquiries regarding religion and prison over the last few years,[31] led courses in university combined with visits to prisons and started a dialogue with experts working in prisons and penal institutions. In 2015, these attempts led to an interdisciplinary project including the Correctional Academy, the Protestant and Catholic Chaplaincy in prison and the Protestant Academy in Vienna. In a first step, different international approaches to religious and spiritual care in prison have been presented and evaluated with regard to the possibility of their application within Austrian correctional institutions. Experts from the Netherlands and Germany working in this field have been invited to Vienna and presented their concept at the Protestant Academy. Furthermore, the author held a lecture about the situation concerning religious diversity and religious care in Spanish prisons. These lectures have been intensively discussed and evaluated by people working in Austrian prisons.

In the second step of this project (2017–2019), the main aim was to document the present situation concerning religious and spiritual care in Austrian prisons. The focus lies on the following questions: which forms of religious care already exist? What are the essential conditions for offering religious care? Which kind of education is required to be able to work in religious and spiritual care in prisons? What are

---

[31] See the author's reference list at the end of this chapter.

the differences and similarities concerning the different kinds of religious care in prisons? In a further step, transparent criteria should be developed regarding the requirements of candidates wishing to engage in prison chaplaincy, the access to penal institutions and the introduction to correctional services. Additionally, the self-understanding of the chaplaincy and/or religious care of each religious group should be displayed so that similarities can be noticed and introduction and supervision, as well as professional educational courses for people working in this area, may be organised jointly.

To obtain a first collection of basic information needed to answer the questions mentioned above, all 16 legally recognised religious groups in Austria have been contacted to provide information concerning their aims and their actions in prisons, their focusses, their forms of religious care, as well as the professional education of the people working in this field, including their desire for further education and training.

2.5.1 First Results and Outlook

One of the basic critiques focussed on the official statistics concerning the religious affiliation in correctional institutions in Austria. In addition to the categorisation of religious groups, the numbers presented give only a vague picture of religious affiliation in Austrian prisons. In 2016, the author of this chapter proposed a comprehensive revision of the statistics and categorisation. After revision by the Ministry of Justice and several prison chaplains, and after clarification of its technical feasibility, this new version of the statistics was implemented in 2018.

On 6 and 7 March 2017, the first interreligious conference of prison chaplains was organised by the Correctional Academy, with participation of the representatives of the Ministry of Justice; the representatives of all legally recognised churches and religious societies, as well as state-registered religious communities, were all invited. In a first step, the results of the survey were presented. Then, the participants gathered in small groups to work on different topics concerning religious care in prison. Two of the results of these working groups were, for example, that any form of proselytism in penal institutions should be prohibited and that every religious group should nominate one person as an official contact for prison chaplaincy. Concerning the requirements of people working in religious care in prisons, it was emphasised that every community has the right to define the criteria. However, a basic psychosocial training such as clinical pastoral care is recommended. The results were documented in minutes.

The representatives of the Ministry of Justice and the prison chaplains jointly agreed that concepts as well as the aims of religious care should be elaborated and disclosed by each religious community, and attempts should be made to develop joint quality standards and general rules for religious care in prisons. A lawyer for the Ministry of Justice suggested that the recommendations should be later implemented in law. The conference further showed that there was a consensus among the different religious groups concerning the clear distinction between religious care, psychotherapy and social work – although it was stressed that the cooperation between these different working fields areas needs improvement. Another idea was that the compulsory one-day introductory course for volunteers in prison should be expanded, including mandatory practical training hours with an experienced prison chaplain, before working independently in a prison. Concerning religious rituals and celebrations, it was emphasised that a "spiritual room" (instead of a multifunctional room for many activities) is of great importance. Further topics that were mentioned during the conference, such as questions of secrecy and management in cases of suicide, will be discussed at forthcoming conferences.

With these results, the first steps have been made to develop a national concept with regard to the management of religious diversity – a request that the author of this article has already been making for several years (Reiss 2015; Reiss 2016a, b, c). In the long term, the hope is that these suggestions will lead to the elaboration of official guidelines of the Ministry of Justice concerning the management of religious diversity, and to a revised version of the correctional orders of the Ministry of Justice. Furthermore, it is planned that the conference of all prison chaplains held in March 2017 should be established as a permanent annual meeting, in which all questions concerning the prison chaplaincy are discussed jointly. Additionally, short annual reports by all prison chaplains should be sent to the Ministry of Justice as well as to the prison governors. For the statistics, an official form will be created in which the activities of the prison chaplaincy will be recorded, in addition to a general evaluation of positive and negative developments of the prison chaplaincy. These reports will be discussed with each prison governor of the respective correctional institution, during the annual conference of prison governors and during the annual conference of prison chaplains. The author has been asked to accompany and supervise the project from the scientific perspective of the study of religions. It is obvious that the management of religious diversity in the Austrian penal system is undergoing radical change, first because, until now, there was only a Catholic chaplaincy and developments happened without any strategy or plan; second, because it is the first time that the question of "religious diversity management" will be addressed and that a national plan will be worked out; and finally, because a joint communication platform has been established for all prison chaplains, whereas previously, each religious community had their own debates with the Ministry of Justice. The first steps towards the development of a national strategy have already been taken, and this may even have an impact on society in general with regard to dealing with religious diversity.

Bibliography

Act on Imprisonment (*Strafvollzugsgesetz – StVG*). (1969). https://www.ris.bka.gv.at/GeltendeFassung.wxe?Abfrage=Bundesnormen&Gesetzesnummer=10002135. Accessed 21 Apr 2017.

Act on the external legal relationships of the Israelite Religious Society (*IsraelitenGesetz*). (1890). https://www.ris.bka.gv.at/GeltendeFassung.wxe?Abfrage=Bundesnormen&Gesetzesnummer=10009176. Accessed 22 Apr 2017.

ARGE Evangelische Gefängnisseelsorge Österreich. (2015). *Informationsbroschüre*. Wien.

Baghajati, C. A. (2010). *Vereinbarung zwischen dem Bundesministerium für Justiz und der Islamischen Glaubensgemeinschaft in Österreich.* http://www.islaminitiative.at/index. php?option=com_content&task=view&id=337&Itemid=23. Accessed 22 Apr 2017.

Concordat between the Holy See and the Austrian Republic with its Supplementary Protocol. (1933). https://www.ris.bka.gv.at/GeltendeFassung.wxe?Abfrage=Bundesnormen&Gesetzesnummer=10009196. Accessed 22 Apr 2017.

Council of Europe. (2006). *Recommendation of the Committee of Ministers to member states on the European Prison Rules.* https://search.coe.int/cm/Pages/result_details.aspx?ObjectID=09000016805d8d25. Accessed 16 Apr 2017.

Federal Act on the external legal relationships of Islamic Religious Societies (*Islamgesetz*). (2015). https://www.ris.bka.gv.at/GeltendeFassung.wxe?Abfrage=Bundesnormen&Gesetzesnummer=20009124. Accessed 22 Apr 2017.

Federal Act on the external legal relationships of the Greek-Oriental Church in Austria (*OrthodoxenGesetz*). (1967). https://www.ris.bka.gv.at/GeltendeFassung.wxe?Abfrage=Bundesnormen&Gesetzesnummer=10009290. Accessed 22 Apr 2017.

Federal Act on the external legal relationships of the Oriental-Orthodox Churches in Austria (*Orientalisch-Orthodoxes Kirchengesetz*). (2003). https://www.ris.bka.gv.at/GeltendeFassung.wxe?Abfrage=Bundesnormen&Gesetzesnummer=20002664. Accessed 22 Apr 2017.

Federal Act on the external legal relationships of the Protestant Church in Austria (*ProtestantenGesetz*). (1961). https://www.ris.bka.gv.at/GeltendeFassung.wxe?Abfrage=Bundesnormen&Gesetzesnummer=10009255. Accessed 22 Apr 2017.

Federal Ministry of Justice. (2016). *Correctional services in Austria.* https://www.justiz.gv.at/web2013/file/2c9484853e44f8f9013ef9d9e2b928dd.de.0/correctional_services_2016_download.pdf. Accessed 21 Apr 2017.

Heynisch, O., & Verheyen, E. Gefahr aus dem Knast. Wie die Russenmafia Verbrechen unter den Augen der Justiz organisiert. In *Südwestrundfunk. Report Mainz*, 22.11.2010., URL: http://www.swr.de/report/-/id=7200620/property=download/nid=233454/18a8q4d/index.pdf. Accessed 16 June 2018.

Hirnsperger, J., Wessely, C., & Bernhard, A. (2001). *Wege zum Heil? Religiöse Bekenntnisgemeinschaften in Österreich: Selbstdarstellung und theologische Reflexion.* Innsbruck/Vienna: Tyrolia.

Hollenstein, O. Wie die Russenmafia den Knast kontrolliert. In *Süddeutsche Zeitung*, 02.12.2012. URL: http://www.sueddeutsche.de/bayern/kartelle-im-gefaengniswie-die-russenmafia-den-knast-kontrolliert-1.1512244. Accessed 16 June 2018.

Islamische Glaubensgemeinschaft in Österreich (IGGiÖ). (2013). *Islamische Seelsorge.* http://www.derislam.at/seelsorge/Gefaengnis/index-start.php?c=content&cssid=%DCber%20Uns&navid=11&par=0. Accessed 23 Apr 2017.

Islamische Glaubensgemeinschaft in Österreich (IGGiÖ). (2017). *Erster hauptberuflicher muslimischer Gefängnisseelsorger in Österreich.* http://www.derislam.at/?f=news&shownews=2074&kid=1. Accessed 23 Apr 2017.

Potz, R., & Schinkele, B. (2016). *Religion and Law in Austria.* Alphen aan den Rijn: Wolters Kluwer.

Reiss, W. (2010a). Anwalt für die religiösen Bedürfnisse. Interreligiöse Seelsorge im Gefängnis. In H. Weiß, K. Federschmidt, & K. Temme (Eds.), *Handbuch Interreligiöse Seelsorge* (pp. 299–308). Neukirchen-Vluyn: Vandenhoeck & Ruprecht.

Reiss, W. (2010b). Schuld und Versöhnung im Judentum, Islam und Buddhismus. In H. Weiß, K. Federschmidt, & K. Temme (Eds.), *Handbuch Interreligiöse Seelsorge* (pp. 162–178). Neukirchen-Vluyn: Vandenhoeck und Ruprecht.

Reiss, W. (2015). Auswirkungen der religiösen Pluralität auf staatliche Institutionen und die Anstaltsseelsorge. In R. Polak & W. Reiss (Eds.), *Religion im Wandel. Transformation religiöser Gemeinschaften in Europa durch Migration. Interdisziplinäre Perspektiven* (pp. 147–186). Vienna: Vienna University Press.

Reiss, W. (2016a). Naikan im Rahmen der Behandlungsmaßnahmen und Diversifikation der religiösen und therapeutischen Betreuung. In W. Reiss (Ed.), *Selbstbetrachtung hinter Gittern. Naikan im Strafvollzug in Deutschland und Österreich* (pp. 65–105). Marburg: Tectum.

Reiss, W. (2016b). Der Umgang mit religiösen Minderheiten in der österreichischen Armee. *Interdisciplinary Journal for Religion and Transformation in Contemporary Society, 2*, 82–113.

Reiss, W. (2016c). Religiös-kulturelle Betreuung im Strafvollzug. Herausforderungen für Staat, Anstalten, Religionsgemeinschaften und Forschung. In K. Appel & I. Guanzini (Eds.), *Europa mit oder ohne Religion? II. Der Beitrag der Religionen zum gegenwärtigen und künftigen Europa* (pp. 203–218). Vienna: Vienna University Press.

Reiss, W. (2017). Management of religions diversity in the Austrian Armed Forces. In H. G. Hödl & L. Pokorny (Eds.), *Religion in Austria 3* (pp. 95–161). Vienna: Praesens.

Reiss, W. (2019). Islamische Seelsorge – aber welche? In M. Klöckner & U. Tworuschka (Ed.), *Handbuch der Religionen* (Vol. 59). EL.

Rosner, S. (2015). Gefangene Radikale. *Wiener Zeitung*, January 16.

Schmidt, A. Russenmafia im Jugendknast. In *DeutscheWelle*, 21.12.2002. URL: http://dw.de/p/304n. Accessed 19 June 2018.

Simoner, M. Wiener Mafia – Die Paten an der blauen Donau, 29 June 2010. In *Der Standard* 29 June 2010. https://derstandard.at/1277337046939/Organisierte-Kriminaltiaet-Wiener-Mafia%2D%2D-Die-Paten-an-der-blauen-Donau. Accessed 19 June 2018.

Unterberger, U. (2012). Religion – die letzte Freiheit. Religionsausübung im Strafvollzug. In W. Reiss & U. Bechmann (Eds.), *Anwendungsorientierte Religionswissenschaft* (Vol. 2). Marburg: Tectum.

Verein für Integrationshilfe. (2015). *Jahresbericht 2015*. http://www.integrationshilfe.at/htm/Jahresbericht2015.pdf. Accessed 23 Apr 2017.

Chapter 3
Belgium: Religions and Prisons in Law

Louis-Léon Christians and Stéphanie Wattier

Abstract A major change has occurred in Belgium, as in other European countries. Religion and prison legal practice and literature are decreasingly focused on individual religious freedom (of inmates). Instead, they are orientated towards addressing radicalisation issues and providing some specific tools for "deradicalisation". Islam, instead of Christianity, has become the main religion to be dealt with in prison administration and correlated case law. However, emphasis is no longer only on the individual, even radicalised, prisoners. A new importance is given to the Muslim chaplains. Their ability to communicate with the (even radicalised) inmates, and to transform them, is becoming of primary importance for the public authorities once again. The (control of the) training of the chaplains has become one of the major issues for the Government. All religious accommodations are now reread against this security background.

3.1 Introduction

In Belgium, the regulation of religion in prison has deeply changed over the past 20 years (Dupont-Boucha 2001; Decroix 1989; Overbeeke 2005). Two major challenges have emerged: the first is the growing number of Muslim prisoners in Belgian prisons; the second is the question of the radicalisation of some of these detainees (Brion 2019; Wattier 2016b; Overbeeke 2019). The terrorist events in Europe and Belgium have exacerbated these two challenges, which in turn have had repercussions on the prison regulations applied to all religions. The increase in the number of Islamic "chaplains" led to a reduction in the number of Catholic chaplains. The strengthening of the security rules has been done in a transversal and "non-discriminatory" way, which uniformly affects all religions. Free access to cells,

L.-L. Christians
Université catholique de Louvain, Ottignies-Louvain-la-Neuve, Belgium
e-mail: louis-leon.christians@uclouvain.be

S. Wattier (✉)
Université de Namur, Ottignies-Louvain-la-Neuve, Belgium
e-mail: stephanie.wattier@unamur.be

© Springer Nature Switzerland AG 2020
J. Martínez-Ariño, A.-L. Zwilling (eds.), *Religion and Prison: An Overview of Contemporary Europe*, Boundaries of Religious Freedom: Regulating Religion in Diverse Societies 7, https://doi.org/10.1007/978-3-030-36834-0_3

formerly usual for Catholic chaplains, is today subject to strict limitations through individual and ad hoc authorisations for all religions. Food and other accommodations are now reread against this security background more than in the context of international religious freedom requirements. Religious issues are no longer really about religion.

3.2   Freedom of Religion in Prison: Legal Aspects

On 12 January 2005, Belgium adopted a Law on the Principles of prison administration and the legal status of prisoners[1]: the so-called Dupont Law. Previously, there had been a royal decree from 21 May 1965 that had a bearing on the general rules of procedure[2], as well as a multiplicity of ministerial circulars, for penal institutions (Ketelaer 2000; Wattier 2015). In its current state of affairs, Belgian penal law still regards the royal decree of 21 May 1965 as applicable inasmuch as the exhaustive list of Articles foreseen by the new law have not yet entered into force owing to political, social and budgetary difficulties. This legislative latency illustrates the difficulty of implementing principles, be it from a political or a budgetary and organisational point of view. A new Royal Decree of 17 May 2019 (M.B. 11 june 2019) specifically determines the status of prison chaplains and finally allows the entry into force of the 2005 law on this subject. This new rule reinforces the chaplains' obligations of democratic loyalty. Among others, s. 7, (4) provides for the obligation of spiritual counsellors "to report to the director of the institution any facts that would constitute a serious threat to security of which they have become aware in the performance of their duties" (Christians 2019).

Until 2005, prisoners were invited, upon their entry into prison, to declare the religious services they wished for, if any (it was not mandatory); these individual written declarations were made available to chaplains, according to the so-called religious ticket system.[3] This is no longer the case. The prisoner can only contact one or more chaplains according to his wishes, by reiterating sporadic requests. The religious ticket system had already been severely criticised in the final report of the reforming commission "Law on Principles of prison administration and the legal status of prisoners", which "wondered rightly whether such practice weren't contrary to Article 8 of the European Convention on Human Rights, that guarantees the right to privacy (…) In the framework of the standardisation principle (= in society as a whole) and by reference to the existing pluralism in a free society, it seems fair to give up the religious ticket system and offer the prisoner the freedom to express his/her wish for consulting at any point in time, either a chaplain or any moral counsellor of his choice. Just like in normal life you may simultaneously be in contact

---

[1] *M.B.*, 1 February 2005, p. 2815.

[2] *M.B.*, 25 May 1965, p. 6272.

[3] Formerly defined in a Royal Decree, 21 May 1965, Article 16 (abrogated).

with several religious or philosophical trends, without necessarily excluding your-self from an interest in a totally opposite direction."[4]

As far as the practice of religious freedom in jail is concerned, Article 71 of the Law on Principles stipulates that "the prisoner has the right to live and practise in accordance with his religion or philosophy individually or communitarily, within the limiting respect of those others' same right" and that "he/she is entitled to reli-gious, spiritual or moral assistance from a representative of his religion or philoso-phy, detached to the prison to that avail."

Article 74, for its part, guarantees in its first paragraph that "[1] the prisoner is entitled to take part without restriction and according to the exercise of his own free will, in the religious or common activities thereto related, as well as encounters and activities organised by the moral counsellors". In a second paragraph, it is seen to that "[1] the prisoner communicates to the chaplain (that is counsellors belonging to recognised denominations) or to the moral counsellor, his intention to take part in the activities mentioned in §1, and is authorised to do so, as long as he commits to abiding by the conditions of order, dignity and tolerance unalienable from these activities". Article 74 further specifies that "the organisation of common activities in the context of a non-denominational religion or philosophy can be subject to concertation in the sense of Article 7. In which case, the chaplains (counsellors from recognised denominations) or moral counsellors should be associated in this consul-tation process."[5] Finally, Article 74, §4, arranges for a special place dedicated to worship-related activities "meeting the prisoner's right to live and practise his reli-gion or philosophy freely" to be fitted in every prison.

The Law on Principles also looks after the prisoners' nutrition by enouncing in its Article 42 that "[1] food should be sufficient in quantity, respect the modern sanitary standards and, if need be, take into account his state of health". A collective letter from the general management of Correctional Establishments (SPF Justice) no. 107 of 16 June 2011 accompanying the entry into force of this text completes its inter-pretation by stating that, "[1] freedom of religion includes the observance of related dietary rules; this implies that the administration should, within reasonable limits, take the necessary dispositions enabling prisoners to respect this aspect of their prac-tice. The term reasonable is to be assessed with respect to the need to acquire specific ingredients, prepare or serve them in a particular way without obstructing the smooth organisation of the penitentiary establishment." (Nounckele 2013)

Furthermore, Article 87 of the ministerial decree of 12 July 1971 on general instructions for penitentiary establishments, as modified by the ministerial decree of 15 April 2002, prescribes that "[if] their convictions demand it, the prisoners shall receive meals meeting the requirements of their religion, as long as these need not be prepared according to ritual forms, and are of the same general standard as those served to other prisoners"; second, "[if] required by their religious convictions, the

---

[4] Final Report, Commission "loi de principe concernant l'administration pénitentiaire et le statut juridique des détenus", *Doc. parl.*, Ch. Repr., sess. ord. 2000–2001, no. 50-1076/1, p. 146.

[5] Article 7: " [i] n each prison, we will try to establish a climate of consultation. To this end, a con-sultation body will be set up in each prison to enable prisoners to express themselves on issues of community interest for which they can contribute".

prisoners receive their meals at other times than the normal ones on request"; third "[if] required by their religious convictions the prisoners may have their meals prepared according to ritual forms and delivered externally. These meals would be delivered through the intercession of the chaplains or Islamic counsellors, and should be of the same general standard as those provided to all other prisoners. The financial contribution of the Treasury for these meals may not exceed the maximum daily rate fixated for prisoners' food by specific instructions"; and fourth, "[if] required by their religious convictions and not compromising the order and security of the establishment, prisoners may keep on demand some worship-related objects in their cells. The Treasury does not intervene for that".

According to an extensive field study carried out by Divine Uwiwese in 2014 (Uwizeye 2014), "in the current state of Belgian Law, prisoners are given the choice between a pork-free diet or one 'with pork'. On the other hand, in some penal institutions, prisoners are given the option to buy meals at the canteen, befitting their religion-related dietary constraints. Two out of three establishments we visited had a canteen with halal as well as vegetarian menus. On the other hand, the "*Consistoire central israélite*" of Belgium, which represents the Jewish penitentiary community of rabbis, cooperates closely with Belgian penal institutions. Some Jewish prisoners would indeed register for *kosher* meals on entry; and the management would then resort to the *Consistoire central israélite* to provide for their meals as prescribed by Jewish principles, according to §3 of Article 87 […]. During the fasting period of Ramadan, some prisons even accommodate their timetable and distribute the food in the evenings to fasting prisoners, still according to Article 87 §3. Others provide their prisoners with cooking rings so as to allow them to eat their meals after sunset. We can attest that allowance is indeed made for the Ramadan's orchestration in Belgian prisons. Despite the carceral living conditions (of promiscuity, overpopulation, etc.), it can be said that the religious practice retains a prominent role in the prisoners' lives."[6]

It should also be added that prisoners belonging to a religion not recognised by the State are nevertheless authorised by penitentiary managers to practise their religion, including in terms of dietary and fasting constraints.[7]

3.3 Regime of State-Recognised Religions in Prison: the Prison Chaplains' Status

The regime for state-recognised religions applies to prison chaplains[8]: each recognised religious authority has the right to suggest the appointment of a fixed number of chaplains, in a proportional way defined by the law for each recognised religion.

---

[6] Uwizeye (2014).

[7] A.M. du 12 juillet 1971 portant instructions générales pour les établissements pénitentiaires, *M.B.*, 10 August 1971, Article 91.

[8] Loi du 4 mars 1870 sur le temporel du culte, *M.B.*, 9 March 1870.

A public legal framework ensues therefrom in terms of heads of religious designations: Catholic chaplains are distinguished from the Protestant, Orthodox, Jewish, Muslim counsellors or chaplains respectively, and from lay humanist counsellors too (El Asri 2015; Van Geyt 2012).

The specific legal status of prison chaplains (social security, holiday, healthcare, unemployment and pensions etc.) has been subject to arduous negotiations for about a decade, particularly because of challenges posed by the Islamic religion (national language capacity, specific training, security issues, representativeness of all Belgian Islamic communities by national origin etc.). For instance, since 2007, chaplains have lost their free access to cell keys, except for ad hoc requests.

The non-recognised religious advisors used to enjoy intermediate rights a law of 26 July 2006[9], which included the abandoning of a principle stemming from European recommendations "for reasons of security in order to ensure protection against potential sectarian actions."[10] They are now covered only by ordinary law for routine visits, with a visiting right restricted to the visiting room (Overbeeke2007).

3.4 Number of Chaplains and Volunteers

There are 64 equivalent full-time chaplains or counsellors for 11,000 prisoners.

Article 72, §1 of the Law on Principles of 12 January 2005 stipulates that "chaplains and counsellors belonging to recognised denominations, as well as moral counsellors from organisations in charge of non-denominational moral services recognised by law, should be appointed in prison according to rules to be determined by the King".

A royal decree determining the framework in which chaplains and Islamic or moral counsellors should operate in prison, as well as their salary scales, was first adopted on 25 October 2005. According to Article 1 of this decree, chaplain nominations were worked out as follows: one chief chaplain for 24 chaplains of the Catholic church; one chief Islamic counsellor for 17 Islamic counsellors in the Islamic religion; 9 moral counsellors of non-denominational philosophy; 6 chaplains for the Protestant religion; 4 chaplains representing the Orthodox religion; 2 for the Jewish religion; 1 for the Anglican church. Article 2 of this royal decree of 25 October 2005 specifies that "only full-time equivalents are referred to in Article 1 of this law". However, certain chaplain services have opted for an increase in the numbers fixed by this legal framework, cutting down on their full-time equivalent. Such is the case for the Catholic, Protestant or Evangelical, as well as lay non-religious philosophical organisations (Belgian Humanist Association).

---

[9] *M.B.*, 28 July 2006.

[10] *Doc. parl.*, Ch. repr., projet de loi portant des dispositions diverses, sess. ord. 2005–2006, no. 1 2518/001, p. 44.

On 11 March 2015, following the attack on the Jewish Museum in Brussels of May 2014, the Minister of Justice adopted an action plan against radicalism in prison. Among the ten measures foreseen by this plan, the need to increase the number of religious representatives in prison was listed. The royal decree of 25 October 2005 was modified by a new royal decree of 10 April 2016, Article 1 of which applies the following apportionment: one chief Catholic chaplain and 24 chaplains for the Catholic religion; 9 for the Protestant religion; one head Islamic counsellor for the Islamic religion and 26 Islamic counsellors; 5 Orthodox chaplains; 2 Jewish counsellors; 2 Anglican counsellors; 9 moral counsellors for organised secularism. In other words, four denominations saw the number of their representatives in prison rise: namely the Protestantism going from 6 to 9 full-time equivalent chaplains; the Orthodox denomination with 4 to 5 chaplains; the Anglican with 1 to 2 and the Islamic denomination with 17 to 24 counsellors.[11]

In its annual report, the general management of penitentiary establishments gives an overview of all staff working in Belgian establishments. The last of such reports dates back to 2015 and was released in June 2016. Religions represent a total of 106 members of staff corresponding to 59.05 full-time equivalents.[12]

Inside prisons, volunteers work alongside the chaplains or designated counsellors. These volunteers are an essential support, all the more so that within the framework of the royal decree of 25 October 2005, chaplains and religious advisors were not allowed to serve in any French- or Dutch-speaking prisons of the country, both totalling since 2009 a more or less stable number of 11,000 prisoners – whose religious convictions have no longer been registered since 2005.[13] Some members of Parliament interested in the number and proportion of Muslim prisoners regularly ask indirect questions to the Minister about the number of halal menus available to prisoners to better evaluate the proportion of Muslim prisoners. On 14 January 2011, the Minister of Justice gave Parliament the following reply:

> Not every penitentiary institution has a halal menu to offer. Among those offering it, the percentage of halal menus served differs according to establishments and their present population. This percentage varies between 20 and 60%. Moreover, certain prisons only offer occasional halal menus (during Ramadan for instance).[14]

In her field study, Divine Uwiwese reports that on 28 June 2014, as far as she was concerned, 212 prisoners out of 616 declared that they were observing Ramadan in Forest prison (which is the largest one in Brussels).

On 13 February 2009, the Minister of Justice had also provided a reply listing the nationalities represented in the prison population:

---

[11] Royal Decree, 10 April 2016 "modifiant l'arrêté royal du 25 octobre 2005 fixant le cadre des aumôniers et des conseillers islamiques appartenant à l'un des cultes reconnus ainsi que des conseillers moraux de philosophie non confessionnelle du conseil central laïque auprès des établissements pénitentiaires et fixant leurs échelles de traitement", *M.B.*, 19 April 2016, Article 1.

[12] Department of Justice, Direction générale des Établissements pénitentiaires, Annual Report, 2015, p. 51, http://justice.belgium.be/sites/default/files/2016-06_epi_rapport_annuel_2015_fr.pdf

[13] See http://statbel.fgov.be/fr/statistiques/chiffres/population/autres/detenu/

[14] *Bull. Q.R.*, 53 – 013 (2010), no. 0128, p. 53.

"The average daily population for 2008 was of 9,890.6 prisoners. 2. In 2008, 57.6% of prisoners on average possessed Belgian nationality, including those naturalised Belgians or possessing a double nationality, who are not kept on separate registers of the DG EPI. On average, 10.7% of prisoners had Moroccan nationality; 4.7% of them Algerian; 2% Turkish; 1.1% Congolese; 0.7% Russian; 0.1% American; 0.1% Chinese; 0.6% Indian. It is hardly possible to reflect faithfully which one is the inmates' mother tongue. And, since the Law on Principles, it is no longer possible to hold statistics on the religions practised by each prisoner in the databases".[15]

3.5 Rules of Conduct for Chaplains

Article 73, §1 of the Law on Principles foresees that [chaplains and counsellors] "have the right to pay a visit within the living zone of the prisoners who apply for it, and to correspond freely inside the prison's walls with them without any check. Within limits set by security, they meet the prisoners who so wish and firstly the prisoners who were confined following a particular security arrangement, an individual regime or a disciplinary sanction." The second paragraph of Article 73 reads that chaplains, counsellors from recognised denominations, as well as moral counsellors from recognised organisations "enjoy the use of an appropriate space for receiving the prisoners, contriving a confidentiality propitious atmosphere".

The royal decree of 21 May 1965 enacting general principles for penitentiary establishments[16] and the ministerial decree of 12 July 1971 enacting general instructions of procedures for penitentiary establishments[17] list a series of behavioural rules, which chaplains and prison counsellors have to obey. Article 44 of the general ROP stipulates that "the religious ministers and moral counsellors should refrain from mixing political allusions with the instructions they provide, or from personal appreciations on the opinions or behaviours of the administrative agents". Besides, Article 48 forbids, among other things, chaplains and prison counsellors from "reveal[ing] facts that they would have been made aware of on account of their function; and they remain liable to this interdiction after being discharged", "to accept on account of their function, gifts, gratifications or any sort or perks excepting the retribution, allocations or indemnities paid to them by the Treasury", "to infiltrate in the establishment alcohol, spirits or any nefarious products", "to promise the prisoners any pardon, sentence reduction, parole or other favourable measures", "to influence the prisoners in their choice of a legal advisor or counsellors". In other words, they are bound by professional secrecy.

Chaplains and counsellors can organise community-based activities or common celebrations once a week in any establishment given prior warning. The enquiry carried out in 2014 by Divine Uwiwese shows for example in the case of the Forest

---

[15] *Bull. Q.R.*, 52 – 062 (2009), p. 273.

[16] *M.B.*, 25 May 1965.

[17] *M.B.*, 10 August 1971.

prison of Brussels, religious and community activities organised as follows: Tuesday is dedicated to the Anglican denomination, Wednesday to the Protestant denomination, Thursday to the Islamic denomination, Saturday or Sunday to the Catholic denomination etc.

On top of that, Article 80 of the general instructions for penitentiary establishments sees to it, that "unless the security and order of the establishment run the risk of being compromised, the director allows third parties to take part in masses or non-denominational celebrations". Divine Uwiwese observed that in most penitentiary establishments, the worship room has a maximum number of seats allowed, for security reasons. She explains on this account that "limitations range from 15 to 40 prisoners per religious or community service. Due to the fear of agents that gatherings in the place of worship could be the kick - off point for fomented movements, management usually limit the number of participants to a community-based worship activity. Prisons being overpopulated, the surveillance staff does indeed apprehend the inmate's potentially harmful movements against the order and security of the establishment. That is why from the attendance of 30 prisoners upwards, security setup is usually reinforced; a minimum of two, rather than a single agent, is necessary for escorting and looking after the group; and if the number of required agents cannot be made available, worship or activities are suspended. Our observers also stressed the lack of surveillance staff, which accounts for the fairly frequent suppression of those activities."

Last, management must organise at least once a year a concertation meeting with the representatives of the denominations and the recognised non-denominational organisations.[18]

3.6   Ongoing Debates

Besides the recurrent debates on prison overpopulation (11,000 actual prisoners for an official capacity of 9000), and the slow but discreet negotiations concerning the chaplains' status, it is essentially Islam that finds itself in the limelight of political attention and of the media. Four debates are at stake respectively on: (a) the proportion of Muslims among the prisoners (see above), (b) prison security issues during Ramadan, (c) proselytism and radicalisation of the Muslim prisoners in prison, as well as (d) the specific roles and training of licensed Islamic counsellors or imams.

On 18 November 2013, the Minister of Justice instructed Parliament as follows:

> It is true that during Ramadan some Muslim prisoners prayed in the covered courtyard. These particular Muslims are prisoners with no record or trace of possible Salafist radicalisation trend. The reason they were allowed to pray there is simply that at the hour of the last prayer of their daily ritual, their timetable placed them at this place. The 'leader' described in the Article is unknown to us; no prisoner matches his physical description. Thus, there are no exacerbated tensions. The director of the Mons Prison summoned the prisoners to let

---

[18] See a circular by the Directeur général EPI: "Cultes et conditions de travail".

them know that the covered courtyard was meant to be a recreation place and not a place of worship for any confession. The message came across. The director had asked for pictures to be taken in order to identify the prisoners who were praying. In his annual reports of 2010 & 2011, state security services indicated that there was no major reason for concern in terms of fundamentalism throughout the various Belgian penitentiary establishments, apart from a few exceptions connected to individuals rather than groups. This being said, we must remain vigilant. The prison population is indeed a vulnerable population, some elements of which are, under certain circumstances, at risk of surrendering to radicalisation opportunities. Over the last years, due among others to a number of legal actions, the proportion of prisoners held on the basis of terrorism has increased, which does require further measures on our behalf, inasmuch as these prisoners may exert a certain fascination in the eyes of younger inmates. The penitentiary administration and local management are aware of this risk and do take the necessary measures whenever appropriate, by applying specific detention regimes for instance. Training and sensitisation campaigns to this issue are also organised. Besides operational initiatives in the prisons themselves, limiting contacts between prisoners and potential recruiters, a cooperation protocol between the state security services and the general management of penitentiary establishments has been concluded, whose purpose it is to facilitate exchanges both ways. State security is also activated within Plan R, involving concertation with different partners on this phenomenon. Plan R for radicalisation is coordinated with the OCAM (Body coordinating the Threat's Analysis), and has been approved by the ministerial commission for intelligence and security (CMRS). The process was launched in 2007 with the training and sensitisation of penitentiary staff on the issue of radicalisation among prison populations. This subject was also at the heart of a permanent concertation process with European partners (from intelligence departments and others) in order to draw lessons from everyone's initiatives in this field. The situation is therefore being carefully monitored by every stakeholder.[19]

A few months later, at the Justice Commission of 3 December 2014, the Minister of Justice declared this time:

Mr. Chairman, in the light of the present circumstances, there are radicalisation risks. These last years, due to various judiciary actions, the number of prisoners held on terrorism-related grounds has risen. This requires a specific attention on your behalf, given the aura enjoyed by the latter in the eyes of several younger inmates. The penitentiary administration and local management are well aware of this risk and do take the necessary measures wherever appropriate, by applying specific detention regimes. Training and sensitisation campaigns to this issue are also organised. Besides operational initiatives in the prisons themselves limiting contacts between prisoners and potential recruiters, a cooperation protocol between the state security services and the general management of penitentiary establishments has been concluded, whose purpose it is to facilitate exchanges both ways. State security is also activated within Plan R, involving concertation with different partners on this phenomenon. Plan R – for radicalisation – where concertation is carried out with various partners touched by the same phenomenon. The plan was approved by the ministerial committee of intelligence and security. The process was launched in 2007 with the training and sensitisation of penitentiary staff on the issue of radicalisation among prison populations. The Ministry of Justice will pay due attention to it, in accordance with the governmental agreement. This topic also lies at the heart of a permanent concertation process with European partners, in order to draw the lessons from everyone's initiatives in this field. Furthermore, let me refer you to the governmental agreement which foresees that intelligence services and the OCAM take a particular interest in the radicalisation phenomenon inside prisons. To that avail, a solution shall be sought, including among others in the frame-

---

[19] Ch. Repr., *Bull. Q.R.,* 53 – B131, no. 1059.

work of the "prison masterplan". Thus, attention is paid to the situation with due diligence by all stakeholders.

On 12 January 2015, the Minister of Justice, Koen Geens, proclaimed his intention to "plan a *smart distribution* of prisoners across the various prisons in the country, according to their respective radicalisation risks, thereby planning to resort increasingly to Islamic counsellors".

Furthermore, after the *Charlie Hebdo* attacks in France, the Minister acknowledged that certain people came out of prison converted to a more fundamental religious trend than when they had entered it, as secular people or non-fundamentalists. According to the Minister, Islamic counsellors play a crucial role inside prisons in fighting radicalisation. In his action plan to cut down fundamentalism inside prisons of 11 March 2015, he therefore planned an increase in the number of Islamic counsellors. When the royal decree of 10 April 2016 was adopted, Islamic denominations shot up from 17 to 24 chaplains or full-time equivalents.[20]

Besides this increase, the Geens plan against fundamentalism in prison is structured around four major pillars. The main one concerns prisoners likely to opt for a fundamental path or those condemned for terrorist acts without being deemed potential recruiters as such. The idea is to let them evolve in a "normal" environment, but monitor them individually or with Islamic counsellors. The most worrisome category of prisoners – those capable of attracting others into the jihadist vocation – is jailed in a specific section dedicated to them in prison. One of these sections will be created in Ittre (26 places) and another one in Bruges (16 places). They are not to be considered high-security zones, but rather sections where personal accompaniment is to be more "targeted". As for prisoners suspected of fomenting terrorist acts, they shall be detained in maximum security cells.

In practice, researcher François Xavier (Xavier 2017) reminds us, after analysing the last circulatory of April 2016[21], the prisoners considered to have a link with "radicalisation" or "fundamentalism" are put into one of four categories by the administrative authorities. The first one (category A for "terrorists") groups "all prisoners who are defendants, sentenced or interned for deeds relating to terrorism"; the second (category B for said "assimilated") one is for "prisoners who have a clear link to terrorism on their commitment order or who, by their acts or words display their belonging to a group of violent fundamentalists"; the third one (category C) covers prisoners deemed "foreign terrorist fighters"; and the fourth one (category D) concerns prisoners "who show radicalisation signs or present the risk of radicalising other prisoners".

---

[20] Royal Decree, 10 April 2016 "modifiant l'arrêté royal du 25 octobre 2005 fixant le cadre des aumôniers et des conseillers islamiques appartenant à l'un des cultes reconnus ainsi que des conseillers moraux de philosophie non confessionnelle du conseil central laïque auprès des établissements pénitentiaires et fixant leurs échelles de traitement", *M.B.*, 19 April 2016, Article 1.

[21] Instructions, "Directeur général de la direction générale des Etablissements pénitentiaires, le 23 janvier 2015, le 2 avril 2015 et en avril 2016 aux directions des prisons", cited by Fr. Xavier, "Le radicalisme en prison", Droit belge & culte, Blog de la Chaire de droit et religion de l'UCL, 17 April 2017, http://ojurel.be/2017/04/17/le-radicalisme-en-prison/

In addition to this, members of prison staff are prepared for the detection of radicalisation through their basic training for new recruits, or through e-learning courses for agents already in place. Finally, the last major pillar of the Geens plan against radicalisation in prison is aimed at optimising contacts between the penitentiary establishments.

It should also be noted that the issue of training Muslim ministers and religious counsellors has recurrently come to the fore over many years. Various initiatives have been taken since 2001. A parliamentary exchange of 25 April 2007, between a deputy and the then Minister of Justice clearly, reflects the stakes and obstacles.

3.6.1 Parliamentary Question

"Mrs Chairman, Minister, in 2000, the Muslim Executive for Belgium (EMB) organised in collaboration with the federal government, a 4-month-long training destined to Muslim chaplains. The application conditions are quite strict: an A2 level degree and 5 years of residence on Belgian territory are, among others, required. Candidates should also pay a 25€ subscription. The training is organised in direct collaboration with prison management. Criminology, law, human and religious science classes are provided as well as miscellaneous curricula. Out of 50 candidates, 18 passed the examination. This training cost about 20,000€. After being screened by the State Security services, about 15 out of the lot met the criteria to be appointed prison chaplains on 4 November 2000. By the end of March 2007, Brahim Bouhna, chairman of the general assembly of the Belgian Muslims (EMB) released to the press the list of the 24 chaplain names, appointed by the Ministry of Justice and paid by the Treasury. Only one name matched the list of graduates. No explanation was given to the remaining graduates. The 24 chaplains were meant to follow further training after their appointment. Two conditions were added for recruitment: the recommendation letter, already required in 2000, must now come from a mosque, and cumulative mandates are now forbidden. The rules seemed to change abruptly. The disallowed graduates tell us, however, that a vast majority of the chosen chaplains nonetheless cumulate many functions, on the one hand, and, on the other hand, that some of the chosen chaplains are religion teachers who failed graduation for lack of language proficiency. If all of this is indeed the case, Minister, one can only marvel at this new example of bad governance from the head of the Belgian Muslim Executive's chief who, after cashing in subscription rights, will have monopolised the time of dozens of applicants and public services, taking part in that training, for nearly 4 months. This Muslim Executive Council seems oblivious to the continuity principle in public affairs management matters. Indeed, it is not because an executive changes that it has a right to make close-cropped table of the sum of previous commitments taken by the previous executive before a number of people or institutions. Are you able to confirm to me that the 2000 examination graduates were excluded from the list put forward by the EMB for the chaplain offices' list in a legal way?"

3.6.2 Answer from the Minister of Justice

"[…]I consider all religious and non-denominational philosophies on an equal plane. By virtue of the separation of powers between the State and the recognised denominations, I cannot interfere with the internal organisation of these denominations and this includes the choice of persons assuming the roles of chaplains in prison. The Belgian Muslim Executive has, just like the other recognised religions and secular movements, put forward to me a list of applications for the chaplaincy and after a security check, I appointed the suggested people who had obtained a security accreditation."[22]

To try to find a solution to the training of Islamic ministers and counsellors[23] (Wattier 2016a), we should take note of the fact that in 2015, the government of the Belgian French Community created a committee designed to focus on the "training of Muslim religious executives and licensed programs". It was set up on 18 March 2015 and drafted its report on 4 December 2015. In its report, the Committee emphasised how "paramount and urgent it is to reinforce the training measures for Muslim religious executives," and that these should be understood in the broadest sense, including "imams, male and female predicators, professors, Islamic Prison counsellors, army members, hospital staff, and youth protection public institutions as well as socio-cultural actors or Muslim intellectuals."[24]

Once this report was handed in, eight concrete proposals were adopted by the Minister of Superior Education and Media of the French Community, to create a "Belgian Islam". One of these proposals was aimed specifically at prison counsellors, as it dealt with "the organisation of theological or societal training for moral counsellors intervening in penitentiary environments […]."[25] These eight concrete

---

[22] CRIV 51 COM 1290 25/04/2007, Commission Justice Chambre, Moslim executive van België, no. 15192.

[23] Wattier (2016a), 377–389.

[24] Commission deputed by Minister Jean-Claude Marcourt, "Propositions au Gouvernement en vue de favoriser un islam de Belgique en Fédération Wallonie-Bruxelles, rapport concernant la formation des cadres musulmans et les émissions concédées", 4 December 2015, p. 5.

[25] The eight proposals are

1. Creation of an "Institute for the Promotion and Coordination of Training Initiatives on Islam".
2. Creation of an "Interuniversity Chair of Practical Islamology" aimed at the reflective and critical analysis of Arab-Muslim thought in its historical and contemporary dimensions.
3. Organisation of language courses for imams recognised by the Executive of the Muslims of Belgium.
4. Organisation of theological or "societal" training for moral counsellors who work in prison and in hospitals.
5. State support for the "University Teaching Certificate of Religious Education" organised by the Catholic University of Louvain and the Executive of the Muslims of Belgium (EMB) – a certificate that is now compulsory for new teachers of Islamic religion.
6. Support for continuing education in "Religious and Social Sciences devoted to Islam in the contemporary world" organised by the Catholic University of Louvain and the Saint-Louis University – Brussels
7. The Minister will transmit to the Government of Wallonia and the Brussels-Capital Region a proposal that is aimed at promoting greater involvement of women among Muslim counsellors.

proposals are both for short- and mid-term horizons: half a million Euros' worth having been allotted by the French Community to achieve them.

The Ministry of Superior Education and Media insisted that "it is about ensuring that the development of a modern Islam in the Wallonia-Brussels Federation, enshrines itself within the respect of the democratic values of tolerance, freedom, equality and free will. It is in this mindset that the training of religious leaders should be framed. It will in the long run be useful to all religious ministers, chaplains, educators and professors alike." He also claimed to have been fully convinced, long ago and well before the Paris and Copenhagen attacks, of the need to aim for a "Belgian and European type of Islam, not an imported one." He intends to explain his approach to the Moroccan and Turkish Ambassadors in Belgium, whose support is sought: "The ambition is to allow the second and third generations as well as new converts to take their destiny into their own hands". And, last but not least, the Minister stressed the importance of "recognising" this modern form of Islam. This implies letting personalities emerge to the forefront of the public stage, including in the media. According to him, "Nothing justifies that Islam, being the second main religion of the country, to this day, still has no access to the dedicated broadcasting programmes licensed by public broadcasting authorities."[26]

3.7   Conclusion

At the end of these long debates, a "public institute for the promotion of training on Islam" was created by a French-speaking decree of 14 December 2016 (M.B. 25 January 2017), whose members were appointed in August 2017. This institute is competent, inter alia, to facilitate and to support (but not to organize by itself) the training of imams and muslim chaplains. In 2019, the representative body of Muslims in Belgium, supported by the Minister of Justice, established an "Islamic training and research academy" (AFOR) which will conduct such training in cooperation with belgian universities. In any case, the implementation of these new programs of training of (Muslim) chaplains and counsellors remains a central and complex issue for the future. The growing individualisation of religious beliefs, along with a widespread suspicion regarding state-trained agents, will complexify the role of official chaplains and imams in prison. Rebuilding collective trust will be the main challenge, not only between inmates and society in general, but also between believers and their own religious authorities.

This measure will involve imposing female representation in the committees responsible for the management of the temporal worship of local Islamic communities, through the conditions of recognition of these by the regions.

8. As Minister of Media, Jean-Claude Marcourt finally hopes that a programme conceding to the Muslim religion will be broadcast, as soon as possible next September, on RTBF. (…).

[26] *Belga*, "Marcourt pose les jalons d'un 'islam moderne' en Belgique francophone", 18 March 2015.

References

Brion, F. (2019). Qui sème le vent… Vers une évaluation du plan d'action contre la radicalisation dans les prisons. In *L'effet radicalisation et le terrorisme. Etat des pratiques et des recherches* (pp. 57–83). Cahiers du GEPS: Politeia Editions.

Christians, L. L. (2019). L'accompagnement spirituel en prison : du soutien individuel au contrôle collectif ? L'arrêté royal du 17 mai 2019. *Droit belge & culte, Blog de la Chaire de droit et religion de l'UCL*. 6 september 2019, http://belgianlawreligion.unblog.fr/2019/09/06/laccompagnement-spirituel-en-prison-du-soutien-individuel-au-controle-collectif-larrete-royal-du-17-mai-2019/

Decroix, V. 1989. Les rapports de l'Eglise et l'Etat au XIXe siècle. La place du religieux dans l'institution pénitentiaire. *Review pénit. et de droit pénal*, 301–377.

Dupont-Boucha, M. S. (2001). Moraliser les détenus. Le rôle des religieux dans les prisons. In *L'Eglise en Luxembourg de Pie VII à Léon XIII (1800–1880). Le choc des libertés* (pp. 207–214). Bastogne, Musée en Piconrue.

El Asri, F. (2015). An outline of the construction of the Islamic Council for Prisons in Belgium. In I. Becci & O. Roy (Eds.), *Religious diversity in European prisons challenges and implications for rehabilitation* (pp. 47–59). Cham: Springer.

Ketelaer, A. F. (2000). Naar een nieuw wettelijk kader voor de morele bijstand in de gevangenissen. *UVV-Info*: 35–39

Nounckele, J. (2013). Régime pénitentiaire et religion. *Droit belge & culte, Blog de la Chaire de droit et religion de l'UCL*. http://ojurel.be/2013/11/07/regime-penitentiaire-et-alimentation-religieuse/

Overbeeke, A. (2005). God achter de tralies. Vrijheid van godsdienst en levensovertuiging in detentiesituaties. In E. Brems, S. Sottiaux, P. Vanden Heede, & W. Vandehole (Eds.), *Vrijheden en vrijheidsbeneming. Mensenrechten van gedetineerden* (pp. 123–150). Antwerpen: Intersentia.

Overbeeke, A. (2007). Veiligheid voor alles? Inperking van het recht op geestelijke verzorging van gedetineerde aanhangers van niet-'erkende' levensovertuigingen [Security for all. Delimiting the right to spiritual assistance for detainees pertaining to 'non-recognised' denominations]. *Panopticon, 4*, 23–40.

Overbeeke, A. (2019). Godsdienstvrijheid en deradicalisering. Het 'forum internum' is niet meer zo heilig. *Nieuw Juridisch Weekblad, 399*, 230–239.

Uwizeye, D. (2014). *La liberté de religion en prison: les droits du détenu* (p. 149). Louvain-la-Neuve: Faculté de droit et de criminologie, Université catholique de Louvain, Master's thesis (L.-L. Christians).

Van Geyt, K. (2012). De religieuze overheid en het ontslag van haar bedienaren. Soeverein in een slinkend rechtsgebied ? *Rechtskundig Weekblad, 13*, 61–65.

Wattier, S. (2015). Le prosélytisme n'est pas un abus en soi, *Droit belge & culte, Blog de la Chaire de droit et religion de l'UCL*. 6 July 2015, http://ojurel.be/2015/07/06/proselytisme-non-abusif-et-prison/

Wattier, S. (2016a). *Le financement public des cultes et des organisations philosophiques non confessionnelles. Analyse de constitutionnalité et de conventionnalité.* Brussels: Bruylant.

Wattier, S. (2016b). Le rôle des représentants des cultes dans la lutte contre la radicalisation religieuse au sein des prisons. *Chroniques de droit public - C.P.D.K., 4*, 611–622.

Xavier, Fr. (2017). Le radicalisme en prison, *Droit belge & culte, Blog de la Chaire de droit et religion de l'UCL*. 17 April 2017, http://ojurel.be/2017/04/17/le-radicalisme-en-prison/

Chapter 4
Bulgaria: Religion in Prison

Daniela Kalkandjieva

Abstract The presence of religion in Bulgarian prisons has never been the subject of systematic investigation. Established in 1878, the young Bulgarian state was not able to rely on the Ottoman legacy but had to build up its prison system anew. Therefore, the efforts of the practitioners and researchers in the sphere of penal law were concentrated on the study of the general principles of the organisation of a modern prison, rather than on specific issues such as religion in prison. At the same time, the establishment of the Communist regime in Bulgaria in 1944 caused a gap in religion-related practices in Bulgarian prisons. The atheist ideology left no space for any respect of the religious rights of prisoners. This changed after the fall of the Communist regime in Bulgaria in 1989. Considering the lack of systematic study of this aspect of modern Bulgarian history, the present article has the modest task of outlining the main stages in the development of religion-related practices in prison. In this regard, it offers an overview of the corresponding legislation during pre-communist times (1878–1944), under communism (1944–1989) and after the fall of this totalitarian regime.

4.1 Introduction

The presence of religion in Bulgarian prisons has never been the subject of systematic investigation. This state of affairs is determined by a set of factors. On the one hand, it is a result of the relatively short history of prisons in modern Bulgaria, which was liberated from Ottoman rule in 1878. During the first years of its existence, the young state had to build its own administration, set up new legislation, create a national financial system and, of course, to replace the old Ottoman system of prisons with a new one that considered contemporary European practices. Therefore, the initial efforts of the Bulgarian authorities were concentrated on the principles of organisation and management of modern prisons. Correspondingly, this issue obtained primary significance for the practitioners and researchers in the sphere of penal law, whereas the specific theme of religion in prisons remained of

D. Kalkandjieva (✉)
Sofia University St Kliment Ohridski, Sofia, Bulgaria

© Springer Nature Switzerland AG 2020   51
J. Martínez-Ariño, A.-L. Zwilling (eds.), *Religion and Prison: An Overview of Contemporary Europe*, Boundaries of Religious Freedom: Regulating Religion in Diverse Societies 7, https://doi.org/10.1007/978-3-030-36834-0_4

secondary importance. The communist *coup d'État* of 9 September 1944 did not provoke a special interest in this subject. On the contrary, the established regime of militant atheism caused a gap in religion-related practices in prison. The new rulers pursued the extermination of religion from all spheres of social life. As a result, the theme of religion in prisons became irrelevant for both lawyers and scholars until the collapse of the communist regime in 1989. Such a lack of systematic study of this aspect of the history of modern Bulgaria presupposes the modest task of this chapter: to outline the main religious practices in prisons since 1878. The overview is organised in accordance with the three major stages in the development of Bulgarian national legislation: the pre-communist period (1878–1944), the communist regime (1944–1989) and the post-Cold War years.

4.2   Religion in Prisons in Pre-Communist Bulgaria (1878–1944)

During the first year of its existence, the young Bulgarian state was administered by a provisional government, appointed by the Russian emperor, who had won the war against the Ottoman Empire (1877–1878). In this way, the first Prison Rules in new Bulgaria were elaborated under the supervision of Count Alexander Dondukov-Korsakov. Acting as Russian Imperial Commissar, he approved them on 29 January 1879. According to this legal act, imprisoned clerics and religious ministers had to be kept separate from the rest of prisoners (article 16).[1] The detained religious ministers were also exempt from any labour duties (article 37).[2] In addition, the rules forbade their chaining (Article 48).[3] Furthermore, the rules distinguished the Orthodox prisoners from those of other faiths. More specifically, they explicitly obliged the former to fast during Lent (article 85).[4] Finally, every regional prison had to maintain an Orthodox church or chapel (Article 118), the management of which was entrusted to a special cleric or one of the guardians (Article 119).[5]

In 1893, the Bulgarian State replaced the Provisional Prison Rules with new ones.[6] This time, they were created by the Bulgarian authorities and issued with the approval of the then ruling Bulgarian Prince Ferdinand Saxe-Coburg-Gotha. The new instructions were much more detailed regarding the issue of religion in prisons, especially regarding the case of Eastern Orthodox Christianity (henceforth

---

[1] *Privremenni pravila za uchrezhdenieto na zatvorite* [Provisional Rules for the organisation of prisons], 2nd edition, Sofia : Darzhavna pechatnitsa, 1882, p. 5

[2] Ibid. p. 9.

[3] Ibid. p. 11.

[4] Ibid., p. 17.

[5] Ibid., p. 21

[6] *Pravilnik za okrazhnite zatvori* [Rules on Provincial Prisons], Sofia: Darzhavna pechatnitsa, 1893. The document was originally published in the *State Gazette*, No. 176, 17 August 1893.

Orthodoxy). They required an Orthodox priest to be appointed in every prison (Article 1),[7] whose duties were specified in a special chapter (Chapter 7, Articles 178–188).[8]

More specifically, the prison chaplain was obliged to perform liturgy and to deliver a sermon every Sunday as well as on Orthodox feasts (Articles 179–180). If it was found necessary by the prison's authorities, on other days, he had to instruct individual prisoners who, according to the authorities, needed moral improvement (Article 180) or who were not aware of the basic Orthodox teaching (Article 181). The priest's duties also included regular visits to hospitalised prisoners or other detained persons who had asked for such meetings (Article 183). He had to be available in the prison at least twice weekly (Article 184). If he learned something important during his talks with prisoners, he had to inform the prosecutor (Article 186). During the church services, prisoners of different genders as well as of different categories of sentences, had to be separated from each other (Article 187). All issues related to the organisation of religious activities had to be arranged jointly by the priest and the director of the prison (Articles 178, 182, 187). Only one Article concerns non-Orthodox religious ministers. According to it, prisoners who did not belong to the majority religion, i.e. Orthodoxy, were allowed to receive spiritual care from their religious ministers on certain previously scheduled days (Article 188).

The Rules of 1893 also addressed the issue of the spiritual needs of the prisoners. If they were literate, then they could read selected types of literature, including religious books (Article 162),[9] which, however, were included in the prison's library only after a preliminary review and approval of the corresponding religious authorities (Article 139). The detainees also had the right to meet the priest in their cells (Article 163).[10] In addition, the rules paid special attention to imprisoned men who had been sentenced to death. They had to be visited by the chaplain at least once a day, but always in the presence of a guard (Article 168).[11] These rules remained almost unchanged until the communist overthrow on 9 September 1944.

In this way, the main religion-related innovations in the prison system of modern Bulgaria mostly concerned the rights of Orthodox prisoners. Under the Rules of 1893, laymen ceased to be subjects of church courts and were sued by civil courts. The only exception was the sphere of marriage and divorce, which remained under the jurisdiction of the Holy Synod of the Bulgarian Orthodox Church until 1946. In a similar way, the family-related issues of the adherents of non-Orthodox faiths remained under the control of the corresponding religious authorities (Muslim, Catholic, Protestant, Jewish and Armenian). At the same time, religious ministers who had infringed the norms of their faiths continued to be sued by the corresponding religious courts (Orthodox, Muslim etc.). Upon the Liberation of Bulgaria in

---

[7] Ibid., p. 1.

[8] Ibid. p. 33–35.

[9] Ibid., p. 31.

[10] Ibid.

[11] Ibid., p. 32.

1878, their punishment was not executed by the church authorities, but by the State ones.[12] At the same time, neither the Orthodox Church, representing up to 85% of Bulgarian citizens, nor the Muslim community – the second biggest religious community in the country (13%) introduced any clauses on religion in prisons in their statutes adopted between 1878 and 1945.[13]

4.3   Religion in Prison Under Communism

The establishment of a communist regime and the adoption of atheism as a guiding ideology in Bulgaria left no space for legal texts regarding the religious rights of prisoners, nor did the spiritual care of prisoners find a place in the new statutes adopted by the Bulgarian Orthodox Church (1951) and the Muslim community (1945, 1949, 1975 and 1986).[14] Despite this neglect, religion turned out to play an important role in the life of many people who happened to end up, for one reason or another, in communist prisons and labour camps. This is especially true for the first years of the rule of militant atheism, when many Orthodox and Catholic clerics as well as Protestant ministers were arrested as enemies of the new regime. Their memoires, as well as journalistic investigations on their detainee experience, which appeared after 1989, reveal that the lack of regulations on religion in prisons did not mean an absence of religious activities. On the contrary, the persecuted clerics not only grew stronger in their faith but sowed the seeds of Gospel in the hearts of their cellmates. Another unexpected outcome of the coexistence of detainees from different Christian denominations was the development of an ecumenical tolerance and solidarity as an act of moral opposition to their godless oppressors. In this regard, it is important to point out that the Christian clerics and ministers detained in the first years of the communist rule had almost no opportunity to communicate with representatives of Judaism and Islam. The reason is rooted in the different policies of the communist regime towards the adherents of the different religious traditions.

---

[12] Stefan, Velikotarnovski Mitropolit, *Tsarkvata i darzhavata v Balgaiya (1878–1918)*, Sofia: Unknown publishing house, 2011, p. 57.

[13] The statutes of the Bulgarian Orthodox Church are available in print: *Ekzarhiyskiy ustav prisposoben v Knyazhestvoto* [Exarchate Statute Adapted to the Principality], Sofia: State Printing House. 1883; *Ekzarhiyskiy ustav prisposoben v Knyazhestvoto* [Exarchate Statute Adapted to the Principality, 1895], Sofia: State Printing House, 1904. The statutes of the Muslim community in Bulgaria can be retrieved from the website of its Grand Muftiship here: http://www.grandmufti.bg/bg/za-nas/normativni-dokumenti/881-ustavi.html

[14] The Statute of the Bulgarian Orthodox Church was imposed by the communist state in January 1951. Its text is available in Bulgarian at: https://www.pravoslavie.bg/Документи/устав-бпц-1950/. In a similar way, the Muslim community had "adopted" a series of statutes in 1945, 1949, 1975 and 1986. Their Bulgarian texts are retractable via the website of the Chief Mufti's Office at: http://www.grandmufti.bg/bg/za-nas/normativni-dokumenti/881-ustavi.html

The Orthodox clergy was the subject of mass persecution before the Paris Peace Treaty, whereas the Protestant pastors and the Catholic priests were attacked after the outbreak of the Cold War.[15] At the same time, after World War II, the majority of Bulgarian Jews left the country to settle in the newly established state of Israel, whereas the few who remained in Bulgaria were supportive of the local Communist Party and many of them shared its atheist ideology. Although some practising Jewish believers were thrown in jail by the communist regime, there are no studies on their experience there.[16] In turn, Muslims also avoided the first waves of persecution by the communist regime, the leaders of which hoped to reduce the Muslim minority in the country by negotiating its emigration to Turkey.[17] Muslims became the subject of repression in the 1950s, when the Bulgarian Communist Party launched a special policy designed to suppress Islam in Bulgaria.[18] In this way, Christians and Muslims *de facto* remained separate in their experience of prisoners under communism.

Another important development linked with religion in communist prisons is revealed by the Bulgarian journalist, Hristo Hristov, who investigates the archives of the totalitarian state secret services. On his website, he has published documents that provide evidence about multiple hunger strikes initiated by the prisoners of Turkish origin whose Muslim names had been forcefully replaced with Bulgarian ones in the 1980s. In May 1989, these prisoners were required by the security services to submit written declarations claiming that they wanted to emigrate from Bulgaria as a condition to receive international passports with their Muslim names restored.[19] The prisoners responded by hunger strikes. They wanted full political amnesty as well as the recognition of their rights to freely use their mother tongue and practise their religion.

---

[15] Daniela Kalkandjieva, *Balgarskata pravoslavna tsarkva i darzhavata (1944-1953)* [The Bulgarian Orthodox Church and the State (1944–1953)] (Sofia: Albatros, 1997), 275–296.

[16] An interview conducted by the author at the Sofia Synagogue in August 2017.

[17] Daniela Kalkandjieva, "Politikata na Balgarskata komunisticheska partiya kam nepravoslavnite religiozni obshtnosti (1944-1953)" [The Bulgarian Communist Party's Policy towards the Non-Orthodox religious communities (1944–1953)], [journal] *Trudove na katedrite po istoriya i bogoslovie* [History and Theology Studies of Shumen University Bishop Konstantin Preslavski, Bulgaria], 2005, vol. 8, pp. 252–264.

[18] Mihail Gruev, *Mezhdu petolachkata i polumesetsa: Balgarite myusyulmani i politicheskiyat rezhim (1944–1959)* [Between the Five-point Star and the Crescent: The Bulgarian Muslims and the Political Regime (1944–1959)], Sofia: IK "Kota", 2003, pp. 175–189; Rumen Avramov, *Ikonomika na "Vazroditelniya Process"* [Economy of the "Revival Process"], Sofia: Sofia Centre for Academic Study/RIVA Publishers, 2017.

[19] Hristo Hristov, "Preimenuvanite otvrashtat s gladni stachki v zatvorite sled mayskite sabitiya prez 1989 godina" [The Bulgarian Turks whose names had been forcefully changed in the mid-1980s responded by hunger strikes in prison], published on the website Darzhavna sigurnost.com on 24 June 2014, available in Bulgarian at: http://desebg.com/2011-01-13-09-25-08/1880-2014-06-24-16-04-08

4.4   Religion in Prisons in Post-Communist Bulgaria

The fall of communism (1989) brought significant changes in the status of religious denominations in Bulgaria. Today, they enjoy free access to the public space. In contrast to the constitutions that were in force during the communist regime and that limited the freedom of religion to the performance of religious rites (Article 78 of the 1947 Constitution; Article 53 of the 1971),[20] the Constitution of 1991 introduced a wider understanding of the freedom of religion. According to Article 37,

1. The freedom of conscience, the freedom of thought and the choice of religion and of religious or atheistic views shall be inviolable. The State shall assist the maintenance of tolerance and respect among the believers from different denominations, and among believers and non-believers.
2. The freedom of conscience and religion shall not be practised to the detriment of national security, public order, public health and morals, or of the rights and freedoms of others.[21]

After 2007, Bulgaria also adopted the European Union's regulations regarding the freedom of religion. In this way, its citizens can follow, individually or in a group, their specific faith traditions and observe the corresponding rites and norms of behaviour. In parallel, the new state authorities made a series of amendments in civil law and adopted new bills and administrative norms to guarantee the religious rights of detained persons in post-communist Bulgaria. Despite these changes, however, the new statutes of religious bodies in Bulgaria continue the pre-communist tradition and do not address the care of their adherents in prison. Instead, this issue is the subject of individual negotiations between the leaderships of the different religious denominations and the state authorities. As a result, the clerics of the Bulgarian Orthodox Church and the ministers of some other faith communities received access to prisoners from the respective religious traditions. In this regard, this chapter offers a review of both the post-1989 Bulgarian legislation on religion in prison and the practices developed by religious denominations in this sphere.

---

[20] The texts of the Bulgarian Constitutions of 1947 and 1971 are published in *Balgarski konstitutsii i konstitutsionni proekti* (Bulgarian Constitutions and Constitutional Projects), Sofia: Darzhavno izdatelstvo "d-r Petar Beron", 1990), pp. 37–81.

[21] The text of the Constitution of 1991 is available in English at the website of the Bulgarian National Assembly: http://parliament.bg/en/const

4.5 Legal Aspects

The first steps for guaranteeing the religious rights of prisoners in Bulgaria took place in 1998, when amendments in the Law on the Implementation of Penalties of 1969 finally addressed this issue.[22] The new texts allowed prisoners to take part in religious services and rites as well as to have access to religious literature (Article 70a). They also envisioned the access of all religious legally recognised religious denominations to prisons and custody places and granted them the opportunity for private meetings with persons under detention (Article 70b [1] and [2]). In addition, the Law guaranteed the right of prisoners and those under temporary arrest to decide themselves whether or not to attend religious services (Article 70b [3]). Furthermore, the amendments of 1998 declared an equal treatment of prisoners without regard for their religious affiliation (Article 70b [4]). Still, this act did not concern all existing religious denominations in the country, but only those that had been officially recognised by the state authorities. In addition, only the representatives of the traditional religion, i.e. Eastern Orthodoxy (1991 Constitution, Article 13 § 3),[23] were recognised as being eligible to be appointed as part of the prison's staff (Article 70b [5]). In 2002, a change in the same law authorised the court or the prosecutor to issue permission for the meetings of prisoners with representatives of religious organisations that have been officially recognised as legal entities (Article 132a [3]). Finally, in 2005, another amendment to the Law on the Implementation of Penalties allowed the approbation councils, which had been set up at the regional courts, to ask the opinion of religious ministers on the cases of individual prisoners (Article 134 [4]).

In 2009, the adoption of a new Law on the Implementation of Penalties and the Detention in Custody provided better conditions for the protection of the religious rights of prisoners in Bulgaria.[24] It takes into account the stipulations of the Religious Denominations Act of 2002, as well as the requirements of legislation of the European Union, which Bulgaria joined in 2007. Although the new penal bill follows the amendments of 1998 and 2005 (Article 167), it also introduces some innovations. If the old texts allowed the payroll of religious ministers only from "the traditional religion" (Article 70b §5), the new ones omit the reference to the traditional religion and introduce a different criterion. More specifically, the new law requires these appointments to consider "the faith which is confessed by the majority of prisoners or persons under detention" (Article 167 §5). In practice, this does not change the result, as the religious demography in Bulgarian prisons is a function of the country's religious demography, i.e. it seems that only the Bulgarian Orthodox Church can benefit from the new formula. At the same time, the state authorities do

---

[22] *The amendments to the 1969 Law on the Implementation of Penalties*, available in Bulgarian at: http://econ.bg/Нормативни-актове/ЗАКОН-ЗА-ИЗПЪЛНЕНИЕ-НА-НАКАЗАНИЯТА_ll_i.158141_at.5.html

[23] The English text of the Bulgarian Constitution is available at: http://www.parliament.bg/en/const

[24] *The 2009 Law on the Implementation of Penalties and the Detention in Custody*, available in Bulgarian at: http://www.gdin.bg/ЗАКОН-ЗА-ИЗПЪЛНЕНИЕТО-НА-НАКАЗАНИЯТА-И-ЗАДЪРЖАНЕТО-ПОД-СТРАЖА_p41_l6.html

not provide official information about the religious affiliation of prisoners, nor do they announce how many non-Orthodox religious ministers have been appointed there.

At the same time, the 2009 Penal Law offers a more elaborate description of the rights of prisoners. It envisions the different treatment of persons under alleviated detention, who now have the right to attend religious services in the city or village where they are serving their term of imprisonment (Article 72 § 3.2). According to another Article (97 §7), publications that propagate religious hatred are cited among the specific types of literature forbidden in the prison. In parallel, the new Penal Law permits restrictions on religious activities in prison in the case of natural disasters, fires, floods etc. (Article 119 §2). At the same time, it treats religious support to prisoners and the persons under custody as part of their social and educational/instructive activities (Article 152 § 2.4). In a similar way, the exercise of freedom of religion in prison is included in the section for creative, cultural and sporting activities (Articles 166 and 167). A no less important novelty concerns the resocialisation of prisoners by giving religious organisations an opportunity to take part in this process (Article 170 §1).

4.6   Remarks on Post-1989 Religion-Related Practices in Prisons

Until recently, the main religious activities in Bulgarian prisons were linked mostly to the national Orthodox Church. The first priest appointed at the Sofia Prison was Father Nikolay Georgiev from the Sofia Diocese. As such, he initiated the building of an Orthodox chapel, which was consecrated on 22 December 1996. In 2000, he also founded the Prison Fellowship Bulgaria for Religious and Social Support of the Detainees.[25] The fellowship started the annual initiative "The Angel Tree", which collects donations for Christmas gifts for the children of prisoners. In 2015, the fellowship started the programme "The Prisoner's Journey", which envisions eight teaching sessions, based on the Gospel of Mark, to be held in the prisons in Sofia, Stara Zagora and Vratsa. The programme is blessed by the Holy Synod of the Bulgarian Orthodox Church and is realised in cooperation with its priests who work at the aforementioned prisons.[26] Currently, Father Nikolay is also Regional Director for Eastern Europe and Central Asia of the Prison Fellowship International.

---

[25] *Prison Fellowship International*, available in Bulgarian at: http://pfbulgaria.org/the-prisoners-journey/?lang=en

[26] Angel Ivanov, "Otets Nikolay Georgiev: "Zatvorite sa nay-golemiya proval na nashata darzhava, tsarkva i obshtestvo" [The prisons are the biggest failure of our state, church and society], published in pravoslavie.bg on 28 February 2017, available at: https://www.pravoslavie.bg/Социална-дейност/отец-николай-георгиев-затворите-са/; "Pateshetvieto na zatvornika – edna nova initsiativa" [The prisoner's journey – a new initiative], published on pravoslavie.bg on 24 April 2015, available at: https://www.pravoslavie.bg/обяви/пътешествието-на-затворника-една-нов/

The representatives of the Bulgarian Orthodox Church are also very active in the provincial prison of Stara Zagora. In 1994, with the blessing of the diocesan Orthodox metropolitan and the support of the prison's administration, one of the local Orthodox priests, Yordan Karageorigiev, initiated the building of the first prison church in Bulgaria (until then, there were only rooms transformed into chapels).[27] Today, the prison has four additional Orthodox chapels at its different buildings and premises.[28] Furthermore, in 2006, a church choir was also set up there,[29] while 32 of its prisoners were rewarded for good discipline with a pilgrimage to an Orthodox monastery.[30] By 2014, the chaplain, Yordan Karageorgiev, had baptised over 1200 prisoners.[31]

Another direction of the efforts of the Bulgarian Orthodox Church was aimed at the religious instruction of prisoners. It organised evangelical lectures and courses in many prisons, e.g. in Stara Zagora,[32] in Lovech[33] etc. In 2007, with the assistance of the state, it also succeeded in opening 35 Orthodox chapels in the 13 central prisons and in other places of detainment.[34] In parallel, it has one priest in each of the 13 central prisons in Bulgaria, who is appointed by the Ministry of Justice on 4-hour working day.[35] Finally, in the summer of 2013, at the request of the Chief

---

[27] Veneta Asenova, "Monitor: Sveshtenik krasti nad 1000 zatvornitsi" [Newspaper Monitor: Priest baptised over 1000 prisoners], published on 8 January 2007, available at: https://www.pravoslavie.bg/Медиен-архив/свещеник-кръсти-над-1000-затворн/

[28] Elena Balabanova, "Okolo 5 hil. lv sa nuzhni za dovarshvaneto na noviya paraklis v Starozagorskiya zatvor" [5000 more Bulgarian levs are necessary for the new chapel in the Stara Zagora Central Prison to be finished], published on the website of the Bulgarian National Radio on 16 December 2016, available at: http://bnr.bg/starazagora/post/100773198/okolo-5-hil-sa-nujni-za-dovarshvaneto-na-novia-paraklis-v-starazagorskia-zatvor

[29] "Zatvornitsi poseshtavat religiozni besedi i kursove po verouchenie" [Prisoners attend religious classes and courses], Source BTA.com, republished by pravolavie.bg on 11 July 2006 at: https://www.pravoslavie.bg/България/затворници-посещават-религиозни-бес/

[30] "Za parvi pat zatvotnitsi poluchavat za nagrada poklonichesko patuvane" [For the first time prisoners have been rewarded with a pilgrimage trip], published at pravoslavie.com on 10 October 2006, available in Bulgarian at: https://www.pravoslavie.bg/България/за-първи-път-затворници-получават-за-н/

[31] Sv. Sinod shte osiguri tsarkovna literatura za zatvornicheskite biblioteki" [The Holy Synod will ensure the supply of religious literature for the prison libraries], published on dveri.bg on 6 June 2013, available at: https://dveri.bg/xhq34

[32] "Zatvornitsi poseshtavat religiozni besedi i kursove po verouchenie" [Prisoners attend religious classes and courses], Source BTA.com, republished by pravolavie.bg on 11 July 2006 at: https://www.pravoslavie.bg/България/затворници-посещават-религиозни-бес/

[33] "Zatvotnitsi zavarshiha kurs po pravoslavno verouchenie" [Prisoners finished a religious course on Orthodoxy], published on 13 October 2011, available online at: https://dariknews.bg/regioni/pleven/zatvornici-zavyrshiha-kurs-po-pravoslavno-verouchenie-790192

[34] Silviya Nikolova, "Vasil Marinov: Golemiyat problem na zatworite e negramotnossta" [Interview with Vasil Marinov, the head of the directorate "Care of the Religious needs of Prisoners"], reprint from newspaper *Duma*, published on 1 February 2007 on pravoslavie.bg, available online at: https://www.pravoslavie.bg/Интервю/васил-маринов-големият-проблем-на-зат/

[35] Ibid.

Prosecutor, the Holy Synod of the Bulgarian Orthodox Church took care of supplying the prison libraries with Orthodox literature.[36]

When Bulgaria joined the European Union, 20 out of the 73 then registered religious communities in the country provided spiritual care to their imprisoned adherents. Those who belong to Catholicism are visited once monthly by a Sofia-based Roman Catholic priest.[37] In a similar way, Evangelical pastors are granted permission to take care of their detained co-religionists. For about 13 years, Pastor Ivodor Kovachev has been developing religious activities in Sofia Prison, where he is in charge of over 50 prisoners.[38] In parallel, the care of Muslim prisoners in Sofia Central Prison is entrusted to graduate students from the Higher Institute for Muslim Studies, who also lead the Friday prayers there.[39] Yet, in the case of this religion the special dietary regime of its adherents presents some serious challenges, e.g. in 2005, a Muslim prisoner with life sentence sued the administration of his prison for being forced to eat pork for about a year.[40]

4.7   Conclusions

The overview of the ways in which religion was presented in Bulgarian prisons since the Liberation of Bulgaria (1878) reveals more elaborate practices in the case of Eastern Orthodoxy – the country's majority religion. After the end of the Cold War, some pre-communist patterns have been quickly restored, e.g. the special support for the activities of Orthodox priests in prisons. At the same time, we observe some new developments in comparison with the pre-communist times. More specifically, the chaplains of religious minorities have received more opportunities to provide effective care of the prisoners who belong to these faith traditions. In this case, however, it seems that the religious rights of the prisoners from the minority religions are not as well observed as those of the Orthodox prisoners, e.g. the regis-

---

[36] "Sv. Sinod shte osiguri tsarkovna literatura za zatvornicheskite biblioteki" [The Holy Synod will ensure the supply of religion literature for the prison libraries], published on dveri.bg on 6 June 2013, available at: https://dveri.bg/xhq34

[37] Silviya Nikolova, "Vasil Marinov: Golemiyat problem na zatvorite e negramotnossta" [Interview with Vasil Marinov, the head of the Directorate "Care of the Religious needs of Prisoners"], reprint from newspaper *Duma*, published on 1 February 2007 on pravoslavie.bg, available online at: https://www.pravoslavie.bg/Интервю/васил-маринов-големият-проблем-на-зат/

[38] "Izpovednikat na prestapnitsite v Tsentralniya Sofiyski zatvor" [The confessor of criminals from the Central Sofia Prison], published on kapelnastvo.com on 22 September 2011, available online at: http://kapelnastvo.com/chap/425

[39] Silviya Nikolova, "Vasil Marinov: Golemiyat problem na zatworite e negramotnossta" [Interview with Vasil Marinov, the head of the Directorate "Care of the Religious needs of Prisoners"], reprint from newspaper *Duma*, published on 1 February 2007 on pravoslavie.bg, available online at: https://www.pravoslavie.bg/Интервю/васил-маринов-големият-проблем-на-зат/

[40] *Judgement No. 73*, the Administrative Court of Stara Zagora, 7 May 2005, available in Bulgarian at: http://www.adms-sz.com/pages/0061d813/28740715.htm

tered neglect to the specific dietary norms of Muslim prisoners. In this regard, the state authorities need to develop new norms to meet the requirements of the 1991 Bulgarian Constitution and the EU Charter of Fundamental Rights for religious freedoms and equal treatment of the existing faith communities. The discrepancies between the paid positions of Orthodox chaplains at prisons and the voluntary ones of the other religious ministers constitute another issue that raises questions about the equal treatment of religions in post-communist Bulgaria. From such a perspective, the issue of religion in prison calls for further research to explore not only the current presence of religion in prison but also the historical experience in that sphere. Without such an analysis, it will be difficult to define to what degree the present problems regarding religion-related activities in Bulgarian prisons are influenced by old stereotypes or are provoked by the process of Eurointegration. In the first case, we will need to identify the past negative practices regarding religion in prison and to elaborate a systematic policy of overcoming them, whereas in the second, efforts should be focused on the harmonisation of the contemporary Bulgarian national legislation and prison system with the European Union's legal acts and guidelines on the protection of the freedom of religion.

Bibliography

Asenova, V. Monitor: Sveshtenik krasti nad 1000 zatvornitsi [Newspaper Monitor: Priest baptised over 1000 prisoners]. Published on 8 January 2007., available at: https://www.pravoslavie.bg/Медиен-архив/свещеник-кръсти-над-1000-затвори/

Avramov, R. (2017). *Ikonomika na "Vazroditelniya Process"* [Economy of the "Revival Process"]. Sofia: Sofia Centre for Academic Study/RIVA Publishers. . http://www.cas.bg/en/books/the-economy-of-the-revival-process-1810.html

Balabanova, E. Okolo 5 hil. lv sa nuzhni za dovarshvaneto na noviya paraklis v Starozagorskiya zatvor [5,000 more Bulgarian levs are necessary for the new chapel in the Stara Zagora Central Prison to be finished]. Published on the website of the Bulgarian National Radio on 16 December 2016., available at: http://bnr.bg/starazagora/post/100773198/okolo-5-hil-sa-nujni-za-dovarshvaneto-na-novia-paraklis-v-starozagorskia-zatvor

Balgarski konstitutsii i konstitutsionni proekti. [Bulgarian Constitutions and Constitutional Projects]. Sofia: Darzhavno izdatelstvo "d-r Petar Beron". 1990.

Ekzarhiyskiy ustav prisposoben v Knyazhestvoto. [Exarchate Statute adapted to the Principality]. Sofia: State Printing House. 1883.

Ekzarhiyskiy ustav prisposoben v knyazhestvoto. [Exarchate Statute adapted to the Principality, 1895]. Sofia: State Printing House. 1904.

Gruev, M. (2003). *Mezhdu petolachkata i polumesetsa: Balgarite myusyulmani i politicheskiyat rezhim (1944–1959)* [Between the Five-point Star and the Crescent: The Bulgarian Muslims and the Political Regime (1944–1959)] (pp. 175–189). Sofia: IK "Kota".

Hristov, H. Preimenuvanite otvrashtat s gladni stachki v zatvorite sled majskite sabitiya prez 1989 godina [The Bulgarian Turks whose names had been forcefully changed in the mid-1980s responded by hunger strikes in prison]. Published on the website Darzhavna sigurnost.com on 24 June 2014, available in Bulgarian at: http://desebg.com/2011-01-13-09-25-08/1880-2014-06-24-16-04-08

Ivanov, A. Otets Nikolay Georgiev: "Zatvorite sa nay-golemiya proval na nashata darzhava, tsarkva i obshtestvo [The prisons are the biggest failure of our state, church and society].

Published in pravoslavie.bg on 28 February 2017., available at: https://www.pravoslavie.bg/
Социална-дейност/отец-николай-георгиев-затворите-са/

Izpovednikat na prestapnitsite v Tsentralniya Sofiyski zatvor [The confessor of criminals from the Central Sofia Prison]. Published on kapelnastvo.com on 22 September 2011, available online at: http://kapelanstvo.com/chap/425

Judgement No. 73, the Administrative Court of Stara Zagora, 7 May 2005, available in Bulgarian in: http://www.adms-sz.com/pages/0061d813/28740715.htm

Kalkandjieva, D. (1997). *Balgarskata pravoslavna tsarkva i darzhavata (1944–1953)* [The Bulgarian Orthodox Church and the State (1944–1953)]. Sofia: Albatros.

Kalkandjieva, D. (2005). Politikata na Balgarskata komunisticheska partiya kam nepravoslavnite religiozni obshtnosti (1944–1953) [The Bulgarian Communist Party's Policy towards the Non-Orthodox religious communities (1944–1953)]. [journal] *Trudove na katedrite po istoriya i bogoslovie* [History and Theology Studies of Shumen University Bishop Konstantin Preslavski, Bulgaria], *8*, 252–264.

Nikolova, S. Vasil Marinov: Golemiyat problem na zatworite e negramotnossta [Interview with Vasil Marinov, the head of the directorate "Care of the Religious needs of Prisoners"]. Reprint from newspaper *Duma*, published on 1 February 2007 on pravoslavie.bg, available online at: https://www.pravoslavie.bg/Интервю/васил-маринов-големият-проблем-на-зат/

Pateshetvieto na zatvornika – edna nova initsiativa [The prisoner's journey – A new initiative], published on pravoslavie.bg on 24 April 2015., available at: https://www.pravoslavie.bg/обяви/ пътешествието-на-затворника-една-нов/

Pravilnik za okrazhnite zatvori [Rules on Provincial Prisons]. Sofia: Darzhavna pechatnitsa. 1893.

Prison Fellowship International. (2019) Available in Bulgarian in: http://pfbulgaria.org/ the-prisoners-journey/?lang=en

Privremenni pravila za uchrezhdenieto na zatvorite [Provisional Rules for the organisation of prisons] (2nd ed.). Sofia: Darzhavna pechatnitsa. 1882.

Stefan, V. M. (2011). *Tsarkvata i darzhavata v Balgaiya (1878–1918)*. Sofia: Unknown Publishing House.

Sv. Sinod shte osiguri tsarkovna literature za zatvornicheskite biblioteki [The Holy Synod will ensure the supply of religious literature for the prison libraries], published on dveri.bg on 6 June 2013., available at: https://dveri.bg/xhq34

The 2009 Law on the Implementation of Penalties and the Detention in Custody. 2009 available in Bulgarian at: http://www.lex.bg/laws/ldoc/2135627067

The amendments to the 1969 Law on the Implementation of Penalties. 1969 available in Bulgarian in http://econ.bg/Нормативни-актове/ ЗАКОН-ЗА-ИЗПЪЛНЕНИЕ-НА-НАКАЗАНИЯТА_l.l_i.158141_at.5.html

Za parvi pat zatvotnitsi poluchavat za nagrada poklonichesko patuvane [For the first time prisoners have been rewarded with a pilgrimage trip], published on pravoslavie.com on 10 October 2006, available in Bulgarian at: https://www.pravoslavie.bg/България/ за-първи-път-затворници-получават-за-н/

Zatvornitsi poseshtavat religiozni besedi i kursove po verouchenie [Prisoners attend religious classes and courses]. Source BTA.com, republished by pravolavie.bg on 11.07.2006 at: https:// www.pravoslavie.bg/България/затворници-посещават-религиозни-бес/

Zatvotnitsi zavarshiha kurs po pravoslavno verouchenie [Prisoners finished a religious course on Orthodoxy]. Published on 13 October 2011, available online at: https://dariknews.bg/regioni/ pleven/zatvornici-zavyrshiha-kurs-po-pravoslavno-verouchenie-790192

Chapter 5
Croatia: Religion in Prison – Equal Access in a Predominantly Catholic Society

Frane Staničić and Siniša Zrinščak

Abstract The chapter investigates the role of religion in prison in Croatia from legal and sociological points of view. As a legal provision, the religious right of prisoners was set up only in the late 1990s and the early 2000s. The intention was to determine whether it was respected by state authorities, in particular in relation to small religious communities and their believers. Based on the analysis of the legal framework and data gathered from the Ministry of Justice, as well as on semi-structured interviews with authorised religious persons from different religions, both majority and minority, it has been concluded that all religious communities have equal access to prisons. However, this general conclusion is followed by a detailed description that shows how the system really works in its different aspects. An inclusive approach revealed in relation to the access of different religions to prisons is discussed in the Conclusion in relation to some particularities of the Croatian case, such as debates about religious presence in public institutions, limited and contested pluralisation in Croatian society in general, weak State performance, etc.

5.1 Introduction

Although the topic of religion in prisons has attracted growing research interest in many European countries, no information (scientific, but not even basic administrative data) exists about religion/religious rights in Croatian prisons. This lack of interest in religion in prisons stands in sharp contrast to vivid public debates about religion in the public sphere, particularly about religious education in public schools, controversies about ethical questions and minority rights (abortion, gay rights etc.) and in general about religion and politics. The fall of the former Yugoslavia and the

F. Staničić (✉) · S. Zrinščak
Faculty of Law, University of Zagreb, Zagreb, Croatia
e-mail: frane.stanicic@pravo.hr; sinisa.zrinscak@pravo.hr

© Springer Nature Switzerland AG 2020
J. Martínez-Ariño, A.-L. Zwilling (eds.), *Religion and Prison: An Overview of Contemporary Europe*, Boundaries of Religious Freedom: Regulating Religion in Diverse Societies 7, https://doi.org/10.1007/978-3-030-36834-0_5

communist regime, and the building of an independent Croatian state, was accompanied by a new role of religion in the public sphere, in particular the dominant Catholic Church. The complete rearrangement of Church–State relations under the new social circumstances during the 1990s provoked debates about the role of religion in a secular and democratic state, and about the rights of different minorities, above all ethnic and religious.

Without intending to carry out a systematic review of the existing knowledge about religion in prison, one could conclude that the growing body of research has been triggered by a rising plurality in many countries. The issue has been how states accommodate the presence of different confessions and if/how the right to demonstrate one's own beliefs in public is recognised by state institutions (e.g. Beckford and Gilliat 1998; Beckford 2011). An aspect of plurality concerns the new religious landscape transformed by immigration. Partly connected, but not fully reduced to that, is an issue of the relations between states, national or dominant religions with a range of privileged rights, and other traditional and new minority religions. It has been shown that the widely used approach based on different models of Church–State relations (e.g. Ferrari 2003a, b; Robbers 2005; Torfs 2007) can be misleading in relation to religion in prison, as in some cases national models can have opposite effects to what has been predicted (Beckford et al. 2005), and as countries belonging to one model can employ different governing approaches to religion in prison (Furseth and Kühle 2011).

The Spanish case can serve as an interesting comparative point for the Croatian situation. Similarities include the historically dominant position of the Catholic Church, as well as the current Church–State arrangements, which are regulated in both countries by international agreements with the Holy See and by agreements between the respective governments and other religious communities (Martínez-Ariño et al. 2015; Zrinščak et al. 2014). The Spanish case demonstrates that the position of different religions in prisons reveals how controversial the process of changing the historical position of the Catholic Church is, and how different groups operate to gain the power to be present in a place such as a prison (Martínez-Ariño et al. 2015; Griera and Clot-Garrell 2015). Despite these similarities, there are some differences between the two countries, which will be explored further in this chapter, to reveal how different social contexts can shape the Church's role in a specific setting.

In the light of that, the main purpose of this chapter is to present basic data on religion in Croatian prisons based on the analysis of legal aspects, administrative data that we were able to collect and semi-structured interviews with priests/ministers of different confessions who act as prison chaplains. Our main aim was to examine if, and to what degree, state authorities respected legal provisions about religious rights in prison, and whether all religious communities had the same access to prisons, and if the rights of prisoners of different confessions were equally respected.

The chapter is divided into six sections. This introduction is followed by analysis of the position of religion from legal and sociological points of view. The two sections that follow describe the legal framework regulating religion in prison and provide basic information about the penitentiary system in Croatia. The fifth and main section is based on the data we collected from state authorities and from semi-structured interviews with authorised religious persons. In the discussion and conclusion sections, we have summarised the results by pointing out the specificities of the Croatian system, which could be further analysed from a comparative perspective.

5.2 Religion, State and Society

The Croatian Constitution guarantees to all people the enjoyment of rights and freedoms, irrespective of, among other things, religion, political or other convictions, freedom of thought and expression, freedom of conscience and religion, and the freedom to demonstrate religious or other convictions (Zrinščak et al. 2014). Furthermore, the Constitution stipulates that all religious communities are equal before the law and separate from the State. However, this Article 41 of the Constitution contains another provision, which states that religious communities are free, in accordance with the law, to set up and manage schools, academies or other institutions, as well as welfare and charitable organisations, and that they enjoy the protection and assistance of the State in their activities (Articles 41/2). This has been further supported by the following legal acts:

1. Four agreements signed between the Republic of Croatia and the Holy See in 1996 and 1998 concerning the position and the role of the Catholic Church as the most dominant religion.
2. The Law on the Legal Status of Religious Communities (LLSRC) of 2002.
3. The agreements between the Government and the respective religious communities.

In addition to the agreements with the Holy See, and following a framework set up in the LLSRC, the Government signed eight agreements covering 19 out of 42 registered religious communities. The agreements were signed with the Serbian Orthodox Church (2003), the Islamic community (2003), the Evangelical Church (2003), the Reformed Christian Church (2003), the Evangelical (Pentecostal) Church, the Church of God and the Alliance of Christ's Pentecostal Churches (2003), the Advent Christian Church (2003), the Reform Movement of the Seventh Day Adventists (2003), the Alliance of Baptist Churches (2003), the Church of Christ (2003), the Bulgarian Orthodox Church in Croatia (2003), the Croatian Old Catholic Church (2003), the Macedonian Orthodox Church in Croatia (2003), the Jewish community Bet Israel (2012), the Coordination of Jewish communities in the Republic of Croatia (2012), the Alliance of Churches "The Word of Life" (2014), the Church of Full Gospel (2014) and the Reformed Protestant Church (2014).

Under the agreements, these religious communities enjoy certain rights stipulated in the LLSRC, which other religious communities are deprived of: religious teaching and confessional instruction in public schools (Article 13), the right to spiritual care in health institutions, and social care institutions (Article 14), *the right to spiritual care in penitentiaries and prisons* (Article 15) and the right to spiritual care of members of armed forces and the police (Article 16) (Staničić 2014, 249). Thus, the Croatian model can be classified as the so-called cooperation model of Church–State relations (Ferrari 2003a, b; Robbers 2005). Although hierarchical (different rights for different religious communities), the Croatian model stands out as the model with, comparatively speaking, a wide range of rights, which a large number of religious communities (the 19 communities that entered into agreements with the State) can enjoy.

The enjoyment of legally prescribed rights must be viewed within the social context, which reveals that Croatia is, at least in terms of numbers, a predominantly Catholic country and a country with a high level of religiosity. According to the 2011 Census data, there were 86.28% Catholics, 4.44% Orthodox, 1.47% Muslims, 0.3% Protestants, 0.01% Jews and 4.57% atheists and agnostics (CBS 2012). The sociological data paint a similar picture: for example, 85.8% of respondents reported believing in God, 80% identified as religious persons, 41% reported attending religious services at least once a month and 53.4% stated that they had a great deal or quite a lot of trust in the Church in 2008 (Črpić and Zrinščak 2014). A comparative analysis suggests that although among 13 Central, Eastern and Southern European countries, Croatia does not belong to the group with the highest level of religiosity (like Poland, Kosovo and Bosnia and Herzegovina), it does belong to the group with high religiosity, together with Italy and Slovakia (Zrinščak and Črpić 2017). Still, this image of a high level of religiosity hides the fact that religiosity is not consistent in all dimensions, that about one third of the population opts for a more individualised approach to religiosity or to the Church's teaching, and that the strong public position of the Catholic Church provokes debates about its allegedly privileged position and access to authorities, and in particular about its position in education (confessional instruction in public schools, although as an optional subject; the Church's opposition to sexual education in schools etc.) (Nikodem and Zrinščak 2012; Zrinščak et al. 2014).

For the purposes of this chapter, the social position of religious minorities is of interest. What differentiates Croatia from most Western, Northern and South European societies is that religious minorities are traditional (such as Orthodox, Muslims and Jews), and their presence in the country is not the result of recent immigration. The historical proximity and similarities of the majority religious group and minority religious groups in terms of language and culture, on the one hand, but their non-visibility in the public space and rather high social distance of the majority religious group towards ethnic/religious minorities, on the other hand, frame what could be labelled as limited pluralisation. This is also conditioned by a history of conflict and tensions on the territory of the former Yugoslavia, and the fact that there is an overlap between ethnic and religious identity among larger minorities (Serbs are predominantly Orthodox, whereas Bosnians are predominantly Muslim). The latter reflects the fact that religion has served as the main marker of separate ethnic identities. This rather controversial picture of the social position of religious minorities is also illustrated by the discrepancy between the wide range of rights they can enjoy, and the social reality where inequalities are observed, and a marked lack of interest, both political and public, in the rights of small religious communities (Zrinščak 2011; Zrinščak et al. 2014). To sum up, our initial hypothesis was to expect differences in the respect of the rights of inmates of different confessions.

5.3 Religion and Prisons: Legal Aspects

Out of the four agreements with the Holy See, the most important one is the *Agreement Between the Holy See and the Republic of Croatia on Legal Issues*, signed in December 1996 and ratified by the Croatian Parliament in February 1997. Under this agreement, the Republic of Croatia guarantees the believers of the Catholic Church the right to religious assistance in prisons, hospitals, health resorts, orphanages and in all other public or private health and welfare institutions (Article 16/1). The agreement also envisaged that the details of the implementation of this provision in public institutions would be set up in a separate document signed by the Church and the State authorities (Article 16/2). This was done, in relation to prisons, in 2002. Under the additional agreement, the Croatian Bishops' Conference has obtained the right to name five chaplains who are to become employees of, and who are to be paid by, the Ministry of Justice. Additionally, penitentiaries, prisons and correctional institutions should provide appropriate places for chaplaincy, whereas all other details of the work of chaplains must be arranged with prison authorities. Chaplains' visits to all prisoners, along with Catholic religious services, should be allowed at least once a week. In addition, prisoners have the right to personal religious literature. The agreement also regulates details related to Christmas and Easter confessions, baptisms and religious marriages in penitentiaries and prisons, as well as some other rights.

The agreements signed between 19 religious communities and the Government regulate the position of the chaplaincy in a similar manner to that of the Catholic Church, although with some differences, which are mainly justified by the size of particular religious communities. Accordingly, the Agreement with the Serbian Orthodox Church allows religious assistance in the army and police forces, prisons, health and welfare institutions. The Serbian Orthodox Church obtained the right to name five chaplains. However, because they aid in all these different institutions, they are not employed by the State or paid from the State budget. Still, prisons have to secure a proper place for them, while visits to prisons and religious services must be allowed at least once a week. The Agreement with the Islamic Community has the same wording as the Agreement with the Serbian Orthodox Church, the only exception being that the Islamic Community has the right to name one imam for all these different institutions. The number of chaplains is not specified in the agreements with the other religious communities as, owing to the small number of their believers, the ministers provide religious assistance if necessary. It is the duty of all religious communities that have signed these agreements to formally designate the authorised religious person(s) who will be providing religious assistance. The designated people usually provide care only for the members of their religious community, but in some cases, they also provide care for other inmates (those of different confession or non-believers) if these inmates express interest in such care.

In all the agreements, it is stipulated that religious assistance will be carried out in accordance with the daily schedule of activities of penitentiaries and prisons according to previous agreement with the management regarding the schedule and the modality of participation of prisoners. Some agreements contain provisions regarding the right of judges and wardens to temporarily exclude prisoners from participating in religious ceremonies and personal spiritual conversations (confession) to maintain order, for example, or for other justified reasons.

In addition, the Law on Execution of Prison Sentences (LEPS) of 1999 stipulates that all prisoners have the right of confession and contact with an authorised religious person (Article 14/1/14). This law is in slight contradiction with the LLSRC, which sets out that religious communities have the right to provide religious assistance to their believers in penitentiaries and prisons, but only under the conditions specified in the agreement between the respective religious community and the Government of the Republic of Croatia. As explained earlier, not all religious communities have such agreements. However, as the LEPS is a special law, and under the maxim *Lex specialis derogat legi generali*, all prisoners have the right to religious assistance by their respective religious community, regardless of whether or not their religious community has signed an agreement with the Government. If a prisoner wishes to have a private conversation with an authorised religious person, he/she must ask permission from the warden (Article 117/4).

This law also stipulates that prisoners have the right to freedom of religion, which includes the use of his/her own religious literature and religious items (religious items can be confiscated in the case of misuse, Article 94/1). Furthermore, an authorised religious person must be allowed, a minimum of once a week, appropriate space and time for religious ceremonies for prisoners under the condition that there are enough prisoners (the number is not defined) of the same denomination (Article 95/1). All prisoners have the right to attend, their denomination notwithstanding, but the warden has the right to temporarily exclude a prisoner from participating if such an action were deemed necessary for maintaining security and order. In addition, the law requires that food is provided according to the prisoner's religious or cultural demands, but only according to the possibilities of each prison (Article 78/1). Still, if a prison is not able to satisfy the prisoner's demand for specific foods, he/she must have the possibility to obtain the specific food in the prison shop and the food is paid by the prisoner himself (Article 78/4).

The Ministry of Justice, acting in accordance with the aforementioned legal sources, issued a circular in 2012 to all penitentiaries and prisons. In this circular, the Ministry specified the rights of prisoners regarding religion, which are derived from the LEPS, agreements with the Holy See, and agreements with other religious communities signed by the Government. It also specified all registered religious communities that are listed in the Register of religious communities of the Ministry of Public Administration. The circular stated that, based on all the above-mentioned conditions, all penitentiaries and prisons are obliged to allow all interested prisoners, who are members of registered religious communities, contact with the representatives appointed by the appropriate religious community, in accordance with the law. As discussed later, it can be hypothesised that what we found to be equal access is probably the main outcome of this circular.

Therefore, at least from a legal point of view, it can be said that when it comes to exercising religious freedom, the Croatian prison system is set up in a way that should guarantee that the religious rights of prisoners are respected and observed.

5.4 The Penitentiary System in Croatia

The penitentiary system in Croatia is under the jurisdiction of the Ministry of Justice. Within the Ministry, there is a Department for the Prison System, which oversees the organisation and supervision of the penitentiary system.

There are four different organisational units of the penitentiary system in Croatia: penitentiaries, prisons, correction facilities and centres. Penitentiaries are organisational units in which prison sentences of more than 6 months' duration are served. There are eight penitentiaries in Croatia. Prisons are organisational units that serve for pre-trial detention and prison sentences of less than 6 months' duration that are imposed in misdemeanour and criminal proceedings. There are twelve prisons in Croatia. Correction facilities are organisational units that serve for the enforcement of corrective measures imposed on minors in criminal proceedings. There are two such facilities: the Centre for Education and the Centre for Diagnostics. At the Centre for Education, the education of all civil servants of the penitentiary organisation system is carried out. The purpose of the Centre for Diagnostics is to determine a treatment plan for an individual prisoner in accordance with his/her status (psychological, social, criminal and medical).

The total number of prisoners as of 31 December 2015 was 3306, with the overall capacity of the system being 3900 prisoners (Aebi et al. 2016). This represents a sharp decrease in the prison population, which was far larger in 2010 (the number of prisoners was 5165 with the system capacity of 3351 prisoners). The surface area effectively available per inmate is 4 m^2. The prison population rate per 100,000 inhabitants is 79.7. Male inmates make up 94.53% of the prison population and only 5.47% of inmates are women (Ministry of Justice 2015: 14). More than 52% of the prisoners are sentenced to a period of 1–5 years. Most prisoners (35.74%) are aged 30 to 40 years, 22.64% are aged between 40 and 50 years. The average age of prisoners is 37 years (Ministry of Justice 2015: 30).

When it comes to the number of members of various religious communities in the penitentiary organisation system, it is hard to even make an estimate, because prisoners are not obliged to disclose information regarding their denomination. The data gathered from the Ministry of Justice for only 7 out of 24 organisational units (accounting for about one third of all prisoners) in the penitentiary organisation system show that 278 out of 1150 prisoners (24%) chose not to disclose such information, 712 were Catholics (61.9%), 55 were Orthodox (4.78%), 44 were Muslims (3.28%), 2 were Baptists (0.17%), 1 was Evangelical (0.09%), 1 was Jewish (0.09%), 2 were of "other" denominations (0.17%) and 55 wee atheists (4.78%). Although fragmented, the data suggest that the small number of members of religious minorities in prison mirrors their proportion in the general population.

5.5   Religion and Prison: How Does the System Work?

This section is based on the data collected from the civil servants of the Ministry of Justice, Department for Penal System, and on the semi-structured interviews with authorised religious persons from the following religious communities: Catholic Church, Serbian Orthodox Church, Islamic Community, Christian Adventist Church and the Evangelical Pentecostal Church in Croatia. The Catholic Church is the biggest and the most dominant religious community in Croatia, whereas others are minority churches, among which the first two (Serbian Orthodox Church and Islamic Community) are traditional and publicly more visible than the latter two communities. The position of all the communities interviewed is regulated either by the agreements with the Holy See (Catholic Church) or with the Government (other communities). The interviews were conducted between March and June 2017. The results are presented focusing on five topics covered in the interviews.

5.5.1   Authorised Religious Persons and Their Visits to Prison

Contrary to the Agreement with the Croatian Bishops' Conference, there are no chaplains among the civil servants in the Ministry of Justice; thus, religious assistance is provided in the same way for all minority religious communities, i.e. by competent priests/imams from the parishes or different organisational units of each specific denomination. According to the data gathered, there are 62 authorised religious persons who provide religious assistance in Croatian prisons (Table 5.1).

Table 5.1   Religious assistance in prison according to different religious communities, 2017

Religious community	Number of authorised religious persons
Catholic Church	27
Serbian Orthodox Church	11
Islamic Community	8
Christian Adventist Church	4
Evangelical Pentecostal Church in Croatia	4
Jehovah's Witnesses	6
Hare Krishna	2

Source: Ministry of Justice

The table confirms that the authorities allow, in accordance with the above-mentioned circular from 2012, all registered religious communities, not only those that signed the agreements, to provide religious assistance in prisons and penitentiaries. In addition to the religious communities surveyed, other religious communities, such as Jehovah's Witnesses and Hare Krishna, also provide religious care. That care is also provided by religious associations: associations that are established under the Associations Act and although they have religious objectives, they are not religious communities. They include the Step of Hope, the Book of Books, Mary's Legion, St. Vinko Paul and the Catholic religious community, Taizé. As the Ministry of Justice lacked information for 3 out of 22 prison institutions, it may be assumed that some other small religious communities, such as Baptist or Jewish communities, also provide their assistance.

On average, there are between 70 and 80 religious events within the penitentiary organisation system in Croatia quarterly, which means that between 280 and 320 religious events take place within the system every year.

The procedure of visits of authorised religious persons is the same for all, regardless of the status of each specific religious community, and it varies only with regard to the way in which religious assistance is given. If a religious community wants to perform religious ceremonies, the visit is announced to the management of the penitentiary, which allows the performance of such ceremonies and communication with the prisoners. The ceremonies are not always formal, for instance, some authorised religious persons (especially Protestants) organise Bible readings, film projections or just discussions. The number of ceremonies and organised visits by religious communities varies depending on the number of prisoners of certain denominations. The management asks the inmates whether they are interested in the announced religious ceremony, and if there is such an interest, the request is approved. There are cases when individual prisoners are under disciplinary procedures and are banned from attending religious services, but they can request an individual visit by the desired religious representative.

Visits from various religious associations, not only the registered religious communities, are also approved, but such visits are not made on an individual basis. These associations usually hold Bible readings for prisoners. The approval criteria are the same as those for the religious communities.

As already mentioned, religious representatives also make individual visits to prisoners. The initiative for these visits must come from the prisoner, and the penitentiary system does not have any influence on prisoners' wishes in this regard. In practice, requests for individual visits are approved, again, regardless of the legal status of the denomination in question. According to the authorised religious persons SURVEYED, there were no cases of denying a prisoner's request for a religious visit.

There is no special registry of visits of authorised religious persons; thus, it is not possible to ascertain the real number of visits (individual and non-individual) of authorised religious persons. However, every entry into the penitentiary facilities is registered.

All of the participants surveyed have stated that they have not experienced any serious problems in their work and that the prison system administration has not hindered them in any way. On the contrary, they have stated that the prison system administration is helpful and tries to ensure that they have everything they need.

5.5.2   Spaces for Religious Ceremonies and Prayer

The availability of spaces for religious ceremonies varies from prison to prison. Some have a designated space that is used exclusively for religious ceremonies. In most of the prisons, there are multifunctional spaces that are used in prisoners' free time as well as for religious purposes, when such spaces are additionally furnished with religious symbols. In other prisons, religious ceremonies and visits are organised in the rooms used for family visits. Because of spatial limitations, special spaces that would be used exclusively for prayer are almost non-existent. Rooms equipped with prayer carpets for Muslim prisoners are available only in some penitentiaries. Owing to the conditions in the penitentiary system, privacy is often doubtful, especially in penal bodies of closed type, in which prisoners spend most of their time in their cells. In such facilities, it is also hard to ensure a space for prayer as prisoners only have two hours for recreation outside of their cells. In the penal facilities of semi-open or open type, such a problem does not exist. The authorised religious persons surveyed did not express any objections regarding the availability or suitability of spaces they are provided with for performing religious ceremonies and giving individual religious assistance. However, they stated that sometimes it was not possible to ensure privacy during such visits as they were held in the common room where all other visits were held.

5.5.3   Religious Literature and Items

All religious communities have the right to donate religious literature to their believers, as well as to prisons and penitentiaries. This opportunity is regularly used by large and small religious communities; thus, libraries in the penitentiary facilities in Croatia are well equipped with religious literature, books and magazines. There are some restrictions owing to security measures, e.g. hardcover books are not allowed, and prisoners are not permitted to write anything in the books.

Prisoners are allowed to have religious literature in their cells if it is in accordance with the list of permitted items and the institution's house rules. Such lists vary from one penal facility to the next, depending on its type (closed, semi-open or open). During their visits, the authorised religious persons usually distribute different religious literature during the religious ceremony. Different religious items (crosses, rosaries, holy pictures) are allowed in accordance with the law. Some prisoners wear crosses and rosaries, whereas others wear religious pearls or other symbols. They are also allowed to furnish their personal space with religious symbols. However, in some prisons it is not allowed to wear rosaries or prayer pearls, or to have religious books (the Qur'an for example, as was stated by the imam) in the cells. The authorised religious persons surveyed stated that prisoners did not complain about their possible inability to have or use religious literature and religious items, whereas some underlined that in general prisoners were not very interested in religious literature.

5.5.4   *Food and Religious Requirements*

The prison system tries to cater for the prisoners' special dietary requirements. Thus, Muslims and Jews can choose a menu that does not contain pork. However, prison menus do not meet the strict requirements for *halal* or *kosher* food. A prisoner who wants to observe religious fasting may do so, but because of rather strict rules regarding food in cells and the strict working hours of prison kitchens and mass halls, it is difficult to properly observe the fast. For example, the imam surveyed stated that Muslim prisoners were usually unable to have *iftar*, although there were instances when it was arranged (for example, for this past Ramadan). The prisoners can always obtain certain groceries from the prison or penitentiary shops or from outside shops, but this is at the prisoner's expense. The authorised religious persons we surveyed indicated that there were no complaints regarding the availability of religiously approved food. There are, of course, general complaints about the quality of the food. In addition, some Muslim prisoners are foreigners and do not speak Croatian, which causes various communication problems, including those related to food.

5.5.5   *Religious Assistance and Prisoners' Rehabilitation*

This is the only section in which the answers from the civil servants in the Ministry of Justice differ from those of the authorised religious persons. Thus, they deserve a closer look. The civil servants claimed that, owing to the separation of Church and State, there was no possibility of including the authorised religious persons, as a part of a planned approach, in the process of rehabilitation of prisoners. However, they felt that every religion could have a positive influence in terms of rehabilitation by forming and ascertaining moral principles. Also, according to them, when prisoners are occupied fulfilling their religious needs, they are less prone to risky behaviour and other non-authorised behaviour. Of course, some prisoners use these rights only to break the monotony of prison life.

   According to the authorised religious persons, the penitentiary organisation system does not fully encourage them to provide religious assistance, but it is allowed and they are provided with all the necessary support. Although there is a generally positive attitude regarding their work, and in some cases, they almost feel part of the team, they see that in fact they are just outsiders. From the perspective of religious communities, much more could be done in terms of their stronger involvement, i.e. by closer and more substantive cooperation. In this regard, the need for an education programme of authorised religious persons was underlined during the interviews. The goal of such a programme would be to help them to prepare for contact with prisoners, which would help them in their work. Namely, the authorised religious persons indicated that they needed more education to improve their communication with the prisoners, and to better adjust their visits to the correctional aims of the prison sentences.

Still, all interviewees share a common perception that they have an impact on the resocialisation of prisoners. Some believe that there are real converts, or to put it exactly, "reborn" persons. This view was expressed particularly by the representative of the Evangelical Pentecostal Church, who stated that personally he saw a lot of cases in which prisoners became "reborn Christians" and respectful citizens after their release. The Catholic priest indicated that at first it had been hard to reach out to the prisoners, that they had been rude, unable to maintain their concentration. However, in time, he managed to establish communication and now there are many more activities involving the prisoners than before. Other authorised religious persons expressed similar views on the matter. The imam stated that some of the ex-prisoners became engaged in the Islamic Community after their release. Their work is also appreciated when there is an assumption that those who request religious assistance, or simply visits, do not actually belong to any specific religious community, as in the case of Roma juveniles, who engage in contact with the Catholic priests, and who – as the priest expressed – are looking for a person who can listen to them without judging them, with whom they can freely discuss their problems.

5.6   Discussion and Conclusion

The main aim of this chapter was to analyse the religious presence in prisons in Croatia as there was previously no information on it. The analysis was based on of the existing contractual and legal provisions, as well as on the data collected in relation to several topics, such as the basic structure of religious assistance in prison, spaces for religious ceremonies and prayers, religious literature and items, food and other religious requirements, and the connection between religious assistance provided by authorised religious persons and the rehabilitation of prisoners. In particular, the research focused on how authorities respect legal provisions regarding the religious rights of inmates, and if, and how, the equality of religious communities, as stipulated by the Constitution and respective laws and agreements, has been respected in terms of equal access of different religious communities to penitentiaries and prisons.

Although we were not able to collect the data for all prisons and penitentiaries, although the research included semi-structured interviews with only five authorised religious persons from different religious communities and although we did not have a chance to make observations in prison or talk to the prisoners themselves, we believe that we can safely claim that legal provisions are respected and that all religious communities have equal access and are treated equally. What is of interest here is that such an inclusive approach is in contrast to public debates about a privileged position of the Catholic Church in public institutions, as well as with a somewhat controversial social position of religious minorities, as described previously. Moreover, this is in contrast to a marked interest of the Catholic Church to be present in education, or to influence laws in certain fields, such as those on abortion or same-sex partnership. Finally, this is also is in contrast to the existing literature on religion in prisons in many European countries, which demonstrates the contested pluralisation in public institutions. As such, the Croatian case can serve as an interesting comparative point of reference for other countries, particularly the post-communist countries and those not studied so far in relation to the topic. What follows is a summary of these particularities, which can serve as tentative explanations to be studied further, especially from a comparative point of view.

The first particularity is because the religious presence in prison is a completely new phenomenon after 45 years of communism. Unlike the systems in all researched Western European countries, and even those in former Eastern Germany (Becci 2012), the communist system did not allow any religious presence in public institutions. Thus, there is no continuity with all the aspects that the tension between tradition and social changes can bring. The system has been set up very recently and in accordance with the new legal framework.

The second aspect concerns what we called a limited pluralisation. Religious minorities are minorities in terms of their number, but are also historic minorities and they are not the result of immigration. Despite the history of conflicts and tensions, in relation to the Serbian Orthodox Church, the history of co-existence in the same territory and the cultural and linguistic proximity are important factors in setting up a favourable legal position of very different religious communities, which is reflected in their access to prisons and penitentiaries.

Limited pluralisation might be the basic reason why prisons, at least from what we were able to observe, were not perceived as a possible contested ground for gaining influence over others, as was observed in the Spanish case with a similar historical position of the Catholic Church (Martínez-Ariño et al. 2015; Griera and Clot-Garrell 2015). Certainly, numbers are at work here, as the percentage of members of religious minorities in Croatian prisons is almost negligible. Although we noted that smaller religious communities show much zeal and eagerness to provide religious assistance within the penitentiary system in Croatia, even when there are no members of those religious communities in the prison or penitentiary they are visiting, this is simply not perceived as a problem or threat by anyone. Thus, prisons appear to be a non-representative example of other public institutions (education system, hospitals, army), which is the third specific feature of the Croatian case.

The inclusiveness of the Croatian penitentiary system was demonstrated by the fact that, contrary to our expectations, access is allowed to all registered communities, and not only to those that signed the agreements with the Government. Although this is in accordance with the Law on Execution of Prison Sentences, our expectation was based on the above-described contradiction between this law and the Law on Legal Status of Religious Communities, but also mainly on the everyday difficulties in implementing the rule of law. Besides the limited pluralisation, and the fact that prison is a peculiar public institution, we hypothesise that the equal access reflects a society that is categorised, according to some authors, as "endorsed religion(s) state" (Fox 2008; Madeley 2015). Croatia endorses one religion in particular (the Catholic Church), but this is legally extended to others, and in some specific social milieus the inclusive endorsement is visible in everyday practice.

The fifth feature could be seen in the somewhat chaotic organisation of the religious presence in prison, which might relate to what is usually termed a weak state. The Ministry of Justice did not have any systematised information about religion in prisons and was surprised to see someone interested in the topic. Although they collected much information for us, some important data are still missing. There is also a weakness noted in relation to religious communities. Thus, contrary to the agreement with the Croatian bishops' conference, no chaplains have been employed by the Ministry of Justice. Catholic priests are not strongly present in prisons and penitentiaries and they visit them only occasionally, as all other religious communities do. The lack of employed chaplains paints a completely different picture of the visibility of religions in a specific institution. We did not obtain any official explanation for this, but the interviewees indicated that this might be an outcome of the shortage of priests – which is also in sharp contrast to the employment of chaplains in the army and police forces (there are 38 army chaplains and 26 police chaplains in Croatia). For representatives of other religious communities, the visits to prisons are just part of their obligations, in many cases additional and indeed quite complicated and challenging tasks.

Sixth, the religious presence can be seen as an outcome of religious freedom and the rights of inmates, and not of the planned actions of both state and religious communities imposing pastoral care (Becci 2012). That is why the religious presence is not part of any rehabilitation programme. Thus, the religious presence in prison, although a demonstration of religious freedom and equality of different religions, is a kind of hidden space, not observed and not discussed from the point of view of separation of Church and State. As already discussed above, this was the single instance in which we noted a difference between the answers of the representatives of the Ministry of Justice and those of religious communities.

Finally, although mainly driven by inmates' religious/spiritual needs, and partly encouraged by prison authorities, the religious presence is mainly secured in a traditional way by maintaining religious services and offering spiritual assistance in the form of prayer, confession or simple conversation. During our limited research, we did not observe any "grey zone of religious life", such as Yoga courses, spiritual awakening, Zen meditation or other similar practices that were found in the Spanish case (Griera and Martínez-Ariño 2014, 9, Griera and Clot-Garrell 2015, 31). However, it is very unlikely that such practices exist in Croatian prisons.

However, it should be underlined again that equal access, along with the other particularities discussed, is based on limited research, and is conditioned by the fact that this is the first ever attempt to study religion in prison from a scientific point of view. In addition, this does not indicate that there is an equal treatment and position of members of religious minorities. Our research did not touch upon that. What is really happening inside Croatian prisons has yet to be uncovered by future research in the field.

Bibliography

Aebi, M. F., Tiago, M. M., & Burkhardt, C. (2016). *Council of Europe annual penal statistics SPACE I – Prison populations survey 2015*. Strasbourg: Council of Europe.

Becci, I. (2011). Religion's multiple locations in prisons in Germany, Italy and Switzerland. *Archives de sciences sociales des religions, 153*, 65–84.

Becci, I. (2012). *Imprisoned religion. Transformations of religion during and after imprisonment in Eastern Germany*. Ashgate: Routledge.

Beckford, J. A. (2011). Prisons et religions en Europe. Les aumôneries de prison: Une introduction au dossier. *Archives de Sciences Sociales des Religions, 153*, 11–21.

Beckford, J. A., & Gilliat, S. (1998). *Religion in prison: Equal rites in a multifaith society*. Cambridge: Cambridge University Press.

Beckford, J., Joly, D., & Khosrokhavar, F. (2005). *Muslims in prisons: challenge and change in Britain and France*. Basingstoke: Palgrave Macmillan.

CBS. (2012). *Population According to Religion – Census 2011*. https://www.dzs.hr/ Accessed 10 June 2017.

Croatian Bureau of Statistics, Statistička izvješća/Statistical reports 1469/2012, p. 14., www.dsz.hr. Accessed 28 June 2017.

Črpić, G., & Zrinščak, S. (2014). Religion, society, politics: Comparative approach. In J. Baloban, K. Nikodem, & S. Zrinščak (Eds.), *Values in Croatia and Europe: Comparative analysis* (pp. 13–41). Zagreb: Kršćanska sadašnjost, KBF Sveučilišta u Zagrebu. (in Croatian).

Ferrari, S. (2003a). The legal dimension. In B. Maréchal, S. Allievi, F. Dassetto, & J. Nielsen (Eds.), *Muslims in the enlarged Europe. Religion and society* (pp. 219–254). Leiden-Boston: Brill.

Ferrari, S. (2003b). The European pattern of church and state relations. *Comparative Law, 20*, 1–24.

Fox, J. (2008). *A world survey of religion and the state*. Cambridge: Cambridge University Press.

Furseth, I., & Kühle, L. M. (2011). Prison chaplaincy from a scandinavian perspective. *Archives de Sciences Sociales des Religions, 153*, 123–141.

Griera, M., & Clot-Garrell, A. (2015). Banal is not trivial: visibility, recognition, and inequalities between religious groups in prison. *Journal of Contemporary Religion, 30*(1), 23–37.

Griera, M., & Martínez-Ariño, J. (2014). *The accommodation of religious diversity in prisons and hospitals in Spain*. http://www.recode.info/wp-content/uploads/2014/01/FINAL-RECODE-28-Griera-and-Martinez_fin.pdf. Accessed 1 June 2017.

Madeley, J. T. S. (2015). Constitutional models and the protection of religious freedom. In S. Ferrari (Ed.), *Routledge handbook on law and religion* (pp. 209–266). Abingdon/New York: Routledge.

Martínez-Ariño, J., García-Romeral, G., Ubasarat-González, G., & Griera, M. (2015). Demonopolisation and dislocation: (re)-negotiating the place and role of religion in Spanish prions. *Social Compass, 62*(1), 3–21.

Ministry of Justice. (2015). *Report on state and functioning of penitentiaries, prisons and correction facilities for 2015*. https://vlada.gov.hr/UserDocsImages//Sjednice/2016/14%20sjednica%2014%20Vlade//14%20-%209.pdf. Accessed 15 June 2017.

Nikodem, K., & Zrinščak, S. (2012). Croatia's religious story: The coexistence of institutionalized and individual religiosity. In D. Pollack, O. Müller, & G. Pickel (Eds.), *The social significance of religion in the enlarged Europe* (pp. 207–222). London/New York: Routledge.

Robbers, G. (2005). State and church in the European Union. In G. Robbers (Ed.), *State and church in the European Union* (pp. 577–589). Baden-Baden: Nomos Verlagsgesellschaft.

Staničić, F. (2014). The legal status of religious communities in Croatian law. *Zbornik Pravnogfakulteta u Zagrebu, 64*(2), 225–254.

Torfs, R. (2007). Religion and state relationship in Europe. *Religious Studies Review, 1*(4), 31–41.

Zrinščak, S. (2011). Church, state and society in post-communist Europe. In J. Barbalet, A. Possamai, & B. S. Turner (Eds.), *Religion and the State. A Comparative Sociology* (pp. 157–182). London: Anthem Press.

Zrinščak, S., & Črpić, G. (2017). Religion, society and politics A comparative analysis of thirteen central, Eastern and Southern European Countries. *Teologiaen Aikakauskirja, 2*, 165–175.

Zrinščak, S., Marinović-Jerolimov, D., Marinović, A., & Ančić, B. (2014). Church and State in Croatia: Legal framework, religious instruction, and social expectations. In S. Ramet (Ed.), *Religion and politics in post-socialist Central and Southeastern Europe: Challenges since 1989* (pp. 131–154). Houndmills: Palgrave.

Legal Documents

Agreement between the Government of Croatia and the Croatian Bishops. Conference on Chaplaincy in Penitentiaries, Prisons and Correctional Institutions 2002

Agreement between the Holy See and the Republic of Croatia on Legal Issues. Official Gazette – International Agreements, No. 3/1997.

Circular of the Ministry of Justice. Department for penal system, Class: 406-07/12-01/29, No: 514-07-01-01-01-01/3-12-1 from 14 May 2012.

Constitution of the Republic of Croatia. Official Gazette, No. 56/1990, 135/1997, 8/1998, 113/2000, 28/2001, 41/2001, 55/2001, 76/2010, 5/2014.

Eight agreements the Government of Croatia signed with 19 religious communities.

Law on Execution of Prison Sentences. Official Gazette, No. 128/1999, 55/2000, 59/2000, 129/2000, 59/2001, 67/2001, 11/2002, 190/2003, 76/2007, 27/2008, 83/2009, 18/2011, 48/2011,125/2011, 56/2013, 150/2013.

Law on Legal Status of Religious Communities. Official Gazette, No. 83/2002, 73/2013.

Chapter 6
Czech Republic: Religious Assistance in Prisons in the Past and Today

Záboj Horák

Abstract The activities of religious communities in prison facilities within the Czech territory were renewed in 1990, after 40 years of absence during communist rule. The relationship between religion and prison is regulated by provisions in constitutional law, international agreements that bind the Czech Republic, other domestic laws, ministerial orders and internal norms of the *Prison Service of the Czech Republic* (the state institution for the administration of prison and similar facilities). Important instruments have taken the form of agreements on spiritual services in prisons between the Prison Service of the Czech Republic, the Ecumenical Council of Churches in the Czech Republic and the Czech Bishops' Conference. Four of these agreements have been signed, the last one in 2013.

Spiritual care in prisons is provided by prison chaplains, who are employees of the Prison Service of the Czech Republic. The chaplains are members of one of 11 religious communities, which recommend them for work in all prison facilities in the Czech Republic.

The prison chaplaincy also cooperates with *Prison Spiritual Care*, a civil association registered under civil law, which also sends volunteers to prison facilities, with the permission of the administration, to provide spiritual care, including counselling inmates. This association represents Christians of almost all denominations in the Czech Republic, whether registered or non-registered.

6.1 Introduction

Allowing religious communities to operate within the Czech prison estate, for inmates to exercise their religious freedom and to receive spiritual guidance to support their social rehabilitation, have a long tradition. It was interrupted only in the

Z. Horák (✉)
School of Law, Charles University, Prague, Czech Republic
e-mail: horakz@prf.cuni.cz

© Springer Nature Switzerland AG 2020
J. Martínez-Ariño, A.-L. Zwilling (eds.), *Religion and Prison: An Overview of Contemporary Europe*, Boundaries of Religious Freedom: Regulating Religion in Diverse Societies 7, https://doi.org/10.1007/978-3-030-36834-0_6

time of communist rule, following the *coup d'état* on 25 February 1948. Within a period of 2–3 years after the *coup d'état*, prison chaplains were individually dismissed without new ones being appointed. Indeed, the last prison chaplains to work under communist rule accompanied the victims of the State's show trials to their place of execution, by hanging, in 1950, for the last time. This lasted until the end of communist rule in late 1989 (Tretera and Horák 2018, p. 84).

The democratic "Velvet Revolution" took place in stages, starting with the brutal attack by communist police on a peaceful student procession commemorating the 50th anniversary of the Nazi closure of Czech universities in Prague, on 17 November 1989, followed by difficult negotiations between the representatives of the civic opposition and the communist regime, against the backdrop of mass demonstrations by the Czechoslovak people, and ending with the appointment of the first non-communist government on 10 December 1989, coinciding with Human Rights Day.

Religious communities were in a good position to enjoy a swift restoration of their activities in prisons, which began as early as 1990. The reason is obvious: both clerical and lay members of religious communities had considerable personal experience of the prison regime from the time of the communist dictatorship. After all, many of them had been imprisoned, even in the 1980s. The first spiritual caregivers to enter prisons in 1990 and the first prison chaplains to enter in 1994 were priests and preachers who had served custodial sentences as prisoners of conscience, often in the prisons where they now worked. They were well acquainted with the local conditions, and familiar with the problems faced by those who had been convicted of various crimes, as well as by most of the prison staff who had taken over from those employed by the old regime (Tretera and Horák 2017, p. 61).

The return of activities by religious communities in the prison estate after the revolution was enabled by Act No. 179/1990 Sb.,[1] which amended the then effective Act No. 59/1965 Sb., on the *Execution of Punishment by Imprisonment*. Ministers of all recognised religious communities, in whose congregational parishes or seats the prisons were located, could visit inmates, regardless of their religious affiliation, with the permission of the prison administration and upon the request of inmates. They talked with inmates about religion, provided them with books and songbooks, and contacted their own religious ministers. They provided such religious help as well as counselling to all inmates who requested it.

Soon after 1990, however, it was obvious that the above-mentioned mode of provision in prison was insufficient and had to be replaced with an organised chaplaincy, employing professional chaplains from different religious communities, who would become members of the prison staff. They would provide chaplaincy services to any inmates who were interested, and co-ordinate spiritual help from outside the prison. The legal outcome of this situation was the first agreement between the

---

[1] Sb. = *Sbírka zákonů*, i.e. the Collection of Laws of Czechoslovakia (since 1993, the Collection of Laws of the Czech Republic).

Prison Service of the Czech Republic, the Ecumenical Council of Churches[2] and the Czech Bishops' Conference,[3] which was reached in 1994.

6.2 Legal Aspects

6.2.1 Constitutional Law

Constitutional acts come first in the hierarchy of norms that regulate freedom of religion. The fundamental constitutional document concerning freedom of religion in the Czech Republic is the *Charter of Fundamental Rights and Freedoms* (hereafter referred to as the Charter).[4] The Charter may be deemed to be the second part of the Czech Constitution (Act No. 1/1993 Sb.). The Charter focuses on the codification of human rights within Czech territory.

Article 15, Section 1, of the Charter states: "The freedom of thought, conscience and religion is guaranteed. Everyone has the right to change their religion or faith or to have no religion." The term "everyone" means all inhabitants of the Czech Republic, whether Czech nationals, nationals of other states, or stateless persons.

Article 16, Section 1, of the Charter reads: "Everyone has the right to freely manifest their religion or faith, either alone or with others, in private or public, through worship, teaching, practice or observance."

The collective dimension to freedom of religion is guaranteed by Article 16, Section 2, of the Charter: "Churches and religious societies govern their own affairs; in particular, they establish their own bodies and appoint their clergy, as well as found religious orders and other church institutions, independent of state authorities."[5]

Exercising the rights mentioned in Article 16, Sections 1 and 2, may be limited by law in the case of measures necessary in a democratic society for the protection of public safety and order, health and morals, or the rights and freedoms of others.[6]

---

[2] The Ecumenical Council of Churches represents 11 churches as its ordinary members and some members as extraordinary members or observers (among them the Federation of Jewish Communities).

[3] The Czech Bishops' Conference represents the Roman Catholic and Greek Catholic Churches. It has 17 members (16 Roman Catholic Bishops and 1 Greek Catholic bishop).

[4] Published under No. 23/1991 Sb. and again under No. 2/1993 Sb.

[5] The designation "churches and religious societies" is a traditional term used in Czech legislation to refer to religious communities. Both designations are deemed equal, whereas it is up to a religious community to determine whether to use either or neither of the two in its name. The designation "churches and religious societies" is used jointly and indivisibly in Czech legal regulations (see Tretera and Horák 2017, p. 19).

[6] Article 16, Section 4, of the Charter.

6.2.2 International Agreements

Second in the hierarchy of rules of law, following constitutional acts, are *international agreements*. The Constitution of the Czech Republic regulates their status with the following words: "Promulgated international treaties, the ratification of which has been approved by the Parliament and which are binding in the Czech Republic, shall constitute a part of the legal order; should an international treaty make provisions contrary to a law, the treaty shall prevail."[7]

High on the list of international treaties, agreed to by the Czech Republic, are the following:

- International Covenant on Civil and Political Rights (1966)
- International Covenant on Economic, Social and Cultural Rights (1966)
- European Convention on Human Rights (1950)

The international agreements create an environment in which the enjoyment of the rights of inmates to individual religious freedom, as well as the collective religious freedom of religious communities to provide spiritual care, can be enforced. These rights are well protected by the Czech courts, but this protection is increased by instruments of international protection, in particular the possibility of appealing to the European Court of Human Rights.

6.2.3 Laws

A special act on religion law in the Czech Republic is *Act No. 3/2002 Sb., on the Freedom of Religious Expression, on the Position of Churches and Religious Societies, and to Amend Some Other Laws (Churches and Religious Societies Act).* Religious communities acquire, according to this act, legal personality through registration by the Ministry of Culture of the Czech Republic. There are 41 registered religious communities in the Czech Republic (as of 22 February 2020).[8] Besides legal personality, a religious community acquires, on registration, certain tax advantages, the right to educate its ministers within its own educational facilities, the right (since 2002) to acquire so-called special rights, and other rights.

Special rights are granted by the Ministry of Culture after fulfilling a set of legally prescribed conditions. These special rights can be divided into seven different groups, including the *right to perform a marriage ceremony with consequences in state law*, which has been granted to 21 registered religious communities, and *the*

---

[7] Constitution of the Czech Republic, Article 10.

[8] About 80% of the members of religious communities belong to the Roman Catholic Church. According to the Czech Bishops' Conference, 3,887,400 baptised Catholics live in the Czech Republic, among a total population of 10.5 million.

right to authorise persons to provide spiritual care in places where detention, imprisonment, preventive detention, protective treatment and protective education are performed. This latter right has been granted to 17 registered religious communities, namely:

1. Roman Catholic Church
2. Greek Catholic Church
3. Evangelical Church of Czech Brethren
4. Czechoslovak Hussite Church
5. Silesian Evangelical Church A.C.[9]
6. Evangelical Church A.C. in the Czech Republic (before 1993, the Slovak Evangelical Church A.C.)
7. Orthodox Church in the Czech Lands
8. Church of Brethren (Evangelical Congregationalists)
9. Unity of the Brethren (Evangelical Church of Herrnhut)[10]
10. Evangelical Methodist Church
11. Apostolic Church (Pentecostals)
12. Unity of Brethren Baptists
13. Old Catholic Church
14. Seventh-day Adventist Church
15. Christian Congregations[11] (founder: Nelson Darby, Ireland)
16. Religious Society of Jehovah's Witnesses
17. Religious Society of Czech Unitarians

According to the principles of individual religious freedom contained in Article 15, Section 1 and Article 16, Section 1 of the Charter of Fundamental Rights and Freedoms, no inmate shall be arbitrarily denied contact with a minister of any religious community, if it is registered. If an inmate asks for a visit of a minister of such a religious community, the prison chaplain who serves in a prison facility contacts that religious community, who recommends his minister for a visit.

As for the status of Muslims: the Centre of Muslim Communities was registered as a religious community (without special rights) in 2004. The number of Muslims in the Czech Republic is relatively low, perhaps no more than 10,000 people. Despite this fact, the Directorate of Prisons in Prague-Ruzyně opened a Muslim chapel and appointed an imam as a voluntary minister (Tretera and Horák 2018, p. 93). The rights of inmates to be visited by an imam are also guaranteed in other prison facilities.

The legal status of the prison chaplaincy is further regulated by the following provisions of the norms concerning prison facilities:

- Act No. 293/1993 Sb., on Detention, Section 15
- Act No. 169/1999 Sb., on Service of a Term of Imprisonment, Section 20

---

[9] A.C. = Augsburg Confession.

[10] This church is known as the Moravian Brethren in English-speaking countries.

[11] This denomination is related to the Plymouth Brethren.

- Act No. 129/2008 Sb., on Preventive Detention, Section 11
- Ministerial orders in respect of the Prison Service
- Executive Order of the General Director of the Prison Service of the Czech Republic No. 28 of 14 May 2015, on the Organisation of Spiritual Services in the Facilities of Prison Service of the Czech Republic

An interesting feature of the Czech system of spiritual care in prison is active ecumenism and a collaboration of the Czech Bishop's Conference and Ecumenical Council of Churches in the Czech Republic from the beginning of the renewal of the spiritual care in 1990 until today. The other interesting feature is the close collaboration of these institutions with the Federation of Jewish Communities in the Czech Republic in relation to the state.

6.2.4   Domestic Agreements

Some of the most useful instruments for guaranteeing religious freedom in prison facilities are agreements on spiritual services in prison reached between the Prison Service of the Czech Republic, the Ecumenical Council of Churches in the Czech Republic and the Czech Bishops' Conference. The agreement of 21 November 2013, which remains in force, uses experience of all three agreements reached by the same parties: the first in 1994, the second in 1999 and the third in 2008. The regulation of the prison chaplaincy according to the above-mentioned agreements is described in the whole article. Therefore, it is not summarised here.

6.2.5   Legal Status of Prison Chaplains and the Chaplaincy

The legal status of prison chaplains and the chaplaincy is based on the principle that any person kept in prison has the right to talk to a minister of any religious community, according to their own choice; none shall be forced upon them. Ministers who visit prisons undertake to render care to anyone, regardless of denomination, even to members of a non-Christian religion, as well as to those who are not members of any religion.

The service of humanist chaplains in prison or in other facilities (hospitals, homes for the elderly) has not been introduced in the Czech Republic, because it has not been requested by inmates or patients. Followers of the humanist movement are not numerous in the Czech Republic. No public discussion has been held on this topic. Maybe one of the reasons is the fact that many people still remember that non-religious ideas were part of the communist ideology connected with the communist totalitarian regime before 1989.

Since the beginning of the chaplaincy, ministers have been providing their services ecumenically, without any confessional restriction. Those who have chosen to carry out their mission of providing spiritual services in prison as their vocation, whether male or female, are referred to as prison chaplains. Once accepted as employees of the Prison Service of the Czech Republic, upon the recommendation of their religious community, they join a *prison chaplaincy*, led by a head chaplain.

The Director General of the Prison Service of the Czech Republic appoints and dismisses the head chaplain and his deputy. There is no requirement concerning which denomination they should belong to. The Czech Bishop's Conference and Ecumenical Council of Churches in the Czech Republic propose candidates for the positions of Head Chaplain and his Deputy to the Director General of the Prison Service.

Other chaplains are appointed and dismissed by directors of prisons. A recommendation from their religious community is required. The other condition is a clean criminal record. Prison chaplains and their activities are funded from the state budget.

The prison chaplaincy cooperates with *Prison Spiritual Care*, a civil association registered under civil law, which also sends its volunteers into prisons, upon the consent of the relevant administration, to provide spiritual care, including counselling inmates. Any person assigned to a task by *Prison Spiritual Care* is obliged to visit a prison facility at least twice per month. This association operates on a voluntary basis and comprises Christians of various denominations, even those registered "without special rights" or not registered at all.

6.2.6   *Denominational Representativeness in Prison*

Prison chaplains can be members of any of the 17 religious communities with the special right to authorise people to provide spiritual care in prison facilities. That said, currently, chaplains are members of 11 different religious communities, who are also employees of the Prison Service of the Czech Republic. Most of them are associates of *Prison Spiritual Care* as well.

There are 52 prison chaplains in total, who operate in 35 prisons and 2 detention centres.[12] Their denominational affiliation is as follows[13]:

Roman Catholic Church: 22
Evangelical Church of Czech Brethren: 9
Seventh-Day Adventist Church: 5
Czechoslovak Hussite Church: 3

---

[12] In the Czech Republic, there are currently 35 prisons (10 of them are detention prisons) and 2 detention centres.

[13] Prison chaplains working in the Prison Service of the Czech Republic. 2019. Webpage of *Prison Spiritual Care*. http://www.vdpcr.eu/v-ze-sti-kaplani.html Accessed 20 May 2019.

Church of Brethren: 3
Orthodox Church: 3
Greek Catholic Church: 2
Methodist Church: 2
Silesian Evangelical Church A.C.: 1
Apostolic Church (Pentecostals): 1
Christian Congregations: 1

There is no system of representation of religious communities in prison facilities, which means that there is no legal norm prescribing how many prison chaplains should belong to a specific religious community.

Each religious community decides which of their ministers will provide spiritual help in prison facilities. The willingness and abilities of a minister to provide spiritual help play an important role. Currently, the head chaplain is a male preacher from the Evangelical Church of the Czech Brethren, whereas his deputy is a Catholic priest. The former head chaplain was a female member of the Catholic Church, whereas her deputy was a preacher in the Church of the Brethren.

There are some female Catholic chaplains. As they cannot be priests, their canonical position in the church is that of a pastoral assistant. The number of pastoral volunteers active in prison is about 200, whereas the number of chaplains is 52.

6.2.7   Regulations Concerning Religious Practice

Regulations concerning religious practice, such as prayers and visits, are guaranteed by the above-mentioned legal instruments.

Accused or convicted persons, who, because of their disposition or beliefs, do not wish to accept the food provided by the prison, can receive their own food at their own expense, if conditions in the prison allow for this.[14]

6.3   Sociological Aspects

6.3.1   Religious Discrimination in Prison

Protection against discrimination in the Czech Republic, in general, is founded on the constitutional provisions within the Charter. Section 1 of Article 3 of the Charter declares that: "Everyone is guaranteed the enjoyment of his or her fundamental rights and freedoms without regard to gender, race, colour of skin, language, faith

---

[14] Ministerial Order No. 345/1999 Sb., Rules of Execution of Punishment, Section 16; Ministerial Order No. 109/1994 Sb., Rules of Execution of Detention, Section 28, Subsection 2.

and religion, political or other conviction, national or social origin, membership in a national or ethnic minority, property, birth, or other status." One of these fundamental rights is religious freedom.[15]

The Czech legal order contains a special regulation regarding anti-discrimination, namely, Act No. 198/2009 Sb., known as the Anti-discrimination Act. In Section 13, the act assigns the role of an anti-discrimination body to the Public Defender of Rights (the Czech Ombudsman), who has the responsibility of combating discrimination on all the grounds covered by EU Equality Directives 2000/43/EC and 2000/78/EC, including religious discrimination.

The Public Defender of Rights is elected by the Chamber of Deputies of the Czech Parliament for a 6-year term, to which he is answerable. Candidates are nominated by the Czech President and the Senate. The body is funded from a ring-fenced part of the state budget. The Public Defender of Rights must provide independent assistance to victims of discrimination, undertake research, publish independent reports and exchange information with anti-discrimination bodies in other EU member states.[16] The office is an independent institution, directly accountable to the Chamber of Deputies of the Parliament. Religious communities play no role in its work (Tretera and Horák 2012, pp. 88–90).

6.3.2   Chaplaincy Operations

Information about the number of chaplains, and their organisation and distribution according to the various denominations in the Czech Republic, was presented in Sect. 6.2.6 of this chapter.

6.3.3   Organisation of Individual Religious Practice

Issues concerning meals and prayers were described in Sect. 6.2.7 of this chapter.

Receiving individual guidance from persons engaged in spiritual care, as well as individual access to religious acts, is allowed. Inmates can also participate in study hours on the interpretation of religious texts, whereas religious communities can provide spiritual and religious literature and songbooks.[17]

---

[15] Articles 15 and 16 of the Charter; see Sect. 6.2.1 of this chapter.

[16] Act No. 349/1999 Sb., on the Public Defender of Rights, Section 21b.

[17] Act No. 169/1999 Sb., on the Service of a Term of Imprisonment, Section 20, Subsection 4 (b – d).

6.3.4   Organisation of Collective Religious Practice (Religious Services and Celebrations)

Religious services in prison are permitted and generally take place during recreational periods. Their exact time is set by the internal organisational rules of the prison.[18]

In many prisons, there are chapels, several of which have only been opened in recent years. The new chapel was opened in the Pilsen-Bory prison during a celebration on 20 December 2016. The Catholic Diocesan Bishop of Pilsen, the Head Chaplain, the Prison Director in Pilsen-Bory, and numerous prison chaplains and inmates were present at this festive occasion.

Religious communities can organise lectures and discussions, particularly on ethical topics, as well as concerts involving groups and individuals.[19]

6.3.5   Church–Prison Relations

The prison administration informs inmates about the provision of spiritual services in the context of the internal rules of the respective prison or in another appropriate manner.[20] If an inmate asks for a visit from a minister, the prison administration is obliged to immediately notify the minister.[21] The prison administration is entitled to deny spiritual services to persons who have committed a breach of duty arising from the legislation on the execution of punishment or internal prison rules.[22]

To resolve major conceptual issues on spiritual activities in prison and similar institutions, the Council for Spiritual Services in Prison Facilities was established.[23] It has nine members: two deputies from the Czech Bishops' Conference, two deputies from the Ecumenical Council of Churches in the Czech Republic, two deputies from the Prison Service of the Czech Republic, two deputies from *Prison Spiritual Care* and the Head Chaplain.

---

[18] Act No. 169/1999 Sb., Section 20, Subsections 2 and 4(a).

[19] Act No. 169/1999 Sb., Section 20, Subsection 4(e).

[20] Act No. 169/1999 Sb., Section 20, Subsection 5.

[21] Act No. 169/1999 Sb., Section 20, Subsection 6.

[22] Act No. 169/1999 Sb., Section 20, Subsection 8.

[23] Agreement of 21 November 2013, on Spiritual Services in Prison between the Prison Service of the Czech Republic, the Ecumenical Council of Churches in the Czech Republic and the Czech Bishops' Conference, Article 3.

6.3.6   Conversion and Proselytism

The rights to conversion and proselytism are guaranteed by the Charter, whose Article 15, Section 1, states: "The freedom of thought, conscience and religion is guaranteed. Everyone has the right to change their religion or faith or to have no religion." According to Article 16, Section 1: "Everyone has the right to freely manifest their religion or faith, either alone or with others, in private or public, through worship, teaching, practice or observance."

On 20 January 2011, *Prison Spiritual Care* approved the Service Code of Ecumenical Cooperation, a document in which the aforementioned issues are dealt with. The code states that the relations between ministers and inmates and the mutual relations between religious communities should be based on the spirit of ecumenism. As such, prison chaplains must refrain from any mission activity that favours their own religious community.[24]

6.3.7   Social Debate

According to a debate posted on the YouTube channel of the Czech Christian Academy in Prague in April 2017, some prison chaplains feel that there is a lack of interest in work of prison chaplains among ecclesiastical leaders. Although church leaders make recommendations regarding their ministry as prison chaplains and are prepared to accept them back into regular church services after their mission in prison, there is insufficient contact between them during the period of the mission. Meanwhile, the current head chaplain believes that the relationship between church leaders and prison chaplains should be as intensive as their relationship with prison authorities. This inter-church problem seems transitional.

6.4   Conclusion

The present system of spiritual care in prison is regarded by state authorities, religious communities and the public as functioning and efficient. It is connected with a high degree of ecumenical cooperation and solidarity between Christians and other religions. Prison chaplains (52) and volunteers for spiritual care in prisons (about 200) support each other. According to the latest debates, the number of chaplains should increase soon. Several chaplains are to be accepted from six religious communities, with the special right to authorise people to provide spiritual care in prison facilities.

---

[24] The Service Code of Ecumenical Cooperation of Prison Spiritual Care. 2017. Webpage of Prison Spiritual Care. https://perma.cc/NYM4-2SNP. Accessed 9 May 2017.

Bibliography

Tretera, J. R., & Horák, Z. (2012). Czech Republic. In Q. C. Mark Hill (Ed.), *Religion and discrimination law in the European Union* (pp. 87–93). Trier: Institute for European Constitutional Law, University of Trier.

Tretera, J. R., & Horák, Z. (2016). Czech Republic. In G. Robbers, W. Cole Durham Jr., & D. Thayer (Eds.), *Encyclopedia of law and religion, volume 4: Europe* (pp. 84–91). Leiden/Boston: Brill/Nijhoff.

Tretera, J. R., & Horák, Z. (2017). *Religion and law in the Czech Republic* (2nd ed.). Wolters Kluwer: Alphen aan den Rijn.

Tretera, J. R., & Horák, Z. (2018). Religious assistance in public institutions: Czech Republic. In R. Balodis & M. R. Blanco (Eds.), *Religious assistance in public institutions, Proceedings of the XXVIIIth Annual Conference Jurmala, 13–16 October 2016* (pp. 83–94). Granada: Editorial Comares.

Tretera, J. R., & Horák, Z. (2019). *Spiritual care in public institutions in Europe*. Berliner Wissenschafts-Verlag: Berlin.

Chapter 7
Czech Republic: Religion and Prison – The History of an Ambivalent Partnership

Lukáš Dirga and Jan Váně

Abstract In this chapter, we shall make a brief excursion into the history of the Czech penitentiary system, focusing on a specific aspect of its evolution: the alternation between periods of a repressive approach to inmates and periods of restoration of a democratic penitentiary system. We shall also describe the changing historical status of religion within the Czech penitentiary system, including a description of the current state of affairs based on available statistical data concerning religion in Czech prisons. Owing to a lack of relevant statistical data, we present, in this chapter, only the available data, namely, data for the period between 2009 and 2016. Despite being rather limited, these data are illuminating in the Czech context. We will also critically reflect on the everyday reality of religious practice in Czech prisons. Based on analysis of key problems encountered by guards, chaplains, and inmates, we will introduce religion as a controversial and ambivalent, yet stable, phenomenon. Among the most problematic issues are those of pragmatic faith, obstacles that prevent prison chaplains from carrying out their jobs and the unsystematic and inconsistent character of penitentiary and post-penitentiary spiritual care.

7.1 The Czech Republic and Its Penitentiary System: A Historical Excursion

The Czech penitentiary system must be understood within its historical context. Its structural changes over time can be linked to two historical perspectives that have alternately prevailed in various periods: a repressive, even dehumanising, approach to inmates, on the one hand, and, on the other hand, a humanistic approach, in a broad sense of the word (Černíková and Sedláček 2002; Tomek 2000). Current trends within the penitentiary system are related to post-communist economic,

L. Dirga · J. Váně (✉)
Department of Sociology, Faculty of Philosophy and Arts, University of West Bohemia, Pilsen, Czech Republic
e-mail: vanejan@kss.zcu.cz

© Springer Nature Switzerland AG 2020
J. Martínez-Ariño, A.-L. Zwilling (eds.), *Religion and Prison: An Overview of Contemporary Europe*, Boundaries of Religious Freedom: Regulating Religion in Diverse Societies 7, https://doi.org/10.1007/978-3-030-36834-0_7

political, legal and educational transformations. Various changes have been implemented within the post-communist Czech penitentiary system, but the Czech penitentiary model has yet to confront several residues of the communist system based on repression and the tough treatment of inmates.

The repressive periods in the history of the penitentiary system have varied in duration and intensity. The First Czechoslovak Republic's (1918–1938) State administration based the new country's penitentiary system on a model inherited from the Austro-Hungarian Empire. The reconstruction of the system, however, was interrupted after Germany invaded the country. It was subsequently replaced by a brutally repressive system of treatment of prisoners during the Nazi Protectorate of Bohemia and Moravia before and during World War II (1939–1945). After the war, attempts were made to implement a less brutal system. However, these attempts were soon brought to a halt by the communist *coup d'état* (1948). With the communists seizing the power, the penitentiary system turned into, for the 41 years to come, a tool of repression used by the totalitarian regime to create and maintain mass terror (Kýr and Janák 2004). The period of communist rule (1948–1989) was, like the period of Nazi occupation, characterised by a dehumanising approach to inmates, legitimised by the so-called class-based approach to incarcerated persons. This paradigm made it possible to subject prisoners labelled as political prisoners to inhumane treatment. Inmates had virtually no rights (neither civil nor human), and there were no institutions able to aid during these times (Tomek 2000, 10). The general violation of human rights was not only tolerated, but, in many cases, the prison staff were asked to actively engage in acts violating prisoners' rights (Schwartz and Schwartz 1989).

The year 1989 represented a breaking point in the modern history of the Czech penitentiary system: the change of political regime, along with the turmoil in prison and growing demand for better treatment in prison (Kýr 2005), initiated a new phase of reconstruction in the penitentiary system. As early as 1990, another attempt to thoroughly reform the model of the Czechoslovak/Czech penitentiary system began. Its main aim was to remove the remains of the communist system (Vacek 2004). In 1991, a new *Czech Penitentiary System Conceptual Framework* was introduced as the key strategic document governing the penitentiary system reform (Netík 1998), which emphasised the need to depoliticise, decentralise[1] and humanise the penitentiary system.

The *Prison Service of the Czech Republic* was founded on 1 January 1993, as an agency to be progressively depoliticised, decentralised and freed from the burden of administrative overload. Reform efforts have been reflected in policy agenda documents issued by both the Prison Service of the Czech Republic (Prison Service of the Czech Republic 2005, 2014) and the Ministry of Justice of the Czech Republic (Ministry of Justice of the Czech Republic 2016). These documents provide guidance for the ongoing transformation of the Czech penitentiary system, which is

---

[1] Decentralisation means that prison management and administration competencies and powers are split among multiple entities (Ministry of Justice of the Czech Republic, General Directorate of the Prison Service of the Czech Republic, directors of individual prisons).

based on the recommendations outlined in the *European Prison Rules* (Prison Service of the Czech Republic 2006).

7.2   Religion in Czech Society and Czech Prisons Throughout History

Religion has played an important role in the Czech penitentiary system. Since the middle of the nineteenth century, prison management policies emphasised educating inmates and humanising prisons. The goal of incarceration was to redeem inmates (instead of enhancing their negative character traits). To that end, inmates were required to attend religious education classes, and they had the right to read religious texts and participate in religious services. Priests working in prisons provided these services (Synek 2013: 39).

The new state (the Czechoslovak Republic, founded on 28 October 1918), took over the penitentiary system from the Austro-Hungarian empire and reformed it.[2] Regular religious services and religious education were provided in all prisons, but participation was voluntary. Priests were supposed to consult with inmates on questions of faith to help them to cope with their sentences, and to write consultation reports for each prisoner's personal file. Multiple churches, including smaller ones, were active in the penitentiary system; the Roman-Catholic Church, however, maintained the dominant position.

The Catholic Church's dominance over the prison system was rooted in its institutional foundations dating back to the Austro-Hungarian era and was further enhanced by the predominant conviction that the church can play a vital role in the correction of severely delinquent individuals. However, in a broader social context, the Catholic Church was visibly weakening, as demonstrated by the entry into the prison system of other religious entities, as well as by the diminishing role of the Catholic Church in such institutions as the school system. This diminishing role followed the establishment of the new state, which inherently implied the search for a national identity distinct from the strongly Catholic Austro-Hungarian identity. For this reason, Czechoslovak politicians were decidedly anti-Catholic, even though most of the population were Catholic,[3] and they worked to curtail the Catholic

---

[2] Legislation and prison administration were gradually transformed, and a progressive system of imprisonment was developed based on three disciplinary classes. Inmates were assigned to lower classes as they made corrective progress. The motion to grant parole (signed into law as early as 1919) can only be filed when the inmate has been transferred to class I, the lowest class.

[3] The formation of Czechoslovakia is intimately entwined with a debate concerning its religious history and identity. In the course of establishing the First Republic in 1918, the role of Catholicism in the new state was hotly debated. This dispute was exemplified by an argument between President Tomáš G. Masaryk and historian Jan Pekař. Masaryk saw the climax of Czech history in Hussitism and the Unity of the Brethren, whereas Pekař saw the foundation of our national identity in the reign of Charles IV and the influence of the Catholic Church (Havelka 1995; Kautman 2015).

Church's influence upon key institutions. As a result, everything Catholic came to be associated with the monarchy, and anti-Catholicism was presented as equal to anti-Austrianism.

In addition to its historical association with the Austro-Hungarian monarchy, the Catholic Church was dominated by high clergy recruited from aristocratic circles. These clergymen demonstrated indifference (at best) towards the national interests, which substantially contributed to the negative perception of Catholicism by political elites of the newly established state (Václavík 2010: 82–84). In response, part of the Catholic clergy broke away from the Catholic Church at the outset of the new state and established a purely national Czechoslovak Church[4] in 1920. The rift between the state and the Catholic Church culminated in 1925.[5] Afterwards, attempts were made to rectify the situation (whereby, for instance, a concordat was established in 1928), and the People's Party became the political representation of Catholicism and an integral part of the political establishment. The 1930 census confirmed that the religious situation had stabilised; however, there were still vast religious differences across regions and between the city and the countryside.[6] Still, we may conclude that the fundamental characteristics of religion and religious institutions in the new state were established in the first 10 years of existence of the Czechoslovak Republic (Horák 2015).

An era of repressive penitentiary practices took place before and during World War II, when the penitentiary system mainly served the purposes of the German Nazi secret police. Nevertheless, spiritual services, including regular masses, continued to be provided in prison. Simultaneously, the relationship between the population and Czech churches, including the Catholic Church, was strengthening as a result of the clergy's tremendous courage and contribution to the resistance before and during occupation (Václavík 2010).

During the repressive Communist rule, the conditions in prison degraded even more. As we have already pointed out, the primary purpose of the penitentiary system under communism was to serve as a tool of repression. Religious organisations were labelled State enemies, and the Catholic Church, which was the largest, most influential, and most internationally recognised religious organisation, was the most affected (Hanuš 2005). Religion was systematically liquidated. Churches were brought under direct and severe supervision exercised by state authorities.[7] Over the

---

[4] In 1971, the Church was renamed the Czechoslovak Hussite Church.

[5] That is, 510 years after the burning of Jan Hus.

[6] In the Czech lands, 75% of the population identified with the Catholic Church, 10% declared themselves as being of no denomination and the rest consisted of other traditional Christian churches. In Moravia, 85% were Catholics, 3% without a denomination, and the rest were accounted for by other traditional Christian churches. Being of no denomination was the second most common attitude towards religion. According to other estimates, though, the percentage was even higher (Mišovič 2001: 83).

[7] The Communist regime established the State Bureau of Clerical Affairs, which was put in charge of granting and revoking state consent for execution of spiritual duties by priests, pursuant to Section 173 of the Penal Code on obstructing the supervision of churches and religious associations. In this way, religious groupings were deprived of their autonomy.

period 1949–1951, virtually all diocesan and auxiliary bishops were interned. Afterwards, religious orders were abolished in two stages. Churches, in particular the Catholic Church, became targets of repeated aggressive campaigns in which they were portrayed as enclaves of political reactionaries (Václavík 2010: 102–103). Although political and ideological pressure subsided after the start of the 1960s, it never completely vanished. In the period of "normalisation" after the Soviet invasion of 1968 (1970–1989), the anti-clerical and anti-religious trend resurged. It would be only a slight exaggeration to say that the normalisation period saw the complete step-by-step transformation of Czech anticlericalism into religious indifference, with the Communist regime keeping the religious environment and religious thinking under firm control. Still, the second half of the 1980s witnessed a partial revival of prestige among traditional religious groupings, notably among Catholics.[8]

In the Communist era, religious services in prison were performed less and less frequently, until they disappeared entirely, the reason being that the position of chaplains in jail administration was fading away. Their entitlements (such as submitting opinions regarding the convicts' potential for improvement) became restricted, and their role became a symbolic one. As the position of religion in communist Czechoslovakia was changing for the worse, constraints were imposed upon inmates' opportunities to engage in religious activities. Eventually, religious activities came to be banned altogether (labelled as "hostile") and replaced by political "education". In re-education programmes, religious education was replaced by political education and by the reading of "appropriate" texts (i.e. texts approved by the regime) (Synek 2013: 50). This situation lasted until 1989.

It is interesting to note that, after the fall of the Communist regime, the status of the Church changed; the Catholic Church had, at the beginning of the 1990s, the highest approval rate in the entire history of Czechoslovakia (founded in 1918). The reason was that most clergy opposed the Communist regime, and both official representatives (e.g. Cardinal František Tomášek)[9] and unofficial ones (e.g. Václav Malý)[10] demonstrated that they were on the side of the nation.[11] Thanks to positive

---

[8] Including, for instance, the gathering of Catholics at the prominent pilgrimage site of Velehrad (attended by 100,000 people), which acquired a significant anti-regime character, or a petition signed by 600,000 people demanding greater religious freedom. (Václavík 2010: 124–125), all of which resulted in the announcement of what became known as the Decade of Spiritual Renewal, which commenced in 1987 (Halík 2014).

[9] František Tomášek (1899–1992) was ordained as Cardinal and the 34th Archbishop of Prague in 1977. Gradually, the tension between him and the Communist regime mounted.

[10] Václav Malý (1950) has been an auxiliary bishop of Prague since 1997. In the Communist era, he was a signatory of Charter 77 and one of its spokespersons. The "state consent with execution of spiritual duties" was taken away from him. In the course of the Velvet Revolution of 1989, he moderated massive anti-regime demonstrations at Letenská Plain and the Wenceslas Square in Prague.

[11] Please refer to the public declaration made by Cardinal Tomášek in the days of the 1989 revolution: "In this groundbreaking moment, the Catholic Church is on the side of the nation!" (Hanuš 2005: 73).

ratings earned on account of its defiance against the Communist regime, the Catholic Church had an unprecedented opportunity to become a high-profile and influential agent in the national reconstruction. Alas, the positive reception of the church in the early 1990s,[12] as supported by data from empirical questionnaire-based surveys (Prudký 2005; Spousta 1999; Tomka and Zulehner 1999, 2000, 2008), gradually declined and finally stabilised in the mid-1990s. One third of the population currently trusts the churches, whereas more than half of the Czech adult populations distrust them.[13]

The change of the political regime after 1989 initiated a reconstruction of the penitentiary system that would comply with the principles governing a democratic society. The *European prison rules* became the core document of the transformation. The rules specify, for example, that religious services are to be institutionalised within the framework of a *Spiritual Services* organisation. "Spiritual services provide inmates with the opportunity to express and apply their constitutional freedom of religion, they help, by emphasising spirituality, to overcome the impact of the criminal environment and to accept the guilt, to change the way of thinking and to improve the quality of human relationships" (Prison Service of the Czech Republic 2005, 16; Prison Service of the Czech Republic 2006).

7.3 Religion in Czech Society and Czech Prisons Today

Religious affiliation represents a differentiating principle, influencing value frameworks governing individual attitudes to life, world, society, or normative systems (Prudký 2009a, 2009b). Therefore, let us now briefly outline some religion-related data concerning the Czech Republic, as established by the 2011 *Population and Housing Census* (hereinafter referred to as the Census).[14] According to the Census, a mere 21% of the population consider themselves religious. Of these, only 14% adhere to a Church or a religious organisation. Most religious people declaring affiliation to some religious organisation (14%) are members of the Roman-Catholic Church, accounting for, in other words, 74% of religious people. (Of the entire population, Roman Catholics represent just 10%.) Thirty-four percent of the population stated that they were unconfessed (which, in absolute numbers, represents

---

[12] In October 1989, right before the Velvet Revolution, 40% of respondents described the Catholic Church as a significant defender of human rights (Mišovič 2001: 111). This trend persisted throughout the mid-1990s, but after that, trust in the Catholic Church declined.

[13] See the recent CVVM poll titled "Trust in selected public institutions as of March 2017", which established that 25% of the population over the age of 15 trust the churches, whereas 64% distrust them.   https://cvvm.soc.cas.cz/media/com_form2content/documents/c2/a4279/f9/po170410.pdf (Accessed 24 August 2017).

[14] 'Population and Religion. Census 2011 (Accessed 16 March 2017, https://www.czso.cz/documents/10180/20551795/17022014.pdf/c533e33c-79c4-4a1b-8494-e45e41c5da18?version=1.0.

3,612,804 persons out of a total of 10,562,214 inhabitants). A significant part of the population (45%, or 4,774,323) refused to answer the question on denomination.

These numbers show that Roman Catholics are the largest religious minority in the country. At first sight, the Catholic Church appears to be an influential institution; it is supported by 10% of the population, on whom it should be able to rely in the case of political and cultural conflicts with the non-affiliated majority. However, as various research projects have documented, the influence of the Czech Catholic Church is not as strong as might be expected given its cultural significance in the history of the nation.

Compared with the rest of Europe, the Czech Republic has a low level of declared religiosity and church attendance and the highest (declared) level of secularity and indifference to religious affairs. Compared with those in the rest of Europe and the USA, Czech, religious groups have little influence and occupy a weak position in public life (Tížik 2012).[15]

In Czech society, churches are entrusted with few and restricted tasks, exacerbating the Czech national indifference (or even hostility; refer to footnote 21) to religion. If church activities are considered legitimate anywhere, it is in the area of charity and caring for the socially vulnerable. Otherwise, though, their engagement in public institutions (schools, the military, the prison system) is merely tolerated, rather than encouraged, and individual faith is considered a private matter.

From the legal perspective, the right of inmates to exercise their religion-related rights in prison (such as attending masses or having access to personal consultations or religious literature) have been guaranteed since 1990. Church organisations and interest groups also participate in the re-education of inmates. In 2008, the Prison Service of the Czech Republic made an agreement with the Czech Bishops' Conference and the Ecumenical Council of Churches in the Czech Republic, entitled *Agreement on Spiritual Services*. The document regulates the activities of religious subjects (mainly prison chaplains) in the context of the Czech penitentiary system: chaplains[16] are entitled to celebrate masses, comment on operational aspects of prison life relating to religion, gather information about inmates and bring into prison items needed to carry out pastoral services properly (this applies mainly to 2 dl of wine) (Synek 2013, 56; Prison Service of the Czech Republic 2008).

The above makes it clear that although, from a long-term perspective, the position of religion in the Czech penitentiary system has strengthened, its role and influence are still limited. When it comes to questions of church affiliation or declared religiosity, Czech society is rather non-engaging, paying no attention to spiritual

---

[15] Tížik combined levels of declared religious affiliation and frequency of church attendance to compare religiosity in 15 European countries and the USA using ISSP data (1995, 2003, 2008).

[16] The Act No. 3/2002 Coll. On Churches and Religious Associations enables churches to "authorise persons performing pastoral duties to render pastoral services in the Armed Forces of the Czech Republic where people are held in custody, jail terms are served, and protective medical treatment or supervised education is carried out". These rights, however, only apply to the churches of the Second Type Registration, i.e. those already established or those complying with special requirements set forth in the Act.

matters (Hamplová 2013). It is thus not surprising that, according to a recent study, Czech prisons still represent a fairly hostile environment for religious organisations (Váně and Dirga 2016). In a recent study, we demonstrated this attitude using the example of prison guards. Before we describe the details of that study, however, we turn to a brief review of existing statistical data on religion in prison in the Czech Republic, followed by a description of existing penological research in the country.

7.4 The Current State of the Czech Penitentiary System

The penitentiary system in the Czech Republic is at the time of writing (March 2017) governed by the Prison Service of the Czech Republic, an organisation reporting to the Ministry of Justice of the Czech Republic. The Prison Service is an armed body headed by the General Directorate of the Prison Service of the Czech Republic and its Director General, appointed and overseen by the Minister of Justice of the Czech Republic.

The Prison Service of the Czech Republic has the following organisational units: General Directorate of the Prison Services, remand prisons, prisons,[17] security detention facilities, the Prison Service Vocational School and the Prison Service Institute of Education. As of 16 March 2017, the Prison Service of the Czech Republic administered a total of 35 prison establishments,[18] including 10 remand prisons, 25 prisons and 2 security detention facilities. As of 15 March 2017, a total of 22,715 persons were incarcerated, including 20,957 men, 1,684 women and 74 detainees in security detention facilities.[19]

In February 2016, the Ministry of Justice of the Czech Republic issued a document defining the governing principles of the development of the Czech penitentiary system and Czech criminal policy, entitled the *Penitentiary System Conceptual Framework Until 2025* (Ministry of Justice of the Czech Republic 2016), which the Government of the Czech Republic approved the same month. The aim of this document is to build a well-functioning and efficient penitentiary system that complies with international standards; integrates with crime prevention programmes, post-penitentiary care, social care and the educational system; and aspires to reintegrate offenders back into society.

The document defines several tools that are supposed to help to achieve the above-mentioned aims, and religion or spiritual pastoral care is one of those tools. The *Penitentiary System Conceptual Framework Until 2025* points out that, from

---

[17] Prisons refer to establishments where unsuspended sentences are served. These are divided into four basic types: minimum-security prisons (type A), medium-security prisons (type B), high-security prisons (type C) and maximum-security prisons (type D).

[18] It is common for multiple types of prison facilities to be located on the same premises. For example, remand prisons are often combined with regular prisons or security detention facilities.

[19] Source: Prison Service of the Czech Republic, http://vscr.cz/generalni-reditelstvi-19/informacni-servis/rychla-fakta/. Accessed 16 March 2017.

the point of view of treating inmates, spiritual care represents an interesting alternative to so-called treatment programmes in that it has a specific (liturgical) character that is immutable and indispensable in the prison environment (Ministry of Justice of the Czech Republic 2016). Overall, however, there is untapped potential for spiritual care in Czech prisons, and a plan exists to increase the staff providing spiritual services in Czech prisons.

7.5 Basic Data Concerning the Functioning of the Ecumenical Prison Chaplaincy in Czech Prisons

Ecumenical Prison Chaplaincy is rendered by the alliance of prison chaplains authorised by their respective churches to perform the service, insofar as the Prison Service of the Czech Republic has approved their engagement. The Prison Service of the Czech Republic employs chaplains. They are organisationally accountable to the directors of their prisons, and, for methodological matters, they report to the Head Chaplain of the Prison Service of the Czech Republic and his deputies. In addition to organising and implementing the spiritual (pastoral) service in local facilities, they also participate in the development and application of educational programmes aimed at effecting a change in inmates' values. Finally, chaplains also render pastoral service to their coworkers and provide advisory services to prison directors in matters regarding a wide spectrum of religious concerns.

Let us now explore the basic statistical data to see what activities the Ecumenical Prison Chaplaincy of the Czech Republic carries out. The management of the Chaplaincy has provided us with updated data (including data for 2016).

Table 7.1 represents data from a worksheet the Chaplaincy uses to report its activities (to the Prison Service of the Czech Republic) and to legitimise its activity inside the Czech penitentiary system.[20] The quantification of individual actions (first carried out in 2015) helps to identify which issues are targeted or need to be targeted (even from the perspective of a rather secular state). The Ecumenical Prison Chaplaincy of the Czech Republic systematically worked with 1497 prisoners in 2016, which means that approximately 6.5% of incarcerated individuals were provided with spiritual care (either face-to-face interviews, consultations after release, or group events, such as lectures and masses).

Although the figure of 6.5% might seem low at first glance, it represents a significant achievement considering the historical unfriendliness of prisons to religion, especially under the still-lingering communist correction paradigm (Váně and Dirga 2016). It is worth noting, however, that the reported face-to-face interviews do not

---

[20] We have, at our disposal, a detailed overview of all operations carried out in individual prisons across the Republic. We can document the level of religious activities as well as the utilisation of spiritual services in individual establishments. We can provide these data upon request.

Table 7.1 Basic statistical data on the activities of the Ecumenical Prison Chaplaincy

Activity	Number of actions
Year 2016	
Number of incarcerated persons the Ecumenical Prison Chaplaincy has systematically been working with	1497
Number of face-to-face interviews	13,914
Contact with released persons	164
Working with the families	117
Contacting the Church community	77
Cooperation with assisting organisations	68
Collective religious practices (lectures, masses, Bible groups etc.)	7055
Average number of participants per event	9
Total participants in these events	53,569
Average number of hours volunteered in prison	713
Year 2015	
Number of incarcerated persons the Ecumenical Prison Chaplaincy has systematically been working with	1225
Number of face-to-face interviews	16,084
Contact with released persons	220
Working with the families	133
Contacting the Church community	80
Cooperation with assisting organisations	68
Collective religious practices (lectures, masses, Bible groups etc.)	6772
Average number of participants per event	8
Total participants in these events	42,642
Average number of hours volunteered in prison	638.5

Source: Ecumenical Prison Chaplaincy of the Czech Republic

necessarily have to be related to religious matters. By contrast, the 7055 group events were related directly to collective religious practice.

Comparing the 2015 and 2016 data (while maintaining full awareness of the fact that it is not possible to draw a general conclusion from this comparison), we find that 2016 recorded a decline in "contact with the released and their families" and in the "number of face-to-face interviews". We observe growth, on the other hand, in the "number of incarcerated persons the Ecumenical Prison Chaplaincy has systematically been working with" and in the number of activities related to the organisation of collective religious practices; the average number of participants in these events remained identical. There was an increase in the average number of hours offered in prison by volunteer chaplains[21] cooperating with the Ecumenical Prison Chaplaincy.

---

[21] These volunteers are members of *Prison Spiritual Care*, a non-governmental organisation registered with the Ministry of the Interior of the Czech Republic as an unincorporated association. Members thereof may include clerics from registered churches as well as members of congrega-

Table 7.2 Number of prison chaplains and selected indicators between 2009 and 2016

Year	2009	2010	2011	2012	2013	2014	2015	2016
Chaplains	34	35	37	37	36	37	38[a]	37[a]
Of which full-time chaplains	8	5	7	7	7	8	8[b]	9[b]
Chaplain's worksheets	20.25	19.55	19.85	20.85	20.85	20.85	20.55	20.95
Volunteering chaplains	215	203	234	226	234	227	216	224
Of which Religious Society of Jehovah's Witnesses chaplains	x	90	63	76	77	82	73	79
Face-to-face interviews	x	x	19,272	24,957	15,011	14,434	16,084	13,914
Collective activities	x	x	x	5554	5996	6203	6772	7055
Systematic care	x	x	x	x	x	1382	1225	1497

Source: Ecumenical Prison Chaplaincy of the Czech Republic
[a]Including the head chaplain
[b]Including the workload of the head chaplain, x no record for the year

Regarding the number of chaplains working in prisons and their workload, we know a bit more: these indicators have been recorded for the Prison Service of the Czech Republic since 2009,[22] as have data concerning the number of volunteering chaplains. Table 7.2 shows that, since 2011, the number of chaplains in Czech prisons has ranged between 37 and 38, which translates, with 35 prisons, into approximately one chaplain per establishment. At the same time, the table shows a slight increase in the number of chaplains employed full time in prisons. This increase, however, is subtle, and we do not consider it to be an indicator of change in the position of religion or chaplains in Czech prisons. The number of chaplains and their workload have effectively remained constant throughout the entire monitored period (2009–2016).

We would like to draw attention to the row dedicated to the Religious Society of Jehovah's Witnesses, which shows that this religious group is seen in a negative way, as a foreign element, despite 0being established in the Czech penitentiary system since the 1920s. The Jehovah's Witnesses were exposed to repeated persecution during World War II, as well as under the Communist regime. The persisting negative attitude towards the group among the public and among traditional churches is reinforced by the group's substantial introversion towards the outside world, as demonstrated by its "information barrier" policy. As such, it impossible to determine the group's organisational structure and internal affairs or to obtain information on its history and the characteristics of individual congregations active in the Czech Republic (Nešpor and Vojtíšek 2015: 445). This naturally makes possible various misinterpretations about the community and further feeds existing prejudices. The negative image was not helped by an episode in 1993, when the top representatives of the Jehovah's Witnesses attempted to deceive the registering authority

---

tions and parishes who voluntarily wish to engage in spiritual and pastoral services in Czech prisons and are authorised to do so by their church executives.

[22]Chaplain worksheets give the total number of working hours of all chaplains working in Czech prisons in a particular year.

Table   7.3 Denominations
represented in 2016

Church	Number of chaplains
Roman-Catholic Church	14 (37.84%)
Evangelical Church of Czech Brethren	7 (18.92%)
Seventh-day Adventist Church	4 (10.81%)
Czechoslovak Hussite Church	2 (5.41%)
Evangelical Brethren Church	3 (8.11%)
Greek Catholic Church	2 (5.41%)
Orthodox Church	1 (2.7%)
Czech Apostolic Church	1 (2.7%)
Christian congregations	1 (2.7%)
Silesian Evangelical Church of the Augsburg Confession	1 (2.7%)
Head chaplain of the Ecumenical Prison Chaplaincy	1 (2.7%)
Total	37

Source: Ecumenical Prison Chaplaincy of the Czech Republic, updated as of 7 November 2016

(the Ministry of Culture) during the religious organisation registration process by betraying some of the fundamental elements of its teachings (Vojtíšek 2004: 100). For a detailed overview of individual denominations active in prisons in 2016, see Table 7.3.

We only have data on the prevalence of various denominations in prisons as of 7 November 2016. We also have information on the structure of the chaplaincy in 2015 (this information, however, does not apply to volunteering chaplains). The lack of statistical data on religion in the Czech penitentiary system illustrates that this field is hard to explore. What we can see, however, is that the Roman-Catholic denomination was the most represented among the chaplains (14 chaplains out of 36, almost 40%). We would also like to draw attention to the strong representation of the Evangelical Church of Czech Brethren, with 7 prison chaplains (18.92%), despite its representation in the total of population of the country amounting to only 0.5%.[23]

There is obviously a serious lack of statistical data on the activities carried out by religious organisations in the Czech penitentiary system (Dirga and Váně 2016), nor can we rely on a sufficiently long data series that would help us unveil the transformations, impacts or influence of religion behind prison walls. This lack of data is striking, given that the Ecumenical Prison Chaplaincy of the Czech Republic has carried out its activities in prisons and remand prisons for over 20 years. However, the data scarcity may reflect the fact that the chaplaincy's influence grew more slowly than its formal integration into the penitentiary system.

---

[23] This figure comes from the 2011 Czech Republic Census.

The role played by religion in the Czech penitentiary system is complex, involving institutional adaptation, the role played by chaplains, attitudes adopted by prison governors and prison guards with respect to the implementation of religious organisations, the attitudes of inmates themselves, and other actors such as non-profit organisations that help with the reintegration of former prisoners into mainstream society (Dirga and Váně 2016).

The lack of relevant statistical data makes it clear that new research is needed on the Czech penitentiary system, especially concentrating on religion and religiosity in prison. To date, however, articles on prison research represent just a tiny proportion of the academic work on prisons in all fields (not only sociology).

7.6   Czech Prison Research

Just as official statistics on religion in prison are lacking, the area is under-researched academically. The development (or lack thereof) of Czech prison research has been deeply influenced by a long series of political events and, above all, by the long period of Nazi and Communist repression, during which it was virtually impossible to carry out any expert penological research. The Penological Research Institute, founded in 1966 and led by Jiri Čepelák, was, in fact, the only institution carrying out penological research and penological educational activities at that time. The Institute was able to carry out its activities until the beginning of the 1980s, when it was abolished for political reasons (Hladík 2012).

Modern penological research was later taken over by the Institute of Criminology and Social Prevention (the former Criminology Research Institute). This institute, in cooperation with the Institute of Education of the Prison Service of the Czech Republic, the Police Academy of the Czech Republic and academic experts, provides for studies concentrating on the Czech penitentiary system. As a result, there was a moderate increase in the number of papers produced by academic researchers. Therefore, it can be expected that Czech prison research will be enriched in the years to come. The research field is still rather underdeveloped when compared with the same field of study abroad, however.

We would like to point out Kateřina Nedbálková's (2006) research on gender and sexuality in women's prisons as a cornerstone of modern Czech sociological research in the field of penitentiary systems. Nedbálková's research follows on from a tradition of research on Czech criminal law and the Czech penitentiary system carried out by Šmausová (1992, 1993, 1994). Since then, prison research has been gaining status and becoming more widely addressed. As evidence of this, let us cite some recent sociological research projects: Dirga and Marhánková (2014) concentrated on the influence of the workplace on the identity of Czech prison guards, and Dirga, Lochmannová and Juříček (2015) focused on the hierarchical structure of inmate populations in Czech prisons.

There is a lack of Czech prison research in general, which logically extends to a lack of studies concentrating on the field of religion and religiosity in Czech prisons. There are a few exceptions, such as Jan Synek's historical analysis of the Czechoslovak penitentiary system during the Communist era (2013) or Jan Váně's and Lukáš Dirga's ethnographic research analysing the forms of religiosity in Czech male prisons (2016).

Considering the above, it is possible to conclude that, despite the current moderate wave of interest, Czech prison research remains underdeveloped, and research on religion in prison is no exception.[24] To address this gap, we conducted a study on religion and religiosity in Czech prisons; we describe the study and its findings in the next section.

7.7 Religion and Religiosity in Czech Prisons: Insights from an Empirical Study

Religion and religiosity in the current Czech penitentiary system have been directly researched in a single sociological study (Váně and Dirga 2016). The researchers concentrated on various forms of religiosity (or on various relationships to religion) in Czech male prisons. Their main aim was to analyse different forms of religiosity and to compare how the key actors of the prison world (inmates, prison guards and representatives of several churches) see the religiosity of inmates. The ethnographic[25] study has shown that religion (specifically, the religiosity of inmates) and its influence on the process of reintegration of former prisoners back into society represents, in the Czech environment, a controversial issue, which has generated ambivalent reactions.

Interviews with chaplains unveiled a whole range of problems connected to the activities they carry out. These can be summed up as follows: (a) the work is challenging and the chaplain workforce limited; (b) the "return on investment" is low, in that inmates usually do not continue to follow the faith after they are released; (c) no long-term integration programmes are provided to released prisoners, whether

---

[24] As for the academic environment, penitentiary system research is carried out mainly at the University of West Bohemia in Pilsen, Palacký University in Olomouc, Masaryk University in Brno or the Police Academy of the Czech Republic in Prague.

[25] We carried out 14 qualitative in-depth interviews with prison guards working in four selected C-type (high-security) prisons in the Czech Republic. These respondents differed by age (ranging from 21 to 48 years) and by the number of years they had been working as prison guards (ranging from 3 to 18). We also carried out five interviews with prison management representatives and four interviews with representatives of the Ecumenical Prison Chaplaincy of the Czech Republic. We were given permission to carry out interviews with 20 inmates. The sentences of the inmates we interviewed ranged from 3 years to life imprisonment. The most problematic aspect of the research was obtaining a permit to enter the prisons to contact prison inmates. To do this, we used our social networks and managed to obtain permits to enter two of the above-mentioned prisons. We spent a total of 7 days, 10 hours per day, inside the two prisons carrying out the interviews and making observations (Váně and Dirga 2016: 645–646).

they are religious or not; and (d) guards are making the chaplains' work difficult (Váně and Dirga 2016, 649).

Prison chaplains refused to endorse the notion that inmates act pragmatically[26] when they participate in religious services or activities organised by the Ecumenical Prison Chaplaincy of the Czech Republic. They embraced, on the contrary, the idea that prisoners are striving to find a new way of life or that faith helps to prevent them from relapsing. Quite often, participants argued that religion represents a return to a familiar setting in an altogether hostile environment. In fact, at least a segment of the prison population looks, while in prison (where failure and frustration accumulate, and identity obtained during socialisation falls apart), for some point of reference or some kind of anchor with which they are familiar from their time outside prison. We believe that this is linked to the fact that people are persuaded that certain institutions (in this case, the Church) exist primarily to help people when in need (in this case, in prison).

Chaplains supported their refusal to believe that prisoners' faith is purely pragmatic by pointing out that participating in religious services or other activities organised by the Ecumenical Prison Chaplaincy of the Czech Republic cannot lead to inmates' release on early parole. The chaplains also disagreed with the assertion that detainees participate in religion-related activities to escape boredom or to transfer information and material goods to or from other inmates or the chaplain.

At the same time, however, the interviews with the chaplains revealed that they were sceptical about what inmates do and say in relation to religion. We believe that this scepticism is well illustrated, on an official level, by the fact that the Ecumenical Prison Chaplaincy of the Czech Republic issued a recommendation (not a requirement) to stop baptisms, or, more precisely, to baptise inmates only after their release. (This recommendation applies to short sentences only; long penalties are exempt from this recommendation.)

The chaplains did not consider the pragmatic character of faith as the most pressing issue. Rather, they were worried about the fact that prisoners rarely remain actively involved in religious life after their release, and, in many cases, they quit religious life altogether. They offered one primary explanation[27]: a lack of long-term integration programmes focused on former prisoners. In other words (not only spiritual) post-penitentiary care is insufficient, and there are no effective programmes to integrate penitentiary and post-penitentiary care. One of the most problematic aspects of this problem, too, is that former prisoners who were baptised, who are getting ready to be baptised, or who used to participate in religious activities in prison find it difficult to successfully integrate into religious activities when released.

---

[26] Through this research, we found that the key respondents feel that there is some ambivalence around the role religion plays in the Czech prison system and that the pragmatic approach many inmates take to faith is becoming a controversial issue. Pragmatic religiosity/faith can be defined as a type of behaviour that, in the context of a collision of discourses, is governed by an instrumental calculation only, without aspiring to the salvation of one's soul (Váně and Dirga 2016: 653).

[27] Further research needs to be carried out on a larger and more heterogeneous sample to clarify this phenomenon.

To address this issue, the Czech Bishops' Conference and the Labour Office of the Czech Republic issued, in 2014, a joint statement about cooperation in the reintegration of former prisoners, but, so far, no action has been taken. Religious former prisoners (we have no record of their number) face, while trying to reintegrate, a lack of trust among congregations, which is nourished by the perception of former inmates' untrustworthiness among potential employers, public authorities and Czech society in general and reflected in the process of searching for work. Cases of successful reintegration can be attributed to individual charisma and effort; no systematic solutions are in place. The above suggests that released prisoners may not see faith as a ticket into mainstream Czech society.

The relationship between prison guards and chaplains is another long-term problem. According to the guards, they accept the presence of prison chaplains because they must. Chaplains, on the other hand, say that it is difficult to coexist with both guards and prisoners. They admit that the position they occupy within the penitentiary system has improved, and they attribute the improvement to the increased education level among prison guards and to the fact that guards and prison governors active during the communist and early post-communist era are now beginning to retire. All the same, the chaplains pointed out that religious inmates have not ceased to be stigmatised, although guards no longer harass them as much as they did in the 1990s.

Thus, if there has been an improvement in the way in which guards treat religious inmates, it has been initiated by management and still exists only on a personal, rather than a systemic, level. Furthermore, the relationship between guards and prisoners contaminates the relationship between chaplains and guards. Chaplains' testimonies reveal the reasons why guards oppose religion within prisons. Chaplains stated that guards opt not to cooperate with them, not on the grounds of atheism (which could have been expected as an attitude remaining from the Communist era) or by claiming that inmates' faith claims are just pragmatic, but simply to make their own jobs easier.

This, however, changes nothing about the fact that chaplains find themselves "between a rock and a hard place" the very moment they begin working in a prison. During the initial phase of the Ecumenical Prison Chaplaincy's involvement in prison, inmates considered chaplains as merely an arm of the guard corps, but this attitude is beginning to change among inmates. Conversely, the mutual lack of trust between guards and chaplain's remains. This mistrust allegedly diminished when the institution of chaplain service was introduced (1998), granting chaplains rights equal to those of prison employees (albeit civil, rather than public, employees). It has, however, not disappeared totally; chaplains in our study mentioned that they are still harassed by both guards and inmates, although not as strongly as before.

Given the above considerations, it is evident that the position of religion in the Czech post-Communist penitentiary system has stabilised. The benefits brought about by this stabilisation, however, are still rather ambivalent. In certain prisons, the influence and benefits brought about by pastoral care are apparent. Let us cite an example: in one of the establishments in our study, an entire floor was turned into a ward for religious inmates and for detainees interested in spiritual matters. This initiative was perceived positively by the inmates, and there was a huge interest in being transferred onto the dedicated floor, where about 60 inmates now live. The ward is also designated for inmates who have been defined as possible targets of violence and inmates with intellectual disabilities. Those who show interest are eligible to stay in this block, but they must pass an interview with an education specialist and with a priest. The priest then makes a recommendation regarding whether the candidate should be admitted to the ward. Furthermore, records of inmates' behaviour and social dangerousness are checked, and a collective assessment (by an educationalist, a member of prison management, a chaplain etc.) follows. Accepted candidates are then assigned to the ward. According to testimonies, the demand exceeds the ward's capacity, and the project is considered successful.

Despite these advances, matters related to the penitentiary system still do not represent a priority for the Roman-Catholic Church hierarchy. Prisons are "just" one of the issues that it has to deal with. Most probably, there are several reasons for this. We will cite those that we established based on indirect answers, hints and observations during our study.

We have already mentioned that several churches work in prison. They have tried to maintain good relations with one another, but, despite their effort, minor conflicts cannot be avoided. The issue of rechristening (by smaller churches) counts among the less visible problems between churches. Additionally, the smaller churches have recently been leaving prisons. This can be explained by the long-term drop in declared religiosity in the Czech Republic and by its intergenerational transfer (Hamplová 2013), which has led to a lack of staff available to provide pastoral care in prisons and other institutions. At the same time, there are conflicts within the corps of prison chaplains concerning competencies and personnel policies (Váně and Dirga 2016). To summarise the position of the prison chaplains we interviewed, and the role religion plays in the penitentiary system: we can affirm that, from the point of view of chaplains, the situation has improved significantly, mainly in relation to prison governors, but also in relation to staff. What is still lacking, however, according to chaplains, is a wise and conscious moral leadership, which would lend appropriate support to prison chaplain services.

If the guards are willing to accept the presence of prison chaplains, this acceptance is a personal attitude, rather than an institutional norm. The most efficient way for chaplains and guards alike to overcome distrust is to strictly follow the prison rules; the chaplains do so to prevent any suspicion that they "are on the same team" as the inmates. If such cases occur, the Ecumenical Prison Chaplaincy emphasises the culpability of volunteering chaplains,[28] rather than official prison chaplains. This implies that prison governors should strive to systematically integrate prison chaplains (i.e. create jobs for them) and not rely on volunteer work.

---

[28] For comparison: as of 31 December 2013, a total of 36 chaplains of 10 churches were active in prison, whereas the Roman Catholic Church, with 14 chaplains, was the most represented. Second came the Evangelical Church of Czech Brethren (8 chaplains). During 2013, a total of 234 voluntary priests of 14 Churches and religious societies with special rights were working in prisons. (Source: Prison Service of the Czech Republic).

It can be concluded that religion has progressively found its place in the penitentiary system and that this tendency has become stronger in the past few years,
although its form varies from prison to prison. The relationship between the State
and the Church is thus primarily influenced by the prison governors and their interest (or lack thereof) in the use of chaplains and their services within prisons.

From our findings, we can conclude that the current state of religion "behind
bars", so to speak, reflects long-term trends in Czech society and, as such, demonstrates a certain amount of ambivalence. On the one hand, churches operating in an
environment that is relatively hostile and among a population that is mostly indifferent and has little trust in traditional churches tend to adopt strategies of operation
that will not annoy the public. When asserting their place in the public domain and
at the institutional level, they avoid providing any pretext for resistance or negative
reaction. This dynamic is evident in the prison system, to which most of the Czech
population does not regularly pay attention; when it does, the prevailing idea is that
the approach to inmates needs to be restrictive (Veselský 2009). Churches have been
incrementally gaining positions in the institutional sphere, if possible, without much
publicity, and they have been doing so primarily in the area of public care, which
society attributes to them anyway. Thus, increasing activity in prison is a way for the
churches to gain influence in a secular society.

Conversely, there is an obvious lack of priests (as well as of active lay believers),
and the indications that we know of suggest that major traditional churches, consequently, might not see the prison system as their key priority. There are multiple
explanations for this fact. First, the lack of staff makes it difficult for churches to
contribute resources to prison environments. Second, it is questionable to what
extent this form of social service is generally recognised as beneficial and, therefore, how it can increase interest in and the prestige of religion and the churches.
Since the Communist regime collapsed, traditional churches have been seeking to
identify their social role and to gain prestige.[29] Indeed, they are constantly dealing
with the problem, not of how to raise socially relevant topics or influence public
agenda, but of how to pursue their own agenda in the public space.

Surveys show that the Catholic Church is failing to develop tools to systematically update its long-term agenda and to regularly incorporate new public issues
into it (Váně 2012, 2015). The Church makes statements on topics of public interest
on a random basis. Topical issues are raised by the personal efforts of individuals,
rather than organised, Church-wide agendas. Unfortunately, such an approach lacks
prospects for systematic accomplishments. An example of such a random impulse
was the establishment of a separate block within a given prison dedicated to

---

[29] At least within the Catholic Church, there were propositions at the start of the 1990s to focus
upon current social topics and thereby contribute to the constitution of post-revolutionary society,
notably the programme known as the "Decade of Spiritual Renewal" prepared and launched by the
Catholic Church as early as 1987. This was a pastoral initiative in which the national renewal was
linked to Czech history, as represented by significant Czech saints as role models whose significance came to be reformulated for current circumstances. The objective of this initiative was to
systematically rethink Czech history through the lens of Czech saints (Halík 2014; Opatrný 2019).

religious inmates (described above); this was the initiative of an individual rather than a product of a targeted church strategy (Dirga and Váně 2016; Váně and Dirga 2016).

It is worth noting, though, that the overwhelming indifference and distrust on the part of the majority of society against institutionalised religiosity make it impossible to proceed quickly with the integration of clerical and religious agendas into the agendas of public institutions. Thus, our conclusion that religion has gradually been finding its place in the prison system in recent years is proof of perseverance and successful efforts, against all odds, on the part of individual prison chaplains.

Bibliography

Černíková, V., & Sedláček, V. (2002). *Základy penologie pro policisty* [Introduction to penology for police officers]. Praha: Policejní akademie České republiky.

Dirga, L., & Marhánková, J. H. (2014). Nejasné vztahy moci – vězení očima českých dozorců. [Prison as a place of ambiguous power relations: The perspectives of Czech prison guards]. *Sociologický časopis/Czech Sociological Review, 50,* 83–105. https://doi.org/10.1306 0/00380288.2014.50.1.31.

Dirga, L., & Váně, J. (2016). Postpenitenciární péče z perspektivy nábožensky založených organizací. [Post-penitentiary care from the perspective of religious organisations]. In V. Černíková & J. Firstová (Eds.), *Postpenitenciární péče. Aktuální otázky* (pp. 104–110). Hodonín: Evropský ústav práva a soudního inženýrství.

Dirga, L., Lochmannová, A., & Juříček, P. (2015). The structure of the inmate population in Czech prisons. *Sociológia/Slovak. The Sociological Review, 47,* 559–578.

Halík, T. (2014). *Obnovíš tvář země. Texty k obnově církve a společnosti z let 1989–1998 [Thou shalt restore the face of Earth].* Prague: Nakladatelství lidové noviny.

Hamplová, D. (2013). *Náboženství v české společnosti na prahu 3. tisíciletí* [Czech religion at the beginning of the 3rd Millennium]. Prague: Karolinum.

Hanuš, J. (2005). *Tradice českého katolicismu ve 20. století* [Traditions of Czech Catholicism in the 20th century]. Brno: CDK

Havelka, M. (1995). *Spor o smysl českých dějin 1895–1938* [Dispute over the purpose of Czech history]. Prague: Torst.

Hladík, O. (2012). Výzkumný ústav penologický – pokus o reformu českého vězeňství [Penological Research Institute – an attempt to reform the Czech prison]. *Historická Penologie, 10,* 47–57.

Horák, J. (2015). *Dechristianizace českých zemí. Sekularizace jako záměr* [De-Christianization of Czech lands. Final objective: Secularization]. Olomouc: Univerzita Palackého v Olomouci.

Kautman, F. (2015). *O českou národní identitu* [Struggle over Czech national identity]. Prague: Pulchra.

Kýr, A. (2005). Vývoj situace vězeňství po 17. listopadu 1989 [The development of the prison system after November 17, 1989]. *Historická Penologie, 3,* 1–3.

Kýr, A. (2008). Protektorátní vězeňství se zřetelem na činnost pankrácké věznice [Prisons in the protectorate: Focusing on the Pankrác prison]. *Historická Penologie, 1,* 27–36.

Kýr, A., & Janák, D. (2004). Nástin vývoje československého vězeňství v letech 1948–1989. [Czechoslovak prison system between 1948 and 1989: An overview]. *Historická Penologie, 5,* 1–4.

Kýr, A., & Kafková, A. (2009). Pankrácká věznice v období historických změn (1889–1993) [The Pankrác prison in the period of historical changes (1889–1993)]. *Historická Penologie, 3,* 2–71.

Ministry of Justice of the Czech Republic. (2016). *Koncepce vězeňství do roku 2025* [Penitentiary system conceptual framework until 2025]. Prague: Ministry of Justice of the Czech Republic.

Mišovič, J. (2001). *Víra v dějinách zemí Koruny české* [Faith in the history of lands of the Bohemian crown]. Prague: Slon.

Nedbálková, K. (2006). *Spoutaná Rozkoš: (re)produkce genderu a sexuality v ženské věznici* [Chained pleasure: (re)production of gender and sexuality in women's prison]. Prague: Sociologické nakladatelství.

Nešpor, Z., & Vojtíšek, Z. (2015). *Encyklopedie menších křesťanských církví v České republice* [Encyclopedia of minor Christian churches in the Czech Republic]. Prague: Karolinum.

Netík, K. (1998). *Koncepce rozvoje vězeňství v ČR* [Czech penitentiary system conceptual framework]. Prague: Policejní akademie České republiky (samostatná příloha časopisu České vězeňství 1998/1).

Opatrný, A. (2019). *Desetiletí duchovní obnovy: 1988–1997* [Decade of spiritual renewal]. Svitavy: Trinitas.

Prison Service of the Czech Republic. (2005). *Koncepce rozvoje českého vězeňství do roku 2015* [Czech penitentiary system conceptual framework until 2015]. Prague: Prison Service of the Czech Republic, General Directorate.

Prison Service of the Czech Republic. (2006). *Evropská vězeňská pravidla* [*European prison rules*]. Příloha časopisu České vězeňství č. 1/2006. http://vscr.cz/generalni-reditelstvi-19/informacni-servis/ke-stazeni-112/publikace/. Accessed 16 Mar 2017.

Prison Service of the Czech Republic. (2008). *Dohoda o duchovní službě* [Agreement on spiritual services]. Prague: Prison Service of the Czech Republic, General Directorate.

Prison Service of the Czech Republic. (2014). *Východiska a záměry nové koncepce vězeňství v České republice* [Starting points and design of the new Czech penitentiary system conceptual framework]. Prague: Prison Service of the Czech Republic, General Directorate.

Prudký, L. (2005). *Církve a sociální soudržnost v naší zemi* [The churches and social cohesion in Czech society]. Prague: UK FSV CESES.

Prudký, L. (2009a). *Inventura hodnot* [Inventory of values]. Prague: Academia.

Prudký, L. (2009b). *Studie o hodnotách* [Study of values]. Prague: Čeněk.

Schwartz, H., & Schwartz, M. C. (1989). *Prison conditions in Czechoslovakia. A Helsinki Watch report*. New York: Human Rights Watch.

Šmausová, G. (1992). Znovuzačlenění, nebo trvalá marginalizace vězňů? O funkcích trestního práva [Reintegration or permanent marginalisation of prisoners? On the functioning of the criminal law]. *Československá Kriminalistika, 25*, 225–235.

Šmausová, G. (1993). Dějiny myšlení a jejich význam pro vězeňství [The history of thinking and its relationship to prison systems]. In P. Hungr (Ed.), *Normativnost a realita práva* (pp. 192–209). Brno: Masarykova univerzita.

Šmausová, G. (1994). Symbolické funkce trestního práva [Symbolic functions of the criminal law]. In V. Kratochvíl (Ed.), *Trestněprávní reforma v České republice* (pp. 6–22). Brno: Masarykova univerzita.

Spousta, J. (1999). January. České církve očima sociologických výzkumů [Czech Churches as Viewed by Sociological Research]. In Hanuš, J. (Ed.), *Náboženství v době společenských změn* [Religion in the era of social changes] (pp. 73–90). Brno: MPÚ/MU.

Synek, J. (2013). *Svobodni v nesvobodě: náboženský život ve věznicích v období komunistického režimu* [Bound but free. Religious life in prisons during the Communist regime]. Vyšehrad: Ústav pro studium totalitních režimů.

Tížik, M. (2012). Religion and national identity in an enlarging Europe. In F. Höllinger & M. Hadler (Eds.), *Crossing borders, shifting boundaries: national and transnational identities in Europe and beyond* (pp. 101–121). Frankfurt am Main: Campus Verlag.

Tomek, P. (2000). *Dvě studie o československém vězeňství 1948–1989.* [Two studies on the Czech penitentiary system 1948–1989]. Prague: Úřad dokumentace a vyšetřování zločinů komunismu.

Tomka, M., & Zulehner, P. M. (1999). *Religion in der Reformländer Ost (Mittel) Europas*. Vienna: Pastorales Forum.

Tomka, M., & Zulehner, P. M. (2000). *Religion im gesellschaftlichen Kontext Ost (Mittel) Europa*. Vienna: Pastorales Forum.

Tomka, M., & Zulehner, P. M. (2008). *Religionen und Kirchen in Ost (Mittel)Europa: Entwicklungen seit der Wende*. Ostfildern: Schwabenverlag.

Vacek, E. (2004). Stručný nástin vývoje vězeňství od roku 1989 do roku 1995 [Penitentiary system development between 1989 and 1995: A short overview]. *Historická Penologie, 1*, 10–12.

Václavík, D. (2010). *Náboženství a moderní česká společnost [Religion and modern Czech society]*. Prague: Grada.

Váně. (2012, January). *Komunita jako nová naděje?* [Community as a new hope?]. Plzeň: ZČU.

Váně. (2015, January). Jak/co jim říci, aby naslouchali? Aneb nastolování témat ve veřejném prostoru českou katolickou církví [How/what to say to make them listen or the Czech Catholic Church is setting agenda in the public space]. *Studia Theologica, 17*, 203–229.

Váně, J., & Dirga, L. (2016). The religiosity behind bars: Forms of inmate's religiosity in the Czech prison system. *Sociológia/Slovak. The Sociological Review, 48*, 641–663.

Veselský, M. (2009). České vězeňství viděné optikou veřejného mínění [Czech prison system viewed by public opinion]. *Naše Společnost, 1*, 3–12.

Vojtíšek, Z. (2004). *Encyklopedie náboženských směrů v České republice: Náboženství, církve, sekty, duchovní společenství* [Encyclopedia of religious movements in the Czech Republic; religion, churches, sects, spiritual communities]. Prague: Portál.

Chapter 8
Denmark: Christianity and Islam in Prisons – A Case of Secular Professionalisation of Chaplaincy

Henrik Reintoft Christensen, Lene Kühle, and Niels Valdemar Vinding

Abstract This chapter presents the historical background and current organisation of religion in the Danish penitentiary system from a legal and sociological perspective. The role and presence of religion in prison were not much discussed until 2006, when the Prison and Probation Service published its first report on religion in prisons. Nevertheless, the Lutheran prison chaplain has been a natural part of the Danish prison system since the establishment of the modern prison in the nineteenth century. Following this historical background, the regulation of religion in prison is presented to show the national and international legal framework regulating the work of chaplains and religious practices of inmates. The Prison and Probation Service produces much information and many statistics on prison life, but not related to religion. The final section presents empirical studies of religion among inmates, showing, for instance, that the proportion of Muslim inmates was the same in 2006 and 2017. Although the proportion was around 20% there are very few Muslim chaplains in prison, and they are a relatively recent addition to Lutheran chaplains from the majority church. The last section examines the majority church chaplains, and shows that they take it upon themselves to cater to the needs of all inmates. Although imams remain contested in the wider society, The Prison and Probation Service welcomes Muslim Chaplaincy (after thorough vetting) because they can oppose potential radicalisation and provide pastoral care to the inmates.

H. R. Christensen (✉) · L. Kühle
Department for the Study of Religion, Aarhus University, Aarhus, Denmark
e-mail: hc@cas.au.dk; lk@cas.au.dk

N. V. Vinding
Department for Cross-Cultural and Regional Studies, University of Copenhagen, København, Denmark
e-mail: lbm993@hum.ku.dk

© Springer Nature Switzerland AG 2020   113
J. Martínez-Ariño, A.-L. Zwilling (eds.), *Religion and Prison: An Overview of Contemporary Europe*, Boundaries of Religious Freedom: Regulating Religion in Diverse Societies 7, https://doi.org/10.1007/978-3-030-36834-0_8

8.1   Introduction

The role of religion in prison became of intense public interest in Denmark in early 2015 as a young man, Omar el-Hussein, opened fire at two public events in Copenhagen. The first was on 14 February 2015 at a public event on freedom of expression, where Omar el-Hussein shot and killed a participant and injured four police officers before escaping. Later the same day, he attacked the great synagogue in Copenhagen, where he killed a man from the Jewish congregation who was volunteering as a guard at a bat mitzvah, and injured two police officers. The terrorist managed to escape but was spotted and shot by the police later during the night. He had been released from prison only 2 weeks earlier, and much of the debate after the attacks focused on his potential radicalisation while in prison. In this regard, the debate mirrors a wider debate on the role of religion and religious diversity in society as a whole.

In this chapter, we explore the situation of religion in Danish prisons and some of the changes that have recently taken place in the Danish penitentiary system regarding religion. The first section presents the historical background and current organisation of the prison system, showing how chaplains have been part of this system since the establishment of the early modern prisons, and how Muslim chaplaincies have made a relatively recent contribution in the Danish context. In this first section, we also introduce major studies on religion and prisons, showing that although this has historically been a very small field of study, it has been augmented with the increased religious, cultural and ethnic diversity found in society and in the penitentiaries. The second section examines the legal dimensions of religion in prisons, scrutinising the Constitution, other Danish laws, international conventions, and EU regulations with respect to participation in religious services, pastoral care and individual religious practices. In this section, we examine the regulation of both chaplains and inmates. The final section then describes how religious services, pastoral care and individual religiosity are practised in the prisons.

We base our presentation on official documents and reports, a study from 2015 conducted by two of the authors (Kühle and Christensen 2015), interviews carried out as part of a study on "Imams of the West" by the third author (Vinding, forthcoming) and various other publications, in particular, Winnifred Sullivan (2009, 2014). We show that most prison chaplains belong to the Evangelical Lutheran Church of Denmark, but their profile is different from that of ordinary parish-based ministers. Their theology accommodates and is suited to the realities of prison life. The same goes for Muslim chaplains, who are only hired after a thorough vetting process that ensures a theology compatible with the aims of the Prison and Probation Service. In that way, the theology that the chaplains represent is much more malleable than that of the religions found in society. Unlike the development in the surrounding society, where religion is becoming increasingly diverse, prison chaplaincy remains predominantly Lutheran. The Prison and Probation Service has prepared several positions as Muslim chaplains, but these have been impeded owing to increasing political suspicion towards imams.

Denmark (along with the other Nordic countries) has a majority church and has been relatively homogenous, with almost 75% of the population being members of the Lutheran church. Nevertheless, all members of society interact with institutions such as hospitals, prisons and the military, which means that the chaplains who primarily belong to the majority church meet all kinds of people as part of their work. Religion in Danish prisons thus revolves around chaplains from the majority Lutheran church, who hold what almost amounts to a monopoly on prison ministry. Only recently have Muslim chaplains been added to the system. Concerning the regulation of chaplains from religious communities other than the Church of Denmark, it seems that the Prison and Prevention Service in Denmark has unfolded a pragmatic professional framework in reports and circular letters, but that this process is diverging from the political securitisation of imams in the wake of the terrorist attack in 2015. The unfolding of different and potentially contradictory logic forms the core of the further development of religion in Danish prisons, from a position of (almost) religious monopoly to a situation of religious diversity.

8.2   Historical Background and Current Organisation

In the early modern prisons established in Denmark in the nineteenth century, the prison chaplain was an important figure, overseeing the spiritual care of inmates, understood literally as the salvation of their souls. During the twentieth century, the position of the prison chaplain became more marginal as prison ideology became secularised. This secularisation process became increasingly visible, for instance, through the gradual abolition of obligatory attendance at religious services in the period between 1924 and the new penal code of 1930 (Kühle 2004, 215), the reduction of space used for prison churches, the increasing use of other personnel groups (teachers, librarians, psychologists, social workers) to deal with the welfare of the inmates. Furthermore, in the 1970s, efforts to discontinue chaplaincy positions (which were paid for by the prison authorities) were made, although they were only partly successful (Kühle 2004, 217). An interesting change came in the 1980s when the majority Lutheran Church began to take an interest in prison chaplaincy, and several new positions, paid for by the Church of Denmark, were established (Kühle 2004, 228).

In 1997, the first steps towards establishing a Muslim prison chaplaincy were taken when a convert to Islam, Leon Soudhari Hansen, was employed in Copenhagen prisons, first as a teacher, and from 2002 formally as a full-time Muslim chaplain.[1] Soudhari Hansen's employment was facilitated by Lutheran chaplains in the Copenhagen prisons and also and perhaps in particular by the doctor in theology Lissi Rasmussen, a "pioneer in religious dialogue in Denmark" and herself a Lutheran chaplain since 2008.[2]

---

[1] https://www.information.dk/2002/05/faengsel-fastansaetter-imam

[2] http://www.kristeligt-dagblad.dk/mennesker/pioneren-i-religionsdialog

In 2015, there were 14 prisons[3] and 44 remand prisons in Denmark, with a prison population of about 3400 (Statistik 2015). A majority (64%) of inmates are of Danish descent, whereas 27% are immigrants and 9% are descendants of immigrants.[4] Many of the immigrants and descendants are not Christians. However, the greatest part of pastoral care is; in every facility (51 in all), a minister from the Evangelical-Lutheran Church of Denmark is either associated or employed. The Prison and Probation Service employs seven Lutheran chaplains (6.5 full-time positions), whereas the Church of Denmark employs about 50 chaplains. However, for many of them, prison service is only a minor part of their job description (Kühle and Christensen 2015, 58).

For Muslims, who make up almost 20% of the entire prison population, there is one imam in Copenhagen, who is employed full time, two or three who are employed part time and an additional few who are brought in *ad hoc*. Until recently, there were four state-funded Muslim chaplains, but the future of Muslim prison chaplains has become increasingly uncertain. Currently, there is only one prison-funded Muslim chaplain and one Muslim advisor, who is employed according to the circular letter on employment and supervision of clergy within the Prison and Probation Service, and in reality, functions as a Muslim chaplain in three prisons. He does not want to be addressed as an imam but prefers to be seen as a "mentor".[5] For Catholics, there is one nun, who visits the Copenhagen facilities 1 day a week. Everything else is *ad hoc*. For Jews, a rabbi may be called in when needed. For Buddhists, Hindus and others, a religious person may be called in when needed.

8.2.1   Changes and Trends

The presence of religion in prison was not discussed much until about 2006, when the Prison and Probation Service published a report on religious diversity in prisons. The report was a large qualitative and quantitative study entitled *Report on the Clerical Services for Inmates, Who Belong to Religious Communities Other Than*

---

[3] Copenhagen prisons are included among the prisons, but consist of several institutions and combine remand and prison facilities.

[4] Official Danish immigration statistics distinguish between immigrants and descendants, with immigrants being "a person born abroad whose parents are both (or one of them if there is no available information on the other parent) foreign citizens or were both born abroad" and a descendant is "a person born in Denmark whose parents (or one of them if there is no available information on the other parent) are either immigrants or descendants with foreign citizenship". (https://www.dst.dk/en/Statistik/dokumentation/documentationofstatistics/immigrants-and-descendants/statistical-presentation)

[5] E-mail from the Prison and Probation Service of 21 November 2016. The term chaplain is not used in Danish. Instead they are "prison pastors" or "prison imams". We have decided to use the English term chaplain in this chapter, although in a few cases such as this one, it obscures certain understandings of the actors in the field. Similarly, the Prison and Probation Service specifically uses the term religious preacher (*religiøs forkynder*) at the same time, as it actively wants to avoid proselytisation.

the Evangelical-Lutheran Church of Denmark. The work group circulated a short questionnaire to all Danish inmates in the various closed, semi-open and open facilities (2353 respondents out of a population of 4057 inmates).[6] The report was made based on the growth of ethnic and religious diversity in prisons, and as a preparation for legislation securing the freedom of religion, among other things.

The publication of this report coincided with a major public debate pertaining to Abu Bashar (Mohamad Samha Al-Khaled), who had worked as a Muslim chaplain at the state prison in the city of Nyborg since 2002. Abu Bashar had played a key role in "the largest foreign policy crisis in Denmark since WWII", the cartoon crisis, as he was one of the imams who in 2005–2006 toured the Middle East to mobilise support for a large-scale protest against the newspaper *Jyllands-Posten* and their publication of the Muhammad cartoons. The media accused him of preaching hatred in his sermons in prisons. Furthermore, his name was associated with terrorism-related arrests in Germany. He was fired in July 2006, but according to the then Minister of Justice, Lene Espersen, this was because of cutbacks in the prison budgets.[7]

The 2006 events resulted in two circular letters published in 2013, one formalising inmates' access to practising their religion, and the other formalising the employment of religious minority chaplains. Overall, the report from the Prison and Probation Service evaluated the role of religion and of imams in prison very positively. The Muslim chaplains were seen as playing an important part as role models, and as important facilitators of integration (Prison and Probation Service 2006). However, the loyalty of Muslim chaplains continued to be questioned, both in the media and in parliament. The debates and changes within the last decade show the strong intertwinement of prisons and prevention of radicalisation. Prevention of radicalisation became a high priority after the publication in 2009 of the first general action plan on the prevention of radicalisation called *A Joint and Safe Future.*[8] The 2009 action plan contained 22 initiatives aimed at countering radicalisation in different societal areas. *Initiative 17: Prevention in Prison* contained four activities: an educational programme for personnel, practical training in local democracy in prison, exit programmes and systems of recognition for "religious preachers" in prisons (2009, 23). The last topic is explained as an effort to ensure that religious preachers (the concept used by the Prison and Probation Service for Lutheran as well as Muslim chaplains) are aware of their obligation to counter radicalisation. In the 2014 action plan, *Prevention of Radicalisation and Extremism,*[9] the number of initiatives has been reduced to 12, and the number of activities has likewise been reduced. There are now four activities within the area of the Prison and Probation Service: two initiatives,

---

[6] "Rapport om gejstlig betjening af indsatte, der tilhører andre trossamfund end den evangelisk-lutherske danske folkekirke"

[7] http://www.ft.dk/samling/20061/spoergsmaal/s303/index.htm

[8] "En fælles og tryg fremtid: Handlingsplan om forebyggelse af ekstremistiske holdninger og radikalisering". Available from: http://uim.dk/publikationer/en-faelles-og-tryg-fremtid-handlingsplan-om-forebyggelse-af-ekstremistiske-holdninger-og-radikalisering-blandt-unge

[9] "Forebyggelse af radikalisering og ekstremisme". Available from: http://www.stm.dk/multimedia/Forebyggelse_af_radikalisering_og_ekstremisme_-_Regeringens_handlingsplan.pdf

further education of key personnel (Initiative 2) and exit programmes (Initiative 7) were also part of the 2009 Action Plan, whereas two initiatives, strategic cooperation between authorities (Initiative 1) and Initiative 4 on early prevention were new. Although more activities have been added, the prevention of radicalisation in prisons is no longer a priority area with its own headline, but a focus area with activities presented under general headlines such as "further education" or "exit programmes".

After the terrorist attack in February 2015, counter-radicalisation budgets were increased, and the Prison and Probation Service returned as a central actor for prevention. Twelve initiatives were described; the prevention of radicalisation in prison is the tenth.[10] The initiative continues the activities of the two previous action plans, but reintroduces the role of the "religious preacher", albeit this time as someone who must be under surveillance to ensure that they do not contribute to the potential radicalisation of inmates (2015, 8). The newest action plan from 2016[11] contains nine new initiatives, among which "Increased efforts against radicalisation in prison" is the sixth. It also contains five activities, one of which is "increased screening and surveillance of religious preachers in prison" (2016, 9). In October 2016, in response to questions on the role of imams in the Prison and Probation Service, the then Minister of Justice Søren Pind stated,

> I would like to stress that religious preachers, including imams, can play an important role in the prevention of radicalisation and extremism among inmates in the prisons. Already today, a lot is done to make sure that the right persons are employed in the Prison and Probation Service, and that includes religious preachers, including imams.[12] (Søren Pind, Former Minister of Justice, 2016)

The rest of the answer by the Minister elaborates on what such a screening and surveillance by the Danish security and intelligence service would imply.

The increased focus on Muslim chaplains correlates with a recent bill (L30),[13] which will it make obligatory for chaplains who are to perform legally valid marriages to participate in a 2-day course on the family, freedom and democracy.[14] The focus has thus shifted towards a closer association between rights and duties, where duties are more clearly associated with support for democracy. In 2012, the Prison and Probation Service remained certain that more positions as Muslim chaplains would soon be established and formalities would be settled by the (then-upcoming) circular letters (Mogensen 2012, 30). According to the regulations in the circular letter, chaplains must hold substantial knowledge of Danish society so that they can assist in the resocialisation of inmates, and that the chaplains should prefer-

---

[10] "Et stærkt værn mod terror". Available from: http://www.fmn.dk/nyheder/Documents/Et-staerkt-vaern-mod-terror-2015.pdf

[11] "Preventing and combatting radicalisation and extremism". http://justitsministeriet.dk/sites/default/files/media/Pressemeddelelser/pdf/2016/National-handlingsplan-Forebyggelse-og-bekaempelse-af-ekstremisme-og-radikalisering.pdf

[12] Parliamentary debates, 26 October 2016 (Spm. no. S 82, Minister of Justice, Søren Pind).

[13] http://www.ft.dk/samling/20161/lovforslag/L30/index.htm

[14] http://www.ft.dk/samling/20161/lovforslag/l30/spm/4/svar/1358525/1687486.pdf

ably be drawn from the recognised communities. This puts significant limits on who can serve as a prison imam. The real limits are set, however, by the change in discourse where Muslim chaplains – in the words of Waseem Hussain, the only full-time employed Muslim chaplain, in a word game untranslatable into English – are seen as *modborgere* (anti-citizens) rather than *medborgere* (citizens), and therefore considered unable to do any good in society.[15]

The focus on the formal skills and qualifications of the Muslim chaplains is in a way mirrored by an increasing emphasis on the formal skills and qualifications of the Lutheran chaplains. The situation, nevertheless, is quite different because the wish for more formalised education of prison chaplains comes from the chaplains themselves, rather than from the Prison and Probation Service or politicians. Since 2006, the education unit within the Church of Denmark has arranged yearly courses and seminars for Lutheran prison chaplains.[16] These courses and seminars contribute to building a stronger qualification, in particular within the field of pastoral care, as well as the formation of a professional identity as a (Lutheran) prison chaplain.

8.2.2   Research on Religion and Prisons in Denmark

A small number of publications on religion in prisons in Denmark have been published. Kühle (2004) included a chapter on religion in prisons in Denmark, focusing on, among other things, how Lutheran chaplains in Danish prisons were acting as facilitators and brokers for religious minorities (Beckford and Gilliat 1998). It was based on interviews with Lutheran chaplains, Muslim chaplains and Catholics and Pentecostals visiting prisons. An edited volume on ethics, law and religion in prisons (Kühle and Lomholt 2006), *The Human Face of Punishment*, included significant contributions by the then Director of the Prison Service, William Rentzmann, and the then Ombudsman, Hans Gammeltoft-Hansen, as well as a series of scholars and researchers from the Nordic countries and the UK.

In 2010, while associated with the Centre on European Islamic Thought, the pastor and prison chaplain Lissi Rasmussen wrote *Life Stories and Crime – An Empirical Study of Ethnic Minority Youth in Copenhagen Prisons*. The study is based on conversations with more than 150 inmates of immigrant background, and analyses of more than 500 individual action plans for inmates. Seven "life stories" hold a central position in the book. Religion as such is not a central topic in the book, which nevertheless shows that for many of the informants of Muslim background, their religious interest is invigorated while incarcerated.

---

[15] "Trist, at man tror, at imamer er modborgere i stedet for medborgere, og at de simpelthen ikke kan bidrage til noget positivt i Danmark" https://www.information.dk/indland/2015/04/faengselsimam-praest-religioes-radikalisering-boer-moedes-religioes-indsigt

[16] http://www.frederikssundkirke.dk/fileadmin/group/771/Dokumenter/Haandbog_FFA_september_2016.pdf

Several master theses with independent data collection have also been written on religion and prisons. Olsen (2006) was written based on interviews with six inmates who had converted to Islam, Muslim chaplains, a Lutheran prison chaplain and an employee of the Prison and Probation Service. Olsen has published his results in several articles (2008, 2014). Mai Møller Nielsen's master's thesis from 2012 discusses the ambiguous and ambivalent expectations of Muslim chaplains, based on interviews with two present and one former Muslim chaplains, as well as e-mail correspondence with the Prison and Probation Service, and analysis of relevant official documents. Besides the religious services central to their job description, Muslim chaplains are expected to provide anti-radicalisation, resocialisation, reintegration, recurrence reduction, and tranquillity in the everyday prison life (Nielsen 2012, 1). Similarly, Line Nielsen (2015) discusses the governance of Muslim practices in closed prisons in Denmark, based on a survey distributed to prison managers, interviews with two Muslim chaplains and a group interview with two inmates in the presence of both the Muslim and Lutheran chaplains. Finally, a comprehensive study of Lutheran chaplains, including survey questions and personal interviews with prison chaplains, highlighted the similarities and differences between prison chaplaincy and other chaplaincies (Kühle and Christensen 2015). Before presenting the results of this study, a closer look at the legal dimensions of religion in prisons is necessary.

8.3   The Regulation of Religion in Prison

Regarding the legal aspects of prison and religion relations in Denmark, a few introductory remarks must be made regarding the general state of regulation and governance of religion in Denmark. Broadly speaking, the 1849 Danish Constitutional Act (*Danmarks Grundlov*) governs the framework of the relationship between the State, the Church of Denmark and "the religious communities other than the Evangelical-Lutheran Church of Denmark", as they are called in Article 69 of the Constitutional Act (My Constitutional Act, 2012, 39).

Article 4 of the Constitutional Act defines the nature of the relationship between the State and the Church, stating: "The Evangelical-Lutheran Church of Denmark (*Folkekirken*) is the established Church of Denmark and, as such, is supported by the State" (My Constitutional Act 2012, 3). Article 4 identifies the confessional specificities of the supported Church and defines the obligation of the State to support the Church. Furthermore, in Article 66, it is specified that "the Constitution of the Evangelical-Lutheran Church of Denmark is regulated by an Act" (My Constitutional Act, 2012, 38). This provision dates back to 1849, but the Act referred to was only presented to and adopted by Parliament in 2017, which codified and modified previous administrative practices of governmental departments.[17] Article 67 mandates that "members of the public are entitled to associate in communities to worship God according to their convictions, but nothing may be taught or done that

---

[17] Lov nr. 1533 of 19 December 2017 http://www.ft.dk/samling/20171/lovforslag/l119/index.htm

contravenes decency or public order" (Ibid.). This is the positively defined freedom to associate and to worship, and Article 70 negatively defines the guarantee that "nobody may be deprived of access to the full enjoyment of civil and political rights or evade the fulfilment of any general civic duty on the grounds of his or her profession of faith" (Ibid., 39). There is no obligation to be a member of a specific religious community, let alone the Evangelical-Lutheran Church of Denmark. Nobody is to be discriminated against because of religion and people may serve in public office regardless of religious affiliation. This, in turn, means that religion in Denmark is public and that people can gather publicly in worship (Christoffersen 2012, 243).

In relation to Islam and other minority religions, the details of the right to form religious communities are formulated in Law 1533 of 19 December 2017, which carries the official name of Law on religious communities different from the Church of Denmark. Again, the English translation falls short of the original Danish, which has the word "deviant" rather than "other" in defining the relationship to the State in contrast to the relationship enjoyed by the Evangelical-Lutheran Church of Denmark. Also, here, the object of regulation by the Act is not the communities themselves, but rather their affairs. The law contains a number of rules on how to become a recognised religious community, which, among various privileges, include members' right to make tax-deductible donations to the recognised religious communities as well as the right to perform legally binding marriages. The recognised religious communities (2018) include 28 Muslim denominations, 38 Christian congregations and 2 Jewish congregations, as well as Buddhist, Hindu, Sikh and Old Norse congregations.

8.3.1 Legal Status of Prison Chaplains and Chaplaincy

In addition to the above-mentioned general principles from the Constitutional Act, the legal status of prison chaplains is governed by very diverse legal instruments – both international and national. Similar to many other countries, there is an international dimension to the regulation of religion. Denmark have ratified the international covenants and Declaration on Human Rights, which declares both freedom of religion and the rights of prisoners. In addition to the UN and EU declarations and covenants, this includes, of course, most importantly, the Rules for the Treatment of Prisoners, United Nations General Assembly, 1977 and the European Prison Rules, drawn up by the Council of Europe originally in 1987, revised in 2006. These are non-legally binding standards on good principles and practices in the treatment of detainees and the management of detention facilities.

The sections on freedom of thought, conscience and religion are relevant as for Article 29: freedom of thought, conscience and religion:

Article 29. Prisoners' freedom of thought, conscience and religion shall be respected.

Subsection 2: the prison regime shall be organised so far as is practicable to allow prisoners to practise their religion and follow their beliefs, to attend services or meetings led by approved representatives of such religion or beliefs, to receive visits in private from such representatives of their religion or beliefs and to have in their possession books or literature relating to their religion or beliefs.

Subsection 3: prisoners may not be compelled to practise a religion or belief, to attend religious services or meetings, to take part in religious practices or to accept a visit from a representative of any religion or belief.[18]

The national legal framework on the rights of prisoners and the exercise of religion in Denmark is governed under the framework of the Constitutional Act, as mentioned above, but specified in several supplementary Acts.

8.3.1.1   The Enforcement of Sentences Act 2012[19]

Article 35 of the Enforcement of Sentences Act specifies the right to participate in religious services and Article 41 specifies the rules of employment on religious affiliation.

Participation in religious services, etc.

Article 35. An inmate has the right to attend services held in the institution. If order and security so require, the head of the institution or the person authorised to do so may, however, refuse certain inmates to participate in religious services and limit the number of participants. If it is decided to limit the number of participants, the prisoner concerned should as far as possible instead be allowed to attend the service via electronic media.

Subsection 2: an inmate has the right to talk to a priest or the like from its religious communities.

and

Article 41. The Minister of Justice lays down rules on prisoners' employment, including the employment service should be organised taking into account the prisoner's religious affiliation.

As for chaplains outside the Church of Denmark – that is, from religious communities deviant from the Church of Denmark – they too are governed by the Enforcement of Sentences Act. What is understood here by "priest" is explained in the commentary to the Enforcement of Sentences Act to be any chaplain or clergy of the recognised or approved religious communities – which includes Catholic priests and nuns, Muslim imams etc.[20]

---

[18] https://wcd.coe.int/ViewDoc.jsp?id=955747

[19] Straffuldbyrdelsesloven, LBK no. 1242 of 11 November 2015 https://www.retsinformation.dk/forms/r0710.aspx?id=170653

[20] Recognition or approval of religion in Denmark is a substantial discussion in and of itself, and is explored elsewhere, but in this context, the recognition and approval mean that the religious community has committed itself to respect basic human rights, responsible ministry, organised worship, clear doctrine etc.

This is important for – among other things – the qualified confidentiality, which is upheld for the priest or minister in the right of inmates to talk to a priest or the like from their religious communities (above; Article 35, Subsection 2). This is absolutely confidential and defined in the Administration of Justice Act 2014 [Retsplejeloven, LBK nr 1308 af 09/12/2014]. It may only be violated by a court in cases of national security, substantial danger to life, or the like:

> Article 170. Against the will of he who is entitled to confidentiality, must no priests in the national church or other religious communities, doctors, defenders, legal brokers and lawyers, which has come to their knowledge in the performance of their business, be asked to testify or bear witness.
>
> Subsection 2: the Court may direct doctors, legal brokers and lawyers, except for defence counsel in criminal cases, to testify when the explanation is considered crucial for the outcome, and the nature and its importance to such party or society exist to justify, the explanation required. Such notice may in civil case not extend to what lawyers have learned in a lawsuit that has been entrusted to him for execution, or in which his advice has been sought.

However, by extension, it means that chaplains who are not part of the recognised or approved religious communities in Denmark may not invoke this qualified confidentiality. As we will show below, this confidentiality is a natural part of the chaplains' understanding of the pastoral care they provide. It enables them to be fully present in their conversations with inmates, as these do not have to worry or fear what they tell the chaplains.

8.3.1.2 Employment of and Oversight with Chaplains Outside the Church

Very much building on the recommendations from the 2006 report, the Prison and Probation Services in Denmark have been aspiring to a well-ordered framework for chaplains from other religious communities, most significantly imams and Muslim chaplains. As early as 2011, with the call for a new imam for Copenhagen prisons, it was apparent that a wider framework for the employment of chaplains was needed. The call both specified the tasks of the new imam as a chaplain and provider of religious services and highlighted the need to vet the candidate and the need for him/her to be cleared by the security services.

In the circular letter from 2013 on the "employment of and oversight with religious preachers in the Prison and Probation Service",[21] how to engage chaplains from other religious communities is clearly regulated. Overall, the circular letter is concerned with establishing clear working conditions for the employment of the chaplains in terms of rights, safe working environments, professional and collegial conditions and ongoing conversations with specialists and experts in the religious field, in lieu of what in the Church of Denmark would be a bishop with theological

---

[21] Published as CIR1H no. 9530 of 26 September 2013, "Circular letter on the employment of and oversight with religious preachers in the Prison and Probation Services", by the Ministry of Justice.

oversight. All of this is destined to enable the chaplain to perform his duties and responsibilities to his fullest ability. In addition, and building on this professionalisation of the imams employed by the Prison and Probation Service, the circular letter also addresses the issues of prison security, proper training, radicalisation risks and extremism in prison. Article 21 specifies that,

> Religious preachers may serve an important function as role models to the inmates and may therefore work as an important connection in the integration of the inmates into Danish society. The task performance in the institutions of the Prison and Probation Service must therefore always be handled in such a way, that the performance of tasks contributes to the promotion of a democratic life stance and to the prevention of extremism and radicalisation of the inmates.[22]

With the specification of the positive contribution of religious preachers and chaplains as role models and conducive to integration of the inmates into Danish society, the wording very much predates the current trend of increased securitisation of Islam in Danish political discourse, as this intensified after the terror attacks of February 2015, which problematised the role of imams in particular. As such, the circular letter of 2013 expresses and exemplifies the balanced efforts of the *Prison and Probation Service* to establish a well-regulated framework for chaplains and religious preachers in prison, while taking the threat of radicalisation and extremism seriously. Such a pragmatic approach is confirmed by Waseem Hussain, the full-time Muslim chaplain, in an interview from 2017, where he discusses how these regulations came about:

> I think it is out of the idea that, well, we have priests for the Christian inmates and now there are so many Muslim inmates that we might consider an imam. That's one. A consideration of equal treatment. And then there is something called the EU directive, which means that there are regulations on the subject, which demands that inmates receive the religious service they need. So, there's that, too. So, I think it is a mix, a little of everything. Denmark likes to live up to these obligations, at least, generally speaking, or at least historically speaking. So, the argument goes, yes, we have rising proportion, and yes, we need more equal treatment, and yes, there was a directive, too, we should address, so maybe it is not such a bad idea. (Hussain 11 April 2017, 1:23–1:24)

8.3.1.3 Regulations Concerning Religious Practice and Religious Freedom

The other important circular letter from 2013 – revised in 2015[23] – summarises the efforts made since 2006 to establish equal access to religious practice regardless of the confession of inmates. The basis of the circular letter is the right of inmates to practise their religion (Article 1.1). This does not grant the right to a designated room for worship, but if possible, a room, possibly shared by different religions,

---

[22] Article 21 of CIR1H no. 9530 of 26 September 2013.

[23] Published with small revisions as CIS no. 9910 of 10 July 2015. https://www.retsinformation.dk/Forms/R0710.aspx?id=167763

should be reserved for this purpose (Article 1.3). As for Muslim prayers, some prisons have prayer rooms and two prisons have regular mosques, but often a common room or sports hall may be used for the Friday prayer. Muslim inmates who wish to perform the five daily prayers are given at least a clean place to do so, they are allowed a rug or mat on which to perform the prayer, and they are given access to bathrooms to make their ablutions before the prayer, as well as time in the work schedule to do so. If there is no service or Friday prayer in the prison, inmates in open prisons should regularly be given the opportunity to participate in religious worship outside the prison (Article 1.8). The prison and probation service are, in addition, obliged to ensure that inmates have access to religious literature (Article 1.4), which according to the circular letter on the "employment of and oversight with religious preachers in the prison and probation Services" §28 should be paid for by the prison.

The circular letter also states that the diet of inmates is in accordance with their religious beliefs (Article 1.7). As for meals, there are special allowances for the dietary practices of Muslim and Jewish inmates. With regard to holidays, everyone, regardless of their confession, should be free from work on their holidays (1.5). In practice, many inmates are allowed 1 or 2 days' leave in relation to Christmas; thus, members of other religious communities are given leave in relation to similarly important holidays. For Muslims, it is most commonly *Eid ul-Fitr* after Ramadan. The Prison Services distribute a calendar every year with the most important religious holidays.

The circular letter also establishes a number of limitations to the rights and access to service and practice. These may be general concerns or specific to the inmate, but must in all cases rest on an objective and factual criterion. There is a ban on the wearing of clothes that may hinder identification (1.6). The right to participate in religious worships is also limited by Article 1.2, which states that the Prison and Probation Service may deny access to religious services or limit the number of participants out of concerns for order and security. In such cases, the Prison and Probation Service should seek to compensate by offering a televised transmission of the religious service, an alternative service or private conversations with their chaplain.

8.4 Religion in Prison

While the Prison and Probation Service publishes statistics on many aspects of prison life on a yearly basis, it does not generally produce statistics on issues of the religious adherence of prisoners. The 2006 report is, however, an exception: it included a large qualitative section where many of the issues relevant here are explored in conversation with inmates, chaplains and other prison employees. First, we take a closer look at the religion of inmates, their religious affiliation, perceived discrimination and the organisation of their religious practices. Then, we turn to the chaplains, examining who they are, what they do, with a special focus on how they organise religious services, what they think of pastoral care, and the differences they see between working in a prison and in an ordinary parish.

8.4.1 Religion Among Inmates

The question of representativeness of denominations in prison was also examined in the 2006 report. The report contained the responses to a questionnaire, with a response rate of 58%. Inmates were given six alternatives when asked which religious tradition they identified with: Christianity (58%), Judaism (1%), Islam (19%), Buddhism (2%), Hinduism (1%) and others (19%). They were invited to fill in comments, and here, 29 specified that they were Catholics, 14 identified as followers of Old Norse religion, 12 as Orthodox Christians, whereas others wrote Santa Claus, Pagan, Pantheism, Rastafarianism, Greenlandic Shamanism or Satanism. Included in the category of "others", some respondents said, "no faith".

Since 2006, religious diversity is likely to have increased, as the number of international inmates has increased from 24% in 2011 to 30% in 2017. There is for instance a substantial group of Romanian citizens in Danish prisons.[24] An unpublished survey (1245 participants) on religious adherence and practice was conducted in 2011 as part of the evaluation of the 2009 Action Plan (Nielsen 2011). According to this survey, the percentage of Muslim inmates remains constant (19%), whereas inmates identifying with Christianity (50%), Judaism (<1%), Buddhism (1%), Hinduism (<1%) have declined, as has the category of "others" (7%), which includes 1 Sikh, 1 Scientologist, 1 Shaman and 5 persons who state that they believe in themselves. The decline in the category of "others" seems to be related to the inclusion of the category "non-believers" (18%) in the survey. Within the last 8 years, 23 persons have been charged with or convicted of terrorism, mostly left-wing and Islamist extremism, and several foreign fighters have been charged and some convicted for travelling to Syria. This also affects the religious composition of Danish prisons, although it may not be apparent in the broad categories used in the surveys.

8.4.1.1 Religious Discrimination in Prison

The 2006 report demonstrates that there are claims of religious discrimination in prison on an individual basis by some inmates. This is taken seriously by the Prison and Probation Service, but the report stresses that a claim of religious discrimination is a tool in the everyday power struggles between inmates and prison employees. Employees argue that Muslims in particular are using arguments from the Quran or claim that they will not be handled by non-believers, to resist the general regulations in prison. The Danish right-wing party, Danish People's Party, has

---

[24] https://www.b.dk/nationalt/3-ud-af-10-indsatte-i-de-danske-faengsler-er-udenlandske-statsborgere

Table 8.1 Inmate satisfaction in Copenhagen prisons/closed prisons/general 2015 (percentages)

	Possibility of practising your religion as you like			Possibility of exercising and doing sports			General possibility of doing things in your free time		
Copenhagen prisons	+	–	?	+	–	?	+	–	?
	55	18	27	38	53	9	32	57	11
Closed prisons	+	–	?	+	–	?	+	–	?
	44	20	36	42	50	7	38	56	6
All prisons	+	–	?	+	–	?	+	–	?
	42	16	42	40	52	8	36	57	8

Source: Brugerundersøgelse (User survey) (2015)

voiced its – politically motivated – concern that non-Muslim inmates are being discriminated against when Muslims are allowed leave for Ramadan. Such a story is, of course, unsubstantiated, and the practice is very much a question of equal access to different religious holidays, but it demonstrates the level of discrimination in Danish prisons.[25]

To secure reasonable conditions for prisoners, the Prison and Probation Service published consumer satisfaction surveys in 2013, 2014 and 2015. Religion is not singled out as an area of concern, but it comes up nonetheless in relation to whether inmates find that they have the possibility of practising their religion. The results to this question are posed in Table 8.1, where it is compared with results concerning the possibility of doing sport and other leisure-time activities. They indicate that inmates judge the access to freely practise their religion generally higher than the access to sports or other leisure activities, in particular in Copenhagen Prisons, which have a full-time Muslim chaplain and three full-time Lutheran chaplains. However, about 16% in general and 20% in the closed prisons are not satisfied with the provisions.

Table 8.2 collects information on the satisfaction of prisoners with the services in prison. Compared with other groups of personnel, the level of dissatisfaction with the chaplains is among the lowest. The level of satisfaction is, however, more within the medium range, which seems to be the effect of the chaplain being of no relevance to one third of the inmates in the closed prisons and almost half of the inmates in general. Unlike the "service" of the prison officers, on which almost all inmates have an opinion, the service of the clergy/chaplains is only of interest or visible for some prisoners.

There is no information about the level of satisfaction in relation to the religious affiliation of prisoners. It is, however, again clear that the level of satisfaction is higher in Copenhagen Prisons, which has the only full-time imam as well as three full-time Lutheran chaplains, than in the closed prisons, which are relatively well provided for regarding Lutheran chaplains but not imams. Regarding access to a

---

[25] http://www.danskfolkeparti.dk/DF_Nej_til_diskrimination_i_danske_f%C3%A6ngsler_under_Ramadanen

Table 8.2 Satisfaction with personnel 2015. Copenhagen prisons/closed prisons/general (percentages)

	Chaplains			Prison officers			Social workers			Psychiatrist		
Copenhagen prisons	+	−	?	+	−	?	+	−	?	+	−	?
	55	11	35	70	26	4	71	15	13	20	15	65
Closed prisons	+	−	?	+	−	?	+	−	?	+	−	?
	51	18	32	65	30	4	61	32	7	31	27	42
Prisons in general	+	−	?	+	−	?	+	−	?	+	−	?
	43	13	44	75	22	3	63	24	13	22	19	59

Source: Brugerundersøgelse (User survey) (2015)

chaplain: 51% indicated that this is the case to a high or very high degree, 18% said that this is not the case, whereas 32% said that the question is not relevant (Brugerundersøgelse [User survey] 2015, 34).

8.4.2 Chaplains in Danish Prisons: Who They Are and What They Do

In 2015, a larger study was carried out of Lutheran chaplains in prisons, hospitals, the military and other Danish institutions, consisting of a questionnaire sent out to the chaplains working in the healthcare system, the penitentiary system, the military, and in various smaller institutions/sectors (for instance, in education, and among the homeless and youth) at the time, and semi-structured interviews with 34 chaplains from all those institutions (Kühle and Christensen 2015). Many chaplains are only part-time chaplains and also work as ordinary pastors in a local church, and some have several chaplaincies in addition to being a pastor of a congregation in the Evangelical Lutheran Church of Denmark. In 2014, the prison chaplains established their own association (The Association of Prison and Remand Prison Chaplains).[26] They sent out a questionnaire to all 58 members of the association. The account given below is based on the 37 responses they received and the five interviews they carried out with prison chaplains (Kühle and Christensen 2015).

The average age of prison chaplains is 53 years. The prison chaplains are thus older than chaplains found in hospitals and the military, and older than the inmates (the average age of immigrant inmates is 35 years, 25 years for descendants of immigrants and 36 years for "ethnic" Danes (Department of Justice 2015, 6). That the chaplains are working with people who are easily 20 or 30 years younger than themselves was reflected in some of the interviews when prison chaplains emphasise that they bring wisdom, experience and unlimited presence to people who are marked by "isolation, lack of control, anger, shame, guilt, and hatred" (interview

---

[26] http://www.frederikssundkirke.dk/fileadmin/group/771/Dokumenter/Haandbog_FFA_september_2016.pdf

with Thomas who works in a 30% position as a chaplain in a remand prison). There is a slight majority of women among the prison chaplains and about one third of the chaplains have worked in other institutions previously, such as hospitals and the military. A third of the chaplains have also completed education other than theology, and four of them have therapeutic training. The therapeutic aspect is important, even for chaplains who have not completed such training.

In her study of the chaplaincy in the USA, Winnifred Sullivan argues that the chaplaincy is changing the religious landscape from denominational dogmatic to a spiritual and existential ethics in what she reports the chaplains themselves call "a ministry of presence". To cater to the spiritual needs of the individual in a religiously diverse American society, chaplains must adapt to the demands of the individual users (for instance, inmates) and the institutions they work in. "If one listens to current users of the concept, a ministry of presence may seem to refer to the simple physical presence of the minister – the minister's or chaplain's willingness simply to 'sit with' a client without anxious expectation" (Sullivan 2014, 175). A ministry of presence is a ministry characterised through its focus on spirituality, pastoral care, innovative liturgies and lack of proselytisation. This last element is important. "If the chaplain does not, in the encounter, positively identify himself with a religious tradition, or demand that his client does so, the assumption is that he cannot be accused of imposition or proselytisation" (Sullivan 2014, 177). Even if the chaplaincy is presented as a generic ministry, it draws on Protestant imaginaries focusing on the presence interpreted through the biblical image of the shepherd, where the chaplain cares for his flock. Or it is inspired by the biblical concept of Incarnation and its willingness to take on the burden of others, and enable the future lives of people (Sullivan 2014, 181). Despite the differences between the religious landscapes in the USA and Denmark (Europe), it is possible to see the same kind of underplayed Christianity here: a Christianity that does not proselytise, and that is not recognisable as Christianity – and perhaps even religion, unless you know what to look for. Overall, the way in which Danish prison chaplains describe encounters with inmates is very often through words and concepts similar to a ministry of presence.

The chaplaincy is primarily based on pastoral care, i.e. confidential conversations between the chaplain and inmate. The survey asked the chaplains how much of their time they spend on pastoral care, and on average they say that two thirds of their working hours are spent talking to inmates. Remand prison chaplains spend more time with pastoral care than prison chaplains, who conduct more religious services. To quote Thomas again, he tells us that his understanding of pastoral care means "to be a companion through a person's personal hell". Although he mentions hell in this regard, it does not necessarily have anything to do with the eschatological concept of hell. In fact, chaplains do not talk much about Christianity unless they feel that inmates want them to. Again, Thomas explains: "There are always three present in the pastoral care conversation: the confidant, me, and God. There is a power in that conversation. It is not just me and him or her, but something more, but I do not necessarily tell that to people". Similarly, Caroline is a chaplain in a remand prison who runs group therapies attended by many Muslims. She has decided to focus on stories from the Old Testament because many of these narratives are shared by Muslims and Christians and she wants to be of use to everybody regardless of their faith and does not want to "thrust Christianity upon anyone". She wants to "focus on being human to avoid the brutalisation" that often happens in prison. She does not want to preach to people and she does not want to convert them to Christianity, but Christian values guide everything she does. "There is a religious dimension in talking to them. In being their neighbour".[27] For the chaplain Paul, it is important to address the individual person without necessarily talking about Christianity. "You cannot just sit and talk about Matthew, Mark, Luke, and John or what you want from the Bible if you do not care for the entire human being and help him or her if they have a problem. That would be deeply unchristian". In their survey, Kühle and Christensen asked chaplains about the religious trends among the people they meet, and 78% of the chaplains state that inmates "seek religious experiences" to some or a high degree. In comparison, only 70% of the hospital chaplains and 60% of the military chaplains agree. Furthermore, 89% agree to some/high degree that bricolage or syncretism is a trend among the people they serve. This applies to 77% of the hospital chaplains and 72% of the military chaplains. Finally, prison chaplains also report the lowest share of rejection of religion among their congregation (21% compared with 27% and 29% for hospital and military chaplains respectively) (Kühle and Christensen 2015, 147). Just as Sullivan describes with regard to American chaplains, Danish prison chaplains also cater to all, and not just to Christians.

This is important, because only few chaplains from other religions are available, with only one imam employed full time and a few more who are part time, and provisions for other minority religions being *ad hoc*. In interviews with the Muslim prison chaplains, and in some of their writings, it is clear that they have also subscribed to the above-mentioned concept of pastoral care. One of the Muslim chaplains, who formerly worked in prisons, now in a hospital, wrote his master's thesis of Islamic Spiritual Care on this subject (Baig 2015). In addition, in 2017, the Danish Humanist Association had plans regarding a new programme on existential care that they would like to offer to hospitals and prisons.

As mentioned above, there is a right to either have a collective religious service, or to have very limited leave to go and participate in a service, if the security issues and logistics allow for it. Most prisons have a weekly Sunday service for Christians, and for Muslims – in the larger prisons – there is Friday prayer and *Khutbah* (preach), and for smaller prisons, only every second week, or at a local mosque outside the prison. This means that apart from their pastoral care work, Lutheran chaplains also perform religious services. In this capacity, they are more explicit about their Lutheran tradition than they are when they carry out pastoral care, although there are also examples of providing devotions for other religions based on the needs of the inmates. Thomas has improvised a devotion to a Russian orthodox

---

[27] With reference to Matthew 22:39 "Love thy neighbour as yourself". However, the Danish translation does not use the word neighbour, but is like the German version with regard to both neighbour (*næste* [Danish] and *Nächsten* [German]) and charity (*næstekærlighed* [Danish] and *Nächstenliebe* [German]). Extensive theological literature and public debate exist on how to understand who exactly our neighbours are and who is entitled to our charity.

inmate, playing some Gregorian chanting and complementing this with a readings from the Bible. Additionally, Paul explains that he wants to turn part of the prison into a monastery where inmates could apply to live the simple life of a monk.

Our survey shows that prison chaplains spend 2 hours per week performing Sunday services and rituals. At the same time, they "only" carryout 14 services per year, which means that they perform some other rituals as well (primarily baptisms and marriages). Nevertheless, the religious services in prison are sometimes different from the services found in the local church. For security reasons, there is a limit to the number of participants in the service. Contrary to services in the local churches, where only 10% of the population go to church on a monthly basis, inmates sign up to participate and are put on waiting lists administered by the chaplains. Additionally, one of the chaplains told us that she had turned the Sunday service into a "faith mass" with only few readings from the Bible, but extensive focus on praying and communion. The Eucharist is very important to inmates, providing them with a sense of peace and redemption that they cannot find anywhere else in the prison. In one of the largest prisons in Denmark, the chaplain has changed the Sunday service in a more meditative direction.

> A month ago, we changed the service giving it a more meditative touch. Inmates have been very enthusiastic. When do they experience silence? Rarely. And when do we experience silence together? Very rarely. But I have changed the sermon and I am now using for instance paintings to give it a meditative feeling, and after the sermon we sit in total silence a few minutes before the musician starts playing something meditative. And after that we have the Eucharist (Paul, full-time prison chaplain).

Regarding one of the other elements, proselytisation, Danish Lutheran chaplains explicitly want to avoid taking advantage of their situation and preaching the gospel. This is probably not surprising, since the Prison and Probation Service takes great care when recruiting chaplains (perhaps especially Muslim chaplains) to avoid those who proselytise. This does not mean, however, that there are no problems in this regard. The Prison and Probation Service is very much concerned with conversion and proselytisation among inmates, especially among Muslim inmates, who may become radicalised in their encounters with other inmates.

Lissi Rasmussen argues that there has been an increased interest in religion these past 10 years (Rasmussen 2010, 151), and that the existential and social crisis stemming from being incarcerated helps this along. After the shootings in Copenhagen in February 2015, the public debate on radicalisation in prison increased significantly. Four days after the attack, Waseem Hussain, argued that the Prison and Prevention Service had done all in its power to avoid something like this, and had even reported the radicalised behaviour of the young man to the security and intelligence services. The root of the problem, rather, was to be found in the outside Muslim communities, who had done little or nothing to prevent the terror. He argued that too many Muslims victimise themselves as part of being Muslim and this draws them towards extremist responses.[28]

---

[28] http://nyhederne.tv2.dk/2015-02-18-faengselsimams-opraab-til-muslimer-i-maa-selv-tage-ansvar

8.5   Conclusion

This chapter opened with a reference to the terrorist attack in Copenhagen in February 2015. The attack sparked a huge political and public debate about radicalisation in prison because the terrorist was perceived to have been radicalised in prison. Part of the debate also focused on the role of Muslim chaplains. Since the employment of the first Muslim chaplain in 1997, the Islamic Chaplaincy has been valued by the Prison and Probation Service, but has been the object of public debates as well. The Prison and Probation Service has been engaged in an effort to ground and secure their practices legally. This has been done in two circular letters, which by usage of the concept of "religious preacher" relates to general attempts to regulate religion. This concept is, however, less fitting in regard to prisons, where supplying pastoral care and talking to prisoners takes up much more time than giving sermons. Following the changes and trends in the regulation of religion in prison over the past 10 years, it had become apparent that the Prison and Probation Service had been regulating and pragmatically engaging the imams in the religious life in prisons as an organic part of the welfare and rehabilitation of inmates. This meant that the employment of imams would be done on equal terms to that of other chaplains, and therefore with a focus on pastoral care, but also that imams were seen a natural and important part of the work in prisons, including work on preventing radicalisation and extremism.

Efforts of the Prison and Probation Service to sustain a public presentation of their positive evaluation of the work of Muslim chaplains seem challenged by political debates and the regulation of prisons by the Ministry of Justice, and by discussions in the Parliament after the terrorist attack in 2015. As part of what may be called a pragmatic professionalisation of the chaplains outside the Church of Denmark, the Prison and Probation Service had already established the vetting of new imams, the need to be cleared by the security services and continued oversight by both the Prison and Probation Services and a group of specialists and experts on religion. This process was adopted into the securitisation debate to the extent that the imams in prisons, employed under these guidelines, were themselves called into question as possible causes of extremism and radicalisation. As such, the trends towards internal professionalisation and public securitisation run parallel, creating a complex image of the policies and regulations, especially regarding imams. The 2006 report from the Prison and Probation Service suggested clearer rules regarding on-the-job content and salary, as well as suggesting the employment of more Muslim chaplains. The clearer rules were implemented in two circular letters, but the latter recommendation was, however, not implemented. It is not clear whether this was due to a lack of proper procedures for employing imams, the inability to find proper candidates, or political scepticism and criticism. It may be that the introduction of debates on radicalisation into the area of prison and probation from 2008 have drawn attention away from other important projects.

Although there is a substantial Muslim population in prison, at least nominally, few prisons have Muslim chaplains associated with them. This means that chaplains employed by the Evangelical Lutheran Church have regained some lost ground, not only in response to the increased suspicion of imams in particular but also because of a greater appreciation of pastoral care that caters to all inmates in general. The role of the chaplain is less bound by dogmatic, and more by pastoral care, then becoming a service open to all. In that way, the religion found in prison and in other institutions might serve as an indicator of a religious change in society.

References

Baig, N. (2015). *Islamic Spiritual Care*. Faculty of Theology, University of Copenhagen: Unpublished Master Thesis.

Beckford, J., & Gilliat-Ray, S. (1998). *Religion in prison:'equal rites' in a multi-faith society*. Cambridge: Cambridge University Press.

Brugerundersøgelse [User survey]. (2015). http://www.kriminalforsorgen.dk/Brugerunders%C3%B8gelsen-2015-7549.aspx

CIR1H no. 9530 of 26 September 2013. Cirkulære om ansættelse af og tilsyn med religiøse forkyndere i Kriminalforsorgen [Circular letter on the employment of and oversight with religious preachers in the *Prison and Probation services*] https://www.retsinformation.dk/Forms/R0710.aspx?id=158465

Christoffersen, L. (2012). Den aktuelle danske religionsretlige model [The Current Danish model of the religion]. In L. Christoffersen, H. R. Iversen, N. Kærgård, & M. Warburg (Eds.), *Fremtidens danske religionsmodel [the Danish model of religion in the future]*. Anis: Frederiksberg.

CIS no. 9508 of 25 September 2013. Cirkulæreskrivelse om reglerne for indsattes adgang til udøvelse af religion i kriminalforsorgens institutioner [Circular letter on access of inmates to practise their religion in institutions under the *Prison and Probation Service*] https://www.retsinformation.dk/Forms/R0710.aspx?id=158402 (historical)

CIS no. 9910 of 10 July 2015. Cirkulæreskrivelse om reglerne for indsattes adgang til udøvelse af religion i kriminalforsorgens institutioner [Circular letter on access of inmates to practise their religion in institutions under the *Prison and Probation Service*] https://www.retsinformation.dk/Forms/R0710.aspx?id=167763

Department of Justice. (2015) "Etnicitet og statsborgerskab" [Ethnicity and citizenship] http://www.kriminalforsorgen.dk/Admin/Public/Download.aspx?file=Files%2FFiler%2FPublikatio ner%2Frapporter%2FIndsatte+i+f%C3%A6ngsler+og+arresthuse+fordelt+p%C3%A5+oprin delsesland+og+institutionstype++2014.pdf

Johansen, M. (2015). Hvorfor er jøder i skudlinjen for terrorangreb i Europa? [Why are Jews in the front line in Europe], *Jyllandsposten* 15.02.2015. Available from: http://jyllands-posten.dk/indland/ECE7453125/Hvorfor-er-j%C3%B8der-i-skudlinjen-for-terrorangreb-i-Europa/ Accessed 10 Aug 2017.

Kühle, L. (2004). *Out of many, one. A theoretical and empirical study of religious pluralism in Denmark from a perspective of power* (PhD dissertation). Aarhus University.

Kühle, L., & Christensen, H. R. (2015). Funktionspræster i Danmark. In *En kortlægning* [Chaplains in Denmark]. Århus: SUN-Tryk

Kühle, L., & Lomholt, C. (2006). *Straffens menneskelige ansigt: En antologi om etik, ret og religion i fængslet* [The human face of punishment. An anthology on ethics, law and religion in prison]. Frederiksberg: Anis.

Mogensen, M. (2012). *Teologisk uddannelse i islam i Danmark – indledende behovs – og interessentundersøgelse blandt udvalgte grupper i det danske samfund med perspektivering til teologisk uddannelse i kristendom* [Theological education on Islam in Denmark – Initial need and interest assessment among selected groups in the Danish society with perspectives to theological education in Christianity]. Available: http://religionsmoede.dk/_Resources/Persistent/8/1/9/5/819567c94fda6faa0cc4418f0adecae83713056b/KMS_rapport_2012.pdf. Accessed 10 Aug 2017.

Nielsen, M. M. (2011). *Evaluering af gejstlig betjening af indsatte i henhold til Regeringens handlingsplan om forebyggelse af ekstremistiske holdninger og radikalisering blandt unge, "En fælles og tryg fremtid", 2009.* [Evaluation of religious service of inmates in relation to the Government's Action Plan on prevention of extremist options and radicalisation among youth, 'A common and secure Future' 2009]. Uncompleted and unpublished sketch.

Nielsen, M. M. (2012). Mellem fængsel og fromhed: Sekularisering, "secularization falsified" eller postsekularisering? Diskurser omkring de danske fængselsimamers forventede funktioner i et mikro-, meso- og makroperspektiv. [Between Prison and Piety: Secularisation, Secularisation Falsified or Post-Secularity]. Master thesis, Aarhus University.

Nielsen, L. S. (2015). *Et 'samfund i samfundet' – en undersøgelse af håndteringen af muslimsk praksis i de danske, lukkede fængsler* [A society in society: an analysis of the management of Muslim practice in Danish closed prisons]. Master thesis, Aarhus University.

Olsen, J. A. (2006). *Religiøs identitetsdannelse i danske fængsler: En religionssociologisk undersøgelse af konvertering til islam under fængselsophold* [Religious identity formation in Danish prisons: A sociological analysis of conversions to Islam during retention] Speciale, Københavns Universitet.

Prison and Probation Service (2006), *Rapport om gejstlig betjening af indsatte der tilhører andre trossamfund end den evangelisk lutherske folkekirke* [Report on religious service of inmates belonging to other faith communities than the Evangelical Lutheran Church of Denmark].

Rasmussen, L. (2010). *Livshistorier og kriminalitet.* In *[Life stories and crime] fra Københavns Universitet*. Det teologiske Fakultet: Center for Europæisk Islamisk Tænkning.

Statistik. (2015). Available from: www.kriminalforsorgen.dk/.../Download.aspx?...Files%2FFiler%2FPublikationer%2F

Sullivan, W. F. (2009). *Prison religion: faith-based reform and the constitution.* Princeton: Princeton University Press.

Sullivan, W. F. (2014). *A ministry of presence: Chaplaincy, spiritual care, and the law.* Chicago: University of Chicago Press.

Chapter 9
Estonia: Regulating Religion in Prisons Since the 1990s

Ringo Ringvee

Abstract The Estonian prison system has gone through considerable reforms during the last quarter of century. The Soviet dorm-type prisons have been replaced by cell-type prisons, chaotic and competitive religious ministry is institutionalised in prison chaplaincy coordinated by the adviser-chief of chaplains at the prisons department at the Ministry of Justice, to name but a few of the changes. Estonia is a highly secularised European country where the majority of the population does not consider themselves religiously affiliated, and the same applies to the prison population. Religious freedom in prisons is guaranteed by various legal acts, although there are several limitations in regard to the rights of others, public order, health, morality and internal rules of the institution. There are cases where prisoners have sued prison administrations for violating their religious freedom regarding religious diets and religious practices in the prison environment. The courts' decisions have supported the interpretation of current legislation that although prisoners have the right to practise their religion, there is no obligation for prisons to provide either specific equipment for religious practices or to serve a specific diet (besides a vegetarian option) if this is an unreasonable burden on the institution. Prison chaplains who are employed as civil servants at the Ministry of Justice Prisons Service provide religious services and pastoral counselling.

9.1 Introduction

Estonia is known as one of the few European countries where most of the population do not consider themselves religiously affiliated. According to the population census data from the years 2000 and 2011, almost one third (29%) of the population older than 15 years of age define themselves as religiously affiliated (PHC Database 2000, 2011). One of the most important changes in twenty-first century Estonia

R. Ringvee (✉)
Religious Affairs Department of the Estonian Ministry of the Interior, Tallinn, Estonia
e-mail: ringo.ringvee@moi.ee

© Springer Nature Switzerland AG 2020
J. Martínez-Ariño, A.-L. Zwilling (eds.), *Religion and Prison: An Overview of Contemporary Europe*, Boundaries of Religious Freedom: Regulating Religion in Diverse Societies 7, https://doi.org/10.1007/978-3-030-36834-0_9

regarding religious affiliation concerns the religious composition of society. The 2011 housing and population census data show that, although ethnic Estonians form 69% of the population, they comprise 45% of the religiously affiliated population. In the 2011 population census, the Orthodox Christians outnumbered Lutherans, the historical majority tradition in Estonia, for the first time in history (Ringvee 2014).

When Estonia restored its independence in 1991, it inherited the Soviet prison system. Since then, the prison system and its principles have gone through radical transformation. The prison reforms have included replacement of Soviet dorm-style prison buildings with a modern cell prison environment, and modifying the criminal subculture inherited from the Soviet period. The number of prisons has declined from 10 in 1991 to 3 in 2018, all of which have a modern prison environment, as new prison complexes have been built (2002, 2008, 2018). The new prisons are bigger, and the buildings, security solutions and the prison cell system are modern. Like other post-Soviet transition countries, long prison sentences and a high number of prisoners have characterised Estonia, although the number of prisoners has declined since 2001 by 37% (Dunkel 2017, 634). In January 2018, there were 2706 prisoners compared with 4712 in 2000 (Prison Service 2018a; Saar 2001, 46). According to available data, the percentage of prisoners who define themselves as religiously affiliated is similar to that of the general population, which is around 30%; 59% of these define themselves as Orthodox Christians, 17% as Lutherans and 6.6% as Muslims.

The Ministry of Justice administers prisons through the Department of Prisons, which has four divisions: Sentence Enforcement, Rehabilitation, Legal Division and Development, and Internal Control Division. The Department is managed by the Deputy Secretary-General for Prisons. The heads of division and the adviser-chief of chaplains of prisons act as Assistants to the Deputy Secretary General (Department of Prisons 2018). The Ministry of Justice established the position of the adviser-chief of chaplains, who supervises religious work and chaplains in prisons, in 2001.

The Estonian Ministry of Justice states on its website in 2018 that every prison in Estonia has space for religious services (chapel). There are chaplains in every prison who provide religious or spiritual relief to prisoners and participate in resocialisation processes (Prison Service 2018b). In January 2018, there were 12 chaplains in the prison service in Estonia. Female prisoners comprise 0.05% of the total prison population, and there is one female chaplain.

9.2   Religion and the State in Estonia

The Constitution of Estonia of 1992 guarantees the freedom of religion or belief and stipulates that there is no state church in Estonia. Religious communities may obtain the status of legal entities in accordance with the Churches and Congregations Act

(1993, 2002) that guarantees religious autonomy for registered religious associations and grants them and their clergy certain privileges and exemptions (for example, protection of confessional secrets). Other privileges include certain tax exemptions, exemptions from general rules with regard to employment, and the right to apply for authorisation of their clergy to perform marriages with civil validity (Kiviorg 2016). Religious communities may also become legal entities in accordance with the Non-profit Associations Act as regular non-profit associations, but in that case, they do not enjoy the exemptions and privileges accorded to religious associations. Religious communities may also operate without any legal entity status. The registration of religious associations takes place at the registrar department of a court and the central Register of Religious Associations situated at the Tartu County Court. Although the Estonian Constitution stipulates that there is no state church and indicates the principle of institutional separation, the separation does not exclude the cooperation between the state and religious associations.

In 1995, the Estonian government established a joint commission with the Estonian Evangelical Lutheran Church, the historical majority church. The aim of this commission was to open a discussion between the state and the historical majority church on different areas of common concerns, such as restitution of the properties nationalised during the Soviet period, religious education in schools etc. In 2002, the Estonian government signed a protocol of common concerns with the Estonian Ecumenical Council of Churches. The protocol mapped different areas, from religious education to chaplaincy services in different institutions, heritage protection and cooperation with local governments where common interests were found. The Estonian Council of Churches was founded in 1989 and it has been the most influential ecumenical organisation in Estonia. The founding members of the Council included the Lutheran, Orthodox, Methodist, Seventh-day Adventist churches and the union of Evangelical Christian and Baptists churches, as well as the Roman Catholic Church, which acts as an observer. Since then, the Council has co-opted to membership the Estonian Christian Pentecostal Church, the Estonian Charismatic Episcopalian Church and the congregation of the Armenian Apostolic Church. The 2002 Protocol of Common Concerns between the Estonian Government and the Estonian Council of Churches listed areas of common concerns and cooperation between the state and the Council of Churches and designated the ministries responsible for the cooperation in different sectors (*Ühishuvide protokoll* 2002). The first of the issues in the list of cooperation between the Ministry of Justice and the Council of Churches is prison chaplaincy. The protocol and its goals were confirmed in 2015 when the Ministry of the Interior, responsible for religious affairs since 1993, signed a cooperation agreement with the Council of Churches assuring continuing cooperation (Kokkulepe 2015). Although religious institutions are self-financing associations, the Estonian Council of Churches has received an annual allocation from the state budget since 1992. These allocations are used to finance activities mentioned in the 2002 Protocol and include the chaplaincy service in various institutions, including prisons.

9.3   Religion in Estonian Prisons

Estonia re-established its independence in 1991 and inherited the prison system of the Soviet period that had been in the process of change since the *perestroika* policies of the late 1980s. The Soviet authorities allowed religion into prisons in 1989 and the first clergy to visit prisons came from the Estonian Evangelical Lutheran Church, the Estonian Methodist Church, the Seventh-day Adventist Church and a Russian-speaking Pentecostal congregation. In 1989, religious voluntary work also started in custodial institutions. Although the larger religious services took place in canteens or social areas, there were also attempts to have spaces for religious activities. In 1989, the first prayer room was opened in Viljandi Juvenile Prison and by 1993, all eight prisons at that time in Estonia had a special room for religious activities (Jürjo 2007, 13–14). Although the Lutheran clergy and volunteers had been involved in prison work since 1989, the Estonian Evangelical Lutheran Church established its Centre for Work with Offenders in 1991. The Centre was not only involved in prison work but also in the resocialisation of former prisoners. From the late 1980s onwards, the Estonian Evangelical Lutheran Church (EELC) received financial as well as training aid from its fellow churches abroad. The role of the Finnish Evangelical Lutheran Church was important in the development of prison and criminal work in the EELC (Üprus 2000, 168–174).

In 1989, three Estonian Pentecostal ministers from Canada and Australia representing the Apostolic Church of Pentecost, the Pentecostal Assemblies of Canada and the Assemblies of God Australia started their mission in Estonia. In 1990, they made their first visits to prisons. By 1992, the mission had become the Estonian Christian Church, which started cooperation with Frank Constantino[1] and his Christian Prison Ministries from the USA. The Prison Service of the Estonian Christian Church with Frank Constantino's Christian Prison Ministries became the second of the two major actors in the prison ministries of the first half of the 1990s, in addition to the Centre for Work with Offenders of the EELC. In 1994, the Estonian Christian Church changed its name to the Estonian Christian Pentecostal Church and in 1995 it became a member of the Estonian Council of Churches. As the Council had its Prison Service, the independent prison work of the Pentecostal Church was merged into a more ecumenical environment. At that time, the cooperation between the Christian Pentecostal Church and the Christian Prison Ministries ended, although Frank Constantino continued to provide financial support for a full-time prison chaplain (Jürjo 2007, 20–22; A Place For You 2006, 113–114).

The chaotic times in society at the beginning of the 1990s were reflected in prison, where the doors were open to anyone claiming to be a religious worker (Jürjo 2007, 13). In prison, as in the rest of the society, religion had become

---

[1] Many missionaries and Christian ministries arrived in Estonia in the 1990s, as in other former Soviet bloc countries. F. Constantino was one of the most important foreigners involved in prison work in Estonia.

unregulated. In this situation, there was also competition between different religious actors from mainstream churches to foreign religious organisations and individual religious entrepreneurs trying to establish their ministries in prisons. The situation concerning religious services in prisons became so tense that in September 1992 the Director General of the Detention Houses Board asked the Archbishop of the Estonian Evangelical Lutheran Church to replace the coordinator of the EELC Consistory's Centre for Work with Offenders. The Director General stipulated that the new person in this post should not be a member of any political party, must have a higher religious education, would also consider the interests of other denominations and would help to stabilise the situation in prisons (Ringvee 2011, 44). In December 1992, the Minister of the Interior met with the representatives of the Ecumenical Estonian Council of Churches to discuss religious work in prisons. Following this meeting, the prisons were closed to all religious workers for a week (Jürjo 2009, 404–405). The aim of the Minister's decision was to obtain an overview of who the people and organisations were that claimed to do religious work in prisons and to get the chaotic situation under control.

In September 1993, the Estonian Council of Churches had a meeting where several decisions concerning religious work in prisons were made. It was decided in this meeting that the ECC should take a more central position in organising religious work in prisons by setting the requirement that competent persons would appoint the clergy who would work in prisons and that the Council would evaluate the voluntary workers. Another decision taken in that meeting was that the two central bodies in prison work would be the ECC with its Prison Service and the Centre for Work with Offenders of the EELC. By 1994, the major problems concerning uncoordinated religious activities were overcome and the coordination of the religious work in prisons was concentrated in the ECC Prison Service. In 1995, the Prison Service of the ECC was reorganised into the Estonian Prison Chaplains' Association, which became an important representative and coordinating body for prison chaplains. The Association was eventually dissolved in 2001.

The uncertainty of the position of chaplains in prisons, as well as the financing of prison chaplaincy ended in 1997, when the Ministry of Justice recognised prison chaplains as part of the prison personnel. From then on, the Ministry rather than the Estonian Prison Chaplains' Association administered religious work in prison. In 2000, the ECC started negotiations with the Ministry of Justice for the post of chief of chaplains to supervise religious work in prisons. The ECC proposal was that chaplains and the chief of chaplains, while working at the Ministry, would get their salary from, and be subordinated to, the ECC (Jürjo 2007, 22). The idea of a chief of chaplains in the Ministry of Justice who would be paid by and accountable to a non-profit association did not receive support from the state authorities. After discussions with the ECC, the Ministry of Justice established a position of chief of chaplains at the Department of Prisons (Ringvee 2011, 44; Jürjo 2009, 404–407).

The basic structure for religious work in prisons and detention houses has remained the same since then. Over the years, religious work in prisons has become more established. In 2012, the Ministry of Justice published a handbook for prison chaplains and a new edition of it was prepared for publication in 2019. The handbook covers all the main areas of chaplaincy service and legislation concerning religious freedom, and stresses the ecumenical and interreligious nature of chaplaincy service in prisons (Handbook 2012).

In the prison structure, the chaplains belong to the resocialisation unit with psychologists, social workers, librarians and others. Chaplains' duties include providing religious services, pastoral counselling and recreational activities and responsibility for the resocialisation programmes. Chaplains should also help to establish connections with resocialisation or rehabilitation services (Estonian Prison System Yearbook 2003, 32–33).

The associations themselves pay the salaries of personnel of religious associations in Estonia, except for chaplains in prison and the Police and Border Guard Board. In these institutions, chaplains have double positions as civil servants who are hired in accordance with the Civil Service Act and as ministers of religion (Põder 2012, 7–9; *Avaliku teenistuse seadus* 2012). Prison chaplains are subordinated to the Ministry of Justice and to the legislation as civil servants and prison staff and as ministers of religion to their respective religious associations in matters concerning their religion. Colonel Tõnis Nõmmik (2005, 27), former chief of chaplains of the Estonian Defence Forces, described the double role of chaplains in the military by saying that although chaplains are ministers of religion, in the Defence Force they are first officers and that is how they are perceived. This view could be extended to all chaplaincies that operate in public institutions such as in prisons or in the Police and Border Guard Board. Opinions that the posts of chaplains are available only for Christian denominations or for the clergy of the member churches of the Estonian Council of Churches are not fully unjustified. In the Defence Forces, for example, chaplains must be affiliated with a member church of the ECC (Kiviorg 2003, 117). However, the situation is more complicated, as different institutions set different requirements for their chaplains. Estonian Defence Forces require that chaplains must be affiliated with a member church of the ECC, whereas in prison there is no such requirement (Estonian Defence Forces 2018). However, the Department of Prisons at the Ministry of Justice set the same requirement for the position of adviser-chief of chaplains (Ministry of Justice 2005).

Over the years, various denominations have been represented in the prison chaplaincy. At the beginning of 2019, clergy from the Estonian Evangelical Lutheran Church, the Estonian Apostolic Orthodox Church, the Estonian Orthodox Church of the Moscow Patriarchate, the Estonian Methodist Church, the Estonian Association of Christian Free Churches and the Estonian Association of Evangelical and Free Churches were represented in the prison chaplaincy service. Although there have also been chaplains from other Christian denominations (Baptist, Seventh-Day Adventist), there has been and are inmates whose clergy has not been represented in the chaplaincy service owing to the limited capacity of the religious communities to provide religious personnel for prisons. This includes, for example, the Muslim inmates who form the third largest religious community in prisons after Orthodox Christians and Lutherans. The religious services for these inmates whose clergy is not represented in the chaplaincy are provided by either visiting clergy or volunteers of their religious tradition. The religious volunteer workers must be affiliated with some religious association that is registered in accordance with the Churches and Congregations Act. Religious volunteer work in Estonian prisons is regulated by a decree of the Minister of Justice of 2002 on the inclusion of volunteer workers in the resocialisation and religious activities in prison (*Vabatahtlike kaasamise juhend* 2002). According to this decree, religious volunteers must be members of a church or congregation and have a recommendation from that church or congregation and approval from the prisons' chief of chaplains.

9.4 Religion in Prison: Legal Framework

There are several different legal acts and regulations setting the legal framework for religion and its practice in prison. The Constitution of the Estonian Republic of 1992 guarantees the general principles of religious freedom, equality and non-discrimination (Põhiseadus 1992). Realisation of religious freedom is regulated by the Churches and Congregations Act (*Kirikute ja koguduste seadus* 2002). In Article 2 §8 of the Churches and Congregations Act, individual religious freedom is guaranteed, "unless it damages public order, health, morals, or the rights or freedoms of others". In §9 (1), the Churches and Congregations Act regulates religious activities in custodial, medical, educational and social welfare institutions, as well as structural units of the Defence Forces. Besides the limitations set out in §8 (public order, health, morals, the rights of others), the rules established in these institutions must also be followed. According to §9 (2) of the Act, the religious association must obtain permission from the director of the prison to conduct religious services in prison. In the context of religion in custodial institutions, §11 of the Churches and Congregations Act is also important, as it protects confessional secrets. However, this right is extended to the religious ministers of religious associations registered in accordance with the Churches and Congregations Act.

The first legal act to replace the former regulations on prisoners' rights and to regulate prisoners' religious freedom was the 1993 Code of Enforcement Procedure (*Täitemenetluse seadustik* 1993), which stipulated that prisoners have the right to participate in religious events and to own and use religious literature and other equipment necessary for these events. The Code of Enforcement Procedure also listed persons with whom prisoners may meet. Prisoners had the right to meet besides their family members other persons whose reputation was not suspected by the prison administration, which gave the prison administration a broad freedom of decision-making. The prison administration had to create conditions where the religious needs could be satisfied and meetings with clergy or with competent representatives of the religious tradition of the prisoners. However, the Code did not specify what was meant by a "competent representative". As a reflection of the general liberal attitude of the 1990s, obstructing the distribution of religious literature in prisons and houses of detention was prohibited and inmates had the right to order religious literature from outside the prison. In 2000, the Imprisonment Act replaced the regulations of the 1993 Code of Enforcement Procedure. The current version of the Code of Enforcement Procedure that became implemented in 2006 does not refer to religion (*Täitemenetluse seadustik* 2005). Since 2004, inmates have had the possibility of stating their religious affiliation to the database of prisoners, detained persons, persons in custody and probationers (Kinnipeetavate Register 2004). All religious activities in prisons are voluntary for the detainees.

The Imprisonment Act of 2000 "provides the procedure for and organisation of execution of imprisonment, detention and custody pending trial, and the definition and conditions of prison service and service as a prison officer" (Vangistusseadus 2000). According to the Imprisonment Act §62, the prison service shall ensure that prisoners have the possibility of satisfying their religious needs. According to §§26 and 27, inmates have the right to meet with their religious minister. According to the Imprisonment Act §26 (1), prisoners have the unrestricted right to receive visits from a religious minister, a criminal defence counsellor, a lawyer, a notary and a consular officer. Prison officials monitor these visits, although according to §27 (2), meetings with the religious minister, as well as with the other professions mentioned above, should not be listened to, although visual surveillance is allowed. According to §95, the same rights concerning visits by the religious minister also apply to persons pending trial. In this context, §11 of the Churches and Congregations Act is important as it protects confessional secrets. The content of the confession or pastoral conversation or the identity of a person shall not be revealed by the minister of religion. The Code of Civil Procedure (*Tsiviilkohtumenetluse seadustik* 2005) sets out in §256 that "[a] minister of a religious association registered in Estonia or support staff thereof shall not be heard or questioned with regard to circumstances confided to them in the context of spiritual care".

Wearing religious garb is not allowed in Estonian prisons. The Imprisonment Act states in §46 that inmates have to wear prison clothing. However, skullcaps are allowed for male Muslim prisoners during prayer as they are considered religious symbols, as are skullcaps and *tefillins* for male prisoners affiliated with Judaism. According to §47 (3) of the Imprisonment Act, prisoners are permitted to observe the dietary regulations of their religion "if possible". A similar principle is stipulated in §267 of the Obligation to Leave and Prohibition on Entry Act (*Väljasõidukohustuse ja sissesõidukeelu seadus* 1998), although the religiously motivated diet must be provided at the expense of the person to be deported. However, the prisoner's right to observe his or her religious dietary rules is not understood as an obligation for the prison to provide such dishes.

The 2000 Internal Rules for Prisons stipulate in §10 the prisoner's right to participate in religious services at prescribed times and recognises the right of the clergy to use the necessary equipment for religious rites, including Eucharistic wine. Prisoners may keep religious symbols and religious materials sent by mail to them (*Vangla sisekorraeeskiri* 2000).

The Internal Rules for the House of Detention of 2000 limited meetings between prisoners and religious ministers to one meeting per week of no more than 2 hours. New internal rules from 2009 removed these limitations (*Arestimaja sisekorraeeskirjad* 2009). According to the Internal Rules for the Houses of Detention §31 (4), there is no time limit for an inmate's meeting with a religious minister, and §62 sets out the requirement not to interrupt the meeting, which should take place in a room prescribed for this purpose. Religious ministers of a legally recognised religious association have the right to meet with an inmate directly and these meetings are not allowed to be listened to. However, they are subject to visual surveillance.

The Internal Rules for the Houses of Detention do not allow valuables, such as jewellery, rings, gold watches etc. for inmates; however, there are exemptions for wedding rings and for religious symbols. Religious symbols may also be sent to prisoners by post. Religious sacred books are permitted too.

9.5 Issues and Debates

Although "chaplaincy" is a commonly used word for religious workers in institutions and there are official posts of chaplains in defence forces, prisons and law enforcement, and it is used in legislation, the word itself does not have any legal definition within the Estonian legal framework or legislation. The requirements for chaplains are set out by the internal rules of the institutions. In prisons, the main duty of the chaplain is to provide spiritual care and religious services. If a prisoner belongs to a religious tradition not represented in the prison chaplaincy, the chaplain should organise a meeting with the required religious authority. Chaplains and religious volunteers are also involved in resocialisation programmes, in organising religious recreation activities and counselling.

In 2007, the Estonian Council of Churches, the Estonian Evangelical Lutheran Church and the Qualification Authority initiated the process to clarify professional standards for chaplains. In 2008, the Estonian Qualifications Authority (*Kutsekoda*) registered the first occupational qualification standard for chaplains (Jürjo 2009, 422–423; Ringvee 2015, 84–86). In 2013, the Estonian Qualifications Authority listed the qualification standards for chaplains and pastoral counsellors in their catalogue of occupational qualifications. However, it seems that establishing the occupational qualification standards had not had a notable impact on chaplaincies in institutions with hierarchical subordination, including prison chaplaincies, as internal regulations set the framework for requirements to fill the post. The certificate of profession is given by the Estonian Chaplains' Professional Association Commission, which includes representatives from the Estonian Council of Churches, the Institute of Theology of the EELC, the Ministry of Justice, the Defence Forces, the Defence League and experts (Chaplains Association 2018).

Over the years, the courts have made decisions on cases concerning religion and religious freedom in the Estonian prison environment. In 2007, a prisoner sued the prison administration for violating his constitutional right to practise religion, as the prison had confiscated his incense sticks that he considered essential for his Buddhist religious practice. Tartu District Court decided in a case no. 3-07-701 (2 May 2007) that confiscation of incense sticks by the prison authorities was justified on the grounds of prison security and did not consider the burning of incense sticks essential for practising Buddhism (Kiviorg 2016, 47). In 2009, the same prisoner applied for permission to use incense sticks for religious purposes in Viru Prison. After a negative answer from the prison administration, the prisoner sued the prison for violation of his constitutional rights for religious freedom and violations in prison procedures. Although the administrative court sided with the applicant's argument, the decision was appealed and in 2010, the Tartu Circuit Court decided in case no. 3-09-1822 that the prison's decision not to allow the use of incense sticks in the prison's maximum-security ward based on the rights and health of the other inmates, as well as prison officials and for security reasons, was justified. Security is one of the main factors in limiting manifestations of religious freedom. Thus, for example, in 2011, the Tartu Circuit Court in case no. 3-09-2036 considered the decision of the prison not to allow a prisoner from the maximum-security ward to participate in a religious service in the prison chapel justified because of prison security.[2]

Another issue that has sometimes created tensions in prison concerns the possibilities of following one's religious food regulations. According to the Imprisonment Act §47 (1), the dietary norms in prison should be in conformity with the general dietary habits of the population. The Imprisonment Act §47 (3) allows prisoners to follow their religious dietary regulations if possible. In 2013, the Tartu District Court made a decision in case no. 3-11-2943, where it affirmed the general understanding that there is no obligation for the prison to provide food in accordance with religious requirements. Providing a special diet based on religious requirements is a challenge for prisons in several respects, including the financial cost of special food, as well as the conditions and skills available for the preparation of the required food. The vegetarian option has been considered to be a sufficient alternative to the regular prison menu. Currently, all prisons have vegetarian and non-vegetarian menu options, although the vegetarian menu is served only on the basis of medical prescriptions or when justified for religious reasons. In case no. 3-11-2943, an Orthodox Christian prisoner had applied for the vegetarian menu for religious reasons. The prison refused the application with the argument that although in Orthodox Christianity there are times of fasting, the Orthodox Church does not require a fully vegetarian diet for regular believers. The court decision was well justified; there have been questions on the rationale of requiring medical or religious justification for the vegetarian menu (Olesk 2015, 689).

Although the Prison Service must provide the possibility of practising one's religion, the positive religious right does not mean that the prison should provide equipment for religious practices. This decision, which echoes that on practising a religious diet in prison, was made by the Tallinn Administrative Court on case no. 3-16-2388 from 2017, when an inmate of Tallinn Prison sued the institution for violation of prison regulations and freedom of religion, as the prison had refused to

---

[2] Court decisions since 2006 are searchable online at www.riigiteataja.ee/kohtulahendid/koik_menetlused.html. Accessed 6 February 2018.

provide him with a lamp so that he could read his sacred book after sunset and before dawn, as his religious tradition required.

Although legal acts protect religious freedom in prisons, it has been noted that there are problematic areas, especially regarding the internal security of prisons, as the legislation does not take into account all its specificities. Thus, for example, according to the Imprisonment Act §26 (1), the inmate has the right to meet with religious ministers, whereas the prison administration has no right to control whether or not the person claiming to be a minister of religion actually is one. In addition, although chaplains and religious volunteers go through background checks, there are no legal grounds for conducting background checks for religious ministers visiting prisons and detention houses at the request of the inmate (Olesk 2015, 689).

9.6 Conclusion

The Estonian prison system has gone through tremendous changes during the last 25 years. These changes also affect religion and religious work in prisons, which have moved away from the enthusiastic and chaotic beginnings towards an institutionalised arrangement managed by the chief of chaplains at the Prisons Department of the Ministry of Justice. There are special spaces for religious activities in every prison and every prison has chaplains who belong to the regular prison personnel. The chaplains have double subordination; although they are clergy of their religious association, they are also subordinated to the Prisons Department of the Ministry of Justice and hired in accordance with the Civil Service Act.

The two main partners for the state providing religious services in prison are the Estonian Evangelical Lutheran Church and the Ecumenical Estonian Council of Churches. The dialogue with these two institutions is more regular than with other religious organisations and has resulted in common cooperation agreements that include prison chaplaincy. The reasons for the closer cooperation between the state and the EELC and the ECC, however, may not be ideologically motivated, but reflect more pragmatic or cost-efficiency reasons, as most of the prisoners who register their religious affiliation in the prisoner's register define themselves as Orthodox or Lutherans or affiliates of Christian denominations represented in the ECC.

Although the main cooperation partner for the State is the ECC, the primary goal of the chaplaincy service is to accommodate the religious needs of all inmates. If a prisoner is affiliated with a religious tradition that is not represented in the prison chaplaincy service, he or she may request a meeting with a religious authority, which prison chaplains have to organise. However, problems may occur when the religious community itself has limited resources with regard to their religious personnel.

Several legal acts regulate religious life in prisons. The legal framework and internal regulations of prisons give considerable protection to religious activities for inmates, especially regarding private meetings of inmates with religious personnel that have the same protection as meetings with defence counsellors, lawyers, notaries and consular officers. Although most of the cases that have come to the courts regarding violations of religious freedom are from inmates, none of these cases has been brought to the European Court of Human Rights. The court rulings in Estonia have stressed the margin of appreciation of the prison administrations.

Sources and Bibliography

A Place for You. (2006). *A Place for You. The first 15 years of Estonian Christian Pentecostal Church*. Tallinn: Eesti Kristlik Nelipühi Kirik.

Arestimaja sisekorraeeskiri. (2011). Arestimaja sisekorraeeskiri [Internal rules of detention house] *Riigi Teataja*, RT I, 30 September 2011, 4. www.riigiteataja.ee/akt/120052017011?leiaKehtiv. Accessed 6 Feb 2018.

Avaliku teenistuse seadus. (2012). Avaliku teenistuse seadus [Civil service act]. *Riigi Teataja* RT I, 6 July 2012, 1. [Civil service act] www.riigiteataja.ee/akt/126032013005?leiaKehtiv. Accessed 6 Feb 2018.

Chaplains Association. (2018). Estonian Council of Churches Website. Eesti Kaplanite Kutseühing [Estonian Chaplains' Professional Association]. http://www.ekn.ee/inc.toovaldkond.php?leh t=T%F6%F6valdkonnad&alamleht=EESTI_KAPLANITE_KUTSE%DCHING. Accessed 6 Feb 2018.

Department of Prisons. (2018). Institutions. http://www.vangla.ee/en/intitutions/prisons-department-ministry-justice. Accessed 6 Feb 2018.

Dunkel, F. (2017). European penology. The rise and fall of prison population rates in Europe in times of migrant crises and terrorism. *European Journal of Criminology, 14*(6), 629–653.

Estonian Defence Forces. (2018). Kaplaniteenistus [Chaplaincy]. http://www.mil.ee/et/kaitsevagi/muud-yksused/kaplaniteenistus. Accessed 12 Feb 2018.

Estonian Prison System Yearbook. (2003). *Vanglasüsteemi aastaraamat/Estonian prison system yearbook. 2002–2003*. Tallinn: Justiitsministeerium/Ministry of Justice.

Handbook. (2012). *Vanglate kaplaniteenistus ja usuline töö vanglas. Kaplaniteenistuse käsiraamat* [Prisons chaplaincy service and religious work in prisons. Handbook of chaplaincy service] (J.-C. Põder, Ed.). Tallinn: Justiitsminsiteerium.

Jürjo, S. (2007). *Erinevate kaplaniteenistuste tekkimine ja areng Eestis aastatel 1988 – 2007*. Master thesis. Theological Institute of the Estonian Evangelical Lutheran Church, Tallinn (Unpublished manuscript).

Jürjo, S. (2009). Chaplaincy. In R. Altnurme (Ed.), *History of the Estonian ecumenism* (pp. 422–423). Tartu/Tallinn: University of Tartu/Estonian Council of Churches.

Kinnipeetavate Register. (2004). Riikliku kinnipeetavate, arestialuste ja vahistatute registri asutamine ja registri pidamise põhimäärus. Vabariigi Valitsuse määrus 13 July 2004 no. 246, *Riigi Teataja*, RT I 2004, 57, 409. https://www.riigiteataja.ee/akt/926888?leiaKehtiv Accessed 6 Feb 2018.

Kirikute ja koguduste seadus. (2002). Kirikute ja koguduste seadus [Churches and congregations act], *Riigi Teataja*, RT I 2002, 24, 135. https://www.riigiteataja.ee/en/eli/511012018004/consolide. Accessed 6 Feb 2018.

Kiviorg, M. (2003). Church and state in Estonia. In S. Ferrari & W. Cole Durham Jr. (Eds.), *Law and religion in post-Communist Europe* (pp. 99––120). Leuven/Pairs/Dudley: Peeters Publishers.

Kiviorg, M. (2016). *Law and religion in Estonia* (2nd ed.). Alpen aan den Rijs: Kluwer Law International.

Kokkulepe. (2015). Siseministeeriumi ja Eesti Kirikute Nõukogu vaheline koostöö kokkulepe 21. 01. 2015 [Agreement of cooperation between the Estonian Ministry of the Interior and the Estonian Council of Churches, 21 January 2015]. www.siseministeerium.ee/sites/default/files/dokumendid/usuasjad/koostookokkulepe_siseministeerium_ja_ekn.pdf. Accessed 6 Feb 2018.

Ministry of Justice. (2005). Adviser-Chief of Chaplains, Job Description. https://www.just.ee/sites/www.just.ee/files/contacts/.../51055053.rtf. Accessed 6 Feb 2018.

Nõmmik, T. (2005). *Vaimulikud kaitsejõududes. Eesti kaitseväe kaplaniteenistus ja selle eellugu.* Tartu: Kaitseväe Ühendatud Õppeasutused.

Olesk, M. (2015). Usuvabadus vanglas. *Juridica, X,* 686–700.

PHC Database. (2000). Estonian Statistics, Database, Population and Housing Census 2000, Religious   Affiliation.   http://pub.stat.ee/px-web.2001/I_Databas/Population_census/PHC2000/16Religious_affiliation/16Religious_affiliation.asp. Accessed 6 Feb 2018.

PHC Database. (2011). Estonian Statistics, Database, Population and Housing Census 2011,   Religious   Affiliation.   http://pub.stat.ee/px-web.2001/I_Databas/Population_census/PHC2011/01Demographic_and_ethno_cultural_characteristics/08Religious_affiliation/08Religious_affiliation.asp. Accessed 6 Feb 2018.

Põder, J.-C. (2012). Kaplan ja kaplaniteenistus. In J.-C. Põder (Ed.), *Vanglate kaplaniteenistus ja usuline töö vanglas. Kaplaniteenistuse käsiraamat* (pp. 6–11). Tallinn: Justiitsministeerium.

Põhiseadus. (1992). Eesti Vabariigi Põhiseadus [The Constitution of the Republic of Estonia]. *Riigi Teataja,* RT 1992, 26, 349. https://www.riigiteataja.ee/en/eli/ee/521052015001/consolide/current. Accessed 6 Feb 2018.

Prison Service. (2018a). Prison Service Website. News and numbers. Prisoners and probationers. http://www.vangla.ee/et/uudised-ja-arvud/vangide-ja-kriminaalhooldusaluste-arv. Accessed 6 Feb 2018.

Prison Service. (2018b). Prison Service Website. Religion. http://www.vangla.ee/en/serving-sentence/religion. Accessed 6 Feb 2018.

Ringvee, R. (2011). *Riik ja religioon nõukogudejärgses Eestis 1991–2008* [State and religion in post-Soviet Estonia 1991–2008]. Tartu: Tartu Ülikooli Kirjastus.

Ringvee, R. (2014). Religion: Not declining but changing. What do the population censuses and surveys say about religion in Estonia? *Religion, 44*(3), 502–515.

Ringvee, R. (2015). *Annotated legal documents on Islam in Europe: Estonia.* Leiden: Brill.

Saar, J. (2001). Penal policy in Estonia, 1991–2000. In R. Vetik (Ed.), *Estonian human development report 2001* (pp. 46–50). Tallinn: Tallinn Pedagogical University.

Täitemenetluse seadustik. (1993). Täitemenetluse seadustik [Code of enforcement procedure]. *Riigi Teataja* RT I 1993, 49, 693.

Täitemenetluse seadustik. (2005). Täitemenetluse seadustik [Code of enforcement procedure], *Riigi Teataja* RT I 2005, 27, 198. https://www.riigiteataja.ee/en/eli/ee/510012018005/consolide. Accessed 6 Feb 2018.

Tsiviilkohtumenetluse seadustik. (2005). Tsiviilkohtumenetluse seadustik [Code of civil procedure] *Riigi Teataja* RT I 2005, 26, 197. https://www.riigiteataja.ee/en/eli/ee/515012018001/consolide. Accessed 6 Feb 2018.

Ühishuvide protokoll. (2002). Eesti Vabariigi Valitsuse ja Eesti Kirikute Nõukogu ühishuvide protokoll 17. 10. 2002 [Protocol of Common Concerns between the Government of Estonian Republic and the Estonian Council of Churches, 17 October 2002]. www.siseministeerium.ee/sites/default/files/dokumendid/usuasjad/eesti_vabariigi_valitsuse_ja_eesti_kirikute_noukogu_uhishuvide_protokoll.pdf. Accessed 12 February 2018.

Üprus, A. (2000). *Õigus halastusele. Eesti kiriku kriminaaltöö ja hingehoiu osa selles.* Tallinn: Logos.

Vabatahtlike kaasamise juhend. (2002). Vabatahtlike kaasamise juhend vanglas kinni peetavate isikute resotsialiseerimisse ja usulisse tegevusse, *Riigi Teataja,* RTL 2002, 129, 1875. https://www.riigiteataja.ee/akt/767345. Accessed 6 Feb 2018.

Väljasõidukohustuse ja sissesõidukeelu seadus. (1998). Väljasõidukohustuse ja sissesõidukeelu seadus [Obligation to leave and prohibition on entry act]. *Riigi Teataja,* RT I 1998, 98, 1575. https://www.riigiteataja.ee/en/eli/518122017007/consolide. Accessed 6 Feb 2018.

Vangistusseadus. (2000). Vangistusseadus [Imprisonment Act], *Riigi Teataja*, RT I 2000, 58, 376. https://www.riigiteataja.ee/en/eli/511092017003/consolide. Accessed 6 Feb 2018.

Vangla sisekorraeeskiri. (2000). Vangla sisekorraeeskiri [Internal rules of prison]. *Riigi Teataja* RTL 2000, 134, 2139. https://www.riigiteataja.ee/akt/106102017007?leiaKehtiv. Accessed 6 Feb 2018.

Chapter 10
Finland: Re-evaluating the Social Role of Religion in Modern Society – Religion in Prisons

Sami Puumala

Abstract This chapter comprises five parts. The first part provides a view of prisons in Finland as a whole, both from a historical perspective and according to the current situation, followed by a discussion of the key objectives of the latest developments in legislation regarding the prison service. This is namely the key objective of imprisonment, to be a process of rehabilitation from the beginning (pretrial detention) to the time after the release from prison – a process that the authorities have to plan in cooperation with the prisoner and in cooperation with the required actors from outside the prison (such as NGOs and faith communities). The second part is a short summary regarding prison sentences: first, a description of the development of prisons in Finland over the last two centuries into a sanction system similar to the prison services of other Nordic countries; second, an examination of the Finnish statutes and other guiding principles regarding religious practice in prisons. The chapter will show that Finnish national statutes and principles are based on international (UN and the Council of Europe) treaties. The section will also describe the organisation of religious practice in prisons. The third part explores current societal debate over prison chaplaincy and the prison ministry in Finland. The fourth part presents empirical research data related to the religiousness of prisoners and religious activities in prison. The presentation is restricted to descriptive statistical analysis. The last part is a discussion of religion in prisons from the perspective of the sociology of religion, which will be closer to a sociological reflection than to a theoretical analysis.

S. Puumala (✉)
Evangelical Lutheran Church of Finland/National Church Council/Division for Diaconia and Pastoral Counselling, Helsinki, Finland
e-mail: sami.puumala@evl.fi

© Springer Nature Switzerland AG 2020
J. Martínez-Ariño, A.-L. Zwilling (eds.), *Religion and Prison: An Overview of Contemporary Europe*, Boundaries of Religious Freedom: Regulating Religion in Diverse Societies 7, https://doi.org/10.1007/978-3-030-36834-0_10

10.1   Introduction

Religion in prisons in Finland is a profoundly interesting and important phenomenon. As a field for research and reflections on religion and society, religion in prisons may function like a double-sided mirror: first, exploring religion in prisons deepens our understanding of prisoners and prisons; second, exploring religion in prisons deepens our understanding of religion, religiosity and religious behaviour. This chapter takes into account the different dimensions that co-create the importance of religion in prisons both at an individual and at a social/societal level:

1. The long history and wide traditions of religious practices in Finnish prisons, which are as old as the modern or even pre-modern prisons in the country – prison chaplains and faith groups have been active since the beginning and still are one of the largest actors to provide activities to prisoners.
2. The heavy emphasis that national legislation and the international treaties (UN and EC prison rules) place on religious rights in prison.
3. Most importantly, religiosity and religious behaviour among Finnish inmates seem to be truly wide phenomena. It almost appears that inmates were one of the most religious and religiously active groups of Finns. Religion really seems to matter to prisoners. On the other hand, inmates deal with many matters of life in connection to religion. Therefore, there is a need for society to understand the religious needs of the prisoners.

This chapter has two aims: first, to provide an overview of the phenomenon, "religion in prison in Finland". The overview is based on historical, legal and sociological data. The second aim is to provide a sociological reflection on the phenomenon. The reflection has two sides:

1. A contemporary societal estimation of the role of religion in prison culminating in the social debate about the prison chaplaincy.
2. A wider reflection on the role and meaning of religion with support from theoretical ideas borrowed from some of the major traditions and creators of sociological theory.

10.2   Sources of Information Used in This Chapter

This chapter presents some findings of a large research project on religion in prisons in Finland. The research data contains five sets of empirical material: statistical materials on prisoners based on random sampling[1] and complementing qualitative

---

[1] Sample = 600 men + 215 women, response rate = 54%. Based on the socio-demographic and criminological background data at the time of the sample, the sample is representative and the overall results can be generalised to all prisoners – the number of non-Finnish prisoners was also representative of their ratio to all prisoners.

interview material,[2] a survey conducted on prison chaplains,[3] a survey conducted on prison governors,[4] a survey conducted on religious communities engaged in prison ministry[5] and a survey of representatives of congregations engaged in the prison ministry.[6] Some of the material was obtained as part of a joint project between the Evangelical-Lutheran Church of Finland and the Criminal Sanctions Agency on religious practice in prison, gathered for the project report.[7] In addition, the second part of the chapter uses data published by the Criminal Sanctions Agency on prisons and prisoners.

10.3 The History and Current Situation of Prison Administration in Finland[8]

The roots of Finnish prison administration go back to the 1600s, when Finland was under Swedish rule. It was a time of developing provincial administration, and provinces were put in charge of arresting those suspected of crimes and sentencing them. Following the birth of the model of a modern prison, the actual Finnish prison administration was developed during the 1800s, when Finland was under Russian rule. This means that most of the prisons in Finland were founded by the Russian administration. The principle still affecting the structure of the prison network also dates back to that time. It is the idea that prisons are divided into provincial prisons located in provincial centres and holding mainly prisoners on remand, and central prisons holding those serving prison sentences. Some central prisons were in cities (originally in Helsinki and Turku, for example, and later in Riihimäki) and some were built in the middle of the countryside (e.g. Sukeva). In rural prisons, prisoners would carry out tasks required by the rural community, such as clearing fields and looking after animals. More open prisons were also established. Prisoners in these labour colonies would participate in the construction of roads and building work and carry out other tasks required by the industrialising society.[9]

---

[2]$N = 35$.

[3]$N = 21$, response rate 100.

[4]$N = 27$, response rate 93.

[5]Respondents were people responsible for prison ministry of the denominations and religious movements who engage in prison ministry at national level, with nine denominations or movements in total.

[6]$N = 310$, not obtained by random sampling.

[7]Työryhmän raportti 2015. (Report of a working party 2015.)

[8]Information sources: data published by the Criminal Sanctions Agency. For more information please see www.rikosseuraamus.fi.

[9]Following the Second World War, Finnish criminal policy underwent a significant change as a rational and humane Scandinavian criminal policy was adopted. This resulted in a dramatic drop in the number of prisoners. Finland, like the other Nordic countries, is among nations with the world's lowest numbers of prisoners in proportion to the population.

The division of prisons into provincial prisons, central prisons and labour colonies was abolished in the 2000s. Nowadays, prisons are divided into closed prisons and open institutions. All prisons have been named after their locations. Some of the closed prisons are used to house both prisoners on remand and those serving prison sentences, whereas some of the larger closed prisons concentrate on holding those serving prison sentences. Most female prisoners are placed at Hämeenlinna prison. It is currently undergoing reconstruction work and will eventually become an institution holding female prisoners only.

A feature of recent development in Finland is the need to modernise the ageing prison stock to create prison conditions that comply with international recommendations. It has been unflattering for a modern Western country such as Finland to be reprimanded by the European Committee for the Prevention of Torture for conditions in certain prisons. The Finnish state administration has acknowledged the need for the modernisation of prisons and has allocated resources for this. In the recent social debate, it has been assumed that, for economic reasons, cuts would have to be made to the prison network (the government was expected to close three or four prisons), but this has not happened. The trend has been to maintain a reasonably extensive prison network to continue to fulfil one of the key objectives of modern imprisonment – placing prisoners in their local area to promote their family contacts.

Finland has 15 closed prisons and 11 open institutions. Open institutions account for one third of all prison places. In recent years, the prison administration system overall has been developed, as the previously separate Prison Service and Probation Service (whose task is the enforcement of community sanctions) were united to form the Criminal Sanctions Agency, which is responsible for the enforcement of punishments. Finland is divided into three Criminal Sanctions Regions: Southern Finland, Eastern and Northern Finland, and Western Finland. The objective of the division into regions is to promote integration within the system: each of the Criminal Sanctions Regions has a regional administration, which includes a regional centre and an assessment centre. The regional centres are responsible for the strategic guidance of the prisons and the assessment centres are responsible for the sentencing plans, which are based on a risk and needs assessment. The goal is to ensure an equal chance for every prisoner in every prison to serve his/her sentence in a way that promotes his/her placement back into society and to live without crime.

The most recent reform in Finnish prison administration legislation took place in 2006. The central idea of the new Imprisonment Act is the systematic and consistent enforcement of imprisonment. It is the authorities' duty to draw up an individual plan for the term of sentence, together with the prisoner. If the prisoner wishes, rehabilitative religious activities may also be included in the plan for the term of the sentence. The aim of the new Act is to promote the implementation of the imprisonment process from start to release, to support the prisoner's return to society and a crime-free life.[10] To achieve this aim, the prison authorities rely on partners that also

---

[10] In the past two decades, the Criminal Sanctions Agency has developed rehabilitative activities in prisons by allocating resources for implementing rehabilitation programmes developed in other countries and in Finland. Criminal Sanctions Agency's researchers and other research institutions

include congregations and Christian organisations. After the public sector actors, religious organisations are the largest group in Finland to offer various types of support to serving prisoners and released prisoners.

In 2016, the average daily number of prisoners in Finland was 3120, and of these, 585 were prisoners on remand. A total of 5531 prisoners were released from prisons in 2016. Of the released prisoners, around 40% served a sentence of a maximum of 3 months. The average length of sentences for those released was 11.1 months. Four prisoners out of 10 were sentenced for violent crimes. Theft offences, robberies and other property offences accounted for a quarter of those sentenced, and narcotics offences accounted for 19%. In the past 10 years, the share of first offenders has risen from 30 to 36%. Just under 30% of the prisoners were in prison for the third to seventh time in 2016. Just under 20% of the prisoners were in prison for at least the eighth time. Women accounted for 7% of all prisoners. The proportion of non-Finnish prisoners has increased by 75% in the past decade, and their share of all prisoners has risen to 17%. The increased number of non-Finnish prisoners is perhaps the most significant trend in recent years. It is also closely connected to issues related to religious practice in prisons.

10.4   The Organisation of Religious Practice in Prisons and Related Statutes and Principles

According to the Constitution of Finland (Section 11), "Everyone has the freedom of religion and conscience. Freedom of religion and conscience entails the right to profess and practise a religion, the right to express one's convictions and the right to be a member of or decline to be a member of a religious community. No one is under the obligation, against his or her conscience, to participate in the practice of religion". Section 22 of the Constitution states that "the public authorities shall guarantee the observance of basic rights and liberties and human rights". Thus, the authorities also have a duty to secure the guarantee of freedom of religion as a basic right in prisons. According to the Freedom of Religion Act (Section 1, Subsection 3), "Everyone has the right to make decisions about their religious status by joining a religious community willing to accept them as members, or to leave such a community".

Finland has ratified the prison rules of the UN and the Council of Europe. National legislation and prison guidelines abide by these rules. According to the Finnish Imprisonment Act (Chapter 11, Section 3), "Where possible, church services, prayer meetings and other religious events shall be arranged in the prison in accordance with the needs of the prisoners. Prisoners shall be provided with the possibility to meet the spiritual representative or other representative of their own

---

have also addressed the rehabilitative activities and the need for such activities. Evaluation procedures and an accreditation system are applied to rehabilitative activities.

religion. A prison shall have premises suitable for the practice of religion. A prisoner who is intoxicated or who disturbs an event referred to in subsection 1 or endangers prison order or safety may be denied the right to participate in the event. If a prisoner is not allowed to participate in common events, his or her possibility of engaging in religious practices shall be attended to in another manner." Equivalent statutes are also included in the Remand Imprisonment Act (7:2) giving remand prisoners the same right to practise religion. Any restrictions on the practice of religion in prison must be based on legislation.

The current interpretation of the Freedom of Religion Act has also provided prisoners with a stronger freedom to distance themselves from religion. Significant changes include the 1971 decree abolishing the requirement for prisoners who are members of the Lutheran Church to attend church services, and the development that took place from 1990 to the early 2000s, which cut back on the number of church and spiritual community volunteers interacting with prisoners on prison wards. Today, prisoners receive information about the opportunities for practising religion and pastoral care regardless of their religious background, membership of religious communities or their religiousness. A prisoner gets that information, when he arrives in prison, together with other information about the prison, provided to him by the prison officers of the arrival ward. Prisoners have the freedom of choice. The duty to observe the right of those choosing to participate lies with the prison authorities.

In compliance with the UN recommendations, closed prisons in Finland employ a full-time Evangelical-Lutheran chaplain, as most of the prisoners belong to the same religion and church, the Evangelical Lutheran Church of Finland. Added to that, representatives of other churches and religions organise religious and spiritual events in prison and meet prisoners in person by permission of the prison governor. The permission may be granted for an individual event or meeting, or until further notice. The latter practice is more common, as most prisons have agreed on annual spiritual events and visits for meeting prisoners with various religious communities. Prisoners can choose to participate in spiritual events organised by their own denomination or by other denominations and religious communities and to meet their representatives. This is a wider interpretation of the minimum requirements stated in the UN and Council of Europe prison recommendations regarding prisoners' rights to contact with their own religious community.

The intention in prisons and in religious communities engaged in the prison ministry has been to arrange for an adequate number of people representing different religious communities, should a prisoner wish to meet such a person. The aim is not to convert anyone – proselytism is not allowed in prison. Should such activities be discovered, the activities of a religious community or an individual representative may be stopped. Religious communities engaged in the prison ministry commit to respecting other religions when applying for permission to work in a prison. Conversion to another religion is rare among prisoners, but "returning" to one's own religion is common. The starting point is the prisoners' needs and willingness to participate in activities, rather than religious communities' desire to engage in prison ministry. An individual may not establish spiritual activity in a prison without being sent and recommended to the prison by a religious community responsible for the activities. Any faith group needs to apply for permission to prison ministry. In the application, the religious community names the member(s) for whom it applies for permission and includes a written recommendation by the community management for those persons. The recommendation demonstrates that those persons enjoy confidence in their faith community as active members and that the faith group considers them proper representatives of their faith in the prison ministry.

Christian communities engaged in the prison ministry maintain an ecumenical cooperative organisation for training their members and laying out general guidelines for religious activities in prisons. The organisation arranges 2-year training courses for volunteers in the prison ministry. The training costs are covered by the congregations and the Criminal Sanctions Agency participates in the training. Other religious groups receive guidance and support with regard to prison visits by local prisons, as so far only Christian communities have organised religious work in prisons; therefore, training has not yet been needed. The latest development concerning other faith groups has been the cooperation of some Islamic communities and the Criminal Sanctions Agency to engage the Islamic communities in the prison ministry. Also, the Christian denominations and some representatives of Finnish Muslims have recently started to plan common training seminars.[11]

10.4.1   Prison Chaplains and Religious Communities Engaged in Prison Work

Thirteen closed prisons employ a full-time Evangelical Lutheran chaplain. Two open institutions and one closed prison employ a full-time deacon. Four open institutions employ a part-time chaplain or deacon. As a rule, prisoners in open institutions attend spiritual events outside the institution, with permission to leave. Open institutions arrange transport on these occasions.

The early history of prison chaplains dates back to prison preachers during the time when Finland was under Swedish rule. As early as the 1500s, it was the clergymen's task to prepare those sentenced to death. In the 1700s, their task was to guide prisoners to confess to their actions. At the beginning of the 1800s, the prison preacher was made a permanent position. Under Russian rule, in the late 1800s, their task was specified as individual pastoral care and the position was connected to the positions of clergymen under ecclesiastical legislation. In the early 1920s, as Finland had become independent, the position was changed to a prison chaplain and a government statute made it a part of the prison administration.

---

[11] Unlike in many neighbouring countries of Finland, there are so few prisoners of faiths other than Christian in most Finnish prisons that there have been poor grounds for developing regular religious activities. Instead of that, there have been case-by-case visits by imams to meet individual prisoners and to arrange religious meetings if the prisoners have expressed such a wish.

This means that in Finland, prison chaplains are part of the prison staff and their salaries are paid by the Criminal Sanctions Agency, but appointments are made and aptitude tests carried out by the Lutheran Church. Prior to aptitude testing, the Criminal Sanctions Agency provides the Lutheran Church with a statement of the applicants it considers most suitable. The position of prison chaplains is enacted in the Church Act (Article 6, Section 12): "Positions may be allocated for prisons and for the pastoral care of the deaf, and for other specific situations. In all issues related to priesthood, the office holder works under the chapter". As a prison employee, a prison chaplain works under the prison management, with the prison governor or assistant manager as their immediate supervisor. In practice, this means that prison chaplains have no ecclesiastical supervisors, although in principle the bishop of their diocese is their supervisor.

There is no uniform job description for prison chaplains.[12] Their key responsibilities include managing ecclesiastical services in prison, with a focus on the pastoral care of prisoners. Their tasks have also included (often a great deal of) participation in other rehabilitative work in prison, as well as other shared prison tasks. The role and job description of a prison chaplain has been influenced by the general development of pastoral care within the Evangelical Lutheran Church of Finland towards therapeutic pastoral care. Prison chaplains are required to take a 3-year specialisation course in pastoral care arranged by the Lutheran Church. (Similar training is arranged for hospital chaplains and family counsellors, as well as others working in special pastoral care positions.) The training is extensive (60 study credits.) Prison chaplains are invited to the training after their appointment to a post in prison.

Many denominations and religious communities participate in religious activities in prisons. The most notable actors are the Evangelical Lutheran Church, the Pentecostal Movement, the Evangelical Free Church, the Seventh-Day Adventist Church, the Salvation Army and the Orthodox Church. Of the revivalist movements, extensive prison work is carried out by the Conservative Laestadians. There are many other smaller local faith groups, whose representatives visit prisoners sporadically (if any inmate desires this), but the former work in prisons regularly. Congregations and other faith communities cover the costs of the activities themselves. Prisons provide guidance on practical matters. This guidance is usually the task of the prison chaplain. Prison chaplains also promote the right of prisoners belonging to other religious communities to profess and practise their religion and maintain contact with representatives of these religions.

Prisoners have a right to observe the customs of their religious tradition within the limits of the law, and practicalities – such as dietary arrangements and fasting: for example, meals with no pork or the opportunity to have meals during Ramadan exceptionally late in the evening, after the cells are closed. Prisoners are allowed to have religious literature and articles in their possession. Religious literature is

---

[12] The Criminal Sanctions Agency and the Lutheran Church have recently agreed to strengthen the coordination of prison chaplaincy – including a common description of the key tasks of all the prison chaplains.

available in prison libraries and religious communities may give prisoners spiritual literature, but religious material will not be delivered to anyone against his/her wishes. Prisoners have the opportunity to follow religious programmes on the radio and television in their cells. According to legislation, prisons must have premises suitable for the practice of religion, usually a church or a chapel. In more modern prisons, efforts have been made to ensure that these premises are suitable for different religions, a separate space called Room for Religions, furnished and decorated in a way that can be modified to suit the needs of various religious traditions.

10.5   Current Debate

In the UN and the Council of Europe prison rules, the practice of religion and pastoral care in prison is outlined by two basic ideas:

1. The guarantee of basic rights,
2. Solutions based on prisoners' needs.

In Finland, the first of these basic ideas is adopted in legislation and the level of adherence in prisons is high. Religious communities and prison chaplains have emphasised that the practice of religion must not be seen as a form of free-time activity, although in practice, some spiritual events are organised in prison in a similar manner to free-time activities. Their emphasis has been on the basic rights aspect of the practice of religion.[13]

Research data on Finnish prisoners provide a clear starting point for solutions based on the needs of prisoners when organising the practice of religion and pastoral care: closed prisons require a full-time prison chaplain. As mentioned earlier, the majority of prison governors share this view. From time to time, it is suggested in social debate that rather than full-time prison chaplains, the practice of religion and pastoral care in prison could be adequately organised through chaplains working part time and visiting prisons from their congregations (as in Sweden, the only Nordic country to have adopted this approach). However, such an arrangement would clearly go against the needs and wishes of prisoners in Finland.

In practice, even the arrangement adopted by open institutions of part-time prison chaplains does not cater for the needs of prisoners, as the remote location of some institutions means that the prisoners have no real opportunity to receive

---

[13] This has also been the opinion of the highest controller of the legality of governmental actors in Finland, the Parliamentary Ombudsman. A prisoner filed a complaint with the Ombudsman, having been made to choose between meeting family members and attending a church service, as they were scheduled for the same time. In his decision, the Ombudsman ordered the prison to rectify the situation so that the prisoner was able to do both. The decisions of the Ombudsman carry the weight of precedents, meaning that this decision has become the guiding norm for prisons in general.

adequate pastoral care outside the institution.[14] Key survival methods for a prisoner include minding one's own business and avoiding conflicts in relation to the prison organisation and other prisoners. It is, therefore, controversial to present arguments (that have sometimes been presented by prison authorities in discussions with the prison chaplaincy and the churches over the past few years) that everything is fine, that there are no additional needs regarding the practice of religion or pastoral care, and that there is no need for prison chaplains, because prisoners do not complain about these issues. Everything may seem to be on track, but, based on empirical data gathered from prisoners, there are problems underneath the surface. Even flimsier is the argument stating that, "supply increases demand", meaning that smaller resources could be adequate for the practice of religion and pastoral care, but demand is generated as more activities are offered. This type of argument would be arrogant and underestimates the needs of prisoners. Fortunately, one comes across it only rarely.

In Finland, the relationship between the prison administration and the (mainstream) church has been close and cooperative. The spirit of cooperation has been manifested in the numerous joint bodies established to promote the practice of religions and pastoral care in prison. The current body performing these tasks was set up by the central management of the Evangelical Lutheran Church of Finland and implemented by a cooperative body of the Criminal Sanctions Agency and the church; Advisory Committee on Spiritual Work in Prisons and Related Activities. Participants include representatives of minority denominations, and cooperation with other religious communities is also possible. The close relationship between the State and the Evangelical Lutheran Church in Finland, as in Norway, Denmark, and some other European countries, also manifests in the way in which resources for hiring prison chaplains are allocated by government officials.

In recent years, the central social debate has been concerned with the initiative of the Criminal Sanctions Agency to transform the positions of prison chaplains from the staff of the Criminal Sanctions Agency to the personnel of the Lutheran Church. In 2012, the Criminal Sanctions Agency proposed this to the Ministry of Justice. However, the negotiations between the church and the ministry did not result in action at the ministry. Instead, on the initiative of the church, and with the approval of the Minister of Justice, an extensive project was launched to survey the issue of the practice of religion in prisons. The project was concluded in 2015 and there has been continuous debate since then. The issue is greater than who should be the employer of prison chaplains. The employment issue is connected to the financing of the prison chaplaincy: who should pay? Unambiguous answers cannot be found, even in the UN or Council of Europe prison recommendations. Western countries have interpreted the issue in various ways. In many countries, the state is considered responsible for resourcing the positions. This is because the state imprisons people

---

[14]An interesting observation in my prisoner material is that there is no difference in attitudes towards the practice of religion and pastoral care between prisoners in closed prisons and open institutions. Both groups have the same need for pastoral care and practice of their religion.

and restricts their rights and opportunities, and it should therefore also be responsible for safeguarding their basic rights.[15]

The prison chaplaincy debate can be seen as a part of a wider social development: in Finland, the distance between the Church and the State has gradually increased, in a societal, peaceful manner. As recently as during the 1980s, President Kekkonen (president from 1952 to 1982) would occasionally intervene in Church matters, such as the appointment of bishops, but in general he would keep a social distance from the Church. During the term of President Mauno Koivisto (1984–1992), the government could no longer really intervene in Church matters, and changes to the Church Act could only be made on the initiative of the Church. With this background in mind, the positions of clergymen in social institutions (prisons, the army, universities and other educational institutions, and hospitals) could be seen to signify continuation of the previous social status and role of religion in the public space. The debate initiated by the Criminal Sanctions Agency regarding the organisation of the employment of prison chaplains can be understood as part of this phenomenon: the distancing trend between the Church and the State.

10.6   Research Data[16]

From prisoners' own self-identification, a Christian background is more common among prisoners than in the rest of the population. Some 90% of female prisoners (66% of all women in Finland) and 78% of male prisoners (56% of all men in Finland) describe themselves as having a Christian background. The division of prisoners into denominations corresponds to that of the rest of the population, with certain exceptions (Fig. 10.1). There are more members of the Pentecostal Movement and members of several denominations, in particular among female prisoners, than in the rest of the population. There are also more members of the Orthodox Church among prisoners than in the rest of the population. The reason for this is that most prisoners from former Soviet countries describe themselves as Orthodox. Among Russian-speaking prisoners, religion, language and culture are entwined – the majority of these prisoners (86%) say that they are Orthodox. For them, religiousness and the desire to belong to their church is strong. This has led to a significant

---

[15] With their arrangements regarding prison chaplains, Nordic countries, with the exception of Sweden, have adopted the approach that government officials should safeguard prisoners' rights to practise religion and pastoral care by allocating resources for employing prison chaplains. However, there are vast differences in the relationship between the State and the Church in Nordic countries. In Finland, the church has, administratively, been more independent of the State than in other Nordic countries. In Sweden, the formal separation of the Church and the State is relatively recent. In Norway, too, the administrative separation of the church from the state has been quite recently strengthened. Only in Denmark can we talk about a formal state church. Then again, the tax system of the Finnish Church – collecting church taxes as part of general taxation – has led to the Finnish Church having the most solid financial base among the Nordic national churches (Kjems 2016).

[16] Data in chapter 10.6 originally published in Työryhmän raportti 2015, used by a kind permission of the Church Council of the Evangelical Lutheran Church of Finland.

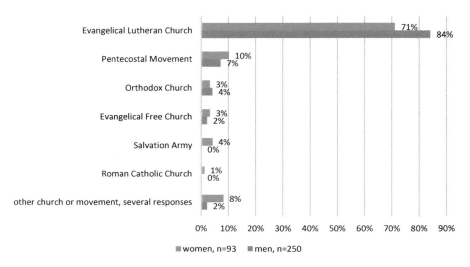

Fig. 10.1 Prisoners' membership in denominations

deficiency in resources in Finnish prisons, regarding Russian-speaking Orthodoxy, as the resources of the Finnish Orthodox Church for Russian-speaking work are meagre.[17]

More than half of all male prisoners and around two thirds of all female prisoners say that they are religious, and almost half of the men and more than half of the women consider their faith to be fairly or very important (Tables 10.1 and 10.2).

Only 4% of women and 7% of men reported a change in membership of a religious community during their time in prison. On the other hand, one third of the respondents reported having experienced a change in their religiousness during their time in prison, and the majority of those mentioned some kind of religious homecoming, or re-seeking contact with their own religious community.

More than half of prisoners wish to have contact with their church (Fig. 10.2). Among the prisoners wishing for contact with Christianity, it is common to wish for contact with several denominations. This is the opinion of a third of the women and a fifth of the men. Male prisoners wish for contact with the Evangelical Lutheran Church more than female prisoners (60% of men, 45% of women). Almost all Russian-speaking prisoners wish for contact with the Orthodox Church. Sixty percent of the prisoners who identify with Islam (90% of them identify as Muslims, and 10% not Muslims but with an Islamic background) wish for contact with the Islamic community, and 80% of them do not consider the branch of Islam to be significant.

---

[17] The Finnish Orthodox Church operates in Finnish. There are only a few Orthodox chaplains, who speak fairly fluent Russian. In some of the largest prisons in Southern Finland, the Orthodox Church has been able to serve the prisoners in Russian, owing to the appointment of a part-time prison chaplain. However, the number of foreign prisoners has grown rapidly during the past few years (Sect. 10.3). Therefore, there is a need for more Russian-speaking chaplaincy resources.

Table 10.1 Prisoners' own views of their religiosity

		Men (%)	Women (%)	Men (n)	Women (n)
Own religiousness	Extremely/very religious	19	25	48	23
	Somewhat religious	37	45	92	41
	Not religious or non-religious	23	11	56	10
	Somewhat/very/extremely non-religious	21	19	52	17
	All	100	100	248	91

Table 10.2 Significance of faith to prisoners

		Men (%)	Women (%)	Men (n)	Women (n)
How important is your faith?	Very important	21	31	56	31
	Fairly important	24	23	64	23
	Important to some extent	29	23	77	23
	Not that important	12	10	33	10
	Not important at all	15	13	40	13
	All	100	100	270	100

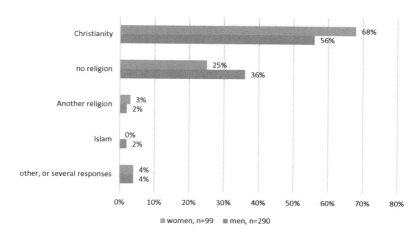

Fig. 10.2 Prisoners want to have contact with their denomination during their time in prison

The significance of religion to prisoners is also manifested in their attitude to the ceremonies, teachings and traditions of their religion. These are considered important by 85–93% (Fig. 10.3).

Participation in services among prisoners is higher than among the rest of the population. Half of the female prisoners and a fifth of the male prisoners attend a service monthly, with a fifth of the female prisoners attending a service weekly.

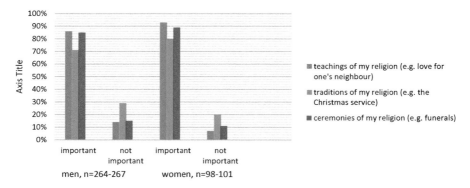

Fig. 10.3 The significance to prisoners of the teachings, traditions and ceremonies of their religion

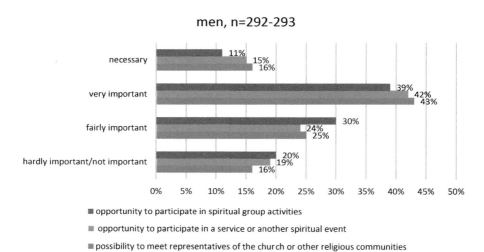

Fig. 10.4 Male prisoners' view of the necessity of different forms of religious activity

Some 70% of all female prisoners and 60% of the male prisoners attend church at least once during their time in prison. Almost half of the men and more than half of the women participate in spiritual group activities in prison. More than half of the prisoners meet with church workers and volunteers. Religious activities (spiritual events, group activities, individual meetings) are considered at least fairly important by 80–90% of prisoners (Figs. 10.4 and 10.5).

Half of all prisoners attend a pastoral care discussion with a prison chaplain during their time in prison (Fig. 10.6). The most common topic in the pastoral care discussions is relationships. Content relating to relationships can be found in nearly all pastoral discussions. Other typical topics of pastoral care discussions include problems related to imprisonment in general and anxiety caused by being a prisoner.

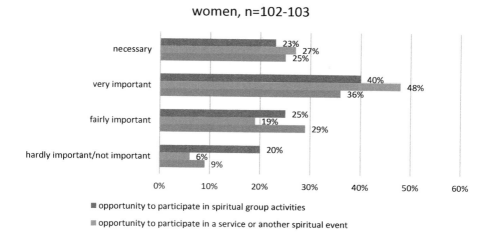

Fig. 10.5 Female prisoners' view of the necessity of different forms of religious activity

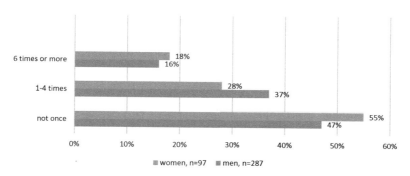

Fig. 10.6 Prisoners' participation in individual pastoral care in prison

Spiritual issues and philosophical questions of life are also regularly discussed in pastoral care.

Prisoners emphasise the difference between talking to a chaplain and talking to a psychologist, social worker or rehabilitation worker, even when the topic of discussion is the same. According to prisoners, the role of the chaplain is different. Discussions with a chaplain are marked with a different kind of confidentiality and freedom. According to prisoners, with a chaplain they can talk about their issues and experiences more as parts of their life as a whole, whereas with other workers the focus is on issues relating to their profession.

Although prisoners do not explicitly speak of the existential dimension in their answers, it is justifiable to say that their discussions with the chaplain have an existential approach, as they discuss the prisoner's life holistically. Structures of religion and pastoral care also offer tools for such discussions with prisoners who have

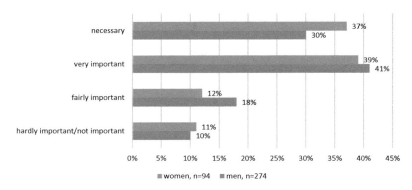

Fig. 10.7 Prisoners' view on the necessity of pastoral care in prisons

distanced themselves from religion. The prisoners' responses create a picture of pastoral care and a chaplain as a kind of existential mirror that the prisoners can use to examine themselves. Prisoners emphasise that an important aspect of pastoral care is the absolute confidentiality based on confessional secret, and that the chaplain represents something other than the prison – even if they are employed by it. As one prisoner said, "Discussions with the chaplain and spiritual activities must be out of reach of the authorities, they must be an area free of authorities". Therefore, it is easy to understand that the majority of male prisoners would prefer chaplains to be employed by the Church rather than the current arrangement (chaplains employed by the prison).

Three quarters of prisoners consider pastoral care in prison very important or necessary, and 90% of prisoners consider it at least fairly important. Non-Finnish prisoners and members of other religions, especially Muslims, also find pastoral care in prison important, and report it to have been helpful (Fig. 10.7).[18]

Compared with other pastors, prison chaplains carry out a large amount of individual pastoral care. On average, a full-time prison chaplain will have 500–800 individual pastoral care discussions every year. Prisoners also consider it important for prisons to have a full-time chaplain. The prisoners stress that when the need arises, it is important to have a chaplain available quickly onsite rather than having to wait around a week for a chaplain to visit. According to inmates, the chaplains should move among prisoners, seeking contact with those incapable of seeking help themselves, particularly those in danger of social exclusion.

---

[18] It is common for prisoners to prefer to participate in the communal practice of religion (religious events and group activities) organised according to their own religious tradition – whereas prisoners of other denominations and religions are more willing to have individual discussions with the Evangelical Lutheran prison chaplain than with a representative of their own faith group. Factors behind this may include the fact that, as a prison employee, a prison chaplain is able to provide better advice on practical life problems than a visiting faith group representative, and the fact that traditions in other denominations and religions may not include the Finnish (Western) tradition of individual pastoral care with a therapeutic approach and involvement in practical issues (e.g. substance misuse, social problems).

Most prison governors also find it important for prisons to have a full-time chaplain and that a range of spiritual activities and pastoral care are available. According to prison governors, it has an impact on the atmosphere and well-being in prison. Like prisoners, prison governors would prefer the administrative arrangement of prison chaplains to be part of the Church organisation rather than the prison organisation. According to the governors, management and resourcing of religious activities is more suitable for the Church than for the State administration.[19]

Then again, when prison governors were asked who was responsible for issues related to the practice of religion for the prison, all governors said it was a responsibility of the prison chaplain. If prison chaplains were not prison staff, certain changes would be inevitable: prison chaplains not employed by the prison would not have the responsibility of a (prison) official to take care of the coordination of all the religious activities in prison, as they now do. This alternative is particularly problematic for minority denominations engaged in prison work. They see that such a change would have a negative impact on the widespread observance of the right to practise religion when different religious groups are concerned. According to minority faith groups, prisons need a full-time chaplain to coordinate and support the prison work carried out by all groups. The other faith groups have not approved of the idea either that prisons should not employ a religious professional (with a required religious education) to ensure the observance of all prisoners' rights to practise their religion.[20]

Prison chaplains prefer to keep their office in State administration, as they feel that it gives them better opportunities for providing versatile support for prisoners. On this issue, the hierarchy of the Evangelical Lutheran Church of Finland has the same view as the prison chaplains. The Church has emphasised the responsibility of the State to ensure the fulfilment of prisoners' basic rights, including the right to practise religion, which means that the state is responsible for resources for the prison chaplaincy.

10.7   Conclusion

There have been no signs of the prison administration or the Criminal Sanctions Agency being anti-religion, anti-Church or anti-chaplaincy. The debate is more concerned with wider changes in the personnel structure and work organisation in prisons, including the role of the institutional chaplain. There may be a trend towards seeing the chaplain's role more narrowly focused on "purely religious

---

[19] However, a third of the governors of closed prisons prefer prison chaplains to be employed by the prison to ensure seamless cooperation within the prison community and the rehabilitative team in particular.

[20] Non-Finnish prisoners are even more adamant than Finnish prisoners about the role of the prison chaplain in providing contact with their own religious communities and the opportunity to practise their own religion.

matters" – which would be a misinterpretation of prisoners' needs and of religion – in a sense of lived religion. This may also be an issue of societal development, in line with the latest theoretical interpretations of secularisation: the progress of secularisation has not followed the assumptions of earlier secularisation theory. In other words, the progress of modernisation has not been followed by the fading of the public role of religion.[21] Rather, religion has remained on the social stage, even if changes have occurred in the forms of religion and its relation to society. Thus, according to one of the most renowned representatives of the secularisation debate, Peter Berger, both secularisation and religion have progressed and developed side by side, as complementary ways of existence in relation to the world, rather than as opposites.[22] This kind of phenomenon can be detected in the role of religion in Finnish prisons[23]: a positive attitude towards the role of religion in the public space, but also a tendency to separate the roles of religious actors and the government.

Finns' attitudes towards religion in the public space are surveyed every fourth year by the Church Research Institute in studies on Finnish religiousness. According to the latest study, 81% of Finns have a positive attitude towards chaplains being present in prisons (54% very positive), and only 4% have a negative attitude.[24] Finns' attitudes and the views of prison governors show that religion continues to play a strong role in the public space in prisons. However, the most fertile ground for religion has always been the semi-private space, the area of the family and close relationships. This also seems to be the case with religion in prisons (see text for Fig. 10.6), as with the rest of the population.

According to my material on prisoners, the collective dimension of religion and the individual dimension of religion are inseparably entwined. They cannot replace

---

[21] E.g. Berger 1973, Luckmann 1967.

[22] Berger 2014, 51–67. According to another noted secularisation theorist, Thomas Luckmann (2008), the factor explaining the existence of religion is humans' experience of insecurity and powerlessness when facing reality. Since early times, religion and churches as institutions in particular, have provided protection for humans' ever-endangered reality. Modernisation has changed the nature of threats, but the fundamental endangerment of humans' existence and the individual's powerlessness is still present. These factors generate and maintain religion, and they can explain why secularisation did not eradicate religion, even with a change in the forms of religion.

[23] See, for example, Francis and Penny 2014, 323–329. In the modern religion–sociological debate various trends are represented by Bruce 2010 and Davie 2010, for example, with the former seeing the progress of secularisation as an inevitable element in the development of Western modernisation, whereas the latter deems it necessary to change the paradigms of social sciences to create approaches that account for the ever-permeating presence of religion in modern society.

[24] Ketola (2016), 203–205. In the past 4 years (2012–2015), the share of those with a positive attitude towards chaplains in prison has remained the same when compared with the previous 4 years, but among those with a positive attitude, the share of those with a very positive attitude has increased from 47% to 54%. As much as 90% of members of religious communities have a positive attitude towards chaplains being present in prisons. This view is also shared by the majority of non-members (58%). Younger people have the most positive attitude. A negative attitude towards chaplains being present in prisons is associated with negative attitudes towards religion and a non-religious identity. In addition to age, positive attitudes are associated with higher income levels, Lutheran values and a commitment to Christianity.

each other, however, which leads to the necessity in prisons of taking adequate action to guarantee both dimensions of the practice of religion. With regard to motivation for religious activity among prisoners, the effect of the individual dimension of religion is stronger than that of the social dimension. The key motivator is the experience of inner help sought in religion – calming oneself down, maintaining hope and the alleviation of negative thoughts and feelings. This may also explain the fact that the prisoners, who most likely turn to religion and pastoral care for help, were the same prisoners who reported greater than average problems in various fields of life, such as social relationships, mental health and substance misuse. The significance of religion in prisons, therefore, can be psychologically interpreted as a means of coping mentally with a life crisis.[25]

Society also sets prisoners a social challenge of coping with strong social deprivation. Prisoners have few possibilities of controlling their surroundings and their roles. The role of a prisoner involves what Erving Goffmann called the deprivation of the self, where their own identity fades and is replaced with an institutional role, until they adopt the institutional role as their primary identity.[26] Imprisonment creates a feeling of powerlessness. Religion offers relief from social deprivation. From a Parsonian perspective, religion adds the possibility of transcendental reference to an unbearable reality. In the dilemma of the meaning of life, religion gives prisoners a chance of faith in meanings that surpass the deficiencies in their current reality.[27] From a Weberian perspective, the function of religion in prison, therefore, is the same as the function of religion in general – but with different weighting coefficients. Religion offers a new self-image to replace the one that has become unbearable, and ways of expressing beliefs and values that promote coping.[28]

From a Durkheimian perspective, in religion a social community manifests veiled in divinity.[29] Prisoners are cut off from the social community. They are not part of normal society, although the normative task of imprisonment is to help prisoners to return to society. Thus, religion in prisons can be seen as a return of the forbidden social. From the Foucauldian point of view, religion in prisons offers opportunities for discursive counter-processes opposing institutional power. With religion, prisoners can strive for discursive control of the social reality that they have lost. Identifying with the pro-social values and role expectations of religion may enable prisoners to change their role in the prison community, in relation to the prison institution and in wider society. Religious symbols are used to create order and meaning in a mentally depressive and socially empty world, where he/she has little control of what happens to him/her. The world, which is deemed insignificant

---

[25] See, for example, Pargament 1997, Greer 2002, Gartner and Larson 1991, Clear and Sumter 2002, Levitt and Loper 2009, Mandhouj et al. 2014.

[26] See Goffman 1961.

[27] See O'Dea and Aviad 1983, 5–7.

[28] See O'Dea and Aviad 1983, 5–6, 11–16.

[29] See O'Dea and Aviad 1983, 12–13.

and distant, is sanctified again to give it significance and to claim ownership through religion.

To conclude: religion in prisons is a wide and diverse phenomenon. Compared with other nations, Finnish inmates seem to be more religious. Prisoners need and use religion for many purposes: spiritual, mental, family related and other social needs. All of these together form the religious needs of the inmates. The individual and collective dimensions of religions are as important, and both must be properly regarded by authorities and religious communities. The religious needs of inmates justify the role of full-time prison chaplains, as well as the wide availability of religious activities by many faith groups. The freedom of choice by any inmate is a guiding principle for participation in these activities.

The latest development in the societal debate related to prison chaplains (see Sect. 10.5) has been the conclusion of the Criminal Sanctions Agency, together with the Ministry of Justice, to maintain the positions of prison chaplains among the staff of the Criminal Sanctions Agency. Thereby, the job description of the prison chaplains can further include wide responsibilities in the rehabilitative activities by the prison and a responsibility to coordinate and ensure the right to religion for all inmates, irrespective of the religion or other world view. On the other hand, the role of faith groups in the prison ministry, especially at the time of the prisoner's release from prison, shall be strengthened. Special attention will be given to the guidance and coordination of the prison chaplaincy and faith groups in the prison ministry. This task will be carried out through cooperation of the Criminal Sanctions Agency and the faith communities.

References

Berger, P. L. (1973). *The social reality of religion*. Harmondsworth: Penguin.

Berger, P. L. (2014). *The many altars of modernity: toward a paradigm for religion in a pluralist age*. Boston: De Gruyter.

Bruce, S. (2010). Secularization. In B. Turner (Ed.), *The new Blackwell companion to the sociology of religion* (pp. 125–140). Malden: Wiley-Blackwell.

Clear, T. R., & Sumter, M. T. (2002). Prisoners, prison and religion: religion and adjustment to prison. In T. P. O'Connor & N. J. Pallone (Eds.), *Religion, the community and the rehabilitation of criminal offenders* (pp. 127–159). New York: Haworth Press.

Davie, G. (2010). Resacralization. In B. Turner (Ed.), *The new Blackwell companion to the sociology of religion* (pp. 160–178). Malden: Wiley-Blackwell.

Francis, L. J., & Penny, G. (2014). Gender differences in religion. In V. Saroglou (Ed.), *Religion, personality and social behavior* (pp. 313–337). New York: Taylor&Francis.

Gartner, J., Dave, B., Larson, D., & Allen, G. D. (1991). Religious commitment and mental health: A review of the empirical literature. *Journal of Psychology and Theology, 19*(1), 6–25.

Goffman, E. (1961). *Asylums: Essays on the social situation of mental patients and other inmates*. New York: Doubleday.

Greer, K. (2002). Walking an emotional tightrope: Managing emotions in a women's prison. *Symbolic Interaction, 25*(1), 117–139.

Ketola, K. (2016). *Osallistuva luterilaisuus. Suomen evankelisluterilainen kirkko vuosina 2012–2015: Tutkimus kirkosta ja suomalaisista*. Kirkon tutkimuskeskuksen julkaisuja 125.

Helsinki: Kirkon tutkimuskeskus. [Committed Lutheranism. The Evangelical-Lutheran Church of Finland 2012–2015: A report on the Church and Finns.]

Kjems, S. (2016). *Comparing the financial situation of seven majority churches in Northern Europe.* Presentation in The 23rd Nordic conference for the sociology of religion. Helsinki.

Levitt, L., & Loper, A. B. (2009). The influence of religious participation on the adjustment of female inmates. *American Journal of Orthopsychiatry, 79*(1), 1–7.

Luckmann, T. (1967). *The invisible religion: The problem of religion in modern society.* New York: Macmillan.

Luckmann, T. (2008). Religion, human power and powerlessness. In E. Barker (Ed.), *The centrality of religion in social life: Essays in honour of James A. Beckford* (pp. 175–187). Aldershot: Ashgate.

Mandhouj, O., et al. (2014). Spirituality and religion among French prisoners: An effective coping resource? *International Journal of Offender Therapy and Comparative Criminology, 58*(7), 821–834.

O'Dea, T. F., & Aviad, J. O.'. D. (1983). *The sociology of religion.* Englewood Cliffs: Prentice-Hall.

Pargament, K. I. (1997). *The psychology of religion and coping: Theory, research, practice.* New York: Guilford Press.

Työryhmän raportti. (2015). *Uskonnonharjoittaminen vankiloissa – Selvitys Uskonnonharjoittamiseen vankiloissa liittyvistä kysymyksistä.* Suomen ev.lut. kirkon julkaisuja 28. Helsinki: Kirkkohallitus. [Report of a working party. The practice of religion in prisons – A report on the issues related to the practice of religion in prisons.]

Chapter 11
France: Worship in Prison – Legal Framework and Religious Experience

Vincente Fortier

Abstract Although the exercise of religion in prison is a fundamental freedom, it is regulated in the light of the specific conditions of the prison environment. The French Code of Criminal Procedure, case law and international texts adopted by France provide the legal framework. But the effective implementation of freedom of religion in prisons faces a number of challenges.

11.1   Introduction

The exercise of worship can be defined as rendering homage to God, or to beings regarded as divine, resulting in a set of requirements and practices, as well as community ceremonies or assemblies. For the believer, worship involves participating in religious services, celebrating feasts, meeting with the minister of worship, observing religious prescriptions (for example, praying, which implies the possession of prayer books and religious objects; or following dietary restrictions).

Freedom of religion, therefore, has two dimensions, one collective, which is carried out "in the form of organised and codified worships and rituals in which the ecclesial authorities are the authorising officers and guardians" (Gonzalez 2013: 1), and without which freedom of religion cannot flourish, and the other dimension is individual. The collective dimension is at the level of the religious institution or group, whereas the second takes place at the level of the believer, allowing the exercise of his/her freedom of religious convictions while respecting his autonomy of will.

Freedom of religion (understood as freedom of the internal and external forum) is a fundamental freedom, the exercise of which is protected and guaranteed by internal provisions (Article 1 of the law of 9 December 1905; Article 2 of the

V. Fortier (✉)
University of Strasbourg/CNRS, Strasbourg, France
e-mail: vfortier@unistra.fr

© Springer Nature Switzerland AG 2020
J. Martínez-Ariño, A.-L. Zwilling (eds.), *Religion and Prison: An Overview of Contemporary Europe*, Boundaries of Religious Freedom: Regulating Religion in Diverse Societies 7, https://doi.org/10.1007/978-3-030-36834-0_11

Constitution of 4 October 1958) and international provisions ratified by France (European Convention for the Protection of Human Rights and Fundamental Freedoms, especially in Article 9; International Covenant on Civil and Political Rights of 19 December 1966, especially in Article 18).

However, certain circumstances may affect the freedom to exercise religion, some of which are relevant to the place where the religion is practised. Because of their nature, their specific characteristics and their population, certain places imply constraints in terms of safety or health standards and, consequently, require adaptation, limitations or even prohibition of the exercise of worship. This is the case with healthcare institutions whose specific requirements take precedence over the free exercise of religion (Fortier and Vialla 2013), but also, in a very different way, in prisons, closed places where the salvation of souls is played out (Béraud et al. 2016; Fornerod 2016; Schmitz 2017).

How is the practice of worship ensured in detention centres? Is the detainee/believer's freedom of worship respected, under what conditions and in what manner? How can we reconcile the security requirements of the prison environment with the requirements of conscience linked, for example, to the possession of objects of worship? What difficulties do believers encounter? How can we articulate the rites and intense moments of the different religions that coexist in prison with the constraints of prison life? Is there equal treatment between different religions?

The problem is complex for at least two reasons: on the one hand, the "public" is captive, but as the Council of State reminded us in 2014,[1] it cannot, in principle, be totally deprived of the right to practise its religion. For example, the High Administrative Court has recently made clear that persons placed in disciplinary cells retain both the right to speak with a chaplain outside the presence of a supervisor, and the right to the authorisation provided for in Article R. 57-9-7 of the Code of Criminal Procedure to receive or keep in their possession the objects of religious practice and books necessary to their spiritual life, even though the provisions of Article R. 57-7-44 state that placement in a disciplinary cell entails the suspension of access to activities.[2]

On the other hand, here undoubtedly more than in any other place, the interpenetration, the superposition of spaces (what is public space and what is private space? How can a private space be defined?), is the source of ambiguities, tensions and sometimes hesitant jurisprudential solutions. It must be added that, in the same space (the prison), different statutes coexist (penitentiary staff subject to a strict obligation of neutrality versus "users" of the prison service in principle free to manifest their religion).

After a brief presentation of the legal framework of worship in French prisons, we will examine how this legal framework is implemented.

---

[1] *Le juge administratif et l'expression des convictions religieuses*, Les dossiers thématiques du Conseil d'Etat 2014 (on-line).
[2] CE, 11 juin 2014, M.S., no. 365237.

11.2 Legal Framework of the Exercise of Worship in Places of Detention

This legal framework is, under French law, Article 1 of the Act of 9 December 1905 on the Separation of Churches and the State, which establishes the obligation of the State to organise the legal regime of freedom of religion. This article states that "the Republic shall ensure freedom of conscience. It guarantees the free exercise of worship under the restrictions set out below in the interest of public order." The very choice of terms (ensuring, guaranteeing) indicates that the State has a positive obligation to adjust this freedom so that it can be exercised in practice.

These arrangements sometimes take the form of maintaining chaplaincies in public services, so that people who are excluded from civilian life because of their status (e.g. military personnel) or condition (e.g. prisoners, hospitalised patients) can worship.

Thus, Article 2 of the 1905 Act, after stating that the Republic neither recognises nor subsidises any religion, and consequently abolishing from the State budget expenditure on the exercise of worship, provides an exception concerning expenditure on the services of the chaplaincy intended to ensure the free exercise of worship in public establishments such as high schools, schools, hospices, asylums and prisons.

This does not infringe the religious neutrality of the State. This positive action of adjusting to denominations is aimed at correcting the imbalance arising from the fact that the persons concerned see their possibility of worshipping compromised or rendered more difficult by particular conditions. Neutrality becomes somewhat "active" even if both terms seem contradictory. This does not result in any particular favour given to one religion over another. The public authorities have an obligation to ensure the free exercise of worship services by persons who, as in hospitals or prisons, are unable to do so on their own. The public body is therefore liable if it does not take adequate measures to guarantee the freedom of worship of those in a particular situation. For example, the Council of State questioned the State's responsibility for not having approved a sufficient number of ministers to allow any detained person to practise the religion that they claim, in the case of an imprisoned person who is a Jehovah's Witness.[3]

Symbolically, the regulation of prison chaplaincies is included in the Code of Criminal Procedure in Chapter X on "Preparatory actions for the reintegration of detainees" in the section entitled "Concerning spiritual assistance". According to Article R 57-9-3, "Every detained person shall be able to satisfy the requirements of his/her religious, moral or spiritual life. Upon his/her arrival in the institution, s/he shall be advised of his/her right to receive a visit from a minister of religion and to attend religious services and worship meetings organised by persons authorised for such purposes." Articles R 57-9-4 to R 57-9-7 provide for the organisation of services, the possibility for detained persons to meet with the chaplain and the

---

[3] CE, 16 October 2013, Keeper of the Seals v/M. F. and others, no. 351115.

authorisation to "receive or keep in their possession objects of religious practice and books necessary for their spiritual life".

Articles D 439 to D 439-5 lay down more specifically the appointment of chaplains and the procedures for carrying out their duties.

One must add to this first set of rules Article 26 of the Penitentiary Act of 24 November 2009, which states: "Prisoners have the right to freedom of opinion, conscience and religion. They may worship as they see fit, under conditions appropriate to the organisation of the premises, without any limitations other than those imposed by the security and good order of the establishment."[4]

Finally, as a source of inspiration, as they do not have binding force, we should mention the European Prison Rules,[5] first adopted in 1973, revised in 1987 and again in 2006, which are aimed at standardising the prison policies of the Council of Europe member states, and at ensuring the adoption of common practices and standards. Rules 29-1 to 29-3 are devoted to freedom of thought, conscience and religion. Rule 29.1 states that "the right to freedom of thought, conscience and religion of prisoners shall be respected". Rule 29.2 states that "the prison system shall be organised, as far as possible, in such a way as to enable prisoners to practise their religion and follow their philosophy, to participate in services or meetings conducted by authorised representatives, to receive them in private and to hold books of a religious nature". Rule 29 (3) prohibits the coercion of prisoners to practise a religion: "Prisoners shall not be compelled to practise a religion or to follow a philosophy, to participate in religious services or meetings, to participate in religious practices or to accept the visit of a representative of any religion or philosophy."

The French texts and the case law clearly guarantee detainees the freedom to worship and respect for their religious convictions, adjusting the general rule so that it can be applied to everyone in an indiscriminate manner without running counter to the conscience imperative. Moreover, the Decree of 30 April 2013[6] created standard internal regulations applicable to penitentiary establishments, Article 18 of which relates to spiritual assistance. The last three paragraphs recognise the right of prisoners to worship, either in their cells or during religious services.

In its note of 16 July 2014 on the practice of worship in detention,[7] the management of the prison administration indicates the obligations it has: the obligation to organise access to worship to guarantee the effectiveness of the religious freedom of detained persons; the obligation to combat all forms of proselytism, as well as radical or sectarian aberrations; the obligation of neutrality of all persons who participate in the public prison service. However, the implementation of this legal

---

[4] JORF no. 0273 2009, p. 20192.

[5] Council of Europe, Committee of Ministers, Rec (2006) 2.

[6] Decree no. 2013-368 2013, on the standard rules of procedure for prisons, *JORF* no. 0103, 3 May 2013, p. 7609.

[7] BOMJ no. 2014, 29 August 2014.

framework remains complex. The religious experience of prisoners and the difficulties encountered by the prison administration show that the practice of worship in prison sometimes fails to meet the requirements of the texts.

11.3 Implementation of the Legal Framework

The prison administration organises and sets the framework for worship in prisons. It organises access to worship services and must enable prisoners to live their religion.

11.3.1 Chaplaincy

Seven denominations are nationally approved to provide chaplaincy services in prisons: the three main Christian religions (Catholic, Protestant, Orthodox), Judaism, Islam, Buddhism and Jehovah's Witnesses. However, the administrative courts considered that the administrative authorities should exercise their discretion and not refer to a mere list of "recognised" religions.

The status of religious staff working in prisons varies. Some are regular chaplains (among which there are both paid and volunteer chaplains, the latter being the most numerous) and others are chaplaincy assistants.

According to the figures provided by the Ministry of Justice, the distribution of religious workers, as of 1 January 2015, among the different denominations, is as follows: 760 for Catholic worship; 317 for Protestant worship; 193 for Muslim worship; 75 for Jewish worship; 52 for Orthodox worship; 111 intervenors for Jehovah's Witnesses; 10 for Buddhist worship; and, finally, 50 intervenors for other faiths (Pentecostals, Adventists, Evangelicals Protestants, Church of the Seventh-Day Adventists, Coptic Church).[8]

These figures are important because they raise the problem of the place given to minority religions in this system. Regarding Islam, there was an increase in the number of religious workers between 2012 and 2015. They were only 151 in 2012.

The procedure for approving prison chaplaincy workers is set out in the circular of 20 September 2012.[9] Chaplains devote all or part of their time to the spiritual care of detained persons; to the celebration of religious services and the organisation of worship meetings; and to the organisation of religious feasts, in conjunction with the administration. The functions are defined in article R. 57-9-4 of the Code of Criminal Procedure.

---

[8]The numbers differ slightly in the table provided by the International Prisons Observatory, French section (workforce on 1 August 2015).

[9]Circular 2012 on the accreditation of paid or volunteer chaplains, volunteer chaplaincy auxiliaries in correctional institutions, and of occasional chaplaincy attendants, NOR: JUSK 1240021C.

The chaplaincies are structured at the local, regional and national levels. The dialogue is constant with the prison administration, whose chaplains are the only interlocutors for all matters relating to their worship.

Detainees may, at their request and as often as they wish, consult with the chaplains of their confession. No measure or sanction shall interfere with this ability. Article R. 57-9-6, paragraph 2, of the Code of Criminal Procedure stipulates that meetings with chaplains "shall take place outside the presence of a supervisor, either in a visiting room, in a room provided for that purpose, or in the cell of the detained person and, if he or she is in the disciplinary district, in a room determined by the head of the institution".

The prison governor may authorise the handing over of the cell keys to the chaplain, considering security features, the configuration of the penitentiary establishment, seniority and regularity of the chaplain's intervention. It is also provided that persons detained engaged in a collective work activity who request to speak with a chaplain shall also benefit from such an interview outside working hours or, exceptionally, by interrupting their activity, provided that such interruption does not affect the activities of other detained persons.

Correspondence with chaplains is also regulated. According to Article R. 57-8-20 of the Code of Criminal Procedure, "Correspondence addressed to chaplains approved by the establishment or dispatched by such persons shall be addressed in a sealed envelope bearing on the envelope all the information necessary to indicate the quality and professional address of the addressee or sender". However, written correspondence between an inmate in one institution and a chaplain or volunteer chaplaincy assistant at another institution remains controllable.

Since Decree No. 2017-756 of 3 May 2017,[10] paid military, hospital and prison chaplains recruited from 1 October 2017 onwards must hold a diploma in civil and civic education or, failing that, undertake to obtain it within 2 years of their recruitment. These provisions are applicable overseas only if the diploma can be obtained by distance education or in the territory itself. A decree of 5 May 2017 sets out the procedures for approving training courses that will be authorised to award this diploma.

As Curtit (2017) points out, this new obligation of training imposed by the public authorities is relatively original in an area where religious authorities have, until now, enjoyed complete autonomy to designate chaplains. The author rightly notes that the requirement of "religious conformity" required by the religious institution is now supplemented by a "civic conformity" imposed by the administration.

Curtit (2017) points out that the requirement for new recruits to obtain a diploma is perceived as an interference of the State by certain Protestant and Catholic religious leaders who have their own recruitment criteria and provide university-level training, which they wish to see approved in the new system of equivalence. On the part of Muslim leaders, this reform is rather well received, but the national hospital chaplain insists on the need to recruit more Muslim chaplains, who still very often

---

[10] JORF no. 0106 2017, text no. 105.

carry out their duties without being paid. The obligation to obtain a diploma is imposed only on paid chaplains, even if they have a small quota of hours, whereas volunteer chaplains who do not receive any public remuneration – but who are in some cases paid by their religious institution – are not concerned, even though they constitute a large part of the staff in hospital or penitentiary chaplainships. "The demand for training and professionalisation of these staff must be accompanied by a continuation of the effort to create new posts by the public authorities in order to guarantee the quality of the service offered, while reducing precarious situations by offering job opportunities in line with university training" (Curtit 2017: 580).

11.3.2   The Religious Experience of Prisoners

As of 13 June 2008, France set up a new administrative authority, the General Controller of places of deprivation of liberty (*contrôleur général des lieux de privation de liberté*), whose mission is to monitor the conditions under which persons deprived of their liberty are taken into care and transferred, to ensure that their fundamental rights are respected. In spring 2011, the General Controller of places of deprivation of liberty, Jean-Marie Delarue, issued an opinion on the exercise of worship in places of deprivation of liberty,[11] in which he highlighted some important difficulties encountered by detainees in their religious practice, in particular the possession of religious books and objects and compliance with dietary requirements.

11.3.2.1   Books and Religious Objects

Article R 57-9-7 of the Code of Criminal Procedure provides that " … detained persons shall be entitled to receive or keep in their possession the objects of religious practice and books necessary for their spiritual life". However, numerous cases of lack of respect for religious objects, or of detainees being prohibited from possessing them, have been reported to the General Controller. The General Controller considered, in his notice, that detainees should be allowed to possess the reference books related to their religion (Bible, Qur'an). This was often denied to them on the grounds that in places of detention and in their cells, prisoners are not allowed to possess hardcover books but only softcover books, for security reasons. The General Controller of places of deprivation of liberty recommended that an exception should be made for religious works and, therefore, that no distinction should be made between hard- and softcover books.

In its note of 16 July 2014, the Prison Administration Directorate stated that religious publications cannot be allowed if they contain "serious threats to the

---

[11] M. AB c. Director of the penitentiary centre of Saint-Quentin-Fallavier, request number 1302502. Notice of 24 March 2011, JO no. 0091 2011. Mr. Delarue was General Controller from 2008 to 2014. The controller general is currently Mrs. Adeline Hazan.

security of persons and institutions, or insulting or defamatory remarks, or signs directed against officers and collaborators of the public prison service as well as detainees", in accordance with Article 43 of the Penitentiary Act of 24 November 2009. It is not necessary to distinguish between hardcover books and others. The documentary resources of prison libraries shall reflect as far as possible the "interests of the entire prison population, in accordance with the Constitution and laws". In other words, all denominations must be represented in comparable proportions and works of proselytising, sectarian or radical nature are prohibited. When a doubt appears about a book, the director of a detention centre submits this question to the referee of the interregional direction in charge of *laïcité* and religions, who can consult the chaplain or another competent service.

With regard to religious journals, an interesting case concerning journals published by Jehovah's Witnesses was referred to Lille Administrative Court on 1 July 2003.[12] The director of a detention centre had refused to distribute the magazines *La tour de garde* (*The Watchtower*) and *Réveillez-vous* (*Wake up*) to detainees who had subscribed to them. The Administrative Tribunal rescinds administrative decisions on the grounds that:

> it has not been established that the content of these reviews posed a danger to public order, the safety of persons or that of the detention centre; that, therefore and subject to this reservation, given that it is not for the administration to promote or prevent the dissemination of religious beliefs, the reason for the decision of the detention centre according to which these reviews are published by a congregation whose sectarian character has been recognised by a parliamentary commission of inquiry is not among those who could legally justify the interruption of their dissemination, insofar as it ignores the principles of neutrality and secularism of the state.

As for religious objects, according to the General Controller's opinion issued in 2011, if their possession is to be supervised, each prisoner should be allowed to keep those whose size, nature and shape are not likely to endanger the security of the prison community or the prisoner himself. This is not always the case, and the General Controller of places of deprivation of liberty had received complaints concerning the disappearance or deliberate degradation of such objects, or contemptuous behaviour. The decision to deprive prisoners of such religious objects is in most cases not a decision to interfere in the religious life of the prisoner and to obstruct his/her practice, but rather ignorance on the part of prison staff of what is religious and what is not. It seems necessary for prison staff to be able to identify prayer objects such as phylacteries, ciboria, prayer mats etc.

In the annexe to its note dated 2014, the prison administration drew up an indicative list of the main religious objects authorised in detention. This document had to be brought to the attention of prison staff. These are calendars with prayer times (Muslim worship), rosaries (Christian, Muslim, Buddhist worship etc.), bell (Buddhist worship), cross (Christian worship), kippa (Jewish worship), reliquary pendant (Buddhist worship), *siwak* (Muslim worship), Buddha statuettes (Buddhist

---

[12] Administrative Court, Lille, chamber 6, 1 2003, no. 001519, *Juris-Data* no. 2003-225856.

worship), *talith* (Jewish worship), prayer mat (Muslim worship), *tefillin* or phylac-teries (Jewish worship) and *vajra* (Buddhist worship).

Prayer is allowed individually in the cell or collectively, in the presence of the chaplain, in the multifaith room. In this regard, and in accordance with Article R.57-9-5 of the Code of Criminal Procedure, each penitentiary establishment has a room dedicated to the practice of worship. Rooms of worship are often used by dif-ferent religions; their decoration should then be as neutral as possible.

11.3.2.2   Dietary Requirements of a Religious Nature

The issue of food and food bans linked to certain religions is another major problem in places of detention. Here again, it is necessary to recall the Code of Criminal Procedure which, in article D 354, provides that: "Prisoners shall be provided with a varied, well-prepared and well-presented diet, in accordance as regards quality and quantity to the rules of diet and hygiene, taking into account their age, state of health, the nature of their work and, as far as possible, their philosophical or reli-gious convictions". This provision is included in Article 9 of the Decree no. 2013-368 2013 on the standard internal regulations of penal institutions.

As the General Controller pointed out in his 2011 opinion, the question of pre-scribed food is all the less negligible because food (quantity and quality) is central to any individual deprived of liberty. Today, with rare exceptions, all places of depri-vation of liberty are able to provide a variety of meals. Few, however, offer foods that comply with ritual prescriptions. The result is, on the one hand, a shift in prac-tices, with people asking for vegetarian menus when they do not wish to deprive themselves of meat, and, on the other hand, real food deficiencies.

According to the above-mentioned opinion of the General Controller, places of deprivation of liberty must be organised to be able to provide menus that meet reli-gious requirements. Whenever food market conditions allow it, the supply of meat or other dishes prepared according to rites approved by religious authorities should be implemented. On the other hand, people who do not follow prescriptions should not have to endure dietary constraints that are not their own. Where it is not possible to do otherwise, the General Controller advocated allowing chaplains to introduce a limited amount of such foods.

The note on the practice of worship in detention of 2014 makes recommenda-tions to access to confessional foods. For example, it states that, during "inbound interviews", prisoners are asked to choose from three types of menu: traditional, meatless and pork-free (a change of diet during detention is always possible). But the prison administration does not offer confessional menus. Nevertheless, prison-ers may purchase products that meet religious standards or receive them on major religious holidays. Indeed, as recalled in the note from the prison administration, "Each penitentiary establishment, whether under public or delegated management, is required to organise this offer of confessional products". Detainees therefore have the opportunity to purchase food in accordance with religious requirements in can-teens. And "if there is no stock, the establishment shall take all necessary steps as soon as a detained person declares his intention to eat according to the precepts of his religion". Chaplains can bring compliant food to arrivals when the canteen does not offer it, while the necessary supply procedures are completed. In addition, the delivery of ritual parcels by chaplains is also foreseen and authorised under certain conditions.

Concerning food and religious requirements, we must recall the decision of the European Court of Human Rights of 7 December 2010.[13] In this case, a Polish Buddhist prisoner had repeatedly requested meatless meals, stating that he adhered strictly to Mahayana Buddhism's rules against meat. The Strasbourg Court emphasises that the refusal of the prison authorities to allow the person concerned to follow a vegetarian diet does fall within the scope of Article 9 of the Convention. Although prepared to accept that a decision to make special arrangements for a particular prisoner may have financial implications for the prison institution, the Court notes that the applicant, Mr. Jakobski, only requested a meat-free regime. His meals therefore did not have to be prepared, cooked and served in a specific way and did not require special products. The Court therefore considers that providing a vegetarian diet would not have caused any disruption in the management of the prison or a decline in the quality of meals served to other prisoners. The Court concludes that the authorities failed to strike a fair balance between the interests of the prison authorities and those of Mr. Jakobski, in violation of his rights under Article 9 of the Convention.

The Grenoble Administrative Court, in a rather audacious judgement of 7 November 2013,[14] declared illegal the refusal of a prison director to serve halal meals to prisoners, taking into account the constraint. According to the administrative judges, "It is constant that the meals served daily at the Saint-Quentin-Fallavier penitentiary centre do not include halal meat, whereas the prisoners are public service users in a forced situation". By refusing to serve halal meals when prisoners are under duress, and because this solution is being implemented in other institutions, which proves that it is not unreasonable, the director of the establishment violated Article 9 of the European Convention for the Protection of Human Rights and Fundamental Freedoms, Article 18 of the International Covenant on Civil and Political Rights, Article 26 of the Law of 24 November 2009 and Article R. 57-9-3 of the Criminal Procedure Code.

However, in three recent judgements, the Council of State considered that the prison administration was not obliged to provide prisoners with food that respected their religious beliefs.

The first decision, dated 16 July 2014,[15] concerns the case handled by the Grenoble Administrative Court on 7 November 2013, which ordered the director of the Saint-Quentin-Fallavier penitentiary centre to regularly offer halal meat menus to Muslim prisoners. The Minister of Justice had appealed this judgement

---

[13] CEDH 2010, case of Jakobski v. Poland, application no. 18429/06.
[14] M. AB c. Director of the penitentiary centre of Saint-Quentin-Fallavier, request number 1302502.
[15] CE 2014, Keeper of the Seals, Ministry of Justice c/M.B., no. 377145.

before the administrative court of Lyon,[16] asking this court and then the Council of State for the execution of the judgement to be suspended while his appeal was examined.

The Council of State granted the Minister's request for a stay of execution. The High Administrative Court notes, on the one hand, that the distribution of meals composed of halal meat within the penitentiary centre would represent a high cost and would entail major changes in the operation of the penitentiary centre that could, in the event of an annulment of the judgement of the Grenoble Administrative Court, be very difficult to challenge. The Council of State inferred from this that the execution of the judgement would have consequences that would be difficult to reverse.

The Council of State also considered that the arguments put forward by the Minister of Justice to contest the judgement, based on the violation of the principle of secularism and the incompatibility of the measure ordered by the administrative court with the requirements of detention, appear, in the state of the investigation, serious.

As a result, the obligation for the administration to comply with the injunction to offer meals composed of halal meat is suspended.

The second ruling of the Council of State dated 25 February 2015[17] specifies that "while the observance of food prescriptions may be regarded as a direct manifestation of religious beliefs and practises within the meaning of Article 9 of the European Convention for the Protection of Human Rights and Fundamental Freedoms, the provisions criticised, which aim to enable prisoners to exercise their religious beliefs in matters of food without, however, requiring the administration to guarantee, in all respects, the right to food that respects these convictions cannot be viewed, in the light of the general interest objective of maintaining good order in penal establishments and the material constraints inherent in the management of these establishments, as an excessive infringement of the right of the latter to practise their religion".

Finally, the judgement of 10 February 2016[18] settled the case initially raised before the Grenoble Administrative Court. The visas of the International Covenant on Civil and Political Rights, the European Convention for the Protection of Human Rights and Fundamental Freedoms, the Charter of Fundamental Rights of the European Union, the Code of Criminal Procedure, the law of 24 November 2009, Article 26 of the Code of Administrative Justice, the Council of State, although considering that "the observance of food prescriptions may be regarded as a direct manifestation of religious beliefs and practises", decided that "it belongs to the prison administration, which is not obliged to guarantee to prisoners, in all circumstances, a diet respecting their religious convictions, to allow, as far as possible in view of the material constraints specific to the management of these establishments

---

[16] Lyon 2014, no. 14LY0013.

[17] CE 2015, no. 375724.

[18] CE 2016, no. 385929, published in the Lebon compilation.

and in compliance with the general interest objective of maintaining good order in prison, the observance of dietary requirements resulting from religious beliefs and practises".

In the present case, the Council of State refers to the assessment made by the Lyon Administrative Court of Appeal, according to which "the [prison] administration provides all prisoners with menus without pork as well as vegetarian menus, which prisoners may request on the occasion of the main religious holidays, menus in accordance with the prescriptions of their religion and, finally, that the canteen system permits to acquire, in addition to the menus available, food or preparations containing halal meat; it has thus taken into account not only the fact that Muslim prisoners are not exposed to the risk of having to consume food prohibited by their religion, but also the fact that the administration ensures that they can, to a certain extent, consume food in accordance with the prescriptions of their religion".

As for the principle of equality, it "does not preclude different situations from being regulated differently or equality being derogated from on grounds of general interest, provided that the resulting difference in treatment is, in either case, related to the object of the norm which establishes it and is not manifestly disproportionate in relation to the differences in the situation likely to justify it". According to the Conseil d'Etat, "the Lyon Administrative Court of Appeal noted that the conditions under which the daily menu offer is organised in the Saint-Quentin-Fallavier penitentiary centre, recalled in point 4 above, are the same for all detained persons, whether or not they practise a religion and irrespective of the religion they practise, including the possibility of using the canteen system".

However, not all prisoners have the financial resources to obtain compliant food. The Council of State recalls that persons detained on condition of income may receive assistance in kind from the State. Considering this possibility, the High Administrative Court considers that "it is for the prison administration, when the arrangements for organising the daily supply of menus it chooses involve, to ensure that the obligations mentioned in point 3 above are respected, that persons detained may obtain supplementary food through the canteen system in accordance with the requirements of their religion, to guarantee to those who lack sufficient resources the possibility of exercising such a right by providing them, within the limits of its budgetary and supply constraints, with appropriate assistance in kind for this purpose".

11.4 Conclusion

In a file entitled "Religion in prison" (12 July 2015),[19] the French section of the International Prison Observatory notes that "religion occupies an important place in prison but rarely as a problem" compared with "the idleness, overcrowding,

---

[19] https://oip.org/analyse/dossier-la-religion-en-prison/

violence and powerlessness that make up the inmate's daily life". Nevertheless, the demand for spirituality is important, as is the phenomenon of the intensification of religious practices, according to the same file. The situations are complex, subtle distinctions must be made, and an amalgam of religious fundamentalism and violent radicalism must be avoided.

Anyway, the fact remains that the exercise of worship in places of deprivation of liberty must obviously be conceived in respect of the principle of secularism. Secularism is not the enemy of religions. The principle involves a double requirement: the neutrality of the State, on the one hand, and the protection of freedom of conscience on the other. State neutrality is, therefore, closely linked to freedom and equality. Without being naïve, but in order not to exacerbate the tensions that threaten social cohesion, we must ensure that all believers, whatever the nature of their belief and the modalities of their expression, are treated with equal dignity.

Bibliography

Béraud, C., de Galembert, C., & Rostaing, C. (2016). *De la religion en prison*. Rennes: Presses Universitaires de Rennes.

Curtit, F. (2017). Un diplôme de formation civile et civique obligatoire pour les futurs aumôniers rémunérés. *Revue Droit & Santé, 78*, 578–580.

Fornerod, A. (2016). *Annoted Legal Documents on Islam in Europe: France*. Leiden/Boston: Brill.

Fortier, V., & Vialla, F. (Eds.). (2013). *La religion dans les établissements de santé*. Bordeaux: LEH éditions.

Gonzalez, G. (2013). L'autonomie ecclésiale dans la jurisprudence de la Cour européenne des droits de l'homme. *RDLF* (29). (www.revuedlf.com).

Schmitz, J. (2017). L'Etat laïc à l'épreuve de l'espace carcéral. *Journal du Droit Administratif, 1*(3), 107–124 & *Cahiers de la LCD* 03: Laï-Cités : Discrimination(s), Laïcité(s) & religion(s) dans la cité (dir. Esteve-Bellebeau & Touzeil-Divina); Article 124.

Other Documents Consulted

Administrative Court, Lille, chamber 6, 1 July 2003, no. 001519, *Juris-Data* no. 2003-225856.

BOMJ no. 2014-08, 29 August 2014.

CE, 16 October 2013, Keeper of the seals v/M. F. and others, no. 351115.

CE, 11 June 2014, M.S., no. 365237.

CE, 16 July 2014, Keeper of the Seals, Ministry of Justice c/M.B., no. 377145.

CE, 25 February 2015, no. 375724.

CE, 10 February 2016, no. 385929, published in the Lebon compilation.

CEDH, 7 December 2010, case of Jakobski v. Poland, application no. 18429/06.

Circular 20 September 2012 on the accreditation of paid or volunteer chaplains, volunteer chaplaincy auxiliaries in correctional institutions, and of occasional chaplaincy attendants, NOR: JUSK 1240021C.

Council of Europe. (2006). Committee of ministers. *Receptor*, 2.

Decree no. 2013-368, 30 April 2013, on the standard rules of procedure for prisons, *JORF* no. 0103, 3 May 2013, p. 7609.

JORF no. 0106, 5 May 2017, text no. 105.

JORF no. 0273, 25 November 2009, p. 20192.

Le juge administratif et l'expression des convictions religieuses, Les dossiers thématiques du Conseil d'Etat, 2014 (on-line).

CAA Lyon, 22 July 2014, no. 14LY0013.

M. AB c. Director of the penitentiary centre of Saint-Quentin-Fallavier, request number 1302502. Notice of 24 March 2011, *JO* no. 0091, 17 April 2011. Mr. Delarue was General Controller from 2008 to 2014.

Chapter 12
France: Islam, a Central Topic of the Research Field Dedicated to Prisons and Religion – A Review of the Literature

Céline Béraud

Abstract In recent years, religion in prison has attracted some interest within the social sciences. This field of research was developed in France at the beginning of the 2000s, at the initiative of the British sociologist of religion James Beckford. At first, Islam attracted most of the scholarly attention, before more general work was undertaken in the early 2010s. Nevertheless, the framing imposed by public policy following the terrorist attacks has led to a tightening of the research conducted on religion in prison institutions around what is commonly called radicalisation.

12.1 Introduction

In recent years, religion in prisons has attracted some interest within the social sciences. This field of research has developed in France, as in other European countries, at the initiative of the British sociologist of religion James Beckford. It has then remained in dialogue with this European research, even though it has focused less on the chaplaincy, at least at the beginning, but has more connections with prison sociology.

At first, Islam attracted most of the scholarly attention before some more general work was undertaken. Following the terrorist attacks as early as March 2012 (Toulouse and Montauban shootings), French prisons have been described as breeding grounds for radicalisation and homegrown terrorism. Inmates' radicalisation process became a popular topic in the media and received scholarly attention.

C. Béraud (✉)
École des Hautes Études en Sciences Sociales, Paris, France
e-mail: celine.beraud@ehess.fr

© Springer Nature Switzerland AG 2020
J. Martínez-Ariño, A.-L. Zwilling (eds.), *Religion and Prison: An Overview of Contemporary Europe*, Boundaries of Religious Freedom: Regulating Religion in Diverse Societies 7, https://doi.org/10.1007/978-3-030-36834-0_12

12.2 Islam, the First Religion in French Prisons

Farhad Khosrokhavar's (2004) pioneering work, presenting Islam as "the first religion in French prisons", received critical comments. Despite the absence of denominational statistics produced by state institutions, the author argued, as if it were obvious, that most detainees in French prisons were Muslim. In the prisons of major cities, the proportion was reported to be as high as 80%. Farhad Khosrokhavar denounced, in contrast, the "derisory institutional framework" that Islam had in prison compared with Catholicism, Protestantism and Judaism. The sociologist also sought to understand the forms of recourse to Islam in detention to draw up a typology of Muslim detainees (from "Islamists" to "converts", via "mentally disturbed"), as well as to analyse the interactions of the latter with different actors in prison (fellow detainees, imams, prison guards and social workers). Portraits of Muslim women were also drawn.

The 2001–2003 survey made by Farhad Khosrokhavar (2004) was initiated by funding obtained by two members of the Centre for Ethnic Studies at the University of Warwick: James Beckford and Danièle Joly. The aim was to carry out comparative research on how Muslim inmates were treated in prison in France, England and Wales, taking into consideration the differences between the British multi-faith approach and the practice of the French *laïcité*. The results of this collective study were published in English and French (Beckford et al. 2005a, b). According to the authors, the French specificity at the time lay in the great difficulty experienced by Muslim inmates in practising their faith. Thus, the prison administration opted to ignore or avoid the question, "until when inmates should display their penchant for radical Islam" (Ibid., p. 22). The lack of facilities and resources for Muslim inmates was salient concerning the organisation of collective prayers, access to various objects (prayer carpets, compasses, copies of the Quran), respect for food prescriptions (halal meat), wearing of headscarves for women etc. According to the authors, no solution was provided by prison authorities at a national level. Local accommodation and other forms of tinkering were dominant and included arbitrary interpretations of the principle of *laïcité* by prison wardens and compromises made by guards. Hence, a strong feeling of discrimination among Muslim inmates, which they swiftly interpret in terms of racism, when they compare their fate with that of Christians and Jews: "It is as if French prisons reproduced – and perhaps also amplified – the feeling of exclusion and powerlessness that is so characteristic of disaffected young Muslims in disadvantaged suburbs." (Ibid., p. 345). The lack of Muslim chaplains (estimated between 39 and 69 at the time for around 195 prisons) led the most fervent Muslims to take action themselves. The issue was also sometimes addressed by some officers, wardens or social workers, who, for instance in the 1990s, set up the first canteens[1] for Ramadan. One must add that, at that time, it

---

[1] Inmates can buy certain everyday items from the prison canteen (food, cigarettes, stamps, personal hygiene products etc.), that is, using their own spending money. The food bought from the canteen during Ramadan supplements the meals supplied free of charge by the prison administration.

was mostly the Catholic and Protestant chaplains who looked after the Muslim inmates. Several Christian chaplains distributed copies of the Quran and prayer diaries, which they had collected in the mosque. Many of them took responsibility for visiting Muslim inmates. The pages in Khosrokhavar's book devoted to the concrete conditions of exercise of their mission by Muslim chaplains are sparse. The study shows that, even when there was a Muslim chaplain in a prison, he may not have always been welcome. Muslim chaplains sometimes had to face indifference from staff, and even forms of obstruction. As for inmates, some preferred not to visit the chaplain either because they viewed him as a representative of the prison administration, or because they intended to live their faith individually without institutional mediation.

Farhad Khosrokhavar then turned his attention to the phenomenon of radicalisation. He devoted a book to detainees who were imprisoned in France for their connection with al-Qaeda, whose interviews he reproduced in full (Khosrokhavar 2006). This book attempted to identify the different paths that may have led these individuals to Islamist terrorism. Despite the importance of these works, religion in prisons remained quite a marginal object of research in France until just before 2010.

12.3   Studying Religious Facts as a Whole

Since the early 2010s, religion in prisons has aroused the interest of historians (Landron 2011, 2013) and, to a lesser extent, of lawyers (Fortier 2014). Thus, Olivier Landron (2011) offered a substantial summary on religion in prisons during the last century,[2] more precisely on the history of relations between Catholicism and the prison world (a few pages are devoted to Protestantism). The book was followed by conference proceedings on the same topic Landron (2013).

This second set of research has also and above all broadened the focus beyond Islam. The proceedings of the study days organised by the Office of Prison Administration on "the religious fact in prison", at Sciences Po (Paris) in Autumn 2013, testify that the movement to broaden the research perspective had already started (DAP 2014), a movement that is, of course, related to the expansion of the religious offer in the prison system. Two lines of research emerged at that time: analysing religious experiences in the very specific context of prisons; studying the challenges posed by religious diversity to the chaplaincies, but also more generally to the daily organisation of prison life.

In 2011, a thematic issue of the journal *Archives de Sciences Sociales des Religions,* published under the supervision of a Swiss colleague, Irene Becci, highlighted the topicality of the question and the now more abundant research conducted

---

[2] Unfortunately, little is said in Landron's first book regarding some important changes concerning Christian chaplaincies that have occurred in the last three decades: effects produced by the presence of an increasing number of lay chaplains (including a large proportion of women); challenges represented by religious plurality and, especially, the presence of Islam in the prison space.

on this theme, even in France. Thus, Rachel Sarg and Anne-Sophie Lamine (2011) analysed the role of religion for inmate converts (whatever their faith) in French prisons: tranquillisation, meaning and self-rehabilitation. The authors insisted on the fact that inmates also make strategic use of religious activities and chaplains to improve their lot by meeting other inmates, gaining some information about prison life and about their trial, and sometimes challenging prison staff.

Based on almost 2 years of field research, a research project financed by the prison administration (Béraud et al. 2013, 2016) has implied a dialogue among the sociology of religion, prison sociology and political sociology. Inspired by the theory of symbolic interactionism, an in-depth ethnographic study was conducted between January 2011 and October 2012, both "from above" (in administrative centres and at the top of religious institutions) and "from below" (in eight French prisons). The study equally explored the points of view of prison administration, of chaplains of all denominations, and of inmates (believers and non-believers), by observing, among other things, cultural activities or chaplains' visits to cells. Face-to-face interviews with prisoners, the Office of Prison Administrations (officials, correctional officers, social workers) or other people working in prisons (doctors, tutors, managers etc.) were also conducted. It was a question of understanding what religion is and represents for inmates (without limiting oneself to a specific denomination), how it is administered by prison authorities and staff, as well as the future of chaplains whose discreet presence has not only withstood the various waves of secularisation but has demonstrated an unexpected vitality nourished by the arrival of "new" entrants. It aims to explore, from a comprehensive sociological perspective, the place and role which prison authorities, chaplains and incarcerated people attribute to religion. In particular, it has led to the question: what might lead some inmates to get involved in religion during their incarceration. It was shown that religion often responds to the failings of the prison institution, which today struggles to either protect or promote the reintegration of inmates.

This is a broad perspective that Rachel Sarg also adopts in her thesis published in 2016. The sociologist proposes to consider all religious offers, "organised and mobilised by inmates". In a theoretical framework influenced by Raymond Boudon and Gérald Bronner, she analyses the prison experience as being marked by a whole series of uncertainties that the practice of religion (beliefs, prayer, worships, chaplains' attendance) could effectively reduce.

The years 2000–2010 constitute a period of reinforced institutionalisation of religious plurality in French prisons (for a long time limited to Catholic, Protestant and Jewish denominations). The management of prison administrations carried out this institutionalisation voluntarily. There is a form of catch-up regarding Islam (tripling the number of Muslim chaplains in those 10 years, the appointment of a national chaplain in 2005, special arrangements for Ramadan made by prison authorities, documents delivered by the Office of Prisons Administration to sensitise staff to the practices and beliefs of Muslim inmates), but this is not limited to that religion. A national Christian Orthodox chaplain was appointed in 2010, followed 4 years later by a female Buddhist national chaplain. In the case of Buddhism, which in France benefits from a favourable appreciation, the prison administration has contributed to increase the offer of chaplaincy services. However, the requests for the creation of a chaplaincy emanating from Jehovah's Witnesses were, for opposing reasons, denied. Only a decision of the State Council on 16 October 2013 caused the administration to yield. Following a dispute lasting several years, the supreme administrative jurisdiction ruled that the insufficient number of inmates professing that they belonged to this religious organisation, labelled as "sectarian" by the watchdog Miviludes (*Mission de vigilance et de lutte contre les dérives sectaires*),[3] could not constitute grounds for denying approval for chaplains. The number of chaplains of these different denominations increased significantly during the first half of the years 2010.

As a matter of fact, competition for the resources to be distributed by prison authorities is severe between the different faiths. Furthermore, it is not easy for newcomers to conform to patterns and norms, which were originally framed for the purposes of Christian chaplaincies (Béraud et al. 2016). The institutionalisation of religious diversity also raises the question of the future of the long-held majority religion, Catholicism, in prisons. The ongoing rebalancing in favour of the "new" entrants leads not only to a certain redistribution of statutes and resources but also to the questioning of institutional routines from which Catholic chaplains had benefited up till then (Béraud 2016).

12.4   Prison, Radicalisation, Terrorism

Prisons are regularly called into question[4] since the wave of terrorist attacks that affected France from 2012 onwards.[5] These accusations reached their climax in early 2015. In fact, Coulibaly and one of the Kouachi brothers, like Nemmouche, Merah and Kelkal before them, had a past of delinquency that had led them to prison, where they were said to have re-embraced religion and, at the same time, moved to violent engagement. Public policy to combat radicalisation identifies prisons as being important places, as can be seen from the antiterrorism scheme of January 2015. Through the additional funds allocated to the prison administration, a major effort is being made to recruit Muslim chaplains, whose preventive action was at that time unanimously underlined. In 2016, Islam became the denomination that received most public funds in prison, ahead of Catholicism. Public funds have also been allocated to research on radicalisation,[6] several projects being conducted in prison.

---

[3] Inter-Ministerial Task Force to Monitor and Combat Abuse by Cults.

[4] In Toulouse and Montauban, Mohammed Merah, 23, a French citizen, killed three soldiers on 11 and 15 March, before shooting three children and a teacher at a Jewish school on 19 March.

[5] Things are, of course, much more complex, which the public authorities seem to have since become aware of. The perpetrators of terrorist acts committed in recent years have not all experienced incarceration and the involvement of religion in prisons cannot be reduced to violence and terrorism.

[6] In total, at the beginning of 2016, more than €425 million of the public budget was allocated to fighting radicalisation; in universities, about 15 chairs have been opened in this field (Crettiez 2016).

Farhad Khosrokhavar's book on radicalisation was published in December 2014, 1 month before the attacks on *Charlie Hebdo* and *Hyper Cacher*. It quickly became a bestseller. Its subject matter is not limited to the prison space, but the author does, however, dedicate a good part of his book to it, the prison being presented as the institution most exposed to the phenomenon, compared with schools, hospitals or the army. The following year, Farhad Khosrokhavar (2016) devoted a chapter to "the radicalised" in a more general book on French prisons. He addresses the forms of frustration and stigmatisation of Islam in prisons and in the rest of society, the processes of ideologisation, and group dynamics (imitation and competition among fellow inmates).

The call of the Centre National de la Recherche Scientifique (CNRS) for "post-attack" projects has enabled new research to be initiated, a second phase of which is currently funded by the Ministry of Justice on the institutionalisation of the Muslim prison chaplaincy (Béraud and Galembert, 2016–2018). The French public authorities have relied heavily on the Muslim Chaplaincy, making of it a key tool in the fight against prison radicalisation since the mid-2000s. However, this way of investing in Muslim Chaplaincy raises questions and produces negative effects. It is, in fact, an instrument that escapes the control of administration, in part because of its dual nature (the chaplain is both a public official and a representative of his religious group) and because of the still weak rationalisation of the relationship between the administration and the chaplains (despite recent efforts to formalise and standardise practices). Moreover, by over-emphasising the Muslim chaplain as the centrepiece in the fight against radicalisation, the administration is publicly showing that it expects him to be the agent of some form of social control over the practices and beliefs of his imprisoned fellow co-religionists. By doing so, it undeniably contributes to weakening his legitimacy among inmates. Two years after the beginning of the research project, the prison authorities seem more aware of these negative effects. They are now much more cautious. The role of Muslim chaplains in the fight against radicalisation is now deemed only indirect. However, several questions arise. How can the state accompany the structuring of the Muslim Chaplaincy while leaving a space of autonomy to its representatives, autonomy that is not only in conformity with the law but is also the guarantee of the effectiveness of their action? The project also analyses the main obstacles to the full institutionalisation of Muslim Chaplaincy, over which the public authorities have little direct control.

Foreign to the Islamic tradition, chaplaincy is still poorly known to Muslims. The internal divisions within the Islamic field linked to the national origins of Muslim leaders but also to the tendency of some to behave as local religious entrepreneurs, jealous of their prerogatives and, therefore, reluctant to see their authority overshadowed by a higher authority, weakens the collective action and complicates relations with the public authorities who manage the religious phenomenon on a model strongly imbued with Catholicism (that of a centralised, hierarchical and territorial model).

Another piece of research conducted in the "post-attack" context, on the "mechanisms of violent radicalisation" led by Xavier Crettiez and Romain Sèze (2017), proposes to explore the processes of violent radicalisation. It is not limited to jihadist engagements, since militant trajectories (Corsican and Basque) leading to nationalist violence are integrated to identify their common and specific causes. The survey has largely taken place in prison establishments. However, according to the authors, they intend to carry out interviews with their respondents, who are imprisoned, not to analyse radicalisation in prison, even if incarceration is recurring in these trajectories.

12.5   Conclusion

After research moved away from the sole issue of Islam in prison, the framing imposed by public policy against radicalisation has led to a tightening of the research conducted on religion in prison institutions around what is commonly called radicalisation. One can regret such a rather reductive tendency. Nevertheless, it is accompanied by a certain renewal of research questions. Thus, it is through the question of radicalisation that the question of gender, which for a long time was a real blind spot in research on religion in prison in France and abroad, was in fact considered for the very first time (Béraud et al. 2017). The involvement of women in a planned attack in Paris in September 2016, as well as the return of some women from Syria, led the prison authorities to rethink the policy of combating radicalisation, which until now had only concerned male inmates.

Bibliography

Becci, I. (Ed). (2011). Prisons et religions en Europe. *Archives de sciences sociales des religions,* no. 153.

Beckford, J., Joly, D., & Khosrokhavar, F. (2005a). *Muslims in prison. challenge and change in Britain and France.* London: Palgrave Macmillan.

Beckford, J., Joly, D., & Khosrokhavar, F. (2005b). *Les musulmans en prison en Grande-Bretagne et en France.* Louvain: Presses universitaires de Louvain, coll. "Atelier de recherche sociologique ".

Béraud, C. (2016). *Ce que l'institutionnalisation de la pluralité religieuse fait au catholicisme. Le cas des aumôneries de prison et d'hôpital.* Paris: Sciences Po, Habilitation thesis to supervise research (ed Didier Demazière).

Béraud C., & de Galembert, C. (2019). *La fabrique de l'aumônerie musulmane des prisons.* Funding by CNRS in the framework of the "post-attacks" funding, then the Direction de l'administration pénitentiaire and Mission de recherche Droit et Justice.

Béraud, C., de Galembert, C., & Rostaing, C. (2013). *Des hommes et des dieux en prison.* Paris: Research funded by DAP and GIP Mission de recherche Droit et Justice.

Béraud, C., de Galembert, C., & Rostaing, C. (2016). *De la religion en prison.* Rennes: PUR.

Béraud, C., Rostaing, C., & de Galembert, C. (2017). Genre et lutte contre la radicalisation. *Cahiers du genre, 63,* 145–165.

Crettiez, X. (2016). Penser la radicalisation. Une sociologie processuelle des variables de l'engagement violent. *Revue française de science politique, 66,* 709–727.

Crettiez, X., & Seze, R. (Eds.). (2017, April). *Saisir les mécanismes de la radicalisation violente: pour une analyse processuelle et biographique des engagements violents. Rapport de recherche pour la Mission de recherche Droit et Justice.*

de Galembert, C., Béraud, C., & Rostaing, C. (2016). Islam et prison: liaisons dangereuses ? Pouvoirs, revue française d'études constitutionnelles et *politiques,* no. 158, La lutte contre le terrorisme, pp. 67–81.

Direction de l'administration pénitentiaire. (2014). *Le fait religieux en prison: configurations, apports, risques.* Paris: Direction de l'administration pénitentiaire, coll. "Travaux et Documents".

Fortier, V. (2014). L'exercice du culte en milieu carcéral. In D. Koussens & V. Amiraux (Eds.), *Trajectoires de la neutralité* (pp. 159–169). Montréal: Presses Universitaires de Montréal.

Khosrokhavar, F. (2004). *L'islam dans les prisons.* Paris: Balland.

Khosrokhavar, F. (2006). *Quand Al Qaïda parle: témoignages derrière les barreaux.* Paris: Ed. Grasset, Paris.

Khosrokhavar, F. (2014). *Radicalisation.* Paris: Ed. de la MSH.

Khosrokhavar, F. (2016). *Prisons de France. Violence, radicalisation, déshumanisation: Surveillants et détenus parlent.* Paris: Robert Laffont, "Le monde comme il va".

Landron, O. (2011). *La vie chrétienne dans les prisons de France au XXe siècle.* Paris: Cerf, "L'histoire à vif".

Landron, O. (2013). *Christianisme et prison. Rencontres, dialogues, confrontations.* Paris: Parole et Silence.

Sarg, R. (2016). *La foi malgré tout. Croire en prison.* Paris: PUF.

Sarg, R., & Lamine, A.-S. (2011). La religion en prison. Norme structurante, réhabilitation de soi, stratégie de résistance. *Archives de Sciences Sociales des Religions, 153,* 85–104.

Chapter 13
Germany: Inequality in Legal Practice – Managing Religion in Prisons

Sarah J. Jahn

Abstract This chapter provides a general overview of religion in German prisons. It starts from the changing and divided history of the German state in the twentieth century and ends with today's situation in prisons. It presents recent topics and trends, in social scientific research as well as in politics. There are different types of prisons, with regional and demographic specificities, and different politics of prison and religion, as well as a huge variety of forms of religious communitarisation, beliefs and religious practice. They all need to be known to understand the greater scope for action that prison officials have to deal with, for managing religion in everyday life. Not only are structures of interest, therefore, but also understandings, societal debates about the governance of religious diversity and religious debates about theological legitimacy. The different meanings of terms such as "chaplaincy" and "religious society" are good examples to explain this entanglement. The German legal framework is "religious friendly", but there is no equality among the various denominations. The possibility of practising religion in prison, as an individual or collectively, depends on the legal status a denomination has, both in prison and in society.

13.1 Introduction and General Presentation

At first glance, it does not seem that religion and prisons belong together nowadays, as it did at a time when religion and the State were not separate. Most so-called Western societies now consider religion as a possible option and a private matter: individuals can decide if they want to be a member of a religious community, and they are granted the freedom of practising their religion. However, it is the call of other people to decide whether one would become a prisoner or not, and everyday life in prison is determined by structures and regulations. Imprisoned people, therefore, cannot do whatever they want; they have less space to observe their privacy.

S. J. Jahn (✉)
Center for Religious Studies (CERES), Ruhr-University Bochum, Bochum, Germany
e-mail: sarah.j.jahn@rub.de

© Springer Nature Switzerland AG 2020
J. Martínez-Ariño, A.-L. Zwilling (eds.), *Religion and Prison: An Overview of Contemporary Europe*, Boundaries of Religious Freedom: Regulating Religion in Diverse Societies 7, https://doi.org/10.1007/978-3-030-36834-0_13

Nevertheless, the possibility of privacy and freedom exists in prison. It is important to know the legal and institutional possibility of such freedom for inmates to understand the relationship between religion and prisons in Germany.

Since 1972, inmates have had the same basic rights (e.g. human dignity, personal freedom, equality before the law, freedom of faith and conscience) as persons outside prison walls. The decision regarding the basic rights of inmates, as given by the Federal Constitutional Court, ensures that every detained person has the same rights as any other person in Germany (2 BvR 41/71). Imprisoned people were fully dependent on actions by prison officials before 1972, but this only applied to inmates in the zones of the Allies because between 1949 and 1990, Germany was separated into the German Democratic Republic (GDR) and the Federal Republic of Germany (FRG). The Federal Constitutional Court only refers to people in the FRG. Also, State–Church relations were completely different in the two parts.

After 1945, State–Church contracts, which regulated specific conditions of the field of cooperation between the state and religious societies, ended in all occupied zones in Germany. In the occupation zones of the Allies, churches could be independent from the State or they could partner with the State, as described in Sect. 13.2. In the Soviet zone, on the other hand, strict subordination prevailed, which, combined with the socialist ideology, led to the marginalisation of religion and official suppression of the Church from society (Beckmann and Kusch 1994).

Today, religious freedom is not only a framework for religion in German prisons, but understanding rehabilitation as the central goal of imprisonment is also an important aspect of the entwined history of religion in prisons. Since the eighteenth century, prisons have increasingly become an institution aimed at preventing crimes (Morris and Rothman 1995). Important impulses for reformation of the penitentiary system and today's understanding of rehabilitation came from Christian clergymen such as John Howard and Heinrich Balthasar Wagnitz (Howard 1792; Wagnitz 1791, 1792). Previously, prisons had been buildings to collect "bad" people and to separate them from the outside world (Foucault 1975). However, historical changes and the current legal framework have allowed detained persons to practise their religion in prison, and religious organisations to take an active part in prison life.

In 2016, Germany had 182 prisons, with 14 of them being houses for day release. Below is an overview of the different types of prisons and the occupancy rate (Statistisches Bundesamt 2017):

As Table 13.1 illustrates, there are different types of prisons in accordance with the numbers of occupants, housing types and gender of inmates. The present chapter gives an overview of religion in prison in general; recent research and topics; and presents the legal and social aspects. Owing to insufficient research and statistical data on religion in German prisons, I present here a specific scope for empirical data from my own research in closed prisons. This research was carried out between 2011 and 2015 in six prison institutions for male offenders with a detention time of at least 3 years (Jahn 2017). I explored the negotiation and organisation of religious diversity in German prisons. The research goal was to analyse how the right to religious freedom is negotiated in the German penal system. Based on the sociology of

Table 13.1 Total number of prisons in Germany, 2016

German prisons 2016		Occupancy capacity			Occupancy rate			Prison type		
Total		Total	Individual cells	Communal cells	Total	Individual cells	Communal cells	Pretrial	Cyp	Others
A/B: 182	Total	73,627	54,720	18,907	62,865	47,176	15,689	12,992	48,485	1388
	Female	4220	3134	1086	3607	2532	1075	727	2814	66
A: 168	Total	62,793	49,777	13,016	55,399	43,050	12,349	12,992	41,032	1375
	Female	3477	2597	880	3070	2095	975	727	2277	66
B: 14	Total	10,834	4943	5891	7466	4126	3340	–	7453	13
	Female	743	537	206	537	437	100	–	537	–

Open (B) and closed (A) correctional institutions; total number of inmates and female inmates; capacity in individual cells and community cells; prison types of pretrial detention, custodial sentence/young offender sentence/preventive custody (cyp) and others law and the study of religion, I conducted field studies and semi-structured guideline interviews with prison staff and inmates in several German prisons. The prison sample was selected in accordance with regional differences (e.g. urban, rural, or religious landscape) to get a broad base of empirical data. In summary, I collected 80 interviews, numerous documents, and conducted six field studies with participants.

13.2   Legal Aspects of Religion in German Prisons

In Germany, the legal system is divided into three sections: public law, private law and criminal law (Robbers 2006). Public law is a collection of norms regulating the relations between the State and state institutions and between the persons involved. It is divided into two main areas: constitutional law and administrative law. The regulations are written down in the *German Basic Law* (*Grundgesetz, GG*) and in the procedural rules for each administrative public body, such as prisons, ministries, municipalities, schools, among others. Prisons in Germany are public bodies. The procedural rules there are *Prison Acts* and house rules. Owing to the federal system in Germany, each federal state (*Bundesland*) has its own *Prison Act*. Also, each prison has its own house rules that correspond to the characteristics of that prison, such as function, important periods to structure the day (such as sleeping, working, eating hours), leisure activities, education offers, special therapies, and staff, among others. Further, the relationship between law and religion is laid down in the *German Basic Law*. Therefore, public law is the only section of interest here.

13.2.1   Public Law and Religion in German Prisons

The legal status of prison chaplains and chaplaincy, the representation of denominations in prison and the regulations concerning religious practices and religious freedom relate to the rules written down in the Basic Law. Specifically, Article 4, Sections 1 and 2 constitute religious freedom, but the incorporated Articles 136 to 141 of the Weimar Constitution also serve as regulation of religious freedom (*Weimarer Reichsverfassung, WRV*). Together, they are known as the *Religionsverfassungsrecht* (Robbers 2001).

As in most of the so-called Western countries, religion and the State are separated in Germany. This separation refers to the individual level (Article 4, Section 1 and 2 GG) and the collective level (Article 137 WRV). The freedom of faith and conscience (Article 4, Section 1 and 2 GG) in the legal text means the following (Federal Law Gazette 2010):

1. Freedom of faith and of conscience, and freedom to profess a religious or philosophical creed, shall be inviolable.
2. The undisturbed practice of religion shall be guaranteed.

Article 137 from the Weimar Constitution – framed on 11 August 1919 – means (ibid):

> Article 137: (1) There shall be no state church. (2) The freedom to form religious societies shall be guaranteed. The union of religious societies[1] within the territory of the Reich shall be subject to no restrictions. (3) Religious societies shall regulate and administer their affairs independently within the limits of the law that applies to all. They shall confer their offices without the participation of the state or the civil community. (4) Religious societies shall acquire legal capacity according to the general provisions of civil law. (5) Religious societies shall remain corporations under public law insofar as they have enjoyed that status in the past. Other religious societies shall be granted the same rights upon application, if their constitution and the number of their members give assurance of their permanency. If two or more religious societies established under public law unite into a single organisation, it too shall be a corporation under public law. (6) Religious societies that are corporations under public law shall be entitled to levy taxes based on the civil taxation lists in accordance with Land law. (7) Associations whose purpose is to foster a philosophical creed shall have the same status as religious societies. (8) Such further regulation as may be required for the implementation of these provisions shall be a matter for Land legislation.

Article 141 WRV is of interest for prisons and prison chaplaincy (Ibid):

> To the extent that a need exists for religious services and pastoral work in the army, in hospitals, in prisons, or in other public institutions, religious societies shall be permitted to provide them, but without compulsion of any kind.

The constitutional framework also applies to prisons and inmates. Generally speaking, each inmate can choose to believe in and practice a religion, or not. Also, religious and philosophical societies can offer services. This can be dubbed the freedom for, and of, religion. Only the collision with other basic rights or institutional limits could limit the power of religious freedom. The limits institutionally given lead to negotiations in everyday prison life. As described in Sect. 13.3, order and security are the main reasons to limit religious freedom in prison. Therefore, the institutional specificities and functions of prisons regulate religious practices and religious freedom more than the general legal framework. To understand the negotiation processes, it is necessary to have a closer look at the terminology. There are different understandings and meanings of "chaplaincy" and "religious society".

The first term is "chaplaincy", which is part of Article 141 WRV, which states that religious societies will be permitted to provide chaplaincy if there is a need. In practice, though, chaplains from Catholic and Protestant churches have contracts with the ministries of justice of the federal states. At the moment, there is a discussion about the possibility of having Muslim chaplains and Islamic chaplaincy because the number of Muslim inmates has increased during the last decade. In 2016, the German Islam Conference (*Deutsche Islam Konferenz*) debated about the chaplaincy for Muslims in public institutions, such as military establishments, hospitals and prisons (DIK 2016). The political debate can be summarised in three main questions:

---

[1] "Religious society" is used as an official technical term in the legal text beside other entities such as "church" or "religious communities." There is no common language in the legal text because of the different historical stages at which the text has been written (Link 2004).

- Need: is chaplaincy for Muslims in such institutions necessary?
- Religious understanding: how could an Islamic chaplaincy be understood from an emic point of view?
- Political and legal framework: what kind of institutionalised chaplaincy should be funded by the State?

As the German Islam Conference is a political arena, all these questions have political connotations and different dimensions, according to the Federal Ministry of Interior. After 1 year of work, the DIK published recommendations for Islamic chaplaincy in prisons (DIK 2017). It recommended a countrywide working group because of the significant differences in practices among the federal states. Not only should the ministerial actors play their respective parts, but religious actors responsible for the practice of the Basic Law concerning religions will also be included in the working group (Ibid, 9). The goal of such a group should be to formulate basic requirements for Islamic chaplaincy (Ibid, 10).

The second term is "religious society" (Jahn 2015a). Article 137, Section 2 WRV of the Basic Law mentions the term *"Religionsgesellschaft"*, which is derived from the State–Church law of the nineteenth century. A synonymous use is found in the terms "religious community" and "church". The case regarding the legal claim of Muslim communities from 2005 specifies these distinctions (BVerwG 6 C 2.04). The religious community is, therefore, understood as a subgroup. In principle, any religious tradition can form a community, but it is not necessarily recognised as a society in the understanding of the public law. It is a union based on private law like any other club – for example, a football club or a theatre club. Public recognition in the form of a corporatist status is, however, only found when certain characteristics of the communion form exist, mentioned in Article 137. The prerequisites are based on the religious communitarian ideology of Christian churches. According to legal scholar Wiebke Hennig, the religious constitutional law has a "structural Christianisation" (Hennig 2010). New religious traditions, such as the Islamic tradition, often encounter problems regarding recognition by the public law. Additionally, public recognition is the duty of the federal states (Article 30 GG); hence, each of the 16 federal states in Germany has different numbers of publicly recognised religious communities.

13.2.2 Structural Aspects of Religion in German Prisons

The federalism is the main structural aspect of religion in German prisons. Federalism is important for the public recognition of religion, but also for the legal and public organisation of prisons. Both are federal tasks. The numbers of prison institutions and detained persons are different in each of the federal states. Every federal state has its own Prison Act. Most of the legal regulations are the same,

Table 13.2 Differences in prison policy (total numbers)

	Bavaria	North Rhine-Westphalia
Chaplains (Catholic, Protestant)	28	54
Doctors	45	61
Psychologists	104	161
Teachers	52	112
Social workers	164	308
Leading administrative positions – i.e. head of the institution	60	95
Middle-range administrative position – i.e. head of the security section	178	280
Low/range positions – i.e. caretaker	316	547
Security personnel	3927	6186
Training positions for further education	483	585
Total	5357	8389
Number of prisons	42	65
Number of spots	12,103	18,807
Inhabitants of the federal state	12,583,528	17,554,329

because every federal law must be coherent with the Basic Law, but there are differences in the preferences of prison goals. Some of the Prison Acts name rehabilita-
 and security as goals, whereas some others, such as those in Bavaria, place
sis on security (BayStVollzG 2007)[2]:

cement of imprisonment serves to protect the public against further offences. It is
enable prisoners to live a life without criminal offences in the future (responsi-
ment).

such as those in North Rhine-Westphalia, emphasise rehabilita-
st important goal (StVollzG NRW 2015)[3]:

n of imprisonment serves the purpose of enabling prisoners to live
nces in the future.

basic decision in practice: whether to simply lock up
n outside prison walls, or to work with them to insti-
s. In practice, these differences are also reflected in
ted in Table 13.2 below. The figures are a cumu-
the federal states. They inform the financial
ecution of terms of imprisonment.[4]

es. The figures refer to 2012 and are
stice.

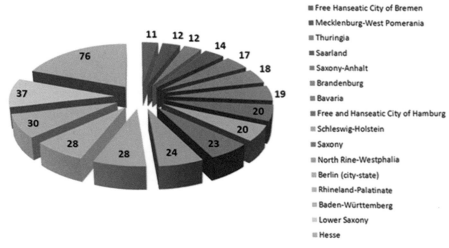

Fig. 13.1 Total number of recognised religious corporations under public law (minimum to maximum)

Similar to penal policies, each state has its own religious policy. In March 2014, numerous religious communities were legally recognised as a corporation under public law (Bundesministerium 2014)

As illustrated in Fig. 13.1, there are huge differences in the recognition of religions under public law across federal states. One good example is Jehovah's Witnesses: because the group wants to be recognised in all federal states as a corporation under public law, it has been fighting for this since 1990. In 2006, they obtained their right in Berlin. In 2017, North Rhine-Westphalia was the last federal state to recognise their legal status (Jehovas 2017a, b).

The public recognition of religious communities is necessary to negotiate legal contracts with the State. Such contracts are signed between the recognised religious community and each federal state. They include special tasks such as prison chaplaincy. As of August 2014, the religious contractors were Protestant and Roman Catholic Churches in every federal state, as well as Jewish and Islamic community in some states. In German prisons, Protestant and Roman Catholic chaplains standard. Chaplains with other religious backgrounds are the exception. law is an integral part in the relationship between religions and the State (2012). It regulates in detail the joint tasks where religion and the state such as chaplaincy and religious education. The rights and obligations contract partners are regulated in a specific contract. However, this questions about the personnel, and the financial possibilities of imple toral care. Some modifications to include offers for Muslims in pri implemented in the last decade, as will be shown in the next section

13.3   Sociological Aspects of Religion in German Prisons

13.3.1   Data on Religious Affiliation and Religiosity

Getting valid statistics on the religious affiliation of inmates is nearly impossible, because inmates do not have to declare their religious affiliations.[5] Nevertheless, for some years now, it has become common practice to ask inmates about their religious affiliations in the initial interview when they enter the prison. Some of the inmates give an answer, and some do not. The data presented in Table 13.3 give an impression of the religious affiliations of inmates in three prisons:

The data are from male inmates of three different prisons for a long-term detention (with a minimum of 3 years). Prison A is located in a rural area in Western Germany, Prison B at the border of a medium-sized town in South Germany and Prison C in a rural area near the Dutch border. Three religious groups can be identified: Catholics, Protestants and Muslims. Catholics are the largest group in every prison; Protestants are the second-largest group in two of the prisons; Muslims

Table 13.3 Categories of religious affiliations (absolute numbers)

Categories	Prison A	Prison B	Prison C
Inmates in total (2012)	547	631	698
Difference	1	0	69
Christian	1		
Catholic	232	266	260
Roman Catholic	2		
Protestant	122	176	140
Evangelical Lutheran	1		
Orthodox	15	33	
Russian Orthodox	2		
Greek Orthodox	1		
Evangelical Free Church	2		
New Apostolic	2		
Mennonite	1		
Baptist	2		
Jehovah's Witness	1		
Muslim	77	59	145
Jew	1		2
Buddhist	4		1
Other	1	6	
Without statement	67	16	81
Without denomination	12	75	

---

[5] This legal fact is due to the freedom of religion and belief (Article 4 GG) and the right to personal data protection (BVerfG 1983, 1 BvR 209/83).

are the second-largest group in Prison C and the third-largest group in Prisons A and B. Other religious affiliations are also shown, but numbers are relatively insignificant. The data could be understood as an approximation and not as a picture of the reality because of the way in which it was collected. Some prisons, such as Prisons B and C, use their own categories from which inmates could choose. Other prisons, such as Prison A, use open questions and collect all given answers. Owing to the use of different methods of data collection, a coherent overview is not possible.

Collecting data for scientific studies is an alternative way of obtaining information on religious affiliation. However, it is difficult to conduct research in German prisons and religion is not a key topic for ministries of justice, which must grant official permission to conduct research (Jahn 2017). In only one known study were data collected in a quantitative way. This interdisciplinary study about religiosity and crime prevention at the University of Tübingen collected data on the religiosity of juvenile inmates in two prisons – one in West Germany and another in East Germany (Kerner et al. 2005). It was a questionnaire with about 200 variables about religion (Ibid, 145–147). Researchers asked about the religious affiliation too, but in a non-comparable way: the data for the West German prison was divided into Christians (54%), Muslims (18%) and others (27%). For the prison in East Germany, a distinction was made between religious affiliation (7.1%) and non-religious affiliation (92.9%). In addition to the affiliation, there were questions about the value given to religion and religiosity. The value question combines 34 items in total. For the comparison, two items were used (Believing in God, Living according to Christian values, and norms): believing in God was more common for young inmates in the West German prison (30.3%) than in the East German one (4.7%). Living according to Christian values and norms is the same, but with lower numbers (9.5% in the West German prison and 3.6% in the East German prison gave a positive answer). Researchers also inquired about religiosity with the item "I consider myself religious." Table 13.4 shows the distribution between religious and non-religious inmates of both prisons and data on the characteristics of religiosity (Ibid, 147).

Table 13.4 Characteristics of religiosity (percentage)

Categories	East German Prison	West German Prison
Inmates in total	260	460
Total respondents	170	201
Religiosity (total)	6.6%	27.8%
Non-religiosity (total)	93.3%	72.1%
Religiosity (Christian)	–	27.3%
Non-religiosity (Christian)	–	72.6%
Religiosity (Muslim)	–	35.2%
Non-religiosity (Muslim)	–	64.7%
Religiosity (Non)	–	24%
Non-religiosity (Non)	–	76%

In contrast to the official numbers given by prisons, the study by the Tübingen researchers gives us a more differentiated perspective about religion because the "religion gap" between the former East German and West German federal states is still wide, not only in terms of belonging, but also of believing (Müller et al. 2013). This can also be seen in prison as a societal institution. The research by Irene Becci on the transformation of religion in Eastern Germany, as well as my own study in prisons across Germany, make it clear that there are regional specificities (Becci 2012; Jahn 2017). However, despite the historical situations regarding religion in both East and West Germany, we cannot make a general statement based on these data because not every inmate comes from the region where he/she is detained. Therefore, not every "none"-inmate is a local. The place of crime and the place of the judicial proceedings are crucial for the distribution of inmates. However, in some cases, inmates are displaced, for example, if they want to pursue professional education, which is offered in some prisons, or if they want to be accommodated closer to their relatives.

13.3.2 Religious Organisations

In contrast to data on individual religiosity, organised religion is much easier to observe. There are a variety of religious organisations in German prisons, but they differ with regard to the degree of institutionalisation and establishment. The prison chaplaincy in Germany is fully served by the Protestant and Catholic Churches – it is an institutionalised offer. As described in the previous section, there is an ongoing debate on the possibility of institutionalised chaplaincy such as the Christian one, served by Muslims or Islamic communities (Harms-Dalibon 2017). Jehovah's Witnesses want to offer an institutional chaplaincy too, but ministries of justice and prisons resist such requests.

There are other types of counselling and care besides chaplains. There are welfare organisations such as *Caritas* and *Diakonie* that offer counselling. Although religious welfare organisations offer more profane counselling, Evangelical organisations combine religious counselling and care activities. Such organisations are established in prisons as volunteers or with contracts for special tasks, such as working with people with addictions. Apart from these well-organised types of chaplaincy, there are also some local initiatives from migrant churches and other religious communities (Nagel 2015). Offers by Jewish communities were not identified during research. In the following, the various religious organisations will be presented with their specific traits in terms of institutionalisation and establishment.

(a) Institutionalised chaplaincy by Protestant and Catholic Churches[6]

---

[6]The following section is an updated comprehension of a German article of mine (Jahn 2011a).

Prison chaplains in the Federal Republic of Germany are employees, civil servants, or volunteers. Employed chaplains and chaplains with the status of a civil servant are common these days, but it depends on who employs them. In Germany, each prison has a Protestant and a Catholic chaplain; they are appointed by each federal ministry of justice in agreement with the regional diocese (Catholic) and regional Church (Protestant). The closed contracts are based on the concordats and contracts between the Holy See, or regional church offices, and the respective federal state. The regulations are based on the legal and political framework, as described in the previous section. In most of the cases, chaplains are employees of the federal State; however, in some cases they are employed by their Church because some chaplains do not want to be an employee of the State, whereas some are too old, because there is an age limit in Germany for becoming a State civil servant.

Protestant and Catholic chaplains are organised in conferences, which represent the Church, the public, and the politic. They are incorporated into the Church structure. Both Churches provide guidelines for the chaplain's work in prisons (*Deutsche Bischofskonferenz* 2006; Evangelische Konferenz für Gefängnisseelsorge in Deutschland 2009). According to the guidelines of the Protestant and Catholic chaplaincy, being a prison chaplain can primarily be described as the service of man and his relationship with God. These chaplains understand themselves to be critical dialogue partners and advocates of prisoners. They understand the prison as part of society and prisoners as part of their own parish. They participate in social debates on law and punishment by writing public statements, organising meetings and further training programmes, and cooperating with other government and non-government bodies. Both Protestant and Catholic prison chaplains have a national conference, which consists of various regional conferences, working groups and special representatives. Both conferences are closely connected with the respective Church. The German Bishops' Conference and the Evangelical Church in Germany (EKD) have their own commissioners for prison chaplaincy. In April 2017, the Catholic Conference had 225 members, who worked as full – or part-time chaplains. The secretary of the Protestant Conference mentioned 230 members. Nowadays, there are fewer chaplains in the prisons. However, for the chaplains, the problem arises in practice because the tasks in the contracts are still the same. Article 4, sentence 1 (extract; Sächsische VE Gefängnisseelsorge 1993) of the agreement between the Free State of Saxony and the Evangelical Lutheran Church for the regulation of the chaplain service in prison states of the following duties[7]:

- Holding regular worship services and individual counselling including visits to the prison cell and individual talks with the prisoners
- Hearing of confessions and administration of the sacraments
- Offering of group work, courses and training hours
- Participation in visits and monitoring of prisoners (special medical care)
- Pastoral counselling and support for relatives of prisoners in partnership, marriage and family affairs

---

[7] Author's own translation of the title.

- Participation in the reintegration and rehabilitation process of prisoners
- Participation in social assistance to prisoners and their families
- Advice in the acquisition of books for prisoners' libraries
- Participation in the training of prison staff
- Public relations

In addition, the chaplains do not only care for inmates of their own faith, but also for other inmates. To be more specific, worship services and other tasks must be prepared irrespective of the number of participating inmates. In rural areas, chaplains with tasks in several parishes and institutions spend most of their time travelling. A Protestant chaplain from a prison in rural Saxony explains:

> I have already 50% in prison and 50% in two church parishes. And by the distance I must …, so I cannot be in the prison every day. That is why I found the rhythm for myself: Wednesdays and Fridays I am in the prison. There are exceptions because I am sometimes there on Tuesdays, Wednesdays, and Fridays. But there are also weeks when I only have one day. Or even when there is so much in the parishes that I cannot find… I try to balance it somehow.

The developments described lead to the situation that more and more ecumenical and volunteer work takes place in prison. In some prisons, Protestant and Catholic chaplains as well as their volunteers, understand themselves to be a chaplaincy team. They share all tasks except for the sacraments. In other prisons, they hold a communal worship service. Although the decline in the percentages of working hours of chaplains refers to the decline of church members in prison, this is related to the decline in the number of church personnel. Above all, Catholic churches have fewer staff who can celebrate the sacraments. Therefore, priests sometimes serve several prisons in one diocese and lay people do the main work. In the Catholic Church, pastoral work is open to both the laity and the clergy, but the ability to perform baptism and confirmation is given only to priests (Bischofskonferenz 2006). Independent of previous professions outside the church, theological competence and additional training are necessary. Additional training is offered by the national conference on behalf of the German Bishops' Conference (Ibid 2006). In contrast to this, the Protestant chaplain needs theological education (Evangelische Konferenz für Gefängnisseelsorge in Deutschland 2009). The training for the Protestant chaplains is education that corresponds to the standards of the community for pastoral psychology. It takes place at the Institute for Special Chaplaincy in Bethel (*Seelsorgeinstitut in der Bildung und Beratung Bethel*) and comprises 6 weeks spread over a period of 2 years. The event is organised jointly by the institute, the church office of the Evangelical Church of Germany (EKD) and the Protestant National Conference for Prison Chaplains. The training takes place primarily for beginners and is open to Catholics and Protestants.

(b) Making of Muslim chaplains, Islamic chaplaincy in prison[8]

---

[8] This section is an updated summary of an article of mine written in German (Jahn 2014).

As already described in the Sect. 13.2, most of the Muslim organisations have not yet been included in the partnership contracts with the State. Owing to Muslim organisations remaining publicly unrecognised, it is not yet possible to offer Muslim inmates religious and social support like that received by their Christian counterparts in prison. In the institutions where I conducted my research, there was no institutionalised and professional Islamic chaplaincy. Either Christian chaplains or employees of the social service in prison are mostly responsible for Muslim inmates. Sometimes, voluntary Muslims and imams of the DITIB (The Turkish–Islamic Union of the Institution for Religion) offer support to Muslim inmates. Imams from DITIB come into the prison and offer the Friday prayer. But in most cases, such an offer is only for Turkish detainees. Also, the visits are irregular and pose problems of understanding between prison officials and imams – not only in terms of language but also in terms of understanding the rules of the prison institution.

However, for some years now, there have been more comprehensive approaches to establishing a Muslim-made Islamic chaplaincy at local and federal levels. The City of Wiesbaden initiated the project "MUSE – Muslim Pastoral Care in Wiesbaden in 2008."[9] The aim of the project is to initiate and institutionalise Islamic chaplaincy at a municipal level in several public institutions such as prisons, hospitals and schools. The federal state of Lower Saxony has had a working group since 2009 to establish Islamic chaplaincy together with Muslim unions. In 2012, there was an agreement on Muslim pastoral care between regional Muslim unions and the Ministry of Justice in Lower Saxony (Niedersachsen 2012). The Free and Hanseatic City of Hamburg concluded a contract on activities in public institutions such as hospitals, prisons and police training centres in 2013 (*Freie und Hansestadt Hamburg* 2013). The federal state of Bremen thereafter signed a contract on religious care in special institutions (Bremen 2014). These examples are initiatives under construction, have no continuity and are not institutionalised. In some places, the cooperation between different groups of interest works well; in other places, as in Berlin 2013, some problems appeared. The German Press Agency reported: "There is a burning dispute over the Muslim prisoners' care between the Berlin Senate and Muslim Associations" (German Press Agency 2013). The initial point was that the Federal Office for the Protection of the Constitution (*Bundesamt für Verfassungsschutz*) raised security concerns about members of the working group.

In her research, Lisa Harms-Dalibon focuses on "the dynamics of the governance of religious diversity as an interplay of national and institution-specific sets of logic by looking at the construction of the Muslim prison chaplaincy in Germany" (Harms 2017) in the federal states of Lower Saxony, Berlin and Hesse. Her research focuses on the emergence of an organised Muslim chaplaincy in Germany. One of her results is that "neither the influence of national legal ideologies nor the institutional location of specific rules and practices are sufficient to fully account for the dynamics of religious diversity inclusion. Rather, both are mediated through a field

---

[9] Author's own translation.

of actors who combine and reshape their environment wherever spaces of negotiation emerge" (Ibid, 17).

I agree with the result of Harms-Dalibon. However, in addition to the questions of governance, the question of theological legitimacy is also posed. Islamic chaplaincy raises the question of whether "Islam" knows chaplaincy as a theological concept and as a practice. The specific discussion not only has an institutional, legal and political dimension, but also a dimension of religious legitimacy. Lawyer Vigor Fröhmcke prominently holds this position. In his dissertation on the legal position of Muslims in the prison system, he argues that:

> Islam does not know such a religious person [...] like the Christian pastor. The Imam is only the leader of the Friday prayer, the most important common worship of the week. He is merely a preacher, since he has knowledge about the strictly ritualised prayer rules. Moreover, he has knowledge of Arabic as the language for the worship service. He is, however, not a professional theologian; he has a civil profession in everyday life. (Fröhmcke 2005)[10]

Fröhmcke understands Christian chaplains as pastors. He has a Christocentric and dogmatic legal perspective (Jahn 2011b). Legal scholar Matthias Rohe has a different view of this topic. He argues that Muslims must be socially integrated into Germany. The inclusion of other traditions and faiths is necessary (Rohe 2014). Additionally, the theologians and editors of the conference proceedings "Islamic pastoral care between origin and future" (Uçar and Blasberg-Kuhnke 2013) state that Islam has chaplaincy. Bülent Uçar and Martina Blasberg-Kuhnke state contrary to the opinion of Fröhmcke:

> If chaplaincy is understood as a religiously motivated and well-founded support, this does not only exist from the beginning in Islam, no chaplaincy is of fundamental importance for religiousness in Islamic understanding. As a differentiated and professional institution with different expertise and dimensions it is, however, a novelty for most Muslims in Germany. (Uçar & Blasberg-Kuhnke 2013)

Cimşit (2013), Arshad (2013) and Seyyar (2013) explain the historical and theological understanding, as well as the historical roots of the Islamic chaplaincy from an inner Islamic perspective, in the same publication. From the viewpoint of the latter authors, chaplaincy in prison is part of Islamic traditions. Abdullah Takim, professor of classical and modern Quran exegesis (*tafsîr*) at the University of Vienna, holds the same opinion. He held a lecture at the meeting of the German Islam Conference (DIK) in 2016. Moreover, he states:

> [T]he Christian-influenced pastoral system should not simply adapt, but should consider the faith of the Muslims, their cultural values, the respective traditions [...] of those Muslims living in Germany, and thus develop a concept with respect to new scientific knowledge. (Takim 2016)

Additionally, he mentions that models should be invented at a local level in collaboration with Muslim communities and public actors under scientific supervision, but the theological training should be carried out in institutes for Islamic theology (Ibid).

---

[10] Author's own translation.

(c) Other religious organisations in prisons

Other organisations are not institutionalised like the two types described in the previous sections. The causes and backgrounds of this situation are different and depend both on their religious self-understanding and on external understanding.

Welfare organisations such as *Caritas* and *Diakonie* are part of the so-called third sector or also known as the private–public partnership in Germany (Jahn 2017). It means that such organisations are not in the public or economic sectors of the State. They are independent and have special social tasks. Both organisations are among the largest employers in Germany. As organisations, they are closely connected with Protestant and Catholic churches and part of the religious history of the country. Both these organisations have a religious self-understanding and a religious origin. But as organisations with social tasks, they offer more profound counselling. Table 13.5 illustrates the different offers they made in the prisons where I conducted research. In every prison, there is only one of the two organisations. Additionally, Table 13.5 shows the professional status of the offer.

One challenge for faith-based welfare organisations is the tension between their religious backgrounds and the increasing economisation of their service and self-understanding (Jähnichen et al. 2010). From the prison's point of view, they are service providers. A psychologist described them as in the following:

> We have contracts here with Caritas regarding addiction counselling. […] We actually just want the addiction counselling. We are not buying the missionary mission or anything like that. […] The service personnel come from outside. […] Caritas is a good provider because it is a big carrier here in the area.

The self-understanding is still based on their religious backgrounds, as the preamble in the guidelines by Caritas illustrates:

Table 13.5 Comparison of offers and professional status of Christian welfare organisations

Prison	Offer	Professional status
1	Caritas: addiction counselling and group for alcohol addicts	Contract and expense allowance
2	Caritas: social training and addiction counselling	Service on demand (fee)
3	Diakonie: addiction counselling, choir	Service on demand (fee or volunteer work)
4	Diakonie: drug and gambling counselling	Service on demand (fee or volunteer work)
	Christopheruswerk (member in *Diakonisches Werk*, a federation of different Protestant-based welfare organisations): counselling for ex-offenders in spe, insolvency consultation and debt counselling	Contract, volunteer work
5	Caritas: counselling office for ex-offenders	Contract, volunteer work
6	Diakonie: offers for several discussion groups	Volunteer work

The service of Caritas is like worship and preaching [...]. On this basis, the German Caritas Association has formulated its self-image in its mission statement. All its actions are designed to protect people in their dignity, to promote solidarity in a plural world, and to work for a life of freedom, justice and peace around the world. This service of love is fulfilled by the works of individual persons, Christian communities, and communities, as well as through the communal Caritas. It thus also contributes to the construction and further development of ecclesiastical structures and to the livelihoods of communities. As a welfare organisation of the Catholic Church, the German Caritas Association is involved in shaping ecclesiastical and social life. Through its work, it contributes to the credibility of the ecclesiastical proclamation in public. (Caritas 2005)

In contrast to professional welfare organisations, non-governmental organisations, such as free churches, make religious offers such as Bible groups, individual religious counselling and religious training courses. Most of these organisations have an Evangelical background (Jahn and Becci 2017). Their self-understanding is based on the Lausanne Covenant, signed during a conference of Evangelical leaders in Lausanne in 1974. The close connection between Evangelisation and social engagement is central there.

In accordance with the theological self-understanding, and the history of Evangelical traditions as independent of the State, as well as from Protestant and Catholic Churches, there are no formal agreements with the State. Evangelical traditions want to be independent and, as such, do not want to have the status of a publicly recognised body under public law. Accordingly, counselling activities in prison are always dependent on the local context. As reaction, any activity – a regular Bible group or individual counselling by persons and groups – must be approved by prison officials. The activities are mainly for offender counselling inside and outside of prisons, and addiction counselling. Even offender counselling is very important for the prison system because there are only a few official offers owing to financial restrictions (Wirth 2010). A typical offer is the so-called contact groups where several volunteers meet inmates in prison. It is a group event with a mix of worship service and something like coffee/teatime. Most of the relationships between inmates and volunteers are built on this basis. After imprisonment, such groups have residential communities where ex-offenders can start new lives. Addiction counselling is the focus of Evangelical activism in prison. Alcohol and alcohol abstinence are a classic topic of Evangelical beliefs (Warner 2009). Like offender counselling, prisons have not institutionalised addiction counselling. In many prisons, the addiction therapy is supported by honorary offers. A psychologist in one of the prisons I studied explains that

Addiction therapy does not exist in a proper sense here. So, there is the addiction advice, which is rather a low-threshold offer. [...] It is the basic course on alcohol. The most important thing is the transfer of knowledge. In my view, if a prisoner is on this "basic course on alcohol", then he has direct contact with the volunteer. And they get to know each other on this basic course.

It is interesting that private–public partnership providers are active in the field of rehabilitation; these sometimes have a very strong religious self-understanding and an individual expectation, all part of the offer and the way of working in prisons

(Jahn 2015b). For research, it is interesting to explore such developments and compare them with tendencies seen and researched mainly in North America (Nagel
2006; Prätorius 2006; Sullivan 2009).

Welfare organizations and Evangelical organizations do not want to be publicly
recognized by the law and do not want to offer a chaplaincy service like Protestant
and Catholic churches. Since 2017, Jehovah's Witnesses is publicly recognized in
all federal states of Germany (Zeugen Jehovas 2017a, b), but cannot offer services
like Protestant and Catholic churches (Jahn 2017). In a position paper by Jehovah's
Witnesses, the following is written:

> "Experience makes it clear that legal determinants are not self-evident for several prison
> officials. It is more or less openly given that the efforts of Jehovah's Witnesses constitute
> rather a burdensome evil. Whether this is due to a not quite correct legal understanding of
> officials or, for example, in a close relationship with the chaplaincies of the both large
> churches, cannot be ascertained for the most part." (*Jehovas Zeugen*, N. N.)

One of the prison officials from my own research explains a common practice with
Jehovah's:

> "So, the [Jehovah's Witnesses] can make a notice on the board. If inmates express interest,
> then we allow the conversation in the visitor centre of our prison where they also get visits
> by relatives. This can also be done in a group. But I do not go so far that they can move
> freely in the prison, like others".

13.3.3   Religious Practice

According to my research, in Prison A and Prison C, in comparison with other prisons that I visited, many inmates declared being affiliated with a religion in the statistical records of the prison. However, only a few inmates use the existing religious
offers, or practice religion in general. Based on interviews with inmates and prison
staff, I concluded that "religion" is perceived mainly as a possible field of interest to
read and share time with others etc. Combined with an intrinsic religious motivation, religious practices are, in relation to other practices, relatively minor. But what
religious practices are common and how does the prison institution react towards
religious practice? The following overview gives an impression of the diverse practices from both the prison institutions towards religious practices and inmates who
want to practise religion.

In general, there is a distinction between individual religious practices, just like
we have with several rituals, and collective practices such as religious services. The
possibility of carrying out individual practices is mostly the result of an individual
decision taken by the prison staff, whereas the possibility of performing collective
practices must be decided at a higher level because more organisation is required in
those cases. Both types have in common that decisions taken regarding certain practices are clear and observed in all prisons, whereas decisions concerning other practices are inconsistent.

Clear decisions are usually made when there is an institutionalised offer such as *halal* food for Muslims. Every prison in Germany has been offering this for some years now. Inmates had to register for it, much like those who have diabetes or need special food because of medical prescriptions. This is not a problem because the prison infrastructure can serve different types of food to many people. Ramadan, however, is a slightly different kind of arrangement from the daily provision of *halal* food. When inmates want to practise Ramadan, the institution arranges it, changing the prison organisation during this period. A prison official said:

> For example, in case we have Muslims during Ramadan [...] we make sure that Muslim prisoners get a hot dish during this period to prepare something to eat when they are allowed to eat.

The organisation of Ramadan illustrates how the institution deals with practices that modify the established order. Individual religious practices are permitted as long as security and order are guaranteed in the institution. Security and order constitute the key institutional logic in prisons to decide whether something would be permitted or not. Prison Act part 1, First Title, Section 4 states:

(1) The prisoner shall participate in the drawing up of his treatment programme and in achieving the objective of treatment. His willingness to this effect shall be awakened and encouraged.
(2) The prisoner shall be subject to such restrictions of his liberty as are laid down in this Act. Unless the Act provides for a special regulation, only such restrictions may be imposed on him as are indispensable to maintain *security* or to avert a serious *disturbance of order* in the penal institution. (Federal Law Gazette I 2012)

Changing the institutional order is up to the will of prison administrators and the feasibility of the changes. Immediate protection of inmates is the primary goal of imprisonment and, therefore, special security instructions are permitted. These are listed in administrative regulations of the Prison Act as well as in the house rules. The administrative regulations apply for every prison in each federal state; the house rules are specific for each prison because of the specificities of each detention centre. Regulations around suicide illustrate this.

There are restrictions imposed on religious practices for security reasons concerns is the *tefillin*. The ban on leather straps is used in accordance with the suicide prevention. A prison guard states:

> He wanted to have these *tefillin*, that is a wooden box and two or three metres long, narrow straps, leather straps, which they then put around their arms at prayer [...]. Unfortunately, we could not approve this for security reasons.

Beside those two clear restrictions, religious books in general and the prayer rug for Muslims are examples where the institutional practice is not consistent. The practice with religious books depends on the library situation in the prison. Generally, most prisons just allow German books who are new, original packed as well as from an official seller for security reasons. A prison official illustrates a typical conflict

> "In religious books, we are a little more critical when it comes to obtaining foreign literature. So, we really prefer German books. There may be a conflict, when a prisoner says he wants a certain book from somewhere else. In reply, we say, 'No, we cannot let that happen because we do not know what's in there.'"

There is no time in prison to control every package, and there are problems with the translation of foreign literature. Some prisons have libraries with good selections of religious books, also in other languages, or they have a collaboration with local libraries. In such cases, inmates do not have problems accessing religious literature.

Permission to have a prayer rug is more complicated and depends on individual decisions. In one of the prisons I visited, the prayer rug was not allowed because its use in the Qur'an was not mentioned as mandatory, as the prison officer informed me. In another prison in my study, an inmate may acquire a prayer rug at his own expense, which is then taken away from him again because the institution is not sure if security regulations allow the use of prayer rugs. In yet another prison, inmates can use their personal prayer rugs without restriction. In this case, arguments about security and the religious nature of the practice do not play a role. These examples illustrate the different arguments used when dealing with a specific religious practice.

Collective religious practices are religious services by Catholic and Protestant chaplains, Bible groups by chaplains or by volunteers from other Christian denominations, and Friday prayers led by an imam. The way in which a collective religious practice works is a good indicator of whether a certain religion is accepted or not. Acceptance in this case does not refer to legal aspects, but to social acceptance. For instance, despite existing legal contracts, Christian chaplains are not accepted in every prison and they often face problems in organising regular worship. In fact, Evangelical groups without any public contract may sometimes enjoy greater social acceptance than churches with legal contracts. In a similar way, most Islamic organisations are not legally recognised, but can offer Friday prayers in some prisons. Contrarily, Jehovah's Witnesses are legally recognised and yet they do not get permission to offer collective practices in prison.

To illustrate the *modus operandi* of social acceptance, I will refer to the different understanding of missionary activities. Evangelical organisations perceive "missionary activity" as the central activity in their religious self-understanding, just as Bleick writes in his definition of Evangelicals that Evangelicalism is synonymous with the "Great Commission" (Bleick and Schäger 2008: 271). Additionally, missionary activities not only mean a dogmatic theological understanding, but also social activism, just as there are activities for inmates and ex-offenders with problems of drug addiction (Jahn and Becci 2017). Evangelical groups offer Bible groups and Alpha courses. They understand the offers to be relations work. An Evangelical pastor said:

> The key question is how we live in relationships. It's the topic of the Alpha course: How do I live in relation to myself? How do I live in relation to my neighbour? How do I live in relation to God? If these whole relationship questions are clarified, good things happen. And of course, a relationship with a church community and a religious community will emerge inevitably.

The prison official said in response to this offer:

> But these providers do not put their religious backgrounds on the table […]. This is oriented in a very secular way in terms of the needs of prisoners here. The task is to look at one's own development self-critically to see quite a lot of conversational contacts and whether one may perhaps change. And that is the main idea.

In contrast, prison managers see the religious practice of Jehovah's Witnesses in a critical way. One prison official argues why they have no offer:

> So, I would not let them go from one prison cell to another as outside happens from one front door to another. Prisoners should not be exposed to anything they would not have to accept outside.

In this case, security is not meant to protect the population from criminal activities, but to protect inmates from the missionary activities of Jehovah's Witnesses, which are carried out by the members as part of their preaching service. Missionary activities are used here as a security-relevant argument, which has negative connotations in the case of Jehovah's Witnesses. In the case of other religious organisations, such as the Evangelical groups, preaching is not seen as a problem, although the mission is a central part of their theology.

13.4   Conclusion

Religion in German prisons is a recent topic in German politics of integration and migration. But this topic also belongs to social scientific research. It is important to advocate for a broader perspective on religion and prisons that does not focus exclusively on Muslims. As described before, the legal framework is religion-friendly, and the possibility of privacy and religious freedom exists in prison. Also, religious organisations play an active part in prison. There is a separation between the state and religion, and there are ways for religious organisations to join common tasks in public institutions such as prisons. But there is no equality between religions. The Protestant and Catholic Churches are partners of the State, whereas other religious organisations must abide by the historically given Christian and theological concepts such as chaplaincy. Recently, there have been public as well as political debates on the possibility of integrating Islam into German public law and German public institutions. There are federal states that have contracts for chaplaincy with Muslim organisations. However, some federal states are more open to new religions. Thus, there is inequality in the field of practice, not only in terms of legal recognition but also regarding institutional practices. The legal text can be interpreted in different ways. Therefore, collective religious practices are a good indicator of how a religion is accepted in the institution and the federal state. The possibility of a prisoner practising religion depends on the status of a religious organisation in that prison.

Religion is both an option in prison and a private matter. Religious practices, combined with intrinsic religious motivation, amount to very little compared with other types of practices. Besides, religious affiliation does not say much about actual individual religious practices in prison. Also, there is a difference between belonging and believing in prison. To conclude, the different data about religious affiliation and religiosity in German prisons show that existing tendencies are similar in general society and in the prison institution: We have the three "big religious groups" and the "nones"; there is also an individualisation process. But there are some interesting findings, such as the presentation of Muslim inmates in Prison C and the high number of Catholic inmates in every prison. Additional studies related to this topic from a practical, criminological, and sociological view hint that there is no clear relationship between religion in society and religion in prisons. To say something valid about religious affiliations and religiosity in prisons, extensive interdisciplinary research is needed. Qualitative studies, such as those by Irene Becci (2012), Harms-Dalibon (2017) and Jahn (2017), could be a starting point for a quantitative survey in Germany.

References

Monographs and Articles

Arshad, M. (2013). Schuld, Vergebung und Seelsorge im Islam. In B. Uçar & M. Blasberg-Kuhnke (Eds.), *Islamische Seelsorge zwischen Herkunft und Zukunft. Von der theologischen Grundlegung zur Praxis in Deutschland* (pp. 39–60). Frankfurt am Main: Lang.

Becci, I. (2012). *Imprisoned religion. Transformations of religion during and after imprisonment in Eastern Germany*. Farnham: Ashgate.

Beckmann, B., & Kusch, R. (1994). *Gott in Bautzen. Gefängnisseelsorge in der DDR*. Berlin: Links Verlag.

Bleick, G., & Schäger, G. (2008). 1.7 Pfingstliche und charismatische Kirchen und Gemeinschaften. In M. Hero, V. Krech, & H. Zander (Eds.), *Religiöse Vielfalt in Nordrhein-Westfalen. Empirische Befunde und Perspektiven der Globalisierung vor Ort*. Schöningh: Paderborn.

Cimşit, M. (2013). Islamische Seelsorge – Eine theologische Begriffsbestimmung. In B. Uçar & M. Blasberg-Kuhnke (Eds.), *Islamische Seelsorge zwischen Herkunft und Zukunft. Von der theologischen Grundlegung zur Praxis in Deutschland* (pp. 13–25). Frankfurt am Main: Lang.

Day, A. (2011). *Believing in belonging: Belief and social identity in the modern world*. Oxford: Oxford University Press.

Foucault, M. (1975). *Surveiller et punir: Naissance de la prison*. Paris: Gallimard.

Fröhmcke, V. (2005). *Muslime im Strafvollzug. Die Rechtsstellung von Strafgefangenen muslimischer Religionszugehörigkeit in Deutschland*. Berlin: Wiss. Verlag.

Harms-Dalibon, L. (2017). Surveillance and prayer – Comparing Muslim prison chaplaincy in Germany's federal states. *Comparative Migration Studies, 8*, 1–22. https://doi.org/10.1186/s40878-017-0051-5.

Hennig, W. (2010). *Muslimische Gemeinschaften im Religionsverfassungsrecht. Die Kooperation des Staates mit muslimischen Gemeinschaften im Lichte der Religionsfreiheit*. Nomos: der Gleichheitssätze und des Verbots der Staatskirche. Baden-Baden.

Howard, J. (1792). *The state of the prisons in England and Wales*. London: Printed for J. Johnson, C. Dilly, and T. Cadell.

Jahn, S. J. (2011a). Gefängnisseelsorge in der Bundesrepublik Deutschland. In M. Klöcker & U. Tworuschka (Eds.), *Handbuch der Religionen* (Vol. 29, pp. 1–31). Landsberg am Lech: Olzog.

Jahn, S. J. (2011b). Gilt der Gleichheitsgrundsatz (Art. 3. Abs. 3 GG) auch für muslimische Inhaftierte? *Religion, Staat, Gesellschaft: Zeitschrift für Glaubensformen und Weltanschauungen, 2*, 425–435.

Jahn, S. J. (2014). Zur (Un-)Möglichkeit, islamischer Seelsorge im deutschen Justizvollzug. *Cibedo-Beiträge, 1*, 20–25.

Jahn, S. J. (2015a). Recht und Religion. In V. Krech & L. Hölscher (Eds.), *Handbuch der Religionsgeschichte im deutschsprachigen Raum* (Vol. 6/1, pp. 389–414). Paderborn: Schöningh.

Jahn, S. J. (2015b). Institutional logic and legal practice: Modes of regulation of religious organisations in German prisons. In O. Roy & I. Becci (Eds.), *Religious diversity in European Prisons* (pp. 81–99). Cham: Springer. https://doi.org/10.1007/978-3-319-16778-7_6.

Jahn, S. J. (2016). Being private in public space? The 'administration' of 'religion' in German Prisons. *Journal of Religion in Europe, 4*, 402–422. https://doi.org/10.1163/18748929-00904005.

Jahn, S. J. (2017). *Götter hinter Gittern. Die Religionsfreiheit im Strafvollzug der Bundesrepublik Deutschland.* Frankfurt am Main: Campus.

Jahn, S. J., & Becci, I. (2017). Evangelikalismus und soziale Fürsorge II: Seelsorge im Strafvollzug. In F. Elwert, M. Radermacher, & J. Schlamelcher (Eds.), *Handbuch Evangelikalismus. Lokal und global in Geschichte und Gegenwart* (pp. 379–394). Bielefeld: Transcript.

Jähnichen, T., et al. (Eds.). (2010). *Caritas und Diakonie im goldenen Zeitalter des bundesdeutschen Sozialstaats. Transformationen der konfessionellen Wohlfahrtsverbände in den 1960er Jahren.* Stuttgart: Kohlhammer.

Kerner, H.-J., et al. (2005). Religiosität, Gewaltaffinität und Rechtsbewusstsein junger Inhaftierter in West und Ostdeutschland. In A. Biesinger (Ed.), *Brauchen Kinder Religion? Neue Erkenntnisse – Praktische Perspektiven* (pp. 141–152). Beltz: Basel.

Link, C. (2004). Religionsgesellschaften. In H. D. Betz (Ed.), *Religion in Geschichte und gegenwart. handwörterbuch für theologie und Religionswissenschaft* (Vol. 7, p. 326). Tübingen: Mohr Siebeck.

Morris, N., & Rothman, D. J. (Eds.). (1995). *The Oxford history of prisons. The practice of punishment in Western society.* New York: Oxford University Press.

Müller, O., et al. (2013). Religiös-konfessionelle Kultur und individuelle Religiosität: Ein Vergleich zwischen West- und Ostdeutschland. *KZfSS Kölner Zeitschrift für Soziologie und Sozialpsychologie, 1*, 123–148. https://doi.org/10.1007/s11577-013-0221-x.

Nagel, A. K. (2006). *Charitable choice – Religiöse Institutionalisierung im öffentlichen Raum.* Münster: Lit.

Nagel, A. K. (Ed.). (2015). *Die zivilgesellschaftlichen Potentiale religiöser Migrantengemeinden.* Bielefeld: Transcript.

Pollack, D., & Müller, O. (2013). *Religionsmonitor. Religiosität und Zusammenhalt in Deutschland.* Gütersloh: Bertelsmann.

Robbers, G. (2001). Religious freedom in Germany. *Brigham Young University Review, 2*, 643–668.

Robbers, G. (2006). *An introduction to German law.* Baden-Baden: Nomos.

Rohe, M. (2014). Bedeutung und Perspektiven der Seelsorge im Justizvollzug. *Forum Strafvollzug – Zeitschrift für Strafvollzug und Straffälligenhilfe, 1*, 53–58.

Seyyar, A. (2013). Die theoretischen Konzepte der Seelsorge aus islamischer Sicht. In B. Uçar & M. Blasberg-Kuhnke (Eds.), *Islamische Seelsorge zwischen Herkunft und Zukunft. Von der theologischen Grundlegung zur Praxis in Deutschland* (pp. 85–100). Frankfurt: Lang.

Statistisches Bundesamt. (2017). *Rechtspflege. Bestand der Gefangenen und Verwahrten in den deutschen Justizvollzugsanstalten nach ihrer Unterbringung auf Haftplätzen des geschlossenen und offenen Vollzugs jeweils zu den Stichtagen 31. März, 31. August und 30. November eines Jahres.* Wiesbaden: Statistisches Bundesamt.

Sullivan, W. F. (2009). *Prison religion. Faith-based reform and the constitution.* Princeton: University Press.

Uçar, B., & Blasberg-Kuhnke, M. (Eds.). (2013). *Islamische Seelsorge zwischen Herkunft und Zukunft. Von der theologischen Grundlegung zur Praxis in Deutschland.* Frankfurt am Main: Lang.

Voas, D., & Crockett, A. (2005). Religion in Britain: Neither believing nor belonging. *Sociology, 1*, 11–28. https://doi.org/10.1177/0038038505048998.

Wagnitz, H. B. (1791). *Historische Nachrichten und Bemerkungen über die merkwürdigsten Zuchthäuser in Deutschland. Nebst einem Anhang über die zweckmäßigste Einrichtung der Gefängnisse und Irren-Anstalten* (Vol. 1). Halle an der Saale: Johann Jacob Gebauer.

Wagnitz, H. B. (1792). *Historische Nachrichten und Bemerkungen über die merkwürdigsten Zuchthäuser in Deutschland. Nebst einem Anhang über die zweckmäßigste Einrichtung der Gefängnisse und Irren-Anstalten* (Vol. 2). Halle an der Saale: Johann Jacob Gebauer.

Warner, J. (2009). Temperance, alcohol, and the American Evangelical: A reassessment. *Addiction, 104*, 1075–1084. https://doi.org/10.1111/j.1360-0443.2009.02616.x.

Wirth, W. (2010). Übergangsmanagement aus dem Strafvollzug. In D. Dölling (Ed.), *Jugendliche Gewaltdelinquenz – Beteiligte und Reaktionen* (pp. 77–98). Heidelberg: DVJJ.

Wißmann, H. (2012). Religionsverfassungsrecht im föderalen Mehrebenensystem. In I. Härtel (Ed.), *Handbuch Föderalismus* (Vol. 3, pp. 183–213). Berlin: Springer.

Internet Resources

Seelsorgeinstitut Bethel. (2017). Homepage. http://www.seelsorgeinstitut-bethel.de/. Accessed 8 Aug 2017.

Freie Hansestadt Bremen. (2014). Vertrag zwischen den islamischen Landesverbänden und der Freien Hansestadt Bremen. www.senatspressestelle.bremen.de/sixcms/.../13/2013_01_04%20. Vertragsentwurf.pdf. Accessed 8 Aug 2017.

Bundeskonferenz der Katholischen Seelsorgerinnen und Seelsorger im Justizvollzug. (2017). Homepage. www.kath-gefaengnisseelsorge.de. Accessed 8 Aug 2017.

Bundesministerium des Inneren. (2014). Religions- und Weltanschauungsgemeinschaften. http://www.bmi.bund.de/PERS/DE/Themen/Informationen/Religionsgemeinschaften/religionsgemeinschaften_node.html. Accessed 22 Aug 2014.

Evangelische Konferenz für Gefängnisseelsorge in Deutschland. (2017). Homepage. www.gefängnisseelsorge.de. Accessed 8 Aug 2017.

German Press Agency. (2013). Quarrel in Islam forum, available via http://www.berlin.de/aktuelles/berlin/3251308-958092-krach-um-muslimische-seelsorge-islamforu.html. Accessed 8 Aug 2017.

Freie und Hansestadt Hamburg. (2013). Vertrag zwischen den islamischen Landesverbänden und der Freien und Hansestadt Hamburg. www.hamburg.de/contentblob/3551370/data/download-muslim-verbaende.pdf. Accessed 8 Aug 2017.

Zeugen Jehovas. (2017a). Informationsportal Jehovas Zeugen in Deutschland. https://www.jehovaszeugen.de/Zweitverleihungen.56.0.html. Accessed 8 Aug 2017.

Zeugen Jehovas. (2017b). Anerkennungsverfahren. http://www.jehovaszeugen.de/Anerkennungsverfahren.65.0.html. Accessed 8 Aug 2017.

Deutsche Islam Konferenz. (2016). Fachtagung, Muslimische Seelsorge in staatlichen Einrichtungen. http://www.deutsche-islam-konferenz.de/DIK/DE/DIK/1UeberDIK/Aktuelles/aktuelles-node.html. Accessed 8 Aug 2017.

Deutsche Islam Konferenz. (2017). Seelsorge in öffentlichen Einrichtungen als Thema der Deutschen Islam Konferenz. http://www.deutsche-islam-konferenz.de/SharedDocs/Anlagen/DIK/DE/Downloads/LenkungsausschussPlenum/20170314-la-3-abschlussdokument-seelsorge.pdf?__blob=publicationFile. Accessed 8 Aug 2017.

Lausanne Movement. (1974). The Lausanne Covenant. http://www.lausanne.org/content/covenant/lausanne-covenant. Accessed 8 Aug 2017.

MUSE – Muslimische Seelsorge e.V. Wiesbaden. (2017). About MUSE. http://muse-wiesbaden.de/?page_id=155. Accessed 8 Aug 2017.

Land Niedersachsen. (2012). Vereinbarung zwischen den islamischen Landesverbänden und dem Land Niedersachsen. https://www.mj.niedersachsen.de/download/73665/zum_Download.pdf.

Takim, A. (2016). „Und meine Barmherzigkeit umfaßt alle Dinge" (Koran 7,156): Das islamische Menschenbild und die Seelsorge im Islam. http://www.deutsche-islam-konferenz.de/SharedDocs/Anlagen/DIK/DE/Downloads/Sonstiges/20160307_vortrag_takim_seelsorge.pdf?__blob=publicationFile. Accessed 8 Aug 2017.

Legal Documents and Grey Literature

Act concerning the execution of prison sentences and measures of rehabilitation and prevention involving deprivation of liberty (Federal Law Gazette I p. 2425; the translation includes the amendment(s) to the Act by Article 4 of the Act of 5 December 2012).

Basic Law for the Federal Republic of Germany in the revised version (Federal Law Gazette Part III, classification number 100-1, as last amended by the Act of 21 July 2010).

Deutsche Bischofskonferenz. (2006). *Denkt an die Gefangenen als wäret ihr Gefangen (Hebr 13,3). Der Auftrag der Kirche im Gefängnis.* Die deutschen Bischöfe, No. 84.

Bundesverfassungsgericht (BVerfG). (1972). *Grundrecht von Strafgefangenen.* Urteil vom 14.03.1972 (Aktenzeichen 2 BvR 41/71).

Bundesverfassungsgericht (BVerfG). (1998). *Recht auf informationelle Selbstbestimmung.* Urteil vom 15.12.1983 (Aktenzeichen 1 BvR 209/83).

Bundesverwaltungsgericht (BVerwG). (2005). *Rechtsanspruch der Religionsgemeinschaften auf Einführung von Religionsunterricht.* Urteil vom 23.02.2005 (Aktenzeichen 6 C 2.04).

Evangelische Konferenz für Gefängnisseelsorge in Deutschland. (2009). *Evangelische Konferenz für Gefängnisseelsorge in Deutschland: Ich war im Gefängnis und ihr seid zu mir gekommen. Leitlinien für die Evangelische Gefängnisseelsorge in Deutschland.* Stuttgart: Kirchenamt der EKD.

Caritas Germany. (2005). *Präambel Satzung des Deutschen Caritasverbandes e. V. vom 16. Oktober 2003 in der Fassung vom 18. Oktober 2005.*

Landtag von Nordrhein-Westfalen (StVollzG NRW). (2015). *Gesetz zur Regelung des Vollzuges der Freiheitsstrafe in Nordrhein-Westfalen.* Strafvollzugsgesetz Nordrhein-Westfalen – StVollzG NRW vom 13. Januar 2015 (GV. NRW, Ausgabe 2015 No. 5).

Prätorius, R. (2006). *Bestrafen – Betreuen – Bekehren. "Restorative Justice" in den USA: eine Abkehr vom punitiven Liberalismus?*, Vortrag auf der Jahrestagung der Gesellschaft für Sozialen Fortschritt, 12/13 October 2006.

Freistaat Sachsen. (1993). *Vereinbarung des Freistaates Sachsen mit den evangelischen Kirchen im Freistaat Sachsen zur Regelung der seelsorgerlichen Tätigkeit in den Justizvollzugsanstalten* (Sächsische VE Gefängnisseelsorge 2.6.2, 25).

Jehovas Zeugen. (2019). N. N. *Positionspapier zur seelsorgerischen Tätigkeit von Jehovas Zeugen in Anstalten.*

Landtag des Freistaates Bayern (BayStVollzG). (2007). *Gesetz über den Vollzug der Freiheitsstrafe und der Jugendstrafe* (Bayerisches Strafvollzugsgesetz – BayStVollzG) vom 10. Dezember 2007 (BayRS 312-2-1-J).

Chapter 14
Italy: Tested by New Religious Diversity – Religion in the Prison System

Francesco Alicino

Abstract As far as the Italian prison system is concerned, the public authorities have always considered the Catholic Church and its religious care providers as indispensable partners for implementing the rehabilitation programme, as established in Article 27 of the Constitution. It remains that in the last decades those authorities have substantially failed to reach this very goal, which is mainly because of their incapacity to make the Italian criminal justice system more efficient and reduce overcrowding in prisons, whose population, on the other hand, is increasingly changing, especially from a religious point of view.

Thus, although almost nowhere in Italy do the life conditions in jail respect human dignity, the prison system currently consists of a modest team providing spiritual guidance for inmates belonging to confessions other than Catholicism. And, as the author tries to demonstrate in this chapter, this situation is not only in contrast with both the constitutional rights and the supranational legal principles (such as those referring to the European Convention of Human Rights and the European Union's Treaties). It also makes Italy's prisons potential breeding grounds for cultural conflicts and religious radicalism, the most illustrative examples of which are given by the questions related to the growing presence of Muslim inmates.

14.1 Introduction

Prisons across Europe are facing an overcrowding crisis, which is a manifestation of at least three trends: tougher sentencing by judges (particularly for drug-related offences), a slow justice system and lack of monetary resources to build new facilities to accommodate the excess number of inmates. In Italy during the last few decades, this situation has deteriorated even further (Fig. 14.1). The greatest proof is the 2013 sentence published by the European Court of Human Rights (ECtHR),

F. Alicino (✉)
University LUM Jean Monnet, Bari, Italy
e-mail: alicino@lum.it

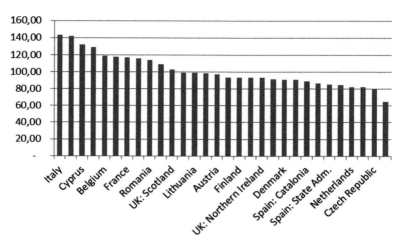

Fig. 14.1 Prison density per 100 places
Source: The European Prison Observatory (2015)

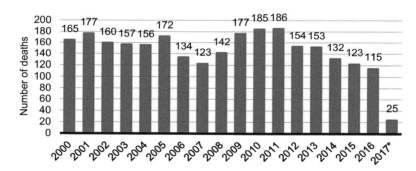

Fig. 14.2 The number of deaths in jail for suicides, health care dysfunction, overdoses and other unclear causes in Italy from 2000 to 2017
Source: Ministero della Giustizia (2017a)

which condemned the Italian State for "widespread violations of human rights of prisoners".[1] On that occasion, the ECtHR gave Italy 1 year to rectify the issue.

This situation becomes even more severe when taking into account the fact that the rate of suicide in Italian prisons is one of the highest in the EU (Fig. 14.2).

In addition, under the pressing process of immigration, the number of foreign inmates in Italian prisons is very high (Figs. 14.3 and 14.4).[2] Once again, this is

---

[1] ECtHR, *Affaire Torreggiani et autres c. Italie, Requêtes* numéro 43 517/09, 46 882/09, 55 400/09, 57 875/09, 61 535/09, 35 315/10 et 37 818/10.

[2] In 2016 in Italy, 27% of the prison population was foreign.

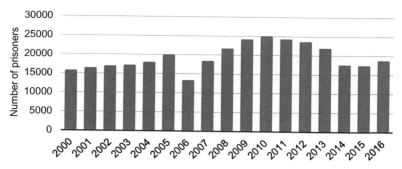

Fig. 14.3 Number of foreign prisoners in custody in Italy from 2000 to 2016
Source: Ministero della Giustizia (2017a)

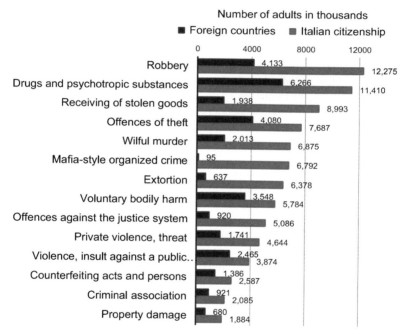

Fig. 14.4 Adult prison population in Italy in 2015, by leading type of crime and nationality (in 1000 people)
Source: Ministero della Giustizia (2017a)

because of the malfunctioning of the Italian justice system, which has a major impact on people without family support and few financial resources.[3]

The foreign detainees are much more numerous in the correctional facilities of those districts where there is a high percentage of immigrants, for example Milan

---

[3] See Vatrella (2015).

and Vicenza, where more than 60% of inmates are foreign-born, whereas in the mountain territories of Trentino-Alto Adige and Valle d'Aosta the proportion reaches nearly 70% (Fig. 14.5).[4]

Now, the difficult conditions faced by Italian detainees are also reflected in the complex relationship between religion and prisons, which generally shows a situation where in a cell there can be, by way of example:

- An inmate cohabiting with people of six different languages and six different cultural habits
- One who prays, as an observant Muslim, five times a day and another who swears five times a minute
- One who eats pork and one who cannot bear to look at it
- One who never washes and one who washes all the time

As an Italian inmate said during an interview, "[i]f you take a bunch of people like a mini United Nations, it is a disaster when there is only one toilet, when everybody brings their own culture to the bathroom" (Ghosh 2013).

As matter of fact, in the last 40 years in Italian prisons the "religious geography" has changed dramatically (Fabretti 2014). Along with other Mediterranean Countries, until few decades ago, Italy was a country of emigration: from the unification of the State in 1861 until the 1970s an impressive number (almost 27 million) of Italian people went abroad, desperately seeking for a job. Today, around 5 million people holding an Italian passport still live abroad, where the total number of people of Italian origin, migrants and their descendants, is about 60 million. Since the 1970s, Italy has become a state of immigration. At the beginning, the number of people coming from abroad was modest. It is only in more recent years that human migration from developing countries has been more visible (Alicino 2017). As such, this phenomenon has had an important effect on the State's religious geography, including in the Italian prison system.

Yet, both the penitentiary facilities and the legislation are still based on the past situation when, from a religious point of view, the Italian prison population was substantially homogenous. To put it in other words, the legislative instruments and the prison system developed for managing claims in a monocultural prison community do not easily fit in with the problems that arise in a completely changed religious context.

One result of this is that the Italian prison system does not necessarily promote the respect of the human rights of all inmates, including those who are part of neo-religious *nomoi* groups (Benhabib 2002; Shachar 2000), usually made up of foreign-born immigrants (Motoli 2013). Thus, the same legislative policy, which seems attractive from some religious and cultural perspectives, can be seen as a disadvantage, if not discriminatory, towards those detainees belonging to denominations other than the historical churches.

---

[4] See also Gonnella (2015).

Region	Number of Prisons	Capacity	Inmates		Foreign-born Inmates	Foreign-born Inmates %
			Total	Women		
ABRUZZO	8	1,587	1,785	73	206	11.54
BASILICATA	3	425	517	18	119	23.01
CALABRIA	12	2,659	2,559	43	523	20.43
CAMPANIA	15	6,107	6,708	334	880	13.11
EMILIA ROMAGNA	11	2.797	3.195	154	1.575	49,29
FRIULI VENEZIA GIULIA	5	476	623	16	223	35.79
LAZIO	14	5.239	5.971	403	2.657	44,49
LIGURIA	6	1,109	1,407	60	735	52.23
LOMBARDIA	18	6.120	7.927	381	3.588	45,26
MARCHE	7	852	812	23	280	34,48
MOLISE	3	263	338	0	82	24,26
PIEMONTE	13	3.838	3.670	139	1.601	43,62
PUGLIA	11	2,347	3,206	155	490	15.28
SARDEGNA	10	2.633	2.110	49	476	22,55
SICILIA	23	5.895	5.912	121	1.310	22,15
TOSCANA	18	3.385	3.244	117	1.510	46,54
TRENTINO ALTO ADIGE	2	506	443	20	307	69,30
UMBRIA	4	1,336	1,447	57	471	32.55
VALLE D'AOSTA	1	181	157	0	101	64.33
VENETO	9	1,845	2,164	130	1,177	54.39
Total	193	49,600	54,195	2,293	18,311	33.78

Fig. 14.5 Prisons and inmates in Italy
Source: Ministero della Giustizia (2017b)

This situation is even more evident when focusing attention on specific issues, such as

- The difference between the legal status of Roman Catholic chaplains and the legal status of religious ministers of other denominations, which are divided into those that have signed an *intesa* (agreement)[5] with the State (para. 2) and those that do not yet have an *intesa* (para. 3)[6]
- The rules concerning religious care[7] and religious freedom in the Italian prison system (para. 4)
- The challenges relating to the growing presence of Muslim inmates in Italy (para. 5)[8]

14.2   Legal Status and Social Role of Roman Catholic Chaplains

Article 26 of the 1975 Penitentiary law (No. 354, *legge penitenziaria*) states that detainees in Italy have the freedom to profess religion, to educate themselves in their own creed and to practise worship. At the same time, Article 1 of the 4 March 1982 law (No. 68) provides that worship, religious education and religious care of Roman Catholicism in Italian prisons are formally entrusted to chaplains. Besides, under Article 16 of the 1975 Penitentiary law, Catholic chaplains are part of the commissions that draw up prison regulations. More generally, chaplains are called upon to support and contribute to the development of human beings, with the result that they often fill the role of promoters, guarantors and defenders of the detainee's fundamental rights, including those referring to freedom of religion (Colaianni 1983).[9]

Compared with the previous legislation – when they were in charge of managing the prison library, the education programme and the correspondence of detainees (Pizzorusso 1973) – Catholic chaplains continue to celebrate sacred rites and provide for religious care. Regarding the Catholic (code of canon) law[10] and the State's current legislation, the core task is that chaplains transmit the gospel and bring religious support in places of detention. Their presence in prisons is therefore

---

[5] See Article 8.3 of the Italian Constitution.

[6] Alicino (2013).

[7] On the notion of "religious care", and its difference from the notion of "spiritual care", in the Italian prison system, see Rhazzali (2015).

[8] Rhazzali (2010); Cucinello (2016).

[9] This right is established in Article 19 of the Italian Constitution, which affirms that "[e]veryone [including a detainee] has the right to profess freely their religious faith in any form".

[10] See Can. 564–572, especially can. 566 (§ 1): "[i]n hospitals, prisons, and on sea journeys, a chaplain, moreover, has the faculty, to be exercised only in those places, of absolving from *latae sententiae* censures which are neither reserved nor declared, without prejudice, however, to the prescript of can. 976".

primarily legitimised by the need for religious care, which allows the chaplain's role to be distinguished from that carried out by psychological assistants and social workers who, as stated by the Italian laws, are also part of the organisational structure of prisons.

In reality, however, prison chaplains remain not only religious figures but also persons potentially capable of listening to the needs of detainees.[11] Chaplains are not only those who celebrate mass and the Catholic sacrament of penance and reconciliation, they are also persons whom detainees trust for moral and material support. In practice, chaplains normally provide the prisoners most in need with daily essentials, such as clothing, food, financial sustenance (for inmates and their families) and access to affordable medication. In doing so, they often find themselves coordinating voluntary activities. This explains the increasing number of the so-called little letter (*domandine*), through which many prisoners from religions other than Catholicism regularly ask the prison officials to meet with a chaplain, and not (or not only) for spiritual purposes.

In this sense, it is also worth remembering what is affirmed in Article 74 of the 1975 Penitentiary law, under which the competent diocesan bishop appoints a local priest as a member of the Council for social assistance (*Consiglio di aiuto sociale*), which provides prisoners with support throughout the retention period and after a detainee has served his/her sentence. Nowadays, these voluntary activities are formally ruled by both Article 78 of the 1975 law (No. 354) and Article 120 of the 2000 Presidential Decree (No. 230) regarding the measures depriving or limiting personal freedom (*Regolamento recante norme sull'ordinamento penitenziario e sulle misure privative e limitative della libertà*).

Chaplains are also involved, officially or unofficially depending on the specific correctional institution, in decisions concerning some benefits – such as the treatment and the use of alternative penalties to prison and of early release – which are aimed at facilitating the reintegration of detainees into society. It should be noted that even the frequency and participation in religious services might be used as a parameter to evaluate the conduct of an inmate to decide whether to grant him/her those benefits. This practice is legally justified by the content of the 1975 Penitentiary law, which states that the judgement about a prisoner's behaviour is mainly based on certain activities, such as those related to education, jobs and religion.[12]

It is also important to remember the 1986 *Gozzini* law (No. 663/1986) – in Italian *legge Gozzini* – which reformed an important part of the State's legislation concerning the prison system. Since then, inmates (especially those who have ties to terrorist organisations or are incarcerated for participating in criminal organisations) have been encouraged to collaborate with public authorities. Under this new legislative scenario, the whole prison personnel, including chaplains and nuns, has also been

---

[11] In fact, this is more suited to the religious nature and mission of the figure of the chaplain. It is not by chance that in France chaplains are called *aumônier*, deriving form *aumône*, which refers to charity and solidarity (Beckford 2011).

[12] See Article 15 of the 1975 Penitentiary Act.

converted into a sort of community of observers: for example, they can inform competent authorities on the behaviour of prisoners.

Along with these developments, in 1984, the Holy See and the Italian government signed the concordat almost completely revising the 1929 Lateran Pacts. This agreement produced some changes in the prison chaplaincy. First, the status of religious care providers passed from aggregated personnel to personnel in charge of spiritual care. Second, the nomination of a chaplain is no longer dependent on a double State–Church agreement: the religious authority now has the power to autonomously appoint someone as a religious care provider, without prior settlement with the Italian authorities.

On the other hand, though, religious care in prison is increasingly considered an individual right, protected by the State. It is no longer an obligation imposed upon prisoners by the joint action of the State and the Catholic Church. Thus, since the second half of the last century, services provided by the Roman Catholic Church, and the presence of chaplains, have implicitly and explicitly dominated the Italian prison system. But it is also evident that, from a socio-cultural point of view, a greater diversification of the prison population and a move towards more individually orientated religious care have been observed since then.

14.3 The Regulation and Presence of Denominations Other Than Catholicism

Since the 1970s and 1980s, Italy has been dealing with social and cultural challenges as a consequence of unprecedented religious and cultural diversification. This situation, until a few decades ago, was unexpected and unimaginable. It has in fact produced needs and problems stressing the issue of secularism (the *principio supremo di laicità*, as the Italian Constitutional Court calls it),[13] with the result that the relationship between the State and religions is becoming increasingly difficult and, at times, harshly contested.

To better understand that relationship, we have to distinguish bilateral legislation from the 1929 Unilateral law (No. 1159). The former is based on both the Lateran Pacts (regulating the relationship between the State and the Catholic Church)[14] and agreements called *intese* (regulating the relationship between the State and some of the denominations other than Catholicism[15]). The latter refers to the status and the role of confessions other than Catholicism that have not yet signed an *intesa*.

---

[13] See the famous sentence No. 203/1989, where the Italian Constitutional Court defined the supreme principle of secularism.

[14] Article 7 of the Italian Constitution.

[15] These are: *Tavola valdese* (Waldensian Evangelical Church); *Chiese cristiane avventiste del 7° giorno* (Seventh-Day Adventists); *Assemblee di Dio in Italia* (Assemblies of God); *Unione delle Comunità ebraiche italiane* (Union of Jewish Communities); *Unione Cristiana Evangelica Battista d'Italia* (Union of Christian Evangelical Baptists); *Chiesa Evangelica Luterana in Italia* (Lutheran

Once the Italian Government and the representatives of a given religion have signed an agreement (Article 7.2 of the Italian Constitution) or an *intesa* (Article 8.3 of the Italian Constitution), these two documents need to be ratified (agreement) or approved (*intese*) by specific acts of Parliament. These acts are "atypical legislation" because, once they enter into force, they can be amended only on the basis of new State–Church agreements or new *intese* between the State and minority religions: no amendment is possible based on unilateral legislation made by Parliament. In this manner, the Catholic Church and some other denominations (those that have signed an *intesa*) have the guarantee that their legal status cannot be altered without considering their will (Bouchard 2004; Ferrari 1993).

In any case, or maybe for this very reason, in Italy the connection between the State and religions remains substantially tailored to the exigencies and the notion of "traditional creeds". Tending to privilege some religious organisations over others, neither bilateral legislation nor the 1929 law can be easily used to regulate "different" (theologically and structurally) denominations. This is particularly the case of the religions whose presence in Italy is relatively recent (Casuscelli 2008), such as Sikh groups, Hindu communities and, above all, Islamic organisations. The problems related to the representatives of denominations other than Catholicism in the Italian prison system are clear examples of that.

As mentioned before, Article 26 of the 1975 law (No. 354) affirms, in accordance with the 1948 Constitution, that detainees have the freedom to profess and practise their faith freely. This translates into the fact that the celebration of the Catholic rites and the presence of at least one chaplain in prison must be assured. The situation, however, is different when it comes to detainees belonging to confessions other than Catholicism. In these cases, such inmates have the right to receive spiritual care carried out by religious ministers, but only upon request and provided that the presence of those ministers is compatible with the public order and the well-being of the prison community.

Besides, it is important to note that within the Italian legal system, the expression "religious minister" does not come from religious terminology. It is a *nomen iuris* that the State's laws use to define the civil status of some figures. At the same time, however, these laws sustain that the recognition of a religious minister results from a connection between the State's legal system and the laws of a given religion. In other words, the State attaches the civil status of religious minister to those who, within a denomination, are already considered as such.

Thus, as far as the civil notion of religious ministers is concerned, the connection between the State's laws and the laws of a given religion is based on two main features:

Church); *Sacra Arcidiocesi d'Italia ed Esarcato per l'Europa meridionale* (Patriarcate of Constantinople); *Chiesa di Gesù Cristo dei Santi degli ultimi giorni* (Church of the Latter Day Saints); *Chiesa Apostolica in Italia* (Apostolic Church in Italy); *Unione Buddista italiana* (Italian Buddhist Union); *Unione Induista Italiana* (Italian Hindu Union).

1. The autonomy of a denomination in deciding who is able to play the specific role of religious minister;
2. The right of the State to formally recognise the status of religious ministers, verifying whether persons appointed as such effectively exercise activities that, within a religious group, distinguish them from "normal" believers (Alicino 2015).

The fact remains, however, that any community with religious aims can operate within the Italian legal system, including prisons, without authorisation or prior registration. The legal source of this is essentially Article 19 in combination with Article 8.1 of the Constitution (Varnier 1995).[16]

All of this may explain the content of Article 58 of the 2000 Presidential Decree (No. 230) affirming that, in cases related to denominations whose relationships with the State are regulated by *intese*,[17] the prison authorities should authorise religious ministers to enter prisons. Prisoners adhering to religions without *intese* also have the right to participate in the religious celebrations of their own faith, as long as they are not in opposition with the order and security of the correctional institute. The display of religious symbols in cells is allowed and individual worship is permitted as well.

In particular, the 2000 Decree establishes the right of detainees adhering to religions without *intese* to enjoy the guidance of ministers of their own faith: these are chosen by the prison authority from the list of religious ministers who are accredited by the Ministry of the Interior. Alternatively, in prisons, the presence of religious ministers may be authorised under Article 17 of the 1975 law (No. 354), which allows them to be considered social operators (who promote and empower the rehabilitation of inmates and their reintegration back into society, thus reducing the risks of poverty and social exclusion).

---

[16] Article 8.1 declares that "[a]ll religious confessions enjoy equal freedom before the law".

[17] On this point, see: Article 8 of the 11 August 1984 Act, No. 449 (*Norme per la regolazione dei rapporti tra lo Stato e le chiese rappresentate dalla Tavola valdese*); Article 9 of the 22 November 1988 Act, No. 516 (*Norme per la regolazione dei rapporti tra lo Stato e l'Unione italiana delle Chiese cristiane avventiste del 7° giorno*); Article 6 of the 22 November 1988 Act, No. 517 (*Norme per la regolazione dei rapporti tra lo Stato e le Assemblee di Dio in Italia*); Article 10 of the 8 March 1989 Act, No. 101 (*Norme per la regolazione dei rapporti tra lo Stato e l'Unione delle Comunità ebraiche italiane*); Article 7 of the 12 April 1995 Act, No. 111 (*Norme per la regolazione dei rapporti tra lo Stato e l'Unione Cristiana Evangelica Battista d'Italia*); Article 7 of the 22 November 1995 Act, No. 520 (*Norme per la regolazione dei rapporti tra lo Stato e la Chiesa Evangelica Luterana in Italia*); Article 6 of the 30 July 2012 Act, No. 126 (*Norme per la regolazione dei rapporti tra lo Stato e la Sacra Arcidiocesi d'Italia ed Esarcato per l'Europa meridionale in attuazione dell'articolo 8, terzo comma, della Costituzione*); Article 10 of the 30 July 2012 Act, No. 127 (*Norme per la regolazione dei rapporti tra lo Stato e la Chiesa di Gesù Cristo dei Santi degli ultimi giorni in attuazione dell'articolo 8, terzo comma, della Costituzione*); Article 7 of the 30 July 2012 Act, No. 128 (*Norme per la regolazione dei rapporti tra lo Stato e la Chiesa Apostolica in Italia in attuazione dell'articolo 8, terzo comma, della Costituzione*); Article 4 of the 30 December 2012 Act, No. 245 (*Norme per la regolazione dei rapporti tra lo Stato e l'Unione Buddista italiana in attuazione dell'articolo 8, terzo comma, della Costituzione*); Article 4 of the 31 December 2012 Act, No. 245 (*Norme per la regolazione dei rapporti tra lo Stato e l'Unione Induista Italiana in attuazione dell'articolo 8, terzo comma, della Costituzione*).

Now, the actual implementation of these provisions leads us to assume that, in theory, the absence of an agreement (*intesa*) between the Italian State and some religious denominations should not affect the right of inmates to worship freely. In practice, this absence makes it very difficult for many detainees to exercise that right, a difficulty that is especially valid for foreign-born inmates.

The following table shows the data made available (and updated to 2014) by the Italian Ministry of Justice concerning the presence of representatives of religious minorities in Italian prisons:

Total number of penal institutions in Italy	231
Jehovah's Witnesses	53
Islamic organisations	33
Orthodox Churches	19
Evangelical Churches	16
Buddhists	14
Jews	5
Adventist Church	3
Christian Catholic and Apostolic Church	2
Evangelical Pentecostal Church	2
Assemblies of God in Italy	1
Waldensian Church	1
Confessions not specified	14

14.4 Religious Practices and Religious Freedom

In any case, religion is one of the most solid pillars of the treatment of inmates in Italy. This is all the more true when comparing the current legislation with the previous rules that, for example, established the obligation for detainees to attend mass and other Catholic rites, with the exception of those who said that they adhered to creeds other than Catholicism.

After the 1948 Constitution entered into force, the relationship between prisons and religion in Italy changed completely, at least from a legal point of view. This is mainly because the 1948 constitutional principles are based on the imperative balance between the "universal" need for peaceful coexistence among different viewpoints, and the equal protection of "fundamental" rights, which implies not only the rights of a religious group to be different from other denominations, but also the rights of individuals within both the State's legal system and religious communities.

As far as the relationship between religion and prisons in Italy is concerned, the impact of this constitutional framework is quite clear. One of the best examples of that is given by the conditions of the inmates, who, although subject to isolation during the so-called pre-trial detention,[18] are allowed to receive assistance from religious ministers. This example is important because it highlights the crucial need to affirm a reasonable constitutionally based compromise between

- The right and the interest of an inmate to exercise his/her religious beliefs
- The State's right and interest in preventing anyone from tampering with the evidence of the related case

By virtue of the special protection given to the fundamental rights, the measure of solitary confinement cannot affect the detainee's religious freedom. This means that a detainee can be prevented from exercising this right, but only on the basis of specific reasons such those referring to the risk of changing significantly the probative value of the evidence, as delineated by the investigation.

The inmate's freedom of religion also plays a key role in matters of alimentation. In this case, we should remember that food-related issues – which include the behaviour surrounding the production, distribution and consumption of food – could be seen as narrative performances of how a community constructs notions of itself and its relationship with the world. Therefore, food may also involve a belief in spiritual, invisible and transcendent entities. In brief, it can infer religion. Moreover, given that food is a fundamental part of our culture, and as religion is one of the great cultural constructs of human society, we can deduce that food and religion are very often strictly interconnected (Alicino 2014).

With regard to the prison system, it should first be noted that there is no legal rule regulating the nutritional regime in Italy. However, the jurisprudences of the Italian Constitutional Court and the Court of Cassation have affirmed that respect for specific diets should be considered a direct expression of the right to the freedom of religion.[19] Hence, inmates should be able to access food in conformity with their own religious convictions. In other words, the Italian penitentiary system shall be organised, as far as possible, to allow detainees to practise their religion and follow their beliefs, which implies feeding them in accordance with their own values and beliefs. Nonetheless, in Italy, these principles remain routinely unimplemented. Even though in the last 40 years the religious geography of prisons has changed dramatically, the penitentiary system is still dominated by the traditional view in relation to food. The Italian prison system continues working as if only practising Catholics constituted the prisoner population. But we know that this is not true, as in many Italian prisons most of the inmates are now believers of confessions other than Catholicism.

Moreover, the presence of numerous believers who do not originate from Catholicism has created the need to reorganise religious worship and religious care in an entirely new way. In Italy, religions other than Catholicism should have their

---

[18] Pre-trial detention refers to detaining of an accused person in a criminal case before the trial has taken place.

[19] See Corte costituzionale; sent. No. 26/1999; sent. No. 526/2000; sent. No. 526/2000; sent. No. 66/2009. See also Cass. pen., Sez. I, sent. n. 41,474, 25 September 2013. See also ECtHR, *Jakóbski v. Poland*, Application No. 18,429/06, 7 December 2010.

spaces in prison. Accepted in principle, this consideration is far from being universally implemented in the present penitentiary system, which, for this very reason, gives rise to a number of problems, ranging from practical ones to those related to the correct implementation of constitutional rights (Olivito 2015). These rights, for example, must give an inmate the concrete opportunity to profess freely his/her religious faith in any form, individually or in association. Yet in the Italian prison system, this opportunity is often hindered by many factors, such as the absence of adequate spaces (necessary for prayer and religious meditation), the deficiency of financial resources (for food processing that meets religious requirements), and the lack of religious ministers (authorised to conduct worship and administer religious services).

In sum, traditionally identified with the Roman Catholic chaplain, the prison population is now composed of a considerable number of members of different religions. It is comprises, for example, Muslims who, as such, would feed and pray in conformity with their religious – *halal* – principles, which, given the grave condition of many Italian penitentiaries and the current legislation, is almost impossible. Some very critical situations stem from this, that, in relation to Muslim inmates, end up producing anxiety, apprehension, discomfort, if not religious conflicts. After all, it is not by coincidence that these are the kinds of circumstances in which many Muslims are involved. This is also because they are the most numerous non-Catholic inmates within the Italian prison population.[20]

14.5 The "Challenges" Related to Muslim Inmates

The 2013 report made by the Italian Ministry of Justice entitled "Mosques in Prison Institutions" (Ministero della Giustizia 2013) affirms that at least 35% of inmates in Italy come from Muslim-majority countries, mostly Morocco and Tunisia. Many of these inmates have been convicted of (or are pre-trial detainees for) drug dealing, theft, falsifying documents and resisting arrest. Just fewer than 9000 are observant Muslims, including 181 imams or spiritual leaders, and 53 out of 202 prisons surveyed have more or less adequate places of worships. In general, the significant lack of adequate space in Italian prisons leads Muslim inmates to pray in their cells or in the yard.

Italy's chronically overcrowded and underfunded prisons are in fact likely places for religious radicalism to proliferate. In this context, extremists can create networks, recruit and radicalise new members, cancelling out attempts at rehabilitation (Ministero della Giustizia 2013). Although those accused of terrorism are rigorously separated from the rest of the inmates to reduce the risk of radical proselytism,

---

[20] On this issue, it is important to note that "[a]s we are speaking of Muslims in Italian prisons, it is legitimate to wonder who these individuals really are", as Rhazzali (2015) does in his essay.

the "common" prisoner population might also include fundamentalists who would have access to fragile, easily influenced individuals (Marranci 2009).

This explains the behaviour of the prison authorities, who appear to be constantly preoccupied with the potential links between Islam and terrorism, which also explains why the spaces for Islamic worship in prison and Muslim religious care providers are under constant vigilance. In this manner, the Italian authorities try to avoid those activities, rather than guaranteeing the right to freedom of religion, becoming potential breeding grounds for religious extremism and a recruitment pool for terrorist organisations.

It should not be forgotten that many inmates find religion behind bars. They find solace in religion, which allows them to recreate their communities of origin. These are people with no strong religious beliefs to begin with, but who might find protection and a new social identity in Islam. For these reasons, experts and scholars call on prison authorities to bring in "moderate" imams, supposed to be capable of providing religious care and, if possible, of creating a new counter-radicalisation strategy in jail.

Having said that, it should be noted that in the Islamic tradition imams are neither priests nor clergymen who, as in Catholic milieus, are purposely "consecrated" to the role of religious ministers. Instead, imams are selected at the local level: generally members of an Islamic community choose someone who at this level is considered knowledgeable and wise, who understands the Quran and is able to recite it correctly and properly. We can therefore argue that – generally – an imam is a respected member of a Muslim group.

In some communities, a Muslim may be recruited to be an imam after having undergone special training. In others, imams are chosen from among the existing members of an Islamic denomination without any specific training programme. Besides, there is no universal governing body to supervise imams, which is done at the community level. This may explain why in Italy, imams, as religious ministers, are almost all self-taught. This also explains the fact that there is no comprehensive list of imams and other Muslim representatives in Italy.

Thus, to remedy a lack of a list referring to Islamic authorities, the Ministry of Justice's Circulars of 6 May 1997 (No. 5,354,554) and 2 January 2002 (No. 508,110) have established a specific procedure to allow applicants to enter an Italian prison and guarantee the freedom of religion of Muslim inmates. This procedure gives representatives from Muslim communities the possibility of communicating with the Ministry of the Interior (and the General Directorate for Prisoners and Treatment – *Direzione generale dei detenuti e del trattamento*) the name of the religious organisation they belong to, their role within this organisation and their mosque of reference. After verification of the documents presented, the General Directorate decides whether or not to authorise the application.

Nevertheless, the most numerous imams in Italian prisons are Muslim detainees. We may call them do-it-yourself imams, who are able to organise worship, prayer functions and representation of co-religionists when dealing with the prison administration. Although these imams do not have theological training, they have charisma and credibility among Muslim inmates. Their role is particularly evident in the institutions where there are sections for Muslim inmates only. In cases like these, the detainee imam organises the prayer sessions and acts as an interface between his co-religionists and the prison authorities (Rhazzali 2015).

In any case, Italy's prisons currently consist of a modest team providing religious care for Muslim inmates, which is almost always guaranteed on a voluntary basis, as well as being at the discretion and capacity of the prison authorities. Combined with the fact that there is no formal agreement between the State and the Islamic communities, the effectiveness of provisions referring to freedom of religions, worship and religious care of Muslim inmates is therefore extremely limited.

For all these reasons, the State must work on projects with the most recognised Islamic organisations in Italy (such as *UCOII*,[21] *AMI*[22] and *COREIS*[23]), to license more imams who may work with Muslim inmates in a more effective way and under the framework of the constitutional principles.[24] On the other hand, the presence of educated religious figures could be an effective tool for challenging and tackling religious fundamentalism and extremist opinions.

In this sense, it is important to note that in 2015, the Department of Penitentiary Administration (DAP) and the *UCOII* signed a Memorandum of understanding. This could be seen as an effort towards a more reasonable and effective approach to the questions raised by the growing presence of Muslim inmates in the Italian prison system (Giustizia 2015), like those referring to religious radicalism.

Likewise, in January 2016 the Italian Minister of Interior established the Council for Relations with Italian Islam (*Consiglio per le relazioni con l'Islam Italiano*), made up of experts in ecclesiastical law, religions and Islam. The Council provides opinions and formulates proposals on the integration of the Islamic population in Italy, including Islamic inmates. In this context, in February 2017, the Minister of Interior and some Islamic organisations signed the National Pact for an Italian Islam, which was aimed at "strengthen[ing] dialogue and active collaboration with the interior ministry administration, continuing efforts to work against expressions of religious extremism and promoting a process of legal organisation of Islamic organisations in harmony with the principles of current regulations on the issue of religious freedoms" (Ministero dell'Interno 2017).

---

[21] *Unione delle Comunità Islamiche d'Italia* (Union of Islamic Communities and Organisations).

[22] *Associazione Musulmani Italiani* (Association of Italian Muslims)

[23] *Comunità Religiosa Islamica Italiana* (Islamic Italian Community).

[24] It is important to note that the provisions regulating religious care in prison are a novelty in the Islamic tradition, occurring only in Western contexts. There is no similar provision in the prison systems of Muslim-majority countries or, rather, there is no form of religious care provided, "except very recently, as a consequence of a more general introduction of prison systems based on European or American models, resulting from the development of a greater awareness and acceptance of the rights of individual freedoms in the societies and political institutions, thanks to the ratification and adoption of the international declarations of human rights" (Rhazzali 2015, p. 137).

14.6   Conclusion

The prison community is the outcome of what the inmates and other actors involved in a penitentiary create. It is a cultural life that is not straightforwardly given by the disciplinary standard set by the correctional institution. It can actually stand in opposition to it.

However, commonalities develop among detainees called symbiosis, which in Italy is also characterised by the common experience of the prison chaplaincy. After all, the established chaplaincy in the history of the Italian prison system has been considered an important instrument in the rehabilitation and integration programme, as affirmed by the State's law (Becci 2011). This is the reason why, as far as prisons are concerned, the State has always seen the Catholic Church and its religious care providers as essential partners for implementing the constitutional principle, under which "[p]unishment cannot consist in inhuman treatment and must aim at the rehabilitation of the convicted person".[25]

In the last decades, Italian public authorities have substantially failed to reach this very goal (Antigone 2015). This is mainly because of their incapacity to make the criminal justice system more efficient and reduce overcrowding in prisons, the population of which is at the same time increasingly changing, especially from a religious point of view (Corleone 2015). This is a result of a long-term policy, through which Italian prisons leave detainees in inhuman conditions that, at the end of the day, has nothing to do with the constitutional provisions, such as that referring to Article 27 of the Italian Charter (Camera Penale di Napoli 2011).

Indeed, as was intended to demonstrate with this chapter, that grave situation is not only in contrast with the constitutional and supranational legal principles (such as those related to the European Convention of Human Rights and the European Union's Treaties). It also makes Italy's prisons potential breeding grounds for cultural conflicts and radical (political, ideological or religious) views, putting them into violent action.

Bibliography

Alicino, F. (2013). La legislazione sulla base di intesa. In *I test delle religioni "altre" e degli ateismi*. Bari: Cacucci.

Alicino, F. (2014). Religion and sustainable food in the age of consumer culture. *Review of Studies on Sustainability, 1*, 101–124.

Alicino, F. (2015). Imams and other religious authorities in Italy. *Stato, Chiese e Pluralismo Confessionale, 12*, 1–28.

Alicino, F. (2017). The place of minority religions and the strategy of major denominations. The case of Italy. *Rivista AIC, 2*, 1–20.

---

[25] Article 27 of the Italian Constitution.

Antigone. (2015). *XI Rapporto nazionale sulle condizioni di detenzione. Oltre i tre metri quadri.* Torino: Edizioni Gruppo Abele.

Becci, I. (2011). Religion's multiple locations in prison, Germany, Italy, Swiss. *Archives de Sciences Sociales des Religions, 153*, 65–84.

Beckford, A. J. (2011). Les aumôneries de prison: une introduction au dossier. *Archives de Sciences Sociales des Religions, 153*, 11–21.

Benhabib, S. (2002). *The claims of culture: equality and diversity in the global era.* Princeton: Princeton University Press.

Bouchard, G. (2004). Concordato e intese, ovvero un pluralismo imperfetto. *Quaderni di Diritto e Politica Ecclesiastica, 1*, 70–71.

Camera Penale di Napoli. (2011). In Centro Direzionale, Palazzo di Giustizia, Camera Penale di Napoli (Ed.), *Il Carcere possibile. Giuda ai diritti e ai doveri dei detenuti.* Napoli.

Casuscelli, G. (2008). La rappresentanza e l'intesa. In *Islam in Europa/Islam in Italia tra diritto e società*, ed Alessandro Ferrari, 285–322. Bologna: il Mulino.

Colaianni, Nicola. 1983. *La riforma dell'ordinamento del personale di assistenza religiosa nell'amministrazione penitenziaria. Diritto Ecclesiastico* I:214-230.

Corleone, F. (2015). La riforma penitenziaria e il fallimento del carcere. *Questione Giustizia, 2*, 43–48.

Cucinello, A. (2016). L'Islam nelle carceri italiane. *Paper Ismu Ottobre*, 1–16.

Di Motoli, P. (2013). I musulmani in carcere: teorie, soggetti. *Studi Sulla Questione Criminale, 8*, 75–98.

Fabretti, V. (2014). Le differenze religiose in carcere. *Culture e pratiche negli istituti di Pena alla Prova del Pluralism. Roma: Universitalia.*

Ferrari, S. (1993). Il Concordato salvato dagli infedeli. In V. Tozzi (Ed.), *Studi per la sistemazione delle fonti in materia ecclesiastica* (pp. 127–158). Salerno: Edisud.

Ghosh, Palash. 2013. Italy's overcrowded prisons: a growing tragedy of epic proportions. *International Business Times*, June 18.

Gonnella, Patrizio. 2015, Detenuti straieri in Italia. http://www.associazioneantigone.it/upload2/uploads/docs/sintesilibro.pdf. Accessed 16 Apr 2017.

Marranci, G. (2009). *Faith, ideology and fear: Muslim identities within and beyond prisons.* London: Continuum.

Ministero dell'Interno, Consiglio per le relazioni con l'Islam Italiano. (2017). Patto nazionale per un Islam italiano, espressione di una comunità aperta, integrata e aderente ai valori e principi dell'ordinamento statale. http://www.interno.gov.it/it/servizi-line/documenti/patto-nazionale-islam-italiano. Accessed 15 Sept 2017.

Ministero della Giustizia. (2015). Protocollo d'Intesa tra il Ministero della Giustizia, Dipartimento dell'Amministrazione Penitenziaria e l'Unione delle Comunità e delle Organizzazione Islamiche in Italia (UCOII). http://www.ispcapp.org/AttiMinistero/docs/Protocollo_Intesa_UCOII.pdf. Accessed 17 April 2017.

Ministero della Giustizia. (2017a). Prisoners in Italy. https://www.statista.com/study/38767/prisoners-in-italy-statista-dossier/. Accessed 17 April 2017.

Ministero della Giustizia. (2017b). Detenuti presenti e capienza regolamentare degli istituti penitenziari per regione di detenzione. https://www.giustizia.it/giustizia/It/mg_1_14_1.page;jsessionid=Olfe31uoyjK4F99uQLz+VpQg?facetNode_1=4_54&facetNode_2=2_5&facetNode_3=0_2&contentId=SST1268354&previsiousPage=mg_1_14. Accessed 15 Apr 2017.

Ministero della Giustizia, Dipartimento dell'Amministrazione Penitenziaria. (2013). Le Moschee negli Istituti di Pena. http://www.ristretti.it/commenti/2014/febbraio/pdf3/moschee_carceri.pdf. Accessed 17 Apr 2017.

Olivito, E. (2015). 'Se la montagna non viene a Maometto'. La libertà religiosa in carcere alla prova del pluralismo e della laicità. *Costituzionalismo.it, 2*, 1–47.

Pizzorusso, A. (1973). I cappellani negli istituti di prevenzione e pena nel diritto vigente e nel progetto di riforma penitenziaria. In *Studi per E. Graziani* (pp. 555–569). Pisa: Pacini Editore.

Rhazzali, M. K. (2010). *L'Islam in carcere. L'esperienza religiosa dei giovani musulmani nelle prigioni italiane*. Milan: FrancoAngeli.

Rhazzali, M. K. (2015). Religious care in the reinvented European imamate Muslims and their guides in Italian prisons. In I. Becci & O. Roy (Eds.), *Religious diversity in European prisons. Challenges and implications for rehabilitation* (pp. 117–140). Cham/Heidelberg/New York/Dordrecht/London: Springer.

Shachar, A. (2000). The puzzle of interlocking power hierarchies: Sharing the pieces of jurisdictional authority. *Harvard Civil Rights – Civil Liberties Law Review, 2000*(35), 385–426.

The European Prison Observatory. (2015). Detention conditions in the European. http://www.associazioneantigone.it/upload2/uploads/docs/PressKit.pdf. Accessed 17 Apr 2017.

Varnier, G. B. (1995). La prospettiva pattizia. In V. Parlato & G. B. Varnier (Eds.), *Principio pattizio e realtà religiose minoritarie* (pp. 8–13). Torino: Giappichelli.

Vatrella, S. (2015). *Penitenti educati. Migranti in una etnografia carceraria*. FrancoAngeli: Milan.

Chapter 15
Latvia: The Position of Religion in the Penitentiary Institutions

Anita Stasulane

Abstract This chapter discusses the position of religion in the Latvian prison system. Starting with a short history of the prison administration in Latvia, the author describes the contemporary legal status of prison chaplaincy, prison regulations regarding religious practices, accommodation of individual religious beliefs and collective religious practices. In Latvia's multi-denominational situation, the overwhelming majority of prison chaplains are Protestants. However, the Roman Catholic Church and the Orthodox Church compensate for this deficiency through the work of volunteer chaplains. By comparing the number of spiritual services provided by permanently employed and volunteer chaplains, the author concludes that volunteer chaplains make a significant contribution to the spiritual care of convicted persons in Latvia. When comparing work with convicted people individually and in groups, data show that individual work constitutes 62% of all activities performed by religious organisations in prison. The chapter highlights some cases of religious discrimination in prison, associated with keeping religious items and food, and discusses ministering in prison.

15.1 General Insight

15.1.1 Historical Background

Latvian prisons are like living history, as some currently functioning prisons in Latvia are located in buildings that are over a hundred years old: Jelgava Prison was built in 1830, while the second-oldest prison in Latvia, known as the White Swan, was built in 1863 in Daugavpils. Several prison buildings were adapted to meet the requirements of prisons because they were built for different uses; for example,

A. Stasulane (✉)
Daugavpils University, Daugavpils, Latvia
e-mail: anita.stasulane@du.lv

Ilguciems Prison is a former horse stall. Liepaja's Karosta Prison (built around 1900) represents the most striking page in Latvian prison history: Until as recently as 1997, it served as a place for military personnel to serve their disciplinary punishment. The types of inmates housed there changed with changes in political power: revolutionaries, sailors from the Tsarist army, deserters from the German Wehrmacht, 'enemies of the people' from Stalin's time, and soldiers from the Soviet and Latvian armies. A museum currently operates at the Karosta Prison, and it is the only military prison in Europe open to tourists.

The largest and most modern prison in Tsarist Russia was the Central Prison in Riga, planned for 1360 prisoners. From 1902 to 1914 the complex was composed of 15 buildings. The First World War brought important changes to Latvia's history. After the proclamation of the Republic of Latvia (1918), the prison inspectorate was created in the image of the earlier governorate's prison inspectorate (Veitmanis 1939, 21). The newly established institution was not able to become a fully fledged state institution owing to the outbreak of the Red Terror throughout Latvia.

Three prisons operated while the Bolsheviks were in power in Riga (January to May 1919): the Central Prison, the Female Prison and the Governorate Prison. These played an important role in the Bolsheviks' repressive regime: 4200 people were imprisoned in Riga's prisons within 5 months. About 60 people died each month from illnesses in Riga's prisons, while the death penalty was handed down in 1000 cases (Šiliņš 2013, 122). It is significant that the Bolsheviks established a law on a new type of incarceration: concentration camps in Latvia. The 'untrustworthy' inhabitants were relocated to two easily guarded islands on the Daugava River and condemned to a slow death. The Bolsheviks created concentration camps in other places in Latvia too: at Pļaviņas, Valmiera, Alūksne and Vecgulbene (Šiliņš 2013, 119–120).

The Republic of Latvia's prison administration system developed further in the summer of 1919, when the Main Prison Board was formed, employing only four people initially. After a month, it was reorganised into the Main Prison Organization Administration, with the number of employees gradually increasing: in 1920, 20 people were employed in the administration (Ieslodzījuma 2016). Up until 1940, about 2000 prisoners were simultaneously serving their sentences in 19 prisons and places of detention. The Prison Department coordinated the chaplain service, which employed ministers whose work as chaplains was their primary employment, ministers who fulfilled their obligations episodically as chaplains, and ministers who undertook their work as chaplains temporarily, combining this work with their service in a congregation (cf. Veitmanis 1939). From 1936 to 1940, prisoners took part in worship services on a voluntary basis. Attendance at a worship service had to be organised at least once a month if a prisoner expressed such a wish. This didn't apply to prisoners who were minors, whose attendance at worship services was compulsory. Not all prisons had chapels, which is why religious services were held in separate rooms. Christian worship services took place in the same chapel, while Jews had their own.

When Soviet forces occupied Latvia in 1940, prisons were utilised for incarcerating 'social class enemies', but a year later they served to imprison 'racial enemies' of the German National Socialists. After the Second World War, the Soviet regime transformed places of imprisonment into sources of unpaid workforce. In the 1980s, without increasing the number of prisons and only building light construction barracks and naming them 'corrective labour colonies', 16,000 people served their sentences in Latvia. Skirotava Prison, which had a capacity of around 500 people, housed more than 2000 prisoners.[1] Everything that could be manufactured was made in the prisons, and the quantities of manufactured goods reached very impressive levels for those times – 300 million roubles. During the Soviet period, the 'spiritual' care mission in prisons was carried out by *politruki*, or political education instructors, who devoted most of their work to strengthening the communist regime and spreading its ideological propaganda.

After Latvia regained its independence in 1991, there were 15 prisons operating in the country. In 1994, the ministry of the interior developed a guideline on the regulatory procedure for the provision of religious services in prison.[2] However, the prisons' spiritual care was limited to uncoordinated and irregular visits by ministers and volunteers. An ecumenical Religious Matters Consultative Board was set up in the prison department's social rehabilitation branch for the more active coordination of pastoral work in prison. In 2003, the prison administration (PA) was allocated a budget for the creation of a chaplain service, and each place of detention got its own chaplain.

15.1.2   Current Organisation of Penitentiary Institutions

Latvia's economic crisis (2008–2010) forced reform on the country's places of detention. Several prisons were consolidated to reduce the numbers of employees in the state administration and cut the administrative costs of maintaining prisons. Currently nine prisons operate in Latvia, with most of them located in the central region of the country. Two prisons (Ilguciems Prison, and Central Prison) are located in Riga and another not far from Riga, in Olaine. Daugavgriva Prison is located in Latvia's second-largest city, Daugavpils, and Latvia's other large cities, Jelgava, Jekabpils, Valmiera and Liepaja, also contain a prison. A correctional institution for minors is located in Cesis.

In 1995, Latvia switched to a progressive system for serving sentences, in which closed, partly closed and open prisons were created, which gave prisoners the possibility of ending up at a level with a less strict regime if they had served out part of their sentence and behaved well. The Sentence Execution Code of Latvia (Saeima 2016) identifies three types of prison: closed, partly closed and open. Men who have

---

[1] In 1988, a prison riot took place at Skirotava Prison, which was suppressed with the help of military forces.

[2] In an interview, one of the chaplains pointed out that the initiative for the creation of Prison's Chaplains' Service came from the Head of the Prisons Department at that time, who invited Baptists from the USA to help introduce a Prison Chaplains' Service into Latvia.

been sentenced to prison for serious or very serious crimes, as well as prisoners transferred from partly closed prisons for gross or systematic breaches of the regime, serve their sentences in closed prisons: Daugavgriva Prison (with open type prison section), Jelgava Prison, Valmiera Prison, and Olaine Prison (with a partly closed and an open type prison sections). Security and continual surveillance of prisoners are present at partly closed prisons, and prisoners with a lower-level sentencing regime[3] serve their time in closed cells. Ilguciema Prison for women (there is also a correctional section for minors) is partly closed, and a partly closed Jekabpils Prison has an open type prison section. Both men and women serve their sentences in open type prison sections (at Olaine Prison, Daugavgriva Prison and Jelgava Prison).

In addition to the aforementioned types of prisons, there are also investigative prisons (Liepaja Investigative Prison and Riga's Central Prison), where suspects, the accused and persons to be tried, and those who have been sentenced to jail are kept imprisoned (Ministru 2003). Correctional centres for minors exist as a separate type of prison, where young people up to the age of 18 serve their prison sentences (Cesis Juvenile Correctional Institution). Female minors serve their sentences at separate sections of women's prisons, which were set up according to the requirements set for correctional institutions for minors (Ilguciema Prison's correctional section for women).

15.1.3   Recent Changes and Trends

Political reform of criminal punishment commenced in Latvia with changes to the Criminal Law (2012), which changed the goal of criminal policy – not only to punish, but to restore justice, protect society, re-socialise convicts and prevent crime. This reform significantly increased the scope for applying penalties not associated with a more general denial of liberty as well, which is why the total prison population has decreased: from 6117 prisoners in 2012, to 4409 in 2015, and to 4202 in September 2016 (Ieslodzījuma 2016). The ministry of justice sees the number of prisoners decreasing by 30% by 2020. However, there remains a high percentage of prisoners in Latvia – 355 per 100,000 inhabitants (Kronberga and Sīle 2016).

The level of recidivism in relation to the total number sentenced has remained at more than 50% for a long time and continues to increase.[4] Prisons reflect the social situation in Latvia in a direct way, especially the youth unemployment problem. A fifth of all prisoners are young people up to the age of 30, while a third of them end up serving multiple prison sentences. Of the young people imprisoned, 52% are battling various addictions: drugs, alcohol, gambling and computer games (Justoviča 2015).

---

[3] In closed or partly closed prisons, prisoners are allocated one of three regime levels: highest, medium or lowest.

[4] In 2015, 44.47% of those imprisoned were first-time offenders (Cf. Ieslodzījuma 2016).

The location of prisons in historical buildings and the technical condition of their infrastructure create a range of problems. Of all the places of detention in Latvia, only the Cesis Juvenile Correctional Institution for minors is in line with modern standards (Luksa 2013). The majority of existing detention centres do not conform to human rights standards, which is why compensation must be paid to prisoners who submit complaints about prison conditions to the European Court of Human Rights and win their case if prison conditions are recognised as being unsuitable.

Many experts and investigatory structure groups, including representatives of the European Committee for the Prevention of Torture (CPT) and the European Human Rights Commissioner, have visited Latvia. European institutions continue to make quite harsh criticisms of Latvia's prisons, even though there has been noticeable progress in the prison system in recent years. Latvia has been reproached for the fact that living space in prisons is less than 4 m² per prisoner.[5] The surveillance of prisoner relations is made more difficult as the ratio of prisoners per prison employee is large.[6]

Because of the infrastructure, the movement of prisoners in prisons is also inefficient and requires large personnel resources to guard and monitor them, which could be avoided with the creation of new prison infrastructure.[7] In 2008, the ministry of justice developed the *Concept for the Development of Detention Centre Infrastructure*, which included four principles: new prisons need to be evenly distributed throughout the nation's territory so that convicted persons are located as close as possible to their family members and to where they live, people should not be moved from prison to prison, cells must be able to accommodate two persons, and there must be suitable spaces for resocialisation and employment.

15.1.4 Current Prison Studies

Knowledge on penitentiaries in Latvia 'develops in the minds of autodidacts who are territorially and institutionally dispersed' (Luste 2011). Because in recent decades the bare-minimum of research funding provided by the state resulted into resorting to (mostly foreign) grants as the sole research funding mechanim, research is only available through participation in international programme projects. The PA participated in the European Commission's Criminal Justice programme project called Suicide Prevention System Development in Imprisonment Places (2014–2016) with the goal of improving suicide prevention. During the project, a group of researchers from Latvia, Romania, the Czech Republic and Slovakia developed recommendations for prison personnel to work with prisoners who demonstrate unstable psycho-emotional behaviour (Europris 2017).

---

[5] Currently, according to Latvian law, a prisoner must be allocated 2.5 m².

[6] In Latvia, there are on average three prisoners to every prison employee, while in some European countries, the ratio is one prisoner to every prison employee (Cf. Seržants 2005).

[7] Liepaja Prison is the most important infrastructure site for a safer society and for the resocialisation of prisoners. It will be the first place of detention built in Latvia since the country regained independence. Construction was planned to commence by late 2017 but it is still postponed. (Cf. Latvijas 2016).

The European Prison Observatory is undertaking research on prison conditions in the EU. Using quantitative and qualitative methods, current conditions in prisons in various European countries are being analysed, and existing conditions are compared with international norms and standards protecting prisoners' basic rights, especially with the European Prison Rules of the Council of Europe. During the project, prison councils,[8] which include prison employees, elected prisoners and chaplains, were highlighted as an example of best practice (Crétenot 2013). The Latvian Centre for Human Rights prepared an overview on prison conditions in Latvia (Kamenska et al. 2013).

The ECOR[9] project (2014–2016) focused on the exchange of best practices, promoting alternatives to the usual detention and the development of a post-penitentiary integration programme.[10] An evaluation of the Ilguciema Prison's long-standing Miriam Christian education and nurturing programme, which was developed in 2002 and is conducted by the prison chaplain, was undertaken as part of the project. The programme is based on a methodology developed by the Association of Protection and Assistance to Convicts (APAC) and is concerned with the restoration of a person's self-esteem, based on Christian values.

Ringolds Balodis has been systematically researching the relationship between church and state in Latvia for an extended period and has also focused on the legal aspects of religion in prison (Cf. Balodis 2003: 141–176, 2002: 420–454, 2000: 227–230). Furthermore, Feliciana Rajevska and Dace Demme have analysed the integration of prisoners, focusing particularly on the employment of convicted persons. The highest level of employment among convicted persons was observed from 2003 to 2007 owing to the increase in emigration of residents to western Europe in search of work. The prison workforce was used more widely due to the shortage of workers in Latvia. Currently, the largest hurdle for prisoner employment is that, since 2005, employers no longer receive income tax rebates for the employment of prisoners (Rajevska and Demme 2010: 161–192).

15.2 Legal Aspects

15.2.1 Legal Status of Prison Chaplains and Chaplaincy

The profession of chaplain is registered under Code No. 2636 19, in the classification list of professions adopted by the Latvian government (Ministru 2010). The Sentence Execution Code of Latvia states that the Chaplain Service shall be subordinate to the PA (Article 46). The Cabinet of Ministers Regulations (CMR) No. 423

---

[8] Prison councils have been operating in nine prisons in the United Kingdom since 2009.

[9] The project European Communities of Restoration has been funded with the financial support of the Criminal Justice Programme of the European Union (cf. European Communities).

[10] The project partner representing Latvia was the non-governmental organisation Integration for Society.

Section 7, 'On the Spiritual Care of Convicted Persons' (Ministru 2006a), also provides for the involvement of chaplains in the development of convicted persons (Article 30).

The Law on Religious Organizations defines chaplains as pastoral staff who perform official duties in places for serving sentences, national armed forces units and elsewhere, where the pastoral care of a regular clergyman is not available (Article 1) (Saeima 1995). On the other hand, CMR No. 134, 'On the Chaplain Service', specifies that a chaplain is a person who has obtained theological education in accordance with the prescribed procedure of the corresponding religious organisation and who has been nominated for the position by one of the following religious organisations: the Latvian Evangelical Lutheran Church, the Roman Catholic Metropolitan Curia of Riga, Latvia's Orthodox Church, Latvia's Pomorian Old Believer Church, Latvia's United Methodist Church, Latvia's Baptist Congregations Association, the Union of Seventh Day Adventist Latvian Congregations, the International Church of God Latvian Pentecostal Union, Latvia's Dievturi[11] Congregation and the Latvian Pentecostal Congregation Centre (Articles 4–5) (Ministru 2011).

These religious organisations are not the only ones that are active in prisons in Latvia. The Sentence Execution Code states that lawfully registered religious, benevolent and charitable organisations shall be permitted to carry out moral development activities (Article 46.1). Furthermore, the Law on the Procedures for Holding under Arrest states that an arrested person has the right to ask the chaplain to request the presence of a clergyman of the arrested person's religious organisation (Article 27) (Saeima 2006).

The activities of the Chaplain Service are defined by CMR No. 134, 'On the Chaplain Service': chaplains undertake the spiritual care of prisoners, those sentenced and prison personnel,[12] provide moral support and consultations on religious and ethical questions, and implement moral education measures (Article 16). A chaplain is hired by the head of the PA (Article 6), while a particular institution has the right to ask the Prison Chaplains' Association for its opinion on a chaplain who has been selected by a religious organisation about the chaplain's suitability for work in the chaplain service (Article 7). The decision about the establishment of a chaplain service was made by the administration of the prison, which notifies religious organisations about a vacant chaplain position, indicating the requirements of the position and the terms of employment (Article 8).

If a religious organisation establishes that a chaplain's professional skills do not match the responsibilities of the position, it shall inform the prison about the aforementioned non-compliance. In evaluating the declaration from the religious organisation, the PA has the right to terminate the employment contract with the chaplain (Article 9). The finances and the supply of materials for the chaplain's activities are

---

[11] *Dievturi* means 'God keepers', a Latvian neo-pagan group.

[12] The chaplain has the right to help prison staff in addressing spiritual problems if they consult with the chaplain.

provided by the relevant state or local council institution from the allocated budget funds or the company that legally employs the chaplain (Article 20).

The title Chaplain for Work in Prison is usually used when advertising the vacant chaplain's position (Profesiju 2017). Chaplains work an eight-hour day in the Prison Administration Resocialisation Section. They perform their work duties in the chapel, but individual consultations take place in the cell of the convicted person. The chaplain's duties are to provide for convicts' spiritual care regardless of religious beliefs or affiliation, to provide convicted person with moral support and consultations on religious and ethical questions, to hold religious services, video sessions, lectures, religious literature study activities, concerts and other events, to present religious education and rehabilitation programmes which will encourage changes in the values orientation of convicted persons, to organise meetings between convicted persons and ministers, to observe a code of ethics and the chaplain work ethic, and to maintain prisoners' confidentiality.

15.2.2 Denominational Representation in Prison

To guarantee the equality of inhabitants, regardless of their attitude towards religion, the Law on Religious Organizations (Article 4) states that state and local government institutions, public organisations and events, and companies shall be prohibited from requesting information from employees thereof and other persons regarding their opinion towards religion or regarding denominational affiliation. The prison administration does not collect data on the religious affiliation of convicted persons.

15.2.3 Prison Regulations on Religious Practices

The Law on Religious Organizations states that religious organisations may perform religious activities in places for the serving of prison sentences if the persons present therein so wish (Article 14). The anticipated time and place for an event shall be coordinated with the administration of the relevant institution. The Sentence Execution Code of Latvia states that the procedures by which convicted persons shall be permitted to see a minister and participate in moral development activities shall be regulated by the internal procedural regulations of the penitentiary institution (Article 46).

To ensure the spiritual care of convicted persons, chaplains at penitentiary institutions organise the activities of religious organisations or perform them in accordance with the normative acts of the Chaplain Service. Religious activities take place in the presence of prison staff (except for confession). Convicted persons meet with the minister at a time allowed by the daily schedule and in accordance with the procedure outlined by the head of the PA. The minister is to visit convicts who have been placed in isolation cells only with the permission of the head of the penitentiary institution (Articles 35–38) (Ministru 2006a).

The CMR No. 423 Section 7, 'On the Spiritual Care of Convicted Persons', also addresses the issue of religious items among those that can be delivered in consignments and parcels. With the permission of the head of the penitentiary institution, the convicted person may possess religious items delivered in a consignment or parcel in his cell or living area (Article 39). The head of the penitentiary institution, within 14 days of the receipt of the religious item, will determine its compliance with the penitentiary institution's internal regulations and, taking the chaplain's opinion into account, make a decision regarding the possession of the item. The chaplain will let the penitentiary head know what religion the convicted person practices and whether the item is necessary for religious purposes.

15.3   Sociological Aspects

15.3.1   Religious Discrimination in Prison

The Latvian constitution Satversme declares that everyone has the right to freedom of thought, conscience and religion, emphasising that church shall be separate from the state (Article 99) (Latvijas 1922). The Law on Religious Organizations states that direct or indirect restriction of inhabitant rights or the creation of privileges for inhabitants, as well as violation of the religious sensibilities of persons or incitement of hatred in connection with the opinions of such people towards religion, is prohibited (Article 4.1). The Sentence Execution Code of Latvia states that discrimination against a convicted person on the basis of religious convictions shall not be permitted (Article 4). Litigation, as well as alternative dispute resolution methods like, for example, negotiations, mediation and conciliation, is used in the settlement of disputes in cases of religious discrimination. If convicted persons believe that religious discrimination has been directed at them at the place of detention, they have the right to turn to the court, asking it to acknowledge the discrimination which has taken place and to seek compensation for losses and moral damages.

In 2009, an ombudsman received an application from a convicted person that spiritual care was not provided in prison and that it was not possible to meet with a priest from the Orthodox Church. However, religious discrimination was not established in this case because the obstacles that prevented the convicted person meeting with an Orthodox priest were created by Latvia's Orthodox Church, which refused to subject their priests to the regulated screening of persons and property. Ministers of other denominations did not refuse to be subjected to the examination of property and could undertake the spiritual care of prisoners (LR tiesībsargs 2009).

In 2011, the constitutional court considered a convicted person's constitutional grievance on the ban on keeping Buddhist prayer beads in prison. The court decided that there had been a restriction on the freedom to express religious conviction

(LR Satversmes 2011). In 2015, the issue of video observation of meetings between chaplains and those serving life sentences at the Daugavgriva Prison came up (LR tiesībsargs 2016). In 2016, an ombudsman received 550 submissions from prisoners,[13] but there were no complaints about religious discrimination in places of detention among them (Berke 2017). One of the interviewed chaplains indicated that when he started visiting places of detention 12 years ago, prison personnel tended to verbally abuse convicted persons about their religious conviction when escorting them to meetings with the chaplain. This situation has since been eliminated owing to the PA's concern for the professional development of its employees (Interviewee No. 1).

In recent years, the courts have reviewed several matters associated with food served in prison which was incompatible with the religious convictions of convicted persons. In 2010, a convicted Muslim's action against the prison for restricting his religious freedom was granted by a supreme court decision (LR Augstākā 2010). In 2012, the issue of whether, in accordance with their religious conviction, imprisoned Hindus were entitled to vegetarian food, which does not contain meat and is not cooked in fat; the issue received widespread media exposure. The convicted person was able to convince the highest court that, as a member of the International Society for Krishna Consciousness (ISKCON), he was unable to eat meat from slaughtered animals (LTV 2012). In 2014, action was taken, based on the application of a convicted member of the ISKCON, whereby meat and fish products were replaced with soya powder when vegetarian food was served in prison. In the applicant's view, soya or soya beans could replace meat and fish, and he objected to a prison policy, by which onions and garlic, which he didn't use due to his religious beliefs, were not excluded from his diet. The court did not find this declaration to be sufficient for establishing a protected expression of religious freedom (Administratīvā 2014).

15.3.2   Ministering in Prison

Up until 2014, the Resocialisation Concept allotted one chaplain per 300 convicted persons, but the current *Guidelines for the Resocialisation of Prisoners 2015–2020* allow for one chaplain per 250 convicted persons. A shortfall in state budgetary allocations is hindering the achievement of this indicator, and so in 2015 there was one chaplain for every 295 convicted persons (Ministru 2015).

In 2016, 16 chaplains (including two females) were permanently employed at the PA: five Lutherans, four Baptists, three Adventists, three Pentecostals and one Catholic (no Orthodox chaplains are employed in the prison system). A spokesman for the PA emphasised that they would like to see more priests (at least deacons)

---

[13] Prisoners complained about their living conditions, torture, inhumane treatment, physical and moral abuse, the rights to freedom and security in serving their sentence, rights to medical assistance, good management principles, and issues associated with serving their sentence.

among the chaplains (Interviewee No. 4), but currently 31% are lay chaplains. In fact, the small number of secular persons has been determined less by the PA's desire to attract more priests than by the low wages. The interviewed chaplains were of the same opinion: that the work of a chaplain in prison was so poorly paid that a secular person would be unlikely to earn a livelihood from it. Ministers, especially Catholic and Orthodox priests, are fully engaged in serving their congregations, but lay chaplains are dissatisfied with the low pay. This is one reason why there were still two vacant full-time prison chaplain positions in early 2017.

When in the *Regulations on the Chaplains' Service* the PA mentions religious organisations in connection with a prison chaplain vacancy, applicants for the position are nominated by these organisations. The CVs submitted by candidates for the positions and recommendations from their religious organisations are reviewed by the Religious Matters Consultative Council, which includes one representative from each of the religious organisations mentioned in the *Regulations on the Chaplains' Service*.[14] The council interviews the applicants for the position and vote to adopt a resolution as to which applicant best satisfies the requirements of the prison chaplain position, but the decision to hire is made by the PA.

The *Regulations on the Chaplains' Service* do not indicate what the proportional division for prison chaplains among the religious organisations should be. Assuming that the religious persuasion of convicted persons is proportional to that of Latvia's general population, one of the chaplains expressed dissatisfaction with the emerging situation: the majority of convicted persons are Lutherans, Catholics and Orthodox, but their spiritual care has ended up in the hands of numerically small denominations (Interviewee No. 2). However, there has been no open discussion on this topic because ecumenism is highly valued in Latvia. The PA spokesman has pointed out that the denominational representation in prisons is also taken into account now when evaluating applicants for prison chaplain: if a chaplain of a certain denomination is already working at a particular prison, priority is given to an applicant from a different denomination (Interviewee No. 4).

Volunteer chaplains, who have been authorised by their denomination, also undertake pastoral work at Latvia's prisons. Chaplains from lawfully registered religious groups that are not mentioned in the *Regulations on the Chaplains' Service* also undertake spiritual care as volunteers. A comparison of the number of spiritual services provided by permanently employed and volunteer chaplains reveals that in 2015, volunteer chaplains conducted 54% of worship services, 49% of concerts of religious music, 39% of individual pastoral discussions and consultations, 35% of religious literature studies and organised 25% of religious film showings (IVP 2016). Data for 2015 do not differ significantly from previous years, revealing that volunteer chaplains account for a significant share of the spiritual care given to convicted persons.

---

[14] A spokesperson for the PA pointed out that Latvia's Dievturi Congregation does not participate in the work of the Religious Matters Consultative Council.

The training system for employees at places of detention only provides prison guards and wardens with an initial qualification. One volunteer chaplain emphasised that the spiritual care concept of his denomination differs from that of other denominations. Firstly, by its individual approach, and secondly, by the involvement of congregation members, people involved in culture and business people in the resocialisation programmes for convicted persons. However, chaplains should have a common understanding about resocialisation and methods of working with convicted persons so that they can become more successfully involved in resocialisation work.

The PA's annual reports do not regularly collate data about the activities of religious organisations in prison. The available data (Cf. IVP 2009) show that in 2008, of all the religious activities held in prisons, 20.71% were conducted by members Orthodox community, 18.46% by Pentecostals, 16.70% by Lutherans, 11.83% by Adventists, 10.77% by Baptists, 9.60% by Catholics, 2.54% by Old Believers, 0.04% by Methodists and 9.35% by others (ISKCON, Jehovah's Witnesses, Muslims, Buddhists and New Generation). The situation changed in 2010: Catholics were the most active and conducted 19.53% of the religious activities, Orthodox 19.18%, Pentecostals 18.44%, Lutherans 11.22%, Adventists 11.49%, Baptists 10.77%, and Old Believers 4.59%, while others (ISKCON, Jehovah's Witnesses, Muslims, Buddhists and New Generation) conducted 4.82% of the religious activities. Even though there is only one Catholic employed by the PA and the Orthodox Church does not even have a permanent chaplain working at a prison, the Roman Catholic Church and the Orthodox Church compensate for this deficiency through the work of volunteer chaplains.

15.3.3 Accommodation of Individual Religious Beliefs and Practices

In 2011, with PA Instruction No. 235, 'On the Organization of Catering for Prisoners', a common menu and common food preparation technology were established at all places of detention. The Sentence Execution Code of Latvia (Article 77.7) states that norms for prisoners' daily food are determined by CMR No. 1022, 'On the Norms for the Material Supply of Prisoners Food and Household Needs' (Ministru 2006b). These regulations provide for special food norms for patients, minors and pregnant women. Prisoners who don't wish to have certain food products in their diet for religious reasons do not have their own food norms catered to. However, the regulations do allow (Article 5) the use of replacement food products, and meat products can be replaced by soya products (Appendix 2, Article 4.10).

A convicted person has the right to possess those items that are necessary for religious rituals or spiritual practices. A chaplain usually evaluates the need for Christian religious items. Conflicts between convicted persons and prison management arise when it is not clear whether a requested item serves a religious purpose.

If the convicted person asks for the religious item of another religion, the chaplain must invite the representative of the respective religion to the prison to ascertain whether the item sought is needed for religious purposes. All PA structural units must observe the same regulations, but, as pointed out by one chaplain who was interviewed, 'Each prison has its own prison superintendent, and the prison superintendent is in reality the king in [his] prison', which is why there tend to be differing approaches to the organisation of spiritual care in places of detention in Latvia, because 'there is one law, but there can be many interpretations' (Interviewee No. 1).

Convicted persons participate in spiritual care events voluntarily. Group events are announced in advance, and convicted persons register for them. A prison's operational section evaluates whether convicted persons' regime would allow them to participate in the events. In addition, convicted persons must register in advance for individual discussions with a chaplain. Data for the six years (2010–2015) clearly shows that individual religious events dominate with 62% over collective events in Latvia's prisons. In comparing work with convicted people individually and in groups, one of the chaplains emphasised the advantage of individual activities:

> 'Serious discussions take place one on one. [...] I go to N prison three times per month and spend all day there – three days per month from morning till evening. And I devote one day to individual discussions only. And each time, about 50 people have registered so I can't talk to all of them in full. I devote about 20–30 minutes to each of them, which is already very little, but I can't do it differently' (Interviewee No. 3).

From the experience of the chaplain, collective events in prison tend to acquire a non-religious character: prisoners who take part in organised charismatic-style worship services make bets on who will go out in front this time and accept Jesus (Interviewee No. 2).

15.3.4   Accommodation of Collective Religious Practices

Despite the disparate dynamics in different years, in the years 2010–2015, the overall number of individual meetings increased from 8497 to 10,023. Of the group events, the number of concerts organised at prisons most obviously increased, having doubled from 169 to 295, whereas activities involving the study of religious literature (from 2216 to 1923) and the number of films shown with a religious theme (from 1813 to 1601) decreased. The amplitude of the fluctuations in the number of worship services hasn't been great: about 100, or around 10 worship services, more or less, per year per prison.

Each Latvian prison has a chapel, and more than one in some cases. For example, there are four chapels in the Central Prison, and one of them was set up consistent with the canons of the Orthodox Church. The regularity of worship services in prison depends on the people involved (both the chaplain and the convicted person) in the particular denomination, for example, a Catholic worship service takes place once a month. One chaplain explained that, in Latvia, there are 'no restrictions on pastoral care, and everything depends on resources, while the prison regime must be observed: people go to either lessons or work on work days and consequently you won't get many people to come to a pastoral event in the middle of the work day. It's either in the evening on work days or on weekends' (Interviewee No. 1). Each denomination has specific days when its volunteer chaplains work at places of detention, so that spiritual care can take place regularly. In this way, prisoners can register to participate in religious events in a timely way.

15.3.5   Church–Prison Relations

In Latvia, the same principles that determine relations between church and state hold in relations between church and prison. The Latvian constitution *Satversme* states that the church is separate from the state. The agreement signed by the Republic of Latvia and the Holy See in 2000 establishes the legal status of the Roman Catholic Church and guarantees the right to administer Catholic spiritual care in prisons and other penitentiary institutions (Article 30.1). Following long discussions on how to regulate relations between the state and other churches, laws on seven religious organisations were adopted and came into effect in 2008. The Law on the Evangelical Lutheran Church states that, according to the Law on Religious Organizations, the Evangelical Lutheran Church's chaplains can also perform official duties in places where prison sentences are served and elsewhere, where the pastoral care of a normal clergyman is not available. In addition, the church shall oversee the spiritual care activities of chaplains (Article 11). The same is also stated in the Law on the Latvian Orthodox Church (Article 12), the Law on Latvian Pomorian Old Believer Church (Article 10), the Law on the Latvian United Methodist Church (Article 10), the Law on the Latvian Baptist Congregations Association (Article 11) and the Law on the Latvian Union of Seventh-Day Adventist Congregations (Article 11). The activities of chaplains in prisons are not defined in the Law on the Riga Jewish Religious Community.

15.3.6   Attempts to Proselytise or Convert

Because the religious affiliations of prisoners in Latvian prisons are not recorded, it is impossible to ascertain the prevalence of proselytism and conversion. Based on his experience, one chaplain explained that being *born again* is characteristic of prisoners of a certain age: it is usually experienced by people in midlife, not by young people:

> Young people who are usually caught up with addictions, and drugs, they don't think about anything yet. They have grown up in poor circumstances and prison isn't anything special for them, and consequently they don't feel any discomfort. [...] Those who end up in prison as adults – for them life has broken down completely. These are the situations when a per-

son doesn't know what to do. Quite often, all of their relatives have given up [on them]. [...] For them, [in midlife] there's a greater wish to change something in their lives. (Interviewee No. 1)

Conversion, too, is not a rare phenomenon in Latvia's prisons. As noted by one of the interviewed chaplains, prisoners 'quite often express the wish [to convert], as a lot of it depends on how you behave towards these people. If you are interested in them, they stick to you. For them it really doesn't matter [from which denomination you are]' (Interviewee No. 3).

In Latvia's multi-denominational milieu, conversion is a sensitive topic and depends on the individual chaplain's attitude. One of the chaplains explained his attitude, based on ecumenical principles:

> If a person comes to me and says that he wants to be christened, I try to find out what his origins are [...] if he doesn't know anything, I ask him which church his grandmother went to: what sort of towers did the church have, what sorts of crosses? This way you can establish what he is [...]. I am not interested in converting people [...], my interest is that the person, on encountering God, returns, starts changing his life. If I see that his roots are different, I tell him that we can continue our pastoral discussions, but if you want to get christened, I recommend that you get in touch with the representative of the other denomination. At times they do this, at other times they don't. [...] We don't have the goal that we have to get them into our church. (Interviewee No. 2)

A chaplain employed by the PA must provide convicted persons with pastoral care taking into account their request to invite a minister from a different denomination or religion to see them. However, most prisoners were born and raised in Soviet times, when religious freedom was severely restricted, which is why most convicted persons don't know which denomination they belong to (many were baptised secretly and religion wasn't practised in the family). One of the volunteer chaplains explained: if a convicted person requests spiritual care, usually only the denominational services of the chaplain working in the prison are offered initially. Chaplains of other denominations or religions are invited if the convicted person is aware of his denominational or religious belonging and insists on his rights to receive spiritual care directly from someone of his denomination. Because most convicted persons are unaware of their denominational heritage, cases of conversion in prison are usually connected with integration into the chaplain's denomination.

The number of Muslims in prison can be roughly determined by the number of requests for Islamic religious items. A PA spokesman pointed out that about ten Muslims were currently serving sentences in Latvian prisons. From his observations, growing interest in Islam was evident among convicted persons a few years ago: prisoners expressed a desire to meet with the leaders of the Muslim community of Tatar origin, and there were cases of conversion as well. In contrast, it is currently difficult to establish how actively prisoners are adopting Islam, since previously the adoption of Islam in prison took place in the presence of two witnesses, but currently Muslims allow for adopting Islam in telephone conversations. A PA spokesman explained that some prisoners adopt Islam to isolate themselves from the general prisoner community and thereby obtain a little more freedom in their situation of captivity.

15.3.7   Current Social Debates and Future Research

Regrettably, society in Latvia is uninterested in what is taking place behind prison walls. That is why there are no public discussions in Latvia on issues facing convicted persons. Prisoners are only mentioned in the media in cases where a court is reviewing the complaint of a convicted person. Society's overall attitude also comes out in pointed comments; for example, in an article on conditions in prisons, the reporter added that 'in prison they feed them better than many pensioners in our country can afford to eat' (Didrihsone 2016).

In interviews with prison chaplains, it became clear that there is no sense in Latvia of societal responsibility for this attitude towards prisoners. Prisoners commit their crimes within a specific social environment: most of them come from broken or disadvantaged families or are orphans, while many offenders are themselves the victims of violence – but this disadvantaged environment was created by society.

The high level of recidivism reveals a lack of social foresight in Latvia: in 2015, 55.53% of convicted persons were repeat offenders (IVP 2016). The state does not fund research on the problem of recidivist crime, and, as observed by a PA employee, 'half of the prisoners want to change their lives, but don't know how to do it. [...] They gain employment, but as soon as it comes to light that they have been imprisoned, they lose their job' (Interviewee No. 4). After serving their sentence, breaking into the labour market is problematic for those prisoners with no prior work experience. To acquire the needed experience, improvements need to be made with respect to job opportunities in places of detention. The state is irresponsibly indifferent, because it offers no tax breaks for companies that hire ex-convicts.

Finally, it should also be noted that there have been no discussions in Latvia about spiritual care in prisons even though there is no reason to think that the religious organisations mentioned in the *Regulations on the Chaplains' Service* are necessarily the only ones qualified to minister to prisoners' spiritual needs. A different attitude towards some religions is evident here, and it is unclear why this attitude exists. If such an attitude cannot be justified, it can be considered discrimination and to be inconsistent with Article 91 of the Latvian constitution.

This chapter has served to reveal how little research has been conducted on prisons in Latvia. Social scientists can be instrumental in producing evidence-based recommendations for prison policy. However, the role of research in policy planning is expressed mainly in the economic context in Latvia. The plan outlined in *Latvija 2030,* Latvia's sustainable development strategy, is for research to be oriented towards market demand, requiring a closer linkage between business and science and the internationalisation of research activity. The strategy envisages the orientation of research institutions towards the supply of services to state and local government institutions, as well as local and foreign companies. Each year, the State Probation Service and the Prison Administration announce the themes of academic research which includes, among others, The importance of spiritual care in the resocialisation process for prisoners: an analysis of the operating practices of the Chaplains' Service in Latvian prisons (comparing individual prisons by district, type of regime, age, gender and other aspects) (Tieslietu 2017). The development of future lines of research should address this specific topic. Unfortunately, the relationship between prison and religion has not received sufficient attention from academics because funding for this type of research is not made available. Moreover, a reduction in funding is evident: if research and development expenditures were 0.55% of GDP in 2007, then this figure already fallen to 0.51% of GDP in 2017, placing Latvia second to last among EU nations (EUROSTAT 2019). In this context, there is little hope that significant research on the role of religion in the resocialisation of prisoners will be conducted in the near future.

A shortfall in funding is not the only hurdle; a lack of social commissioning is also notable. The view that religion could have a significant role to play in the creation and maintenance of morality, including in the rehabilitation of prisoners, is not a common view in Latvia's post-Soviet secularised society. Taking into account the poor forecast regarding possibilities for the development of research in Latvia, it can be predicted that, in future as well, only studies conducted in other countries will be taken into account in evaluating the efficacy of religious programmes and developing prison policy in Latvia.

Bibliography

Administratīvā rajona tiesa Rēzeknes tiesu nams. (2014). Lietas Nr. A420375513 spriedums. https://www.tiesas.lv/nolemumi/pdf/151793.pdf. Accessed 20 Mar 2017

Balodis, R. (2000). *Valsts un Baznīca*. Rīga: Nordik.

Balodis, R. (2002). *Baznīcu tiesības*. Rīga: Mantojums.

Balodis, R. (2003). Church and state in Latvia. In S. Ferrari & W. Cole Durham Jr. (Eds.), *Law and religion in post-communist Europe* (pp. 141–176). Peeters: Leuven/Paris/Dudley.

Berke, E. (2017). E-mail message to author, April 20, 2017.

Crétenot, M. (2013). From national practices to European guidelines: Interesting initiatives in prison management. http://www.prisonobservatory.org/upload/EPOinterestinginitiatives.pdf. Accessed 20 Mar 2017.

Didrihsone, L. (2016). Ūdens un maize? No kā patiesībā sastāv cietumnieku maltīte?. http://apollo.tvnet.lv/zinas/udens-un-maize-no-ka-patiesiba-sastav-cietumnieku-maltite/728588. Accessed 20 Mar 2017.

European Communities of Restoration – in prisons and as alternatives to detention. http://restorative-justice.eu/ecor/. Accessed 20 Mar 2017.

Europris. (2017). Suicide Prevention Guidelines. http://www.europris.org/suicide-prevention-guidelines/.

EUROSTAT. (2019). News release. https://ec.europa.eu/eurostat/documents/2995521/9483597/9-10012019-AP-EN.pdf/856ce1d3-b8a8-4fa6-bf00-a8ded6dd1cc1 Accessed 20 Mar 2017.

Ieslodzījuma vietu pārvalde. (2016). 2015. gada publiskais pārskats. http://www.ievp.gov.lv/images/stories/2015-parskats.pdf. Accessed 20 Mar 2017.

Interviewee No. 1. Interview by the author. Tape recording. Riga, March 10, 2017.

Interviewee No. 2. Interview by the author. Tape recording. Riga, April 14, 2017.

Interviewee No. 3. Interview by the author. Tape recording. Riga, April 16, 2017.

Interviewee No. 4. Interview by the author. Personal interview. Riga, April 18, 2017.

IVP. (2009). Arhīvs. http://www.ievp.gov.lv/index.php/publikacijas/arhivs Accessed 20 Mar 2017.

IVP. (2016). 2015. gada publiskais pārskats. http://www.ievp.gov.lv/images/stories/2015-parskats. pdf. Accessed 20 Mar 2017.

Justoviča, P. (2015). Realitātes stāsts: kā cietumā rehabilitējas jaunietis. http://www.lsm.lv/ lv/raksts/cilvekstasti/dzive/realitates-stasts-ka-cietumos-rehabilitejas-jaunietis.a116906/. Accessed 20 Mar 2017.

Kamenska, A., Pūce, I., & Laganovska, K. (2013). Prison conditions in Latvia. http://www.prisonobservatory.org/upload/PrisonconditionsinLatvia.pdf. Accessed 20 Mar 2017.

Kronberga, I., & Sīle, S. (2016). Apcietinājuma izpildes prakses tendences Latvijā. http://providus. lv/article/apcietinajuma-izpildes-prakses-tendences-latvija. Accessed 20 Mar 2017.

Latvijas Avīze. (2016). Liepājā par 74 miljoniem eiro taps jauns cietums. http://www.la.lv/liepajapar-74-miljoniem-eiro-taps-jauns-cietums/. Accessed 20 Mar 2017.

Latvijas Satversmes Sapulce. (1922). Latvijas Republikas Satversme. https://likumi.lv/doc. php?id=57980 Accessed 20 Mar 2017.

LR Augstākā tiesa. 2010. Spriedums Lieta Nr. A42446907. http://at.gov.lv/files/uploads/files/ archive/department3/2010/10_ska-160.doc. Accessed 20 Mar 2017.

LR Satversmes tiesa. (2011). Spriedums lietā Nr. Nr.2010-50-03. http://www.satv.tiesa.gov.lv/wpcontent/uploads/2016/02/2010-50-03_Spriedums.pdf. Accessed 20 Mar 2017.

LR tiesībsargs. (2009). Gada ziņojums. http://www.tiesibsargs.lv/uploads/content/legacy/ Tiesibsarga%20gada%20zinojums_2009.pdf. Accessed 20 Mar 2017.

LR tiesībsargs. (2016). LR tiesībsarga 2015. gada ziņojums. http://www.tiesibsargs.lv/uploads/ content/legacy/Tiesibsarga_2015_gada_zinojums.pdf. Accessed 20 Mar 2017.

LTV. (2012). Ieslodzītais tiesājas ar cietumu par to, lai tiktu nodrošinātas veģetāras ēdienreizes. https://www.youtube.com/watch?v=p7obaO2VxhE Accessed 20 Mar 2017.

Luksa, M. (2013). Latvijā būs jauni cietumi. http://www.lvportals.lv/visi/likumi-prakse/253797-latvija-bus-jauni-cietumi. Accessed 20 Mar 2017.

Luste, M. (2011). Nojaucot cietuma mūrus. http://providus.lv/article/nojaucot-cietuma-murus. Accessed 20 Mar 2017

Ministru kabinets. (2003). Izmeklēšanas cietumu iekšējās kārtības noteikumi. MK noteikumi Nr. 211. https://likumi.lv/doc.php?id=74350&from=off. Accessed 20 Mar 2017.

Ministru kabinets. (2006a). Brīvības atņemšanas iestādes iekšējās kārtības noteikumi. MK noteikumi Nr. 423. https://likumi.lv/doc.php?id=136495. Accessed 20 Mar 2017.

Ministru kabinets. (2006b). Noteikumi par ieslodzīto personu uztura un sadzīves vajadzību materiālā nodrošinājuma normām. MK noteikumi Nr.1022. https://likumi.lv/doc.php?id=150405. Accessed 20 Mar 2017.

Ministru kabinets. (2010). Profesiju klasifikators: 1.pielikums Ministru kabineta 2010.gada 18.maija noteikumiem Nr.461. http://www.lm.gov.lv/upload/darba_devejiem/prof_klasif_0112.pdf. Accessed 20 Mar 2017.

Ministru kabinets. (2011). Noteikumi par kapelāna dienestu. MK noteikumi Nr.134. https://likumi. lv/doc.php?id=226332. Accessed 20 Mar 2017.

Ministru, K. (2015). Par Ieslodzīto resocializācijas pamatnostādnēm 2015.-2020. gadam. MK rīkojums Nr.580. https://likumi.lv/doc.php?id=276740. Accessed 20 Mar 2017.

Profesiju pasaule. (2017). Kapelāns darbā ieslodzījuma vietās. http://www.profesijupasaule.lv/lv/ cat/49/79/193. Accessed 20 Mar 2017.

Rajevska, F., & Demme, D. (2010). Sociālā integrācija. In N. Muižnieks (Ed.), Cik integrēta ir Latvijas sabiedrība? Sasniegumu, neveiksmju un izaicinājumu audits (pp. 161–192). Rīga: LU Akadēmiskais apgāds.

Saeima. (1995). Reliģisko organizāciju likums. https://likumi.lv/doc.php?id=36874.

Saeima. (2006). Apcietinājumā turēšanas kārtības likums. http://www.saeima.lv/L_Saeima8/lasadd=LIK_1669.htm Accessed 20 Mar 2017.

Saeima. (2016). Latvijas Sodu izpildes kodekss. https://likumi.lv/doc.php?id=90218 Accessed 20 Mar 2017.

Seržants, K. (2005). Cietumi nelīdz… vai palīdzēs miljoni?. http://www.tvnet.lv/zinas/kriminalzinas/285044-cietumi_nelidz_vai_palidzes_miljoni. Accessed 20 Mar 2017.

Šiliņš, J. (2013). *Padomju Latvija 1918–1919*. Rīga: Vēstures izpētes un popularizēšanas biedrība.

Tieslietu ministrija. (2017). Tieslietu ministrijas priekšlikumi noslēguma darbu tēmām 2017.gadā. http://www.lu.lv/fileadmin/user_upload/lu_portal/jf/studijas/zinas_bak/TM-priekslikumi2017.pdf. Accessed 20 Mar 2017.

Veitmanis, K. (1939). *Ieslodzījumu vietas 1918–1938*. Rīga: Kriminālpolitiskais departaments.

Chapter 16
Montenegro: Religion in Prisons

Nikola B. Šaranović

Abstract The topic of this paper is religion in the Montenegrin penitentiary system, i.e. the legal and institutional framework, as well as the practice of exercising freedom of religion in Montenegrin prisons. It contains a section on the constitutional guarantees, legal solutions and international standards and a chronology on how the conditions for the exercise of freedom of religion have improved. Contracts between state and church and religious communities are also discussed with reference to their communication with prisoners, as well as monitoring mechanisms, both national and international, of the system of criminal sanctions in Montenegro, including the conditions for exercising the right to freedom of religion. With regard to conditions in prison, emphasis is placed on the premises for religious rituals and equipment of prison kitchens to prepare adequate meals according to prisoners' religious affiliations. The main design for the construction of a multifunctional building that would serve the needs of prisoners, including those related to religion, is also outlined. Furthermore, the chapter addresses the strategic framework for the fight against violent extremism, with a discussion of the measures and activities under the remit of the Institute for the Execution of Criminal Sanctions. The topic of religion in prison is addressed in connection with Montenegro. It is an area in which good cooperation between the state and church and religious communities has been established. The conditions for exercising freedom of religion are subject to regular, open and constructive communication between the management of the Institute for the Execution of Criminal Sanctions and the authorised representatives of church and religious communities.

For their help in the preparation of this paper the author thanks Mr. Miljan Perović and Mr. Kemal Zoronjić, respectively director and deputy director of the Institute for the Execution of Criminal Sanctions of Montenegro.

N. B. Šaranović (✉)
Master of Law, Society and Religion and Master of Law (E.U. Law), Podgorica, Montenegro
e-mail: nisha@t-com.me

© Springer Nature Switzerland AG 2020   257
J. Martínez-Ariño, A.-L. Zwilling (eds.), *Religion and Prison: An Overview of Contemporary Europe*, Boundaries of Religious Freedom: Regulating Religion in Diverse Societies 7, https://doi.org/10.1007/978-3-030-36834-0_16

16.1   Introduction

Religion in prison is a topic that has to do with more than just the place and role of religion in society since the religiosity of prisoners cannot be treated in the same way as the religiosity of free citizens. In the situation in which prisoners find themselves, the deepest inner freedom is expressed in radical outer limits; it is the freedom of spirit as opposed to the imprisonment of the body, the freedom of religion of those who are deprived of liberty.

Regardless of the criminal offence for which they were sentenced and the severity of the sentence imposed, prisoners are more or less isolated from free society by the same walls. In some contexts, these walls should be insurmountable obstacles. In others, however, they should be more like a membrane that stops harmful but allows for useful 'traffic'.

Such 'traffic' lies in the stem of the word 'religion': the Latin term *religare* means 'reconnecting'. It refers to the relationship a human being has with God, to which prisoners are entitled either alone or in a community with others, by prayers, sermons, customs or rituals. The regulation of this right in Montenegro is the topic of the following sections.

16.2   Data on Religious Denominations in Montenegro

Before introducing a legal framework for the freedom of religion in Montenegro, and bearing in mind that prisons in a way represent 'society in its own small world', we will briefly present basic information about the religiosity of the citizens of Montenegro. According to the last census, conducted in 2011, 620,029 citizens identified themselves as follows: 446,858 or 72.07% as Orthodox, 21,299 or 3.44% as Catholic, 118,477 or 19.10% as Muslim, 894 or 0.14% as Adventist, 451 or 0.07% as Agnostic, 118 or 0.02% as Buddhist, 1460 or 0.24% as Christian, 145 or 0.02% as Jehovah's Witness, 143 or 0.02% as Protestant, 6337 or 1.02% as other, 16,180 or 2.61% non-identified, and 7667 or 1.24% as Atheist.[1]

Because the census deals with the 'quantity' of religiosity, the 'internal image' or 'quality' of religiosity is more evident in a survey conducted in 2008 within the

---

[1]According to the first post-socialist census in 1991, 425,133 out of the 615,035 inhabitants, or 69.12% of the population, declared themselves Orthodox, 118,016, or 19.18%, declared as Muslims, and 27,153, or 4.41%, as Catholic. Data from the Census of Montenegro in 2003 provide a more detailed overview and show that of 620,145 inhabitants, 460,383, or 74.23%, self-identified as Orthodox, 110,034 (17.74%) as Muslim, 21,972 (3.54%) as Catholic, 383 (0.061%) as Protestant, 58 (0.009%) belonged to pro-oriental cults, 12 (0.001%) identified as Jewish, and 2424 (0.39%) as belonging to other denominations. There were also 13,867 (2.23%) undeclared, 5009 (0.80%) unknown, and 6003 (0.96%) were non-religious.

framework of the European Values Study.[2] Speaking generally about religiosity, 88% of respondents said that they believed in God, and 87% declared themselves as religious, which ranks Montenegro among the countries with the most religious population in Europe.[3] The survey also indicated that 28% of respondents believe in a personal God, 50% believe in some sort of spirit or life force, 78% believe that religion is important in life, 67% believe that God is important in their lives, and 70% find strength and comfort in their faith. Furthermore, 62% of respondents are somewhat or very interested in the sacred and the supernatural, 38% believe in heaven and 31% believe in hell, 29% believe in life after death, and 16% believe in reincarnation. Of those included in the survey, 35% believe in amulets and 67% believe in sin, and 29% recognise some force in all major religions. On the other hand, 9% of respondents do not believe in any kind of spirit or life force, while 8% declared themselves to be non-religious and 5% identified as atheist.

When it comes to professing religiosity, 8% of respondents attend religious ceremonies once a week (not including baptisms, burials, and weddings), 23% pray to God beyond religious ceremonies more than once a week, and 11% attend religious ceremonies once a week (excluding baptisms, burials, and weddings).

16.3   Religion as a Basic Human Right and Freedom

As a basic human right and freedom, religion is protected and promoted under Article 46 of the constitution of Montenegro, under the heading 'Freedom of thought, conscience and religion', which reads as follows:

> Everyone shall be guaranteed the right to freedom of thought, conscience and religion, and the right to change his/her religion or belief, and freedom, either alone or with others and in public or private, to manifest his/her religion or belief in worship, sermons, customs or rituals. No one is obliged to declare their religious or other beliefs. Freedom to express religious beliefs may be restricted only if necessary to protect human life and health, public order and peace, as well as other rights guaranteed by the Constitution.

In terms of their content and scope, the basic legal standards for the protection and promotion of rights and freedoms are in accordance with international standards enshrined in the Universal Declaration of Human Rights, the Covenant on Civil and Political Rights, and the European Convention on Human Rights and Fundamental Freedoms, which regulate this area in almost the same way. Apart from the direct

---

[2] The aforementioned survey is especially valuable given the fact that Montenegro was included in the research programme for the first time. The programme itself was launched in 1981, using a sample of 1000 citizens of Europe, and is implemented every ninth year. In the fourth wave, it encompassed nearly 50 European countries/regions and 70,000 inhabitants, as a 'unique research project on how Europeans feel about life, family, work, religion, politics and society'.

[3] While acknowledging the 1% difference, we can say that the belief in God and religiosity in Montenegro match, especially when compared to countries in the region and beyond.

constitutional guarantees, the highest legal act of Montenegro allows for the possibility of an additional guarantee, as envisaged in Section 9 under the title 'Legal system'. It prescribes that ratified and published international treaties and generally accepted rules of international law are an integral part of the internal legal order, having supremacy over national legislation and being directly applicable when they regulate matters differently than the national legislation.

In close connection with the collective aspect of freedom of religion is the constitutional article about religious communities. Article 14 of the constitution reads as follows: 'Religious communities are separate from the state. Religious communities are equal and free to perform religious rites and religious activities.'[4] The separation of religious communities from the state should be interpreted as a constitutional principle of the delimitation of responsibilities of the state and religious communities, in the spirit of the European democratic tradition and the 'doctrinal formula of separationism',[5] which, in turn, does not exclude cooperation between the state and religious communities in matters of common interest, again in the spirit of modern trends in Europe, where the current ruling system is the cooperative separation of state and religious communities. In this sense, the view that 'at the sub-constitutional level, the picture may look different than suggested by the typology of church-state relations',[6] which in our country is most obviously mirrored in the agreements signed with religious communities, will be presented later.[7] Cooperation between the state and religious communities itself, however, is best developed in the area of the execution of criminal sanctions.

---

[4] 'Montenegro is defined as a secular state where religious communities are separate from the state. The Constitution (art. 14) guarantees to the religious communities active in the territory of Montenegro equal rights and freedom in the practice of ceremonies and religious affairs. The state does not intervene in the internal organisation or organisation of religious affairs, but has left such affairs to be a competence and responsibility of the respective religious communities, i.e. religious communities are autonomous in regulating their organisation and affairs. There is no state religion in Montenegro.' *Initial Report of Montenegro on the Implementation of ICCPR 2012.*

[5] Ibán, Iván C. 2013. God in Constitutions and Godless Constitutions. In *Law, Religion, Constitution: Freedom of Religion, Equal Treatment, and the Law*, Farnham: Ashgate, p. 52.

[6] Van Bijsterveld Sophie C. 2000. Church and State in Western Europe and the United States: Principles and Perspectives, *Brigham Young University Law Review*, p. 991.

[7] 'The exercise of religious rights is specifically regulated by the Law on the Legal Status of Religious Communities (Official Bulletin of SRMNE 9/77 and 26/77) and Law on Celebration of Religious Holidays (Official Bulletin of RMNE 56/93). Pursuant to the Law on the Legal Status of Religious Communities, establishment of religious communities and organisations i.e. religious communities is free; their establishment or termination of activity need to be registered with the administrative authority competent for the interior affairs at the territory of the local government where such community that has either been established or terminated its activity has its seat. The Law explicitly prohibits abuse of religious communities and their institutions, as well as religious activities or religious feelings, for political purposes. In addition, the Law prohibits prevention or obstruction of practice of religious ceremonies and religious affairs i.e. manifestation of religious feelings. Sanctions are envisaged for non-compliance with these and other legal provisions. Given the guaranteed freedom of religion, forced enlisting in a religious community is also prohibited, as well as forced participation in religious ceremonies.' *Initial Report of Montenegro on the implementation of ICCPR 2012.*

16.4   Religion in the Normative Framework of the Execution of Criminal Sanctions

The law on the Execution of Prison Sentences, Fines and Community Service regulates the execution of criminal sanctions in Montenegro. The Montenegrin normative framework is harmonised with European prison rules, according to which freedom of thought, conscience and religion of prisoners must be respected. Similarly, prisons should be organised in such a way that prisoners can practise their faith or observe their religious beliefs, attend services or meetings with authorised representatives of their religion or belief, and have books or literature relating to their religion or belief. On the other hand, prisoners cannot be forced to profess a faith or religious beliefs, attend prayers or religious gatherings, participate in religious ceremonies or meet with representatives of a particular religion or belief.

The law prohibits discrimination against convicted persons on whom sanctions were imposed on the basis of religion or belief.[8] It also stipulates that a prisoner has the right to religious rituals and to participate in religious activities in accordance with the law, for which purpose the Ministry of Justice can conclude agreements with church and other religious communities. The Institute for the Execution of Criminal Sanctions shall provide adequate space and conditions for performing religious ceremonies and activities, including the performance of individual religious ceremonies, and the representative of church and other religious organisations may, with the approval of the prison warden, visit a prisoner who is receiving treatment at the Institute or in a medical institution. House Rules[9] contain detailed rules defining the manner of organisation of religious ceremonies and activities of prisoners.[10]

Participation in religious ceremonies and activities may be prohibited in case it is necessary to maintain order in the prison or for other security reasons, or if this right is abused.[11] Furthermore, the law stipulates that prisoners shall be allowed to possess religious literature and items used for religious purposes, of which, however, they can be deprived when misused.[12] When it comes to dietary requirements, the law stipulates that a prisoner is entitled to three meals per day, which are made in accordance with the religious and cultural needs of prisoners.[13] Individual

---

[8] Article 5, 'Prohibition of discrimination.'

[9] 'Religious ceremonies may be performed in churches, temples, official premises, at cemeteries, private homes, etc. without authorisation from competent authorities; their performance outside the mentioned premises requires authorisation from the competent authority. Persons placed in health, social welfare or similar institutions may practise their religion to the extent granted by the house rules of the given institution. Upon personal request, such persons may receive visits by priests for the purpose of performing religious ceremonies. Persons serving prison sentences are guaranteed the right to practise religious life.' *Initial Report of Montenegro on the implementation of ICCPR 2012.*

[10] Article 67 of the law.

[11] Article 68, 'Prohibition of participation in religious activities.'

[12] Article 69, 'Religious literature and items.'

[13] Article 44, 'Diet.'

religious services are accommodated upon request for prisoners being held in solitary confinement as a disciplinary measure.[14]

The religious identity of prisoners is taken into consideration on the occasion of their release from prison: if the last day of the sentence is a religious holiday, the prisoner is released on the last working day before the religious holiday.[15] Religious identity is respected in the case of death of a prisoner as well: if the deceased prisoner's family does not agree to arrange a funeral or if a prisoner has no close family, he or she is buried at the expense of the institute in the cemetery of the municipality where the prison is located, with respect for the dignity of the deceased and the respective religious and other traditions observed.[16]

The House Rules stipulate that collective religious rituals and other activities shall be conducted under the supervision of security officers and individual religious rituals only under visual oversight. Prisoners who wish to establish contact with representatives of a church or other religious organisation must submit a written request. Such requests are subject to the decision of the prison warden, with prior opinion of the treatment unit obtained. In addition, prisoners are released from work duty on religious holidays, in accordance with the Law on Religious Holidays. Prisoners are not allowed to abuse religious rights and freedoms for the sake of spreading religious and ethnic intolerance and hostility.

16.5   Agreements

Prisoners' right to freedom of religion is provided for in agreements signed between the state and church and religious communities. The first such agreement was signed between Montenegro and the Holy See on 24 June 2011, as a Fundamental Treaty, and a year later the government concluded agreements regulating the relations of mutual interest with the Islamic (30 January 2012) and Jewish (31 January 2012) communities. The difference is reflected in the fact that the Basic Agreement between Montenegro and the Holy See is a bilateral international agreement that is approved and published, pursuant to Article 9 of the constitution of Montenegro, which makes it an internal part of the legal order of Montenegro and gives it primacy over national legislation, making it directly applicable when matters are regulated differently from domestic legislation. The common feature of these agreements is their political rationale, i.e. commitment of the parties to the improvement of relations between the state and religious communities, in the spirit of 'benevolent separation'.[17]

Another common feature is the right of churches and religious communities to conduct pastoral activities in prison. Thus, the Fundamental Treaty recognised the

---

[14] Article 116, 'Execution of disciplinary measures.'

[15] Article 97, 'Release.'

[16] Article 54, 'Death of prisoners.'

[17] Schanda, Balász C. 2010. Recent Developments in Church-State Relations in Central Europe. In *Law and Religion in the 21st Century: Relations Between States and Religious Communities*, Farnham: Ashgate, p. 165.

right of the Catholic Church to provide pastoral care for Catholics in prison.[18] This right is also recognised for the Islamic community, with the additional provision of a special diet and the preparation of appropriate food for Islamic believers.[19] Furthermore, the Agreement with the Islamic Community envisages that detained or imprisoned persons of Islamic faith can be prevented from participating in religious rituals by the public prosecutor or the presiding judge for justified reasons. Also, the director of the Institute for Execution of Criminal Sanctions may temporarily prohibit participation in a religious ceremony in order to maintain security and order and shall inform the representatives of the Islamic community thereon, while personal conversations on spiritual matters cannot be denied for longer periods of time.[20] Equivalent provisions for Jews are contained in the agreement governing the relations of mutual interest between the government of Montenegro and the Jewish community in Montenegro.[21]

---

[18] Article 17 of the Charter of Fundamental Rights: 'Montenegro recognises the Catholic Church's right to pastoral care of Catholic believers who are in armed forces and in police services, and those who are in prisons, hospitals, orphanages and all institutions for health and social protection, whether public or private type.'

[19] Article 18 of the Treaty on the Regulation of Relations of Mutual Interest between the Government of Montenegro and the Islamic Community in Montenegro: 'Montenegro recognises the Islamic community's right to care for their members who are in the army and police, and those who are in prison for the execution of criminal sanctions, hospitals, other medical institutions and institutions for social assistance. Special diet, implying the appropriate food for the needs of Islamic believers, will be provided in the army, police, prisons for the execution of sanctions, hospitals and other medical institutions, and institutions for social protection and assistance, as well as institutions providing meals for students.'

[20] Article 19 of the Treaty on the Regulation of Relations of Mutual Interest between the Government of Montenegro and the Islamic Community in Montenegro: 'The state prosecutor or the presiding judge may, for justified reasons, prohibit the participation of detained or imprisoned persons in religious ceremonies. If this is necessary for the purpose of maintaining security and order, the director of the Institute for the Execution of Criminal Sanctions may temporarily prohibit participation in a religious ceremony of a person serving a prison sentence, informing the representatives of the Islamic community in Montenegro thereon. Personal spiritual conversation from Paragraph 2 of this article shall not be denied over the period longer than the duration of the reasons why the prisoner was refused the right to participate in religious ceremonies.'

[21] Article 16 of the Agreement on the Regulation of Relations of Mutual Interest between the Government of Montenegro and the Jewish Community in Montenegro: 'Montenegro recognises the Jewish community's right to care for their members who are in the army and police, and those who are in prison for the execution of criminal sanctions, hospitals, other medical institutions and institutions for social assistance. Special diet, implying the appropriate food for the needs of Jewish believers, will be provided in the army, police, prisons for the execution of sanctions, hospitals and other medical institutions, and institutions for social protection and assistance, as well as institutions providing meals for students.' Article 19: 'The state prosecutor or the presiding judge may, for justified reasons, prohibit the participation of detained or imprisoned persons in religious ceremonies. If this is necessary for the purpose of maintaining security and order, the director of the Institute for the Execution of Criminal Sanctions may temporarily prohibit participation in a religious ceremony of a person serving a prison sentence, informing the representatives of the Jewish community in Montenegro thereon. Personal spiritual conversation from Paragraph 2 of this article shall not be denied over the period longer than the duration of the reasons why the prisoner was refused the right to participate in religious ceremonies.'

16.6   Strategic Documents for Fighting Violent Extremism

To gain a broader picture of religion in Montenegrin prisons, an unavoidable topic
is the question of violent extremism, which has been a matter of current interest at
the European and global level in recent years, especially in the context of the
'migrant crisis'. Consistent with its international approach, Montenegro has
improved its strategic and normative framework to combat violent extremism in a
brief period of time, which is an important segment of combating and preventing
radicalisation in prisons.

Thus, in December 2015, the government of Montenegro adopted a Strategy for
Combating Violent Extremism for the period 2016–2018, which establishes a
framework for a comprehensive and effective response to the challenges posed by
the growing problem of radicalisation and violent extremism around the world. This
document is, inter alia, based on the guidelines of the United Nations, the European
Union priorities and regional priorities in the framework of the Cooperation Process
in South-East Europe, as well as solutions developed under the auspices of the EU
Radicalisation Awareness Network and the Global Forum for Combating Terrorism.
In March 2016, the government adopted an Action Plan for the Implementation of
the Strategy for Combating Violent Extremism, which elaborates the strategic
objectives through the prescription of specific activities, the competent authorities
for their implementation, deadlines, the necessary budgetary resources and outcome
indicators. These measures include the establishment of an 'exit strategy' intended
to help individuals leave violent extremism, i.e. drawing up a support plan for individuals leaving radical/terrorist groups, assessing the risks of identified individuals/
returnees from extremist/terrorist groups to plan for their reintegration, drawing up
a plan of reintegration of individuals within the prison facilities (facilitating psychological or religious counselling to individuals), providing for adequate support to
individuals at risk of radicalisation, which implies identification of individuals at
risk of radicalisation by producing a list of indicators for early recognition of radicalisation, preparing a plan of deradicalisation of individuals at risk of radicalisation
through a comprehensive social, psychological and educational approach, launching awareness-raising campaigns at the local level, and creating and implementing
programmes for vulnerable groups. Training of specialists for early recognition –
prevention of radicalisation – is envisaged as an ongoing measure.

16.7   Institutional Framework

The competent institution for the execution of criminal sanctions in Montenegro is
the Institute for the Execution of Criminal Sanctions, a body within the Ministry of
Justice.[22] The institute is composed of the following organisational units: the

---

[22] Decree on the Organisation and Manner of Work of State Administration of Montenegro.

Correctional Center, Remand Prison, Prison for Short Sentences, Prison Bijelo Polje, Public Health Service and the Centre for the Training of Personnel.[23] The institute carries out the following criminal sanctions: imprisonment, 40-year prison sentences, juvenile imprisonment, mandatory treatment for alcoholics, security measures of mandatory treatment for drug addicts, and measures to ensure the presence of the accused in criminal proceedings – detention and psychiatric observation and expertise.

The Ministry of Justice oversees imprisonment and other sanctions. Pursuant to the Law on the Execution of Prison Sentences, Fines and Community Service, prisoners have the right to file complaints with the head of the institute regarding the protection of their rights and interests over the term of their imprisonment, including imprisonment of 40 years. The institute shall investigate complaints and render decisions on them no later than 15 days after their receipt, submitting their decisions to the concerned prisoners without delay (in accordance with the law governing administrative procedures). Prisoners are entitled to appeal decisions of the director of the institute to the Ministry of Justice, no later than 8 days after the day on which the decision was received. In this case, the Ministry shall render judgment about the appeal within 15 days of the day of receipt of the appeal. If judgment is not rendered within the prescribed time frame, such behaviour may be challenged before the competent court.

In addition, all persons deprived of liberty have the right to submit complaints to the ombudsperson. The ombudsperson has the right, without prior notification, to inspect premises in penitentiaries, organisations, institutions and other places where persons deprived of liberty may be held, as well as to visit, without prior notification and approval, detained persons and ensure that their rights are being upheld. In the absence of an official or other person, the ombudsperson may, personally or through an interpreter, talk to persons deprived of liberty, as well as to other persons who can provide necessary information.

An important institution in this segment is the Ministry for Human and Minority Rights. Within this ministry, there is Directorate for Relations with Religious Communities, which is responsible for the affirmation and development of freedom of religion and which organises meetings of the combined commissions for the implementation of agreements with the church and religious communities.[24]

---

[23] Rulebook on job classification and internal organisation of the Ministry of Justice of Montenegro.

[24] The Directorate for Relations with Religious Communities carries out the tasks relating to the drafting of laws and regulations in connection with the condition of religious communities; cooperation and interaction between the state and religious communities and improving their position in society; affirmation and development of freedom of religion; protection of religious components in the cultural and ethnic identity of minority nations and other minority national communities; development and affirmation of the value of religious culture; support and help in religious architecture and the protection of cultural heritage; assisting in the protection of the legal and social status of religious communities, the exercise of their legal rights, and the regulation and improvement of the social and material position of the clergy; maintaining a register of religious communities, as well as other appropriate tasks within the scope of the Directorate.

The ombudsperson also functions as a national preventive mechanism against torture. The religious rights of prisoners were examined in a report of this body in 2013, which stated that the prison in Bijelo Polje respected the needs of members of all religious communities in the planning, preparation and delivery of meals, but that special conditions for religious ceremonies were not met. Similarly, there were no special rooms provided for the profession of religions. It was also reported that no special rooms were allocated for the profession of religion in the prison for short sentences in Bijelo Polje and that the institution did not meet the specific dietary requirements of Muslims. As for the prison for short sentences in Podgorica, it was reported to provide food in accordance with religious needs, but there were no special rooms for the profession of religion and fulfilment of religious obligations. The same was reported for the Spuž penal and correctional facility.

16.8   Current Situation

On 31 December 2016, the total number of prisoners in the Institute for the Execution of Criminal Sanctions was 1123. Priests and religious officials make around 10 visits per month, mainly related to religious ceremonies (celebrating important religious dates and holidays, as well as weekly prayers and rituals) but also to individual prisoners. The number of visits depends on prisoners expressing the need to meet religious authorities.

Particular attention is paid to the diet of prisoners and its compatibility with the religious needs of prisoners, in line with legal acts. Recognising the special importance of a quality diet provided in prisons, the institute has recently allocated significant funds for the construction and equipping of new prison kitchens, so that all the necessary standards, including Hazard Analysis and Critical Control Point (HACCP), a preventive approach to ensuring food safety, and halal, are met. In addition to a prison doctor, there is also a nutritionist and a chef for halal food in prison.

To promote the resocialisation and integration of prisoners, the Institute for the Execution of Criminal Sanctions has established collaborative relations with church and religious communities. To improve the resocialisation of prisoners, a project for the construction of a multifunctional facility has been launched which would accommodate the needs of prisoners, including those related to religious life. The building is designed to meet all the required standards in prisons when it comes to cultural and educational activities, as well as to the religious needs of prisoners.

There is direct communication with religious officials who visit the institute to perform religious rituals. The institute management makes efforts to further enrich activities in this respect through additional and direct communication between religious persons and prisoners, with a view to improving the social reintegration of prisoners and their treatment.

Recently, special attention has been paid to properly furnish the rooms for individual and group religious services and expand the availability of literature with religious content. To this end, the Orthodox Church and other religious communities donated books to the institute.

16.9 Conclusion

Although still in the process of a 'complex transition'[25] and 'consolidation of church-state relations',[26] Montenegro is a country that respects freedom of religion. As a post-socialist country, where the revitalisation of religion has occurred in all its forms, although it is a secular state in terms of the system of separation, Montenegro is a post-secular society in terms of the religiosity of its citizens.

Multiple constitutional guarantees in line with international standards, quality criminal law protection, the ongoing reform of the legal framework, and the process of developing a contractual relationship with the church and religious communities are the indicators of the attention being paid to all aspects of freedom of religion in Montenegro. This is perhaps most obviously reflected in the area of the execution of criminal sanctions. There are almost no open issues between the state and church and religious communities in this regard.

The system of enforcement of criminal sanctions in Montenegro is constantly improving; this includes improvements in conditions for exercising the freedom of religion in prison. The state's approach to this issue previously was simultaneously reactive and proactive. Reactivity was reflected in the actions taken to remedy short-comings identified in relevant reports on the situation in Montenegrin prisons, while a proactive approach was reflected in timely preparations for eventual challenges, such as radicalisation and violent extremism among prisoners. In this approach, both aspects of religion – individual and collective, as well as all aspects of religiosity – are respected, from adequate nutrition and participation in rituals to the availability of appropriate religious literature.

Of course, it should be noted that this study examined the normative, institutional and spatial-technical conditions for the exercise of freedom of religion in Montenegrin prisons and conducted a brief review of practices so far. The influence of religion on the resocialisation and reintegration of prisoners is a special topic which deserves to be the subject of multidisciplinary research. This research should be qualitative and include prisoners, prison staff, and religious officials, so as to 'measure' the relationship between religion as the independent variable and reintegration/socialisation as the dependent variable. Such research would be useful not only for prisoners, prison management and judicial authorities, but also for society as a whole.

---

[25] Barberini, Giovanni C. 2010. States and Religions in Post-Communist Europe. In *Law and Religion in the 21st Century: Relations Between States and Religious Communities*, Farnham: Ashgate, p. 147.

[26] Shanda, Balász C. 2010. States and Religions in Post-Communist Europe. In *Law and Religion in the 21st Century: Relations Between States and Religious Communities*, Farnham: Ashgate, p. 165.

Bibliography

Ibán, I. C. (2013). God in constitutions and godless constitutions. In W. Cole Durham et al. (Eds.), *Law, religion, constitution: Freedom of religion, equal treatment, and the law* (pp. 37–56). Farnham: Ashgate.

Schanda, B. C. (2010). Recent developments in church-state relations in Central Europe. In R. B. States & R. Communities (Eds.), *Law and religion in the 21st century*. Ashgate: Rinaldo Cristofori and Silvio Ferrari. Farnham.

Van Bijsterveld Sophie, C. (2000). Church and state in Western Europe and the United States: Principles and perspectives. *Brigham Young University Law Review, 3*, 989–995.

Chapter 17
The Netherlands: Oligopoly Dynamics in the Penitentiary System

Kees de Groot and Sipco Vellenga

Abstract The way the Dutch penitentiary system deals with religion reflects a relatively long history of religious diversity. Representatives of organised denominations – religious or secular – are allowed to participate in a system that gives chaplains (called 'spiritual counsellors') a status as civil servants, while they are directed by their own head of the chaplaincy (religious or humanistic). This system favours, or even promotes, the formation of organised worldviews. Thus far, Roman Catholics, Protestants, Jews, Humanists, Muslims, Hindus and Buddhists have succeeded in obtaining a position in this system. Representatives of other religions are also welcome as chaplains, but they are not salaried by the state and integrated in the judicial system; they remain visitors with special privileges. The first salaried Muslim chaplains entered prison in the 1990s. Therefore, the 'prison imam' is less associated with direct political motives in countering radicalisation among Muslim detainees. Indirectly, the Dutch system regulates religion by promoting the formation of distinct categories, such as 'Humanistic' – resulting from a campaign for the interests of the non-religious detainees – and 'Muslim' – an umbrella term for all the different detainees who have an affinity with Islam, now considered as belonging to one 'background community'.

We would like to express our gratitude to Mohamed Ajouaou, Ryan van Eijk and Niels den Toom for their careful reading of and insightful comments on an earlier version of this chapter.

K. de Groot (✉)
Tilburg University, Tilburg, The Netherlands
e-mail: c.n.degroot@tilburguniversity.edu

S. Vellenga
University of Groningen, Groningen, The Netherlands

© Springer Nature Switzerland AG 2020
J. Martínez-Ariño, A.-L. Zwilling (eds.), *Religion and Prison: An Overview of Contemporary Europe*, Boundaries of Religious Freedom: Regulating Religion in Diverse Societies 7, https://doi.org/10.1007/978-3-030-36834-0_17

17.1   Introduction

The Netherlands is a country with a relatively long history of religious diversity. This is reflected in the way the penitentiary system deals with religion. In recent decades, three developments have emerged: the increasing absence of religious affiliation among the population at large (68%), the continuing resonance of labels such as faith (42%) and spirituality (31%), and the growing presence of Islam (6% of the population) (Bernts and Berghuijs 2016). Whereas people without religion are clearly underrepresented in prison (31%), Muslims are overrepresented (20%) (table). The diffuse phenomenon of spirituality, furthermore, contrasts with the strict religious categories that are used in the discourse that governs the organisation of the prison chaplaincy.

We will focus on the way the prison chaplaincy has been established in the Netherlands.[1] What are its origins and how does it manifest itself in the current religious and judicial context? The Muslim chaplaincy shall serve as a case illustrating the way the Dutch systems deals with religious newcomers. European countries differ in how they deal with the right of Muslim detainees to spiritual care. Whereas in Denmark imams are almost excluded from prison chaplaincy because of alleged affinities with radical Islam (Kühle 2016), in France the appointment of prison imams has increased since 2006, as part of a strategy to counter radicalisation among detainees (de Galembert 2016). Our suggestion is that the Dutch system of prison chaplaincy demonstrates how a system of regulated access to a religiously plural prison chaplaincy serves to promote and regulate spiritual care for religious minorities such as Muslims. In this way, we use the broad perspective of religion–state relations to shed light on the particular case of the Muslim prison chaplaincy (Martikainen 2014).

We will describe the national tradition of managing religious diversity, the sociogenesis of spiritual care, the system of delegating authorities and the formation of the Muslim prison chaplaincy. We will conclude with a remark on the position of the chaplaincy in regulating religious diversity in the context of the penitentiary system.

17.2   Dealing with Diversity

Unlike most European countries, the Dutch context is not characterised by a 'quasi-monopoly' of one or more churches that are challenged by newcomer religions such as Islam (Roy 2015). From its inception in the sixteenth century onwards, the Netherlands has been composed of various religious communities: different Protestant groups, Catholics and Jews. In the course of the nineteenth century, the

---

[1]Although in the Netherlands, the Dutch equivalent of 'chaplaincy' is only used for the Christian variety, we will follow the inclusive usage that has become customary. A strict translation of the Dutch, inclusive, term for what chaplains, or 'spiritual counsellors', practice is 'spiritual care'.

newly constructed Kingdom of the Netherlands developed into a constitutional monarchy, favouring the Reformed Church, but allowing religious freedom. Between 1816 and 1942, the Netherlands was probably the largest Muslim kingdom on earth, as it incorporated the Dutch East Indies, currently Indonesia. In the European part, religious freedom promoted the emancipation of orthodox Protestants, Roman Catholics and Jews. A religiously plural political system was constructed, corresponding with a religiously plural civil society, known as pillarisation: religious diversity was used as a means to govern the country (Lijphart 1968). During World War II (WWII), 75% of Dutch Jews were deported and killed. Despite efforts to overcome the divisions in religion and politics, oppositions between Catholics, Protestants, liberals and socialists continued. The post-war reconstruction of the Netherlands was an effort in state building along denominational lines. The state supported faith-based organisations in education, media, politics and leisure. In the 1960s, the confessional character of some of these organisations started to fade as they became more intertwined with the state and state-related organisations. Other confessional organisations persisted, in particular those that were relevant to the content of the worldview they represented, such as broadcasting organisations, schools and political parties. Church participation and membership started to decline, starting with the Dutch Reformed Church. Other religions and new religious movements entered the scene – in particular Islam because of migration from Turkey and Morocco in the post-WWII period – but this did not change the trend towards religious decline.

Currently, at the beginning of the twenty-first century, the Netherlands can be considered a secular and religiously heterogeneous country, with a tradition of public policy that favours organised religion. Nearly 70% of the Dutch population consider themselves as having 'no religion' (Bernts and Berghuijs 2016). One quarter of the Dutch identify themselves as Christians, most of them as Catholics, others as mainline Protestants or other Christians. Muslims constitute 5% of the population; the remaining 2% identify as Buddhists, Hindus, Jews or other.

All these distinct religious minorities co-exist with diffuse categories of people who are religiously indifferent or who do not consider themselves part of a community with a particular worldview. Nearly one-third of the population identify as 'spiritual persons'. Some of them exist in milieus where paranormal activities, Westernised Buddhism and alternative psychology are popular. The boundaries between these categories are not clear-cut; a Muslim may quite well be interested in new spirituality. Yet this hyper-diversity appears, not in a vacuum, but in a context defined by a particular social and religious history. Current arrangements of religious diversity build on structures designed to deal with the diversity of Protestants, Catholics and Jews.

Although the government does not regulate religion, it does favour religions, or secular worldviews, which are organised. In this sense, the Dutch model may be called an oligopoly (Yang 2010). It reflects a way of dealing with state–religion relations which is both different from the monopolies, until recently, of the Anglican state Church in England and Wales and the Roman Catholic Church in France with its formal tradition of *laicité* (Beckford et al. 2005). It differs as well from a free religious market in a country with competing religions, such as the United States. It is certainly not like countries with a similar degree of secularisation, like the Czech Republic, which have had a tradition of expelling religion from the public domain. Oligopoly dynamics reflect a longer tradition of multi-faith management, which has developed in a Christian context. Therefore, the situation is different from one in which a monopolist either succeeds in continuing its position by facilitating other religious communities (Furseth 2003, 2014) or gradually loses this position (Martínez-Ariño et al. 2015).

17.3   The Sociogenesis of Spiritual Care

The prison chaplaincy started as an obligation specified for the two main categories of detainees: Protestants and Catholics. With the introduction of the penitentiary system, prisoners in the northern part of the Netherlands were obliged to attend Protestant church services, while prisoners in the south were obliged to attend Catholic Mass. In 1824, the first prison chaplains were appointed by the king, receiving a state allowance. Their primary mission remained moral guidance, evangelisation and conversion, even when the Protestant and Jewish judiciary chaplains became civil servants. In 1949, the minister of justice appointed a head of the Protestant chaplaincy and a head of the Roman Catholic chaplaincy which served to integrate a specialised type of spiritual care within the penitentiary system (Abma et al. 1990; van Iersel 1991). Organised religions could request access to institutions in order to tend to the needs of their members in connection with issues where the state was not allowed to interfere due to the separation of church and state: the care of souls. In 1954, the organisation of those without a religious affiliation, the Humanist Association, started its efforts to obtain access to organised spiritual care in total institutions. Non-religious chaplains gained recognition under the heading of Humanism, which gave rise to the new profession of humanistic counsellors who were not only supposed to counsel detainees but also to lead meditation meetings as an equivalent to church services (Brabers 2006). Thus, the historical religious diversity contributed to the formation of a rudimentary system that would provide for spiritual care to a religiously diverse population. At the end of the twentieth century, Muslims entered this system (Kloosterboer and Yılmaz 1997).

In the Netherlands, the official term for prison chaplaincy, including Islamic prison chaplaincy, is 'spiritual care'. This term refers to an interdenominational and professional concept of chaplaincy and has become prevalent since the 1970s, reflecting a tendency to deal with religious diversity in a particular way (Snelder 2006). The term 'spiritual care' (*geestelijke verzorging*) was invented, first in hospitals, as an umbrella term for the activities of chaplains from all denominations: 'spiritual counsellors' (*geestelijk verzorgers*) was the name given to its practitioners. In Dutch, this label refers not to the neologism 'spirituality' but to the category of spirit and mind (*geest*). It entails the suggestion that the spirit, like the body, needs care. The new term proved successful both in opening up the care of souls in institutional settings to representatives from a wide range of religious and secular worldviews and in uniting them as practitioners of the same profession. It did not, however, gain currency among the general public and remained somewhat artificial (ter Borg 2000).

Catholic and Protestant hospital chaplains united in a professional association (Association for Spiritual Counsellors in Care Institutions) with distinct Catholic and Protestant sections. In the following decades, Humanist, Jewish, Islamic, Hindu and Buddhist sections were added. In 2013, the professional Association for Spiritual Counsellors opened its ranks to chaplains operating in the army, prisons and the private sector and modified its name accordingly. Those providing spiritual care are supposed to be recognised by their background community as, for example, pastor, rabbi, or humanistic counsellor. Recently, an agency was even established that scrutinises candidates who seek to operate as spiritual counsellors without an institutional affiliation with an organised worldview (Vereniging van Geestelijk VerZorgers 2015). The state-recognised Register for Spiritual Counsellors accepts certified spiritual counsellors who have been recognised by a Council for Spiritual Counsellors Not Delegated by a Background Community (RING-GV).

This recent development stands in contrast to the concept of spiritual care as it prevails in prisons and the army. Here, spiritual care is always a particular, denominational, type of spiritual care. The spiritual counsellor is therefore, by definition, *also* a representative of a particular community. To promote the match between supply and demand, detainees are asked who they prefer. In 2007, 2008, 2009, 2010 and 2017 a survey was conducted among either a sample of or all detainees. Partly based on this survey, the Minister of Justice and Security decides on the appointment of chaplains. With the prison population in 2017, this resulted in around 150 prison chaplains (not all working full time).

Table Religion, Preference, Chaplains (%)

	General population (2015)	Registered worldview among prisoners (2010)	Preference among prisoners (2010)	Spiritual counsellors (2010)	Preference among prisoners (2017)
Roman Catholic	11,7	23,2	24,1	29,0	20,5
Protestant	12,8	13,5	16,3	24,4	12,1
Other Christian (GIN)/Greek/ Russian Orthodox	0,8	1,0	1,4	0,0	2,8
Jewish		0,8	1,5	2,0	1,8
Muslim	4,9	20,7	19,0	18,0	28,6
Humanist		0,9	11,4	19,7	9,9
Hindu		2,1	2,6	4,0	1,5
Buddhist		0,4	1,8	3,0	1,8

(continued)

Table Religion, Preference, Chaplains (%)					
	General population (2015)	Registered worldview among prisoners (2010)	Preference among prisoners (2010)	Spiritual counsellors (2010)	Preference among prisoners (2017)
Other	2,0	0,3	2,6		
No (need)	67,8	31,1	19,6		21,0
Unknown		6,0			
	100,0	100,0	100,3	100,1	100,0

Sources: *God in Nederland 1966–2015* (Bernts and Berghuis 2016) (general population)
Voorkeurspeiling Geestelijke Verzorging (Henneken and Mol 2010)
Uitslag Voorkeurspeiling Dienst Geestelijke Verzorging (Brief Minister van Justitie en Veiligheid aan de Voorzitter van de Tweede Kamer) (8 January 2018) (Dekker 2018)
(Only detainees in prisons and remand centres are taken into account in this table. The distribution of spiritual counsellors reflects all custodial institutions)

The preceding table allows us to make the following observations. Compared with the general Dutch population, Muslims and Catholics are overrepresented in prison. Those who indicate no religious affiliation are underrepresented. This is a common finding: religion correlates strongly with the region of origin. Twenty percent of the detainees were born in the former Netherlands Antilles (predominantly Catholic), Surinam (partly Catholic), Morocco or Turkey (both Muslim-majority countries) (Directie Beleid en Bestuursondersteuning 2017).

The survey also reveals that humanistic spiritual counsellors are preferred by more detainees than those registered as such themselves. Apparently, there is also a demand for spiritual care among those who did not register as being affiliated with a denomination.

The staff is distributed more or less according to the detainees' preferences as expressed in the preceding survey, but the share of humanistic counsellors currently exceeds the proportion in the preferences, whereas the share of Islamic counsellors is lower than is warranted by the preferences. The most recent survey (2017) indicates an even increasing demand for Islamic and a decreasing demand for Protestant spiritual counsellors. Recently, Greek and Russian Orthodox spiritual counsellors have been appointed.

The denominational system has not gone undisputed, in particular in light of the increasing religious diversity and the deinstitutionalisation of religion. Recently, a (Western) Buddhist chaplain suggested modifying the denominational system altogether in order to adjust to religious hyper-diversity or 'multiple religious belonging' (van Zessen and Koolen 2013). The Roman Catholic Chaplain General countered this position by defending the current system, which has succeeded in preventing the state from interfering with the content of spiritual care by appointing authorities who represent particular religions and worldviews (van Eijk 2015). An alternative position is held by Hans Schilderman (2015), Professor of Religion and Care at Radboud University Nijmegen, who recommends that chaplains take their professional affairs into their own hands, just as 'liberal professions', such as lawyers and physicians, have done. This would fit with developments in the professional association mentioned earlier. It is unclear, however, how this recommendation would work in the penitentiary system. It plays down how spiritual care is rooted in lived religion and relinquishes the position religious authorities have in the current system. Until now, prison chaplaincy continues to be built on organised religious groups, reflecting the influence of the historical pillarisation system.

17.4 The Penitentiary System and Delegating Authorities

The Custodial Institutions Agency distinguishes five types of penitentiary institutions: (1) *remand centres* for adults held in pre-trial detention or serving short-term sentences; (2) *prisons* for adults convicted of an offence; (3) *correctional institutions for juvenile offenders* for young people between 12 and 18 years of age, up to a maximum of 23 years old, convicted of an offence; (4) *forensic psychiatric centres* for adults who have been convicted and require psychiatric care (patients); (5) *detention centres* for foreign nationals living illegally in the Netherlands, for those who have been refused access at the border, and for drug couriers. Over 80% of the people in custody are in remand centres and prisons.

Since 2012, the number of detainees has decreased by 24%. At the end of 2016, an average of 10.902 people were detained in penitentiary institutions (Directie Beleid en Bestuursondersteuning 2017). Owing to the substantial decline in the number of serious crimes, the reduction in the duration of prison terms, replacement of imprisonment by community service and the outplacement of convicts in care institutions, Dutch prisons are not overcrowded, as is the case in other European countries. Moreover, from an international perspective, the percentage of those accused who are convicted is low in the Netherlands (Smit et al. 2016). From 2005 to 2015, the prison population rate decreased from 132 per 100,000 to 82 according to the International Centre for Prison Studies (van Eijk 2016). This is still higher than the Nordic and German (79) rates, but lower than the rates in France (98), Italy (106), Spain (132) and Poland (217), not to mention the USA, where the rate is 716 per 100,000.[2] For the period 2015–2021, the Ministry of Justice and Security projects a scenario in which the number of registered crimes will decline by 5% and the capacity of the penitentiary system will decline by 21%.

In this connection, detainees can take advantage of an ample supply of professional services and facilities that are on offer in penitentiary institutions, ranging from psychological programmes to vocational training. Most prisoners have their own individual cell and enjoy privacy. During the day, detainees follow a well-structured programme (get up, eat, train, work, play sports, be outside, and undergo therapy). Group activities organised by the prison chaplaincy during the week must fit in a tight schedule (Oliemeulen et al. 2010). Sunday services, on the other hand, give some detainees a welcome opportunity to get out of their cells (van Dun 2011; Oskamp 2004).

---

[2] The Ministry of Security and Justice uses adjusted figures (51 detainees per 100,000 inhabitants), which results in the lowest ranking in Europe, together with Finland (Directie Beleid en Bestuursondersteuning 2017).

The legal basis of the   care practised from various backgrounds, be it a religion or other worldview. After a lengthy debate, the individual right to gain access to the care of souls, or its equivalent, remained the basis: people should be able to receive the usual pastoral care they are able to receive from their priest, minister or equivalent in daily life, even when circumstances hinder contact between individuals and representatives of their religion or worldview (Hirsch Ballin 1988). Since 1994, the Law on Spiritual Care in Health Care and Judicial Institutions mandates that penitentiary institutions ensure that suitable spiritual care be available for patients and inhabitants of any religion or worldview who remain in detention for any length of time beyond 24 hours. This law is based on Article 6 of the Dutch constitution: '1. Everyone shall have the right to profess his religion or belief freely, either individually or with others, without prejudice to his responsibility under the law' (Grondwet voor het Koninkrijk der Nederlanden 2008). Hence, the state should not hinder the exercise of religion. This freedom of religion is not absolute, as the article continues: '2. Rules concerning the exercise of this right other than in buildings and enclosed places may be laid down by an Act of Parliament for the protection of health, in the interest of traffic and to combat or prevent disorders.' At the same time, the state cannot interfere with religion. The Law on Spiritual Care is included in the Penitentiary Principles Law (Article 41): detainees are entitled to practise their religion; the director of the penitentiary institution is responsible for facilitating suitable spiritual care (Penitentiare beginselenwet 2017).

To facilitate the profession of religion and belief in total institutions such as prisons and the army, a system has been developed with a strict division of authority. The criteria to gain access to this system, however, are less formalised and precise, but are implied by practice over time, following the historic example of the Christian churches. Faith communities of a certain size, which have existed over a longer period of time, do not undermine the state and form a legal body, are eligible for accreditation. This means that the head of this particular chaplaincy will be part of the management team of the Department for Spiritual Care (*Dienst Geestelijke Verzorging*) at the Ministry of Security and Justice. This department is directed by a regular civil servant. The 'head chaplains' direct their own spiritual counsellors as far as matters of content are concerned, whereas the entire management team and its director take care of the formal aspects. Spiritual counsellors are themselves both incumbents and civil servants. Besides these chaplains, detainees may receive visits from others who provide spiritual care. In these cases, the prison director will decide on special privileges, such as access outside visiting hours and having the right to use a separate room. In such cases, the local department for spiritual care will play an advisory role (Fig. 17.1).

Thus, spiritual care leans heavily on organised and lived religion. Detainees should be allowed to express and practise their religion as they would in regular life. Grounded in the European Convention on Human Rights (Article 9), this has been, and remains, the juridical foundation of spiritual care in prisons (van Eijk 2013). The state allows religions to exercise pastoral care and its equivalents using delegated authorities (*zendende instanties*), which enable the Ministry of Justice and Security to communicate with 'a religion'. These authorities cooperate in a Department for

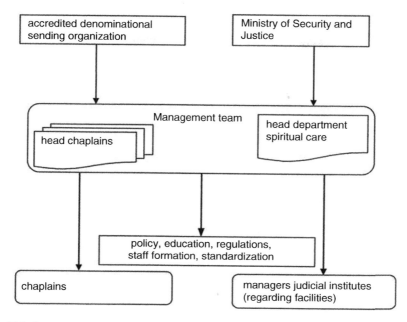

Fig. 17.1 Simplified organisational model of prison chaplaincy in the Netherlands. (Ajouaou and Bernts 2015a)

Spiritual Care, which has been expanded with representatives from the Islamic community (Ajouaou and Bernts 2015b), the Hindu community and representatives of Buddhism, alongside the Catholic, Protestant, Jewish and Humanistic sections, which had been established earlier. In this context, the path of pillarisation has been pursued into present times. In practice, however, Catholic and Protestant chaplains have worked for detainees of other faiths as well (Spruit et al. 2003).

Within these sections, the plea for an orientation that is both confessional and professional dominates. Spiritual care, then, is practised as part of a specific religious tradition, is open to those who are not part of this tradition, and follows professional and academic standards that are common to all practitioners. The chaplains' primary activities are specified as initial interviews, informal conversations, individual counselling, group counselling, regular religious services, incidental meetings, and providing spiritual aid in times of crisis (Eerbeek and Van Iersel 2009). They must be academically qualified and competent in theological hermeneutics, communication, pastoral counselling, ritual performance and leadership. This orientation reflects the habitus shaped by the field itself: spiritual counsellors are representatives of a religious community, which is supposed to have sufficiently trained these counsellors to be suitable in a position in the military or judiciary system. Thus, the government can indirectly exclude independent, 'radical' or 'sectarian' spiritual counsellors. Thus, there is self-regulation of the religious field. The state relies on the background communities and the academy to recruit, educate and select candidates. Through academic education, mandates by background communities, the setting of civil service and the juridical boundaries, job descriptions, professional training, and interdenominational teamwork, the system promotes the formation of practitioners of the 'care of souls' (Weber 1989): religious and secular guidance, counselling and support. Thus, the government is not at all or to a lesser extent confronted with a variety of ritual, ethical and educational specialists from all kinds of backgrounds, all claiming to support detainees in professing their religion in their own way.

At the operational level, prison chaplains tend to rely on a 'ministry of attentiveness' (*presentiepastoraat*). According to this model, an essential skill of pastors, and of helping professions as such, is the ability to accompany others in an attentive way (Baart 2001; Klaver and Baart 2011). Less frequently, prison chaplains report that they try to widen prisoners' worldview (the dialogical model) or that they share their own religious motivations (the kerygmatic model) (Flierman 2012). Detainees themselves report that their belief or convictions support them in getting through their detention time, accepting life as it is and working on their own development. As they practise their religion, they value the contact with relatives (Oliemeulen et al. 2010).

The Dutch prison chaplaincy shows a formal continuation and expansion of the confessional paradigm while operating in a pluralistic religious and secular context. The keyword in the legitimisation of spiritual care in the state-regulated context is increasingly, besides freedom of religion and belief, *security* (Todd 2013). The link with organised religions, and the complex incorporation of their representatives into the governmental bureaucracy, serves to warrant the legitimacy of this service. Moreover, since 9/11, the focus on the perspective of security has also penetrated the Ministry of Justice, which in 2010 was renamed the Ministry of Security and Justice. This security policy extends to the Department of Spiritual Care, which now requires that chaplains serve to promote peace and order in prisons (van Eijk 2013). From the perspective of religions, however, this is not the goal of spiritual care. Chaplains, as advocates of human dignity, may indeed consider it their duty to protest the actions of prison authorities.

Increased secularisation and pluralisation have been answered by the expansion of the confessional model, resonant with the Dutch version of oligopoly dynamics: *organised religious pluralism*. At the same time, prison chaplains also reach people of faiths other than their own and try to prove their usefulness. As such, the umbrella term 'spiritual care' reflects the idea that all these different religious and secular representatives share a common ground which enables them to operate in multifaith teams, a strategy that can be labelled *generalised pluralism*.

17.5   The Formation of an Islamic Chaplaincy

The case of the Muslim chaplaincy demonstrates how the institutional dynamics of the oligopoly system work and how state and religion are formally separate but practically intertwined.

In the 1960s, Dutch companies started to recruit labourers from the Mediterranean countries. In the 1970s, the proportion of Muslims in the Netherlands increased further as labour migrants from Morocco and Turkey invited their families to join them. The diversity in the general population was reflected in the prison population. During the 1970s and 1980s, Christian spiritual counsellors served as 'brokers' for imams. In 1982, a list of accredited (Turkish) imams facilitated the entrance of imams in penitentiary institutions (Kloosterboer and Yılmaz 1997). The first Muslim chaplains in custodial institutions were appointed in the early 1990s. These were hired by the government on a freelance basis, since the Islamic chaplaincy did not yet meet formal requirements such as mastering the Dutch language or having a delegating authority, a head of chaplaincy and academic training. For this reason they could not become public servants. To serve the increasing Muslim prison population, workarounds were designed. Research carried out in 2002 (Spruit et al. 2003) indicated that Muslim chaplains were present in 26 of the 41 custodial institutions. This was already comparable to the presence of Catholic and Protestant chaplains.

In 2005, representatives from various Islamic backgrounds succeeded in forming one organisation that could serve as a delegating authority and filed a request to the Minister of Justice. Not all trends were represented; Alevites, for example, withdrew (Kloosterboer and Yılmaz 1997). After negotiations, the Contact Organ Muslims and Government (CMO) was recognised in 2007 by the Dutch government as the Islamic delegating authority(Boender 2013). This has favoured a greater relative proportion of the Muslim chaplaincy in the total supply of spiritual care. Subsequent surveys among inmates also indicated a larger demand for the Islamic chaplaincy than was offered (Henneken-Hordijk and Mol 2010). In 2017, among Islamic spiritual counsellors, there were six female employees. The majority of Islamic spiritual counsellors, male and female, work in regular prisons and detention centres; a few are active in the two special terrorist departments, which are part of the prisons in Vught and De Schie. Probably 33 prisoners are incarcerated in these departments, likely 28 Jihadists and 5 extreme-right radicals.

Prison imams are appointed as public servants to offer detainees religious counselling and spiritual care. Although this profile differs from the traditional function of the imam (one who leads prayer) in Muslim communities, this term was settled on (Ajouaou 2010). In official documents, the term Islamic spiritual counsellor prevails, also because usually only male counsellors are called imams. The application procedure is strict. Job requirements and selections minimise the appointment of imams with a radical background, and supervision and professionalisation minimise the chance that they will radicalise on the job (Section Islamic Spiritual Care 2016).

Besides the profile of the prison imams, what they provide is also important. Three particular elements are important. First, the fact that these imams try to meet the religious needs of prisoners as adequately as possible. This concerns not only beliefs but also the component of praxis, such as provision of halal food, prayer times, religious feasts, wearing headscarves and wearing a beard. Although the freedom of religion guarantees that Muslims can have halal meals *de jure*, the director may appeal to practical circumstances in order to defend the de facto limitation of the provision of halal food (Post 2005). The generous facilitation of the religious preferences of detainees by prison imams is probably partly inspired by the motive that religiosity should not become a point of contention for prisoners. At the same time, prison imams try to convey to Muslim detainees Islamic views that exclude radicalisation or offer a counterbalance to it. Distinguishing religiosity and ideology, they try to facilitate the confession of *religion* as much as possible and, at the same time, offer a moderate Islamic *ideological* view which undermines radical ideologies (Ajouaou 2016).

Islamic prison chaplaincy extends to the social dimension. Imams are often involved in maintaining or regaining contact with parents, partners and children. As representatives of the world outside, they also work selectively with volunteers who wish and are able to contribute to resocialisation during detention and care after detention. Radical volunteers are refused. Dutch Islamic prison chaplains do not honour requests from foreign powers or networks that wish to get in touch with Muslim detainees (Ajouaou 2015).

Finally, next to these ideological and social elements, practical activities are relevant. Prison imams see it as their responsibility to ensure that the treatment of detainees is humane. According to their job description, they must contribute to a denominational policy 'in promoting a humane detention climate and care tailored to the detainees within the facility'. (Spiritual Care Department 2016: 1) If they notice incidents pertaining to the violation of human dignity, they are supposed to contact staff members or prison directors. Prison directors, however, may also regard chaplains as (regular) members of the staff. Since 2016, special staff members of the Custodial Institutions Agency have been trained to detect radicalisation among detainees. The magazine for the partners of the agency includes chaplains as supporters of these special staff members (van Meer and Ledegang 2017). This task may conflict with the confidentiality of spiritual care and with the goal of their presence, which is defined along internal religious lines, such as 'leading the faithful' (Ajouaou 2010) for Islamic or 'sanctifying life' (van Eijk 2013) for the Catholic chaplaincy.

17.6 Conclusion

The Dutch system of spiritual care displays a particular way of dealing with the principle of separation between church and state and with the fundamental right of freedom of religion and belief. The state can enter into dialogue with religious communities, but it does not control them. To a certain extent, these communities enjoy the freedom to have and develop their own visions. Addressing the topic of governance and religion, Marco Ventura (2016), an expert on religion and law, makes a distinction between governance *by* religion, governance *of* religion and governance *through* religion. The work of spiritual counsellors, such as prison imams, in the Netherlands can be treated as an example of governance *through* religion. The state facilitates a service that is organised according to oligopoly dynamics: an expansive system of delegating authorities working together in a Department for Spiritual Care at the Ministry of Security and Justice, directing spiritual care in the entire penitentiary system. These delegating authorities represent a limited variety of religious and secular sections of the population. Religious groups considered radical are actually excluded.

On the one hand, the Dutch system incorporates and regulates representatives of large religious communities; on the other hand, it allows chaplains to approach detainees as persons from their own perspectives, rather than as representatives of a political ideology. Because of the last element, prison chaplains and prison imams have the opportunity to counterbalance the sometimes understandable but one-sided approach of the state in a period of securitisation (Vellenga and De Groot 2019).

Although this system is relatively open to newcomers, it also tends to create religious categories that have never existed as such before, such as Humanists and Muslims, as distinct, more or less homogeneous communities, each with their own spiritual counsellors (Burchardt 2017). The institutional logic, and the Christian tradition it is embedded in, promote church-like organisations and practices tailored to the traditional care of souls and weekly liturgy. This contrasts with the fluid presence of religion in everyday life, even in closed settings such as life in prison.

Bibliography

Abma, J. F., Blom, E. J. M., Loman, G., Dautzenberg, A. J., & Blom, M. B. (1990). Geestelijke verzorging in penitentiaire inrichtingen; een orientatie op een karakteristiek werkveld. *Justitiële Verkenningen, 16*(6), 102–124.

Ajouaou, M. (2010). Imam achter tralies. Casestudie naar islamitisch geestelijke verzorging in Nederlandse penitentiaire inrichtingen met bouwstenen voor een beroepsprofiel. PhD Thesis, Universiteit van Tilburg.

Ajouaou, M. (2015). How Islamic religious services can contribute to preventing and countering religious radicalization in prisons. The Dutch model. Unpublished paper Radicalization and Violent Extremism Conference, Barcelona,14 October 2015.

Ajouaou, M. (2016). Interview by Sipco Vellenga, 28 October 2016. Amsterdam.

Ajouaou, M., & Bernts, T. (2015a). The effects of religious diversity on spiritual care: Reflections from the Dutch correction facilities. In I. Becci & O. Roy (Eds.), *Religious diversity in European prisons* (pp. 31–45). Cham: Springer.

Ajouaou, M., & Bernts, T. (2015b). Imams and inmates: Is Islamic prison chaplaincy in the Netherlands a case of religious adaptation or of contextualization? *International Journal of Politics, Culture, and Society, 28*(1), 51–65. https://doi.org/10.1007/s10767-014-9182-y.

Baart, A. (2001). *Een theorie van de presentie*. Utrecht: Lemma.

Beckford, J. A., Joly, D., & Khosrokhavar, F. (2005). *Muslims in prison. Challenge and change in Britain and France. Migration, minorities and citizenship*. Hampshire/New York: Palgrave MacMillan.

Bernts, T., & Berghuijs, J. (2016). *God in Nederland 1966–2015*. Utrecht: Ten Have.

Boender, W. (2013). Embedding Islam in the 'moral covenants' of European states: The case of a state-funded imam training in the Netherlands. *Journal of Muslims in Europe, 2*(2), 227–247. https://doi.org/10.1163/22117954-12341265.

Brabers, J. (2006). *Van pioniers tot professionals: de dienst humanistisch geestelijke verzorging bij de krijgsmacht (1964–2004)*. Utrecht: De Tijdstroom.

Burchardt, M. (2017). Diversity as neoliberal governmentality: Towards a new sociological genealogy of religion. *Social Compass, 64*(2), 180–193. https://doi.org/10.1177/0037768617697391.

de Galembert, C. (2016). Les aumôniers musulmans dans la politique de lutte contre la radicalisation. Paper presented at the international symposium the making of Muslim chaplaincies in prison – Comparative approaches, Paris, 25 November 2016.

Dekker, S. (2018). Uitslag voorkeurspeiling Dienst Geestelijke Verzorging ed. Ministerie van Justitie en Veiligheid. Den Haag.

Directie Beleid en Bestuursondersteuning. (2017). *DJI in getal* (pp. 2012–2016). Den Haag: Ministerie van Veiligheid en Justitie, Dienst Justitiële Inrichtingen.

Eerbeek, J., & van Iersel, F. (2009). Positie en werkwijze van het justitiepastoraat in de inrichtingen. In A. H. M. van Iersel & J. D. W. Eerbeek (Eds.), *Handboek Justitiepastoraat. Context, theologie en praktijk van het protestants en rooms-katholiek justitiepastoraat* (pp. 101–112). Budel: Damon.

Flierman, F. (2012). *Geestelijke verzorging in het werkveld van justitie: een empirisch-theologische studie*. Delft: Eburon.

Furseth, I. (2003). Secularization and the role of religion in state institutions. *Social Compass, 50*(2), 191–202.

Furseth, I. (2014). The ambiguity of secular and religious space. The Norwegian penitentiary system. In R. van den Breemer, J. Casanova, & T. Wyller (Eds.), *Secular and sacred? The Scandinavian case of religion in human rights, law and public space* (Research in contemporary religion) (Vol. 15, pp. 152–169). Göttingen: Vandenhoeck & Ruprecht.

Grondwet voor het Koninkrijk der Nederlanden. 2008.

Henneken-Hordijk, I., & Mol, G. (2010). *Voorkeurspeiling Geestelijke verzorging*. Den Haag: Ministerie van Justitie en Veiligheid.

Hirsch Ballin, E. M. H. 1988. *Overheid, godsdienst en levensovertuiging: eindrapport van de Commissie van advies inzake de criteria voor steunverlening aan kerkgenootschappen en andere genootschappen op geestelijke grondslag (ingesteld bij ministerieel besluit van 17 februari 1986, Stcrt. 1986, nr. 51)*. 's-Gravenhage, The Netherlands: Ministerie van Binnenlandse Zaken, Stafafdeling Constitutionele Zaken en Wetgeving.

Klaver, K., & Baart, A. (2011). Attentiveness in care: Towards a theoretical framework. *Nursing Ethics, 18*(5), 686–693.

Kloosterboer, D., & Yılmaz, C. (1997). *Justitie, islam en de imam: een onderzoek naar de behoefte aan geestelijke verzorging onder moslimgedetineerden* (Islam & samenleving) (Vol. 1). Den Haag: Nederlandse Islamitische Raad (NIR).

Kühle, L.. (2016). The development of Muslim Chaplaincy in Denmark. Paper presented at the International Symposium 'The making of Muslim chaplaincies in prison – Comparative approaches', Paris, 25 November 2016.

Lijphart, A. (1968). *The politics of accommodation: pluralism and democracy in the Netherlands*. Berkeley [etc.]: University of California Press.

Martikainen, T. (2014). Immigrant religions and the context of reception in advanced industrial societies. In H. Vilaga, E. Pace, I. Furseth, & P. Petterson (Eds.), *The changing soul of Europe. Religions and migrations in northern and southern Europe* (pp. 47–65). Farnham/Burlington: Ashgate.

Martínez-Ariño, J., García-Romeral, G., Ubasart-González, G., & Griera, M. (2015). Demonopolisation and dislocation: (Re-)negotiating the place and role of religion in Spanish prisons. *Social Compass, 62*(1), 3–21.

Oliemeulen, L., van Luijtenaar, M., Al Shamma, S., & Woldf, J. (2010). Geestelijke verzorging in detentie. In *Visie van ingeslotenen op behoefte en aanbod*. Den Haag: WODC, ministerie van Justitie.

Oskamp, P. (2004). *Overleven achter steen en staal: vieringen en geloofsbeleving in de bajes onderzocht*. Zoetermeer: Meinema.

Penitentiare beginselenwet. 2017. ed. Overheid der Nederlanden.

Post, M. (2005). *Detentie en culturele diversiteit: de effectuering van de rechtspositie door etnische minderheden in detentie*. Utrecht: Universiteit Utrecht.

Roy, O. (2015). Conclusion and perspectives. The diversification of chaplaincy in European jails: Providing spiritual support for new inmates or countering radicalism? In I. Becci & O. Roy (Eds.), *Religious diversity in European prisons* (pp. 187–190). Cham: Springer.

Schilderman, H. (2015). Van ambt naar vrij beroep. De geestelijke verzorging als voorziening in het publieke domein. *Tijdschrift voor Religie, Recht en Beleid, 6*(2), 5–23. https://doi.org/10.5553/TvRRB/187977842015006002002.

Section Islamic Spiritual Care (2016). Religious profile of the head of Islamic spiritual Care at the Ministry of security and justice.

Smit, P. R., Moolenaar, D. E. G., van Tulder, F. P., & Diephuis, B. J. (2016). *Capaciteitsbehoefte Justitiële Ketens t/m 2021. Beleidsneutrale ramingen.* Den Haag: Wetenschappelijk Onderzoek- en Documentatiecentrum.

Snelder, W. (2006). Beknopte geschiedenis van de VGVZ tot 2000. In J. Doolaard (Ed.), *Nieuw handboek geestelijke verzorging* (pp. 84–100). Kampen: Kok.

Spiritual Care Department (2016). *Function document.* The Hague: Ministry of Security and Justice.

Spruit, L., Bernts, T., & Woldringh, C. (2003). Geestelijke verzorging in justitiële inrichtingen. In *Rapport Kaski 502.* Nijmegen: ITS/KASKI.

ter Borg, M. B. (2000). *Waarom geestelijke verzorging? Zingeving en geestelijke verzorging in de moderne maatschappij.* Nijmegen: KSGV.

Todd, A. (2013). *Military chaplaincy in contention: Chaplains, churches and the morality of conflict* (Explorations in practical, pastoral and empirical theology). Farnham: Ashgate.

van Dun, Th. (2011). *Invoeren in vieren: ritueel-liturgische strategieën: een onderzoek naar de katholieke kerkdiensten in inrichtingen van justitie in Nederland.* Tilburg University, [S.l.].

van Eijk, R. (2013). *Menselijke waardigheid tijdens detentie.* Oisterwijk: Wolf Legal Publishers.

van Eijk, R. (2015). Goed geregeld. Geestelijke verzorging bij justitie. *Tijdschrift voor Religie, Recht en Beleid, 6*(1), 69–81.

van Eijk, R. 2016. Global facts and trends. An overview. In *For Justice and Mercy. International reflections on Prison Chaplaincy,* eds. R. van Eijk, G. Loman, and Th. de Wit, 177–189. Publicatiereeks van het Centrum voor Justitiepastoraat, vol. 8. Oisterwijk: Wolf Legal Publishers.

van Iersel, A. H. M. (1991). De voorgeschiedenis van het justitiepastoraat. "Ik was in de gevangenis". In G. W. M. de Wit (Ed.), *Het justitiepastoraat in Nederland: uitgave ter gelegenheid van veertig jaar Hoofdaalmoezenier en Hoofdpredikant bij de Inrichtingen van Justitie in Nederland 1949–1989* (pp. 3–18). 's-Gravenhage: Bureau Hoofdaalmoezenier/Bureau Hoofdpredikant, Ministerie van Justitie.

van Meer, M., & Ledegang, N. 2017. Alle puzzelstukjes op tafel. DJIZien. Magazine voor ketenpartners http://djizien.dji.nl/djizien/artikel/alle-puzzelstukjes-op-tafel/index.cfm. Accessed 19 July 2017.

van Zessen, N., & Koolen, B. (2013). Geestelijke verzorging in de gevangenis. *Tijdschrift voor Religie, Recht en Beleid, 4*(1), 29–43.

Vellenga, S., & De Groot, K. (2019). Securitization, Islamic chaplaincy, and the issue of (de)radicalization of Muslim detainees in Dutch prisons. *Social Compass, 66*(2), 224–237. https://doi.org/10.1177/0037768619833313.

Ventura, M. (2016). Governance by, of and through religion. Paper presented at the EUREL conference governance and religion, Luxembourg, 29–30 September 2016.

Vereniging van Geestelijk VerZorgers. 2015. Beroepsstandaard Geestelijk Verzorger. https://vgvz.nl/wp-content/uploads/2016/06/beroepsstandaard_definitief.pdf. Accessed 1 Aug 2017.

Weber, M. (1989). *Max Weber Gesamtausgabe I/19.* Tübingen: J.C.B. Mohr.

Yang, F. (2010). Oligopoly dynamics: Consequences of religious regulation. *Social Compass, 57*(2), 194–205.

Chapter 18
Norway: Religion in the Prison System

Helge Årsheim

Abstract This chapter provides a basic overview of the regulation of religion in the Norwegian prison system. After a brief introduction, the chapter maps the role of religion in Norwegian correctional facilities from a historical perspective and examines the changing demography of the prisoner population. In the main section of the chapter, the legal and institutional framework for the management of religion in Norwegian correctional facilities is examined in some detail, with an emphasis on how the regulation of religion during imprisonment interacts with other regulations of religion in Norway, what specific international and domestic provisions regulate religion during incarceration, the role of clergy and other religious leaders, and the management of religion as an operational issue for prison staff, including the growing concern with prisons as hotbeds of radical and violent extremism.

18.1 Introduction

The regulation of religion in Norwegian prisons must be considered against the paradoxical background of a gradually diminishing role for religious institutions in public life, significant drops in church attendance and belief in God among the majority population, combined with growing religious diversity and the increased political salience of religion in late modernity (Furseth 2015). Managing religion within the confines of correctional institutions has to take into account all these changes, accommodating the equal access of religious clergy to inmates and safeguarding their rights to manifest their religion or belief, while also monitoring the spread of religious doctrines and perceptions that can inspire violent and radical extremism. Moreover, this management must always take into account the specific security challenges represented by forced incarceration, while also attending to the often complicated behavioural, social and psychological challenges facing the majority of the prisoner population.

H. Årsheim (✉)
University of Oslo, Oslo, Norway
e-mail: helge.arsheim@teologi.uio.no

© Springer Nature Switzerland AG 2020   285
J. Martínez-Ariño, A.-L. Zwilling (eds.), *Religion and Prison: An Overview of Contemporary Europe*, Boundaries of Religious Freedom: Regulating Religion in Diverse Societies 7, https://doi.org/10.1007/978-3-030-36834-0_18

Although Norway has recently experienced an increase in the regulation and litigation of religion, from the legal regulation of the ritual circumcision of baby boys and the conscientious objector status of medical doctors to the denial of services based on religious adherence and a ban on the full-face veil in all educational institutions,[1] this trend has yet to reach the role of religion in correctional facilities, which has so far not been subject to litigation in the Norwegian legal system. In the absence of such litigation, this chapter primarily examines legislative changes and their rationale in preparatory works, seen in relation to international and domestic guidelines and circulars, to paint as complete a picture of the regulation of religion in Norwegian prisons as possible. After a brief historical introduction and a note on the demographic changes in the prisoner population, the chapter introduces the general legal framework on religion in Norway, preparing the ground for a more detailed assessment of the specific legal rules that govern religion during incarceration.

18.2   Historical Backdrop

Antecedents to the current organisational structure and principles for punishment in the Norwegian correctional services can be traced back to the founding of the Oslo Penitentiary, the first purpose-built prison in Norway, in 1851 (Schaanning 2007: 272). Prior to this invention, imprisonment was mostly organised in fortresses, labour camps and other, more ad hoc arrangements. With the advent of organised incarceration, the institutional foundations of prisoner rehabilitation and criminological research developed within the confines of the Oslo Penitentiary as a collaboration between wardens, doctors and pastors, with the latter entrusted with the strongest obligation to turn the morally lost and depraved prisoners into well-functioning and moral members of society (*op. cit*: 275). Over the course of the twentieth century, the purpose of incarceration changed gradually into a medical approach that saw crime as a treatable disease, and into a more socially oriented form of rehabilitation that emphasised work and education for the inmates in combination with a more comprehensive attention towards the psychosocial needs of each individual prisoner.

This latter perspective informed the 1958 Prison Act,[2] which paved the way for an 'import model' for prisoner rehabilitation that invited specialised entities in the civil service to participate in educational and labour-oriented services within the

---

[1] For an overview of these and other recent regulations and litigation on religion in Norway, see EUREL. *Norway – Current debates*, http://www.eurel.info/spip.php?rubrique962, accessed 29 June 2017.

[2] Unfortunately, few Norwegian acts or preparatory works are available in English. For the sake of consistency, I have relied on the database of unofficial translations maintained by the law library at the University of Oslo, http://app.uio.no/ub/ujur/oversatte-lover/, accessed 29 June 2017. The majority of Norwegian legal materials cited in the text were retrieved from https://lovdata.no/, accessed 29 June 2017.

confines of correctional facilities. The influence of this model has turned prisoner rehabilitation services in Norway into a complex subfield where a variety of ministries and other public bodies participate in providing the services offered in Norwegian prisons. Under this division of labour, prison chaplains are no longer appointed by prison management but in cooperation with the Church of Norway (CoN), which remains the official employer of the chaplains. From the 1970s, the idea that rehabilitation could also be achieved through community service and other alternative forms of sentencing has gained a considerable foothold in Norway, sparking the creation of numerous facilities dedicated to rehabilitation outside the formal confines of the correctional service, including several religiously oriented organisations that have developed extensive rehabilitation programmes. Since the passing of the current Execution of Sentences Act in 2001, these alternative correctional services have been conjoined with the regular prison system under the joint, coordinating Norwegian Correctional Service.

18.3   Religion in Norwegian Prisons

The interface between the Norwegian correctional system and religion is broad and growing, encompassing (a) the general legal framework and policy on religion in Norway, including the influence of international law, (b) specific regulations on the right to religious freedom and freedom from religious discrimination among the prisoner population, (c) the role of chaplains and other religious workers in the rehabilitation and care for inmates, and (d) the role of religion as an operational issue for prison staff, including the growing concern that religious radicalism may spread within correctional facilities. A key question for the following discussion is the extent to which the approaches to 'religion' under regulation in each of these aspects overlap and correspond with one another.

Interactions between all of these aspects take place in relation to a prisoner population that is increasingly diverse, in terms of both nationality and religious convictions. The scope of these changes is hard to determine, as the Personal Data Act (2000) prohibits the registration of 'sensitive' data, including religious affiliation, unless specifically required by law, or if the individuals under registration give their express consent. Owing to this restrictive regulation, there is no official statistic on religious adherence among the Norwegian prison population, as also reported for other countries in this volume. Provisional numbers from personal estimates by prison chaplains suggest that the relative proportion of Norwegian inmates with a Muslim background amounts to somewhere between 20% and 25% of the prison population (Furseth and Kühle 2011: 128), although these numbers are highly uncertain. No estimates are available for the remainder of the prison population, but from 2007 to 2017, the proportion of prisoners with Norwegian citizenship plummeted from 85% to 68% (Statistics Norway 2017),[3] with a sharp rise in inmates from other European countries, which currently make up more than 60% of the non-Norwegian prisoner population. Owing to this development, paired with the general downturn in religious belief and adherence among the majority population, the religious diversity in Norwegian prisons, while not known, is likely to be considerable.

18.3.1 General Legal and Policy Framework on Religion

The Norwegian constitution has guaranteed the freedom of religion since 1964, through an amendment that was adopted during the 150-year celebration of the 1814 constitution, while also fulfilling the international obligations incurred through the ratification of the 1950 European Convention on Human Rights. Following amendments in 2012 that separated the CoN from the state, Article 16 provides that

> All inhabitants of the realm shall have the right to free exercise of their religion. The Church of Norway, an Evangelical-Lutheran church, will remain the Established Church of Norway and will as such be supported by the State. Detailed provisions as to its system will be laid down by law. All religious and belief communities should be supported on equal terms.

Article 2 of the amended constitution also provides that 'our values will remain our [sic!] Christian and humanist heritage'. While this article is largely considered salutary and without influence on the surrounding legal regulation of religion, the formulation of Article 16 has led to some public debate due to the continued special treatment offered to the CoN, both in financial terms and in terms of the regulations within the specific Church Law (1996) governing everything from the structure of parishes to the procedure for building and maintaining church buildings.

Apart from the constitutional guarantee of religious freedom, the principal legal instrument on religion in Norwegian law is the 1999 Human Rights Act, which incorporated the provisions of the International Covenant on Civil and Political Rights (ICCPR), the International Covenant on Economic, Social and Cultural Rights (ICESCR) and the European Convention on Human Rights (ECHR) in domestic law.[4] While the Human Rights Act does not formally rank as a constitutional bill of rights, the amended Article 92 of the constitution provides that 'the authorities of the State shall respect and ensure human rights as they are expressed in this Constitution and in the treaties concerning human rights that are binding for Norway', effectively giving the provisions of these conventions constitutional authority. The principal legal rules on religion in the international instruments

---

[3] Statistisk sentralbyrå. *Fengslinger,* 2014. https://www.ssb.no/sosiale-forhold-og-kriminalitet/statistikker/fengsling, accessed 13 June 2017.

[4] Through later amendments, the Convention on the Elimination of All Forms of Discrimination against Women (CEDAW) and the Convention on the Rights of the Child (CRC) have also been included in the Human Rights Act.

incorporated by the Human Rights Act are Article 18 of the ICCPR and Article 9 of the ECHR, both of which guarantee the freedom of religion or belief, including their 'manifestation' through external worship, teaching, observance and practice. The scope of these norms for the regulation of religion in Norwegian prisons has so far not been addressed in Norwegian jurisprudence.

Norwegian policymaking has long been dominated by a welfarist approach that assumes organised religious communities are beneficial to social wellbeing (Leirvik 2016). Since the adoption of the 1969 Religious Communities Act, registered religious communities have been financially supported by the state at a per-capita rate similar to the public funds made available to finance the CoN, a support that has also been made available to non-religious 'life stance' communities since 1981.[5] The public funding of religious communities enjoys strong political support, although the conditions for funding have long been a subject of debate, partly fuelled by scepticism towards the role of mosques as hotbeds of fundamentalist Islam, but also by increasing criticism of the gender discrimination of the Catholic Church.

Although public support for organised religious activity has long been strong and vocal, the external 'manifestations' of religious practice have increasingly become topics of public concern. Beginning in the late 1990s and up to the present, several debates have erupted on the acceptability of everything from the Islamic call to prayer, the wearing of the hijab and niqab in public, at work and in schools, and the foundation of religious private schools, to the accommodation of ritual slaughter, and the length of the beards of Muslim men working in security services. Among these debates, which have largely incorporated larger European worries about 'creeping sharia', the only issue directly relevant to the regulation of religion in prison is the provision of certified halal food to Muslim inmates, a form of accommodation that has been specifically derided by the populist right-wing Progress Party.

18.3.2   Specific Regulations of Religion in Norwegian Correctional Facilities

The regulation of religion in the Norwegian prison system has evolved from § 20 of the Prison Act (1958), which made no mention of the individual religious freedom of inmates but provided that a chaplain should be hired at each facility, to a more general assertion of the obligation of the Correctional Service to allow each inmate to 'manifest religion or belief' in the current Execution of Sentences Act (2001) § 23. According to the preparatory works to the bill, religious manifestations are expected to take place outside working hours and other organised activities, preferably during breaks and leisure time. While the guarantee does not explicitly invoke

---

[5]This expansion took place with the adoption of the unfortunately translated Act Relating to Allocations to Religious Communities. Unregistered communities may also apply for support, but they have to include virtually the same items of information as registered communities.

the freedom of religion as it is spelled out in the constitution or the Human Rights Act, the use of the term 'manifestation' suggests that these surrounding legal rules are relevant to the interpretation of the provision. The guarantee is conditional and subject to the discretion of the prison warden, who is entitled to limit the manifestation of religion or belief for practical and security purposes, effectively granting wardens a considerable administrative discretion in the determination of what constitutes the threshold for 'practical' or 'security' purposes. Other provisions in surrounding legislation may also limit access to religious manifestations within correctional facilities.[6] The interpretation of Norwegian legislation on religion in prison is also guided by the principles outlined in the Prison Recommendations (2006) issued by the Council of Europe (CoE), which guarantee not only the freedom of religion or belief and its manifestations, but also the rights of inmates to participate in religious services, to have access to religious literature, and to receive visits by religious leaders.[7] Similar, even broader guarantees informing the interpretation of religious freedom of inmates in Norwegian prisons can be inferred from the UN Standard Minimum Rules for the Treatment of Prisoners (1955).[8] The potential influence of the more recently adopted United Nations Nelson Mandela Prison Rules (2015) has yet to be addressed in official policy documents.[9]

Practical conditions for the recognition of the religious freedom of inmates in Norwegian prisons must be considered against the backdrop of the 'normalcy principle' informing the purpose of imprisonment in the Norwegian correctional system. According to this principle, the terms of imprisonment should be based on three different yet interrelated modes of normalcy – medical, statistical and cultural/moral (Vollan 2016: 448). Medical and statistical conditions refer to the complicated set of challenges facing inmates in terms of mental and physical health, behavioural problems, social and drug issues and educational troubles. Helping inmates with these conditions, which tend to be overrepresented among the prisoner population, is the province of health care and social workers who are responsible for the preparation of prisoners to 'normal' life after incarceration. While the purpose of securing medical and statistical 'normalcy' refers to the correction of a certain set of static principles that will always be challenging in any society, the principle of cultural/moral normalcy is far more dynamic, fluid and uncertain, shifting in tandem with social changes.

---

[6] These conditions are listed in the *travaux preparatoires*, Ot. prp. nr.5 (2000–2001) *Om lov om gjennomføring av straff mv. (straffegjennomføringsloven)* at 13.1.

[7] Council of Europe: Recommendation Rec (2006) of the Committee of Ministers to Member States on the European Prison Rules (Adopted by the Committee of Ministers on 11 January 2006 at the 952nd meeting of the Ministers' Deputies), Section 29.

[8] Standard Minimum Rules for the Treatment of Prisoners. Adopted by the First United Nations Congress on the Prevention of Crime and the Treatment of Offenders, held at Geneva in 1955, and approved by the Economic and Social Council by its Resolutions 663 C (XXIV) of 31 July 1957 and 2076 (LXII) of 13 May 1977, Sections 41–42.

[9] For an introduction to how the Nelson Mandela rules approach religion, see Temperman 2017.

While religion has always played a vital role in the fostering of cultural/moral normalcy, the shift from a legal framework that stressed the role of the prison chaplain to one emphasising the individual rights of each inmate to religious 'manifestations' indicates the gradual transformation of the role of religion, from key service provider to individual rights guarantee, reflecting the dynamic nature of 'cultural/moral' normalcy. Hence, where the Prison Act secured access to prison chaplains so inmates could receive guidance on their path towards cultural/moral normalcy, the Execution of Sentences Act secures access to religious manifestations because this right is one among many basic conditions for the realisation of cultural/moral normalcy in society. This is not to say that the role of prison chaplains and other religious leaders in guiding inmates has been abandoned, but rather that it has gone through a subtle shift, in which the role of individual choice and autonomy has been strengthened at the expense of formal religious authority, a shift which corresponds well with the general 'juridification' of religion in society (Årsheim and Slotte 2017).

Importantly, the shift from religion as a resource for rehabilitation to religion as a basic right for each inmate also corresponds to a gradual shift in the purpose of punishment, from the idea that incarceration in and of itself should foster *normalisation* – that the Correctional Service should be obliged to change the attitudes and conceptions of each individual inmate, and towards *normalcy*, the idea that the primary task of the Correctional Service is to provide terms of imprisonment that do not deviate too strongly from the conditions of life outside prison. This is a far cry from the early modern purpose of imprisonment, but corresponds well with the UN Standard Minimum Rules Section 60(1), which prescribes that prison authorities 'should seek to minimise any differences between prison life and life at liberty which tend to lessen the responsibility of the prisoners or the respect due to their dignity as human beings'. The central idea behind this principle is derived from a human rights–based approach that considers inmates to have legitimately forfeited their rights to liberty but should retain the full spectrum of their other rights as secured by human rights law (Vollan 2016: 458).

While there has been no jurisprudence on § 23 of the Execution of Sentences Act, the equality and anti-discrimination ombudsman, which oversees the extensive legal framework on anti-discrimination,[10] has issued its opinion in three cases of alleged religious discrimination among inmates. In a 2007 case (Case No. 07/1598), the ombudsman criticised the practice at Ringerike Prison of disallowing Muslim inmates to bring food back to their cells in order to eat after sunset during Ramadan, a practice that was quickly abandoned following press reports. In two cases decided in 2016 (Case Nos. 15/273 and 15/2355), the ombudsman concluded that neither the confiscation of newspaper clippings featuring the logo of Islamic State (IS) nor the

---

[10] Anti-discrimination provisions have been scattered across a variety of acts since the 1970s, partly as a consequence of the ratification of international instruments like the Convention on the Elimination of Racial Discrimination (CERD) and the Convention on the Elimination of All forms of Discrimination against Women (CEDAW), and partly as a response to homegrown legal activism. An anti-discrimination act that summarises the provisions of all the other acts is currently under review by parliament and entered into force in 2018.

confinement of inmates not participating in religious services to their cells during service constituted religious discrimination since both practices were motivated by security or staffing concerns.

In addition to the formal prison system, Norwegian authorities oversee a facility for the administrative detention of asylum seekers at Trandum, a former military base close to Oslo Airport, Gardermoen. The conditions at Trandum have been subject to extensive criticism for years owing to regular reports of harsh conditions that possibly violate the human rights of asylum seekers.[11] Detention at Trandum is regulated by the 2008 Immigration Act § 107, which stipulates that detainees have the right to manifest religion or belief, but this right can be limited or revoked to maintain order or security. Unlike in the regular prison system, detention at Trandum is not overseen by the Correctional Service but by the Police Immigration Service, a separate branch of the Norwegian police force set up to deal with the management of immigration, from registration upon arrival to the transportation of unsuccessful asylum seekers and other irregular migrants. Hence, circulars, regulations and guidelines governing incarceration in the regular Norwegian prison system are not in effect in Trandum.

18.3.3   Chaplains and Other Religious Workers

Although access to chaplains and other religious workers is not explicitly laid out in the Execution of Sentences Act, this right can clearly be inferred from domestic and international laws on the issue (see earlier discussion). While prison clergy had formerly come exclusively from the CoN, recent decades have seen an expansion of counsellors of other religions and worldviews, particularly imams, although no exact figures exist owing to the ad hoc nature of the arrangements. There is no state funding or specific policy on the recruitment of these counsellors, whose access to the prisons is governed by the Execution of Sentences Regulation (see subsequent discussion). Despite this growth in counsellors from other traditions, the clear majority of chaplains are still ordained by the CoN. The duties and responsibilities of CoN chaplains are outlined in the Prison Chaplain Regulation (2016). While the earlier version of this regulation was overseen by the Ministry of Culture, the recent disestablishment of the CoN transferred the responsibility for this regulation to the General Synod of the CoN, effective as of 1 January 2017. The regulation lays out the basic legal framework for prison chaplains hired by the CoN, including their duties to conduct religious services and provide counselling and other duties that are similar to those of parish priests. While prison chaplains from the CoN are formally bound to these rules, their role has also grown into one of gatekeeper and facilitator of access of religious counsellors from other denominations, not least imams who

---

[11] The Parliamentary ombudsman has expressed several concerns with the human rights conditions at Trandum after visits, see SOM-2012-2408, SOM-2008-1966 and case No. 2006/225, which resulted in an urgent message to parliament, Dok.nr. 4:01 (2006–2007).

have catered to the growing proportion of Muslims in Norwegian prisons (Furseth 2006).

In a report on the conditions of imprisonment from the equality and anti-discrimination ombudsman issued in 2017, the ombudsman expressed its concern with the lack of established structures and platforms of cooperation for the facilitation of religious services to the prisoner population. To rectify the situation, the ombudsman recommended a model in which chaplains from a variety of religious traditions should be hired by the Correctional Service and not by the religious organisations themselves, modelled on similar arrangements in the health sector and the armed forces.[12]

The Execution of Sentences Regulation (2002) § 6–5 provides that visits by religious leaders, counsellors or clergy should be conducted under the same control regime as other prison visits, subject to the wardens' discretion. To better facilitate access for representatives of other religious communities to an increasingly diverse prisoner population, the Ministry of Justice and the Ministry of Culture developed a set of guidelines for coordination on religion or belief in correctional facilities in 2009,[13] in line with the ambitions for administrative cooperation outlined in the Execution of Sentences Act § 4. The guidelines emphasise the importance of adhering to international prison standards while also clarifying the responsibilities of various public entities involved in the carrying out of sentences. The guidelines stress that the provision of religious services in prison is primarily limited to organisations officially registered under the Religious Communities Act (1969) and is conditional to provisions in general Norwegian legislation.

In addition to these formal, general criteria, the guidelines stress that the value basis of the Correctional Service is 'humanist', working from the premise that humans are 'unique and inviolable'. This starting point entails that the provision of religious or belief services in prison should be conducted with 'respect for individuals and human rights' regardless of the identity or background of each prisoner. The warden is authorised to bar access to prisons for representatives from religious or belief communities whose services do not conform to the 'ethical values, purposes and rules' of the Correctional Service, effectively granting wardens extensive administrative discretion not only on the basis of security or other practical conditions, but also on the content and format of the services offered. Representatives are required to speak Norwegian or English, with the exception of personal conversations with individual inmates and in prayer, liturgical readings or other rituals, which can be conducted as the religious community in question sees fit.

Over the course of recent years, prison authorities have become more active in fighting violent radicalism in Norwegian prisons through increased recruitment of religion or belief counsellors. In the 2014 Action Plan to Counter Violent Extremism

---

[12] See 5.8 in Likestillings – og diskrimineringsombudet. *Innsatt og utsatt. Likestillings- og diskrimineringsombudets rapport om soningsforholdene til utsatte grupper i fengsel.* http://www.ldo.no/nyheiter-og-fag/brosjyrar-og-publikasjonar/rapporter/soningsrapport/, retrieved 26.06.2017.

[13] Justis- og politidepartement, Kultur- og kirkedepartementet. *Rundskriv:Samarbeid om tros- og livssynstjenester i fengsel.* (Ref. 200,607,578, 1.7.2009).

issued by the Norwegian government, the Correctional Service was tasked with the responsibility of establishing a team of counsellors in Oslo and the surrounding area, citing successful experiences with cross-religious cooperation among religious leaders in fighting extremism. Since then, the Service has developed a circular that stresses the obligations of prison staff to 'uncover' traces of violent extremism and communicate worrisome tendencies to other official entities in the security apparatus and to better accommodate the needs of inmates to manifest their religion or belief. Significantly, the circular hypothesises that the better accommodation of a plurality of religions or belief systems in prison may have a 'balancing effect' among different worldviews in the prisoner population, which in turn may prevent the spread of violent extremism.

18.3.4   Religion as an Operational Issue

In addition to the regulations that specify the rights of inmates to receive visits from clergy and to manifest religious and other beliefs, the role of religion in Norwegian prisons has become a key concern as an operational issue among prison staff. As the prisoner population has become more diverse, the 'governance' of religion has become a major theme for officers working in the Correctional Service.[14] To guide officers in their management of religion, the Correctional Service regularly runs courses on cultural and religious sensibilities and has issued a set of guidelines that seeks to pinpoint the major differences between Norwegian and 'foreign' concepts of what religion is and what it means to be religious in society.[15] The guidelines stress the collective, external aspects of 'other' religions, in contrast to Norwegian, privatised notions of religion that emphasise the internalisation of beliefs. Prison officials are reminded of the strong internal differences among different denominations within the same faith and the foundational nature of religion in the lives of many inmates.

Besides the religious differences among inmates, prison staff have increasingly also become acquainted with a diversity of organisations offering religious services and activities for prisoners, ranging from organised pilgrimages for both staff and inmates,[16] via the facilitation of a festive evening meal during Ramadan sponsored

---

[14] By 'governance' in this setting I am referring to the key aspects of non-legal forms of steering exercised primarily (but not exclusively) by civil servants, including '… regulation or steering, guidance by a variety of means, not only by rules. It includes only those mechanisms of action coordination that provide intentional capacities to regulate, including co- and self-regulation' (Bader 2007, 873).

[15] Kriminalomsorgen. *Utenlandske statsborgere i kriminalomsorgen. Håndbok for ansatte* (2015), see 5.3.4. 'Kunnskap om religionens betydning i fengsel'.

[16] Kriminalomsorgen. *I pilegrim for en bedre fremtid.* http://www.kriminalomsorgen. no/i-pilegrim-for-en-bedre-fremtid.365962-237613.html, accessed 28.06.2017.

by the Moroccan embassy,[17] to the organisation of a spiritually infused 'retreat' for inmates in cooperation with the Salvation Army,[18] which runs a comprehensive prison outreach programme. The retreat programme, which is offered primarily for long-term prisoners in Halden Prison, provides prisoners with a three-week period of silence, working with their own 'lives, experiences and hopes'. This period of introspective reflection is followed up with collective worship services, counselling, communal meals and meditation and has recently also been expanded to cover pilgrimages where inmates trek from Dovre to Trondheim and the medieval Nidaros Cathedral.[19] This programme resonates well with a broader interest in Norway in pilgrimages as a form of therapeutic, remedial practice typical of the 'subjective turn' in modern culture (Mikaelsson 2012: 270).

Over the course of the last decade, the role of extremism and radicalisation has come to the forefront of public debate in Norway, leading to the adoption of new guidelines on how to deal with this issue in the Norwegian prison system.[20] Although the guidelines take a 'neutral' view of radicalism, they are still dedicated mainly to the fight against right-wing and Islamic extremism, the two radical ideologies with the deepest footprint in the Norwegian prisoner population. The guidelines stress the inherent potential of poor prison conditions acting as independent 'radicalisers', triggering discontent and frustration that make inmates susceptible to extremist views that can evolve into radicalism in the longer term. To prevent this process from taking place, the guidelines emphasise the need for respect and accommodation of the religion or belief of inmates, to keep tensions and grievances at a minimum. This accommodation, however, can in no way encroach upon basic security concerns, although the latter should be sought by acting 'flexibly' and reasonably with inmates who might negatively react to prison officers of different ethnicity or gender identities.

In more concrete terms, the guidelines suggest prison officers pay close attention to behavioural change related to religion, vocal support for 'final solutions' based on religion, verbally legitimating threats or violence in the name of religion, in addition to ten specific items related to the detection of 'Islamism'.[21] The guidelines

---

[17] Kriminalomsorgen. *Oppmuntring i fastetid.* http://www.kriminalomsorgen.no/oppmuntring-i-fastetid.541270-237613.html,accessed 28.06.2017.

[18] Kriminalomsorgen. *Stor interesse for retreat i Halden fengsel.* http://www.kriminalomsorgen.no/stor-interesse-for-retreat-i-halden-fengsel.5303780-237613.html, accessed 28 June 2017.

[19] Frelsesarmeen. *Retreat i Halden fengsel.* http://www.frelsesarmeen.no/no/vart_arbeid/fengselsarbeidet/hoyre_kolonne/vare_tilbud/Retreat+i+Halden+fengsel.d25-SxdjK57.ips, accessed 28 June 2017.

[20] Kriminalomsorgens Høgskole og utdanningssenter KRUS. *Radikalisering og voldelig ekstremisme. Håndbok for ansatte i Kriminalomsorgen med særskilt fokus på håndtering i fengsel* (2016).

[21] These items include 'ambition/wish to establish a new world order based on the Islamic Sharia, connected to the idea of an Islamic caliphate; 'Ummah thinking' emphasising brotherhood and mutual responsibilities; increased emphasis on purity and purification and corresponding increased distance from or break with all Western influence and everything considered 'un-Islamic' in the

recommend the establishment of contact with clergy or others who may assist in developing alternative ideas, conceptions and modes of action as an antidote to the radicalisation process. Significantly, however, the extensive guidelines provide no input on the formation of a 'team of counsellors' on religion or belief, as requested by the Ministry of Justice in the action plan to fight terrorism adopted in 2014 (see earlier discussion).

One of the more concrete outcomes of the new emphasis on radicalism is the establishment of INFOflyt (INFO flow), a system for the sharing of information on high-risk individuals among the police, the Correctional Service and the security services. In INFOflyt, these entities can register 'sensitive data' that would normally be off limits in information-sharing systems, including religious adherence. The condition for registration is that it must fulfil the conditions in the Execution of Sentences Act § 4f, which specifically lists the prevention of 'violent extremism' as one of the legitimate reasons for the registration of sensitive information like religious adherence.

Taken together, the many different operational issues raised by religion illustrate the complexity of regulating religion in prison: while the freedom to manifest religion through worship, teaching and observance and the right to meet with clergy and other counsellors are principles of the 'humanist' foundations of the Correctional Service, religion can also generate anything from joyful and constructive experiences on the path to rehabilitation to a significant cultural obstacle and, most dramatically, to a considerable security risk that merits exceptional and drastic measures.

18.4   Conclusion

The regulation of religion in Norwegian correctional facilities has come a long way from the first prison chaplains set out to rectify the ways of intractable inmates in the Oslo Penitentiary in the mid-1800s. Over the course of these 150+ years, the notion of 'religion' and the regulatory challenges that come with its management have shifted decisively in nature and scope. Perhaps most significantly, there is no longer any unique, singular 'sacred canopy' that can provide a coherent and reliable measurement of 'moral/cultural normalcy' in Norwegian society, nor is there a state-run church that can take part in administrative cooperation among public entities in the correctional system. As the contents of 'religion' have increasingly become a private, individual matter, prison wardens have increasingly seen the need

---

religion; doomsday/apocalyptic thinking; glorification of self-sacrifice, vengeance, martyrdom and jihad; extensive use of 'da'wah' (missionary work); rhetoric focusing on the Western 'war on Islam' and on Jewish conspiracies; 'takfiri' thinking, entailing that none other than your own group are worthy of life, including other branches of Islam; resistance to Western democratic principles, modernity and economic systems; defence of the Islamic State, of al-Qaida and of terrorism in 'the name of battle'.

to accommodate the rights to religious manifestations of each singular inmate. However, while the original sacred canopy offered by an excessively monocultural and mono-religious surrounding society may have ruptured, the rise of new and assertive forms of religious belonging and self-understandings has led both to the provision of religious programmes for rehabilitation and introspection like the retreats in Halden Prison and to the need to manage and control the spread of extremist radicalism among prisoners.

In this management, prison wardens are granted exceptionally broad autonomy, with the authority to refuse virtually any aspect of religious manifestations, including the right to bar specific religious communities or their representatives from access to prisons on the basis of the content of their message. Although the discretion granted to wardens for security purposes is a general feature of prison management, the possibility to curtail religious manifestations is particularly striking given the strong protection offered to the freedom of religion or belief in international instruments, which stress that this right cannot be set aside even in 'time of public emergency which threatens the life of the nation'.[22] How far this administrative discretion goes, however, is uncertain, as the scope of the Execution of Sentences Act § 23 has yet to be challenged before the courts. However, if the recent grievances brought before the anti-discrimination ombudsman and the gradual changes in the direction of increasingly specific and targeted means of control intimated in the guidelines to fight radical extremism are anything to go by, we are likely to see litigation on this right in the very near future.

Bibliography

Årsheim, H., & Slotte, P. (2017). The Juridification of religion? *Brill Research Perspectives in Law and Religion, 1*(2), 1–89.

Bader, V. (2007). The governance of Islam in Europe: The perils of modelling. *Journal of Ethnic and Migration Studies, 33*, 871–886.

Furseth, I. (Ed.). (2015). *Religionens tilbakekomst i offentligheten? Religion, politikk, medier, stat og sivilsamfunn i Norge siden 1980-tallet*. Oslo: Universitetsforlaget.

Furseth, I. (2006). Flerreligiøsitet i norske fengsler. In L. Kühle & C. Lomholt (Eds.), *Straffens menneskelige ansigt? En antologi om etik, ret og religion i fængslet* (pp. 213–238). København: Anis.

Furseth, I., & Kühle, L. (2011). Prison chaplaincy from a Scandinavian perspective. *Archives de Sciences Sociales des Religions, 56*, 123–141.

Leirvik, O. (2016). Religion som velferdsgode? *Kirke og kultur, 120*, 309–311.

Mikaelsson, L. (2012). Pilgrimage as post-secular therapy. In T. Ahlbäck & B. Dahla (Eds.), *Post-secular religious practices* (pp. 259–273). Åbo/Turku: Donner Institute for Research in Religious and Cultural History.

Schaanning, E. (2007). Fra sjelesorg til sjelsgranskning. Prestens rolle i Botsfengslet. *Kirke og kultur*: 272–287.

---

[22] ICCPR article 4.

Temperman, J. (2017). Freedom of religion or belief in prison. *Oxford Journal of Law and Religion, 6,* 48–92.

Vollan, M. (2016). 'Mot normalt'? Normalitetsprinsippet i norsk straffegjennomføring. *Tidsskrift for strafferett, 16,* 447–461.

Chapter 19
Poland: Religious Assistance and Religious Practices in the Prisons

Michał Zawiślak, Michał Czelny, and Aneta Abramowicz

Abstract The aim of this chapter is to discuss the level of guarantee of religious freedom of prisoners, both in historical and legal perspective. The answer to the question of whether believers of different religions have similar access to religious services and similarly guaranteed right to practise their own religion, e.g. religiously motivated diet, has fundamental importance. The analysis of prisoners' right to practise their own religion was conducted with regard to the constitutional principle of equality of rights of churches and other religious denominations, including the practice of their application.

This chapter points out that Catholic pastoral care is present in all prisons in Poland. However, nowadays, other religious denominations are exercising their right to provide religious assistance in prison. The authors also highlight the problem of the non-legally-binding regulations governing pastoral care in prisons. The chapter shows the danger of limiting the right to perform religious activities due to a lack of professional training of prison staff.

19.1   Historical and Sociological Overview of Prison Pastoral Care

19.1.1   The Beginnings of Pastoral Care in Prison (1772–1918)

The beginning of pastoral care in prison in Poland dates back to the feudal period, with an instruction dated 18 September 1550 issued by the Chancellor of the Crown, Stanisław Ocieski (Czacki 1800; Bedyński 1994).

M. Zawiślak (✉) · M. Czelny · A. Abramowicz
Department of Law on Religion, The John Paul II Catholic University of Lublin,
Lublin, Poland
e-mail: lexis@kul.pl

© Springer Nature Switzerland AG 2020
J. Martínez-Ariño, A.-L. Zwilling (eds.), *Religion and Prison: An Overview of Contemporary Europe*, Boundaries of Religious Freedom: Regulating Religion in Diverse Societies 7, https://doi.org/10.1007/978-3-030-36834-0_19

The Asylum of Saint Michael in Rome[1] established by Pope Clement XI in 1703 became an inspiration for establishing similar community homes for young prisoners in Warsaw, with the Community Home of Saint Michael established in 1732 and founded by Rev. Gabriel Peter Baudouine and the Community Home established in 1736 and founded on the initiative of Bishop Adam Rostowski.

In 1767, the Marshal of the Crown, Stanisław Lubomirski, established the so-called *Więzienie Marszałkowskie* [Marshal Prison] in Warsaw, for which he formulated the first prison rules (prison law) in Poland. The Marshal Prison functioned in this way until 1795, when the first prison chapel was established (Bedyński 1994, 13–14; Nikołajew 2012, 21).

The second half of the nineteenth century saw the establishment of the permanent presence of a chaplain in many prisons in the Kingdom of Poland (Tymowski, Kieniewicz, Holzer 1990, 227–258).[2] The statistical data for 1881 show that for the 20 prisons of the Russian part of Poland (former Kingdom of Poland), there were 19 Roman Catholic priests, 15 Protestant pastors, 4 Orthodox priests and 2 (Orthodox) deacons (Bedyński 1994, 25; Kaczyńska 1989; Szymański 2016, 67).

19.1.2   Pastoral Care in Second Republic of Poland, 1918–1939, and During Communist Regime, 1945–1989

After the end of the First World War, the first reference to the religious activities of religious ministers in prison is found in the Decree of the Chief of State of 8 February 1919, which was concerned with temporary prison regulations.[3] It determined the chaplain's formal position (Article 3), where prisoners were allowed to receive the spiritual support of a priest of their own denomination (Article 11) (Bedyński 1994, 29; Maleszyk 2016, 25; Nikołajew 2012, 27). On this basis, 109 Roman Catholic chaplains were appointed by the state, with churches or chapels being built in 117 prisons (Bedyński 1994, 30; Nikołajew 2012, 28–29). These regulations were introduced because authorities were trying to prevent the secularisation of prisoners (Maleszyk 2016, 26).

Another legal act from that period was the Ordinance of the Minister of Justice of 20 April 1926 on meeting prisoners' religious needs and on the educational,

---

[1] This was a youth detention centre aimed at moral improvement. It was the first time that the function – prison chaplain – appeared.

[2] The Kingdom of Poland was created in 1815 by the Congress of Vienna as a sovereign state of the Russian part of Poland (Tymowski, Kieniewicz, Holzer 1990, 227-258). The kingdom lost its status as a sovereign state in 1831 (in the defeat of the November Uprising) and was gradually politically integrated into Russia over the course of the nineteenth century; it became an official part of the Russian Empire in 1867. See more in Tymowski, Michał, Kieniewicz Jan, Holzer Jerzy. 1990. *Historia Polski*, 227–258. Warszawa: Editions Spotkania.

[3] Dekret naczelnika Państwa z dnia 8 lutego 1919 r. w sprawie tymczasowych przepisów więziennych, *Dziennik Ustaw* [Official Journal] 1919, No. 15, item 202.

school and outside-school activities in prison,[4] which made religious leaders (not only Catholics, but from all recognised religious denominations) directly responsible for religious influence on prisoners, where all prisoners had the right to satisfy their religious needs. Moreover, young prisoners up to 21 years old were required to participate in religious education. The chaplains had to administer the sacraments and teach young prisoners about religion and ethics (Bedyński 1994, 30–31; Nikołajew 2012, 28; Maleszyk 2016, 26; Szymański 2016, 71). These rules were confirmed in the Ordinance of the President of the Republic of Poland of 7 March 1928 on the organisation of the prison system,[5] where a separate section (Chapter V of that Ordinance was titled 'Spiritual, Educational and Outside-School Care') was dedicated, among other things, to religious care in prison (Migdał 2011, 175–178; Nikołajew 2012, 29; Szymański 2016, 71–72).[6] In 1925 there were a total of 117 prison chapels and churches, with 125 permanent prison chaplains (Migdał 2011, 178).

Another important legal act was the Ordinance of the Minister of Justice of 10 June 1931 on prison rules,[7] which organised the issues related to the access of prisoners of various denominations to the services organised under prison chaplaincy conditions and treated religious care as a basic educational and penitentiary instrument. The available sociological surveys of that period indicate that the most numerous groups of prisoners, apart from the Roman Catholics, included the followers of Judaism and the Orthodox Church. Pursuant to the provisions of the ordinance, an organisation called the Prison Committee was established (Bedyński 1994, 31–32; Nikołajew 2012, 29–30; Maleszyk 2016, 26–27; Plisiecki 2016, 52–54; Szymański 2016, 72–74; Lasocik 1993, 86; Migdał 2011, 398–403).[8] The Prison Committee constituted an institution appointed by the Minister of Justice in larger prisons. It was a social body, its main task being cooperation with the prison administration concerning the influence on the carrying out of a sentence and post-penitentiary support.

By the middle of 1945, the prison rules of 1931 were effectively in force, although based on the instruction of the Minister of Public Security of 11 June 1945 on prison

---

[4] Rozporządzenie Ministra Sprawiedliwości z dnia 20 kwietnia 1926 r. o zaspokajaniu potrzeb religijnych więźniów i o działalnosci oświatowej, szkolnej i pozaszkolnej w wiezieniach, *Dziennik Ustaw* No. 9, item 10.

[5] Rozporządzenie Prezydenta RP z dnia 7 marca 1928 r. w sprawie organziacji więziennictwa, *Dziennik Ustaw* No. 29, item 272.

[6] See: Migdał, Jerzy. 2011. *Polski system penitencjarny w latach 1918–1928*, 175–178. Gdańsk: Wydawnictwo Arche; Nikołajew, Jerzy. 2012, 29; Szymański, Andrzej. 2016, 71–72.

[7] Rozporządzenie Ministra Sprawiedliwości z dnia 10 czerwca 1931 r. w sprawie regulaminu więziennego, *Dziennik Ustaw* No. 71, item 577.

[8] The prison chaplain was crucial in this issue. See Bedyński, Krystian. 1994, 31–32; Nikołajew, Jerzy. 2012, 29–30; Maleszyk, Ryszard. 2016, 26–27; Plisiecki, Marek. 2016. *Opieka duchowa w założeniach więziennictwa II Rzeczypospolitej*. In *Wolność sumienia i religii osób pozbawionych wolności. Aspekty prawne i praktyczne*, eds. Jerzy Nikołajew, Konrad Walczuk, 52–54. Warszawa: Wydawnictwo Unitas; Szymański, Andrzej. 2016, 72–74; Lasocik, Zbigniew. 1993. *Praktyki religijne więźniów*, 86. Warszawa: Wydawnictwo Naukowe PWN; Migdał, Jerzy. 2011, 398–403.

rules,[9] the chaplain was expelled from the prison staff (Bedyński 1994, 61–70; Nikołajew 2012, 34–35). Religious and moral values were replaced by the communist ideology of the state. Pastoral service in prison was restored by the decision of the *Departament Więziennictwa i Obozów* [Department of Prison System and Camps] as of 1 April 1946, but it was only provided by Roman Catholic priests, because of the limited presence of other denominations (after the Second World War, Poland became a religiously homogeneous country; Nikołajew 2012, 35).

The functioning of prison pastoral care was the subject of an agreement concluded by and between the government and the Polish Episcopate, dated 14 April 1950.[10] One of its provisions specified that the religious care of prisoners might be provided by chaplains appointed by the relevant department authorities at the request of an ordinary bishop (Point 17). The forms of pastoral care in this agreement included the celebration of Holy Mass on Sundays and other holy days, sermons, confession and Holy Communion (annex). However, the content of these provisions was ignored by the government at that time (Bedyński 1994, 72–76; Maleszyk 2016, 29; Nikołajew 2012, 36).

In another agreement, Announcement of the Joint Commission of the Representatives of the Government and the Polish Episcopate of 8 December 1956 on the principles of settling mutual relations, dated 8 December 1956, between the government and the Polish Episcopate,[11] the provisions concluded in 1950 were confirmed. Moreover, principles were established for the pastoral care of prisoners and for the appointment of prison chaplains. However, the prison authorities did not issue any relevant delegated legislation to this agreement (Bedyński 1994, 76–81; Nikołajew 2012, 37; Maleszyk 2016, 29). The ordinance on the performance of religious services in prison adopted by the circular of the Minister of Justice of 14 December 1956[12] still limited the religious prisoner's right to that of being provided with spiritual care and departed from the principles adopted in the agreement of 1950 (Bedyński 1994, 83–84; Migdał 2008; Nikołajew 2012, 37–38). In accordance with the anti-religious position of the government, the Holy Mass was celebrated in the years 1956–1980 only in 22 prisons (out of a total of 122 prisons), and in subsequent years the number of celebrations of Holy Mass was reduced. The religious

---

[9] Instrukcja Ministra Bezpieczeństwa Publicznego z dnia 11 czerwca 1945 r. w sprawie regulaminu więziennego, not published.

[10] Porozumienie między Rządem RP a Episkopatem Polski [Agreement Between the Government of the Republic of Poland and the Polish Episcopate]. In *Listy pasterskie Episkopatu Polski 1945–1974*. 91–97. Paris: 1975; The Agreement may also be found in: *Państwowe prawo wyznaniowe Polskiej Rzeczypospolitej Ludowej. Wybór tekstów źródłowych*, 1978. Edited by Marian Fąka. 26–30. Warszawa: Wydawnictwo ATK.

[11] Komunikat Komisji Wspólnej przedstawicieli Rządu i Episkopatu z dnia 8 grudnia 1956 r. o zasadach uregulowania wzajemnych stosunków. [Announcement of the Joint Commission of the representatives of the Government and the Polish Episcopate of 8 December 1956 on the principles of settling mutual relations]. In Raina, Peter. 1994. *Kościół katolicki a państwo w świetle dokumentów 1945–1989*, vol. 1, 575–576. Poznań: W Drodze.

[12] Zarządzenie Ministra Sprawiedliwości z dnia 14 grudnia 1956 r. [Circular of the Minister of Justice of 14 December 1956] No. 80. not published.

activity of the prisoners was limited to individual prayer and contemplation in prison cells (Bedyński 1994, 85–87; Nikołajew 2012, 39).

Changes in prison pastoral care occurred only in 1981 as a result of the social and political events that took place in Poland during August 1980. Due to the workers' protests and prison revolts, the Circular of the Minister of Justice of 17 September 1981 on the Performance of Religious Practices and Services in Prisons, Detention Suites and Social Adaptation Centres was introduced,[13] although the implementation of these provisions encountered difficulties. It occurred during the period of martial law, when prisons were still overcrowded and full of political prisoners[14]: political prisoners (who were suspected of supporting democracy, especially the 'Solidarność' movement) who were put in jail without legal basis. It is a more specific description for political prisoners not sentenced to jail but still there for political reasons. Only on 1 September 1987 did the Polish Bishops' Conference create the office of *Naczelny Kapelan Więziennictwa* [Chaplain Chief of the Prison System] (Bedyński 1994, 95–96; Nikołajew 2012, 40–41; Wojtas 2016, 450–457).[15]

19.1.3 Political Transformation and Its Influence on the Shape of Prison Pastoral Care after 1989

The political transformation of Poland in 1989 resulted in significant changes in the entire prison system. The religious life of prisoners was regulated by two legal acts,[16] Act of 17 May 1989 on the Guarantees of the Freedom of Conscience and Religion and Act of 17 May 1989 on the Relations between the Polish State and the

---

[13] Zarządzenie Ministra Sprawiedliwości z dnia 17 września 1981 r. w sprawie wykonywania praktyk i posług religijnych w zakładach karnych, aresztach śledczych i ośrodkach przystosowania społecznego, społęcznego [Circular of the Minister of Justice of 17 September 1981 on the Performance of Religious Practices and Services in Prison, Detention Suites and Social Adaptation Centres] *Official Journal of the Minister of Justice* 1981 No. 5, item 27.

[14] The circular allowed for two forms of religious services: celebration of Holy Mass and confession. Those services were to be performed in chapels or other suitably prepared locations (Bedyński, 1994, 87–89; Nikołajew, 2012, 39–40).

[15] A priest, Jan Sikorski (1990–2001), assumed that task, and another priest, Paweł Wojtas (2001–2016), was his successor. Currently this post is held by a priest by the name of Adam Jabłoński (Bedyński 1994, 90, 95–96; Nikołajew 2012, 40–41; Wojtas 2016, 449–450).

[16] Ustawa z dnia 17 maja 1989 roku o gwarancjach wolności sumienia i wyznania [Act of 17 May 1989 on the Guarantees of the Freedom of Conscience and Faith], *Dziennik Ustaw* 2005, No. 231, item 1965. and Ustawa z dnia 17 maja 1989 roku o stosunku Państwa do Kościoła Katolickiego w Rzeczypospolitej Polskiej [Act of 17 May 1989 on the Relations between the Polish State and the Roman Catholic Church in the Republic of Poland], *Dziennik Ustaw* 2013, item 1169.

Roman Catholic Church in the Republic of Poland,[17] as well an ordinance of the Minister of Justice on rules for carrying out prison sentences.[18]

The above regulations included the necessity of establishing prison chapels or reactivating the old ones. The chaplain staff began to stabilise (first on the central level, then in the districts), while in 1990, the Minister of Justice appointed the chief prison chaplains from the Roman Catholic, Orthodox and Evangelical-Augsburg Churches. Prisoners were able to follow their religious practices and have objects of worship, as well as to attend religious services in an undisturbed and peaceful way. The possibility was also introduced of visits to prisons by the religious ministers of other denominations (e.g. Jehovah's Witnesses) (Nikołajew 2012, 41–44; Bedyński 1994, 103–114).

Later, two ministerial regulations[19] were published, supplementing and clarifying the provisions of Article 17, Paragraphs 1–3of the concordat concluded on 28 July 1993 between the Holy See and the Republic of Poland.[20] Religious freedom of prisoners was also guaranteed in the Constitution of the Republic of Poland of 2 April 1997[21] and in the Executive Penal Code of 6 June 1997.[22]

---

[17] Ustawa z dnia 17 maja 1989 roku o stosunku Państwa do Kościoła Katolickiego w Rzeczypospolitej Polskiej [], *Dziennik Ustaw* 2013, item 1169.

[18] Rozporządzenie Ministra Sprawiedliwości z dnia 2 maja 1989 roku w sprawie regulaminu wykonywania kary pozbawienia wolności [Ordinance of the Minister of Justice of 2 May 1989 on the Rules for Carrying Out Prison Sentences], *Dziennik Ustaw* No. 31, Item 166 as amended.

[19] This refers to the Rozporządzenie Ministra Sprawiedliwości z dnia 5 listopada 1998 r. w sprawie szczegółowych zasad wykonywania praktyk religijnych i korzystania z posług religijnych w zakładach karnych i aresztach śledczych [Ordinance of the Minister of Justice of 5 November 1998 on the Detailed Principles of Religious Practices and Use of Religious Services in Prisons and Detention Suites], *Dziennik Ustaw* No. 139, Item 904. Rozporządzenie Ministra Sprawiedliwości z dnia 2 września 2003 r. w sprawie szczegółowych zasad wykonywania praktyk religijnych w sprawie szczegółowych zasad wykonywania praktyk religijnych i korzystania z posług religijnych w zakładach karnych i aresztach śledczych [Ordinance of the Minister of Justice of 2 September 2003 on the Detailed Principles of Religious Practices and Use of Religious Services in Prisons and Detention Suites], *Dziennik Ustaw* No. 159, Item 1546.

[20] 1. The Republic of Poland shall ensure conditions for the exercise of religious practices and for the benefit of religious assistance to persons remanded in prison, institutions for rehabilitation and for social reintegration, and also to persons in health and social care institutions and in other establishments of a similar nature.

2. The persons referred to in Paragraph 1 shall be guaranteed in particular the opportunity to participate in Holy Mass on Sundays and holy days, to attend catechism classes and other spiritual retreats, and the benefit of individual religious assistance, always within the scope of the conditions of their confinement, as mentioned in Paragraph 1 above.

3. To exercise the rights of persons referred to in Paragraph 1, the diocesan bishop shall appoint chaplains through whom the respective civil institution shall draw up an appropriate contract. *Dziennik Ustaw* 1998, No. 51, Item 318.

[21] *Dziennik Ustaw* 1997, No. 78, Item 483 as amended.

[22] *Dziennik Ustaw* No. 90, Item 557 as amended.

19.2 Organisation of Religious Assistance

According to data from the National Population and Housing Census in 2011, membership in the Roman Catholic Church was declared by 33,728,700 people, which constitutes 87.6% of all Polish citizens.[23]

Pursuant to Article 53 of the Constitution of the Republic of Poland,[24] freedom of conscience and religion shall be ensured to everyone (Misztal 1993,104–107; Piechowiak 1996, 10–12).[25] People being held in prison and custody suites,[26] including minors , are ensured the right to exercise their freedom of conscience and religion. Currently, the following legally recognised churches provide their followers with particular entitlement to enjoy their freedom of religion by statute: Roman Catholic Church,[27] Polish Orthodox Church,[28] Evangelical-Augsburg Church,[29] Polish Reformed Church,[30] Polish Catholic Church,[31] Seventh-Day Adventist Church,[32] Christian Baptist Church,[33] Evangelical Methodist Church,[34] Old Catholic

---

[23] Central Statistical Office. 2015. National-ethnic, linguistic and denominational structure of the Polish population – National Population and Housing Census 2011, 92. Warszawa: CBOS.

[24] Article 53, Para. 1. Freedom of faith and religion shall be ensured to everyone.

Para 2. Freedom of religion shall include the freedom to profess or to accept a religion by personal choice as well as to manifest such religion, either individually or collectively, publicly or privately, by worshipping, praying, participating in ceremonies, performing of rites or teaching. Freedom of religion shall also include possession of sanctuaries and other places of worship for the satisfaction of the needs of believers as well as the right of individuals, wherever they may be, to benefit from religious services. Konstytucja Rzeczypospolitej Polskiej z dnia 2 kwietnia 1997 r. Dziennik Ustaw No. 78, Item 483 as amended.

[25] Regarding the concept of the freedom of religion, see Misztal, Henryk. 1993. Kościelne pojęcie wolności religijnej a ustawa o gwarancjach wolności sumienia i wyznania. *Kościół i Prawo* 11:104–107; Piechowiak, Marek. 1996. Wolność religijna – aspekty filozoficzne-prawne. *Toruński Rocznik Praw Człowieka i Pokoju* 3:10–12.

[26] A custody suite is a place of temporary isolation for persons suspected of committing a crime, while the prison is a place where prison sentences are served. See Nikołajew, Jerzy. 2012. *Wolność sumienia i religii skazanych i tymczasowo skazanych*, 50–51. Lublin: Wydawnictwo KUL.

[27] Art. 32 Ustawa z dnia 17 maja 1989 r. o stosunku Państwa do Kościoła Katolickiego w Rzeczypospolitej Polskiej, *Dziennik Ustaw* 2013, Item 1169 as amended.

[28] Art. 28 Ustawa z dnia 4 lipca 1991 r. o stosunku Państwa do Polskiego Autokefalicznego Kościoła Prawosławnego w Rzeczypospolitej Polskiej, *Dziennik Ustaw* 2014, Item 1726.

[29] Art. 23 Ustawa z dnia 13 maja 1994 r. o stosunku Państwa do Kościoła Ewangelicko-Augsburskiego w Rzeczypospolitej Polskiej, *Dziennik Ustaw* 2015, Item 43.

[30] Art. 12 Ustawa z dnia 13 maja 1994 r. o stosunku Państwa do Kościoła Ewangelicko-Reformowanego w Rzeczypospolitej Polskiej, *Dziennik Ustaw* 2015, Item 483.

[31] Art. 17 Ustawa z dnia 30 czerwca 1995 r. o stosunku Państwa do Kościoła Polskokatolickiego w Rzeczypospolitej Polskiej, *Dziennik Ustaw* 2014, Item 1599.

[32] Art. 18 Ustawa z dnia 30 czerwca 1995 r. o stosunku Państwa do Kościoła Adwentystów Dnia Siódmego w Rzeczypospolitej Polskiej, *Dziennik Ustaw* 2014, Item 1889.

[33] Art. 18 para. 1 oraz art. 20 ust. 3 Ustawa z dnia 30 czerwca 1995 r. o stosunku Państwa do Kościoła Chrześcijan Baptystów w Rzeczypospolitej Polskiej, *Dziennik Ustaw* 2015, Item 169.

[34] Art. 19 para. 1 Ustawa z dnia 30 czerwca 1995 r. o stosunku Państwa do Kościoła Ewangelicko-Metodystycznego w Rzeczypospolitej Polskiej, *Dziennik Ustaw* 2014, Item 1712.

Mariavite Church,[35] Pentecostal Church,[36] Catholic Mariavite Church,[37] and the Union of Jewish Religious Communities.[38]

The provisions of the 17 May 1989 Act on the Guarantees of the Freedom of Conscience and Religion[39] include the right of prisoners to engage in religious practices. Therefore, every legally recognised religious denomination[40] has the right to provide its followers with pastoral care. Religious denominations should exercise the right to the organisation of pastoral care according to the principle of the equality of religious denominations expressed in Article 25, Paragraph 1 of the Constitution of the Republic of Poland.[41] According to constitutional provisions, it is not possible now in Poland to create or promote a particular model of religious rehabilitation programmes or to introduce or promote a single-religion prison system (i.e. Catholic, Protestant or Muslim). This is the main reason not to introduce into the legal system a model of prison religious care under the control of one of the religious denominations or to introduce a single-religion prison system (Nikołajew 2015).

[35] Art. 16 para. 1 Ustawa z dnia 20 lutego 1997 r. o stosunku Państwa do Kościoła Starokatolickiego Mariawitów w Rzeczypospolitej Polskiej, *Dziennik Ustaw* 2015, Item 14.

[36] Art. 19 para. 1 Ustawa z dnia 20 lutego 1997 r. o stosunku Państwa do Kościoła Zielonoświątkowego w Rzeczypospolitej Polskiej, *Dziennik Ustaw* 2015, Item 13.

[37] Art. 16 Ustawa z dnia 20 lutego 1997 r. o stosunku Państwa do Kościoła Katolickiego Mariawitów w Rzeczypospolitej Polskiej, *Dziennik Ustaw* 2015, Item 14.

[38] Art. 16 Ustawa z dnia 20 lutego 1997 r. o stosunku Państwa do gmin wyznaniowych żydowskich w Rzeczypospolitej Polskiej, *Dziennik Ustaw* 2014, Item 1798.

[39] Article 4 Para. 1 Point 3 'the right to possess and use the objects required for worshipping and performing religious practices shall also be exercised by persons (…) staying in prison, community homes and educational institutes, as well as custody suites and juvenile shelters', and Article 2 Item 2, 'While exercising their freedom of conscience and belief, citizens may in particular participate in religious activities and ceremonies according to the principles of their religion, as well as perform their religious duties and celebrate religious holidays', *Dziennik Ustaw* 2005, No. 231, Item 1965, as amended.

[40] There are now in Poland 165 registered religious denominations. All of them have the right to provide their followers with pastoral care.

[41] According to the position of the Constitutional Tribunal resulting from the judgement of 2 April 2003 (K. 13/02, OTK –A 2003, No 4, Item 28), 'the principle of equality of churches and religious associations shall mean that all churches and religious associations having a significant common feature should be treated equally. At the same time, this principle assumes different treatment of churches and religious associations that do not have a significant common feature from the point of view of a given regulation'.

19.2.1   The Right of Religious Denominations to Organise Religious Assistance

The organisation of religious assistance in prisons has been guaranteed for the following religious denominations: Catholic Church, Polish Orthodox Church, Polish Catholic Church, Seventh-Day Adventist Church, Christian Baptist Church, Evangelical-Methodist Church, Old Catholic Mariavite Church, Pentecostal Church, Catholic Mariavite Church, Union of Jewish Religious Communities, Evangelical-Augsburg Church and Evangelical-Reformed Church.

Moreover, in reference to the Catholic Church, the right to organise pastoral care in prison is guaranteed under Article 17 of the Concordat.[42] Other religious denominations have the right to provide religious assistance pursuant to the provisions of the Act of 17 May 1989, including Eastern Old Believers Church,[43] Muslim Religious Union,[44] and Karaim Religious Union.[45] The right to organise religious assistance in prison is also ensured for registered religious denominations.[46]

As regards the Catholic Church, the Polish Orthodox Church and the Union of Jewish Religious Communities, the right to religious assistance in prison can be exercised in all prisons, juvenile homes and educational centres. In the case of other religious denominations, this right can be exercised according to the Act of 17 May 1989[47] and is regulated equally in the acts defining the legal status of religious denominations in an individual way (Abramowicz 2016).

---

[42] Article 17, Paragraph 1. 'The Republic of Poland shall guarantee the conditions to perform religious practices and use religious services for persons staying in prison, educational centres, juvenile homes, healthcare institutes, nursing homes, as well as in other homes and centres of this type.'

2. The aforementioned entities shall be provided, in particular, with the possibility of participating in Holy Mass on Sundays and holidays, catechesis and retreats, as well as with the possibility of attending individual religious services in compliance with the purposes of these entities' stay in facilities indicated in section 1.' Konkordat pomiędzy Stolicą Apostolską a Rzeczpospolitą Polską podpisany w dniu 28 lipca 1993 r., *Dziennik Ustaw* 1998, No. 51, Item 318.

[43] Rozporządzenie Prezydenta Rzeczypospolitej z dnia 22 marca 1928 r. o stosunku Państwa do Wschodniego Kościoła Staroobrzędowego, nie posiadającego hierarchii duchownej, *Dziennik Ustaw* No 38, Item 363 as amended.

[44] Ustawa z dnia 21 kwietnia 1936 r. o stosunku Państwa do Muzułmańskiego Związku Religijnego w Rzeczypospolitej Polskiej, *Dziennik Ustaw* No. 30, Item 240 as amended.

[45] Ustawa z dnia 21 kwietnia 1936 r. o stosunku Państwa do Karaimskiego Związku Religijnego w Rzeczypospolitej Polskiej, *Dziennik Ustaw* No. 30, item 241 as amended.

[46] There are currently 165 registered religious denominations in Poland. Kościoły i związki wyznaniowe wpisane do rejestru kościołów i innych związków wyznaniowych. 2017. https://mswia. gov.pl/pl/wyznania-i-mniejszosci/relacje-panstwa-z-kosci/13964,Relacje-panstwa-z-Kosciolami-przydatne-informacje-dokumenty-i-akty-prawne.html. Accessed 20 April 2017. See also: Stanisławski, Tadeusz. 2016. Finansowe koszty zapewnienia wolności sumienia i religii osób pozbawionych wolności. In *Wolność sumienia i religii osób pozbawionych wolności. Aspekty prawne i praktyczne*, eds. Jerzy Nikołajew, Konrad Walczuk, 168–169. Warszawa: Wydawnictwo Unitas.

[47] *Dziennik Ustaw* 2005, No. 231, item 1965, as amended.

In practice, the following Christian religious denominations have been providing pastoral care: Catholic Church (including the Greek Church), Polish Orthodox Church, Evangelical-Augsburg Church, Pentecostal Church, Seventh-Day Adventist Church, Christian Baptist Church, Evangelical-Reformed Church, Polish Catholic Church, Old Catholic Mariavite Church, Jehovah's Witnesses, Fellowship of Christian Churches, Christian Congregation, and the Church of God in Christ. Non-Christian religious denominations are providing pastoral care as well: Gideons International, World Spiritual University Brahma Kumaris, Sangha Kandzeon Buddhist Association and the International Society for Krishna Consciousness.

Regular activities in prison are conducted by representatives of the following churches: Catholic Church, Polish Orthodox Church (in all six dioceses of the Polish Orthodox Church, 47 chaplains perform their service) (Migdał 2008, 390–391; Lenczewski 2016, 459–470), Evangelical-Augsburg Church (within the framework of the Evangelical-Augsburg Church, prison chaplains perform their service in the area of four out of six dioceses of this church) (Migdał 2008, 390–391; Janik 2016), Pentecostal Church, Seventh-Day Adventist Church, Christian Baptist Church, Bible Society and Jehovah's Witnesses (Migdał 2008, 390–391; Niewiadomska 2016, 9:116).

19.2.2   Structure of Prison Pastoral Care

The Catholic Church, the Evangelical-Augsburg Church, the Polish Orthodox Church and the Pentecostal Church have created a separate structure dedicated to prison pastoral care (Nikołajew 2015, 69).

The organisational structure of the Central Board of the Prison Service [*Centralny Zarząd Służby Więziennej*] establishes a separate organisational and administrative unit for the prison ministry of the Catholic Church. Pastoral care by the Polish Orthodox Church is coordinated by the National Chaplain of Orthodox Pastoral Care and the National Priests of Polish Prisons of the Polish Orthodox Church. In the case of the Pentecostal Church, missionary activity in the prison environment is conducted in various ways (e.g. holiday gift packages, special meetings, charity concerts, outside help, assistance following release from prison) by a specialised unit – the Prison Mission (Nikołajew 2015, 69–70).

Since 1 October 1997, the Board of Prison Pastoral Care [*Rada Duszpasterstwa Więziennego*] has been operating within the Central Board of the Prison Service. It constitutes an advisory body of the General Director of the Prison Service within the scope of the exercise of religious freedom of people held in prison and custody suites. Its permanent members include the national prison chaplains of the Catholic, Evangelical-Augsburg and Polish Orthodox Churches. Their task is to coordinate the activities of their churches on the premises of the prisons. If needed, the board composition may be supplemented by the General Director of the Prison Service with national chaplains of other religious denominations (Janik 2016, 486; Lenczewski 2016, 470–471; Nikołajew 2012, 198–199).

Moreover, the structure of the Prison Service includes the Prison Office [*Biuro Penitencjarne*],[48] and the scope of its activity includes cooperation with representatives of churches and other religious denominations within the scope of the performance of religious services and supervision of the exercise of prisoners' right to freedom of religion (Lenczewski 2016, 471; Nikołajew 2012, 200).

In some prisons, representatives of various religious denominations cooperate with each other. One example may be provided by the Social Prison Board [*Społeczna Rada Penitencjarna*] operating in the prison district in Cieszyn [*Zakład Karny Cieszyn*], which gathers representatives of the Catholic, Evangelical-Augsburg, Pentecostal and Seventh-Day Adventist Churches. Its main task is to enable the prison administration and the chaplains of various denominations to take actions based on the principle of tolerance and equality (Nikołajew 2015, 69).

19.2.3 Religious Practices and Religious Services in Prison

Pursuant to Article 102 point 3 of the Executive Penal Code of 6 June 1997, people who are imprisoned may exercise their freedom of religion (Malec 1989, 21–24; Bedyński 1994; Meler 2003, 59–67; Migdał 2008).[49] In all prisons, chaplains from the Catholic Church and other recognised religious denominations perform their service in the form of voluntary agreement (free of charge)[50] or on the basis of a regular labour contract (paid by the state) (Krukowski 2008, 116–117; Borecki 2007, 144). In most cases, chaplains provide pastoral care free of charge (Nikołajew 2012, 208–209; Różański 2016, 240–244; Jaworski 2016, 230; Rakoczy 2008, 227).

In 2015, a total of 184 chaplains were hired by the state in the prison service, including 28 on a full-time basis (labour contract), mostly Roman Catholic

---

[48] The legal basis is constituted by § 4 Paragraph 9 of the Statute of the Central Board of Prison Service. See: Załącznik do Zarządzenia Ministra Sprawiedliwości w sprawie nadania Statutu Centralnemu Zarządowi Służby Więziennej z dnia 1 lipca 2015 r. *Official Journal of the Minister of Justice* of 2015, item 174 as amended.

[49] Regarding prisoners' right to freedom of conscience and religion, see inter alia: Malec, Jan. 1989. Posługi religijne w zakładach karnych. *Przegląd Penitencjarny i Kryminologiczny* (14–15):21–24; Lasocik, Zbigniew. 1993. *Praktyki religijne więźniów*, Warszawa: Wydawnictwo Naukowe PWN; Bedyński, Krystian. 1994. *Duszpasterstwo więzienne w Polsce – zarys historyczny*, Warszawa: First Business College; Meler, Sławomir. Prawo więźniów do wolności religijnej. *Przegląd Więziennictwa Polskiego* 38:59–67; Duszpasterstwo *więzienne w pracy penitencjarnej*, eds. Jan Świtka, Małgorzata Kuć. 2007. Lublin: Wydawnictwo KUL; Migdał, Jerzy. 2008. *Polski system penitencjarny w latach 1956–2008 w ujęciu doktrynalnym, normatywnym i funkcjonalnym. Kontynuacja czy zmiana?* Gdańsk: Arche.

[50] Article 17, Paragraph 3 of the Concordat reads as follows: 'A diocesan bishop shall refer chaplains with whom a relevant institution shall conclude a relevant agreement.' This provision does not specify, though, whether this agreement is voluntary (free of charge) or not. See: Krukowski, Józef. 2008. Realizacja Konkordatu z 1993 r. w polskim porządku prawnym. In *Konkordat Polski w 10 lat po ratyfikacji. Materiały z konferencji*, eds. Józef Wroceński, Helena Pietrzak, 116–117. Warszawa: Wydawnictwo UKSW; Borecki, Paweł. 2007. Zasada równouprawnienia wyznań w prawie polskim, *Studia z Prawa Wyznaniowego* 10:144.

chaplains (Stanisławski 2016, 172). The number of jobs for religious assistance is continuously increasing (Nikołajew 2012, 201; Mezglewski 2012, 116)[51] owing to the large number of Catholics in prison (Nikołajew 2013, 126). Chaplains of other religious denominations perform their services both on a regular basis paid by the state or free of charge. The number of jobs for non-Catholic chaplains is much smaller (around 33 in total)[52] because the number of prisoners of religions other than Catholicism is also much smaller (Zawiślak 2017, 115).

People beginning their prison sentence or provisional detention are notified of the possibility of attending religious practices in prison immediately after their arrival at their institution. In practice, the first conversation about this subject with a new arrival at a prison/detention centre is held by the prison service officer. The officer goes over the scope of rights and obligations as well as the internal rules within the scope of performing religious practices and services (Nikołajew 2012, 140).

Within the framework of the religious practices of Polish prisoners, sacramental activity is the most significant (Nikołajew 2012, 385). The best-protected right is that of free prayer in a residential cell. The religious customs connected with Christmas wafer breaking, the blessing of food on Easter Saturday, participation in rosary services and confessions are followed without obstacles (Nikołajew 2012, 142). Prisoners of other faiths can also freely practise their religion (i.e. ablutions, daily prayer), especially in their prison cells.

Individual and collective prayer, as well as participation in services and catechetical meetings organised in prison, constitute the most readily available forms of religious activity for prisoners (Meler 2003, 64).[53]

Prisoners are allowed to attend services and listen to sermons, in accordance with their religion. Every prison has a broadcasting centre through which radio messages and broadcasts are transmitted, while on Sundays and church holidays prisoners may listen to Holy Mass (Bielecki 2016, 403–414; Wierzbicki 2016, 417–431; Paszkowski, Krzywkowska 2016, 435–445.).[54] Jews, Muslims and other believers

---

[51] See also: Mezglewski, Artur. 2012. Finansowanie nauczania religii w placówkach publicznych oraz wynagrodzeń kapelanów z budżetu państwa. In *Finansowanie związków wyznaniowych w krajach niemieckojęzycznych i w Polsce. Die finanzierung der Religionsgemeinschaften in den Deutschsprachugen Ländern und in Polen*, eds. Dariusz Walencik, Marcin Worbs, 116. Opole: Colloquia Teologica.

[52] In 2004, a total of 173 chaplains were hired by the state: 131 Catholic chaplains, 19 Orthodox chaplains and 14 Evangelical-Augsburg Confession chaplains. See http://www.racjonalista.pl/kk.php/s,4322/k,2%2029 Accessed: 15 October 2017.

[53] Meler, Sławomir. 2003. Prawo więźniów do wolności religijnej. *Przegląd Więziennictwa Polskiego* 38–39:64.

[54] Regarding religious practices in particular prisons: Bielecki, Marek. 2016. Praktyki religijne osadzonych w zakładzie karnym w Zamościu. In *Wolność sumienia i religii osób pozbawionych wolności. Aspekty prawne i praktyczne*, eds. Jerzy Nikołajew, Konrad Walczuk, 403–414. Warszawa: Wydawnictwo Unitas; Wierzbicki, Konrad. 2016. Praktyki religijne osób pozbawionych wolności w zakładzie karnym w Chełmie. In *Wolność sumienia i religii osób pozbawionych wolności. Aspekty prawne i praktyczne*, eds. Jerzy Nikołajew, Konrad Walczuk, 417–431. Warszawa: Wydawnictwo Unitas; Paszkowski, Marek and Justyna Krzywkowska. 2016. Prawo osadzonych do opieki duszpasterskiej i wykonywania praktyk religijnych na przykładzie zakładu karnego w Barczewie. In *Wolność sumienia i religii osób pozbawionych wolności. Aspekty prawne i praktyczne,* eds. Jerzy Nikołajew, Konrad Walczuk, 435–445. Warszawa: Wydawnictwo Unitas.

are also allowed to attend religious services. Prisoners of faiths other than Catholicism usually listen to Catholic radio messages (Zawiślak 2017, 116).

Prisoners may freely possess religious objects in their cells. In practice, even the stricter standards of conduct used for so-called dangerous prisoners do not limit their possession of these objects. A typical example of this is a condemned man who, though in a high-security prison, possessed a Bible, rosary and religious magazines.[55]

All people in prison or custody suites are allowed to exercise their constitutional right to education. Schools and educational institutions operating within prisons and custody suites are organised at all educational levels, i.e. primary, secondary, basic, grammar and post-secondary, except for university education. Religious education takes place in prison institutions without any limitations for all recognised religious denominations.

Article 38 § 1 of the Executive Penal Code of 6 June 1997 allows for cooperation with associations, foundations and other organisations, as well as with churches, for the purpose of resocialisation. Moreover, the law allows for the appointment of representatives of churches and religious associations as members of the General Board for Social Reintegration and Assistance for Convicts [*Rada Główna do Spraw Społecznej Readaptacji i Pomocy Skazanym*].[56] While in prison, prisoners use the charity of religious denominations, such as holiday gift packages, special meetings and charity concerts (Osowska-Rembecka 2016, 134), as well as participation in the charitable activities of the Catholic Church (Osowska-Rembecka 2016, 143).

The prison administration keeps no records on the religious affiliations of their prisoners. Personal files do not include religious affiliation, and prisoners are not required to declare anything on this subject. In practice, the administration must allow contact between a prisoner and the religious minister selected by the prisoner from the list. The list is compiled by the prison authorities at least once a year. All recognised religious denominations can submit a religious minister for inclusion on the list at any time. During their stay in prison, prisoners may change their religious affiliation without notice. The prison administration cannot require confirmation from religious ministers that prisoners belong to a specific religious community (Nikołajew 2012, 167).

In practice, prisoners have the right to participate in the meetings of different religious groups simultaneously and to accept the charity offered by those groups (such as holiday gift packages, special meetings and charity concerts), regardless of personal religious affiliation (Nikołajew 2012, 167; Zawiślak 2017, 117). All prisoners can participate in the meetings of any religious groups regardless of whether or not they are even affiliated with those groups.

---

[55] Judgement of the Regional Court in Gliwice of 18 December 2013, II C 131/12, LEX no. 1,720,749.

[56] See: § 2 Paragraph 4 Rozporządzenia Prezesa Rady Ministrów z dnia 21 sierpnia 1998 r. w sprawie określenia szczegółowych zasad i trybu powoływania oraz działania Rady Głównej do Spraw Społecznej Readaptacji i Pomocy Skazanym, a także rad terenowych do spraw społecznej readaptacji i pomocy skazanym, *Dziennik Ustaw* No. 113, Item 723.

19.2.4 Restrictions on Religious Practices in Prison

In the prisons of Lublin Province, four complaints about religious discrimination were recorded between 1 January 2006 and 30 June 2009. The first one involved a citizen of Belarus being held in the prison in Zamość District [*Zakład Karny Zamość*] and concerned the limited right to attend a religious meeting. The second involved a prisoner in the prison in Chełm District [*Zakład Karny Chełm*] and concerned the difficulty with which the prisoner was able to meet with a Muslim religious leader. The third involved a prisoner (Polish citizen) who said that '*members of the Orthodox church and Ukrainians enjoy greater consideration than Poles/emphasis in original*' because of their religious affiliation. In the fourth case, a Russian citizen from Chechnya complained about the non-consideration of his religious dietary requirements (halal) in the prison in Zamość District (Nikołajew 2012, 174; Zawiślak 2017, 117). In all these cases, the prison authorities deemed the complaints unfounded.[57]

In the Lublin detention ward, a temporary detainee refused to remove his clothes and eat meals prepared by prison authorities, claiming religious reasons (Nikołajew 2012, 173; Zawiślak 2017, 117–118). The prisoner, Abd Elsam B., refused to stay in the prison cell because he had to pray while facing the toilet. He then refused to remove his clothes, citing religious reasons. The prisoner was condemned by the prison authorities because he breached internal prison security rules and also demanded that his meals be prepared in accordance with his the dietary rules of his religion. The director of the detention ward refused his demand because the meals prepared for him would then be less healthy. It is important to note that the detainee did not file a complaint and did not exercise his right to appeal to a court or to contact the Egyptian embassy (Nikołajew 2012, 173). However, it must be stated that this prisoner's case illustrates an illegal restriction on his right to practise his religion as he himself desired.

Catholic prisoners are guaranteed the preparation of vegetarian meals every Friday and on all religious holidays requiring a fast, i.e. Ash Wednesday and Good Friday. In the case of *Jakóbski v. Poland*, the European Court of Human Rights ruled that Poland violated Article 9 of the European Convention on Human Rights due to its failure to prepare vegetarian meals for a Buddhist inmate.[58] According to the complainant's religion, he was supposed to have a simple meat-free diet. He merely asked to be granted a vegetarian diet, which excluded meat products. The court noted that his meals did not have to be prepared, cooked and served in a prescribed manner, nor did he require any special products. He was offered no alternative meals, nor was the Buddhist Mission consulted on the issue of the appropriate diet (Maffei 2013, 490–496).[59]

---

[57] The report on the method of complaint consideration in the District Prison Service Inspectorate in Lublin in the first 6 months of 2009, July 2009, p. 4. See Nikołajew, Jerzy. 2012, 174.

[58] ECHR, Judgement of 7 March 2011, case of *Jakóbski v. Poland*. (Application no. 18,429/06). See Para. 52.

[59] Maffei M.C. (2013) The Vegetarian Diet in Prison: A Human Right? The Case of Jakóbski v. Poland. In: Boschiero N., Scovazzi T., Pitea C., Ragni C. (eds) International Courts and the Development of International Law. T.M.C. Asser Press, The Hague, The Netherlands 489–496.

In the case of *Wojciechowski v. Poland*, the European court decided that Article 3 of the European Convention on Human Rights (concerning the prohibition of torture) was violated in the context of overcrowded housing conditions; however, Article 9 of the Convention was not violated.[60] The complainant argued that as a temporary detainee, he had a limited right to participate in Holy Mass. Evidence in the case indicated that the complainant was able to practise his religion. In 2008, the prison unit where the complainant was being held did not have the capacity to enable all prisoners to participate in collective religious services, so those who wanted to attend such services had to enrol with their tutor. Their names were then entered into a computer system, and participants were selected on a rotating basis.

All these cases clearly demonstrate that prison staff is not well prepared for ensuring prisoners the right to practise one's religion (Zawiślak 2017, 119). According to Poles' religious affiliations (87.6% Catholic), it is obvious that the Catholic Church and other Christian denominations have a stronger and more established presence in prisons. However, the law provides many opportunities to take part in religious practices and fully respects religious pluralism.

19.3 Conclusion

In practice, the restriction of prisoners' religious freedom is affected by the absence of detailed internal regulations in prisons or by a lack of knowledge of religious practices, mainly of Muslim and Jewish prisoners, by the prison staff. The prison staff are mostly Catholics and do not fully understand the needs of prisoners of other religions, mostly because they receive no training on this matter. Some discriminatory treatment of prisoners on religious grounds still takes place in Poland's penitentiary system. Incidentally, both prison authorities and other prisoners treat Muslims with suspicion. Until now, no religions have questioned the legal framework of religious freedom in Polish prisons.

Internal prison regulations are becoming more and more 'sensitive' to the religious needs of prisoners and show an increasing awareness of the growing pluralism of Polish society. On the other hand, analysis of solutions resulting from certain internal regulations in individual penitentiary units clearly shows that – despite the growing awareness of the rights of prisoners and the evident cooperation of the state with religious denominations to meet prisoners' needs – certain problems remain, and existing solutions continue to have shortcomings with regard to the level of guarantee of prisoners' religious freedom or observance of the principle of equality and equal rights.

---

[60] ECHR, Judgement of 26 June 2016, case of Janusz Wojciechowski v. Poland (application no. 54511/11).

Bibliography

Abramowicz, A. (2016). Duszpasterstwo w instytucjach penitencjarnych a zasada równouprawnienia związków wyznaniowych. In J. Nikołajew & K. Walczuk (Eds.), *Wolność sumienia i religii osób pozbawionych wolności. Aspekty prawne i praktyczne* (pp. 131–146). Warszawa: Wydawnictwo Unitas.

Bedyński, K. (1994). *Duszpasterstwo więzienne w Polsce – zarys historyczny.* Warszawa: First Business College.

Bielecki, M. (2016). Praktyki religijne osadzonych w zakładzie karnym w Zamościu. In J. Nikołajew & K. Walczuk (Eds.), *Wolność sumienia i religii osób pozbawionych wolności. Aspekty prawne i praktyczne* (pp. 403–414). Warszawa: Wydawnictwo Unitas.

Borecki, P. (2007). Zasada równouprawnienia wyznań w prawie polskim. *Studia z Prawa Wyznaniowego, 10*, 115–160.

Czacki, T. (1800). *O litewskich i polskich prawach.* Warszawa: J.C.G. Rakoczy.

Janik, P. (2016). Działalność ewangelickiego duszpasterstwa więziennego w Polsce. In J. Nikołajew & K. Walczuk (Eds.), *Wolność sumienia i religii osób pozbawionych wolności. Aspekty prawne i praktyczne* (pp. 475–488). Warszawa: Wydawnictwo Unitas.

Jaworski, Z. (2016). Gwarancje wolności religijnej dla osób przebywających w zakładach penitencjarnych i wojsku według Konkordatu z 1993 roku. In J. Nikołajew & K. Walczuk (Eds.), *Wolność sumienia i religii osób pozbawionych wolności. Aspekty prawne i praktyczne* (pp. 223–235). Warszawa: Wydawnictwo Unitas.

Kaczyńska, E. (1989). Ludzie ukazani. In *Więzienia i system kar w Królestwie Polskim 1815–1914.* Warszawa: Państwowe Wydawnictwo Naukowe.

Krukowski, J. (2008). Realizacja Konkordatu z 1993 r. w polskim porządku prawnym. In J. Wroceński & H. Pietrzak (Eds.), *Konkordat Polski w 10 lat po ratyfikacji* (pp. 87–129). Warszawa: Wydawnictwo UKSW.

Lasocik, Z. (1993). *Praktyki religijne więźniów.* Warszawa: Wydawnictwo Naukowe PWN.

Lenczewski, M. (2016). Posługa duszpasterska kapelanów PAKP w zakładach karnych i aresztach śledczych w Polsce. In J. Nikołajew & K. Walczuk (Eds.), *Wolność sumienia i religii osób pozbawionych wolności. Aspekty prawne i praktyczne* (pp. 459–473). Warszawa: Wydawnictwo Unitas.

Maffei, M. C. (2013). The vegetarian diet in prison: A human right? The case of Jakóbski v. Poland. In N. Boschiero, T. Scovazzi, C. Pitea, & C. Ragni (Eds.), *International Courts and the Development of International Law* (pp. 489–496). The Hague: T.M.C. Asser Press.

Malec, J. (1989). Posługi religijne w zakładach karnych. *Przegląd Penitencjarny i Kryminologiczny* (14–15), 21–24.

Maleszyk, R. (2016). Historyczne aspekty kształtowania się prawa więźniów do wolności religijnej. In J. Nikołajew & K. Walczuk (Eds.), *Wolność sumienia i religii osób pozbawionych wolności. Aspekty prawne i praktyczne* (pp. 15–33). Warszawa: Wydawnictwo Unitas.

Meler, S. (2003). Prawo więźniów do wolności religijnej. *Przegląd Więziennictwa Polskiego, 38*, 59–67.

Mezglewski, A. (2012). Finansowanie nauczania religii w placówkach publicznych oraz wynagrodzeń kapelanów z budżetu państwa. In D. Walencik & M. Worbs (Eds.), *Finansowanie związków wyznaniowych w krajach niemieckojęzycznych i w Polsce. Die finanzierung der Religionsgemeinschaften in den Deutschsprachugen Ländern und in Polen* (pp. 111–122). Opole: Colloquia Teologica.

Migdał, J. (2008). *Polski system penitencjarny w latach 1956–2008 w ujęciu doktrynalnym, normatywnym i funkcjonalnym. Kontynuacja czy zmiana?* Gdańsk: Arche.

Migdał, J. (2011). *Polski system penitencjarny w latach 1918–1928.* Gdańsk: Arche.

Migdał, J. (2012). *Polski system penitencjarny w latach 1928–1939.* Gdańsk: Arche.

Misztal, H. (1993). Kościelne pojęcie wolności religijnej a ustawa o gwarancjach wolności sumienia i wyznania. *Kościół i Prawo, 11*, 104–107.

Niewiadomska, I. (2016). Polski model resocjalizacji penitencjarnej. *Teka Komisji Prawniczej. Polska Akademia Nauk Oddział w Lublinie, 9*, 100–122.

Nikołajew, J. (2012). *Wolność sumienia i religii skazanych i tymczasowo skazanych*. Lublin: Wydawnictwo KUL.

Nikołajew, J. (2013). Reguły Minimalne i Europejskie Reguły Więzienne a prawo więźniów do wolności sumienia i religii w Polsce. *Studia z Prawa Wyznaniowego, 16*, 111–135.

Nikołajew, J. (2015). Zadania struktur duszpasterstwa więziennego w zakresie indywidualnej wolności religijnej. *Opolskie Studia Administracyjno-Prawne, XIII*(4), 57–76.

Osowska-Rembecka, A. (2016). Programy oddziaływań penitencjarnych na przykładzie Okręgowego Inspektoratu Służby Więziennej w Warszawie. *Przegląd Więziennictwa Polskiego, 92*, 134.

Paszkowski, M., & Krzywkowska, J. (2016). Prawo osadzonych do opieki duszpasterskiej i wykonywania praktyk religijnych na przykładzie zakładu karnego w Barczewie. In J. Nikołajew & K. Walczuk (Eds.), *Wolność sumienia i religii osób pozbawionych wolności. Aspekty prawne i praktyczne* (pp. 435–445). Warszawa: Wydawnictwo Unitas.

Piechowiak, M. (1996). Wolność religijna – aspekty filozoficzne-prawne. *Toruński Rocznik Praw Człowieka i Pokoju, 3*, 10–12.

Plisiecki, M. (2016). Opieka duchowa w założeniach więziennictwa II Rzeczypospolitej. In J. Nikołajew & K. Walczuk (Eds.), *Wolność sumienia i religii osób pozbawionych wolności. Aspekty prawne i praktyczne* (pp. 49–62). Warszawa: Wydawnictwo Unitas.

Rakoczy, B. (2008). Ustawa o stosunku Państwa do Kościoła Katolickiego w Polsce. In *Komentarz*. Warszawa: Wolters Kluwer.

Różański, M. (2016). Kapelan więzienny. Prawne podstawy duszpasterzowania. In J. Nikołajew & K. Walczuk (Eds.), *Wolność sumienia i religii osób pozbawionych wolności. Aspekty prawne i praktyczne* (pp. 237–248). Warszawa: Wydawnictwo Unitas.

Stanisławski, T. (2016). Finansowe koszty zapewnienia wolności sumienia i religii osób pozbawionych wolności. In J. Nikołajew & K. Walczuk (Eds.), *Wolność sumienia i religii osób pozbawionych wolności. Aspekty prawne i praktyczne* (pp. 167–174). Warszawa: Wydawnictwo Unitas.

Szymański, A. (2016). Kapelani więzienni w II Rzeczypospolitej – zarys problematyki. In J. Nikołajew & K. Walczuk (Eds.), *Wolność sumienia i religii osób pozbawionych wolności. Aspekty prawne i praktyczne* (pp. 63–81). Warszawa: Wydawnictwo Unitas.

Wierzbicki, K. (2016). Praktyki religijne osób pozbawionych wolności w zakładzie karnym w Chełmie. In J. Nikołajew & K. Walczuk (Eds.), *Wolność sumienia i religii osób pozbawionych wolności. Aspekty prawne i praktyczne* (pp. 417–431). Warszawa: Wydawnictwo Unitas.

Wojtas, P. (2016). Działalność katolickiego duszpasterstwa więziennego w Polsce. In J. Nikołajew & K. Walczuk (Eds.), *Wolność sumienia i religii osób pozbawionych wolności. Aspekty prawne i praktyczne* (pp. 449–458). Warszawa: Wydawnictwo Unitas.

Zawiślak, M. (2017). The limitations of religious practices in Polish prisons. *Review of Comparative Law, 30*(3), 107–123.

Chapter 20
Romania: Physical Captivity and Spiritual Freedom – Historical, Sociological and Legal Aspects of Religion in the Prison System

Gabriel Bîrsan

Abstract The main purpose of this chapter is to highlight key aspects of the relation between religion and the Romanian penitentiary environment. An in-depth look into the history of the correctional system on today's Romanian territory reveals that religion has always been an important part of penal history, although its role and importance in the punishment process have shifted over time. Besides identifying the events and people who have influenced the modelling of the penitentiary system and the practice of religion in the carceral environment over time, this chapter documents the status of religion in Romanian prisons, the way religious freedom is respected, the impact of religion on detainees and future prospects.

20.1 Introduction

The topic of religion in prison has been hotly debated in recent decades in the West. Researchers wish to understand the role played by religion in the prisons of late-modern societies and what forms of religiosity may be identified among actors in the prison world (Beckford and Gilliat 1998). Above all, they are interested to see how religious freedom is respected in prisons, how religion is lived behind bars, and how it transforms the lives of inmates. Recently, the growing diversity of the religious affiliations of inmates, including minority faiths, is one of the main areas of interest among sociologists of religion (Becci and Roy 2015). This diversity has made principles such as democracy, freedom or human rights – the pillars of Western

G. Bîrsan (✉)
Doctoral School of Theology and Religious Sciences, University of Strasbourg, Strasbourg, France
e-mail: gabriel.birsan@etu.unistra.fr

© Springer Nature Switzerland AG 2020
J. Martínez-Ariño, A.-L. Zwilling (eds.), *Religion and Prison: An Overview of Contemporary Europe*, Boundaries of Religious Freedom: Regulating Religion in Diverse Societies 7, https://doi.org/10.1007/978-3-030-36834-0_20

civilisation – harder to support and defend both inside and outside prisons (Crépeau and Sheppard 2013; Koenig and De Guchteneire 2007; Beckford 2013; Jones 2001). Religious diversity in prisons can be seen as one of the causes of discrimination, proselytism and radicalisation (Mulcahy et al. 2013), phenomena that are intensely fought over by national and supranational institutions (e.g. Radicalisation Awareness Network [RAN] and Prison and Probation Working Group [P&P][1]). Diversities and minorities are also associated with increased security limitations, so the need to understand and prevent security risks, whose origins might be in the religious diversity from inside prisons, could be another impetus for increased research on this theme.

In Romania, however, sociologists have shown limited interest in the subject of religion in prison. The factors that have led, in the Western world, to research and debate on the theme of religion in prison have been for a long period almost totally absent in Romania.

The study of the relationship between religion and imprisonment in Romania remains in its early stages due not only to the fact that during the communist period religion was completely removed from public life, but also, and especially, to the fact that the young Romanian democracy has not fully developed the reflex to defend religious freedom, wherever it is manifested. The specialised literature in sociology is poor; the literature issued by the various denominations has been more fruitful and insightful. Lately, this topic has begun to be debated, but only as a secondary theme, in the context of the overcrowding crisis of the Romanian penitentiary system, which has attracted international media coverage and because of which the Romanian state risks sanctions from European institutions.

On the other hand, the particularities of Romanian society have made the penitentiary environment in Romania hard to characterise as religiously diverse. There are no official statistics on prisoners by confession, but, in line with the national proportions (86.45% Orthodox, INS[2] 2013), the Orthodox religion would be expected to be the one professed by more than 85% of detainees. Traditional minorities – Catholics, Muslims, Jews – are small in number and have a very long history of adaptation to and cooperation with the Romanian state. Foreigners represent only 1.1% (WPB[3] 2016) of the total number of detainees. Thus, Romanian researchers also lacked the religious plurality from inside prisons to conduct thorough studies on religion in Romanian prisons.

Broadly speaking, with a delay of several years to several decades, the Romanian penitentiary system, and implicitly the regulations of the practice of religion in

---

[1] The RAN and P&P constitute a hub of networks connecting people involved in preventing radicalisation and violent extremism throughout Europe. They were launched in 2011 by the European Commission, https://ec.europa.eu/home-affairs/what-we-do/networks/radicalisation_awareness_network/about-ran/ran-p-and-p_en, 5 September 2017.

[2] Institutul Naţional de Statistică România—National Institute of Statistics Romania, www.insse.ro.

[3] The World Prison Brief, Institute for Criminal Policy Research is an online database providing free access to information on prison systems around the world, http://www.prisonstudies.org/.

prison, followed the same stages of development as in Western countries (Bruno 2006a) but managed to develop its own characteristics, determined by the historical past. For several centuries, under the influence of Byzantine culture, state and religious authorities almost equally divided between them the right to judge and punish. Starting in the nineteenth century, Romanian prisons almost entirely aligned with Western standards on the role of religion in prison. Initially, the rules of empiricism stripped religion of its historical role of explaining, controlling and punishing crime, and in the twentieth century religion in prison became simply a constitutionally defended right.

20.2 Brief History of Romanian Penitentiary System

A foray into the history of the Romanian detention system reveals vast differences in the portrayal of punishment and the role of prisons in different historical ages. Prisons have served different functions over the course of their existence. At times prisons were at the heart of society owing to the mere fact that places of detention were located in churches, monasteries or public institutions. Sometimes, prisons were used more to protect than to punish those imprisoned, whereas at other times prisons were simply used as points of transit, but most of the time, prisons were synonyms with death. In the nineteenth century, prisons began to be used as places of atonement for sentences that deprived criminals of their liberty and not necessarily as a means of excluding them from society. In the twentieth and twenty first centuries, prisons finally aspired to become civilising institutions that embraced concepts such as human rights whose main purpose was to rehabilitate and resocialise delinquents for the benefit of the whole society.

20.2.1 Ancient and Medieval Eras

Most historical sources that present the history of the Romanian penitentiary system start with the Dacians. In the absence of any information about the existence of a code of laws applicable in the actual territory of Romania before the first century BC and considering the elements of culture, morality and social organisation (patriarchal slavery) which dominated the Geto-Dacian world, scholars assume that criminals were subjected to corporal punishment or used for domestic or public works rather than being incarcerated (Chiş 2003).

Dacia's conquest by the Roman Empire (AD 105–106) brought the Roman laws and implicitly the Roman system of punishment in the new province (*Dacia Felix*). The first forms of detention appeared: sites of forced labour, such as stone quarries and gold, silver or salt mines (Bruno 2006a).

The period between the withdrawal of the Roman administration (AD 274) and the creation of the Romanian feudal states (fourteenth century) is not covered by many historical data, but one thing is certain: the local penal practice, and the entire local system of laws, suffered from a thorough Roman, then Byzantine, influence. Combining local traditions with the customs of Romans, Byzantines and other migrants led to the emergence of an unwritten code of laws called *Jus Walachicum* (also known as *Romanian Law*, *Land Law* or *Divine Law*) (Dianu 1901; Dinulescu 2006). This set of unwritten laws functioned identically in all Romanian provinces (Walachia, Moldavia and Transylvania) until the fourteenth century. From this period until the early twentieth century, laws of Western influence were imposed on the process of trial and sentencing of guilty persons in Transylvania, at the time under the influence of Hungarian rule.

The first written laws regarding the regulation of punishments (called *pravile*) appeared in Wallachia and Moldavia only in the middle of the seventeenth century, but they were infrequently obeyed, the will of judges (either a prince or nobility and clergy delegated by him) and the power of custom (the *land law*) remaining the main sources of jurisprudence.

Pursuant to both written and unwritten laws, punishments were almost entirely of a corporal and pecuniary nature, the death penalty being the most common sentence for serious offences (Filitti 1934). Prisoners who managed to avoid the death penalty were condemned to forced labour in a mine, which was virtually equivalent to a death sentence.

Imprisonment was not a punishment in itself. Prison was simply a place where those accused were detained awaiting sentencing and its execution. Detention was brief, a few days, often only a few hours, its role being similar to today's preventive arrest. Prisons were also intended to compel the fulfilment of an obligation or to obtain the testimony, almost always obtained by torture, of those about to be judged (Bruno 2006a). The organisation of prisons was not regulated by any law, and there was no central administration, management being left to the discretion of the authorities who oversaw them – prince, noblemen or abbots of monasteries. Inmates were not supported by public funds; prisons were maintained either by those arrested, who had to pay their own way, meaning their own detention costs, or by charitable citizens who donated money, food and clothing. From the point of view of location and appearance, prisons were just holes in the ground or basements in castles, monasteries or high dignitaries' domains (Chiş 2003).

Transylvania, being under Hungarian, Austrian and, for a short period, Turkish administration – all empires with a developed and complex culture of punishment – saw its prisons develop more quickly. From the very beginning, fortresses and other important public buildings were built with space for prison cells. Starting in the sixteenth century, in all major cities, prisons were housed in buildings specially designed for this purpose. Local councils also developed prison regulations, and so detention was based on written orders or administrative decisions (Bruno 2006a).

20.2.2   Reformation and Modernisation of Prisons – Eighteenth to Twentieth Centuries

The eighteenth century was characterised by the interest of local authorities in the prison systems developed in other countries. The Western education received by the rulers of Romanian principalities led to the implementation of the ideas of great criminologists like Cesare Beccaria or John Howard in both Wallachia and Moldavia. Detention became a means of punishment in itself and in addition, at least in theory, a way of rehabilitation in the eyes of society. One of the consequences of implementing these ideas was that detention conditions were significantly improved; for example, a special department for a centralised administration of prisons was founded, the accused were judged solely on the basis of evidence, conditional release was introduced, new prisons were built, women were separated from men, and infirmaries were set up in large prisons (Chiş 2003; Bruno 2006a.)

However, the most significant reformation of the penitentiary system took place after the introduction in Wallachia (1831) and Moldavia (1832) of *organic regulations*.[4] Thus, during the nineteenth century, major reforms were carried out: first, statutes of organisation for the entire prison system were written; more prisons were built for different categories of inmates by gender, type of offence, and length of detention; the death penalty and torture were abolished (Constantiniu 2016); the institutions of *prosecutor* and *advocate* were introduced; the costs of sustaining prisoners were covered by the state; and prisoners were paid for their work (Filitti 1936).

The main creator of the modern Romanian penal system was Ferdinand-François-Marie Dodun des Perrières, a French criminologist brought to Moldavia by Prince Grigore Ghica in 1855 to organise Moldavian prisons. He had founded many prisons that remain in operation to this day and formulated the most important prison laws and regulations. The reforms he initiated in Moldavia were extended to Wallachia. He unified prison services and formulated the first penal code (1864) following the unification of the Romanian principalities in 1859. Further, he authored two major documents considered to be the foundation of the modern penitentiary system: *Regulations on the Organisation of Prisons and Charity Service Establishments in Romania* (1862) and *Prison Law* (1874).

The union between Romania and Transylvania (1918) marked the beginning of the twentieth century. Romanian society was dominated at that time by a strong nationalist sentiment that inevitably had ripple effects in how prisons were run. Thus, prisons were in the service of national uniformisation: in Transylvanian prisons, where Hungarian prisoners formed the majority, the Hungarian language was banned and all prison guards had to be of Romanian origin. A new prison law was passed in 1929. Its significant contribution was the establishment of a Superior

---

[4]*Organic regulations* were quasi-constitutional organic laws enforced by the Imperial Russian authorities in Moldavia and Wallachia, with slight differences from one principality to another, which remained in force until 1858.

Council of Prisons, composed of recognised scholars. Their participation in the most important congresses of criminology introduced Romania to the international scientific criminological community. In 1936, a new penal code appeared, and in 1938 the Regulation on the Procedure for the Enforcement of Punishments was issued, at that time one of the most advanced European regulations concerning the role of prisons. The idea of social rehabilitation of prisoners was laid out in detail and forcefully argued in a separate chapter called 'Education Measures'. Unfortunately, capital punishment was reintroduced the same year by the authoritarian regime of King Carol II.

20.2.3   Prisons During Communist Regime (1947–1989)

During the communist regime, the Romanian penitentiary system entered the era of *re-education* and of *creating a new man*, goals equivalent to terror, extreme privations and dehumanisation. During the Stalinist period (Ciuceanu 2001), between 1947 and 1964, the number of political prisoners and deported people greatly increased, forced labour colonies were established, the capacity of prisons was greatly expanded and prison staff was militarised.

Through the intervention of international institutions, in 1964, political prisoners were released and detention conditions generally improved. This trend continued after the rise to power of Ceauşescu in 1965. The new penal code of 1969 abolished forced labour camps but set up factories close to prisons where prisoners were used as the labour force. Compulsory labour transformed the prison into a profitable state institution, as prisoners' living expenses fell below their income (Bruno 2006a). Ceauşescu's regime did not invest at all in new prisons; on the contrary, many of the existing ones were demolished. Following the political decision not to exceed an annual prison population of 15,000, it was decided to abolish more than 70% of prisons (Decree No. 225/1977), leaving only 16 imprisonment institutions in operation.

Even if prison conditions improved over time (modern practices like sanitation facilities in all cells, medical facilities in all prisons, food standardisation, and so forth were imposed by international regulations to which Romania was a signatory), inmates' quality of life was very poor, and respect for even the most elementary human rights was arbitrary. Consequently, this period still saw many victims. According to various statistics, the penitentiary system during the communist regime registered approximately two million prisoners, of which half a million died (Frunză 1990, Lățescu 1995, IICCMER[5] 2016).

---

[5] *Institutul de Investigare a Crimelor Comunismului și Memoria Exilului Românesc – The Institute for the Investigation of Communist Crimes and Memory of the Romanian Exile*, https://www.iiccr.ro/.

20.2.4   Post-Communist and Present Organisation of Penitentiary System

In December 1989, the communist regime fell, but its practices in prisons continued, as in the broader Romanian society, for another few years. The death penalty was abolished in January 1990, but the first signs of rupture with the communist era were seen after the opening of Romanian authorities to the international environment. Due to Romania's accession to the Council of Europe in 1993 and the ratification by the Romanian parliament of the Convention on Human Rights and Fundamental Freedoms in 1994, inspections and reports of international institutions such as the European Institute for Crime Prevention and Control, the Committee Against Torture and its Convention Against Torture and Other Cruel, Inhuman or Degrading Treatment or Punishment, and Amnesty International forced the Romanian government to take measures to humanise prisons. Ten years later, the prison staff was demilitarised, and in 2006 Romania aligned prison practices with those in Europe, as seen in its integration into the European Union in 2007 (Șerban 2008). Since 2010, a series of laws have been issued, including a new penal code (2014).

Currently, the most serious problem faced by the penitentiary system is overcrowding. As of 21 April 2017, the 45 penitentiary facilities with a capacity (based on 4 m²/inmate) of 19,108 spots accommodated 27,251 inmates (ANP 2017[6]), an occupancy rate of 142.62% or a deficit of more than 8000 spots. This crisis, in addition to the overall poor living conditions in prisons, meant that, as of late 2015, Romania had the most convicted criminals according to the European Court of Human Rights (ECHR), violating 243 times Article 3 of the Human Rights Convention on the prohibition of torture and inhuman or degrading treatment or punishment (Puiu 2016). The ECHR issued the first warning 5 years ago, pronouncing against Romania a semi-pilot decision in the *Case of Iacov Stanciu v. Romania* (24 July 2012). Because the deadline imposed by the ECHR for resolving the overcrowing problem was coming to an end and the overcrowding was as bad as before, some politicians proposed in February 2017 a bill in favour of amnesty/pardon for several categories of offences/prisoners. This move greatly angered civil society and led to massive street protests, which postponed the solution to the problem of prison overcrowding.

20.3   Status of Religion in Romanian Prisons

During the Middle Ages, across Europe, judgements and punishments were carried out in accordance with the rules and restrictions imposed by the Church and often even within the walls of the Church (Dammer 2002), so it is no exaggeration to

---

[6] *Administrația Națională a Penitenciarelor - National Administration of Penitentiaries*, http://anp. gov.ro/.

assert that prisons themselves were imprisoned within the confines of religion. Since the Enlightenment, roles have reversed, and religion has come to enter, literally and figuratively, into prison, to provide convicts with spiritual armour aimed at deflecting moral disease. As will be seen, Romanian prisons followed the same pattern.

20.3.1 Religion in Prison During the Medieval Romanian States

Until the nineteenth century, religious beliefs and their institutional representation (the Church) had an overwhelming influence over the entire process of judgement and punishment of convicted people in Romania. The expression *religious beliefs* refers to Christianity and, after the eleventh century, to Orthodox Christianity. The Catholic Church had an influence in Transylvania only starting in the fourteenth century.

First of all, the laws establishing punishment were religiously inspired. The first collection of laws in today's Romanian territory was the *Jus Walachicum*, also called *Divine Law*. According to a highly regarded Moldavian scholar of the eighteenth century, the old Romanian common law was founded on the 'laws of Byzantine emperors and on decisions of Church Councils' (Cantemir 1716). The first written collections of laws were called *pravile*: Pravila of Vasile Lupu (1646) and Pravila of Matei Basarab (1652). *Pravila* is a Slavic word meaning *law*, which in the old Romanian language designated a body of laws, both secular and ecclesiastical, synonymous with the term *nomocanon*. Because the laws had a pronounced religious character, it follows that the penalties, implicitly those involving detention, constituted the effect of a violation of religious norms. Certain traditions regarding imprisonment, more related to popular religiosity than to the teachings of the Church, were also contained in Jus Walachicum: during Holy Week, before Easter, and on the day of Christmas Eve all prisoners not yet judged were released; on Sundays, prisoners received subsidies (food and clothing) from the faithful who went to church (Iorga 1930).

Secondly, the function of the judge was most often carried out by clergy. Rulers frequently entrusted the right to judge common crimes to nobles or bishops and abbots of monasteries (Dianu 1901; Berechet 1926). This happened for several reasons: a cleric was considered morally superior to other judges, copies of the written laws (*pravile, nomocanons*) were kept in monasteries, and clergy was one of the few categories of people who could understand and interpret those texts. In addition, monastic judgement was quite effective because there is little evidence of complaints against monks, which probably encouraged rulers to delegate more often the right of judgement to monasteries (Bruno 2006a).

Thirdly, monasteries, especially in the medieval period, were the toughest places of detention, where most often political opponents and the most dangerous criminals were held. As an example, Prince Vlad the Impaler, better known as Vlad Dracula, built Snagov Monastery (1457) specifically for the incarceration of his political enemies. Monasteries were also used for the incarceration of women and juvenile offenders (Bruno 2006a).

Almost all monasteries built in Wallachia and Moldavia in the sixteenth and seventeenth centuries, over 20 in number, were used as prisons at some point. This state of affairs changed in the early eighteenth century during the reign of Nicolae Mavrocordat, considered one of the leading reformers of the ancient Romanian penal system. Firstly, he forbade priests and monks from judging. In addition, he gave new meaning to monastic imprisonment, considered modern for those times: prison guards had to respect the human dignity of convicts and treat them with kindness so they could correct their behaviour rather than worsen it. In 1716, Nicolae Mavrocordat built the Văcărești Monastery, one of the most modern prison monasteries in all of Europe, where inmates were taken to religious services every day and treated like beggars, crippled or homeless persons (Gorescu 1930; Marinescu 2011).

20.3.2 Modern Romanian State: The Evolution of Religious Assistance in Romanian Penitentiary System

This period of refinement of the Orthodox medieval penal system lasted nearly a century and a half, until the implementation of the ideas of Ferdinand-François-Marie Dodun des Perrières. Through his reforms, he reconfigured power relations in society, taking from the main political actors (princes, nobles, priests) the most important element of their sovereignty: the right to punish. Along with the laws concerning prisons adopted after the official creation of the Romanian state (1859), the Orthodox medieval penal system – dominant for centuries – was replaced by a modern, secular and bureaucratic one. The birth of the modern Romanian prison system occurred amid a continuing secularisation of society and a systematic abolition of the Church's responsibilities in the public sphere.

The 1864 General Regulation for Central Prisons, the 1874 Prisons Law, the 1874 General Regulation of the Central House of Correction for Minors or the Regulation of the Military Prison Târgşor from 1895 contained special chapters dedicated to religious services in prison and setting out the duties of priests (Costescu 1916). Thus, religious care was established in prison and the institution of the prison chaplain was created. In a first phase, religious assistance was provided only to the inmates of the Orthodox confession. It was assured by ordinary priests who had no special training in accomplishing their mission in the carceral environment (Sucilă-Pahoni 2012). In 1928, Romania adopted the model of recognised religions, the Orthodox Church retaining, however, a distinct status. The new laws on prisons from 1929 and 1938 ensured inmates' access to religious assistance granted to all recognised religions. According to Article 21 of the Law Regulating Religions of 1928, the recognised religions were the Orthodox Church, the Greek-Catholic Church, the Catholic Church, the Calvinist Reformed Church, the Lutheran Evangelical Church, the Unitarian Church, the Armenian-Gregorian Church, the Mosaic religion (Judaism) and Islam.

20.3.2.1 Religion in Communist Prisons

After 1947, as a result of the communist regime, atheism became state policy and religions were barely tolerated. The communist state used all possible means to compel religions to limit their activities. All catechetical activity was seen as a threat to the communist society. Therefore, all priests were forced to renounce all missionary activity in public spaces. Religious assistance was completely removed from public institutions, including prisons. Chaplains were forced to renounce their mission, being transferred as parish priests. Those who opposed such policies were arrested, and some even died while in prison.

Paradoxically but also tragically, during the communist regime, religion had an even greater presence in prisons than ever before because of the persecution by the communist state of clerics of all confessions who publicly expressed their discontent with communism. Records show that more than 1725 Orthodox and 400 Greek-Catholic clerics (Bălan 2000; Tismăneanu 2006) were jailed in communist prisons, in addition to an unknown number of Roman Catholic and Protestant clerics. A significant number of them died in prison. The fact that, until 1977, the prison for women of Mislea functioned in the former monastery of the same name is also worth mentioning. This prison is famous because, during the communist regime, notorious women of Romanian society were incarcerated there (Spânu 2010).

As a result of being tortured and the extremely difficult conditions of detention, for many prisoners, religion was genuinely the last refuge. Thus, a current of resistance or dissidence by faith emerged, which produced a certain kind of religious literature that after the fall of communism gave birth to a movement called the *saints of prisons*.

20.3.2.2 Religion in the Post-Communist and Present-Day Penitentiary System

After 1989, the tradition of religion's presence in public institutions was restored (Patriciu 2014). This tradition was reinstated by the new constitution, which remains in force at present:

> Article 29 (5) of Romania's constitution of 1991: 'Religious denominations shall be autonomous from the state and shall enjoy support from it, including the facilitation of religious assistance in the army, hospitals, prisons, nursing homes and orphanages'.

Religious assistance in prison is guaranteed by the constitution, by general laws concerning the penitentiary environment and by special laws related to the issue of religion in prison, but the effective reintroduction of religious assistance in prison was made by the signing of protocols between the state and, initially, the Romanian Orthodox Church. A first such protocol was signed in 1993 and has since been periodically renewed (Conovici and Secal 2012). It states that a religious assistance office will 'coordinate religious assistance activities for Orthodox detainees and detainees of other denominations'. The same agreement foresees that 'in units where more than 300 inmates belong to a recognised denomination, a representative of the respective denomination can be hired'. The status of the prison chaplain also specifies that the latter 'takes care of the prisoners of the other religious denominations who must also benefit from religious assistance from the religion to which they belong'. With time, the dominant position of the Romanian Orthodox Church with respect to religious assistance in public institutions has attenuated, at least in theory. At the moment, almost all recognised denominations, 18 in total, have separate collaboration agreements with the National Administration of Penitentiaries.

Religious assistance is also clearly mentioned by Law No. 275/2006, updated by Law No. 254/2013, on the carrying out of sentences and detention measures ordered by judicial bodies during criminal proceedings. According to Article 58 of the latter law:

(1) Freedom of conscience and opinion, as well as the freedom of religion of convicted persons, cannot be restricted.
(2) Convicted persons have the right to freedom of religion, without prejudice to the freedom of religion of other convicted persons.
(3) Convicted persons may participate, by free consent, in services or religious meetings organised in prison, receive visits by representatives of that denomination and obtain and hold religious publications as well as religious items.

Government Decision No. 157/2016, which approves the rules of implementation of Law No. 254/2013, contains more numerous and more detailed directives concerning the practice of religion and religious assistance in prison:

Article 124: Freedom of conscience, of opinion and of religion

(1) The National Administration of Penitentiaries, through its subordinate units, allows the access of representatives of religions and religious associations recognised by the law in the penitentiary environment, in order to meet the need for religious assistance among detainees, under Article 58 of the law, based on the written approval of the director of the penitentiary.
(2) The director of the penitentiary may prohibit access of representatives of religions or religious associations recognised by law for a maximum period of 6 months under the conditions stipulated in Article 141.
(3) Inmates may declare, by their free consent, a confession or religious affiliation upon entering the detention facility and subsequently during the carrying out of punishment.
(4) The change of the religious affiliation during the period of detention shall be revealed by a statement on own responsibility and by the confirmation act of belonging to that religion.
(5) Representatives of religions or religious associations having access to the penitentiary may distribute to detainees publications and religious objects which can be kept in a reasonable number. Reasonable is determined by the number and size of publications, books and religious objects in the possession of a detainee, without affecting the shared living space of other detainees.
(6) Prisoners participating in religious or moral-religious activities may request confidential meetings with representatives of religions or religious associations recognised by law, under conditions established by the administration of the penitentiary.
(7) Prisoners shall not be compelled to practise any religion or to adopt any faith, to participate in religious meetings or reunions, or to accept visits from a representative of a particular religion or of a religious faith.
(8) Where a change of religion is concerned, detainees shall be allowed to participate in the meetings of that religion or faith, with the agreement of their representatives and taking into account the specific security measures of the facility, detainees' daily schedule and the number

of participating inmates. Prisoners are informed that changing religion is a major decision that can affect their relationship with family members or others.

Article 201: Religious assistance

(1) Detainees have the right to religious assistance under conditions established by the regulation on religious assistance in places of detention approved by order of the Minister of Justice.
(2) Representatives of religious organisations, associations and denominations may carry out religious services and activities and visit detainees without affecting the activities of the penitentiary with the approval of the director of the place of detention.
(3) The provisions of Article 124 shall apply accordingly.

Moreover, discrimination of any kind, including religious discrimination, is banned (Article 6 of Law No. 254/2013); places for practising religion can be arranged in prison (Article 232 of Decision No. 157/2016); contact between inmates and 'national, international, governmental or non-governmental organisations and individuals who contribute or support … religious assistance' (Article 289 of Decision No. 157/2016) is encouraged.

Since 2006, religious assistance in prison has been the subject of an independent law. The Regulation Concerning Religious Assistance in Prison, introduced by Order of the Minister of Justice No. 610/C/2006, established a set of rules concerning the access of inmates to religious assistance. It states that religious assistance is guaranteed but not compulsory, inmates are not required to declare their religion at the moment of incarceration or at any time during the period of their detention. It guarantees the access of recognised denominations in prison and forbids prison administrative personnel from interfering in religious programmes proposed to inmates by the recognised denominations. This regulation underwent minor changes in 2013 (Order No. 1072/C/2013).

The most recent document governing religious assistance in prisons to come into force is the Regulation on the Religious Assistance of Persons Deprived of Liberty in the Custody of the National Administration of Penitentiaries of 10 November 2016, approved by Order No. 4000/C/2016. The innovations introduced by this law over previous ones are the right of detainees to request meals prepared according to the prescriptions of the religions or religious associations to which they belong; the possibility for prisoners to receive food in detention, according to their religious beliefs, from the religious denominations or religious associations to which they belong; religions or religious associations recognised by law can provide religious assistance in prison through volunteers and missionaries; and physical or legal persons can make donations to the administration of places of detention to support moral-religious activities.

20.3.2.3   Religion in Prison: Statistical Perspective

Currently, the penitentiary system in Romania, composed of 45 penitentiary facilities, includes 9 churches – distinct buildings all with interior and exterior characteristics of a church – and 34 chapels inside prisons. They all belong to the Romanian Orthodox Church but can be used by other denominations with the consent of the Orthodox authorities. There are also two multi-confessional spaces.

The Romanian penitentiary system employs 37 Orthodox chaplains. To these can be added several dozen collaborating priests, who are members of all denominations. All penitentiary priests are guided and represented by a coordinator priest who is appointed by the Romanian Orthodox Church.

Prisoners are not obliged to declare their confession when they are imprisoned, so there are no official statistics on inmate confessions. Some researchers have come up with several statistics concerning the confessional breakdown of inmates. In 1893, 35,012 Orthodox, 3291 Jews, 1316 Catholics and 630 Muslims were being held in penitentiaries (Merei 2015). Over a century later, in 1998, the distribution by confession of inmates was more diversified and directly proportional to the religious distribution in Romanian society as a whole (INS 2002): 45,578 Orthodox, 2139 Roman Catholics, 1627 atheists, 1069 reformed, 435 Greek-Catholics, 432 Muslims, 357 Pentecostals, 118 Baptists, 101 Adventists, 10 Buddhists and 181 from other religions (Chiș 2003).

20.4 Status of Prison Chaplains

Priests have been a constant presence in Romanian penitentiaries, regardless of the time period. Chaplain as a profession emerged in the nineteenth century, but it took on a certain importance right after the fall of communism.

Nowadays, Law No. 195/2000 regarding the establishment and organisation of military clergy regulates the status of prison priests or prison chaplains. Pursuant to Article 4 of this law, all priests employed by the National Administration of Penitentiaries are considered military and their main activity is to provide religious assistance, 'in a patriotic spirit', to military and civilian personnel of the prisons in which they operate. They assure religious assistance to inmates based on the other laws governing religious assistance to inmates.

> Article 9 (1) of Law No. 195/2000: 'The recruitment of military priests is made … among the consecrated or ordained personnel only from among those having Romanian citizenship, recommended by a legally constituted religion, licensed in Pastoral Theology and having at least two years of experience in church activity.'

The foregoing article sets forth that, like any other cleric working in a public institution, the penitentiary priest is subject to two-man management or *res mixta* (Tăvală 2016). Canonically, the penitentiary priest is permanently linked to the religious authority which granted him permission to apply for his position. Administratively, he serves entirely under the rules and regulations of the institution which employs and pays him, the salary of the penitentiary clergy being paid completely by the prisons in which they perform the function of chaplain. In addition, the status of military cleric confers upon penitentiary priests all privileges enjoyed by regular soldiers, for example, a military grade and pay and retirement benefits. By virtue of this status, a penitentiary priest can also serve in prison management, which some have done. He can be a member of commissions that decide on conditional releases, and he can draw up reports according to which the conditions of detention of an inmate can be improved or worsened. Incidentally, even an ordinary priest can to a certain extent influence the decision of a court regarding the severity of punishment imposed on a judged person: isolated cases of well-known people who have avoided imprisonment on the basis of *certificates of goodwill and good Christian behavior* released by priests have been reported in the press.

Although it may seem that the current status of penitentiary priests is similar to that of the Middle Ages, the situation on the ground is very different. In addition to service duties, penitentiary priests must cope with the pressures and demands, in most cases illegal, coming from inmates and from their superiors. Most importantly, they must cope with their conscience. Unfortunately, thus far, there is no scientific work that deals with the status and role of clerics in penitentiaries from a sociological perspective, such details being only sporadically reported in the press.

Penitentiary priests are evaluated annually and regularly attend training sessions and symposiums organised by the National Administration of Penitentiaries in cooperation with recognised religious groups and non-governmental organisations (NGOs). The chaplain coordinator participates annually in international meetings with his counterparts from other countries, the last one having taken place in Strasbourg, France, in June 2016.

20.5   Efficacy of Religious Care in Prison

Religion is a very important component of the carceral identity of detainees. However, the relation of detainees to religion differs from therapy or an opportunity for social and moral rehabilitation of oneself or a strategy for making life easier in prison (Sarg and Lamine 2011) or a macro-level experience (Clear et al. 2000).

These issues have never been researched in connection with Romanian prisons. Some researchers tend to describe the relation of detainees to religion more as a means of venting bitterness (Pocotila 2014). Some relate the tendency of detainees to switch from their Orthodox confession to another religion to the advantages that can be gained from such a switch: for instance, non-Orthodox detainees are taken out of the prison once a month for religious service, which does not happen for Orthodox detainees since most prisons have an Orthodox chapel (Hohotă 2015). Changing religion is as simple as making a statement:

> Article 4 (3) of the Regulation of 10 November 2016: 'The change of confession or religious affiliation during the period of detention is revealed by a statement on own responsibility and by the act of confirming membership in the religion.'

Some inmates have made such declarations in newspapers or on TV shows, depending on their conviction, that religion helped them morally during their period of incarceration. In the absence of thorough sociological research, the question of the efficacy of religious assistance in prison remains unanswered.

20.6 Regulations Concerning Religious Practices

The first regulation permitting prisoners to use religious books dates back to 1862 (Merei 2015). Today, the possession and use of books and religious objects by detainees are permitted by Article 58 (3) of Law No. 254/213. The number and nature of these books and objects are specified by the internal regulations of each prison.

The same internal regulations dictate the timetable for religious services and pastoral visits. For Orthodox detainees, religious services are scheduled according to Orthodox calendar holidays. The fact that Orthodox chaplains are permanent employees of prisons means that Orthodox detainees, but not only them, have access to religious assistance almost every day. For detainees of other confessions, scheduled pastoral visits from a representative of a recognised religion or religious association are possible upon written request. The approval of access to a place of detention for representatives of religious denominations and associations recognised by law is given in writing by the director of the prison. Directors also have the right to forbid, by reasoned decision, access to religious representatives for a maximum of 6 months. The general rules on access of representatives of religious cults to prisons are contained in Article 2 of the Regulation of 10 November 2016.

Regarding nourishment, according to the regulations on force regarding dietary standards in prison, the daily menu in Romanian prisons includes various meals suitable for vegetarian diets and for inmates whose religion requires a special menu. Article 50 (1) of Law No. 254 of 19 July 2013, on the execution of sentences and detention measures ordered by judicial bodies during criminal proceedings, states that

'the administration of each penitentiary shall ensure appropriate conditions for preparing, distributing and serving food according to the standards of food hygiene, depending on the age, state of health, nature of work performed, *respecting the religious beliefs assumed by the condemned person by a statement on own responsibility*'.

Order No. 2713/C/2001, which contains guidelines on the application of food standards in times of peace for the staff of the Ministry of Justice General Directorate of Penitentiaries, provides that the provision of meals to individuals in detention who identify as belonging to a certain religion can be adequately ensured, replacing, as far as possible, food products not accepted by their group with others that are permitted. These inmates are fed according to Food Norm No. 17. In compliance with norm, pork products can be replaced by beef, lamb or poultry (Stanciu and Mihăilescu 2016).

20.7 Religious Discrimination, Proselytism and Radicalisation in Romanian Prisons

Religious discrimination in prison is legally forbidden pursuant to Article 6 of Law No. 254/2013. Proselytism and radicalisation, although not subjects of precise legal provisions, are condemned and discouraged both inside and outside of prison.

Representatives of the majority religion and those of minority religions have always levelled accusations of discrimination and proselytism at each other, especially in the early years after the fall of communism.

Until 1997, when the presence of Orthodox priests in prisons began to increase, those accused of proselytism were certain Evangelical and non-Trinitarian denominations – Adventists, Pentecostals, Mormons and Jehovah's Witnesses – which, on the background of international support, have visited prisons very often to distribute religious materials and attract followers (Bruno 2006b). One of the reports concerning religious life in prison has the following statement:

> Helsinki Watch Report 1992, p. 25: 'One of the changes in prison life during the last two years has been permission to hold regular religious services. Many of the prison directors were proud that various foreign religious organisations had been to their prisons and most directors agreed that religious services were a positive event in prison life. Orthodox and Catholic as well as a host of Evangelical religious services appear to be conducted periodically. Helsinki Watch also observed reading materials from Evangelical denominations in the cells of several prisoners.'

However, the Orthodox Church could also be involved in such practices. A 2004 report published by APADOR-CH[7] denounces the monopoly of the Romanian Orthodox Church in prisons. According to this report, an earlier order of the coordinator chaplain, still in force in 2004, forbids detainees from switching from one religion to another while incarcerated, arguing that they are in a state of stress and, therefore, cannot judge clearly. Secondly, the organisation which drafted this report considered unacceptable the presence of Orthodox priests in the prison at meetings of detainees with representatives of other denominations. Moreover, APADOR-CH disagrees with some duties of the Orthodox priests since these responsibilities may discriminately affect detainees of other denominations (APADOR-CH 2004). Orthodox priests have the right, sometimes even the obligation, depending on their position in the prison leadership hierarchy, to be members of conditional release committees. They can also influence, by giving a positive or negative opinion, the appointment of room leaders selected from among detainees.

As for Islamic radicalisation, the only reference to such behaviour in Romanian prisons is a recent statement of the director of the National Administration of Penitentiaries (Mediafax 2017):

> 'Radicalisation is a phenomenon that is not visible today in the penitentiary system. We have prisoners of Islamic religion with tendencies towards radicalisation, but this is not a phenomenon for the time being. We are only preparing ourselves, nationally and internationally, to prevent such events and not to let them develop in the Romanian penitentiary system. There are protocols of collaboration with institutions with competence in this area, but this package of measures is not yet necessary because this phenomenon does not exist in the penitentiary system. We are only preparing to prevent it.'

---

[7] Asociaţia pentru Apărarea Drepturilor Omului în România-Comitetul Helsinki – Association for the Defense of Human Rights in Romania - Helsinki Committee, http://www.apador.org/.

20.8 Monitoring Religious Assistance in Prison

Religion in Romanian prisons is not independently monitored. However, information about religious life in prison, other than that provided by Romanian authorities, can be found in reports and surveys covering the entire penitentiary system drawn up by foreign and domestic organisations.

One of the most active NGOs when it comes to monitoring prisons is APADOR_CH. Other sources of continuously updated information on the prison system in Romania are the institutions of the Council of Europe aimed at defending human rights, the European Institute for Crime Prevention and Control (HEUNI), for example (Walsley 1995). A critical view of the state of religion in prisons can also be found in the US Department of State annual report on religious freedom. The media also reports violations of human rights when necessary, but its approach is only rarely taken into account by authorities.

This picture will be completed, of course, by complaints of inmates at the ECHR regarding the violation of their religious rights by the Romanian government. To date, Romania has been accused seven times at the ECHR, and found guilty once, of violating Article 9 (thought, conscience and religion) of the Convention:

1. *EZE v. ROMANIA*, No. 80,529/13, 21 June 2016 – Food that is incompatible with the prescriptions of Islam; the Court decided that there is no need to examine the admissibility or the merits of the complaint under Article 9 of the Convention.
2. *SANATKAR v. ROMANIA*, No. 74,721/12, 16 July 2016 – Insufficient space to deploy a prayer mat because of overcrowding; the Court decided that there was a violation of Article 3 of the Convention as regards conditions of detention in prison, but with no implications regarding freedom of religion.
3. *VARTIC v. ROMANIA*, No. 14,150/08, 17 December 2013 – The applicant complained that authorities' refusal to provide him with a vegetarian diet imposed by Buddhist rules violated his freedom to manifest his religion as provided by Article 9 of the Convention; the Court decided that Article 9 of the Convention was violated since the national authorities did not provide the complainant with a vegetarian diet in accordance with the requirements of the Buddhist religion as practised by him.
4. *AUSTRIANU v. ROMANIA*, No. 16,117/02, 12 May 2013 – Confiscation of cassette players used by prisoners to listen to religious tapes; the Court decided that there had been no interference with freedom of religion. The Court decided instead that Article 3 of the Convention was violated.
5. *LEONTIUC v. ROMANIA*, No. 44,302/10, 4 December 2012 – The detainee contests the mention, over the course of the trials, of his religious affiliation; the Court found this accusation unfounded.
6. *IORGOIU v. ROMANIA*, No. 1831/02, 17 July 2012 – Impossibility of practising Orthodox worship in prison, the exercise of worship being subject to the *goodwill* of the prison administration. The Court found this accusation unfounded.

7. *ALI v. ROMANIA*, No. 20,307/02, 9 November 2010 – Closing the prayer room. The Court considered this complaint admissible but that there was no need to examine it, given the context and the jurisprudence.

20.9   Conclusion

After this short description of the practice of religion in the Romanian penitentiary system, some subjects still deserve further attention.

At first glance, one might say that the Romanian Orthodox Church has a monopoly on religious assistance in prison because Orthodox priests are the only chaplains employed by the penitentiary system and because they occupy a gendarmerie-like function. In some respects, this may be true, and improvements are needed, but the historical tradition that links the two institutions and the percentage of Orthodox inmates in Romanian prisons are used to justify the majority presence in prisons of Orthodox clergy. Moreover, this model is used by other European countries. Catholicism in Italy (Alicino 2016) and in Spain (Martínez-Ariño et al. 2015; Griera and Martínez-Ariño 2017) and Catholic and Protestant denominations in Germany (Eick-Wildgans 1993; Jahn 2015) enjoy a privileged status based on agreements concluded with the government, which guarantees them the right to a presence in penitentiary institutions. Their ministers hold full-time or part-time positions and are integrated into the organizational chart along with the rest of the prison staff.

Secondly, there is still not enough literature based on sociological surveys and empirical data regarding religious assistance in prisons. Religious freedom is undoubtedly respected, and the Romanian government strives to align its legislation on religious assistance with standards established in other European countries. However, religious assistance remains only at the level of a right protected by the constitution and is not the subject of policies, facilitated by state in collaboration with the recognised religions, aimed at reintegrating the detainees into society and diminishing the rate of recidivism. At this point, religious assistance is valued only in confessional terms, directed only at the spiritual life of inmates and only for the period of their incarceration, with no implications for their future lives as free persons. Nevertheless, the experience of other societies demonstrates the exact reverse of this situation. In the USA or Great Britain, for example, where prisoner re-entry constitutes the central criminal justice challenge, 'the potential of religion as a mechanism of social control and tool to influence behavior in areas of crime policy and offender rehabilitation has received an increasing amount of public and political attention' (Sumter 2006). In these countries, authorities have collaborated with religious institutions to create an institutional support network through which those recently released from prison might more easily find jobs, living arrangements and emotional counselling (McRoberts 2002; Walters-Sleyon 2013).

The main problem of modern penitentiary systems in Romania is the same as in other countries – overcrowded prisons and record numbers of recidivist prisoners. The Romanian penitentiary system has been in crisis for several years because of overpopulation, and the unofficial data estimates range between 45% and 75% (Dâmboeanu 2008, 2011). In this context, well-thought-out and scientifically documented religious policies of reintegration into society could be a viable solution, implemented at little cost. There is sufficient empirical evidence indicating that religious beliefs lead to a reduction in crime and recidivism among prisoners (Hewitt 2006; Mears et al. 2006; Dodson et al. 2011; Adamczyk et al. 2017). These findings suggest that faith is a major factor in reducing crime problems. That is where religious programme research may hold a valuable key to developing criminal justice system solutions.

Bibliography

Adamczyk, A., Freilich, J. D., & Kim, C. (2017). Religion and crime: A systematic review and assessment of next steps. *Sociology of religion: A quarterly review, 00*, 01–34. https://doi.org/10.1093/socrel/srx012.

Alicino, F. (2016). *Prison and religion in Italy. The Italian constitutional order tested by a new "Religious Geography".* http://www.dirritticomparati.it/prison-and-religion-in-italy-the-italian-constitutional-order-tested-by-a-new-religious-geography/. Accessed 15 Aug 2017.

ANP [National Administration of Penitentiaries]. (2017). *Accommodation capacity on 21.03.2017.* http://anp.gov.ro/documents/10180/12939320/Capacitatea+de+cazare+a+unit%C4%83%C5%A3ilor+si+efectivele+acestora+la+data+de+21.03.2017.xlsx/0d205c53-321c-4d39-aed8-5f9337ecb8c0. Accessed 4 Apr 2017.

APADOR-CH. (2004). *Sistemul penitenciar în România 1995–2004 [The Penitentiary System in Romania 1995–2004].* http://www.apador.org/publicatii/10%20ani_ro-2005.pdf. Accessed 4 Apr 2017.

Bălan, I. (2000). *Regimul Concentraționar din România. 1945–1964 [Concentrationary regime in Romania. 1945–1964].* București: Fudanția Academică Civică.

Becci, I., & Roy, O. (2015). *Religious diversity in European prisons.* Cham: Springer.

Beckford, J. A. (2013). Religious diversity in prisons: Chaplaincy and contention. *Studies in Religion/Sciences Religieuses, 42*(2), 190–205. https://doi.org/10.1177/0008429813479293.

Beckford, J. A., & Gilliat, S. (1998). *Religion in prison: Equal rites in multi-faith society.* Cambridge: Cambridge University Press.

Berechet, Ș. (1926). *Judecata la români până în secolul al XVIII-lea [Judgment in romanians' history until XVIIIth century].* Chișinău: Tipografia eparhială "Cartea românească".

Bruno, Ș. (2006a). Istoria și reforma închisorilor românești [History and Romanian Prison Reform]. *Revista română de sociologie XVII, 5–6,* 485–512.

Bruno, Ș. (2006b). *Mediul penitenciar românesc Cultură și civilizație carcerală [Romanian penitentiary environment Carceral culture and civilisation].* București: Institutul European.

Cantemir, D. (2007). *Descriptio Moldaviae – Descrierea stării de odinioară și de astăzi a Moldovei [Descriptio Moldaviae – Description of the state of yesterday and today of Moldavia].* București: Institutul Cultural Român. (First edited in 1716).

Chiș, I. (2003). *Istoria penitenciarelor – ieri și azi [Prison history – yesterday and today].* Iași: A.N.I.

Ciuceanu, R. (2001). *Regimul penitenciar din România. 1940–1962 [The penitentiary system in Romania. 1940–1962].* București, Editura Institutului Național pentru Studiul Totalitarismului.

Clear, T. R., Hardyman, P. L., Stout, B., Lucken, K., & Dammer, H. R. (2000). The value of religion in prison an inmate perspective. *Journal of Contemporary Criminal Justice, 16*(1), 53–74. https://doi.org/10.1177/1043986200016001004.

Conovici, I., & Secal, A. (2012). *Organizaţii cu profil religios angajate în economia socială a României 2012 Raport preliminar [Religious organisations engaged in the social economy of Romania 2012 Preliminary report]*. http://www.ies.org.ro/library/files/raport-preliminar-religioase-februarie-completare2note.pdf. Accessed 10 Apr 2017.

Constantiniu, F. (2016). *O istorie sinceră a poporului român [A sincere history of the Romanian people]*. Bucureşti: Univers Enciclopedic Gold.

Costescu, C. C. (1916). *Colecţiune de Legi...începând dela 1986 şi aflate în vigoare astăzi privitoare la Biserică. [Collection of Laws regarding church from 1866 until today]*. Cartea Românească: Bucureşti.

Crépeau, F., & Sheppard, C. (2013). *Human Rights and diverse societies: Challenges and possibilities*. Newcastle upon Tyne: Cambridge Scholars Publishing.

Dâmboeanu, C. (2008). Cercetarea fenomenului de recidivă din perspectiva 'Carierei infracţionale' [Investigation of the relapse phenomenon from the perspective of the 'Criminal career']. *Revista Română de Sociologie, 5–6*, 395–404.

Dâmboeanu, C. (2011). Fenomenul recidiviei în România [The phenomenon of relapse in Romania]. *Calitatea Vieţii, 3*, 295–312.

Dammer, H. R. (2002). Religion in corrections. *The Encyclopedia of Crime and Punishment, 3*, 1375.

Dianu, G. I. (1901). *Istoria închisorilor din România. Studiu comparativ. Legi şi obiceiuri [History of prisons in Romania. Comparative study. Laws and customs]*. Tipografia Curţii Regale: Bucureşti.

Dinulescu, C. (2006). Reflecţii istoriografice asupra izvoarelor dreptului vechi românesc [Historiographical reflections on old Romanian law sources]. *Revista de ştiinţe juridice*, 188–193.

Dodson, K. D., Cabage, L. N., & Klenowski, P. M. (2011). An evidence-based assessment of faith-based programs: Do faith-based programs "work" to reduce recidivism? *Journal of Offender Rehabilitation, 50*(6), 367–383. https://doi.org/10.1080/10509674.2011.582932.

Eick-Wildgans, S. (1993). *Anstaltseelsorge. Möglichkeiten und Grenzen des Zusammenwirkens von Staat und Kirche im Strafvollzug*. Berlin: Druncker & Humboldt.

Filitti, I. C. (1934). Vechiul drept penal românesc [Old Romanian penal law]. *Revista de drept penal şi ştiinţă penitenciară*.

Filitti, I. C. (1936). Penitenciarele române de la 1828 la 1834. Ocupaţia rusească şi Regulamentul Organic [Romanian prisons from 1828 to 1834. Russian occupation and the Organic Regulations]. *Revista de Drept Penal şi Ştiinţă Penitenciară*.

French Justice Ministry. (2007). http://www.juriscope.org/uploads/etudes/Droit%20penal_Pratiques%20cultuelles%20en%20milieu%20carceral_2007_Synthese.pdf. Accessed 4 Apr 2017.

Frunză, V. (1990). *Istoria stalinismului în România (The history of Stalinism in Romania)*. Bucureşti: Editura Roza Vânturilor.

Gorescu, O. (1930). *Văcăreştii Mânăstire. Văcăreştii Penitenciar [Văcăreştii Monastery. Văcăreştii Prison]*. Bucureşti.

Griera, M., & Martínez-Ariño, J. (2017). The accommodation of religious diversity in prisons and hospitals in Spain. In F. C. Gonzalez & G. D'Amato (Eds.), *Multireligious society. Dealing with religious diversity in theory and practice* (pp. 251–266). New York: Routledge.

Helsinki Watch Report. (1992). *Prison conditions in Romania*. https://www.hrw.org/sites/default/files/reports/ROMANIA926.PDF. Accessed 9 Apr 2017.

Hewitt, J. D. (2006). Having faith in faith-based prison programs. *Criminology and Public Policy, 5*(3), 551–558.

Hohotă, V. G. (2015). *La construction des identités carcérales dans le discours des prisonniers. Approche comparée français et roumain — Thèse de doctorat*. Bourgogne: Université de Bourgogne.

IICCMER (Institutul de Investigare a Crimelor Comunismului şi Memoria Exilului Românesc). (2016). *Sistemul Penitenciar din România: 1945–1989 [Penitentiary system in Romania: 1945–1989]*. http://www.iiccr.ro/pdf/ro/investigatii_speciale/sistemul_penitenciar_1945_1989.pdf. Accessed 6 Apr 2017.

INS (Institutul National de Statistică [National Institute of Statistics]). (2002). *Populaţia după etnie şi religie – medii şi judeţe [Population by ethnicity and religion – medium and counties]*. http://www.insse.ro/cms/files/RPL2002INS/vol4/tabele/t5.pdf. Accessed 31 Aug 2017.

INS. (2013). What does the 2011 Census tell us about Religion? http://www.insse.ro/cms/files/publicatii/pliante%20statistice/11_Pliant%20religii%20eng.pdf. Accessed 5 Sept 2017.

Iorga, N. (1930). *Anciens documents de droit roumain* (Vol. I. II). Bucureşti: Imprimeria 'Datina Romanească'.

Jahn, S. J. (2015). Institutional logic and legal practice: Modes of regulation of religious organizations in German prisons. In I. Becci & O. Roy (Eds.), *Religious diversity in European prisons: Challenges and implications for rehabilitation* (pp. 81–100). Cham: Springer.

Jones, P. (2001). Human rights and diverse cultures: Continuity or discontinuity? In S. Caney (Ed.), *Human rights and global diversity* (pp. 27–50). Abingdon: Routledge.

Koenig, M., & de Guchteneire, P. (2007). *Democracy and human rights in multicultural societies*. Hampshire/Burlington: UNESCO/Ashgate.

Lăţescu, G.-B. (1995). Gulagul românesc în cifre [Romanian gulag in numbers]. In R. Rusan (Ed.), *Memoria ca formă de justiţie [Memory as a form of justice]* (pp. 14–17). Bucureşti: Fundaţia Academia Civică.

Marinescu, O.-D. (2011). *Mănăstirea Văcăreşti din Bucureşti de la origini pînă în prezent [Monastery Văcăreşti from Bucharest from its origins to present days]*. Bucureşti: Editura Basilica.

Martínez-Ariño, J., García-Romeral, G., Ubasart-González, G., & Griera, M. (2015). Demonopolisation and dislocation: (re-) negotiating the place and role of religion in Spanish prisons. *Social Compass, 62*(1), 3–21. https://doi.org/10.1177/0037768614560875.

McRoberts, O. M. (2002). Religion, reform, community: Examining the idea of Church-based prisoner reentry. *Urban Institute*. 20. http://webarchive.urban.org/UploadedPDF/410802_Religion.pdf. Accessed 5 Aug 2017.

Mears, D. P., Roman, C. G., Wolf, A., & Buck, J. (2006). Faith-based efforts to improve prisoner reentry: Assessing the logic and evidence. *Journal of Criminal Justice, 34*(4), 351–367. https://doi.org/10.1016/j.jcrimjus.2006.05.002.

Merei, L. E. (2015). *Regimul juridic al sistemului penitenciar în România în a doua jumătate a secolului al XIX-lea, începutul secolului al XX-lea [Legal status of prison system in Romania in the second half of XIXth and early XXth century]*. Phd thesis. Chişinău: Academy of Sciences of Moldova.

Mulcahy, E., Merrington, S., & Bell, P. (2013). The radicalisation of prison inmates: Exploring recruitment, religion and prisoner vulnerability. *Journal of Human Security, 9*, 4–14. https://doi.org/10.12924/johs2013.09010004.

Patriciu, V. (2014). La presence des cultes dans les institutions publiques dans la société roumaine entre 1989 et 2006. *Teologia, 2*, 25–37.

Pocotila, A. (2014). Preot de penitenciar: 'Aici, sufletul ţi se destramă, bucată cu bucată' [Penitentiary priest: 'Here, your soul breaks apart, piece by piece']. *România Liberă*, April 18.

Puiu, A. (2016). Hotărârea-pilot e inevitabilă [Pilot-decision is inevitable]. https://www.luju.ro/international/cedo/hotararea-pilot-e-inevitabila-romania-inghesuie-mai-multi-detinuti-pe-metru-patrat-decat-italia-in-momentul-declansarii-procedurii-pilot-in-cauza-torreggiani-bul-garia-si-ungaria-au-incasat-inca-de-anul-trecut-hotarar. Accessed 4 Apr 2017.

Sarg, R., & Lamine, A.-S. (2011). La religion en prison Norme structurante, réhabilitation de soi, stratégie de résistance. *Archives de sciences sociales des religions*, (153), 85–104.

Şerban, A. (2008). Considerations about the new law on the execution of punishments and measures ordered by the court during the trial no. 275/2006. *Curierul judiciar, 6*, 62.

Spânu, A. (2010). Aşezământul Mislea de la mănăstire la închisoare. Un dublu sens al cuvântului "fortificat" [Establishment Mislea from monastery to prison. A double meaning of the word 'fortified']. In L.-V. Lefter, A. Ichim, & S. Iftimi (Eds.), *Monumentul XII Lucrările Simpozionului Naţional Monumentul – Tradiţie şi viitor Ediţia a XII-a, Iaşi-Chişinău, 2010* (Vol. II, pp. 221–238). Iaşi: Muzeul Unirii.

Stanciu, M., & Mihăilescu, A. (2016). Alimnetația în penitenciare [Nourishment in prisons]. *Calitatea Vieții, 1*, 20–41.

Sucilă-Pahoni, C. (2012). O privire critică asupra Legii Penitenciarelor de la 1 februarie 1874 [A critical look over the prisons law from 1874]. *Crisia, 42*, 99–109.

Sumter, M. (2006). Faith-based programs. *Criminology and Public Policy, 5*(3), 523–528.

Surmei, C. (2017). Bilanț ANP: Avem deținuți cu tendințe spre radicalizare, dar nu este un fenomen [ANP Balance Sheet: We have detainees with tendencies towards radicalisation, but it is not a phenomenon]. *Mediafax* 22 February 2017. http://www.mediafax.ro/stirile-zilei/bilant-anp-avem-detinuti-cu-tendinte-spre-radicalizare-dar-nu-este-un-fenomen-16170508. Accessed 6 Apr 2017.

Tăvală, E. (2016). Law and religion in the workplace: Romanian report. In M. R. Blanco (Ed.), *Law and religion in the workplace* (pp. 327–337). Granada: Editorial Comares.

Tismăneanu, V. (2006). *Comisia Prezidențială pentru analiza dictaturii comuniste din România. Raport final [Presidential Commission for the Study of the Communist Dictatorship in Romania. Final Report].* http://old.presidency.ro/static/rapoarte/Raport_final_CPADCR.pdf. Accessed 4 Apr 2017.

Walsley, R. (1995). *HEUNI paper No. 4. Developments in the prison systems of Central and Eastern Europe*. Helsinki: European Institute for Crime Prevention and Control, affiliated with the UN.

Walters-Sleyon, G. (2013). Studies on religion and recidivism: Focus on Roxbury, Dorchester, and Mattapan. *Trotter Review, 21*(1), 22–48.

WPB (World Prison Brief). (2016). http://www.prisonstudies.org/country/romania. Accessed 5 Apr 2017.

Chapter 21
Spain: Religion in Prisons – Socio-Legal Perspectives

Julia Martínez-Ariño

Abstract This chapter offers an overview of the situation of religion and religious diversity in Spanish prisons from a legal and a sociological perspective. After a brief introduction to the recent history of religion in the penitentiary system in Spain that focuses mostly on the second half of the twentieth century, the chapter presents the current situation after the democratisation of the country in the last quarter of the twentieth century. An overview is provided of the main developments that have led to a pluralistic legal framework and a situation of institutionalised organisational pluralism in which the traces of the Catholic past are still very present and visible. Qualitative and ethnographic data provide information about the actual situation, concerning concrete issues such as the organisation of the chaplaincy and the accreditation of chaplains, the arrangement of spaces and the presence of symbols, the organisation of religious celebrations and rites, and other related activities. The chapter draws on rich empirical data collected for the GEDIVER-IN project (The "GEDIVER-IN: The management of religious diversity in hospitals and prisons in Spain" project was funded by the National Research Programme of the Spanish Ministry of Economy and Competitiveness and co-directed by Joan Estruch and Mar Griera).

21.1 Introduction

Research on religion in prison in the Spanish context is scarce and has mostly focused on the legal aspects regulating prison chaplaincy (Moreno Antón 1994; Rodríguez Blanco 2009). This limitation was one of the main reasons for setting up the research project[1] this chapter is based on. The main aim was to offer an in-depth

---

[1] The GEDIVER-IN project was directed by Joan Estruch and Mar Griera. The main researchers were Anna Clot, María Forteza, Gloria García-Romeral and Julia Martínez-Ariño.

J. Martínez-Ariño (✉)
Faculty of Theology and Religious Studies, University of Groningen,
Groningen, The Netherlands
e-mail: j.martinez.arino@rug.nl

© Springer Nature Switzerland AG 2020
J. Martínez-Ariño, A.-L. Zwilling (eds.), *Religion and Prison: An Overview of Contemporary Europe*, Boundaries of Religious Freedom: Regulating Religion in Diverse Societies 7, https://doi.org/10.1007/978-3-030-36834-0_21

sociological perspective on the presence and regulation of religion in prison (and hospitals), based on empirical research. This enabled capturing not only the formal aspects and regulations but, more importantly, the negotiations around religion and religious diversity in the everyday life of institutions (Griera et al. 2015).

Public institutions are regulated by legal and administrative texts, but their functioning depends on other elements. Next to formal rules, norms and decisions, negotiations between actors at different levels also shape the functioning of such organisations. In this chapter, a symbolic interactionist perspective is adopted that understands organisations as 'negotiated orders' (Watson 2015) rather than as stable formal structures and rules. From this perspective, 'actors negotiate and elaborate local and situated agreements to strategically implement new organizational arrangements in institutional contexts' (Grenier 2011: 6). Negotiated orders are patterns of activities and meanings that emerge from regular interactions of individuals and groups in organisations. This approach rejects seeing organisations as operating under two completely distinct logics: formal and informal procedures. Rather, the focus is on how actors within these organisations negotiate, break, stretch or ignore the existing rules (Watson 2015). The approach is interested in understanding how the local 'micropolitics of the negotiated order' (Fine 1984: 241) interact with the formal structures and norms of the organisation, to generate new and fluid orders that need to be constantly worked (Strauss 1978). From this perspective, it is possible to understand how negotiations between different actors in a certain legal and institutional framework can also directly or indirectly shape the ways in which religious diversity is addressed in particular contexts. This perspective is better equipped to capture small daily – but relevant – moments, gestures, interactions, negotiations and feelings, as well as power relations and unequal capacities to shape the life of institutions. This is important because all these elements frame the aspirations and opportunities of religious minorities in public institutions. Thus, this chapter examines how religion in prison is governed and accommodated as the result of the implementation of formal legal and regulatory frameworks and procedures but also as the result of fluid negotiations between actors directly in the field that interact within the context of a particular organisational culture (Fine 1984).

As is the case for many other countries in this volume, the presence and legal and institutional regulation of religion in Spanish prisons have changed significantly over the last four decades. The transition to democracy, on the one hand, and the 2004 terrorist attacks in Madrid, on the other, are two turning points in the public and political attention to religion in Spain (Griera et al. 2014), in the particular case of prisons too. This chapter examines these transformations, offering an overview of the current situation in prisons that does not ignore recent historical developments. After a few historical notes on the interaction between religion and the penitentiary during the Franco regime (1939–1975), the chapter continues with a more extensive analysis of the current context. This later section offers a brief revision of the main legal texts that regulate religion in prison and an in-depth account of the institutional arrangements actually at work in Spanish penitentiaries. This section shows both formal organisational arrangements as well as emerging patterns that result from the interaction between actors and interests.

21.2   Religion in the Spanish Penitentiary System: Some Historical Notes

The relationship between the Spanish state and the Catholic Church during the Franco regime was one of 'organic integration' in which the functions of both institutions were not clearly separated. This organic integration, characteristic of confessional systems, was also the formula under which chaplaincy was run in Spanish public institutions, including prisons. This situation only changed with the disestablishment of the Catholic Church in the 1978 constitution and other legal transformations that occurred at the end of the 1970s and 1980s (see legal developments in the next section), which dissolved the figure of chaplains as civil servants of penitentiary institutions (Moreno Antón 2006), among other things.

The best example of this organic integration is to be found in the 1948 Prison Services Rules, a 230-page document regulating all aspects of prison life during the first years of the Franco dictatorship. In this document, religion is present both as an element of prison life and as a crucial 'actor'. Articles regulated the religious practice and instruction of inmates but also the roles that different religious actors played in prison. For instance, attendance at Catholic mass was mandatory for all prison managers and staff as well as inmates, in the latter case with the only exception of those who had proved that they belonged to a different religion, in which case they were allowed to communicate with a minister of their own religion. Catholic religious instruction at different levels of knowledge was mandatory and constituted a key element considered by the treatment board of each prison as part of the criteria to decide upon each prisoner's situation.

Catholic chaplains were employed by the state as civil servants and were integrated in state structures through the Penitentiary Chaplaincy Corps. In 1970, the law restructuring all penitentiary corps established the number of prison chaplains at 41 civil servants.[2] Catholic chaplains were, together with prison doctors, teachers and managers, part of the prison bodies in charge of observing and classifying prisoners (Lorenzo Rubio 2011). Chaplains also played a crucial role safeguarding 'a moral sense of life in prison' (Gómez Bravo 2008: 30) during this period. This task was accomplished, among other ways, through censorship of cultural products, in particular the books of prison libraries. Thus, Catholic chaplains during this period not only fulfilled religious tasks, such as pastoral care, but also developed secular administrative functions.

Religious authorities had an even more prominent role in this period in the women's penitentiaries. The 1948 Prison Service Rules gave Catholic nuns a prominent role in the functioning of penitentiary institutions. Female Catholic orders managed female prisons, and Catholic nuns played a crucial indoctrination role for the offspring of female Republican political inmates who were not religious (Rubio 2014). Again, here, their roles exceeded the strictly religious functions and expanded over a number of spheres of the everyday life of the prison. Moreover, the 1948

---

[2] https://www.boe.es/buscar/doc.php?id=BOE-A-1970-1455

document explicitly stated that each woman was to have a black headscarf in her wardrobe that she would have to wear to attend religious services. Religion and religious actors impregnated the life of prisons, as is also obvious in pictures from that time.

21.3 Religion in Spanish Prisons After Democratisation: Legal and Institutional Transformations

The situation nowadays differs significantly from that depicted in the previous section. The position of religion in general, and of the Catholic Church in particular, in Spanish society and institutions changed radically with the transition to democracy at the end of the 1970s. The Catholic Church is no longer an established church, and the scope of its influence has declined significantly. At the same time, the prison system has also transformed. Currently, the executive capacity of the penitentiary system in Spain is divided in two, one for the Catalan Autonomous Community and one for the rest of the state territory.[3] The signing of the Statute of Autonomy of Catalonia in 1979 led to the transfer of the penitentiary executive competence from the central state to the Autonomous Community in 1984 (Tamarit Sumalla 2016). The body in charge of the Spanish prison system is the General Secretary of Penitentiary Institutions of the Spanish Ministry of the Interior, which covers a total of 71 regular prisons, 3 units for mothers, and 32 open centres according to the most recent data available.[4] In Catalonia, the Penitentiary Services of the Catalan Justice Department is the body in charge of the prison system, composed of ten closed prisons and four open centres.

As of December 2019, there were 50,129 inmates in the Spanish penitentiary system, 3811 of which were women (7.6% of the total incarcerated population). Out of the total, 12,601 were foreigners (25.1%). In the same month, there were 8388 inmates in the Catalan prison system, of which 562 were women (6.7%). Foreigners from both EU and non-EU countries composed 3869 (46.1%) of the total. While data about nationality do not serve as an indicator of religious affiliation, it shows the diversity of the incarcerated population. The lack of information on the religious affiliation of inmates is the result of a legal ban, also valid for the population as a whole. As opposed to the penitentiary administration of other countries discussed in this volume, the Spanish one does not collect data on inmates' religious belonging. One can only use estimates or the number and diversity of chaplains and other religious actors entering prisons (Table 21.2) as a proxy for religious diversity among prisoners.

---

[3] In this chapter, reference is made to Spanish and Catalan prisons and the Spanish and Catalan systems as two legally differentiated systems. Therefore, when reference is made to Spanish prisons, we refer to all of them, except for those that belong to the Catalan system.

[4] Data of April 2018, according to the website of the Secretaría General de Instituciones Penitenciarias: http://www.institucionpenitenciaria.es/web/portal/centrosPenitenciarios/

The only currently available empirical data on religious affiliation in prison are survey data (*n* = 1638) published a few years ago (Gallego et al. 2010). The results show that religious diversity is present among inmates, with Catholicism being the majority religion. At the time the survey was conducted, 39.1% of the prisoners identified themselves as non-practising Catholics, whereas 23.1% defined themselves as practising Catholics. The distribution among other categories is as follows: 12.2% self-identified as evangelical Christians (Protestants), 5.7% as Muslims, 6.2% as members of other religions and 13.8% as atheists or agnostics. Moreover, according to these data, almost 60% of inmates had been in contact with the pastoral service (Catholic prison chaplaincy), which was very positively valued. While these data are already ancient, they can serve as an indicator of a diversifying population. Moreover, our empirical observations during fieldwork in several Spanish and Catalan penitentiaries attest to an increasing and diversifying scope of religious groups and subgroups offering activities for inmates. But how does this demographic and socio-cultural transformation translate into, or become reflected in, legal and institutional settings that are in place?

21.3.1 A Pluralistic Legal Framework

The legal framework regulating religion in prisons in Spain is composed of three strands of legislation, on top of the general international and European rules, which Spain follows: one related to the regulation of religion in general, another one general penitentiary legislation, and the third one related specifically to religion in the penitentiary system.

First, the democratic transition in Spain introduced significant changes in the relationship between church and state. The 1978 constitution disestablished the Catholic Church and recognised the right to religious freedom, further developed in the 1980 Religious Freedom Act. The Spanish legal system became a pluralistic one, more similar to those of other European countries. Moreover, cooperation agreements were signed between the Spanish state and the Catholic Church (1979 Concordat Agreements), on the one hand, and the national federations of the Islamic, Protestant and Jewish communities in 1992, on the other hand, to further concretise the rights recognised in the Religious Freedom Act, including in public institutions.

Second, general penitentiary legislation also recognises the right to religious freedom in the context of prisons. The 1979 Prison Act, the 1996 Prison Rules of the Spanish penitentiary system, and the 2006 Prison Rules of the Catalan penitentiary system establish the general conditions for the respect of the right to religious freedom. This includes protection against discrimination for religious reasons, the right to receive religious care of the confession requested and to be visited by a religious minister of that tradition, the right not to attend a religious service against one's will (something which was the case during the Franco regime), the right to use a space for religious activities and, as much as possible, institutional respect for the religious, philosophical and personal convictions of inmates when serving food.

Third, the aforementioned transformations were also reflected in the specific legal framework regulating the presence of religion in the penitentiary system. Despite Catalonia's having the administrative competences for the penitentiary system, the legal and regulatory framework at work is the same as in the rest of the Spanish penitentiary system. Only smaller decrees establishing cooperation agreements differ between both penitentiary systems. In what follows, these specific regulations and agreements will be presented briefly, divided into three groups: general regulations concerning religion in prison, agreements concerning one specific religious group, and agreements regarding detention centres for foreigners.

First, there are few general regulations concerning religion in prison, and they were developed mostly after the 2004 Madrid terrorist attacks (Martínez-Ariño et al. 2015), for both the Spanish and Catalan penitentiary systems, mainly because of the fear of radicalisation in prison. The 1/2005 Instruction of the Catalan Department of Justice (further developed in internal documents in 2007 and 2014[5]) and the 710/2006 Royal Decree developing the 1992 Cooperation Agreements with the Jewish, Protestant and Islamic federations for the Spanish penitentiary system (further developed in the 6/2007 internal instruction) regulate the conditions for access to prisons, the accreditation procedure and training for religious personnel and volunteers, the procedures for inmates to request religious care, the spaces for religious activities and the times for their use, the creation of the figure of the coordinator of the chaplaincy in each Catalan prison, the financial conditions for the chaplaincy service, and the content and activities of the service. Members of religious groups without a cooperation agreement with the state can be accredited to access the penitentiary system, provided they belong to a religious group officially registered with the Ministry of Justice.

Second, a much more prolific set of agreements with individual religious groups has developed since the late 1980s until today, following the religious diversification of Spanish society. The first agreements were signed with the Catholic Church in 1987 for Catalan prisons (further updated in 2006, 2008, 2015 and 2019) and in 1993 for the Spanish ones. These agreements establish the conditions for the provision of a Catholic chaplaincy and include funding to cover the personal and material costs of the service. This is the main difference to the agreements signed later on with religious minorities, although some of the latter have recently included a monetary allocation.

In 1995 an agreement between the Catalan Department of Justice and the Catalan Federation of Protestant/Evangelical churches followed, which has been automatically renewed and regularly updated through smaller agreements, the last one dating from 2019. From 2009 onwards, these agreements include a budgetary allocation for the non-religious activities for inmates of the Catalan Evangelical Council. In a similar way, the Ministry of the Interior signed an agreement with the Spanish Federation of Evangelical Organisations of Spain (FEREDE) in July 2015, in this

---

[5] 'Regulació de l'accés als centres penitenciaris de voluntaris i professionals en l'àmbit comunitari' de 20 de març de 2007 i 'Regulació de l'accés als centres penitenciaris dels representants religiosos que compleixen funcions de direcció religiosa catòlica, evangèlica i islàmica de 2014.'

case indicating explicitly that no public funding would be provided. The agreement encourages representatives of different Protestant churches to collaborate in their prison work by establishing a single coordinator and spokesperson as contact with the direction of the centre.

In 2007 in Spain and 2008 in Catalonia, specific agreements were signed with representatives of the Spanish and Catalan Islamic federations regarding the provision of Islamic religious care in penitentiary centres. These agreements are automatically renovated every year, the last update for Catalan prisons being in 2019 and for Spanish penitentiaries in 2017. More recently, Royal Decree 561/2017 was signed approving funding for the provision of Catholic (598,000 euros) and Islamic (9000 euros) chaplaincies in Spanish prisons, demonstrating the existing structural imbalance between religious groups.

In the area of interfaith dialogue, the Catalan Department of Justice signed an agreement with the Permanent Religions Working Group (GTER, its initials in Catalan) in 2007 and 2009 to organise interreligious activities in penitentiaries (2230 euros). Similarly, in 2011, the Catalan Department of Justice and the UNESCO Center for Catalonia (UNESCOCAT) association signed an agreement to offer interreligious activities in penitentiaries through AUDIR – UNESCO Association for Interreligious and Interconvictional Dialogue with a budgetary allocation of 11,967 euros. The activities included in the agreement are the establishment of interreligious groups in various prisons, the organisation of round tables to discuss cultural and religious diversity, and activities in prison libraries.

Finally, although officially not considered an agreement with a religious organisation, the 2011 agreement signed between the Catalan Department of Justice and the World Prem Association for the supply of yoga classes, among other cultural activities for the social reintegration of inmates, needs to be mentioned. As shown by researchers (Griera 2017; Griera and Clot-Garrell 2015b), the practice of yoga is increasingly present in Catalan penitentiary institutions. And while these are officially not considered religious activities and members of associations offering such activities are not required to go through the same accreditation procedures as religious actors, ethnographic analysis shows that such activities are not merely performed and understood as physical or cultural activities but do have a religious/spiritual component that cannot be ignored. As Griera and Clot-Garrell show, these activities have been normalised and incorporated into normal functioning without much controversy or even discussion.

Third, a more recent set of agreements has been approved for the provision of religious care in detention centres for foreigners. Established by the 7/1985 Law of Rights and Freedoms of Foreigners in Spain (replaced by the 4/2000 Law on the Rights and Freedoms of Foreigners and Their Social Integration), these centres are legally not part of the penitentiary system. However, in practice they can be treated as similar types of institutions, and people detained in these centres have the right to religious freedom. Three almost identical agreements were signed between the Ministry of Interior and the national Protestant (2014), Catholic (2014) and Muslim (2015) representatives for the provision of religious care in these detention centres. These agreements establish the content and conditions for the provision of religious

Table 21.1 Legal framework regulating religion in Spanish and Catalan prisons

General legislation	1978 – Spanish Constitution
	1979 – Concordat agreements
	1980 – Religious Freedom Act
	1992 – Cooperation agreements with Jewish, Protestant and Islamic federations
General prison legislation	1979 – Prison Act
	1996 – Spanish Prison Rules
	2006/329 Decree on Catalan Penitentiary Rules
Religion in prison legislation	2005 – Instruction 1 of Catalan Department of Justice regulating the right to receive religious care in a penitentiary context
	2006/710 Royal decree to develop agreements with Muslims, Jews, Protestants
	2007/6 Instruction on religious groups
	1987 General agreement for Catholic chaplaincy signed between Catalan Department of Justice and Diocese of Catalonia (updated in 2008 and 2006)
	1993 Agreement on Catholic chaplaincy in Spanish prisons (last update: 2019)
	1995 Agreement on Protestant chaplaincy signed between Catalan Department of Justice and Catalan Evangelical Council
	2007 Agreement on Islam in Spain
	2007/08 Agreement with Islamic Council of Catalonia (last update: 2019)
	2007 and 2009 Agreement GTER
	2009 Agreement Evangelical Council of Catalonia (last update: 2019)
	2011 Agreement between Catalan Department of Justice and World Prem (Yoga)
	2011 Agreement between Catalan Department of Justice and AUDIR – UNESCO
	2015 Agreement on Protestants in Spain FEREDE
	2017 Royal decree on funding for Catholic and Islamic chaplaincies Spain
	2014 Agreement on Protestant chaplaincy in detention centres for foreigners
	2014 Agreement on Catholic chaplaincy in detention centres for foreigners
	2015 Agreement on Islamic chaplaincy in detention centres for foreigners

Source: Own elaboration

care in a similar way to the agreements signed for regular prisons, but in this case it is the General Police Directorate that grants permission to pastors, priests and imams (Table 21.1).

21.3.2   *Institutionalised Pluralism and Traces of the Past*

This section focuses on the specific organisational arrangements that result from the implementation of the regulatory framework and its negotiation between, and enactment by, actors in the field. Attention is devoted to (a) chaplaincy, (b) spaces and symbols, (c) religious celebrations and rites, and (d) other religious/spiritual activities.

21.3.2.1   Chaplaincy: Recognition and Control Through Accreditation and Funding

Chaplaincy, the institutionalised service providing inmates with religious care, offers interesting insights into how religion is understood and organised in public institutions. Formal aspects, such as the type of professional affiliation of chaplains and other care providers, the accreditation procedures in place, the religious actors that are accredited to provide such a service, and the funding of the service, reveal the place allocated to religion.

Data on the number of religious specialists and volunteers offering their services in the Spanish and Catalan penitentiary systems are, as in other cases covered in this book, not fully reliable. The fact that people providing religious and spiritual care in these contexts change regularly makes it difficult to have up-to-date information. Also, differences in the ways the different 'types' of care provider are classified and counted generate doubts as to the quality of the data. However, in this project, data on the number of accredited religious actors in Spanish and Catalan prisons were compiled during the fieldwork carried out between 2011 and 2014. These data include not only chaplains and other official religious leaders but also other people assisting in the provision of religious care. The main finding is that while Catholic actors (chaplains and volunteers) continue to be the majority, chaplaincy has diversified significantly, and minority religious actors are present in many prisons. Moreover, groups like Protestant churches and Jehovah's Witnesses are investing large numbers of human resources in the penitentiary milieu. This diverse situation has most likely become even more so today, but since these data are from 2011 and no comprehensive update has been done since, it is not possible to have a fully updated picture (Table 21.2).

Table 21.2 Accredited religious actors and their distribution among Spanish and Catalan prisons (2011)

	Authorised religious actors	Prisons with religious presence (out of 80 prisons)	Percentage of prisons with religious presence (%)
Catholics	318	80	100
Muslims	24	23	28.7
Protestants	268	50	62.5
Seventh-Day Adventists	15	7	8.7
Orthodox	21	19	23.7
Jehovah's Witnesses	245	42	52.5
Jews	1	1	1.2
Buddhists	1	1	1.2
TOTAL	893	80	–

Source: Martínez-Ariño et al. (2015: 11)

However, more recently, the Spanish Penitentiary Administration created the 'Management of Religious Care in Penitentiary Institutions' database, which offers more or less systematic information for Spanish prisons (excluding here those belonging to the Catalan system). Data available on the number of accredited people need to be treated with caution, since religious care providers are constantly being added and dropped throughout the year, which makes the figures highly variable. According to this database for 2016, there were a total of 704 ministers or assistants accredited to provide religious care in Spanish prisons (excluding Catalan prisons); 164 belonged to the Catholic Church, 251 to the Federation of Evangelical and Protestant churches, 250 to the Jehovah's Witnesses, 17 to independent Evangelical churches, 1 Russian Christian Orthodox priest, 7 Romanian Christian Orthodox priests, 1 representative of the Jewish communities, 11 people representing the Muslim communities of the Spanish Islamic Commission and 2 others belonging to other Muslim communities (Table 21.3).

Despite the data not being fully reliable and thus not providing a full picture of the situation in prison, they show the pluralisation both of the prison population and the chaplaincy system. Prisons in Spain no longer cater exclusively for the majority Catholic population. More and more, representatives of other religious groups access the prison system to provide care for inmates of different religious affiliations. Chaplaincy is thus organised in a denomination-specific structure in which ministers and other religious actors (e.g. assistants, volunteers) are authorised and accredited to provide care for inmates of their own denomination. As opposed to other contexts, like in the UK (see chapter in this book), no interfaith or multifaith chaplaincy has been developed in Spain.

Funding for chaplaincies is provided both by the Spanish as well as the Catalan penitentiary administrations. In both cases, the Catholic Church enjoys a substantially higher budget that covers salaries and other costs. In 2016, the amount allocated for the Catholic prison chaplaincy in the Spanish system rose to 598,500 euros

Table 21.3 Religious actors that have provided religious care by religious tradition or denomination in prison from Spanish penitentiary system in 2016

Religious group/denomination	Accredited people
Catholic Church	164
Protestant/Evangelical Churches	251
Jehovah's Witnesses	250
Independent Evangelical Churches	17
Russian Orthodox Church	1
Romanian Orthodox Church	7
Jewish Community of Spain	1
Spanish Islamic Commission	11
Other Islamic communities	2
TOTAL	704

Source: Secretaría General de Instituciones Penitenciarias (2017)

(SGIP 2017) and in Catalonia to 60,000 euros. This amount differs significantly from the over 120,000 euros that the Catalan administration allocated to the Catholic chaplaincy in 2008, before the economic crisis affected public expenditures. Certain religious minorities also receive some public funding. The Islamic Commission of Spain received 5760 euros (SGIP 2017), an amount that was increased to 9000 euros in the most recent update of the collaboration (Royal Decree 561/2017). In the case of Catalonia, next to the funding to Catholic Chaplaincy, the agreements with different religious minorities mentioned earlier also include funding: 18,000 euros to the Catalan Evangelical Council in 2019 and 2020 and 20,000 euros for the Islamic Council of Catalonia in 2019 and 2020.

Funding and the signing of agreements with the penitentiary administration are a means for religious groups to gain recognition as well as obtain material and symbolic support. However, they also imply more institutional and legal control. When agreements are signed in which funding is provided, this entails the establishment of criteria about who can provide the chaplaincy, what activities can be conducted in the penitentiary context, and which supervision mechanisms, such as end-of-year reports, are implemented to make sure that the agreement is respected. These agreements and funding schemes are a means of standardising chaplaincy services.

While these official data on formal arrangements and agreements provide an interesting picture of the situation, incorporating the perspective of prisons as negotiated orders makes it possible to capture more subtle and variable details that are in play. For example, by inquiring into how the chaplaincy works in practice and observing it first hand, it became evident in our research that Catholic actors enjoy a wide variety of informal 'benefits' that are taken for granted and, thus, remain unseen (Griera and Clot-Garrell 2015a). The simple gesture of greeting between prison guards and different religious actors revealed a lot about the type of relationship established. Catholic chaplains are seen and greeted as members of the staff, while minority religious actors are mostly seen as external or alien to the institution. The way the latter are received very much depends on which guards are working on a particular day and the sympathies these guards might feel for them. Moreover, in some cases, the Catholic chaplain's accreditation card allows access to certain prison modules to which those of minority religious actors do not. This is a result of institutional inertia, due both to the previous condition of chaplains as civil servants and to the different relation of trust that religious minority representatives receive.

21.3.2.2 Spaces and Symbols: Locating Religion

The provision of spaces or rooms for the development of chaplaincy and religious celebrations is also a key element in the organisation of religion in prison. In Spain, the situation varies from prison to prison, and these diverging arrangements are dependent upon the year of construction of the prison. Prisons built before the disestablishment of the Catholic Church in 1978 contain a Catholic chapel, whereas those built therafter can sometimes have a dedicated space for religious celebrations and sometimes not. In the former, chapels have often been transformed into plurifunctional spaces, often retaining their structure and decoration as Catholic chapels. In some cases, though, certain arrangements are made, such as the construction of a screen to cover religious symbols. In the most recently built prisons, either no specific room has been constructed for religious purposes or a 'neutral' space has been constructed. The latter is often called a 'silence room' and represents an attempt to cater for diverse religious needs.

The Observatory for Religious Pluralism in Spain, a public foundation dependent on the Ministry of Justice to deal with religious issues, makes recommendations for the management of multi-confessional spaces in prison. Drawing on existing legislation, which establishes that a chapel or a room needs to be provided to guarantee the right to religious freedom in prison, the Observatory (2011) recommends arrangements of multi-confessional rooms. While no more specifications are offered, there is a clear tendency to promote a pluralistic approach to the arrangement of spaces for religious purposes. In Catalonia, 'silence rooms' are the predominant spatial arrangement in newly built penitentiary centres. The 1/2005 Catalan Instruction established that each prison should have a multi-confessional space adapted to the needs of the different religious communities. No further technical specifications are given. However, the option for 'empty' and 'neutral' silence spaces, where different religious groups can conduct their services and activities and decorate them accordingly on a temporary basis, predominates. These spaces usually contain chairs and a table that are not fixed to the floor and, thus, adjustable and removable. Yet, these spaces are often not used exclusively for religious purposes, and other activities, such as theatre rehearsals or meetings, may take place there in the absence of alternative spaces.

The presence or absence of religious symbols is another sign of the place occupied by religion in public institutions. Following the secularisation of state institutions, most religious symbols were removed from facilities. And while there is a lack of specific regulation in this regard, some court decisions have allowed the presence of religious symbols in public spaces or buildings alleging their cultural nature and the fact that the majority of the population perceives them as cultural artefacts (Arlettaz 2016). In practice, we encountered multiple examples of Catholic religious symbols in penitentiary centres, both inside and outside the chapel or space dedicated to religious uses. Sometimes they are fixed statues, in other cases they are mobile artefacts, such as crucifixes, that are stored in closets and taken out only during religious celebrations. Interestingly, these symbols and images often remain unseen by prison staff, since they are taken for granted as remnants of a past tradition (Griera and Clot-Garrell 2015a; Martínez-Ariño et al. 2015). The presence of religious symbols and artefacts differed slightly in the case of the Catalan prisons visited, where no permanent religious symbol outside the designated space was to be found, be it a chapel or a silent room, but temporary symbols such as a Christmas tree were present.

All these various spatial arrangements regarding the presence of religion, whether in terms of spaces or symbols and artefacts, show that religion is not completely removed from penitentiary institutions. But it occupies a more circumscribed position than it used to enjoy during the period of organic integration between the

Catholic Church and the state before 1978. Understanding prisons as negotiated orders makes it possible to see how a loophole in the regulation of religious symbols combined with references to the institution's 'tradition' facilitates a quite stable and unquestioned material presence of Catholicism in the facilities of some prisons. And since these arrangements are not fully stable, they need to be continually negotiated. An example of this is the fact that the presence in one prison of a statue of a Madonna in a multipurpose room went completely unquestioned, but crucifixes had to be stored in a wardrobe. Yet the Madonna was not unseen or irrelevant to everyone. The fact that Jehovah's Witnesses were celebrating their activities in that room with their back to the Madonna is but one of the emergent arrangements to deal with the material presence of a religious symbol that can be found in this organisational context.

21.3.2.3 Celebrations and Religious Rites

Religious celebrations and rites are legally allowed in the Spanish and Catalan prison systems. Collective religious celebrations are considered a central element of religious practice and are, thus, included as components of the chaplaincy service. In practice, religious celebrations and rites in prison take place regularly in Spain. Both the Catalan and Spanish systems facilitate the organisation of collective prayers and other religious celebrations, especially when it comes to the main celebrations of the major religious traditions (Martínez-Ariño et al. 2015).

However, a deeper look into the conditions under which this happens shows that nuances need to be made. While in principle no religious celebration is banned, except when it can endanger the security of the institution and the people in it, the conditions in which different celebrations are conducted vary significantly. Very often, these differences are not a matter of formal procedures but more the result of the role that informal routines, institutional inertia and personal relations play in the organisation of prison life. Catholic celebrations, for instance, are so deeply engrained in the normal functioning of prisons and so familiar to staff that they are incorporated in the regular functioning of these institutions; examples include the celebration of Easter Passion with theatrical representations, the organisation of special Christmas dinners and the celebrations of the prison patron saint week in September, in which the institution acts proactively in a top-down manner together with the Catholic chaplain and in which members of prison boards and staff participate actively. In contrast, the celebrations of religious minorities, which happen at the demand of inmates and 'visiting ministers' (Gilliat-Ray 2010), but very rarely at the initiative of the institution itself, are still perceived as a 'foreign practice' that often destabilises the normal routine. For example, the celebration of baptisms by Evangelicals that requires the use of a swimming pool (or a similar element) is accommodated and performed, but they are seen as foreign, and the institution and its staff do not actively take part in them, as happens with Catholic celebrations.

Ramadan deserves special mention here. The presence of Muslims in Spain has seen continuous growth in recent decades, largely as a result of immigration

(Moreras 2006). According to data from the Observatory of Religious Pluralism in Spain (2018), as of December 2017, there were a total of 1569 Islamic places of worship in Spain, which represented more than 22% of the places of worship of religious minorities in Spain. Of these, and according to the latest available data collected by the ISOR research group (2014) for the General Direction of Religious Affairs of the Catalan Government, a total of 256 oratories (19% of the total number of places of worship of minority religions) were operational in 2014 in Catalonia.

The overall increase in the number of foreign citizens in Spanish (6153 in 1996, 17,282 in 2000 and 12,601 in 2019, according to data from the Spanish penitentiary administration) and Catalan prisons (3361 foreign inmates in 2006, 4818 in 2011 and 3869 in 2019, according to data from the Catalan penitentiary administration) over the last two decades, many of them coming from Muslim-majority countries, especially Morocco, but also Pakistan or sub-Saharan countries, has prompted new requests regarding Islamic religious practices among inmates. Ramadan constitutes the main Muslim festivity celebrated within prisons, after Catholic Christmas and Easter celebrations. It is one of the cornerstones of the current regulation of religious diversity in such institutions because it requires the reorganisation of daily routines in an institutional context where routines are organised around meals, sleeping hours, and so forth. It poses a challenge to prisons as it becomes an increasingly regular practice for many of these institutions.

To take a closer look at how Ramadan is organised, this chapter will dig deeper into the Catalan case, where in-depth research was conducted. One interesting aspect of the institutional arrangements around the celebration of this festivity is that data on the number of inmates who request to be able to practise Ramadan in Catalan prisons have only been recorded since 2004. This date is important, since it is the year of the Madrid attacks. However, celebrations of Ramadan had started a few years before, around the year 2000. Graph 21.1 shows the evolution of the number of inmates who registered in their prisons as wanting to celebrate Ramadan. The numbers show a sustained positive trend passing from 700 inmates in 2004 to more than double in 2012. Yet the percentage that these represent as part of the overall Catalan prison population remains stable around 14% or 15%. Another relevant aspect of the existing data is that the number of women who request following a differentiated regime during the month of Ramadan is very small. This could be due to several factors, namely the low number of imprisoned Muslim women, the fact that Ramadan may be more widely celebrated by men, the fact that Islamic religious leaders devote less attention to female detention centres or the fact that prisons themselves put less emphasis on this celebration in women's prisons.

The existing data refer to the initial number of inmates who request following a differentiated treatment regime, not necessarily those who follow the practice throughout the whole month. And while at the beginning prison guards sometimes controlled who was following it entirely and who was stopping in the middle, they have gradually realised that it is not their task to do so; they are just facilitators, not guardians of religious practices.

Research showed us that there is no single way in which Ramadan is organised and practised in the everyday life of prisons. Yet there is an attempt to coordinate

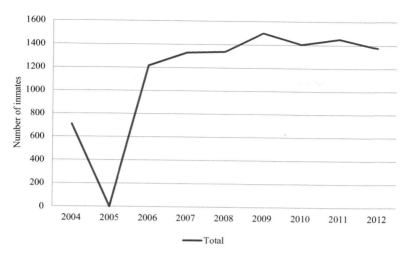

Graph 21.1 Inmates requesting to observe Ramadan in Catalan prisons (2004–2012, no data available for 2005). (Source: Own elaboration based on data from the Department of Justice of the Generalitat de Catalunya)

some practices in order to ensure that inmates can fulfil their religious duties during this period. One of the most important moments is the determination of the day when Ramadan starts. Since this is something that cannot be predicted well in advance, the coordinator for religious affairs in the Catalan penitentiary administration sends a first communication to all centres roughly a month in advance indicating the approximate expected date of start and reminding them that they should start preparations for the month. Two weeks later, the centres receive a second reminder and finally, once the Catalan Islamic and Cultural Council informs the coordinator of the precise day of the start, he sends an urgent communication, usually SMS, letting the prisons know that Ramadan is starting. While this generated some anxiety among prison administrators and staff, who are used to working in an organisational culture with little room left to improvisation, it is slowly being routinized, and more and more individual prisons know how to handle this period and are less hesitant to rearrange some of the prison routines. Additionally, while there are no specific guidelines as to how to organise the month, the central penitentiary administration celebrates regular annual meetings with the Catalan Secretary of Religious Affairs and imams to discuss the main issues and pass on the information to prison directors and administrators. In the past, when the practice was less known, each centre was encouraged to set up a commission in charge of facilitating the celebration of Ramadan and providing a detailed report at the end of it to the central administration. However, as this celebration becomes more normalised, these commissions have lost their function and the report now consists only on the statistics of inmates who request celebrating Ramadan.

During this month, prisons usually attempt to group together in cells those inmates celebrating Ramadan. This allows for an easier organisation of the celebration, particularly when the time to break the feast comes during the night. Inmates are allowed to bring their food to their cells to eat outside regular prison meal hours. Moreover, the Catalan administration has over the years arranged for the provision of special sweets during this period, offered by the Catalan Islamic and Cultural Council and the Moroccan Consulate. Moreover, some prisons also organise cultural activities during these days, such as movies. The celebration of the last day of Ramadan is also organised in most penitentiary centres. Muslim inmates play a large role in establishing the needs of the month due to the limited religious literacy of many prison administrators. The latter often ask Muslim inmates about specific practices and the concrete needs for particular days. The fact that there is almost always a Muslim prisoner working in the prison kitchen and the prison supermarket helps prison administrators ensure that meals and products that are adequate for this period will be available. Thus, celebrations can vary from prison to prison, also depending on the overall leadership style of the prison management and on the agreed-upon practical arrangements.

From an understanding of prisons as negotiated orders, religious celebrations are an exceptional example of the idea of negotiated orders. Formal regulations do not govern celebrations to the last detail, which allows and forces actors to negotiate the actual organisation of these celebrations, including the spaces that can be used, whether or not the celebration will be publicised through a general announcement using a megaphone in the prison, and whether or not members of prison management will be present at those celebrations. Whether Ramadan sweets will find their way to prisons depends on the capacity of managers and administrators and religious actors to agree on the conditions for this. No formal rule will ensure or prevent it.

21.3.2.4   Other Religious/Spiritual Activities

Next to what can be considered 'traditional' religious celebrations, the penitentiary milieu in general, and the Catalan one in particular, is witnessing a spread of other forms of religious or spiritual practices that do not fall within traditional categories. For example, in Catalan prisons, activities such as yoga quarantines (Griera 2017), Reiki classes and Buddhist meditation take place regularly. Interestingly, these appear in an annual report of the Catalan prison administration (Departament de Justícia 2017) next to other secular activities, such as after-school support, sewing, theatre or education for culture, but not together with other religious activities. As my colleagues have shown (Griera and Clot-Garrell 2015b), holistic practices, such as reiki, yoga and meditation, have been normalised and are stripped from their religious/spiritual content and are seen rather as means for the rehabilitation and reintegration of prisoners in a perspective that emphasises self-regulation and individual wellbeing.

Moreover, in the Catalan case, interreligious activities in prison have spread. There are many examples of this development, such as interreligious prayers for peace, the planting of trees inside prisons as a sign of interreligious understanding, and the offer of advice in matters of religion to prison libraries. This is what the interreligious group GTER does. Also, in 2015, the UNESCO Association for Interreligious Dialogue implemented a programme to spread and raise awareness about religious diversity and interreligious dialogue.

Thus, the presence of religion in Spanish prisons, in this case specifically in the Catalan prison system, is not restricted to the chaplaincy. Other activities, whether interreligious events or practices related to new age spirituality, have found their way into prisons. Understanding prisons as negotiated orders allows one to observe how ideas about religious activities can change from one situation to another and how different actors may take advantage of new opportunities to reposition themselves, by, for example, emphasising their role in promoting interreligious dialogue rather than as representatives of a single religious group.

21.4 Conclusion

Spanish prisons have undergone significant legal and institutional transformations with regard to the presence and regulation of religion over the last four decades. These changes are also evident in the daily presence and negotiations of religion. During the Franco regime, Catholicism impregnated all aspects of life in the institution and was a regulating principle. Chaplains and nuns were official prison authorities. This is no longer the case. Although religion, and Catholicism in particular, remains present in many ways in prison life, its scope of influence is more limited. Moreover, next to the secularisation of penitentiaries, a trend towards religious diversification of the prison population characterises the current situation. The latter, together with numerous legal developments, has led to a situation of institutional pluralism, where prisons cater for diverse religious needs. These changes result from formal transformations but also from daily interactions, where different religious and secular actors negotiate to pursue their interests.

The design and implementation of pluralistic legal and institutional frameworks reflect wider European developments. Despite some particularities in the ways this institutional pluralism is implemented in Spain, similarities can be found with other countries discussed in this book. For example, members of a variety of religious traditions are allowed and accredited to provide religious care in prison, and this is being normalised to a greater extent. Moreover, next to 'traditional' religious groups, less institutionalised 'spirituality groups' offering different types of activities are becoming normal in the Spanish prison landscape, similar to the situation in other countries.

However, aside from these similarities, the imprint of the Catholic past, and its particular entanglement with state institutions during the Franco regime, is of a different nature and relevance in the Spanish case. Although most formal aspects of the former 'organic integration' between the Catholic Church and the Spanish state in prisons, such as the Penitentiary Chaplaincy Corps or mandatory attendance at mass, have disappeared, less evident and more subtle aspects remain in place.

Catholic celebrations are part of the 'normal' prison calendar, and Catholic actors often enjoy more freedom of movement and trust from prison staff members than their minority religions' counterparts. Studying prisons as negotiated orders, and not simply as stable structures and formal rules, allows the capture of elements that would otherwise have remained invisible to the researcher's eye.

Bibliography

Arlettaz, F. (2016). No es religión, es cultura: A propósito de las implicaciones religiosas de signos, gestos y palabras. In J. Gracia & D. Jiménez (Eds.), *Tristes tópicos. Representaciones sociales desenfocadas* (pp. 275–288). Zaragoza: Universidad de Zaragoza.

Becci, I., & Roy, O. (2015). *Religious diversity in European prisons: Challenges and implications for rehabilitation.* Cham: Springer.

Departament de Justícia. (2017). *Activitats de voluntariat als centres penitenciaris.* Retrieved from: http://justicia.gencat.cat/ca/ambits/reinsercio_i_serveis_penitenciaris/Voluntariat-en-lambit-penitenciari/#bloc6. Accessed 30 May 2018.

Fine, G. A. (1984). Negotiated orders and organisational cultures. *Annual Review of Sociology, 10,* 239–262.

Gallego, M., Cabrera, P. J., Ríos, J. C., & Segovia, J. L. (2010). *Andar 1 Km en línea recta: La cárcel del siglo XXI que vive el preso.* Madrid: Universidad Pontificia de Comillas.

Gilliat-Ray, S. (2010). From 'visiting minister' to 'Muslim chaplain': The growth of Muslim Chaplaincy in Britain, 1970–2007. In E. Barker (Ed.), *The centrality of religion in social life: Essays in Honour of James A. Beckford* (pp. 145–157). Burlington: Ashgate Publishing, Ltd.

Gómez Bravo, G. (2008). La redención de penas y el penitenciarismo de postguerra. *Sociedad y Utopía: Revista de Ciencias Sociales, 31,* 19–32.

Grenier, C. (2011). The appropriation of new arrangements of public organisations: Locally negotiate to strategically act. *Administratie Si Management Public, 17,* 6–32.

Griera, M. (2017). Yoga in penitentiary settings: Transcendence, spirituality, and self-improvement. *Human Studies, 40*(1), 77–100.

Griera, M., & Clot-Garrell, A. (2015a). Banal is not trivial: Visibility, recognition, and inequalities between religious groups in prison. *Journal of Contemporary Religion, 30*(1), 23–37.

Griera, M., & Clot-Garrell, A. (2015b). Doing yoga behind bars: A sociological study of the growth of holistic spirituality in penitentiary institutions. In I. Becci & O. Roy (Eds.), *Religious diversity in European prisons* (pp. 141–157). Cham: Springer.

Griera, M., Martínez-Ariño, J., & García-Romeral, G. (2014). Beyond the separation of church and state: Explaining the new governance of religious diversity in Spain. *MMG Working Papers, 14*(08).

Griera, M., Martínez-Ariño, J., Clot-Garrell, A., & Garcia-Romeral, G. (2015). Religión e instituciones públicas en España. Hospitales y prisiones en perspectiva comparada. *Revista Internacional de Sociología, 73*(3), 1–13.

Lorenzo Rubio, C. (2011). Evolución del sistema penitenciario franquista: del redentorismo al cientifismo correccionalista. Crónica de una pretensión. In A. B. Alonso, J. de Hoyos Puente, & R. S. Arias (Eds.), *Nuevos horizontes del pasado. Culturas políticas, identidades y formas de representación: Actas del X Congreso de la Asociación de Historia Contemporánea.* Santander: Ediciones de la Universidad de Cantabria.

Martínez-Ariño, J., García-Romeral, G., Ubasart-González, G., & Griera, M. (2015). Demonopolisation and dislocation: (re-)negotiating the place and role of religion in Spanish prisons. *Social Compass, 62*(1), 3–21.

Moreno Antón, M. (1994). La asistencia religiosa católica en centros penitenciarios: Comentario al Acuerdo de 20 de Mayo de 1993 entre la Presidente de la CEE y el Ministro de Justicia. *Revista española de derecho canónico, 51*(136), 199–216.

Moreno Antón, M. (2006). La asistencia religiosa en España. In I. Martín Sánchez & J. G. Navarro (Eds.), *La libertad religiosa en España y Argentina* (pp. 99–119). Madrid: Fundación Universitaria Española.

Moreras, J. (2006). Migraciones y pluralismo religioso. Elementos para el debate. *Documentos CIDOB. Migraciones* 9: 1.

Observatorio del Pluralismo Religioso en España. (2011). *Guía técnica para la implementación y gestión de los espacios multiconfesionales.* Madrid: Observatorio del Pluralismo Religioso en España.

Rodríguez Blanco, M. (2009). Asistencia religiosa penitenciaria de las confesiones minoritarias con acuerdo de cooperación. In I. Martín Sanchez & M. Gonzalez Sanchez (Eds.), *Algunas cuestiones controvertidas del ejercicio del derecho fundamental de libertad religiosa en España* (pp. 183–207). Madrid: Fundación Universitaria Española.

Rubio, C. L. (2014). Femmes et mères dans les prisons de Franco. Une approche de l'endoctrinement religieux et des privations matérielles dans le système carcéral espagnol pendant la dictature. *Champ pénal/Penal field* 11 [online]. DOI: https://doi.org/10.4000/champpenal.8750

Secretaría General de Instituciones Penitenciarias. (2017). *Informe General de 2016.* Madrid: Ministerio del Interior. Retrieved from http://www.institucionpenitenciaria.es/web/export/sites/default/datos/descargables/publicaciones/Informe_General_2016_acc.pdf. Accessed 20 May 2018.

Strauss, A. L. (1978). *Negotiations: Varieties, contexts, processes, and social order.* San Francisco: Jossey-Bass Inc. Publishers.

Tamarit Sumalla, J. M. (2016). El sistema penitenciari català: fonament i exercici de la competencia. *Revista d'Estudis Autonòmics i Federals, 23*, 235–273.

Watson, T. J. (2015). Organizations: Negotiated orders. In J. Wright (Ed.), *International encyclopedia of the social and behavioral sciences* (Vol. 17, pp. 411–414). Elsevier. Retrieved from https://www.mysciencework.com/publication/show/d5f0f0a2ba960f6a87bff9726693d605 Accessed 15 September 2017.

Legal Documents and Agreements

1948 – Reglamento de los Servicios de Prisiones.

1970 – Ley sobre reestructuración de los Cuerpos Penitenciarios.

1978 – Constitución Española.

1979 – Instrumento de Ratificación del Acuerdo entre el Estado español y la Santa Sede sobre asuntos jurídicos.

1979 – Ley Orgánica 1/1979 General Penitenciaria.

1980 – Ley Orgánica 7/1980 de Libertad Religiosa.

1987 – Acord marc relatiu a l'assistència religiosa catòlica als centres penitenciaris.

1992 – Ley 26/1992 por la que se aprueba el Acuerdo de Cooperación del Estado con la Comisión Islámica de España.

1992 – Ley 25/1992 por la que se aprueba el Acuerdo de Cooperación del Estado con la Federación de Comunidades Israelitas de España.

1992 – Ley 24/1992 por la que se aprueba el Acuerdo de Cooperación del Estado con la Federación de Entidades Religiosas Evangélicas de España.

1993 – Acuerdo sobre asistencia religiosa católica en los establecimientos penitenciarios.

1995 – Conveni marc per a la prestació del servei d'assistència espiritual i religiosa evangèlica als interns dels centres penitenciaris de Catalunya.

1996 – Real Decreto 190/1996 Reglamento Penitenciario.

2005 – Instrucció 1/2005, del Departament de Justícia, de regulació del dret a rebre atenció religiosa en el medi penitenciari.

2006 – Decret 329/2006, de 5 de setembre, pel qual s'aprova el Reglament d'organització i funcionament dels serveis d'execució penal a Catalunya.

2006 – Real Decreto 710/2006 de desarrollo de los Acuerdos de Cooperación firmados por el Estado con la Federación de Entidades Religiosas Evangélicas de España, la Federación de Comunidades Judías de España y la Comisión Islámica de España, en el ámbito de la asistencia religiosa penitenciaria.

2007 – Instrucción del Ministerio del Interior sobre Confesiones Religiosas.

2007 – Convenio de colaboración del Estado con la Comisión Islámica de España para la financiación de los gastos que ocasione el desarrollo de la asistencia religiosa en los establecimientos penitenciarios de competencia estatal.

2008 – Conveni entre el Departament de Justícia i la Conferència Episcopal Tarraconense, en representació de les diòcesis de Catalunya.

2008 – Conveni de Col·laboració entre l'Administració de la Generalitat de Catalunya, mitjançant el Departament de Justícia i el Departament de la Vicepresidència, i el Consell Islàmic Cultural de Catalunya, per tal de garantir el dret de l'assistència religiosa dels interns als centres penitenciaris de Catalunya.

2009 – Conveni filial entre la Direcció General de Recursos i Règim Penitenciari de Departament de Justícia de la Generalitat de Catalunya i el Grup de Treball Estable de les Religions (GTER) a través de l'Associació Amics del GTER.

2009 – XV Conveni filial entre el Departament de Justícia i el Consell Evangèlic de Catalunya.

2011 – Conveni de col·laboració entre el Departament de Justícia i l'Associació World Prem.

2011 – Conveni filial entre la Direcció General de Recursos i Règim Penitenciari de Departament de Justícia de la Generalitat de Catalunya i el Centre Unesco de Catalunya (UNESCOCAT).

2012 – Pròrroga i modificació del Conveni de col·laboració de la Generalitat de Catalunya mitjançant el Departament de Justícia i el Consell Evangèlic de Catalunya.

2012 – Pròrroga i modificació del Conveni de col·laboració de la Deneralitat de Catalunya mitjançant el Departament de Justícia, la Direcció General d'Afers Religiosos del Departament de Governació i Relacions Institucionals i la Federació Consell Islàmic de Catalunya.

2014 – Convenio de colaboración entre el Ministerio del Interior y la Conferencia Episcopal Española para garantizar la asistencia religiosa católica en los centros de internamiento de extranjeros.

2014 – Convenio de colaboración entre el Ministerio del Interior y la Federación de Entidades Religiosas Evangélicas de Española para garantizar la asistencia religiosa evangélica en los centros de internamiento de extranjeros.

Real Decreto 2015

2015 – Convenio de Colaboración para la Asistencia Religiosa Evangélica en Centros Penitenciarios dependientes de la Secretaría General de Instituciones Penitenciarias.

2015 – Pròrroga del conveni de col·laboració entre l'administració de la Generalitat de Catalunya i la Conferència Episcopal Tarraconense.

2015 – XVI Conveni filial entre l'Administració de la Generalitat de Catalunya i el Consell Evangèlic de Catalunya.

2016 – Conveni entre el Departament de Justícia i la Conferència Episcopal Tarraconense per a l'assistència religiosa catòlica als centres penitenciaris de la Generalitat de Catalunya.

2017 – Real Decreto 561/2017, de 2 de junio, por el que se regula la concesión de diversas subvenciones directas del Ministerio del Interior.

Chapter 22
Sweden: Silent Religious Retreat as Rehabilitation Treatment in Prison

Per Pettersson

Abstract In this chapter, the Kumla Prison Monastery is discussed as an example of the ambiguous policy and practice of Swedish secular state institutions in relation to the field of religion. Kumla is the largest prison in Sweden, and one of the most protected and secure ones. It holds convicts serving long sentences. This prison conducts a very special activity, probably unique in the world: the 'Monastery', which allows convicts to undergo a long silent spiritual retreat, as initiated by Ignatius of Loyola, a sixteenth-century Catholic priest. Although Swedish official policy is that state authorities should be religiously neutral, this use of religion in prison illustrates a certain ambiguity of the Swedish secular state institution.

22.1 Introduction

A very special phenomenon in the Swedish prison system is the Monastery division at Kumla Prison, established in 2001, which is probably unique in the world.[1] Kumla is the largest and one of the most protected and secure prisons in Sweden, hosting convicts serving long-term sentences. The Monastery has as its aim to provide an opportunity to more deeply reflect on one's life and to acquire a deeper understanding

---

[1] In November 2018, the management of Kumla prison declared that they had to temporarily close down the Monastery due to the acute lack of space in the Swedish prisons. This was a total surprise for all involved in the Monastery. The management of the Kumla prison said that they regretted to have to take this decision. The facilities are presently used to host 15 inmates. The Swedish prisons are overfilled, and a number of new prisons are being built, but it is unclear when the Monastery will be reopened.

P. Pettersson (✉)
Professor of Sociology of Religion, Service Research Center, Karlstad University, Karlstad, Sweden

Uppsala Religion and Society Research Centre, Uppsala University, Uppsala, Sweden
e-mail: per.pettersson@kau.se

© Springer Nature Switzerland AG 2020   359
J. Martínez-Ariño, A.-L. Zwilling (eds.), *Religion and Prison: An Overview of Contemporary Europe*, Boundaries of Religious Freedom: Regulating Religion in Diverse Societies 7, https://doi.org/10.1007/978-3-030-36834-0_22

of oneself during a month-long silent retreat, following the tradition of sixteenth-century Catholic priest Ignatius of Loyola.

This chapter places the presence of religion in Swedish prisons in the larger Swedish context and discusses the special use of religion by a Swedish state authority. The motivation and argument of the Swedish Prison and Probation Service (*Kriminalvården* in Swedish) for managing the Monastery is analysed in relation to the Swedish official policy that state authorities should be religiously neutral and not be directly involved in religious activities. The case of Kumla Monastery is discussed as an example of the ambiguous policy and practice of Swedish secular state institutions in relation to the field of religion.

22.2 Religion in Sweden, Ambiguous Complexity

Sweden has a population of 9.9 million (2016), of which 61% belong to the old state church, the Church of Sweden, 5% are members of different minority Christian Protestant denominations, 2% belong to the Roman Catholic and Orthodox Churches and 2% belong to other religions, primarily Islam. Altogether 70% of the population belong to some kind of organised religion (Church of Sweden Statistics 2016; Swedish Commission for Government Support to Faith Communities statistics 2015).

Sweden is often referred to as one of the most secularised countries in the world in terms of regular participation in worship and belief in traditional church teachings (Zuckerman 2008). However, the Swedish religious situation is complex and ambiguous, most clearly highlighted by the widespread high level of membership of the Church of Sweden and the persistent role of the majority church. Statistics from 2016 show that 44% of all children born are baptised in the Church of Sweden, 27% of all 15-year-olds participate in its confirmation teaching programme, 34% of all marriages take place in a Church of Sweden church and 74% of all dead are buried within Church of Sweden settings (Church of Sweden Statistics 2016). This complexity of high levels of secularisation in some respects and relatively high levels of religious affiliation and practice in other respects is similar to the other Nordic countries and is sometimes called the Nordic paradox (Bäckström et al. 2004).

Increasing levels of immigration are changing the homogeneous religious landscape. Today, around 23% of the Swedish population is either born abroad or are children with both parents born abroad. Religion migrates along with people, and in particular the increasing presence of Muslims is changing the religious scene. In the suburbs of major cities, the situation with publicly visible religious pluralism is quite different from the general national situation (Andersson and Sander 2005; Pettersson 2014). Thus, the impression one gets of Sweden today as being secularised or religious depends on the choice of indicators as well as the geographical area under consideration.

22.3   State, Church and Prisons from Past to Present

Sweden, Norway, Denmark, Finland and Iceland have historically formed a Protestant Nordic Region. Since the time of the Reformation, Lutheran national churches have been dominant in the five Nordic countries. In Denmark and Iceland they are still state churches, but in Finland, Sweden and Norway, church and state are now separate.

The historic Swedish state–church context meant an almost total integration between church and state, a unitary society in which all citizens were obliged to be baptised and belong to the Church of Sweden, and thereby also a strong connection between the Church, the legal system and the prison system. During the nineteenth century, the church–prison relationship was elaborated by a parliamentary decision of 1841 to introduce the cell system in Swedish prisons (Larsson 2011). The previous model with inmates living together collectively in groups was regarded as morally devastating. The intention behind introducing the cell system was to create an isolated individual environment in which inmates are encouraged to reflect on their life and thereby acquire personal insight, repent, and change their attitude and way of life (Levenskog 1997). Cell punishment was seen as a kind of penance and was to be based on Christian tradition and roots. To achieve this aim, pastoral counselling and the chaplain took on an important and central role. The chaplain would have regular pastoral counselling with each individual inmate and organise common worship with the inmates every Sunday. He was also tasked with organising compulsory education for inmates up to the age of 35, primarily teaching Christianity. Additionally, the chaplain was responsible for the prison library and served as a mediator between inmates and the greater society, especially close to the time of release from prison.

Alongside other European countries, Sweden underwent a continuous process of secularisation during the late nineteenth and twentieth centuries, by which the state as well as individuals liberated themselves from the former power of the Church. A series of continuous reforms took place, gradually reducing the power of the state Church. A first major change in church–state relations took place in 1862, when the municipality administration was split into two: a church administration and a civil administration (Bexell 2003). In 1873, a new law made it possible to leave the established Church and become a member of another Christian denomination recognized by the state. But only two denominations took advantage of the law, the Roman Catholic Church and the Methodist-Episcopal Church (Bexell 2003).

A number of reforms followed, gradually contributing to the separation of church and state, which theoretically can be interpreted as part of the general functional differentiation process of society (Luhmann 1982; Dobbelaere 2002). As part of the reduced role of the church in relation to the state, the role of the chaplain and pastoral counselling in prison was reduced, and new ideas on prisons and punishment were introduced. A prison reform of 1945 abolished the cell system and reintroduced collective living in Swedish prison organisation, although in a different form modernised compared to the past (Levenskog 1997).

It was not until 1951 that the Act on Freedom of Religion was introduced, giving the citizens of the country the right to freely practise a religion of their own choice or to abstain from being a member of any religious body (SFS 1951: 680). The central role of the Church of Sweden in public schools and social services lasted until the 1960s, and local Church of Sweden parishes handled the administration of civil registration until 1991, when it was transferred from the Church to the Swedish tax authorities.

The final major change in church–state relations took place on 1 January 2000, with almost full legal separation. The Church of Sweden changed status from being a state authority to becoming the largest voluntary organisation in Sweden. A new Act on Faith Communities as well as a special Church of Sweden Act were introduced (SFS 1998b:1593, SFS 1998a:1591). This legislation aimed at placing the various faith communities in Sweden on a more equal footing, while simultaneously preserving continuity with respect to the position of the Church of Sweden as the historical national church. Today, the Swedish state is officially neutral in relation to all faith communities, although a few remaining legal regulations marking a special position of the Church of Sweden indicate that the close connection between State and Church has not fully disappeared.

Along with the long and continuous process of separation between state and church that played out in the twentieth century, an official discourse developed stressing the religious neutrality of the state and religion as belonging to the private sphere. When it comes to the presence of religion in state institutions like prisons, it is taken for granted that the entire state administration should be religiously neutral and purely secular. The principle of a secular state is usually motivated by reference to religious diversity, the Act on Freedom of Religion and Swedish constitutional law, 'Instrument of Government', which states: 'Every citizen shall be protected in his relations with public institutions against any coercion to divulge an opinion in any political, religious, cultural or other such connection. He shall further be protected in his relations with the public institutions against any coercion to participate in a meeting for the formation of opinion or a demonstration or other manifestation of opinion, or belong to a political association, religious community or other association for the manifestation of opinion referred to in sentence one' (SFS 1974:152 Article 2 § 2). Nevertheless, religious service functions remain integrated in a number of state institutions, mostly coordinated by the Church of Sweden as the basic provider, in close cooperation with the respective public institution. This is the case concerning the presence of organised religion in, for example, public hospitals, the military, public schools and prisons (Pettersson 2015).

The continuing role of the Church of Sweden can be explained by its history as a fully integrated part of the state and by the fact that its local organisation geographically covers the whole of Sweden. The Church is thereby implicitly still occasionally and in certain contexts regarded more or less as a public utility (cf. Martin 1978, Lundstedt 2006). This public service function, which includes a kind of responsibility for all people in the given geographical area, irrespective of beliefs or nationalities, is also part of the self-understanding of the Church of Sweden, as expressed in the following Church order: 'The parish is responsible for the church activities of all who reside in the parish' (Kyrkoordningen 2007:2 §1). This includes serving anyone in a public institution in which the Church operates, e.g. in prisons. The Kumla Monastery, analysed in this chapter, is a significant example of the integration of the Church of Sweden's service functions in a public institution.

22.4 'Spiritual Care' in Swedish Prisons

As described earlier, there is a long historical tradition of religious presence in Swedish prisons, dominated by Church of Sweden chaplains, but today other faith communities are also represented as a consequence of the legal regulation of Freedom of Religion. The Prison and Probation Service stresses that all inmates are entitled to pursue their faith or religion and to follow the order of their faith while they are in prison (Kriminalvården 2018).

Each prison institution has a local council for 'spiritual care' called the Board for Spiritual Care (Swedish: *Nämnden för andlig vård*, NAV), organised by the prison authority and responsible for the spiritual welfare of inmates. At the national level, the Christian Council of Sweden (SKR) has overarching oversight for spiritual care in prison, including all religions. The Christian denominations coordinate their respective prison chaplains and SKR coordinates Muslim imams serving in prisons. In 2002, a declaration of mutual support and exchange in relation to the chaplaincy was adopted between SKR and SMI. SKR organises a national committee for criminal welfare policy, development of spiritual care and further education of prison chaplains and provides advisors to support the prisons and the faith communities.

Most prison institutions have a priest or deacon from the Church of Sweden serving, and in most prisons there is also a pastor from one of the traditional Swedish Christian minority churches. At the larger institutions there may be additional priests from the Catholic Church, an Orthodox church, or a Muslim imam. Larger prisons have special chapels for worship or religious meetings. Around 180 religious ministers provide religious care in Swedish prisons. Most of them are priests and deacons from the Church of Sweden, other represent Christian minorities and around ten are Muslim imams. The Church of Sweden employs and pays for their own chaplains, while the chaplains from minority Christian and Muslim communities are funded by the state and employed by their respective faith community (Larsson 2011, 11).

The chaplains' task is to meet the inmates' needs for private conversation, counselling, and guidance on moral and existential issues and to provide religious services and other activities. Part of the prison chaplain's work is to help those in prison or remanded into custody to establish contact with a representative of their faith or religion. This means, for example, that a Church of Sweden clergy will assist an inmate in contacting an imam or a Catholic priest. Chaplains also coordinate volunteers visiting prisons, organise conversation and study groups for inmates, and assist prison personnel in cases of conflict, accident or death in prison.

22.5   Kumla Monastery

A special form of prison environment and method of rehabilitation within the Swedish prison system is a unit in the Kumla prison called The Monastery, which is probably unique in the world. Kumla is the largest Swedish prison, with room for 405 male inmates, and one of the Swedish prisons with the highest degree of security and protection (Kriminalvården 2018). In 2001, a specially designed unit for silent retreats was established within the Kumla Prison. The unit is called The Monastery and holds nine accommodation rooms and seven meditation rooms. A Church of Sweden priest, Truls Bernhold, was employed by the Prison and Probation Service to oversee retreat activities. He had personal experience from taking part in a retreat in England according to the *Spiritual Exercises of Ignatius of Loyola* (1491–1556). Bernhold decided to hold retreats at Kumla in line with the model that he had experienced in England. Ignatius of Loyola is known as the founder of The Society of Jesus, The Jesuit Order. *Spiritual Exercises of Ignatius of Loyola* were first published in 1548 and consist of a set of meditations, prayers and mental exercises, which should be practised over a 4-week period. Loyola's exercises aim to help individuals acquire personal insight by thinking, meditating, contemplating, praying and examining their conscience.

Building on Loyola's model, Bernhold developed a 30-day-long silent retreat that remains the core activity at Kumla Monastery. It aims to provide an opportunity to reflect deeper on one's life and to obtain a deeper understanding of oneself by taking part in the retreat. As stated by the prison authority in the information brochure: *'Do you long to find inner peace? Do you want to see the truth behind yourself and develop insight into who you are? Then maybe Klostervägen (Monastery Path) is something for you.'* (Klostervägen 2011). Klostervägen is open only for male inmates.

Taking part in a retreat at the Monastery requires being sentenced to a long prison term. Male inmates from any prison in Sweden who have been sentenced to at least 2 years in prison can apply to participate in a retreat at the Monastery. The retreat follows the tradition of Ignatius of Loyola and is led by a Christian chaplain. The prison authority as well as the responsible retreat chaplains, however, stress that each inmate is free to practise any religion of his own choosing within this common framework, and it is claimed that the retreat should not be regarded as a course in Christian faith (Klostervägen, 2011).

During the years since the Monastery was created, a model and practice have developed whereby, after application and acceptance, the convict takes part in two 1-week-long retreats before being eligible for a 30-day retreat. Six months after the long retreat, a 1-week follow-up retreat is offered. Until recently, the chaplain lived together with the inmates during the whole retreat period, even during the 30-day retreat. But rules on working hours for employees have recently imposed a division of work hours in the Monastery among chaplains. During the period 2001–2014, around 600 inmates had taken part in short retreats and around 170 in 30-day retreats

(Roxell et al. 2016). The Kumla Monastery has inspired one of Sweden's women's prisons, Hinseberg Prison, to organise a bi-annual 6-day retreat for women. This chapter will, however, focus on the retreats at Kumla Prison.

During the long retreat, participants spend a whole month in total silence, apart from a daily individual counselling session of 30 min with the retreat chaplain. Every morning starts with an introduction by the retreat leader in which a word from the Bible is given to use for meditation or contemplation. Every evening ends with a moment of prayer or holy communion. Four biblical themes are selected for the 30 days, one theme for each of the 4 weeks. The first week focuses on God's creation, one's own place in that creation and what has gone wrong. During the second week, the life of Jesus is described and held up as a model of life with respect to values and personal choice. The third week focuses on the crucifixion and death, and the participating individuals are inspired to emotionally experience the suffering and pain of Jesus. The fourth week is filled with life and hope for the future by focusing on the resurrection of Jesus, and participants reflect on the personal strength and personal choices needed in their respective personal lives. Special symbolic rites have been developed that stress significant steps in the individual participants' process during the retreat. An example of this is that during the first week, there is a moment when each participant writes a confession on a piece of paper, followed by a common ritual burning of all the papers in a fire (Roxell et al. 2016).

As described, the 30-day retreat and the Monastery are clearly Christian in their form. Most of the convicts participating in the retreats have a Christian cultural background, but Muslims, Buddhists, atheists and people of other religious backgrounds have also participated. In each of the long retreats, two previous participants act as assistants, seeing to practical issues and serving as guiding support for the participants. One of the most active assistants is a Muslim (Roxell et al. 2016).

Interestingly, the idea of the Kumla Monastery recalls the idea of the cell punishment model that was introduced in 1841, as described earlier in the historical overview. Both models aim to create a prison environment that would stimulate an individual inmate's personal reflections on his life. But the Kumla model is even more elaborate, since the retreat prescribes 1 month of almost total silence. And there is one important difference compared to the historic past: taking part in the silent retreat is a voluntary choice on the part of the inmate. In the 19th century model, the isolated cell and enforced religious teaching was the default option, but the Kumla model prescribes that inmates voluntarily apply to take part in the Monastery retreat. This opportunity and individual choice could be regarded as a psychological advantage for individual inmates that have very limited freedom of choice how to live their life in prison. They cannot escape from the prison, but they can make a choice to be further removed from the general prison population in a kind of exclusive environment that is even more isolated than the general prison. This seemingly contradictory option probably gives a sense of freedom by being a voluntary choice.

22.6   Development of a 'Monastery Path' Programme

Taking part in the Kumla Monastery retreat has proved to be a very successful way for many long-term convicts to take control of their lives and to find a new way to live and manage their lives. Several convicts have appeared in the media over the years, talking about their positive experience in the 30-day retreat and what it has meant to them in finding a new way in life.

Even if no scientific evaluation has been conducted on the long-term effects of the Monastery, the positive experiences reported caused the prison authority to invest in the Monastery model of rehabilitation. Truls Bernhold was asked to give lectures about the Monastery at national meetings of the Prison and Probation Service. Subsequently, the idea emerged of developing a longer and more elaborate rehabilitation programme. This task was given to the now-retired minister Bernhold, and a three-step programme known as the Monastery Path was launched in 2008.

The Monastery Path starts with the Kumla Monastery activities as described earlier. A second step of the programme is established at a specially designed Monastery section at Skänninge prison, which is a prison with a lower degree of security than Kumla Prison, 100 km south of Kumla. Only convicts that have participated in a long retreat at Kumla can apply to the Monastery at Skänninge. The aim at Skänninge is to build on and support the personal spiritual growth and individual responsibility that has been reached at Kumla in a supportive environment.

Skänninge Monastery has room for 18 inmates divided into 3 units, named Ignatius, Franciskus and Ingrid. As in common monasteries, the inmates are called monastery brothers. Their daily activities differ; they can consist of studies, garden work, cleaning, and so forth. There is a daily morning prayer, evening gathering, a weekly holy communion and a chaplain available for individual counselling. However, there are no retreats at Skänninge. There is a special monastic rule at Skänninge with the aim of helping 'to find a direction and staying on the path towards the goal. The intention is to make it easier to listen to your inner voice when you come up against everyday disruptions. The activities are to be characterised by self-respect, respect for others and the sanctity of life' (Klostervägen 2011). This is said in the information brochure, which further stresses that it is important 'To strengthen the spirit of community in the entire monastery, it is important to do things together, for example meals, prayers, group discussions and crafts' (Klostervägen 2011).

In 2010, a third step of the Monastery Path was established at Mariagården in Vadstena, which continued until 2015. Mariagården was not a prison but a treatment home (*behandlingshem*), intended as a place for convicts to spend the last year of their sentence before moving to their own place to live. Convicts could apply to Mariagården if they had around 1 year left and had taken part in the Monastery Path. Mariagården was also open to convicts who had taken part in the Twelve Step Programme as a form of rehabilitation (Roxell et al. 2016). Presently, Mariagården is not operational, presumably for financial reasons, and the third step before release in some kind of rehabilitation environment is arranged according to the individual's needs and not an integrated part of the Monastery Path.

Over the years, since the Kumla Monastery opened in 2001, some studies have been conducted on the Monastery, but very little research and no real evaluation (e.g. Johansson 2012). This is largely because of the high degree of security around Kumla Prison and the strict legal requirement of maintaining individual convicts' integrity. But in 2014, the Prison and Probation Service granted three researchers funding for a qualitative study of the Monastery Path, in which 10 staff members and 14 inmates who had participated in a 30-day retreat were interviewed. The study did not aim to evaluate the Monastery Path but to provide an insider's view of what went on in the Monastery. The report ends with a number of recommendations to the Prison and Probation Service for improving the Monastery Path (Roxell et al. 2016).

22.7 Ambiguity on the Religious–Secular Divide

The Kumla Monastery and the Monastery Path are a typical example of the continuous negotiation taking place when it comes to the place of religion in Swedish secular public contexts (Pettersson 2011b). Even if the Monastery is a very special case, the general situation in Swedish prisons is that religion constitutes an integrated part of the prison organisation, taken for granted and regarded as uncontroversial, not as being in conflict with the secular character of state institutions. The situation is the same in hospitals and the military, and in some ways also in public schools (*Grunddokument med riktlinjer för de kristna kyrkornas arbete med andlig vård inom hälso-och sjukvården* 2004/2017; Elmberg 2010; Skolverket 2012).

There is, however, a tension between the official national policy and political rhetoric of state secularity, on the one hand, and the practice of collaborating with religious agents at the local level in these institutions, on the other. This tension is visible in the official presentation brochure *Klostervägen* (Monastery Path) produced by the Swedish Prison and Probation Service and available as a PDF document on their website. The first page states: '*The Monastery Path, for those who want to find out who they really are – we break the vicious circle*', and subsequent pages describe the Monastery Path, that it uses tools such as silence, the Bible and meditation/reflection. At the same time, its secularity is stressed, and it is said that the Monastery Path is not a course in Christian faith (Klostervägen 2011).

The contents of the official informational brochure demonstrate the negotiation between the state as secular and the integrated religious practice. The prison authority needs to stress the positive aspects of the Monastery and, thereby, legitimise religious practice as a tool for rehabilitation. At the same time, secular authorities need to minimize the religious character of the Monastery Path programme in order to legitimise its integration into the prison as a secular state institution.

22.8   From Religion as Authority to Religion as Service –
Focus on the Value in Use

The Kumla Monastery and the Monastery Path represent a significant example of religious complexity in Swedish as well as Nordic society in general when it comes to the presence of religion in public contexts (Kühle et al. 2018). According to traditional secularisation theory, the role of religion and religious agents would disappear as part of societal functional differentiation and specialisation (Weber 1978). From having been integrated in societal power structures, religion was predicted to lose its public social significance.

But on the contrary, developments since the 1980s have shown that religion returned in different ways as a public resource in Swedish society (cf. Casanova 1994; Bäckström et al. 2011). The ongoing rationalisation and functional differentiation processes have also implied a specialisation of religious institutions. They have lost their overarching political function at the centre of societal power structures and have become potential social resources and service providers in certain areas and with special, sometimes unique, competence (Beckford 1989; Pettersson 2000; Casanova 2006). Consequently, religious institutions are regarded as attractive complementary resources and service providers in certain areas.

In contemporary European society, religious organisations appear and act in parallel with other organisations at a social meso-level and are being increasingly evaluated according to their ability to meet the needs of individuals and other organisations. They are evaluated in relation to the actually perceived quality of their services and to a lesser extent in relation to their traditional authority and legitimacy. The rhetoric defending chaplaincies in state institutions like prisons, hospitals and the military is often motivated by arguing that the presence of religious agents is part of the state service functions in relation to people in these institutions and their freedom to practise their religion.

Along with the neoliberal trend towards outsourcing public welfare services, which has been a kind of paradigm for the dominant Swedish political parties since the early 1990s, there has been an increasing state demand for faith-based organisations' special competence in certain areas. The Kumla Monastery is an example of meeting this demand. Religion is used as a resource to fulfil the 'secular' needs of the state: to rehabilitate inmates. The Monastery demonstrates a specialisation of traditional services of the Church by adapting the concept of 'retreat' to the needs and context of the prison. Implicitly, the religious tradition is regarded as a service with a focus on the demonstrated 'value in use' (Sandström et al. 2008). The focus is on the effect, and not primarily on the credibility of the teaching of the Church, its beliefs and so forth.

It is no coincidence that it was a Church of Sweden priest who was first tasked with launching the Monastery at Kumla. The former state church is still a majority church among the population, and it is not regarded as odd, exclusive or controversial, and not too 'religious'. The Church of Sweden is one of the historical European Christian churches that have lost their former power but have re-emerged as potential value-creating resources (Pettersson 2011a). Like other similar majority churches, it serves a kind of mediating function between the state and other denominations and religions and is often regarded as a representative of all religions in a certain local geographical or institutional context.

22.9 Conclusion

Relationships between state and church in Sweden have slowly and continuously evolved over the last 150 years, going from almost complete unity to a religiously neutral state and increasing religious pluralism. The Church of Sweden has lost its formal power, high participation in activities, totally dominating membership, and so forth. However, this change has gone hand in hand with the continuous presence of religion in certain more specialised aspects.

Even if the Swedish state is principally secular, religion is in many ways integrated into its social practice, as shown by the presence of religious activities in the prison system in general and specifically in Kumla Prison and the Monastery Path. These persistent forms of religious presence in state institutions can be analysed and understood as a consequence of the general societal process of functional differentiation and specialisation (Luhmann 1982; Dobbelaere 2002). Secularisation in this respect does not mean the disappearance of religion, but that religion fulfils more specialised and occasional functions (Pettersson 2013).

When interpreting the state policy expressed in the acts on relations between the state and faith communities as well as in practice, it is obvious that the Church of Sweden and other faith communities are regarded as important resources in the Swedish welfare system that serve complementary functions in society at large. The study of religion in Swedish prisons demonstrates the specialised presence of religious agents in the prison context as well as tension in relation to the official secular policy of the Swedish state.

Bibliography

Andersson, D., & Sander, Å. (Eds.). (2005). *Det mångreligiösa Sverige. Ett landskap i förändring* *(The multireligious Sweden. A Landscape in Change)*. Lund: Studentlitteratur.

Bäckström, A., Beckman, N. E., & Pettersson, P. (2004). *Religious change in Northern Europe. The case of Sweden.* Verbum: Stockholm.

Bäckström, A., Davie, G., Edgardh, N., & Pettersson, P. (2011). *Welfare and religion in 21st century Europe: Volume 2.* Farnham: Ashgate.

Beckford, J. (1989). *Religion and advanced industrial society.* London: Unwin Hyman.

Bexell, O. (2003). *Sveriges kyrkohistoria, part 7 Folkväckelsens och kyrkoförnyelsens tid* *(The church history of Sweden, part 7 the time of revival movements and church renewal).* Stockholm: Verbum.

Casanova, J. (1994). *Public religions in the modern world.* Chicago, IL: University of Chicago Press.

Casanova, J. (2006). Rethinking secularization: A global comparative perspective. *The Hedgehog Review*, 8(1–2), 7–22.

Church of Sweden Statistics. (2016). *Kyrkan i siffror* (The church in numbers). Available online at: www.svenskakyrkan.se

Dobbelaere, K. (2002). *Secularization: An analysis at three levels*. Brussels: Peter Lang.

Elmberg, S. (2010). *Militär själavård (Military chaplaincy)*. Stockholm: Försvarsmakten.

Grunddokument med riktlinjer för de kristna kyrkornas arbete med andlig vård inom hälso-och sjukvården 2004/2017. Fastställt av Samarbetsrådet för andlig vård inom hälso- och sjukvården den 8 mars 2004, uppdaterat den 15 maj 2017. (Basic Document with Guidelines on the Christian Churches Spiritual Care in Medical and Health Care. Approved by The Cooperation Council for Spiritual Care in Health Care March 8, 2004, updated 15 May 2017). Accessible online as a PDF document at: http://www.akademiska.se/Verksamheter/Sjukhuskyrkan/

Johansson, P. (2012). *Spirituality within the prison walls*. Master thesis, Institutionen för socialt arbete. Östersund: Mittuniversitetet.

Klostervägen. (2011). *Klostervägen – for those who want to find out who they really are*. Information brochure. Order number 9283. Kriminalvården: Norrköping. Accessible online at: https://www.kriminalvarden.se/globalassets/fangelse/klostervagen_english.pdf

Kriminalvården. (2018). The Swedish prison and probation service website, www.kriminalvarden.se

Kühle, L., Schmidt, U., Jacobsen, B. A., & Pettersson, P. (2018). Religion and state: Complexity in change. In I. Furseth (Ed.), *Religious complexity in the public sphere. Palgrave studies in religion, politics, and policy* (pp. 81–135). Cham: Palgrave Macmillan.

Kyrkoordningen. (2007). *The church order*. Stockholm: Verbum förlag.

Larsson, Göran. (2011). *Andlig vård inom Kriminalvården. En kunskapsöversikt* (Spiritual Care in the Swedish Prison and Probation Service. An overview). Kriminalvårdens utvecklingsenhet, projektnummer 2009:124. Kriminalvårdens reprocentral, beställningsnummer 6016. Norrköping: Kriminalvården.

Levenskog, Y. (1997). *Institutionssjälavård i Sverige 1932–1989. Med särskild hänsyn tagen till fängelsesjälavården* (Pastoral care in public institutions in Sweden 1932–1989. With specific respect to pastoral care in prisons). Uppsala: Bibliotheca Theologiae Practicae.

Luhmann, N. (1982). *The differentiation of society*. New York: Columbia University.

Lundstedt, G. (2006). *Biskopsämbetet och demokratin* (Ministry of the Bishop and Democracy). Skellefteå: Artos & Norma bokförlag.

Martin, D. (1978). *A general theory of secularization*. Oxford: Basil Blackwell.

Pettersson, P. (2000). *Kvalitet i livslånga tjänsterelationer. Svenska kyrkan ur tjänsteteoretiskt och religionssociologiskt perspektiv* (Quality in Lifelong Service Relationships. The Church of Sweden in Service Theoretical and Sociology of Religion Perspective). Stockholm: Verbum.

Pettersson, P. (2011a). Majority churches as agents of European welfare: A sociological approach. In A. Bäckström, G. Davie, N. Edgardh, & P. Pettersson (Eds.), *Welfare and religion in 21st century Europe: Volume 2* (pp. 15–59). Farnham: Ashgate.

Pettersson, P. (2011b). State and religion in Sweden: Ambiguity between disestablishment and religious control. *Nordic Journal of Religion and Society, 24*(2), 119–136.

Pettersson, P. (2013). From standardized offer to consumer adaptation. Challenges to the Church of Sweden's identity. In F. Gauthier & T. Martikainen (Eds.), *Religion in consumer society: Brands, consumers and markets* (pp. 43–57). Farnham: Ashgate.

Pettersson, P. (2014). Values and religion in transition – a case study of a Swedish multicultural public school. In E. Pace, H. Vilaça, I. Furseth, & P. Pettersson (Eds.), *The changing soul of Europe: Religions and migrations in Northern and Southern Europe* (pp. 193–207). Farnham: Ashgate.

Pettersson, P. (2015). Is the Swedish state secular when religious service functions are integrated in state institutions? *Studia Z Prawa Wyznaniowego, 18*, 23–42.

Roxell, L., Alm, S., & DeMarinis, V. (2016). *Röster om att gå i tystnad – en beskrivning och analys av Kriminalvårdens Klosterverksamhet (Voices on entering silence – description an analysis of the prison and probation service monastery activity). Kriminalvårdens digitaltryck, beställningsnummer 7146.* Norrköping: Kriminalvården.

Sandström, S., Edvardsson, B., Kristensson, P., & Magnusson, P. (2008). Value in use through service experience. *Managing Service Quality, 18*(2), 112–126.

SFS. (1951). *680 Religionsfrihetslagen (The freedom of religion act).* Stockholm: Sveriges riks- dag.

SFS. (1974). *152 Regeringsformen (The instrument of government).* Stockholm: Sveriges riks- dag.

SFS. (1998a). *1591 Lag om Svenska kyrkan (The Church of Sweden act).* Stockholm: Sveriges riksdag.

SFS. (1998b). *1593 Lag om trossamfund (The act on faith communities).* Stockholm: Sveriges riksdag.

SFS. (2008). *567 Diskrimineringslag (discrimination act).* Stockholm: Sveriges riksdag.

Skolverket. (2012). *Mer om...Skol- och förskoleverksamhet i kyrkan eller annan religiös lokal. Juridisk vägledning. Granskad februari 2012* (More about... School – and pre-school activity in churches or other religious premises. Juridical guide. Examined February 2012). Skolverket. Accessible at www.skolverket.se

Swedish Commission for Government Support for Faith Communities, Statistics. (2015). *Nämnden för statligt stöd till trossamfund, Statistik 2012.* Accessible at: www.sst.a.se

Weber, M. (1978). *Economy and society, volumes 1–2.* Berkeley: University of California Press.

Zuckerman, P. (2008). *Society without god.* New York: New York University Press.

Chapter 23
Switzerland: Religions and Spirituality in Prison – Institutional Analysis

Aude Zurbuchen, Anaïd Lindemann, and Irene Becci

Abstract The Swiss prison system presents particular specificities regarding the place it gives to religion and spirituality, in part because of the changes in the religious landscape in recent decades, as well as the federal system, which gives each Canton a margin of manoeuvre in managing religious diversity. On the one hand, the secularisation of Swiss society, including the loss of importance of the recognised churches (Catholic and Reformed) in daily life and the organisation of society, had considerable impacts on their role and status in prison. On the other hand, religious pluralisation, increased in particular by migratory flows, poses important challenges for chaplaincies and prison administrations. This chapter is aimed at analysing the particularities of the Swiss case in its historical, demographic and legal dimensions, while giving an important place to empirical case studies.

23.1 Introduction

The aim of this chapter is to provide an overview of the different ways in which the issues of religion and religious diversity arise in Swiss prisons. First, we examine the historical evolution of chaplaincies in these institutions and then contextualise it in view of the plurality of the religious affiliation of the prison population, the legal framework, the role of religious and spiritual actors in prison, as well as the different profiles of these actors. We illustrate this general framework through the example of the Bellechasse Penitentiary, an institution for men in the Canton of Fribourg

A. Zurbuchen wrote most of the empirical parts, A. Lindemann dealt with the state of the art, among other parts, and I. Becci supervised the work, orientated the literature and edited the introduction and conclusion. The text has been translated by Muriel Bruttin and commented on by Dr. Zhargalma Dandarova, whom the authors thank warmly, together with Dr. Joëlle Vuille who has corrected the passages on the legal aspects. The authors remain solely responsible for the content of this text.

A. Zurbuchen · A. Lindemann (✉) · I. Becci
Institute of Social Sciences of Religions, University of Lausanne, Lausanne, Switzerland
e-mail: Anaid.Lindemann@unil.ch; irene.becciterrier@unil.ch

© Springer Nature Switzerland AG 2020
J. Martínez-Ariño, A.-L. Zwilling (eds.), *Religion and Prison: An Overview of Contemporary Europe*, Boundaries of Religious Freedom: Regulating Religion in Diverse Societies 7, https://doi.org/10.1007/978-3-030-36834-0_23

for the enforcement of sentences and penal measures and deprivation of liberty for the purpose of assistance, and the example of the prison of La Tuilière of the Canton of Vaud, divided into a men's and a women's sector. Using these examples, we look at the wide variety of ways in which religious questions are present, depending on the complex setting of a penitentiary institution. The second part of this chapter is devoted to an immersion into the prison universe and the religious/spiritual phenomena that take place, using extracts of ethnographic observations collected in 2016 by Aude Zurbuchen in different institutions (which we do not name to guarantee the anonymity of the people concerned). These vignettes allow us to highlight the adjustments made by the religious/spiritual actors and the issues with which they are confronted.

23.2   General Framework

23.2.1   Historical Developments

Until the last century, in Switzerland, the chaplaincies held by the recognised churches were structurally integrated into the prisons, and the functions of the chaplains, mostly men (Becci et al. 2011a: 6), were multiple: right-hand men of the direction, they performed all sorts of social tasks, positioned themselves as interlocutors with lawyers, or even offered local language courses. Since the 1980s, however, their prerogatives and the centrality of the Christian religion within the prison universe have gradually narrowed.

This situation, which involved a renegotiation of the place and role of chaplaincies in prison, is one of the results of the secularisation and pluralisation of Swiss society (Baumann and Stolz 2009). First, Swiss society freed itself from the influence of Christian religious institutions by specialising in the fields that constituted it, such as education, medicine or, in the subject that interests us, punitive institutions and security. Second, the relationship with religion has gradually become individualised, multiplying the variety of religious practices and beliefs of social actors and within religious traditions (Stolz et al. 2015). Migratory flows have also reinforced this process of religious pluralisation, bringing new religious affiliations.

Since then, chaplaincies have been assigned a role that is more centred on spiritual support for detainees, rather than solely religious assistance related to a Church (Becci et al. 2011b). The NRP58 study "Religion in Swiss Prisons"[1] (Becci et al. 2011a) demonstrated the transformation of the profession of chaplains since the 1980s. Today, prison chaplains "devote most of their time and energy to listening to detainees" (Ibid.: 6). At the same time, the content of the messages carried by the chaplains are marked more by universalism than by a purely Christian orientation.

---

[1] *"La religion dans les prisons suisses"*, study co-directed by Irene Becci, Claude Bovay and André Kuhn between 2007 and 2011 and funded by the Swiss National Science Foundation SNSF.

This universalisation (or "neutralisation" of the religious message) is seen by some scholars as a new strategy for regulating religion in Swiss prisons (Becci 2015: 5–19). Finally, following the process of differentiation between the punitive role and the objectives of rehabilitation within the penitentiary institutions, the field of action of chaplains is now confined to the field of rehabilitation. In other words, chaplaincy has gone from "a structural status to an individual status (…). The example of the transformation of Catholic or Protestant chaplains to the status of spiritual accompaniment of people reflects more broadly the loss of structural influence of these churches in this context" (Becci 2016: 38).

As an example, the institution of Bellechasse, which was founded in 1898 and contains about 200 places, presents a particularity that is revealing about the loss of influence and centrality of religious institutions in prisons: next to the main building is a church, which, a few years ago, was frequented by some detainees, before security requirements forced the erection of a barrier separating the Catholic religious building from the penitentiary building, thus ending detainee attendance at this church. Currently, the only space that the chaplains of this establishment have as their own space is a storage cupboard.

23.2.2 Inmate Population

In 2017 (the latest official figures), the number of adult prisoners in penal institutions amounted to 6863, of whom 69% were sentenced and 24% were held in pre-trial detention. The remaining 7% comprises people detained either subject to coercive measures related to the Aliens Act (*Loi sur les étrangers*), or for other reasons. These detentions represent an occupancy rate of 92% of the 106 establishments in Switzerland (SFO 2019 report). However, an expert report revealed that some of the establishments in Switzerland are also concerned by the prison over-crowding observed in other European countries (Aebi et al. 2016). According to the report by cantonal experts on questions of enforcement of sentences and measures, prisons in the cantons of Geneva and Vaud were overcrowded by 130,3% and 139.5% respectively (report of the KKJPD 2017). Attempts to compensate for this overcrowding have been observed, for example, in the institution of La Tuilière, which was opened in 1992. The men's sector officially has 28 places, but has in fact 35 beds (pre-trial detention and psychological preventive detention) and the women's sector has 54 places augmented to 61 beds, which makes this prison rather small in Switzerland. Thus, La Tuilière officially has 82 spots, but actually had 96 beds in 2017.

Among these incarcerated individuals, men are overrepresented, accounting for 94% of the prison population, with an average age of 34. People of foreign nationality also constitute a high percentage: they make up almost 70% of the prison population compared with 25% of the general resident population in Switzerland. The numerically significant presence of foreigners is largely due to violations of the Aliens Act, but also to the fact that the foreign population in the country is itself composed of a higher percentage of young men than the population of Swiss nationality (Becci 2016: 32). The result is a very marked cultural diversity in penal institutions, which also has an impact on religious diversity.

However, it is very difficult to provide accurate statistics on religious and spiritual affiliations, as the census procedures and criteria vary from region to region and from institution to institution. Data from the 2010 analysis of two high-security men's prisons, one in French-speaking Switzerland and one in German-speaking Switzerland, show that half of the detainees say that they belong to a Christian denomination and 29% to a Muslim faith (Ibid.: 28). The NRP58 provides figures based on four prisons in the French-speaking and German-speaking areas, in which Muslim men sometimes constitute more than half of the prisoners, whereas Muslim women are a minority (5%) among the detainees. It should be noted, finally, that the different tendencies within each religious tradition are only grossly counted for Christians (Catholics, Protestants, Orthodox), or not at all counted for Muslims. As for new spiritualities, any person claiming this is automatically categorised under "other". In addition to the pragmatic necessities that guide this categorisation, it is one of the symptoms of the relative adaptation of institutions of deprivation of liberty in the face of current religious diversity (Becci et al. 2016).

In a report on penitentiary policy published by the Canton of Vaud,[2] where La Tuilière is located, one can read the following figures for religions declared within the institutions of the Canton: 2% without confession, 1% Hindus, 1% Buddhists, 5% atheists, 47% Christians (whose diversity is represented in the report by the following categories: Christian, Protestant, Catholic, Orthodox), 43% Muslims (whose diversity is not represented in the report) and 1% is declared under "other".

23.2.3   Legal Provisions

Freedom of conscience and belief is enshrined in a complex legal framework, which makes the guarantees of exercising it extremely heterogeneous on Swiss territory. Indeed, freedom of conscience and belief is inscribed in all legislative strata, from supranational law to the internal regulations of prisons (Vuille and Kuhn 2010). Figure 23.1 explains this hierarchical organisation. At the supranational level, freedom of thought, conscience and religion is guaranteed by the European Convention on Human Rights (ECHR)[3] and by the International Covenant on Economic, Social

---

[2] *Rapport sur la politique pénitentiaire au Conseil d'État vaudois.* Janvier 2016: 75

[3] Article 9 (freedom of thought, conscience and religion): (1) Everyone has the right to freedom of thought, conscience and religion; this right includes freedom to change his religion or belief and freedom, either alone or in a community with others and in public or private, to manifest his religion or belief, in worship, teaching, practice and observance. (2) Freedom to manifest one's religion or beliefs shall be subject only to such limitations as are prescribed by law and are necessary in a democratic society in the interests of public safety, for the protection of public order, health or morals, or for the protection of the rights and freedoms of others.

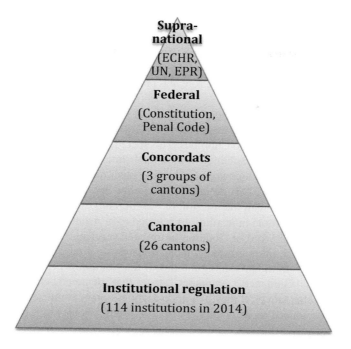

Fig. 23.1 Legislative stratification on the freedom of conscience and belief

and Cultural Rights of the United Nations, both of which are ratified by Switzerland. The European Prison Rules (EPRs), with which Switzerland has worked closely and to which it is committed (Ullrich 2007), complete the supranational system by stating in particular that "the prison system should be organized, as far as possible, in such a way as to allow detainees to practise their religion and follow their philosophy". Strictly speaking, however, EPRs are not binding. They are rather a set of rules that the states voluntarily agree to follow.

However, with the exception of these two minimal rules and contrary to the criminal law and procedure, the right of enforcement of penalties lies with the Cantons. This cantonal prerogative is distributed between two levels: an intermediate level with the three regional concordats that have jurisdiction to issue regulations, directives and recommendations for the grouped Cantons, even though they do not always resort to this jurisdiction in every area; and the purely cantonal level, where each Canton has the jurisdiction to issue its own regulations. For example, the Tuilière and Bellechasse institutions are both part of the Latin Concordat. As Switzerland is made up of 26 Cantons, there are 26 regulations on the exercise of freedom of conscience and belief in prisons, which makes a general analysis difficult. These cantonal regulations vary according to their requirements depending on their density, ranging from very succinct standards to detailed provisions, and according to the place given to the exercise of that freedom, which may be structurally included in the general rules on the execution of sentences or constitute specific provisions (Fink 2017). It should also be noted that Switzerland is technically not a secular state, as two churches (Roman Catholic and Protestant Reformed) are legally recognised as public institutions and their institutional location is defined by each Canton; this influences the role and presence of chaplaincies within prison facilities.

For example, the specific legal framework of the Canton of Fribourg, in which the Bellechasse institution is located, recognises two churches, the Roman Catholic and the Evangelical Reformed Churches. This recognition gives these two Churches "the right to exercise the chaplaincy in the establishments of the State and the communes" in general.[4] The framework convention governing the practice of the chaplaincy in the Cantons (2005) defines it as having the "vocation to animate and support, in accordance with the mission of the churches, the spiritual quest and the religious life of the people in institutions referred to in Article 1, in particular by the announcement of the Word of God, the liturgy and service to one's neighbour. It is a framework open to all interested persons, regardless of their religious sensitivity and convictions".[5] In the prison regulations of the Canton of Fribourg,[6] Article 37, entitled "Spiritual Guidance, Chaplaincy", states that "detained persons may request to see a prison chaplain or, if they belong to a confession not represented by a prison chaplain, a recognised representative of their religion". However, it is not specified here who recognises this representative and how.

In the cantonal law regarding the relationship between State and Churches passed in the 1990s, the term "spiritual assistance" does not appear, as it only regulates the question of ecumenical chaplaincy, which concerns only the churches recognised by the Canton of Fribourg. With regard to the regulation of prisons and the regulations regarding detainees and internees, the term "spiritual assistance" includes the chaplaincy and recognised religious representatives. However, vagueness remains around the way in which a religious representative is "recognised" and by whom.

In contrast, the Canton of Vaud recognises three religious communities and does not mention "spiritual" assistance. Indeed, in a report on the Canton's prison policy from January 2016, one can read: "As the Catholic, Protestant and Jewish communities are recognised by cantonal law [Vaudois], their framework of intervention is clear. It is less so for representatives of other religions. Representatives of these religions may, however, receive authorisations for ordinary visits from the administrative authorities of the institutions to meet certain detained persons who have requested such visits.[7]"

The regulation on the status of pre-trial detainees and sentenced persons placed in pre-trial detention facilities and the 2008 detention regimes (RSDAJ) also

---

[4] Law on relations between Churches and the State passed on 26 September 1990 (ordinary system). Article 23 RSF 190.1

[5] Framework convention passed on 3 April 2005. Article 2 RSF 190.5.

[6] Passed on 12 December 2016. ROF 2007_022

[7] *Rapport sur la politique pénitentiaire au Conseil d'État vaudois*. Janvier 2016: 75.

provides that "prisoners may call upon representatives of churches and religious communities of the establishment".[8] If an inmate calls upon a representative of a church or community recognised by the Canton but not appointed by the facility, he must first obtain the notice of an appointed representative.[9] For a representative of a religious community not recognised at the cantonal level, nothing is specified in the aforementioned regulation. In this perspective, we can note the discriminatory nature of this regulation (Becci et al. 2011a: 9), which recognises only three communities: Catholic, Protestant and Jewish. If one looks at the regulation of the organisation and the staff of the establishment (ROP),[10] one discovers the same discrimination. Indeed, in Sect. IV entitled *Chaplains*, Article 59, entitled "Other confessions", we can read that "ministers of another religion may be permitted to visit detainees of their religion, with the prior authorisation of the director or judge for the accused". We can note that in the various regulations to which this facility is subject, there is no mention of spiritual assistance; only the term chaplaincy is used.

At the institutional level, each facility has its own regulations. The degree of precision varies considerably from one institution to another, depending on the size and needs of the institution. Some provide for the modalities of organisation and appointment of spiritual and religious assistance, which can be set up by an internal chaplaincy in the prison or depend on external persons who are called upon in case of need. Some texts set out the aims, tasks and purposes of this assistance, whereas others remain silent on these issues. Concretely, spiritual or religious offers take different forms, ranging from the provision of religious services to individual or family visits, or taking into account certain food restrictions. Specific requests that do not fall within the general offer may be dealt with on a case-by-case basis, depending on the will and the room for manoeuvre of the management of the institution. According to the results of the NRP58 study, it appears that prison administrations often try to find pragmatic arrangements for managing this diversity, as demonstrated by certain arrangements put in place to satisfy Muslim prisoners (Becci et al. 2011a: 8).

There is a flexible but equally vague form of adjustment in the regulation of the detainees[11] of the Bellechasse prison, which introduces "religious representatives" alongside the chaplains under Article 56 entitled "Spiritual Assistance". This category of actors needs to have been previously recognised "by the competent confessional or religious authorities" (Article 56, paragraph 2). As in the case of the prison regulations, no indication is given of the criteria that give rise to the status of recognised representative, nor are there details regarding which are the competent authorities. The statuses of chaplain and religious representatives give the right to talk to prisoners without supervision, and without these interviews being counted as visiting hours.

---

[8] Regulation passed on 16 January 2008. Article 92, al. 2, RSV 340.02.5.

[9] Regulation passed on 16 January 2008. Article 66, RSV 340.02.5.

[10] Regulation passed on 12 January 1992. RSV 340.11.5.

[11] Regulation passed on 9 December 1998. RSF 341.1.12.

Although the cantonal legal heterogeneity and the relative autonomy of the institutions offer the potential for adaptability in responding to the needs of the very diverse prison population, they also open up the possibilities of the unequal treatment of certain religious minorities. Indeed, spiritual and religious support in prisons has undergone important changes in response to the processes of secularisation and religious pluralisation in Switzerland, while presenting certain difficulties in adapting totally to these changes.

23.2.4 Profile of Religious and Spiritual Actors

The NRP58 research group was able to identify five categories of spiritual and religious actors in prisons, each with a certain degree of institutionalisation and distinct objectives: chaplaincies, other Christian actors, holistic actors, Muslim representatives and compatriots. In addition to Catholic and Protestant chaplaincies, representatives of other religious and spiritual traditions do not have a clearly defined status and their right of access to detained persons is subject to different treatment.

(a) Chaplaincies

In spite of the loss of influence of the churches mentioned above, the fact remains that prisons are marked by a Christian heritage. As a result, the most institutionalised group of practitioners is Christian chaplaincies run by recognised churches. This means that their staff are generally remunerated through state subsidies,[12] that premises can be specially allocated to them in institutions and that their access to detained people is very easy. On the other hand, they attempt to achieve a certain neutrality: they address themselves to all detained people, regardless of confession, and aim to provide spiritual care and individual support that is neutral in terms of religious content. This strategy of universalising the mission of chaplaincies is sometimes felt in religious services, which depart from purely Christian messages. At the same time, the chaplains aim to engage in constructive reflections that encourage future reintegration of detainees, by attempting to reconstitute identity and social connections. They also work on mediation and conflict resolution (Becci 2016). In addition, they are usually considered to be trusted persons and privileged interlocutors, as little institutional stake is played out in their exchanges with prisoners. In a sense, a chaplaincy today plays a role of control, in spite of itself, by ensuring peaceful cohabitation within the prison in which it is integrated and helping prisoners to support the experience of confinement (Becci et al. 2011b: 5).

---

[12] Because of the federal organisation of Switzerland, each of the 26 Cantons has the possibility of choosing their own individual way of regulating relations between the State and religions. As a matter of fact, there are 26 systems, ranging from a total separation of the State and religious institutions (Geneva) and a recognition system where some religious groups have state subsidies or recognition (Vaud).

To illustrate the diversity of settings, we mention two cases. At Bellechasse, the chaplaincy service is made up of three chaplains, representing the two Churches recognised by the Canton, namely the Roman Catholic and Reformed Evangelical Churches. In addition to meeting with prisoners on a daily basis (in corridors, cells, workplaces and places of leisure or sport), the Catholic chaplains, who are hired 1 and 1.5 day a week respectively, are trying to set up a regular mass, every 6 weeks, which depends on the rate of inmate attendance, according to the interviews conducted. The Reformed chaplain does not officiate at worship because of the very limited number of Protestant detainees in the institution. However, he joins and plays an active role in the Christmas and Easter masses. The chaplains do not have their own space, and the religious celebrations take place in the available spaces (hall, cafeteria, corridor). The chaplaincy is also in contact with a visiting officer of the Salvation Army.

At La Tuilière, there are two chaplains: a Reformed chaplain, who is also a pastor, and a Catholic chaplain, both of whom are employed on a part-time basis, working 2.5 days a week. The intervention of any other religious actor is delegated to the chaplains, considered by the prison's management as specialists of the religions within the institution. At present, when a detainee makes a request, the chaplains bring up and discuss this request at management meetings. If the request is deemed inadmissible, the request in the form of an ecclesiastical visit (not counted as an ordinary visit) is not possible. The roles and tasks of chaplains are defined in a cantonal report as follows: "In the prisons of Vaud, Catholic and Protestant chaplains are resource persons who take care of the detainees' spirituality and ensure a space for this aspect of human life. In this sense, they meet the detainees in a broad way, irrespective of either religious belonging or beliefs. Later on, they can intervene in a more specific way in religious matters and pass these requests onto representatives of other religions."[13]

(b) Other Christian actors

Informally institutionalised, some other Christian actors – such as the Bellechasse Salvation Army visiting officer – benefit from easier access to detainees than the simple status of visitor, yet are not given the same leeway as their Catholic and Protestant counterparts. These Christian groups are mainly evangelical, among which the Salvation Army is the most frequently present. Other Christian traditions are represented, such as Baptists and Pentecostals. Their target audience consists of all detainees, regardless of their religious affiliation. Their main activities in penal institutions are the organisation of collective events such as plays or Christmas markets, as well as individual interviews with prisoners. However, their presence is not a response to requests from detainees, but the result of negotiations with chaplaincies and prison administrations (Becci et al. 2011b: 9). Their easier access is

---

[13] *Rapport sur la politique pénitentiaire au Conseil d'État vaudois.* Janvier 2016: 75. The translation is ours.

permitted through their personal network and their historical involvement in the life of penitentiary institutions.

(c) Holistic actors

The so-called holistic actors, who are also close to having an institutionalised status, include representatives of yoga practice, meditation and new spiritualities. These actors have begun to invest in prison spaces since the early 2000s. Technically belonging to no religious community, these new actors do not intervene in terms of managing religious diversity: they are generally defined as "spiritual" agents, whereas prison administrations consider their services rather as health practices or sports activities. As a result, their presence is deemed useful and desirable for detainees, making access to them relatively simple and official. Indeed, some holistic practitioners are permitted to use an institution's premises to give their teachings.

(d) Muslim representatives

Muslim representatives, for their part, have a special position: although Islam is often an important part of the religious affiliation of inmates, if not the majority in certain institutions, imams and other Muslim representatives are subject to the status of visitors and intervene at the request of the prisoners. They must systematically announce their arrival in advance and work in common or borrowed spaces. In addition, as Islam is not officially recognised in any of the Cantons,[14] their work is not remunerated and they work mostly on a voluntary basis. For these reasons, they can spend at most 2.5 h a week in the prison. Imams, usually well-trained young men and affiliated to local Muslim congregations, explain their commitment as philanthropy. Various profiles of Muslim representatives were identified by the NRP58 research group, namely the imam, sufficiently well trained to preach and direct prayer; the chaplain, who focuses his activity on individual accompaniment in addition to religious service; the Big Brother, who focuses on engaging in discussions with prisoners to the detriment of religious service; the mediator, who intervenes at the request of the institution as a cultural mediator; and finally the visitor, who visits for the sole purpose of exchanging with the prisoners. On the other hand, imams are totally absent from the female prison system: only exchange-based women's groups are set up for Muslim inmates and run by volunteers. Institutions explain this choice by referring to the fact that women are not required to participate in Friday prayers (Becci et al. 2011b: 7).

Beyond this unequal treatment in access and working conditions between Muslim representatives and institutional chaplaincies, important adjustments have been made to allow Muslim worship to be carried out and certain Islamic rules to be observed by the prisoners who wish to follow them.

---

[14] In the Swiss Constitution, it is stipulated that the Cantons have the possibility of recognising religious groups, granting them some rights and a symbolic acknowledgement. For the moment (2017), only a few Cantons have recognised the Israelite community, but none of them has recognised Islam.

At Bellechasse, an imam completes the picture of the regular religious actors of the institution already mentioned (the three chaplains and the visiting officer of the Salvation Army). Present for more than 10 years in the institution, the imam has seen his situation regularised and is allowed to be present twice a week: on Tuesday evenings for a maximum of four individual interviews of 15 min each, which are carried out at the prior request of the prisoners, and on Friday for prayer, for which the participants, who register in advance each time, must be declared Muslims. His presence, however, is not institutionalised, and his status remains indefinite, although he is sometimes qualified as a Muslim chaplain.

At La Tuilière, the chaplains are in contact with a Muslim federation, which is itself recognised as a privileged interlocutor by the Canton. This organisation proposed an imam, who was introduced by the chaplains to the prison directors. He now comes regularly, once a month for prayer in the men's area, without being paid. He cannot conduct individual interviews with inmates unless the chaplains feel that they cannot meet the inmate's needs. Here, the rule of the exception is applied to interviews, as otherwise it would be necessary to answer the requests of about a 100 detainees every week, explains the chaplain. As for female Muslim inmates, their small percentage means that the imam does not intervene in the women's sector, but may have an individual interview with a female inmate when she comes for the monthly prayer.

(e) Compatriots

Finally, the so-called compatriots are the least well-off in terms of visibility and recognition. These religious actors, who are only contacted by the entourage or the detained persons themselves, belong to minority and migrant Churches. They are of the same origin or speak the same language as their audience, and are usually from Africa, South America or Asia. Their access to penitentiary institutions is administratively difficult: they are subject to the protocol of visitors and can be received only in the collective visiting room. Their visits are deducted from the quota of visits per prisoner.

Table 23.1 summarises, in a synthetic and therefore necessarily non-exhaustive manner, and not taking into account the porosity of certain categories, the various profiles presented above.

23.3   Diversification of the Spiritual Offer in Prisons

In recent years, ethnographic research in prison has also brought to light a series of practices that could be described as spiritual in the sense of being detached from any regulation of religious institutions. For example, we were able to report on holistic practices around yoga classes, for example, or individual esoteric initiatives. This type of activity is not considered by the prison administration as religious and therefore remains formally linked to sectors that are more in the domain of the psychological (certain therapies), the social (encounters with other members of the spiritual

Table 23.1 Summary of the religious profiles

Profile	Religious denomination	Addressees	Roles/tasks	Status and accessibility
Chaplains of recognised churches	Reformed Catholic	All detained persons	Religious services	Official and paid
			Accompaniment/ listening	Integrated into the facility, usually with own offices and rooms, assistance from volunteers
			Spiritual support	
			Individual interview	
			Ombudsmen	
			Constructive education and rehabilitation	
Other Christian actors	Evangelicals (Salvationist, Baptist, Pentecostal etc.)	All detained persons	Organisation of collective punctual events	Unofficial–official
			Individual interviews	Access facilitated by their network and historical link
			Evangelism (implicit)	Paid by their own Churches
				In the process of institutionalisation
Muslim actors	Muslim (no current details)	Muslim detainees	(a) Imam: ensures preaching and directing prayer	Protocol of visitors
			(b) Chaplain: individual accompaniment and Friday service	Unpaid (volunteer)
			(c) Big Brother: listening	2.5 h per week maximum
			(d) Mediator: cultural mediator, at the request of the institution	
			(e) Visitor: exchange	
Muslim volunteer	Muslim (no current details)	Muslim detainees	Discussion and group sharing	Regular meetings
			Communication usually in the mother tongue	

(continued)

Table 23.1 (continued)

Profile	Religious denomination	Addressees	Roles/tasks	Status and accessibility
Holistic	Do not belong to any religious community	All detained persons	Define themselves as spiritual actors offering yoga, meditation and new spiritualities	In the process of institutionalisation
			Establishments define them as a health practices	
Compatriots	Migrant churches (pantheists, Kimbanguists, Buddhists)	Inmates of the same origin and mother tongue	Listening	Unidentified
				Collective visiting rooms
				Access difficult administratively
				Never solicited by the institution

milieu) or cultural (e.g. the library). The study of the growth of these new spiritualities in prison, in continual negotiation with religious as well as secular actors, is still in its infancy. In this text, we will only present a situation that illustrates the fuzzy outlines of this spirituality that can, in this case, arise in the very heart of historical chaplaincy.

The NRP58 has shown the transformation of the profession of chaplains since the 1980s. Today, prison chaplains "devote most of their time and energy to listening to detainees" (Becci et al. 2011a: 6). To this central role of listening is added a willingness to act by taking into account the transformation of the religious landscape, as demonstrated by the approach of two prison chaplains whom we followed. Indeed, in 2015, they began to train in mindfulness meditation, recognised today in the field of psychotherapy and personal development for its effects in particular on depression, stress and anxiety (Garnoussi 2011: 260). By training in this method, the chaplains followed their intention to bring to the detainees, first, a "tool" without a "specific label" that could help them to gain "some control over their emotions, their body and their actions" in an environment that the chaplains consider to be highly anxiety-inducing, especially in the preventive sector, in which detainees live intensely the process of dispossession of the self (Sykes 1958; Clemmer 1940). One of the chaplains who initiated this process explains that they started from the "feeling [that the prisoners] would need this". This need having been identified as spiritual, the chaplains wanted to respond to it. According to the chaplain, "this approach of meditation, it is the idea of starting from the needs of people. That's where it comes in. Take these needs seriously and go into a 'take care'." The chaplain, although recognising the Buddhist origins of this practice, considers that it is a "tool that has no particular label" and that can be reinvested by each according to his own tradition, a tool that can therefore be offered to all, regardless of religious tradition. Their initiative, however, was not successful, at least in the collaborative form that the chaplains wished to set up with the medical service of the institution, because the latter considered that all the prisoners who had registered for meditation had contraindications that did not allow them to pursue this practice, which it considered part of the psychotherapeutic field.

Such an approach on the part of the chaplains raises questions about the evolution of their place in the institutions, evolution influenced notably by the presence of a religious diversity whose composition no longer corresponds to the dominance of recognised churches, as also shown by the case cited above of the Reformed chaplain who does not officiate at mass because of a lack of participants. Issues of openness and discrimination are also on the agenda. A Protestant chaplain told us, for example, in an interview, that the approach taken by the management of the institution in which he works is to let the chaplains make decisions about the detainees' requests to meet a representative of a religion other than those represented by the chaplains assigned to them, thereby conferring upon the chaplains a subjective and discriminating power. A chaplain, he explained, could not recommend certain communities whose functioning or theology he does not appreciate.

23.4   Immersion Through Participant Observation

23.4.1   *Mass in Prison: Prison A*[15]

On this misty Saturday in a Swiss penitentiary, two masses will be officiated at by an abbot, the chaplain not being entitled to officiate: the first in the pre-trial sector, and the second in the sector of the enforcement of sentences, as inmates in these two sectors are not allowed to have contact with each other. The chaplain and the abbot, with a briefcase in hand, enter the prison without being controlled. Once the chaplain has retrieved his set of keys, which give him access to the various sectors of the prison, the two men undertake a winding course through the prison, punctuated by the opening and closing of the doors. They finally join a guard who proposes that they set up in a small room or at the end of the corridor, in an enlarged space, as the chaplains do not have their own space within the building. After a few exchanges, they chose to use the room, which will be more intimate and quieter. Ten prisoners of this sector registered on a form that the chaplain gave at the beginning of the week to the social service. But the social service did not post it until Friday, and in a place that was not very visible according to a discussion with the guard and then with the eight detainees present: if the sheet had been posted earlier, they would have been greater participation, says the chaplain. The same problem of communication will arise in the sector of execution of sentences, all the more emphasised by the fact that only two prisoners will participate in the mass.

---

[15] For reasons of anonymity, the names of the prisons are not revealed.

Before the arrival of the detainees, the chaplain and the abbot arrange the space, pushing four tables together surrounded with chairs, an arrangement that is meant to allow for greater conviviality and encourage exchange. The abbot takes out a variety of blue terracotta objects from his briefcase and places them on a white doily: a small cross, a saucer in which he places the host, a cup and a candle holder with a small candle. These objects, as well as the abbot's attire, are the only elements that indicate that a mass will be celebrated. The abbot pours white wine into the cup, which he alone will drink to avoid, he tells us, the risk of making a detainee undergoing alcohol rehabilitation drink. Before the ceremony begins, the chaplain, alternating between English and French, reminds prisoners of the daily presence of the chaplains, as well as their availability for individual interviews, upon request, and the possibility of requesting a Bible, of which he has copies in several languages. After the chaplain has specified that the mass will be said in French, the abbot, who has clothed himself in dawn and stole, begins. After about 10 min, he proposes to those present to take to the floor to pray. A detainee takes the plunge and says a long prayer in English. The chaplain later comments that this detainee is, in his opinion, evangelical, although he calls himself a Catholic. The chaplain reads a passage from the Bible dealing with transfiguration. One of the detainees follows the reading in an English-language Bible. The session concludes, and an informal exchange takes place in which the importance to the detainees of a more regular celebration of mass is brought up. The chaplain also returns to this question with the guard who was present in an adjoining room during the mass.

23.4.2 Ecumenical Worship in Prison: Prison B

The chaplains have a room of about 16 m², which they call a chapel. From the outside, nothing distinguishes this room from any other room of the prison. Inside, besides an ecumenical altar, there are some plants, one or two candles, the chaplains having agreed to certain symbolic gestures common to both traditions, notably that of lighting candles. In a small library, there are Bibles translated in several languages. On the walls, a virgin with the child, a map of the world, a poster with the declaration of a principle of peace common to different religious traditions. In a wardrobe that also serves as a cloakroom, there is a stock of mineral water bottles, as indicated by the alignment of small sealed red plugs, which was previously blessed. This water, which sometimes also serves to water the few plants present, is drunk by some detainees, who sometimes also sprinkle some of it in their cells, says the chaplain. Hence, the impressive quantity of bottles.

This Saturday morning, in addition to a visit to the two women's sectors (preventive and enforcement) and to the men's sector, the Reformed chaplain gave two "masses/worship" to the detainees, according to an ecumenical formula that was agreed upon with the Catholic chaplain, one to the "preventive" (that is to say the prisoners awaiting trial), the other to the "condemned". The following Saturday, the "mass/worship" will be followed by the detainees, and will take place every other

Saturday. Although the "preventives" are brought by the guards, it is the chaplain who goes to look for the condemned. The two "masses/worship" are structured in the same way. Preceding the solemn part, questions are raised concerning the organisation of the prison, the injustices felt and lived, the lack of information. The chaplain begins the ceremony with a piece of music, dominated by bird songs, a piece that he chooses according to his tastes, and says a brief introductory prayer. Participants then get up and take a candle that they light and choose to put at the foot of a Virgin, point towards a candleholder in the shape of a cross or towards an icon. The candle is lit for the people about whom the participants are thinking. There follows a moment of recollection, preaching and a moment of the Lord's Supper, which is "simplified", according to the words of the chaplain. Before leaving the chapel, the discussions interrupted by the mass resume. During her visits to the sectors, the chaplain's interactions with the detainees concern practical questions related to the problems encountered in their prison life.

23.5   Conclusion

The overview we have just outlined of religious diversity in the prison environment in Switzerland indicates the many imbrications that need to be taken into account when dealing with this issue. On the one hand, there are complex institutional arrangements, and on the other, multidimensional societal developments. Our reflection leads us to at least two conclusions. First, it is undeniable that prisons have become a secularised space, in the sense that Churches are no longer part of the direction of the organisation, and yet, on the other hand, religion has not disappeared. It has become more pluralistic and this plurality itself at different levels.

In conclusion, we suggest an interpretation based on the proposition of Becci, Burchardt and Giorda (2017), who identified ideal types in urban spaces and came up with at least three different ways of seeing religious actions in a situation of plurality. Starting from a given space and not from a particular religious tradition, and by noting the diversity that is there to put it into perspective through actions, historical religious actors do not appear to be passive, paralysed by the threat of secularity or pluralisation, but actively involved in an attitude of "place keeping". This is the case, for example, of the aforementioned chaplains who propose to introduce into their activities a practice such as mindful meditation. By profiling themselves in a field that the institution considers the reserve of the therapeutic domain, that is to say, the medical service, they seek to update their work by innovating. Conversely, other actors, such as the imam of Bellechasse, place themselves in a strategy of "place making", which was identified by Vasquez and Knott (2015) as a spatial strategy among urban actors of the diaspora. The latter create connections of belonging to a context by their bodily, discursive and sensory presence. Third, the strategy of "place seeking" is specific to religious actors whose presence is ephemeral or not particularly rooted spatially, but rather in reference to a spiritual dimension of the quest. This area is currently poorly visible in prison, whereas outside it seems ubiquitous. We thus find a paradox that questions the level of porosity of the penitentiary institution within society. The question of whether the prison setting reflects, accentuates or reverses trends in the external world and what this signifies remains to be fully explored.

Bibliography

Aebi, M. T., Tiago, M. M., & Burkhardt, C. (2016). Annual penal statistics. SPACE I – Prison Populations. Survey 2015. Council of Europe. Switzerland: University of Lausanne. http://wp.unil.ch/space/files/2017/03/SPACE_I_2015_Report_170314.pdf. Accessed 4 Apr 2017.

Baumann, M., & Stolz, J. (2009). *La nouvelle Suisse religieuse. Risques et chances de sa diversité.* Genève: Labor et Fides.

Becci, I., Rhazzali, K. M., & Schiavinato, V. (2016). Appréhension et expérience de la pluralité religieuse dans les prisons de Suisse et d'Italie: une approche par l'ethnographie. *Critique Internationale, 3*(72), 73–90.

Becci, I. (2015). Institutional resistance to religious diversity in prisons: comparative reflections based on studies in eastern Germany, Italy and Switzerland. *International Journal of Politics, Culture, and Society, 28*(1), 5–19.

Becci, I. (2016). La régulation de la pluralité religieuse contemporaine. Les institutions pénitentiaires entre sécurisation et spiritualisation. In B. Amélie, D. François, & N. Sarah (Eds.), *Réguler le religieux dans les sociétés libérales ?* (pp. 23–43). Genève: Labor et Fides.

Becci, I., Bovay, C., & Kuhn, A. (2011a). La religion dans les prisons suisses: aumônerie en mutation et émergence de nouveaux acteurs. Rapport du PNR58 "Collectivités religieuses, état et société". http://www.nfp58.ch/files/downloads/nfp58_themenheft02_fr.pdf. Accessed 4 Jan 2016.

Becci, I., Bovay, C., Kuhn, A., Schneuwly Purdie, M., Knobel, B., & Vuille, J. (2011b). Enjeux sociologiques de la pluralité religieuse dans les prisons suisses. PNR 58 "Collectivités religieuses, État et Société". http://www.pnr58.ch/files/news/100_Schlussbericht_Becci_fr. Accessed 4 Jan 2016.

Becci, I., Burchardt, M., & Giorda, M. (2017). Religious super-diversity and spatial strategies in two European cities. *Current Sociology, 65*(1), 73–91.

Clemmer, D. (1940). *The prison community.* Boston: Christopher Publishing House.

Fink, D. (2017). *La prison en Suisse : Un état des lieux.* Lausanne: Presses polytechniques et universitaires romandes.

Garnoussi, N. (2011). Le *Mindfulness* ou la méditation pour la guérison et la croissance personnelle: des bricolages psychospirituels dans la médecine mentale. *Sociologie, 3*(2), 259–275.

Stolz, J., Könemann, J., Schneuwly Purdie, M., Englberger, T., & Krüggeler, M. (2015). *Religion et spiritualité à l'ère de l'ego.* Genève: Labor et Fides.

Sykes, G. M. (1958). *The society of captives: a study of a maximum security prison.* Oxfordshire: Princeton University Press.

Ullrich, P. (2007). Informations sur l'exécution des peines et mesures. *Bulletin Info* 2. Bern: Office fédéral de la justice OFJ. https://www.bj.admin.ch/dam/data/bj/sicherheit/smv/smvbulletin/2007/ib-0702-f.pdf. Accessed 10 Jan 2017.

Vuille, J, & Kuhn, A. (2010). "L'exercice de la liberté de conscience et de croyance dans les établissements de privation de liberté en Suisse". *Jusletter.* Weblaw AG. www.jusletter.ch. Accessed 28 Nov 2016.

Vasquez, M. A., & Knott, K. (2015). Three dimensions of religious place making in diaspora. In *Religion and migration.* Cheltenham: Edward Elgar.

Online Publications

Criminalité et droit pénal: Panorama. (2019). Bern: Federal Office of Statistics. https://www.bfs. admin.ch/bfs/en/home/statistics/cataloguesdatabases/publications.assetdetail.7846626.html

Monitorage des capacités de privation de liberté: Connaissances spécialisées & analyses. (2017). Fribourg: KKJPD. https://www.kkjpd.ch/files/Dokumente/Themen/Strafvollzug/170731%20 Bericht%20Kapazit%C3%A4tsmonitoring%202016%20f.pdf

Rapport *"Criminalité, droit pénal: panorama"* publié par l'Office fédéral de la statistique (OFS) en février 2016 sur. https://www.bfs.admin.ch/bfs/fr/home/statistiques/criminalite-droit-penal. assetdetail.241888.html

Rapport sur la politique pénitentiaire au Conseil d'État vaudois. Janvier 2016. http:// www.vd.ch/fileadmin/user_upload/themes/securite/penitentiaire/documentation/ Rapport_sur_la_politique_p%C3%A9nitentiaire_du_CE.pdf

Chapter 24
Turkey: Religious Assistance in Prisons – State Monopoly of Religious Service

Ahmet Erdi Öztürk and İştar Gözaydın

Abstract This chapter examines the religious facilities in the prisons of Turkey where a secular state has been defined constitutionally in 1923, despite the population's being largely composed of Sunni Muslims. Secularism in the Turkish context does not correspond to a separation of religion and state, but rather signifies state management of religion in the public sphere, including prisons. The *Diyanet* is an administrative unit of Turkey, established in 1924 to fulfil functions in connection with only the Sunni Islamic faith and to manage places of worship. In this regard, since the early 1950s, the Diyanet has been overseeing religious services in Turkish prisons, but even under pro-Islamic Justice and Development Party governments, the services could not fully manage this. Therefore, on the one hand, this chapter explains the Turkish understanding of secularism and the role of the Diyanet with its functions in prison, according to various legal regulations. On the other hand, it highlights the differences and similarities between legal regulations and reality, based on personal observations.

24.1 Introduction

Beckford and Gilliat (2005) underline that even though many aspects of prison life, such as living conditions, social relations and rehabilitation, have been scrutinised by journalists, political actors and academic researchers, religion has been largely ignored. Yet, starting from that cornerstone study, many dimensions of the role and situation of religion have been explored by scholars. In this regard, the role of religion and its influence on offender rehabilitation (O'Connor and Perreyclear 2002), the systematic religion programmes in prison (Clear et al. 1992) and the functions of the prison chaplaincy (Beckford 1999) are some of the topics explored in the literature. Religion in prison has become a popular subject (Furseth 2003; Beckford

A. E. Öztürk (✉)
London Metropolitan University, London, UK

İ. Gözaydın
Helsinki Citizens' Assembly, İstanbul, Turkey

© Springer Nature Switzerland AG 2020
J. Martínez-Ariño, A.-L. Zwilling (eds.), *Religion and Prison: An Overview of Contemporary Europe*, Boundaries of Religious Freedom: Regulating Religion in Diverse Societies 7, https://doi.org/10.1007/978-3-030-36834-0_24

and Gilliat 2005), yet most studies focus on prisons of demographically and politically Christian countries. At first glance, the functions of the chaplaincy in Christian practices are not dissimilar from what exists in Muslim contexts, but this cannot be a justification for not focusing on the role of religion in countries where Muslims and members of other religions form the majority. First, institutional religion is only one aspect of religion as a subject of study, but that is not all there is to it: religion is a multidimensional, complex phenomenon. Another aspect of the issue relates to prison systems and the difficulty of penetrating and researching the prison systems in different countries (Liebling 1999; Mahon 1999; Waldram 2009).

It is hard to know which one of these reasons is the main explanation of the fact that even though religious services and activities go back to the 1950s, there is no study on the situation and role of religion in Turkey's prisons. This is surprising, because the topic 'religion and ...' is one of the most popular, since the beginning of the last quarter of the twentieth century, in various academic disciplines such as political science, international relations, sociology and history, since relations between religion, state and society has certain unique historical and structural characteristics in Turkey. Furthermore, there is no clergy in Islam, contrary to church organisation in Christianity, which is one of the primary factors that enable the state to treat religion as a public service. Therefore, it provides another area of study for scholars.

Turkey has been a Muslim-majority and constitutionally secular country since 1937. In other words, Turkey has been defined officially as a *laik* (a Turkish term that is used instead of *laïque* or secular) state, albeit with a Sunni Muslim–majority population. However, *laiklik* (*laïcité* or secularism) in the Turkish context is distinctive, a product of Turkey's historical experience and development (Somer 2007; Gözaydın 2009; Kuru 2009; Öztürk 2016). One of the main pillars of *sui generis* Turkish *laiklik* stems from its ideological state apparatus, which is older than Turkish *laiklik*; the Presidency of Religious Affairs (*Diyanet İşleri Başkanlığı*, henceforth the Diyanet). The Diyanet was established in 1924 as an ideological state apparatus with the primary purpose of ensuring the close management and control of religion by state elites within a secular state structure. That is, the Diyanet is an administrative unit required by law to maintain a *laik* structure. Nevertheless, it has been responsible for the management of religion, particularly the regulation of Islamic faith and practice, religious education, and the construction and maintenance of places of worship from the early republican period (Gözaydın 2009; Lord 2017; Öztürk 2016). To sum up, since the very beginning of the Turkish Republic, religion has been controlled and regulated via the Diyanet in various spheres: mosques, public schools, private religious education centres and prisons.

Since the 1950s, the Diyanet has been officially entrusted with the tasks of rehabilitating prisoners and convicted individuals and rendering them fit for society. Its missions have been gradually enlarged over the years. In this process, domestic laws and international agreements have always been considered, with cooperation between the Ministry of Justice and the Diyanet being, thus, totally legal and accountable (Işık and Demir 2012, 20). In 2009, there were 42 special praying rooms in prison and 417 preachers had been commissioned in prison upon request by public prosecutors (Yıldız and Karanfil 2015). Furthermore, according to the 2017 numbers, 221,607 individuals are in 381 prisons throughout Turkey. Among these prisoners, 4 per cent are female, and young prisoners (under 18 years old) make up only around 1 per cent of the population. There are no data on prisoners' religious characteristics, but 2.1 per cent of all prisoners were identified as foreigners.[1] At this point, it should be noted that, even though Turkey is a *laik* country, except when someone objects to such a designation. This means that every Turkish citizen is born a Muslim in the eyes of the state. From this point of view, it is possible to argue that, except for the 2.1 per cent foreign prisoners, all non-foreign prisoners are considered Muslim, except for certain situations, and the Diyanet is the only authorised structure for their religious assistance. Furthermore, because of the Turkish understanding of *laiklik*, it is illegal for religious communities and groups to provide religious assistance, not only in prison, but in any other areas as well.

In light of these explanations, the structure of this chapter is as follows. It begins with an overview of the evolution of Turkish *laiklik* with the Diyanet and examines the transformation of the Diyanet. Then it explains the legal development processes regarding cooperation between the Ministry of Justice and the Diyanet in connection with religious services in Turkish prisons. Finally, it offers personal observations on the differences and similarities between regulations and reality.

24.2   Turkish *laiklik* and the Key Role of the Diyanet

The Law on the Abolition of the Ministry of Sharia and Pious Foundations, and General Staff, No. 429, dated 3 March 1924, which also established the Diyanet, entered into force after a motion by the deputy Halil Hulki Efendi of Siirt (a city in Southeast Turkey) and his 50 colleagues had been debated and accepted in Parliament. In the motion, the following arguments were raised: 'The involvement of religion and the army in political events invites problems. This reality has been accepted as a ground rule by all civilised nations and governments' (Gözaydın 2009, 12). The main function of the Diyanet institution, according to this law, is to conduct the affairs of Islam related to belief and worship and to manage mosques. Concerning administrative law, the ministry, which is technically the highest office in the central administrative hierarchy, is politically the unit of execution. In a *laik* state like the Turkish Republic, which was struggling to establish a bureaucratic structure, it was politically logical for the executive cadre to decide not to assign religious affairs to a unit within the ministerial cabinet. This cadre, by assigning religious affairs to an entity within the technical administration, assumed control over the place of religion in social life and defined its functions in secular terms by positioning it within a secular structure.

---

[1] For detailed explanations and the date, please see http://www.prisonstudies.org/country/turkey.

The Diyanet was also kept within the administration in the 1961 constitution (Article 154). Following prolonged debate, the related law finally entered into force on 15 August 1965, having been ratified by the Grand National Assembly of Turkey on 22 June 1965, as Law No. 633 on the Foundation and Duties of the Diyanet (Gözaydın 2009). According to this law, the duties of the Diyanet are 'to execute affairs concerning belief, worship and moral foundations of the Islamic religion, inform the public on religion, and to administer places of worship.' As stated by Ali Bardakoğlu, one of the former directors of the organisation, 'The Diyanet, as a public entity, has a special role in producing and conveying religious knowledge' (Bardakoğlu 2008, 368). The Diyanet was featured in Article 136 of the 1982 constitution as the Diyanet under the general administration, in line with the principle of secularism, staying outside all political views and ideas and having the objective of national solidarity and unity, undertaking the functions assigned by its special statute. Until the Justice and Development Party/*Adalet ve Kalkınma Partisi* (AKP) period after 2002, the governments paradoxically used the Directorate of Religious Affairs against the religion and its possible effect on the socio-political field (Öztürk 2016).

Unarguably, the Diyanet plays an essential role in the production and reshaping of religiousness in Turkey's Republican period. However, an important criticism of the Diyanet is that the organisation exclusively serves Sunnies, and even only its Hanafi branch. Obviously, other Islamic groups exist in Turkey, such as Alevis, Shafiis or Jafaris, though their exact numbers are unknown. Nevertheless, the critics claim that the organisation's Islamic interpretations, or the resources that it publishes, only serve the Hanafi current, and that only the Hanafi interpretations of religious texts are taught in schools. Furthermore, religious services for Armenian, Jewish and Greek citizens are covered by their own congregations due to the Lausanne Peace Treaty clauses.

Among these different religions and sects, Alevism represents a problematic issue regarding religious service. The prime minister's office, in a legal process, expressed its views on this matter as follows: 'Alevism is a Sufi-based interpretation and practice of Islam. Alevism and Bektashism, principally, are structures with the belief of 12 imams and esoteric elements. Therefore, Alevism, unlike Bektashism, Mevlevism, Yesevism and Qadiriyya, is not a belief system of *fiqh* or faith; it is a mystical structure, a sect, derived from a historical process.' However, the Ministry of National Education, again during a legal process, claimed that Alevism is a sub-identity of Islam.[2] Meanwhile, the Diyanet claims that it does not treat Alevis and Sunnis differently, as these two groups do not differ on religious matters other than some local traditions and beliefs. The prime minister's office continues to emphasise that the services provided are 'for every member of the Islamic faith, general and above the different religious denominations'.[3] This is the official line of the

---

[2] For a related report see Hilal Köylü, 'Alevileri Kızdıracak Görüş', *Radikal Newspaper*, 7 April 2005, 9.

[3] Official writing dated 19 August 2005 and numbered B.02.0. BHİ -622.01/16,320 by the Prime Minister's Office.

Turkish Republican administration that is employed consistently. According to the former chairman of the Diyanet, Sait Yazıcıoğlu, 'the Diyanet was founded to provide all Muslims, Alevi or Sunni, with service in Turkey. The principles of Islam regarding belief, worship and morality are well defined. The Quran that all Muslims of any denomination recognise as the ultimate Holy Scripture is evident. Informing the public on religion in line with Quranic rules, thereby providing religious and national unity, are the functions of the Directorate of Religious Affairs, assigned by law.'[4] Yet, as stated by the current Director of Religious Affairs, Prof. Mehmet Görmez, 'We cannot assign a religious status; this status may only be defined by the followers of this belief themselves. We have always had two fundamental principles that we have never renounced. One of them is to define Alevism as a non-Islamic belief, and the other is to define *cemevis* as an alternative to mosques, as a temple of another belief…'.[5]

Therefore, another point of contention is the legal status of *cemevis* ('houses of gathering' in Turkish, premises where Alevi-Bektashi religious rituals are held). *Cemevis* are considered to be 'cultural centres',[6] 'a token of cultural wealth with a distinctive cultural and mystical identity that must be preserved',[7] and there have been discussions on whether they are alternatives or equivalent to mosques.[8] However, the decisions taken by the European Court of Human Rights regarding minority religious groups established that the freedom of religion, as guaranteed by the European Convention on Human Rights, does not give a legal permission to states on the legitimacy of religious beliefs or the ways in which religious beliefs are expressed. Pursuant to three decisions taken on the issue in *Manoussakis and others* vs. *Greece* (26 September 1996),[9] *Hasan and Chaush* vs. *Bulgaria* (26 October 2000),[10] and the *Metropolitan Church of Bessarabia and others* vs. *Moldova* (13 December 2001),[11] no state has the authority to question any parties' definition of their own beliefs. Accordingly, on 26 April 2016, the European Court of Human Rights, with its decision No. 6269/10, judged that Turkey violated Articles 9 and 14 of the European Convention on Human Rights. The international judicial authority judged acceptable the demands of services regarding the Alevi Islamic belief to be given as public service, the *cemevis* to be given the status of places of worship, the

---

[4] Sait Yazıcıoğlu, 'Alevilerle Sünniler arasında fark gözetmiyoruz' (series of interviews by G. Şaylan, Laiklik Nedir, Ne Değildir), *Cumhuriyet Newspaper*, 10 March 1990, 6.

[5] http://www.milliyet.com.tr/cemevi-diyanet-in-kirmizi/siyaset/detay/2172767/default.htm

[6] This statement was made by Recep Tayyip Erdoğan in a speech he delivered in Berlin. See *Akşam Newspaper*, 3 September 2003 http://www.aksam.com.tr/arsiv/aksam/2003/09/03/politika/politiaprn4.html

[7] Press statement by the Republic of Turkey Prime Minister's Office Directorate of Religious Affairs, 3 February 2005.

[8] See Ahmet Kerim Güntekin ve Yüksel Işık, 'Diyanet İşleri Başkanı Ali Bardakoğlu ile Söyleşi", *Kırkbudak*, 3 (summer 2005), 10–11.

[9] No. 59/1995/565/651

[10] Application No. 30,985/96

[11] Application No. 45,701/99

Alevi religious leaders to be instated as public officers, schools to be open in order to raise religious leaders (*dede – baba*) to transmit their Islamic beliefs to subsequent generations of the Alevi community, and the allocation of an annual share from the public budget for the services to be provided.

Despite all issues presented, the Diyanetis a structure compatible with the *Realpolitik* of the Republic. It is unlikely that a political actor taking over the government would renounce a powerful organisation such as the Diyanet. Furthermore, the problem is the monopoly of the structure that provides religious services, which is also directly about the religion assistance in prison. When a public service institution ceases to be a monopoly, the receivers of that service may receive it from an institution of their own choice. Politically, in case of a problem that would threaten the public order, the law enforcement agencies would primarily have to deal with issues when the subject of that service is religion. However, it should not be disregarded that the independent judiciary organs should administer such a process to preserve the order of law.

24.3   Role of Diyanet and Official Religion Activities in Turkish Prisons

As noted in the preceding section, according to the Turkish understanding of *laiklik* and regulations that were first formulated at the beginning of the Republican period, the Diyanet is the only institution or state apparatus that has the legal right to grant and regulate religious services for Turkish citizens in prison. In this regard, prisons fall under its mission. That is, having explained the role and duties of the Diyanet may give us a general picture of the management of religions in Turkish prisons.

In his study, Yıldız noted that even though real religious assistance in Turkish prisons date back to 1974 (Yıldız and Karanfil 2015), the official documents and protocols of the Diyanet demonstrate that the origins of relations between the Diyanet and penal institutions (*Ceza İnfaz Kurumları*) date back to the 1950s (Işık and Demir 2012). In 2012, the Diyanet published a *Guidebook of Penal Institutions' Religious Services* (*Ceza İnfaz Kurumları Din Hizmetleri Rehberi*), written by Diyanet scholars Harun Işık and Abdullah Demir, on the historical and legal process of the Diyanet's religious assistance to Turkish prisons. This guidebook is the only detailed resource that explains the philosophy, aims and historical background of the Diyanet's activities in Turkish prisons. In the introduction of the guidebook, the former director of the Diyanet between 2010 and 2017, Prof. Dr. Mehmet Görmez, mentions that one of the fundamental duties of the Diyanet is to provide true religious assistance to prisoners. Furthermore, he states that the legal protocol and collaborative work between the Diyanet and the Ministry of Justice are compatible with international standards. According to him, giving religious assistance to prisoners contributes to their moral and spiritual well-being and helps to improve their religious knowledge (Öztürk 2018).

In their guidebook, Işık and define crime, in traditional terms, as a problem that exists in all societies, a pending problem that exists in all societies and will continue to exist. Furthermore, they describe the role of the Diyanet as that of an educator. According to them, the Diyanet has been charged by the Turkish state with the task of rehabilitating prisoners and detainees since the 1950s (Işık and Demir 2012, 8). The second aim of Diyanet activities in prisons is to help prisoners reintegrate into society after they serve their sentence (Işık and Demir 2012, 9). From this point of view, it is possible to argue that both the Diyanet and the Ministry of Justice see religion as a moral education and a physiological rehabilitation tool, which is compatible with Turkey's state mentality and its *laiklik*.

Starting from the mid-1950s, according to the general reports of the Diyanet, protocols between the Diyanet and the Ministry of Justice and the unique guidebook, it is possible to divide Diyanet activities in prison into four different time periods. Between 1959 and 1983, the first relations and first collaborative works between the Diyanet and Ministry of Justice concerning religious service in Turkish prisons are established. The period between 1983 and 2001 is characterised by tight cooperation (compact cooperation). Between 2001 and 2011 is the period under the First Legal Protocol. Finally, the Second Legal Protocol period started in 2011.

At this point, it would be useful to explain what is meant by tight cooperation and the First and Second Legal Protocol periods. All three of these terms are directly relevant to Turkish political life and the role of religion in the socio-political sphere, and they are the original names that were given to the official report of the Diyanet. At this point, even though religious assistance in prison dates back to the 1950s, its real implementation started after the 1980 military coup, since under military rule and the 1982 constitution the Diyanet's authority and duties were expanded. The Diyanet had a new function, which may be defined, basically, as supporting and promoting a new type of nationalism using the tenets of Islam. Therefore, this compact period witnessed greater visibility and stepped-up operations with respect to religious assistance in Turkish prisons. On the other hand, the legal protocol periods and their names are directly related to the negotiation period between Turkey and the European Union (EU). One of the negotiation requirements that must be fulfilled by Turkey for it to become a member of the EU concerns conditions in its prisons. In this context, the protocols present all the details and describe shareholder (the Diyanet and Ministry of Justice) duties.

As mentioned earlier, religious assistance in Turkey has a history going back more than a half-century. In this regard, an official letter (No. 17,565) sent to the Diyanet by the Ministry of Justice in 1959 marked the start of relations between the two state institutions regarding religious assistance in Turkish prisons. In this letter, the Ministry of Justice asked the Diyanet to hold religious educational conferences in prison at least twice every week. Although the Diyanet honored that legal request, it could not act on it due to a lack of staff members and preachers (Bulut 1997, 53). In 1964, the Ministry of Justice repeated its request with another official letter (No. 8521), and the Diyanet started to organise religious educational conferences in large city prisons such as Istanbul, Ankara, Adana and İzmir (Bulut 1997, 54). In 1974, the Ministry of Justice issued an administrative regulation entrusting the Diyanet with the task of sending preachers to all prisons (Işık and Demir 2012, 30).

The second period of relations between the Diyanet and the Ministry of Justice concerning religion assistance in Turkish prisons started after the military coup of 1980. In 1981, the Office of Commander in Chief sent an order (No. 7130–818-81) to the Directorate of the Diyanet and the Ministry of Justice on the regulation of religious assistance in prisons, which had become overcrowded after the military order. In this order, the Office of Commander in Chief sent a new curriculum which included 74 weekly hours of religious culture and knowledge of ethics to be implemented by the Diyanet in Turkish prisons. Compatible with the mentality of the coup and the new regime, this new curriculum included faith and worship subjects, family values and nature, Kemalist ideas about religion and *laiklik*, patriotism, and history lessons about Muslims and Turks (Işık and Demir 2012, 31). That is, as mentioned previously, as an ideological state apparatus, the Diyanet was once more instrumentalised by the state to impose its ideology, including in prisons. After the coup period, both in the late 1980s and the 1990s, the unstable conditions of the Turkish political system directly affected religious assistance in Turkish prisons.

The year 2001 marked another turning point with regard to religious services in Turkish prisons. During the negotiation processes between Turkey and the EU, the Ministry of Justice and the Diyanet signed a cooperation protocol to improve the conditions of religious care for prisoners. According to this protocol, prison preachers must start providing a religious education, which must include the reading of the Quran, the life of the Prophet Muhammad and Islamic history, for 6 hours a week. Participation in these lectures was not obligatory (Işık and Demir 2012, 33). Even though 2001 was a milestone in religious assistance in Turkish prisons, 2002 represents another important year when political authorities started to affect religious issues in a different way. As noted previously, 2002 marked the beginning of consecutive single-party governments under AKP, which has a pro-Islamic leadership cadre. In this regard, AKP governments have taken an interest in religious issues, including religious assistance in prisons. Therefore, in 2002, 2005, 2006 and 2007, the AKP governments imposed various regulations to improve religious assistance conditions in prison.

Despite the protocols and regulations that had been in place since the mid-1950s, the most sweeping and comprehensive regulations were imposed in 2001 under the First Legal Protocol. According to this protocol, the Diyanet was entrusted with many new tasks. The first task of the Diyanet was to provide religious and moral guidance to detainees and prisoners and correct some previous mistakes. Others included developing the religious and moral feelings and thoughts of detainees, inspiring prisoners to love people, family, the nation and homeland, conducting religious services, providing moral development and spiritual guidance activities in prison, teaching the Quran upon request by detainees and prisoners, preparing a memorial and celebration programme suitable for religious days and weeks, and helping prisoners fulfil religious obligations. Finally, the Diyanet is also in charge of providing religious books in prison libraries, restructuring the religious curriculum in those courses, and helping those in need during prayer times (Işık and Demir 2012, 33–35).

Even though various protocols were signed between the Ministry of Justice and the Diyanet after the 1950s, several issues and conflicts have arisen in religious assistance in prison. Diyanet officials started providing religious assistance in prison on a weekly or monthly basis in the early 2000s. Since then, more than 10,000 copies of the Quran and other religious books have been distributed in prisons. As noted previously, in 2009, there were 42 'chaplains' in prisons and 417 preachers had been commissioned in prisons following requests by public prosecutors. Unfortunately, numbers for more recent years are not available, not even in databases or on the websites of the Diyanet or the Ministry of Justice.

Finally, it is worth mentioning non-Muslim prisoners' conditions in Turkish prisons. According to 2017 numbers, around 2 per cent all prisoners are affiliated with a religion other than Sunni or Alevi Islam, but there are no regulations concerning religious assistance for them. In this regard, all processes are based on demands of prisoners and initiatives taken by the head of the prisoners. For instance, when a Jewish prisoner asks to obtain a Torah, the head of the prisoners can provide it. Furthermore, for more precise demands or religious assistance, the head of prisons could establish a bureaucratic relation with the embassy or other representatives of the prisoner's country and to secure religious assistance for prisoners.

24.4   Conclusion: Some Issues

The Diyanet currently appears to be the only official authority that has a right to provide any religious services in Turkish prisons. This situation has a unique historical background that started in the mid-1950s and gradually developed by initiatives of both the Diyanet and the Ministry of Justice. This collaboration reached a peak during the AKP period and under the negotiation processes with the EU. Yet, there have been some glitches. On the one hand, first of all, the lack of clergy in Islam, in contrast to the institution of the church in Christianity, makes it unreasonable to expect a similar religious service mentality in Turkey. On the other hand, it is obvious that current religious services only take into account Sunni Muslims. Yet Turkey has a population of around 15 to 20 per cent Alevi Muslims, another 5 per cent of other Muslim groups and non-Muslim components living as Turkish citizens under equal constitutional rights and freedoms. In this regard, one could argue that religious services in prisons are not provided on a basis of fairness and impartiality. Secondly, based on personal observation, one could claim that most detainees and prisoners remain unaware of the religious services available to them in prison because of a lack of guidance and information. That is, religious services in Turkish prisons seem to be conducted only on paper, not in practice.

Bibliography

Bardakoğlu, A. (2008). The structure, mission and social function of the presidency of religious affairs (PRA). *The Muslim World, 98*(2–3), 173–181.

Beckford, J. A. (1999). The management of religious diversity in England and Wales with special reference to prison chaplaincy. *International Journal on Multicultural Societies, 1*(2), 55–66.

Beckford, J. A., & Gilliat, S. (2005). *Religion in prison: 'Equal rites' in a multi-faith society.* Cambridge: Cambridge University Press.

Bulut, M. (1997). 'Diyanet İşleri Başkanlığının Yaygın Din Eğitimindeki Yeri.' *Yayınlanmamış Doktora Tezi), AÜSBE, Ankara.*

Clear, T. R., Stout, B. D., Dammer, H. R., Kelly, L., Hardyman, P. L., & Shapiro, C. (1992). Does involvement in religion help prisoners adjust to prison? *Age, 19*(07), 16.

Furseth, I. (2003). Secularization and the role of religion in state institutions. *Social Compass, 50*(2), 191–202.

Gözaydın, İ. B. (2009). *Diyanet: Türkiye cumhuriyeti'nde dinin tanzimi.* İletişim Yayınları.

Işik, H., & Demir, A. (2012). Ceza İnfaz Kurumları Din Hizmetleri Rehberi. In *Diyanet İşleri Başkanlığı Yayınlar-913.* Ankara: Diyanet İşleri Başkanlığı Yayınları.

Kuru, A. T. (2009). *Secularism and state policies toward religion: The United States, France, and Turkey.* Cambridge: Cambridge University Press.

Liebling, A. (1999). Prison suicide and prisoner coping. *Crime and Justice, 26,* 283–359.

Lord, C. (2017). Between Islam and the nation; nation-building, the ulama and Alevi identity in Turkey. *Nations and Nationalism, 23*(1), 48–67.

Mahon, N. B. (1999). Introduction: Death and dying behind bars – Cross-cutting themes and policy imperatives: 213–215.

Nielsen, J., Akgönül, S., Alibašić, A., & Racius, E. (Eds.). (2002). *Yearbook of Muslims in Europe* (Vol. 2). Leiden: Brill.

O'Connor, T. P., & Perreyclear, M. (2002). Prison religion in action and its influence on offender rehabilitation. *Journal of Offender Rehabilitation, 35*(3–4), 11–33.

Öztürk, A. E. (2016). Turkey's Diyanet under AKP rule: From protector to imposer of state ideology? *Southeast European and Black Sea Studies, 16*(4), 619–635.

Öztürk, A. E. (2018). Transformation of the Turkish Diyanet both at Home and Abroad: Three Stages. *European Journal of Turkish Studies. Social Sciences on Contemporary Turkey, 27.*

Somer, M. (2007). Moderate Islam and secularist opposition in Turkey: Implications for the world, Muslims and secular democracy. *Third World Quarterly, 28*(7), 1271–1289.

Yıldız, M., & Karanfil, I. (2015, June 15). Çocuk Ve Gençlik Ceza İnfaz Kurumlarındaki Hükümlülerde Din Hizmetlerine Katılım Ve Değerler Sistemleri İlişkisi Üzerine Bir İnceleme. *Dini Araştırmalar, 18*(46), 66–96.

Waldram, J. B. (2009). Challenges of prison ethnography. *Anthropology News, 50*(1), 4–5.

Chapter 25
United Kingdom: The Public Reconstruction of Religion and Belief in Prisons – Negotiating Diversity, Rights and Constraints

Andrew J. Todd

Abstract This chapter presents an up-to-date portrayal and evaluation of religion and chaplaincy in prison in the United Kingdom, with a particular emphasis on the situation in England and Wales. It draws on current policy, practice and research, considering the interaction of these and how together they shape prison religion and chaplaincy. The chapter charts the development of multi-faith chaplaincy against the background of increasing diversity of belief amongst prisoners. Particular issues include the provision of chaplaincy, including its growing diversity; the policy framework for chaplaincy and developing structures for its management; the scope and significance of conversion in prison and its impact on prisoner identities; the relevance of the humanist-led emergence of non-religious pastoral carers; and an evaluation of the significance of 'extremism' in prison and its projected impact on chaplaincy. The chapter concludes by examining how public policy, related to both equality of opportunity and to the prevention of 'extremism', tends to construct chaplaincy (as a resource to fulfil policy requirements), faith communities (as 'service providers') and religion (as a publicly regulated human right). The conclusion emphasises, however, how such constructions also accommodate considerable diversity of belief and practice, seen in the diversity of identities associated with prisoners' religion and the breadth of pastoral care offered by chaplains.

A. J. Todd (✉)
Anglia Ruskin University, Cambridge, UK

Cambridge Theological Federation, Cambridge, UK
e-mail: at851@cam.ac.uk

© Springer Nature Switzerland AG 2020
J. Martínez-Ariño, A.-L. Zwilling (eds.), *Religion and Prison: An Overview of Contemporary Europe*, Boundaries of Religious Freedom: Regulating Religion in Diverse Societies 7, https://doi.org/10.1007/978-3-030-36834-0_25

25.1   Introduction: Chaplaincy and Religion in Prison

The UK prison estate includes 118 prisons in England and Wales (12 for women), 15 prisons in Scotland (of which 4 accommodate women) and 4 in Northern Ireland (one for women). The prison population in England and Wales as of 7 April 2017 was 85,517, including 3973 women.[1] In Scotland on the same date, the population was 7484 (including 341 women).[2] In Northern Ireland, as of 31 March 2017, the prison population was 1434 (including 46 women).[3] Most of the research considered in this chapter relates to the largest of the prison estates, that of England and Wales.

The provision of chaplains in prison in the UK has been regulated since the Gaols Act of 1823. Current provision is enshrined in the 1952 Prison Act (Sections 7 and 9), which requires that there be an Anglican chaplain in every prison in England and Wales.[4] The chaplain is one of three senior posts in each prison under this act, complementing the appointment of a governor and medical officer.[5] Further provision is made in the act (section 10) for the appointment of ministers of denominations other than the Church of England, should the number of prisoners of those denominations warrant it. This provision was not amended by the 2017 Prisons and Courts Bill (as drafted on 23 February 2017).[6] Provision in Scotland is governed by the Prisons (Scotland) Act of 1989, where the Presbyterian Church of Scotland has played a significant role but where current legislation refers to 'the chaplaincy team'.

Chaplaincy in prison (as other aspects of the work of prisons) was overseen until recently by the National Offender Management Service (NOMS), which became, on 1 April 2017, Her Majesty's Prison and Probation Service (HMPPS). Specific provision for religious practice and chaplaincy is made in the 'Religion' section of the Prison Rules (1999); Standing Order PSO4550, 'The Religion Manual', published in 2000; and its successor 'Prison Service Instruction', published in 2011, as PSI51, 'Faith and Pastoral Care for Prisoners', reissued in 2016 as PSI 05/2016 (NOMS 2016a). Also important is the Service Specification for Faith and Pastoral Care for Prisoners (NOMS 2015). This provision will be discussed further in what follows.

What the legislation and policy documents already referred to indicate is that provision is made in UK prisons for prisoners to follow their religion and for chaplains, as representatives of faith communities, to play a part in the treatment of

---

[1] https://www.gov.uk/government/statistics/prison-population-figures-2017.   Accessed   12 April 2017.

[2] http://www.sps.gov.uk/Corporate/Information/SPSPopulation.aspx. Accessed 12 April 2017.

[3] https://www.justice-ni.gov.uk/articles/weekly-situation-reports-october-2015.   Accessed   12 April 2017.

[4] Provision is also made for (Anglican) assistant chaplains.

[5] As research has shown (Todd and Tipton 2011), the status of the chaplain, as one of the three senior appointments in a prison, has been eroded during the period since the 1952 act, although managing chaplains may still be members of the senior management team of a prison.

[6] This Bill fell with the dissolution of Parliament in May 2017.

Table 25.1 Prisoner population by religion (England and Wales), 2016

Religion	Number of prisoners	Percentage of prison population (%)
Christian	41,940	49.1
Muslim	12,506	14.6
Buddhist	1558	1.8
Sikh	732	0.9
Hindu	421	0.5
Jewish	406	0.5
Other	1437	1.7
No religion	26,349	30.8
Not recorded	92	0.1

prisoners. Thus, for example, chaplains (under the 1952 act) must carry out 'statutory duties', meeting all prisoners received by the prison, and visiting those held in segregation, or in healthcare units, daily. Such visits are always at least offered, although prisoners may refuse them. Further, PSI 05/2016 (NOMS 2016a) and the accompanying service specification (NOMS 2015) indicate a clear responsibility for prisons to provide 1 h per week of worship (or equivalent) and 1 h per week of religious education (or cultural activity) for each prisoner according to their religion or belief.

The religion of prisoners is recorded in the UK. Thus, for example, Allen and Dempsey (2016: 13) provide the following figures for England and Wales (Table 25.1).

The report offers the following comparison:

At the end of March 2016 just under half of the prison population was of a Christian faith – a decrease of 9 percentage points compared to June 2002. The proportion of Muslim prisoners has increased from 8% in 2002 to 15% in 2016. The proportion of prisoners with no religion in 2016 (31.4%) was down 0.6 of a percentage point compared to 2002. (Allen and Dempsey 2016: 13)[7]

In the same report, the situation for Scotland is summarised thus:

As at 30 June 2013 just over 4,600 prisoners (58% of the prison population) in Scotland indicated that they held religious beliefs. Of these, 93% were Christian (of various denominations). Muslim prisoners accounted for 4.4%. Together Buddhist, Sikh, Jewish, Hindu and other religions accounted for 2.7% of the religious prison population. Just over 3,270 prisoners (42% of the prison population) held no religious beliefs. (Allen and Dempsey 2016: 21)

The preceding overview indicates that prisons are affected by an increasing diversity of faith and belief positions and identities in society. The chapter will consider the details of this fact. This trend has given rise to a developing model of multi-faith chaplaincy in the UK that is part of the Prison Service's response to increasing

---

[7]For a further and more detailed picture of growing diversity of belief amongst prisoners, see: http://www.brin.ac.uk/figures/religion-in-prison-1991-2015/. Accessed 28 April 2017.

diversity. Of significance here is the wider legal framework that shapes public organisations' provision of equal opportunity and respect for diversity, notably the 2010 Equality Act, which is rooted in earlier equality legislation and in the European Convention on Human Rights (ECHR), via the 1998 Human Rights Act. The 2010 act gathers earlier anti-discrimination legislation into a single act and establishes a range of 'protected characteristics', including religion and belief, so that the act safeguards the right both to practise one's belief and to change it. The act gives rise, in turn, to the Public Sector Equality Duty (PSED),[8] which sets parameters on how public sector organisations should promote equality and reduce inequality. This policy is discussed in relation to prisons and chaplaincy in NOMS (2016b: 11–14).

Particular issues to be considered concerning the impact of greater diversity of belief in prison include changes in the provision of multi-faith chaplaincy (Sect. 25.2.1), the development and restructuring of the delivery of multi-faith chaplaincy (Sect. 25.2.2), conversion amongst prisoners (Sect. 25.2.3) and the move by the British Humanist Association towards involvement of non-religious pastoral volunteers alongside chaplains in prison (Sect. 25.2.4).

Other trends (to be considered in Sect. 25.3) are the continued governmental concern with prisons as sites of 'extremism' and 'radicalisation', the evolution of measures designed to tackle this, especially following the Counter-Terrorism and Security Act of 2015, and the impact (actual and potential) on prison chaplaincy, an area that has given rise to further research.

Drawing on the chapter's investigation of the aforementioned trends and issues, the conclusion (Sect. 25.4) will give careful consideration to the wider socio-political structural issues, in particular the changing relationship between the state, faith communities, the Prison Service and prison chaplaincy. This will lead to a consideration of how religion is currently constructed in the prison context at the macro-level by public policy but in a different way at the micro-level of day-to-day prison life.

25.2 Diversity of Faith and Belief and Multi-Faith Chaplaincy

The diversity of belief amongst prisoners, portrayed in Allen and Dempsey (2016: 13), to some extent mirrors the diversity of the wider society. The percentages of prisoners in England and Wales registered as Christian (49.1%) are somewhat lower than the figures for the 2011 Census of England and Wales (59.3%)[9]; the percentage of those registered as being of no religion (30.8%) is higher than the census figure (25.1%). More striking are the figures for prisoners registered as Muslim (14.6% as

---

[8] https://www.gov.uk/government/publications/public-sector-equality-duty. Accessed 1 May 2017.
[9] https://www.ons.gov.uk/peoplepopulationandcommunity/culturalidentity/religion/articles/religioninenglandandwales2011/2012-12-11. Accessed 12 April 2017.

compared with a census figure of 4.8%) and as Buddhist (1.8% compared with the census figure of 0.4%). The issues related to the number of Muslims in prison will be dealt with here and in three other sections of this chapter: the growth of Muslim chaplaincy in Sect. 25.2.1; the numbers of Muslim prisoners here and in Sect. 25.2.3 on conversion, which will also consider Buddhist prisoner numbers; and questions to do with 'extremism' in Sect. 25.3.

The disproportionality between numbers of Muslims in the general population and in the prison population is not primarily to do with conversion in prison (see Sect. 25.2.3 in what follows), but rather with complex patterns of criminality and perceptions of criminality affecting different ethnic groups. Marranci argues, drawing on a careful analysis of statistics, that patterns of criminality for Muslims are not significantly different from those of the general prisoner population, in terms of proportions of different crimes. He further indicates that only 1% of the Muslims in prison are detained in connection with terrorism-related crimes (Marranci 2009: 5). His examination of socio-economic, demographic and educational factors is cogent and persuades the reader that the criminality of different ethnic Muslim groups has more to do with those other factors than with their religion (Marranci 2009: Ch. 3). In particular, Marranci points to the likelihood of Muslims of specific social and ethnic groups (such as second-generation Muslims of South Asian origin) living in areas of relative economic and educational deprivation and suggests that this 'facilitates' criminal behaviour (Marranci 2009: ch.3).

In addition, the *Lammy Review* (Lammy 2017) examines disproportional outcomes for those from black, Asian and minority ethnic (BAME) backgrounds within the criminal justice system. Such ethnic groups comprise a number that includes a high proportion of Muslims. The review indicates that 'Those who are charged, tried and punished are still disproportionately likely to come from minority communities. Despite making up just 14% of the population, BAME men and women make up 25% of prisoners, while over 40% of young people in custody are from BAME backgrounds' (Lammy 2017: 3). It highlights particular areas of disproportional treatment for those from BAME groups, in comparison with those who are white, including higher arrest rates, being less likely to plead guilty (and therefore receive a lower sentence) because of a lack of trust in the system, a greater likelihood of being sentenced to prison if found guilty of certain offences, particularly drug-related ones, and poorer treatment in prison. Lammy identifies and addresses (through recommendations) the structural issues within the criminal justice system that underlie disproportional treatment and a lack of trust in the system amongst BAME people. These include under-representation of those from BAME backgrounds amongst those employed within the criminal justice system and a lack of appropriate monitoring. The review further concludes that 'BAME individuals still face bias, including overt discrimination, in parts of the justice system' (Lammy 2017:69). All these factors may contribute to the higher proportion of Muslims in prison, in comparison with the proportion in the general population.

25.2.1 *Provision of Multi-Faith Chaplaincy*

The first area of consideration in relation to diverse belief in prisons is the provision of a 'multi-faith chaplaincy'. This term is in common usage in prisons in the UK. It may be summarised as the provision of chaplaincy services to meet the needs of prisoners of different faiths and beliefs. Such provision is characterised by the appointment of chaplains of different faiths and beliefs to serve as members of the multi-faith team, both to provide faith-specific services to those with whom they share a faith and to share in the team's responsibility for the pastoral care of all in the prison (both prisoners and staff) of whatever faith or belief. It is also character-ised by the provision of appropriate spaces (e.g. chapels, multi-faith rooms, mosques, offices) to enable faith-specific and generic pastoral care services. The history of the multi-faith chaplaincy is summarised in Todd (2013:144–45)[10]:

> Prison chaplaincy in England and Wales has undergone more than a decade of change, which has transformed it from being an Anglican dominated service, to a multi-faith one. Significant aspects of the change (…) have included: publication of PSO4550, 'The Religion Manual' in 2000; the appointment of a new Chaplain General in 2001, with a brief to help prisons 'better meet the needs of a multi-faith community'; the decision, also in 2001, to appoint full-time Muslim chaplains; the appointment of a new Prison Service Chaplaincy Council in 2003; the first ever national conference of 450 chaplains of all faith traditions, also in 2003; and the publication in 2011 of PSI51, 'Faith and Pastoral Care for Prisoners' (Ministry of Justice, 2011) to replace PSO4550. This period has seen the devel-opment in prisons of multi-faith chaplaincy teams; of multi-faith spaces in addition to his-toric chapels, including, for example, multi-faith rooms and mosques; and of the multi-faith use of chapels.

The evaluation of the shift from an Anglican dominance has been considered by various authors (Beckford 1999, 2007; Beckford and Gilliat 1998; Beckford et al. 2005; Gilliat-Ray 2008; Todd 2013). Further, it is widely recognised that Beckford and Gilliat's work (1998) was a significant catalyst in the development of multi-faith chaplaincy in prisons in England and Wales, especially in the move away from Anglican 'brokerage' of chaplaincy involvement for other faith communities and towards those from minority faith groups becoming more fully included as chap-lains, who had previously been designated 'visiting ministers' (Beckford and Gilliat 1998; Gilliat-Ray 2008).

Provision of chaplains has certainly become more diverse between 2000 and 2017, and particularly since the appointment of the first employed Muslim chaplain in 2001. A summary of numbers of chaplains in England and Wales, as of 2009, was provided in Todd and Tipton (2011: 9) with the agreement of NOMS (Table 25.2).

Numbers of chaplains paid seasonally or unremunerated were more difficult to determine. Todd and Tipton reported the NOMS estimate of between 700 and 800 serving in these ways, representing a wide range of denominations or faiths.

Current numbers of chaplains are difficult to ascertain, particularly because all those chaplains who are paid sessionally (according to the hours they work) are

---

[10] Cf. (Beckford 2007)

Table 25.2 Employed chaplains, full- or part-time (England and Wales), 2009

Religion	Numbers of chaplains
Anglican	134
Muslim	92
Roman Catholic	77
Free Church	50
Sikh	2
Hindu	2
Total	357

currently being offered a fixed-term contract of employment.[11] The number of full-time-equivalent chaplains employed in England and Wales on 31 December 2016 was 338, across all religious and belief affiliations.[12] Because this is a full-time-equivalent figure, counting part-time posts as fractions (e.g. 0.5 for half-time), it probably represents an increase over the 2009 figure of 357, which counted total numbers of part-time chaplains.

The increasing diversity of chaplaincy is confirmed by the diversity amongst managing chaplains (also discussed in the aforementioned interview), who lead teams of chaplains in each prison or group of prisons. They currently include 69 chaplains from different Christian churches and denominations (including now two Orthodox Christians), 33 Muslims (around 32% of managing chaplains), one Sikh and one Latter Day Saints chaplain.[13] This appears to also confirm the continuing move away from an Anglican dominance of prison chaplaincy.

It should be noted, however, that there remain some inequalities in chaplaincy provision such that:

> those religious faiths perceived as minor, such as pagan, Hindu or Sikh, [feel] something of a new marginalised group within the multi-faith chaplaincy community. This was commonly expressed in terms of hours available, access to resources and often not feeling part of the core chaplaincy team. (Todd and Tipton 2011: 37–38)

This picture is confirmed and expanded by Beckford, who draws on his interviews with Hindu, Muslim and Sikh chaplains. He identifies four remaining or newly emergent areas of contention, two of which concern specifically the provision of chaplaincy: '(…) the provision of facilities and resources for chaplaincies on an equitable basis (…) and the conditions in which Hindu, Muslim and Sikh chaplains do their work' (Beckford 2013: 202).

One might reasonably conclude that one structural feature of remaining inequalities is precisely the provision of chaplaincy in proportion to the numbers of

---

[11] This uncertainty was confirmed by the Chaplain General to HM Prisons in a telephone interview on 13 April 2017 and again in an email dated 12 October 2017.

[12] Information supplied by the Chaplain General; telephone interview 13 April 2017.

[13] Figures supplied in an email from the Chaplain General dated 12 October 2017.

prisoners of a particular faith within the prison population. This continuing principle, going back to the 1952 Prison Act, appears to disadvantage numerically small faith groups and their chaplains, whose small number of hours and share of resources militate against their full involvement in chaplaincy.

It should be noted, however, that Muslim chaplaincy represents a different picture from that of other minority faith groups. A number of researchers have noted the growth of Muslim chaplaincy in prisons in England and Wales, notably Beckford (2007, 2013), Beckford et al. (2005), Gilliat-Ray (2008) and Gilliat-Ray et al. (2013). Of especial note is that Muslim chaplaincy has grown faster than chaplaincy of any other faith group since 2001 (the date of appointment of the first full-time Muslim chaplain). Todd (2013) attributes the differential growth, in part, to government interest and investment in the role that Muslim chaplains might play in 'anti-extremism' policy and practice (considered further later in Sect. 25.3). Government interest in this role of Muslim chaplaincy appears to have worked in combination with the interest in equality of opportunity to accelerate the growth of the Muslim chaplaincy in particular.

In keeping with the foregoing discussion, in addition to historic tensions arising out of chaplains of different faiths working together in teams and sharing resources, Todd and Tipton (2011: 37) identified a continuing unease in prisons around the perceived disproportionate amount of resources and attention given to the Muslim chaplaincy, which arose from the particular attention paid to Muslim prisoners by the government and the Prison Service. This unease was widely reported by chaplains.

25.2.2   The Delivery of a Multi-Faith Chaplaincy

The second area to be explored in relation to the increasing diversity of beliefs in the prison population is services delivered by multi-faith chaplaincy teams and their regulation. As indicated earlier, this delivery is shaped by current policy and the Public Sector Equality Duty (PSED). The core document is PSI 05/2016 (NOMS 2016a), which sets forth the following desired outcomes:

> The faith and religious needs of prisoners are met. The pastoral needs of prisoners are addressed, in part, through Chaplaincy provision. (NOMS 2016a: 3, Sects. 1.7 and 1.8)

This document is divided into Part 1 (NOMS 2016a: 5–33), 'General Faith Provision' (which sets out 20 expected outputs for chaplaincy), and Part 2 (NOMS 2016a: 34–104), 'Faith Specific Provision' (which offers advice on the practices and requirements of a range of faith and belief groups). The outputs in Part 1 cover the following areas:

> Chaplaincy Faith Provision [see below, on Output 1, for what this means]; Reception into prison; Change of Religious Registration; Corporate Worship or Meditation; Segregation and Healthcare; Religious Festivals; Community Faith Groups; Religious Artefacts and Dress; Access to Religious Classes and Cultural Activities; Promotion of Religious Classes

and Cultural Activities; Supervision of Corporate worship or Meditation; Pastoral Care; Segregation; Healthcare; Discharge/Chaplaincy and faith community support through the gate; Serious Illness or Death in Custody; Serious Illness or Death of a Relative; Self-Harm; Marriage and Civil Partnership; Official Prison Visitors Scheme. (NOMS 2016a: 1)

Each output is in the following form: 'Output 1. The Chaplaincy provision reflects the faith/denominational requirements of the prison.' (NOMS 2016a: 5); or 'Output 4. Prisoners have the opportunity for corporate worship or meditation for one hour per week' (NOMS 2016a: 8).

The faith and belief groups for which guidance is provided in Part 2 of the Prison Service Instruction are as follows:

Bahá'í; Buddhism; Christianity; Christian Science; Church of Jesus Christ of Latter-Day Saints; Hinduism; Humanism; Islam; Jainism; Jehovah's Witnesses; Judaism; Paganism; Quakerism; Rastafari; Seventh Day Adventist Church; Sikhism; Spiritualism; Zoroastrianism. (NOMS 2016a: 1)

There are some apparent anomalies in the preceding list, for example that neither the Church of Jesus Christ of Latter-Day Saints nor the Seventh Day Adventist Church is included under the heading 'Christianity'. This is partly due to the fact that both churches have distinctive practices that need to be accommodated by the prison. It may also be about a perception of which churches have historically been regarded as Christian in the UK. The 'Christian' faith advisers in Annexe C are Anglican, Catholic, Free Church and Orthodox (NOMS 2016a: 45).

Each annexe relating to one of these faiths introduces that faith and may include advice on the following items (as appropriate to the faith): corporate worship or religious practice, rites, festivals, places of worship, private worship or religious practice, sacred texts or religious books, religious artefacts, diet, dress, hygiene, marriage, death and funerals. In addition, the annexe identifies the relevant 'Faith [or Belief] Adviser for further guidance' and whether that person is a member of the Prison Service Chaplaincy Council – a representative body of advisers from different faiths, established in 2003. Annexes may be subdivided to offer details of different subgroups (e.g. denominations) within a faith community.

The Prison Service Instruction also specifies 'mandatory actions' for prisons such that 'Governors must ensure faith provision is available to all prisoners in accordance with the Service Specification "Faith and Pastoral Care for Prisoners"' (NOMS 2016a: 4, Sect. 1.10). It is therefore the service specification (NOMS 2015) that establishes the outputs from PSI 05/2016 as the minimum service provision (NOMS 2015: 1).

The mandatory actions for governors raise the further question of monitoring the delivery of a multi-faith chaplaincy as part of its regulation. This is now accomplished through the 'Assurance and Compliance' process, which evaluates the compliance of an individual chaplaincy and prison with the requirements of PSI 05/2016 (NOMS 2015), mandated by the service specification (NOMS 2015). Evaluation is largely against the specific outputs of the PSI, as well as more general areas, such as provision of places of worship and meditation and matters to do with the chaplaincy team (the team itself, budget management, team integration with the prison and learning and development) (HMPPS 2017). The outcome, in relation to each output, is either confirmation of compliance or an action point designed to lead to greater compliance. This is an evidence-based process that contributes to the evaluation of the prison's performance by HM Inspector of Prisons. In keeping with this wider role, the Assurance and Compliance process leads to so-called RAG scores for chaplaincy, which are a contribution to the RAG score of the prison (HMPPS 2017). These scores are so called because they are characterised by the colours of a traffic light: red, amber, green (or a combination of these colours such as amber-red), with green being a satisfactory outcome and red indicating a definite and immediate requirement for action.

The research carried out by the Cardiff Centre for Chaplaincy Studies (Todd and Tipton 2011) was one of the drivers for the development of the Assurance and Compliance process.[14] That report identified considerable variance in the delivery of chaplaincy in different sites, such that Recommendation 5 was 'that, in order to create consistency and parity, the tension between creativity and consistency, and integration and distinctiveness be given due attention' (Todd and Tipton 2011: 40). The aim of this recommendation was to reduce both the risks to the consistency of chaplaincy provision across the Prison Service and the reputational risk of idiosyncratic chaplaincies in particular prisons led by chaplains with a very individual leadership style, but without eliminating creativity.

A further outcome of that recommendation has been recent changes to the national management of chaplaincy in England and Wales. Advisers based at Prison Service headquarters (HQ) were previously complemented by regional chaplains responsible for the coordination of chaplaincy within regions. Following Todd and Tipton (2011),[15] the role of HQ Advisers was developed, to carry a regional responsibility, alongside their specialisation within the team (such as training). Their regional role has replaced that of the regional chaplains, a role which no longer exists. Further, the HQ Advisers, within their regional role, introduced and conduct the Assurance and Compliance evaluation (since 2013). These changes are designed to significantly enhance the coherence of the management of chaplaincy, and its delivery across different prisons, and to encourage a more direct relationship between headquarters and individual establishments.[16]

---

[14] Evidence for this impact of the research was supplied by the Chaplain General to HM Prisons in an interview conducted by the author on 16 May 2016, during which the evolution of the Assurance and Compliance process was discussed.

[15] That changes were a direct impact of the research was also confirmed by the Chaplain General in the interview on 16 May 2016, in which he charted the historical stages from the reception of the research report to the establishment of a new management structure.

[16] Interview with Chaplain General, 16 May 2016.

25.2.3   Conversion in Prison

A further area of research concerns the reality and significance of conversion in prison. This issue is raised, inter alia, by the difference between the numbers of Muslim and Buddhist prisoners as a percentage of the prison population and the census percentage of members of those religions. It is clear from research evidence that conversion to a number of faiths or beliefs (including reconversion) does happen in prison and has a particular character in this context. One aspect of this is captured well by Maruna et al. in their study of conversions to Christianity. They provide a careful account of conversion as 'narrative identity change' and the reconstruction of the prisoner's 'self-narrative':

> (...) the conversion narrative 'works' as a shame management and coping strategy in the following ways. The narrative creates a new social identity to replace the label of prisoner or criminal, imbues the experience of imprisonment with purpose and meaning, empowers the largely powerless prisoner by turning him into an agent of God, provides the prisoner with a language and framework for forgiveness, and allows a sense of control over an unknown future. (Maruna et al. 2006: 161)

Focusing on conversion, or reconversion, to Islam expands this picture, although the numbers need careful treatment. It seems clear, as discussed in Sect. 25.2, that the high percentage of Muslims in the prison population (14.6%) is not itself the result of conversion.

Nonetheless, prisoners do turn to Islam in prison in different ways. Marranci himself argues that those registering as Muslim on entry to prison commonly rediscover the practice of their religion, which the majority have not been following to any great extent outside prison. He concurs with Spalek (2000), Spalek and El-Hassan (2007) and Beckford et al. (2005), who assert that 'Islam becomes extremely important as part of the prisoners' identity' (Marranci 2009: 89), but he argues for a diversity of Muslim identities in prison (Marranci 2009: Ch. 5), against what he describes as the 'essentialising' approach of writers such as Spalek and El-Hassan (2007).

A further significant study is that by Liebling et al. (2012), which reveals that in certain settings conversion to Islam becomes salient. The study focuses primarily on staff–prisoner relationships and was conducted 12 years after a comparable research project. However, significant attention is paid to faith and religion. The research site, Her Majesty's Prison Whitemoor,[17] is unusual amongst prisons in having a very high proportion of Muslim prisoners. The 2014–2015 Independent Monitoring Board report on the prison indicates that, 'Excluding the specialist Fens Unit, Muslims represented around half of Whitemoor's residents (...)' and that 'Not only were Muslims the largest religion, they were also the biggest power bloc, displacing the greater multiplicity of gangs that had previously existed (...)' (IMB 2015: 4–5).

---

[17]The Prison is part of the 'High Security Estate (HSE). On 31 May 2015 the prison held 447 prisoners, against an operational capacity of 458. Just under one-third were Category A (141), and of them 14 were High Risk Category A' (IMB 2015: 2).

Liebling et al. indicate that a significant proportion of Muslim prisoners in this setting converted in prison. Out of their interview sample of 52 prisoners, 23 identified as Muslim, while 12 further identified as in-prison converts to Islam (Liebling et al. 2012: 77). They offer the following analysis of 'the main motivations for turning to faith':

- sense-making, searching for meaning, identity, and structure;
- dealing with the pains of long-term imprisonment; seeking 'brotherhood'/family or 'anchored relations';
- seeking care and protection;
- gang membership; rebellion: Islam was 'the new underdog religion'; and
- coercion [by fellow prisoners]. (Liebling et al. 2012: 58)

Liebling et al. complement Marranci (2009), providing details of the diverse reasons for adopting or maintaining a Muslim identity in prison. They significantly extend the picture of conversion offered by Maruna et al. (2006). A significant point here is that, in H.M.P. Whitemoor, being a Muslim contributes significantly to group as well as individual identity, where belonging to a group offers both identity and security. Liebling et al. offer further analysis of the advantages and disadvantages of four 'faith-identity manifestations', two 'positive' ('The Muslim Brotherhood'[18] and 'The Devout Muslim') and two 'negative' ('The Muslim "Gang"' and 'Radical Islamist Offenders') (2012: 97). Their consideration of 'radical extremism' at Whitemoor, also important, is discussed in what follows.

Much less well documented, but of significant potential significance, is conversion to Buddhism amongst prisoners. As indicated previously, 2016 figures were 1558 Buddhist prisoners in England and Wales, or 1.8% of the prisoner population (Allen and Dempsey 2016: 13). This compared with the 2011 census figure for Buddhists amongst the population of England and Wales of 0.4%. A *Daily Telegraph* report from 2009 indicated, based on the Ministry of Justice figures, that, 'in 1997 there were only 226 Buddhists in prisons in England and Wales, but by the end of June 2008 that figure had risen by 669% to reach 1737–2% of the 79,734 prison population' (Beckford 2009).

That article highlighted meditation, and its contribution to coping with incarceration, as a significant factor in conversions in prison to Buddhism citing Lord Avebury, patron of Angulimala, the Buddhist Prison Chaplaincy Organisation,[19] in support of this view.

This hypothesis is confirmed anecdotally by a number of prisoners and chaplains. One prison chaplain reported to the author of this chapter in April 2017 that 8.4% of prisoners in that prison were registered as Buddhist and that many were coming to the end of long sentences and reported having been converted through learning to meditate in another prison earlier in their sentences. This is suggestive

---

[18] It is important to note that 'The term "brotherhood" here meant belonging to the group. It had no broader meaning and was not linked in any interview to any specific organisation' (Liebling et al. 2012: 58; footnote 45).

[19] http://angulimala.org.uk/. Accessed 28 April 2017.

of a new pattern of conversion, which would account for the high number of Buddhist prisoners (in comparison with the national population), which needs to be investigated through systematic research.

Although reasons for conversion or adherence to a religion in prison are shown by the foregoing evaluation to be diverse, nonetheless they include the contribution religion can make to a prisoner's sense of identity, enabling him or her to cope with prison life and address the reasons for incarceration. This is in keeping with the link between faith and pastoral care, which is central to the identity of prison chaplaincy and enshrined in the titles of the 'Service Specification for Faith & Pastoral Care for Prisoners' (NOMS 2015) and the PSI 05/2016 'Faith and Pastoral Care for Prisoners' (NOMS 2016a). It is also in keeping with an increasing emphasis on chaplains supporting desistance from crime. Thus, recent training of managing chaplains has addressed this area, including how chaplains could draw on their own faith tradition in working with prisoners towards their desistance from crime, including following release from prison.[20]

25.2.4   Humanism and Multi-Faith Chaplaincy

A further recent development in the multi-faith chaplaincy and the response to diversity of belief concerns the development by Humanists UK, formerly the British Humanist Association (BHA),[21] of the Non-Religious Pastoral Support Network (NRPSN)[22] and training for Non-Religious Pastoral Volunteers[23] to serve across the public sector, including in prison.[24] In April 2017, the network had 157 members (including 18 non-BHA members) and a waiting list of 212. Fourteen non-religious pastoral carers were serving in 12 prisons in England and Wales; a further 16 volunteers awaited security clearance.[25] The policy that has evolved with establishing the NRPSN and associated training programme is that carers offer support to those who would regard themselves as non-religious and would value talking with someone who also identifies in that way. At the same time, these carers are prepared to work with, and as part of, the chaplaincy team in support of all prisoners (although they do not necessarily embrace the title 'chaplain'). It is now clear, therefore, that the non-religious pastoral carers are trained neither to expect to provide support to all registered as being of 'nil religion' in prison nor not to provide support to those whom they encounter seeking support who are registered as belonging to a religion.

---

[20] Interview with Chaplain General 16 May 2016.

[21] https://humanism.org.uk/. Accessed 28 April 2017.

[22] http://nrpsn.org.uk. Accessed 28 April 2017.

[23] http://humanistcare.org.uk/. Accessed 28 April 2017

[24] Hospitals are another particular area of attention for the NRPSN, as are, to a lesser extent, the armed forces and universities. http://humanistcare.org.uk/. Accessed 28 April 2017.

[25] Numbers supplied by Simon O'Donoghue, head of pastoral care at the BHA, in an email to the author dated 13 April 2017.

Rather, they work with others to provide support according to the needs and expressed wishes of those they encounter. This is captured in the NRPSN Code of Conduct:

> Non-Religious Pastoral Carer – An individual accredited by the NRPSN who is appointed and recognised as part of the pastoral, spiritual and religious care team within a public, charitable, or private institution. His or her job is to seek out and respond to those who are expressing pastoral, spiritual, or religious care needs by providing the appropriate support using a cohesive system of values or beliefs, but which does not self-classify as a religious community, or facilitating that support, through contacting, with the patient's permission, the representative of the appropriate religion or belief. (NRPSN 2017)

Of sociological significance is that Humanists UK has approached participation in public sector pastoral care in ways that are, of necessity, akin to those adopted by religious groups. The features that resemble participation by faith communities are the identification of a sponsoring body (Humanists UK/BHA), provision by that body of training for volunteers (with training for professionals planned[26]) and development of a code of conduct and network for recognised practitioners (the NRPSN).

Where there is ambivalence is in the identification of the belief group to whom non-religious pastoral carers offer particular support (within their wider support for all prisoners). The overarching sponsoring body is Humanists UK, and humanism is recognised in PSI 05/2016 (NOMS 2016a: 56–57; Annexe G[27]). However, prisoners cannot at present register as humanist upon reception into the prison (although the mechanism for official recognition is in process[28]). In conversations involving chaplains (including the HQ team) and Humanists UK representatives (to which the author was party), it became clear that the remit for non-religious pastoral carers could not be all those registered as being of 'nil religion', for two reasons. One was that the existing model of chaplaincy (inherited from Anglicanism) was that chaplains, working as a team, provide for all prisoners, irrespective of their beliefs. The second reason is that it is far from clear why people identify as of 'no religion'. It certainly does not equate straightforwardly with being an atheist or humanist. In the 2011 census of England and Wales, 14.1 million people (25.1%) reported that they had no religion[29]; much smaller numbers self-declared as atheist (29,267) or humanist (15,067).[30] Woodhead (2016) clearly demonstrates that the category is complex and includes those who believe in God or who would identify as 'spiritual', as well as atheists and agnostics.

The current working compromise is that non-religious pastoral volunteers work as part of the chaplaincy team to support all prisoners. Their special remit is to

---

[26] http://nrpsn.org.uk/professional-entry-route/. Accessed 28 April 2017.

[27] This identifies the chief executive of the BHA as the belief adviser for humanism.

[28] Telephone interview with Chaplain General, 13 April 2017.

[29] https://www.ons.gov.uk/peoplepopulationandcommunity/culturalidentity/religion/articles/religioninenglandandwales2011/2012-12-11. Accessed 28 April 2017.

[30] http://webarchive.nationalarchives.gov.uk/20160105160709/http://www.ons.gov.uk/ons/rel/census/2011-census/key-statistics-for-local-authorities-in-england-and-wales/sty-what-is-your-religion.html. Accessed 28 April 2017.

support those who self-identify as non-religious and as valuing pastoral care from someone of a similar viewpoint. This maintains the multi-faith chaplaincy model, which provides specific support to those of identified faith or belief groups and pastoral care to all prisoners. This model provides fuller support, therefore, to the 'religious', who now effectively include those who actively declare themselves as non-religious.

25.3 'Extremism' and 'Radicalisation' in Prison

Section 25.1 indicated, as a continuing trend and research focus, government concern that prisons may act as sites for 'extremism' and 'radicalisation', especially Islamist extremism. Much of the recent government provision flowing from this concern stems from the Counter-Terrorism and Security Act of 2015. This gave rise to the 2015 Prevent Duty Guidance (HM Government 2015), which specifies responsibilities across the public sector. Further, the government review of Islamist 'extremism' in prison (Ministry of Justice 2016) gave rise both to a plan, announced in 2016, to place prisoners identified as 'extremists' in special units (BBC News 2016) and to the announcement in 2017 of a new Counter-Extremism Taskforce to work in prisons (HM Government 2017).

These actions elucidate public policy and practice. They confirm that the UK government continues to view 'radicalisation' in prison as a 'threat' (HM Government 2017), where this threat includes the transmission of 'extremist' ideas between prisoners, such that they become radicalised. Further, the reporting of government action signals media interest in this area and a shared rhetoric with government. Research in this area confirms this picture and indicates that concern about 'extremism' and 'radicalisation' may also be shared, to different degrees, by prison staff and prisoners. Spalek and El-Hassan (2007) present a contrast between media rhetoric highlighting risks of 'radicalisation' in prison and the positive contribution conversion to Islam can make to prisoners. The picture presented by Liebling et al. (2012), albeit in the unusual setting of HMP Whitemoor, is more nuanced:

> Staff sometimes viewed any outward appearance of Islam as evidence of radicalisation, rather than a manifestation of faith, and these 'signs' were written up in security reports. Staff perceived Islam as a radical religion; they overestimated extremism; this 'pushed prisoners together', reinforced their views and gave them more power. (Liebling et al. 2012: v)

However, they also show evidence of a real risk from powerful 'extremist' prisoners:

> There was considerable ignorance and confusion (even among recently converted prisoners) about the Islamic faith. Those with extremist views could fill a gap in knowledge with misinformation and misinterpretation or could point to illegitimate staff practices as a reason for upholding oppositional views. Support for moderate interpretations of Islam was 'muted' at the time of the research. (Liebling et al. 2012: iv)

They further identify a complex picture in which other risks to prisoners outweighed the risks of 'radicalisation', which were nonetheless interwoven with the former:

> While the risks of alienation, loss of meaning, and violence, were more pressing than the (also real) risks of radicalisation, failure to address the former issues might make the risk of radicalisation higher. (Liebling et al. 2012: iii)

One might reasonably conclude that risks of 'radicalisation' at H.M.P. Whitemoor, but potentially elsewhere, are real but unduly exacerbated when concern about 'extremism' becomes dominant, when different Muslim faith identities are conflated, and those which have a benefit for prisoners (in relation to coping with incarceration and desistance) are ignored.

Chaplains in general, and Muslim chaplains in particular, being co-opted into the prison's role of preventing 'extremism' goes back at least 10 years and is charted in Todd (2013). Two roles emerge that also feature in the most recent policy documents. One is mentoring prisoners, to reduce the likelihood of their developing 'extremist' views (HM Government 2015: 16; Sect. 112). This positive role was recognised in Todd (2013), which cites Gilliat-Ray (2008) and first-hand research evidence (Todd 2013: 153). The other chaplaincy role is that of monitoring 'extremism' and 'radicalisation', which also appears in the Revised Prevent Duty Guidance (HM Government 2015: 15; Sect. 107). Todd (2013) highlighted research evidence for the way this latter role can change the relationship between chaplain and prisoner, leading, on occasion, the latter to regard the former with suspicion. The first-hand research evidence of Todd (2013: 154–55), the HM Chief Inspector of Prisons (2010: 35) and Liebling et al. (2012: 46; footnote 34) were cited in support of this.

A key argument of Todd (2013) was that this role of monitoring 'extremism' had the potential to significantly reshape the chaplain's role (cf. Gilliat-Ray et al. 2013: 108–114). The risk, which current policy documents would suggest still exists, is that the chaplain's perceived 'neutrality' or independence within the system will be compromised (Todd 2013: 152–57). This 'neutrality' enables the trust that chaplains establish with prisoners and staff to serve as the basis for their humanitarian role (Todd and Tipton 2011).

25.4 Conclusion: Chaplaincy, Public Policy and the Construction of 'Religion'

In conclusion, this chapter examines how the public policy underpinning the developments discussed earlier tends to shape religion within prisons in the UK today. Two areas of policy are significant: equal opportunity and respect for diversity (Sect. 25.1) and the prevention of 'extremism' and 'radicalisation' (Sect. 25.3). Todd (2015) argues that these two areas of policy play a particularly significant role in 'formatting' religion in prison and in the armed forces, as part of a comparison of how the economic, cultural and symbolic capital value (Bourdieu 1986) of chaplaincy are negotiated in the two social settings.

Of significance in recent policy is the concept of duty. This constructs a relationship between government and public sector institutions, in which the latter must fulfil both the Public Sector Equality Duty and the Prevent Duty. This relationship further constructs chaplaincy as a resource in fulfilling these two duties. Thus, in relation to equality of opportunity and respect for diversity, NOMS (2016a) and NOMS (2015) provide a mandatory framework for how chaplaincy enables prisoners of different faiths and beliefs to practise and change their religion or belief. The outputs specified are then monitored through the Assurance and Compliance process (Sect. 25.2.2). That this is a political imperative is confirmed by transcript extracts from interviews with two prison governors (cited in Todd 2013: 150), one of whom spoke of the need to 'tick [the] box' of statutory multi-faith requirements, the other of whom spoke of practising faith as a human right. Resourcing the fulfilment of the Prevent Duty is similarly a political imperative, as another governor (cited in Todd 2013: 154–55) made clear, referring both to the need to involve chaplains and to the risk to their neutrality that was involved.

And if multi-faith chaplaincy is a resource for enabling the prison to fulfil its public duty, then this also redefines the role of faith communities in relation to the prison. Public duties tend to frame faith communities as those who supply and authorise the resource represented by chaplains. A particular faith community becomes, therefore, something akin to a 'service provider'. This emerging role is discussed in Todd (2016), which contrasts it with an older (and still concurrent) way of construing the role of faith communities as representing their members' or adherents' needs.

If chaplains tend to be perceived as resources in the fulfilment of public duties and their faith communities tend to be framed as 'service providers' who supply chaplaincy for such purposes, then this constructs religion in prison in a very specific way: as that to which prisoners have the right, as long as they manifest their religion within publicly defined boundaries, be those the more permissive boundaries designed to promote equality or the more restrictive boundaries designed to prevent 'extremism' and 'radicalisation'. And chaplains are employed to enable religion within the boundaries, but also to monitor the boundaries. Part of the significance of the case of humanism (Sect. 25.2.4) is to illustrate how non-religious pastoral volunteers need to conform to this model. They need to be trained to provide an equality-promoting service similar to that set for religious chaplains within documents such as the Service Specification 'Faith & Pastoral Care for Prisoners' (NOMS 2015), PSI 05/2016, 'Faith and Pastoral Care for Prisoners' (NOMS 2016a) and to be subject to a code of conduct and security clearance, in support of the public management of security and risk. Furthermore, such volunteers require the support and authorisation of the 'service provider' body – in this case Humanists UK.

However, one should not conclude that this represents the whole picture. The constructions of chaplaincy, faith communities and religion discussed earlier offer an effective picture of the shape of a multi-faith prison chaplaincy at the macrolevel. Further, those constructions affect chaplaincy at the micro-level of everyday practice, as chaplains respond to the monitoring process and Assurance and Compliance or take decisions about the security implications of particular aspects of the religious practice of prisoners. But those parameters also provide for significant diversity at the micro-level within the limits they set. This is seen in the diversity of faith identities, discussed in relation to conversion in Sect. 25.2.3. It is seen in the way that the 'lived religion' (McGuire 2008) of prisoners overflows the boundaries of prescribed religious practice, as is seen in the act of candle lighting in the prison chapel, about which Phillips concludes that 'The ubiquity of candle lighting helps to frame the chaplain as offering a ministry where any distinctions between the religious and the secular are blurred or impermanent' (Phillips 2013: 163).

Above all, the diversity of chaplaincy practice at the micro-level, held within the policy-driven macro-level boundaries, is symbolised by the designation of the chaplain's work in Service Specification 'Faith & Pastoral Care for Prisoners' (NOMS 2015) and PSI 05/2016, 'Faith and Pastoral Care for Prisoners' (NOMS 2016a) is about faith *and pastoral care* [emphasis added]. For it is in the day-to-day work of pastoral care that chaplains cross boundaries of faith communities and of faith itself, such that their humanitarian care and concern for all prisoners and for staff remain the role most highly valued by both groups (Todd and Tipton 2011).

Bibliography

Allen, G., & Dempsey, N. (2016). *Prison Population Statistics, 4 July 2016*. House of Commons Library, Briefing Paper Number SN/SG/04334. http://researchbriefings.files.parliament.uk/documents/SN04334/SN04334.pdf. Accessed 11 Apr 2017.

BBC News. (2016). Extremists to be put in special prison units, *BBC News*, 22 August 2016. http://www.bbc.co.uk/news/uk-37151089. Accessed 28 Apr 2017.

Beckford, J. (1999). Rational choice theory and prison chaplaincy: The chaplain's dilemma. *British Journal of Sociology, 50*(4), 671–685.

Beckford, J. (2007). Prison chaplaincy in England and Wales: From Anglican brokerage to a multi-faith approach. In M. Koenig & P. de Guchteneire (Eds.), *Democracy and human rights in multicultural societies* (pp. 267–282). Ashgate: Aldershot/Burlington VT.

Beckford, M. (2009). Buddhism is fastest-growing religion in English jails over past decade, *Daily Telegraph*, 5 August 2009. http://www.telegraph.co.uk/news/religion/5977093/Buddhism-is-fastest-growing-religion-in-English-jails-over-past-decade.html. Accessed 27 Apr 2017.

Beckford, J. (2013). 2013. Religious diversity in prisons: Chaplaincy and contention. *Studies in Religion/Sciences Religieuses, 42*(2), 190–205.

Beckford, J., & Gilliat, S. (1998). *Religion in prison: Equal rites in multi-Faith Society*. Cambridge: Cambridge University Press.

Beckford, J., Joly, D., & Khosrokhavar, F. (2005). *Muslims in prison: Challenge and change in Britain and France*. Basingstoke: Palgrave Macmillan.

Bourdieu, P. (1986). The forms of capital. In J. E. Richardson (Ed.), *Handbook of theory and research for the sociology of education* (pp. 241–258). New York: Greenwood Press.

Gilliat-Ray, S. (2008). From 'visiting minister' to 'Muslim chaplain': The growth of Muslim chaplaincy in Britain, 1970–2007. In E. Barker (Ed.), *The centrality of religion in social life: Essays in honour of James A. Beckford* (pp. 145–157). Aldershot: Ashgate.

Gilliat-Ray, S., Ali, M. M., & Pattison, S. (2013). *Understanding Muslim chaplaincy*. Farnham: Ashgate.

HM Chief Inspector of Prisons. (2010). *Muslim prisoners' experiences: A thematic review*. Available at: http://socialwelfare.bl.uk/subject-areas/services-client-groups/adult-offenders/hminspectorateofprisons/muslim10.aspx. Accessed 1 May 2017.

HM Government. (2015). *Revised prevent duty guidance: For England and Wales.* Revised 16 July 2015. https://www.gov.uk/government/publications/prevent-duty-guidance. Accessed 12 Apr 2017.

HM Government. (2017). *New counter-extremism taskforce to help tackle extremism behind bars.* Press release. https://www.gov.uk/government/news/new-counter-extremism-taskforce-to-help-tackle-extremism-behind-bars. Accessed 12 Apr 2017.

HM Prison and Probation Service (HMPPS). (2017). *Chaplaincy HQ assurance and compliance check sheet.* Supplied courtesy of the Chaplain General to HM Prisons.

Independent Monitoring Board (IMB). (2015). *HMP Whitemoor: Annual Report 2015 (1 June 2014– 31 May 2015).* http://www.imb.org.uk/wp-content/uploads/2015/09/Whitemoor-2014-15.pdf. Accessed 27 Apr 2017.

Lammy, D. (2017). *The Lammy review: An independent review into the treatment of, and outcomes for, Black, Asian and minority ethnic individuals in the Criminal Justice System.* https://www.gov.uk/government/uploads/system/uploads/attachment_data/file/643001/lammy-review-final-report.pdf. Accessed 12 Oct 2017.

Liebling, A., Arnold, H., & Straub, C. (2012). *An exploration of staff-prisoner relationships at HMP Whitemoor: 12 years on.* Revised Final Report. Cambridge Institute of Criminology Prisons Research Centre. London: Ministry of Justice. https://www.gov.uk/government/uploads/system/uploads/attachment_data/file/217381/staff-prisoner-relations-whitemoor.pdf. Accessed 27 Apr 2017.

Marranci, G. (2009). *Faith, ideology and fear: Muslim identities within and beyond prisons.* London/New York: Continuum.

Maruna, S., Wilson, L., & Curran, K. (2006). Why god is often found behind bars: Prison conversions and the crisis of self-narrative. *Research in Human Development, 3*(2&3), 161–184.

McGuire, M. B. (2008). *Lived religion: Faith and practice in everyday life.* Oxford/New York: Oxford University Press.

Ministry of Justice. (2016). *Guidance: Summary of the main findings of the review of Islamist extremism in prisons, probation and youth justice.* https://www.gov.uk/government/publications/islamist-extremism-in-prisons-probation-and-youth-justice/summary-of-the-main-findings-of-the-review-of-islamist-extremism-in-prisons-probation-and-youth-justice. Accessed 12 Apr 2017.

National Offender Management Service (NOMS). (2015). *Service specification for faith & pastoral care for prisoners.* https://www.gov.uk/government/uploads/system/uploads/attachment_data/file/494370/2015-11-11_Faith_and_Pastoral_Care_P3.0_FINAL.pdf. Accessed 26 Apr 2017.

National Offender Management Service (NOMS). (2016a). *PSI 05/2016: Faith and pastoral care for prisoners.* https://www.justice.gov.uk/offenders/psis/prison-service-instructions-2016. Accessed 26 Apr 2017.

National Offender Management Service (NOMS). (2016b). *Chaplaincy HQ bulletin.* December 2016. Supplied courtesy of the Chaplain General to HM Prisons.

Non-Religious Pastoral Support Network (NRPSN). (n.d.). *Code of conduct.* http://nrpsn.org.uk/wp-content/uploads/2016/02/CodeofConduct.pdf. Accessed 28 Apr 2017.

Phillips, P. (2013). *Roles and identities of the Anglican chaplain: A prison ethnography.* Unpublished Cardiff University PhD. http://orca.cf.ac.uk/view/cardiffauthors/A134628F.html. Accessed 5 May 2017.

Spalek, B. (2000). *Islam, crime and criminal justice.* Cullompton, Devon: Willan Publishing.

Spalek, B., & El-Hassan, S. (2007). Muslim converts in prison. *The Howard Journal of Criminal Justice, 46*(2), 99–114.

Todd, A. J. (2013). Preventing the 'neutral' chaplain? The potential impact of anti-'extremism' policy on prison chaplaincy. *Practical Theology, 6*(2), 144–158.

Todd, A. J. (2015). Religion, security, rights, the individual and rates of exchange: Religion in negotiation with British public policy in prisons and the military. *International Journal of Politics, Culture, and Society, 28*(1), 37–50.

Todd, A. J. (2016). Chaplaincy public sector policy in the UK: International lessons to be learnt for religious-spiritual counselling and care. In A. Ayten, M. Koç, N. Tınaz, & M. A. Doğan (Eds.), *Religious-spiritual counselling & care* (pp. 91–109). Istanbul: Center for Values Education (DEM) Press.

Todd, A., & Tipton, L. (2011). *The role and contribution of a multi-faith prison chaplaincy to the contemporary prison service*. Report to the National Offender Management Service. http://orca.cf.ac.uk/29120/. Accessed 20 Feb 2020.

Woodhead, L. (2016). The rise of 'no religion' in Britain: The emergence of a new cultural majority. The British Academy lecture read 19 January 2016. *Journal of the British Academy, 4,* 245–261. http://www.britac.ac.uk/sites/default/files/11%20Woodhead%201825.pdf. Accessed 28 Apr 2017.

Chapter 26
Russia: A Short Word on Religion in Prisons

Mikhaïl Chakhov

Abstract This chapter provides the little information that is available on religions in prison in Russia: the general legal framework, the state of freedom of religion, the organisation of the prison chaplaincy, and the involvement of religious institutions in the pastoral care and education of detainees.

Very little is known about religion in prisons in Russia: few authors have done any research on this topic, in a country where the Law on Freedom of Conscience and Religious Associations dates from 1997 and the place of religions in prison is yet to be fully institutionalised and established. However, it seems important to add this chapter, though it is rather short, to a European overview, the specific situation of Russia and its place in the general history of Europe being of high interest.

According to Article 14 of the Russian Code of Execution of Criminal Sanctions, prisoners are guaranteed freedom of conscience and freedom of belief, and this includes the right to profess, and practise individually or with others, any religion, or to profess and practise none, to choose freely to have and to disseminate religious or other beliefs, and to act in accordance with them.

The implementation of the right to freedom of conscience and freedom of belief must be voluntary and must not violate the internal order of the penitentiary or affect the rights of others.

Based on the requests and choice of prisoners, ministers of religion can be invited to join religious organisations officially recognised by the law. A necessary condition for a meeting between a prisoner and a minister of religion must be initiated by the prisoner; legislation limits the missionary activities and proselytism of religious denominations in penitentiary establishments.

Russian legislation provides for voluntary registration of religious associations to obtain the right to become a legal entity and the rights granted by law. Registered religious associations are called 'religious organisations', and unregistered religious

M. Chakhov (✉)
Professor at the Academy of National Economics and Public Service under the President of Russia, Moscow, Russia

© Springer Nature Switzerland AG 2020

421

J. Martínez-Ariño, A.-L. Zwilling (eds.), *Religion and Prison: An Overview of Contemporary Europe*, Boundaries of Religious Freedom: Regulating Religion in Diverse Societies 7, https://doi.org/10.1007/978-3-030-36834-0_26

associations are called 'religious groups'. The central religious organisation must include at least three local religious organisations. For the Orthodox Church, the parish is the local religious organisation (with a legal personality), the diocese (parochial) and the Church – these are the central religious organisations (in Russian: централизованная религиозная организация, *tsentralisovannaya religiosnaya organisatsiya*, which is impossible to translate properly because there is no accurate equivalent legal term in English) (Chakhov 2012.)

Personal meetings of detainees with ministers of religion are not limited in number but must not last more than 2 hours each. At the request of detainees and with the written consent of the concerned minister of religion, meetings between detainees and clergymen (including the exercise of religious rites and ceremonies) may take place in person, out of earshot of other people and without video surveillance.

Until recently, there was no state-sponsored prison chaplaincy in Russia. All pastoral activities were the responsibility of ministers of religious organisations. Around 1200 Orthodox priests practise their pastoral service in prisons. However, the Russian Government Ordinance of 17 October 2014 on the regional bodies of the Federal Service for the Enforcement of Criminal Sanctions created the function of Deputy Chief for the organisation of work with believing prisoners. These are deputies of the heads of regional agencies of the Federal Criminal Enforcement Service; pursuant to the ordinance of the Government of Russia on 17 October 2014, 'In the regional agencies of the Federal Service for the Execution of Criminal Sanctions are created the functions of deputies of chiefs for the organisation of work with believing prisoners" (*pomochnik natchalnika po organizatsii raboty s ver-ouytchimi zakliuchennimi*). Priests who take up these functions become lay civil servants employed by the state. They number 85 for all of Russia and are officially designated by the title of 'chaplain'.

Prisoners are entitled to participate in religious rites and ceremonies and to possess objects of worship and books of religious literature. The penitentiary administration furnishes the premises for worship. The law established that the federal and regional agencies of the Federal Penal Enforcement Service shall enter into cooperative agreements with the central religious organisations to guarantee prisoners' freedom of conscience and freedom of belief.

These agreements were concluded between the Federal Criminal Enforcement Service and the Russian Orthodox Church,[1] the Russian Council of Muftis, the Federation of Jewish Communities in Russia and the Traditional Buddhist Sangha in Russia. The programme on the main directions of cooperation was signed with the Union of Baptists of Russia.

There is a Department for Pastoral Service in Prisons in the Russian Orthodox Church.[2]

In 2013, there were 581 active religious premises in Russian penitentiary establishments, including 517 for the Russian Orthodox Church, 51 mosques, 7 Buddhist

---

[1] The agreement is available here : http://www.patriarchia.ru/db/text/1414718.html (in Russian).

[2] Official website http://anastasia-uz.ru/, in Russian.

buildings and 4 Catholic churches. There were also about 780 prayer halls, including 453 for Orthodox Christians, 228 for Muslims, 56 for Baptists, 28 for evangelical Christians, 10 for Buddhists, 8 for Jews and 1 for Catholics.

In 2013, there were 232 Sunday schools (Orthodox) in prisons, as well as 85 Bible and Koranic schools, in which more than 7800 prisoners were educated.

The ministers of religion cooperate in the administration of penitentiary institutions for the spiritual and moral education of the prisoners, for the restoration of positive social contacts, and to prepare the prisoners for their release. The ministers of religion take part in commissions for early release. About 100 ministers of religion are members of the public councils of the regional bodies of the Federal Service for the Enforcement of Criminal Sanctions.

The Russian Orthodox Church has established foundations in some of its parishes for the support and assistance of released detainees. There is also an Orthodox ecclesiastical social programme for the prevention of drug addiction, alcoholism and juvenile recidivism.

The Russian Mufti Council is responsible for the spiritual and moral education of Muslim detainees convicted of extremist and terrorist activities. This education is meant to teach them respect for the law and bring them to repentance.

The Russian Baptist Union has founded more than 100 rehabilitation centres to assist released detainees. In the six regions of Russia, the Union of Baptists run the social project Youth Against Drugs to promote a healthy lifestyle and prevent drug addiction.

26.1   Conclusion

Although still young and relatively small, the presence of religions in prisons is growing and becoming more widely recognised. The different religious institutions are setting up their respective pastoral services in order to provide spiritual assistance to the population of detainees. Religious diversity is increasingly present and accepted.

Bibliography

Chakhov, M. (2012). Status of religious organisations, *Eurel – Russia*. http://www.eurel.info/spip.php?rubrique487&lang=en